Wild Flowers
of the World

Paintings by BARBARA EVERARD

Text by
BRIAN D. MORLEY, Ph.D., F.L.S.

CONSULTANT EDITORS:
W. T. Stearn, Sc.D., V.M.H., F.L.S., F.I.Biol.,
British Museum (Natural History)

Peter S. Green, B.Sc., F.L.S.,
Royal Botanic Gardens, Kew

CRESCENT BOOKS · NEW YORK

Renanthera coccinea from South East Asia, plate 126

517101335
Copyright © MCMLXX by Rainbird Reference Books Limited
Library of Congress Catalog Card Number: 79-116143
All rights reserved
This edition is published by Crescent Books
a division of Crown Publishers, Inc.
by arrangement with G.P. Putnam's Sons

Designer: George Sharp

Printed in Hong Kong

CONTENTS

FOREWORD

Diverse as are the plants assembled in gardens, numerous as are their countries of origin, they represent only a small part of the world's floristic richness; yet even so, fortunate and far-travelled must be the botanist and flower-lover who sees in a wild state as many as can be found in well-stocked botanic gardens like Kew and the New York Botanical Garden. Keble Martin's *Concise British Flora in Colour* in one volume gives a pictorial survey of the plants of the British Isles, a relatively impoverished area of the world's flora; Bonnier & Douin's *Flore complète illustrée en Couleurs de France, Suisse et Belgique*, in 13 volumes, does the same for France, Switzerland and Belgium; and there is also Harold W. Rickett's book *Wild Flowers of the United States*. The vast number of flowering plants known, estimated at about a quarter million species, for the earth as a whole, makes it impossible to provide similar guides in colour to them all. Instead, the present work samples them on a regional basis; it tries to indicate, by means of coloured illustrations of some distinctive, characteristic or otherwise interesting plants, the special features of the major botanical regions of the world. These illustrations will supplement, it is hoped, standard horticultural and botanical works and give pleasure to flower-lovers who can follow only in imagination the travels and the toils of the botanical explorers and collectors who have helped to make known this wealth of plants; for tourists they may be a foretaste of those to be sought. The general arrangement is accordingly first geographical and then systematic, thus portraying together related plants of the same area. Any choice of plants, when only a few can be taken from so many, must be somewhat arbitrary and extremely vulnerable to criticism; the emphasis has been on their variety of structure and colour.

The plates are the work of Mrs Barbara Everard, who during her stay in Malaya from 1947 to 1951 made many paintings from life of wild and cultivated tropical plants, which have been used here, and who has subsequently illustrated European plants. Other illustrations have been made from living plants cultivated at Kew, Wisley or elsewhere; when such plants were not available they have been based on specimens in the Kew and Edinburgh herbaria supplemented by colour transparencies of living plants or coloured illustrations in *Curtis's Botanical Magazine* and other reliable works. The accompanying text is the work of Brian D. Morley, now at the National Botanic Gardens, Glasnevin, Dublin, partly revised and rewritten by Peter S. Green of the Royal Botanic Gardens, Kew, and William T. Stearn of the British Museum (Natural History) London, who acted as consultant editors.

Grateful acknowledgement is made to the Director, the Royal Botanic Gardens, Kew, the Regius Keeper, the Royal Botanic Garden, Edinburgh, the Director, the Royal Horticultural Society's Garden, Wisley and their staffs for the facilities granted to Mrs Everard or Dr Morley or to both.

INTRODUCTION

Medieval, Roman and even Greek society all had strange concepts of the lands beyond their everyday reach and peopled these places with monstrous men, and weird plants and animals, and even today there is a tendency to fictionalize foreign floras. In this context it is not inappropriate to remember the words of Alfred Russell Wallace, written in 1869: 'The reader who is familiar with tropical nature only through the medium of books and botanic gardens, will picture to himself in such a spot many other natural beauties. He will think that I have unaccountably forgotten to mention the brilliant flowers, which, in gorgeous masses of crimson, gold or azure, must spangle these verdant precipices, hang over the cascade, and adorn the margin of the mountain stream. But what is the reality? . . . In every direction the eye rested on green foliage and mottled rock. There was infinite variety in the colour and aspect of the foliage, there was grandeur in the rocky masses and in the exuberant luxurience of the vegetation, but there was no brilliancy of colour, none of those bright flowers and gorgeous masses of blossom, so generally considered to be everywhere present in the tropics.' Perhaps the plates which follow will help create a more accurate, if somewhat arbitrary, popular impression of the wild flowers of the world; a world which is all too rapidly being destructively changed.

We have long regarded vegetation as something to be indefinitely exploited for food, clothing and other uses, but natural plant life is not inexhaustible. Conservation of all wild life is necessary for future generations and this need has been so often repeated that the phrase almost loses currency. The time for warnings has gone; the destruction of many wild habitats and their inhabitants, including human groups, has already taken place and continues. Existing complacency over conservation is a frightening measure of a lack of interest in our children and grandchildren.

Once a particular wild animal or plant is made extinct, literally millions of years of evolution become undone; nothing can retrieve the situation. There is no comfort in thinking that extinction is a natural process and therefore inevitable for the organisms extinguished, because, while natural processes are involved, the activity of man, for one reason or another, accelerates and multiplies the means by which extinction can occur. Each day brings nearer the reality of a world populated only by those plants and animals which can compete and co-exist with man, such as the house fly, the clothes moth, the rat and most weeds! A number of rare and unusual plants are featured on the following plates, precisely those in need of protection, illustrating the sort of beauty we could conserve if the effort was made.

The one hundred and ninety-two plates are arranged in twelve geographical groupings, with appropriate captions facing each plate. The choice of the twelve regions was governed by the flora each possessed, and the need to represent as much of the geographical world as possible and the availability of live material from various geographical areas. Two areas which have been consciously under-represented are the Soviet Union and the Middle East. Each area is arranged according to a broad taxonomic plan which has a general basis on that given in J. Hutchinson (1959) *The Families of Flowering Plants* (2 vol.), but which of necessity is sometimes departed from for technical reasons. The use of Hutchinson's taxonomic classification does not imply the author's acceptance of the scheme in its entirety and some of his family limits are not adhered to, but it is used here as a skeleton because

botanical details will be easily found in the two volumes of Hutchinson, which are still in print, by those who may wish to read further into the subject. The choice of families represented in each area was partly governed by the floristic makeup of the area, the need to feature a rough cross-section of the world's flowering plant families and, most difficult of all, depended on the presence of attractive or interesting plants in a family. The families *Gesneriaceae*, *Bignoniaceae* and *Orchidaceae* have, for example, been repeatedly chosen from different areas as they contain attractive species. Sometimes a common but characteristic plant has been chosen for an area, on other occasions a rare plant has been chosen, or a curious plant featured. There are one or two species which have never before been illustrated in colour, several which have not yet been described for science and certainly more which have not been recently featured in a colour picture book. Large plants have not been ignored. To those who might have chosen plants other than those illustrated, the author tenders his apologies.

Wild flowers, their names and lineage.

The term 'wild flower' is ambiguous and has been met by including only Angiosperm families, that is all plants excluding bacteria, algae, fungi, lichens, mosses, ferns and the Gymnosperms, pines, ginkgos and cycads. Technically an Angiosperm is a plant having seeds protected by an enveloping organ called the carpel. As will be seen, there is still plenty to illustrate.

Whenever possible, living material was used in the preparation of the plates, from collections grown in the Royal Botanic Gardens, Kew and the Garden of the Royal Horticultural Society, Wisley. But only a fraction of the world's wild flowers are grown in botanic gardens and it was necessary to use references such as herbarium sheets, colour slides, other illustrations and written descriptions for the preparation of many plates.

Botanists have found that of all the parts of the plant readily available for study, the flower provides the most constant and convenient material for classifying most wild flowers. The flower also helps to establish relationships in terms of lineage, between one family and another.

Names are given to plants so that they may be distinguished from each other, and these identities communicated from person to person. As there are about three thousand different languages in the world according to W. T. Stearn (1966) *Botanical Latin* and because confusion would occur if plants were named in a variety of tongues, scientific plant-names are nearly always of Latin or Greek origin or at least of Latin form. The use of Latin dates back to the time when this language was the international academic form of communication, and when plants were regarded with more medicinal than botanic interest. Latin names often simplify the process of remembering plants, particularly when there exist a number of colloquial names for a single plant, even within the same language. For example one hundred and twelve common names for *Arum maculatum* have been listed, as used in the British Isles in an informative book by C. T. Prime entitled *Lords and Ladies*—which is one of the commoner names in question.

By definition, a group of individual plants essentially similar to one another, but distinguishable from others by an association of characters, is called a *species*. Of course, opinions differ as to what comprises a recognizable specific difference, and plants also vary enormously in the extent to which they diverge from one another. In general, however, the species has proved to be a workable unit.

Groups of species often share similar characters, and such groups are called *genera*. All buttercups, for instance, have the same general characters despite differences in details, and they are grouped into the genus *Ranunculus*. The genus-name followed by the specific epithet, always in that order, gives the species-name which is in universal botanic use. Thus, the scientific name of the Daisy, *Bellis perennis*, consists of the generic name *Bellis*, which is applicable to all plants referred to the genus *Bellis*, and the specific epithet *perennis* only applicable to one species within the genus *Bellis*. For special precision the name of the person who first published the name is cited after the species name. Sometimes an abbreviated form of the person's name is given, particularly if he was well known, and so the Daisy becomes *Bellis perennis* L., as Linnaeus (whose family name is not, as commonly stated, a latinized form of Linné, which name he adopted on ennoblement) named this species. Such author reference is given in the index accompanying the plates which follow, and has technical importance, particularly where two authors have given the same plant different names, or different plants the same name.

For example, *Phacellanthus* Steudel ex Zollinger & Moritzi (1854) was a genus in the *Cyperaceae*, sedge family, which is now included in the sedge genus *Gahnia* J. R. & G. Forster; the accepted *Phacellanthus* is that described by Siebold and Zuccarini (1846), and is a genus in the broomrape family, *Orobanchaceae*, found in the Far East. Similarly *Nymania* K. Schumann (1905) was a genus in the *Euphorbiaceae*, now included in the euphorbiaceous genus *Phyllanthus* L.; while the accepted *Nymania* is that described by S. O. Lindberg (1868) and is a genus in the *Sapindaceae*.

A form of citation that arouses the curiosity of people consulting monographic botanical works is the frequent use of the exclamation mark as follows, 'Columnea urbanii Stearn, Morley 272, 22/9/65, Top Hill, Manchester Parish, Jamaica, UWI!'. It is not that the collector experienced wild elation at finding the plant, although he may have done so; the sign ! indicates that the specimen has been seen and examined.

The origin of plant names is a subject full of the unexpected and full of novelty. The names of species may refer to characteristic habitats, such as *uliginosus* which relates to marshes, *frigidus* which relates to cold places, and *nemorosus* or *nemorum* which relates to woodlands. The names may refer to geographical provenance, such as *occidentalis* relating to anything western, *neapolitanus* relating to Naples, and *monspeliensis* relating to Montpelier, as Monspelium was the old name for that city. Names may describe colours or tints, such as *luteus*, yellow; *aureus*, golden; *sulphureus*, sulphur yellow; *argenteus*, silvery; *albidus*, whitish; *albescens*, turning white. Sometimes these descriptions defeat their own purpose in referring to obscure objects as far as many people are concerned, such as *cascarillus*, the colour of the inner bark of *Cascarilla*, a tree related to the quinine-yielding genus *Cinchona*. Very often names refer to textures or shapes, such as *spinosus*, spiny or *dentatus*, toothed. Sometimes the structure of parts is referred to, such as in the genus *Dimorphotheca*, where two sorts of fruit are borne on the fruiting head.

Generic names are often based on the names of botanists or mythological figures. *Juanulloa* (*Solanaceae*) is derived from a combination of the names Jorge Juan and Antonio Ulloa; *Dillenia* (*Dilleniaceae*) commemorates the botanist Johann Jacob Dillenius (1684-1747); while *Adonis* (*Ranunculaceae*) and *Daphne* (*Thymelaeaceae*) are derived from the names of the god and goddess. The author of a generic name may be ingenious, as was

Karl Ernst Otto Kuntze (1843-1907) with the orchid genus *Sirhookera*, named after the famous British botanist Sir Joseph D. Hooker. An author may be inconsiderate as far as pronunciation is concerned, as with *Radlkoferotoma* Kuntze, a daisy commemorating the botanist Ludwig Adolph Timotheus Radlkofer (1829-1927) or with *Neoturczaninowia*, in the *Umbelliferae*, the brain-child of B. M. Kozo-Poljansky (1890-1957). There are however limitations to the simplification of names, and this has been reached with the publication of *Aa*, a genus of some fifteen tropical American orchids described by Heinrich Gustav Reichenbach (1823-1889). Possibly the simplest of all plant names is *Poa fax*. Anagrams are sometimes the source of plant names such as *Gifola* Cassini, *Ifloga* Cassini, *Logfia* Cassini, and *Oglifa* Cassini from the genus *Filago* L. (*Compositae*). *Jacaima* (*Asclepiadaceae*) is an anagram of the name of a well known Caribbean island, to which the only known species is confined.

Just as species are grouped into more inclusive units called genera, genera are grouped into still larger units called *families*. The process of placing species in genera, and genera in families, is called classification, and produces a hierarchical system of stored information. Classification organizes the natural diversity of wild flowers into units which can be easily comprehended and communicated; thereby a plant of which the name is unknown may be placed in relation to already known specimens. This has more than an academic value where plants possess economic or medicinal uses or both.

The arrangement and definition of families, genera and species by one botanist are not necessarily the same as those of another, but even allowing for the different viewpoints and personalities of botanists, there is reasonable agreement on a general understanding of the families of wild flowers at the present time. Hutchinson briefly indicates some of the different classifications of the past in the first volume of his *The Families of Flowering Plants* ed. 2, p. 2-17 (1959).

The basic floral structure of an Angiosperm is a whorl of sepals, followed by an inner whorl of petals, then whorl(s) of stamens, and finally the carpels (which become the seed-vessels) in the centre of the flower. This floral plan has been variously altered by evolution during the passage of time, so that it is possible to distinguish basic and derived characters in many groups. The following trends are thought to have occurred, and are selected from a list given in Hutchinson.

1. Spirally inserted leaves are thought to be more primitive than whorled or opposite leaves.
2. Bisexual flowers more primitive than unisexual.
3. Solitary flowers more primitive than inflorescences or flower clusters.
4. Petal-bearing flowers more primitive than those without petals.
5. Flowers with unfused petals more primitive than those with fused petals.
6. Symmetrical (regular) flowers more primitive than asymmetrical (irregular) flowers.
7. Flowers with petals inserted at or below the base of the ovary more primitive than those with petals inserted above the base of the ovary.
8. Unfused carpels more primitive than fused carpels.
9. Many carpels in flowers more primitive than few or single carpelled flowers.
10. Food reserves in seeds a more primitive trait than seeds lacking food reserves.
11. Flowers with many stamens more primitive than flowers with few stamens.
12. Unfused stamens more primitive than fused stamens.
13. Single fruits more primitive than aggregate fruits such as that of the pineapple or strawberry.

14. Perennials probably more primitive than annuals or biennials.
15. Land plants more primitive than aquatics as far as flowering plants are concerned.
16. Normally photosynthetic (autotrophic) plants more primitive than heterotrophic plants such as saprophytes, or parasites like the broomrapes, *Orobanche*, and dodders, *Cuscuta*.

Using such criteria established by the work of many botanists, Angiosperms may be arranged into a system crudely reflecting the evolutionary relationship between groups. In some groups the above criteria may not hold true; reversals may occur, as in borages, *Boraginaceae*, where a deep furrow divides the two fused carpels into four units, giving the superficial appearance of separate carpels. Such redirection of the expression of a plant character bedevils the work of the plant namer, or taxonomist. In the following paragraphs a group of families called an order is meant when the suffix -*ales* is used e.g. *Rosales*; a particular family meant when the suffix -*aceae* or -*ae* is used, e.g. *Rosaceae, Palmae*. Plate number references are given for the families mentioned, in the index.

Some botanists believe that, because plants have evolved from one or a few progenitors, it should be possible to classify them in a way that roughly depicts their 'evolutionary tree'. This is possible when we classify the plant kingdom as a whole, the algae, mosses, horsetails, ferns, Gymnosperms and Angiosperms form a series progressing from relative simplicity to complexity, which almost certainly reflects stages and eras in the evolution of plants. But when we apply the same concept to classification within the Angiosperms, family relationships have only theoretical value, for they are based on the supposition that the existing characters of the plant reflect evolutionary affinities and past evolution. Four broad types of family relationship can be mentioned.

A. There are recognizably primitive families, based on the characters listed earlier. The *Magnoliales* comprising: *Magnoliaceae, Illiciaceae, Winteraceae* and *Schisandraceae*; and the *Ranales* comprising: *Paeoniaceae, Ranunculaceae*, and *Nymphaeaceae*; are the most primitive dicotyledons. The most primitive monocotyledons are the *Butomales* comprising: *Hydrocharitaceae* and *Butomaceae*; and the *Alismatales* comprising *Alismataceae* and *Scheuchzeriaceae*.

A1. There are relatively advanced families, the culmination of progressive modification through a series of families. Typical are the *Boraginaceae*, being more advanced but allied to the *Geraniales* and *Polemoniales*. *Scrophulariaceae, Acanthaceae* and *Gesneriaceae* are more advanced families from descendants similar to *Solanaceae* and *Convolvulaceae*. *Compositae* are derived from ancestors like *Campanulaceae*; *Cruciferae* are derived from ancestors like *Papaveraceae*.

A2. Other apparently advanced families have unknown origins and are not clearly related to any other group; such are the *Euphorbiaceae, Salicaceae, Piperaceae* and *Cactaceae*.

A3. Some families appear to be related to a maximum of two others, in what appears to be an intermediate position of development. The *Polemoniales* comprising: *Polemoniaceae* and *Hydrophyllaceae*, link the simple *Geraniaceae, Oxalidaceae, Tropaeolaceae* and *Balsaminaceae* with the more advanced *Boraginaceae*, and possibly *Labiatae*: the *Polemoniales* are unlikely to have any other relationship within the bounds of botanical reasoning. Another example is the *Juncales*, which appear to link the *Liliaceae, Trilliaceae, Pontederiaceae, Smilacaceae* with *Cyperaceae*. The *Juncales* have a typical lily-flower, but the floral parts are typically chaffy and like the parts of grass and sedge flowers.

B. There are families, neither advanced nor primitive, which appear to be related to a whole plexus of other families. The *Loganiales* comprising: *Buddlejaceae, Strychnaceae, Oleaceae,*

Loganiaceae and *Spigeliaceae* seem to have a plexus of affinity with the *Apocynales* comprising: *Apocynaceae, Periplocaceae* and *Asclepiadaceae*; the *Rubiaceae*; the *Bignoniales* comprising: *Cobaeaceae, Bignoniaceae* and *Pedaliaceae*; and the *Verbenales* comprising *Verbenaceae* amongst other families. In many ways the *Loganiales* appear to be a penultimate plexus from which the more advanced *Apocynales, Rubiales, Bignoniales,* and *Verbenales* have radiated.

Similar examples could be cited from the *Passiflorales* relating the *Cucurbitales* and *Loasales,* or the *Liliales* relating the *Agavales, Typhales, Iridales, Amaryllidales, Alstroemeriales* and *Juncales.*

C. There are families which have a number of affinities with other groups, none of which, however, appear ancestral to them. The *Caryophyllales* (the *Caryophyllaceae, Aizoaceae* and *Portulacaceae*) are generally accepted to have a plexus of relationships with *Lythrales* (the *Lythraceae* and *Onagraceae*); *Primulales* (*Primulaceae* and *Plumbaginaceae*); the *Polygonaceae*; *Plantaginaceae*; *Chenopodiaceae*; and the tropical *Phytolaccaceae*. However, the origins of the *Caryophyllales* lie far back in the past, as there are no clear links with the *Ranales* or *Magnoliales* from which they probably arose.

The same could be said for the origin of *Geraniales*, and of *Campanulales*, both groups nevertheless being important centres from which evolutionary trends appear to have radiated.

D. Finally there are families which are neither advanced nor primitive and which have no apparent relatives. Such are the *Casuarinaceae*; the *Garryaceae*; *Loranthaceae*; the tropical parasitic family *Balanophoraceae*; the *Santalaceae* and the *Coriariaceae*. The inability to establish family relationships in groups such as mistletoes or balanophoras is partly because they are parasites with a highly specialized way of life, causing them to differ radically from most other non-parasitic plants.

Wild flowers and cultivated flowers.

The concept of the wild flower as a subject for study may have its origin in man's cultivation of plants specially interesting to him for economic or aesthetic reasons. Plants are inherently variable and man soon came to appreciate that domestication often channels this variation into directions he could exploit. Archaeological investigation shows that man cultivated food and medicinal plants in prehistoric times, with cereals probably being grown as long ago as 7000 B.C. in the Near East. The cultivation of ornamental plants probably arose from their use in religious and sacrificial ceremonies with repeated selection of attractive plants from nature, and persistence in cultivation of the less demanding types. It is not impossible that prehistoric man cultivated ornamentals for their inherent beauty just as we do today.

With the passage of time cultivated plants tend to diverge from their wild relatives owing to conditions of cultivation, and indeed, new types may arise and be preserved in this artificial environment, which would soon die out in the wild. Thus, the wild flower and the cultivated one may become distinguishable but there are flowers grown as ornamentals which occur in an identical state in nature while at the other extreme there are ornamentals never found in the wild state. The changes that can occur in plants are more quickly realized under cultivation than in the wild because of reduced natural selection. Botanists have also made the point that wild flowers generally have a population structure in which inter-breeding takes place, the integrity of the species being maintained by barriers to out-breeding, which is not so in cultivated plants where the populations are at the mercy of man.

Cultivation of ornamentals has been closely linked with social organization and a healthy economic condition; it is an attendant feature of affluence. There is little evidence of flower cultivation in subsistence or nomadic societies, or societies where social strife is prevalent. The centres from which flower cultivation radiated are in what are now China, Mexico, Peru, Egypt and the Near East and recently western Europe. Each of these areas supported a sedentary and economically affluent society at some time in the past, during which flower culture became popular.

Where wild flowers grow.

The habitat
The environment in which wild flowers grow is the air layer up to approximately 100 feet (30 m.) above ground level, sometimes higher, and the earth down to 20 feet (6 m.) below ground level. In watering and tilling the soil, a gardener attends to but a few of the many factors which combine to form this environment.

Unlike animals which are mobile and derive their food either directly or indirectly from plants, these same plants make their own food from inorganic materials. Through the agency of sunlight and the green colouring matter chlorophyll, which occurs in the tissues of most plants, they compound water and nutrients from the soil and carbon dioxide from the air into foods and materials which form the basis for structures as large as trees and as small as duckweeds.

The environment can be divided into that above the soil in which the shoot grows, and the soil itself in which the roots grow.

Above the soil
Light is the source of energy which 'drives' the chemical food-making process called 'photosynthesis'. In daylight hours all green plants photosynthesize for some duration, but at night this process is discontinued, and the non-stop process called 'respiration' becomes detectable. Respiration is essentially the reverse of photosynthesis, being the process whereby food is chemically broken down in order to release energy for use in growth and the 'ticking over' of the plant.

Anyone who has tried unsuccessfully to grow plants under the shade of beech trees or who has noted the lack of undergrowth in shady woods, will appreciate the sensitivity of plants to shading. Not only must a certain intensity of light be available for photosynthesis to occur, but the amount and duration of light must allow the production of food in excess of that required by respiration, if the plant is not to die. No plant can tolerate conditions where respiration constantly burns up all the food manufactured by photosynthesis, for growth processes require an increasing supply of food.

To avoid the effects of insufficient light, many north temperate woodland herbs blossom vigorously in the spring, telescoping their life-cycle into the period before the foliage appears on the trees above. In summer, when the trees are in full leaf, the spring flowers have reproduced and are dying away for another season.

In tropical areas many plants avoid low light intensity by growing on the branches of those plants which would otherwise over-shade them, or by climbing over the crowns of trees many feet above the ground. These 'epiphytes' or 'lianes' as they are respectively called, rarely appear in temperate areas because there is usually insufficient moisture to support such luxuriant vegetation.

The life-processes inside plants are chemical in character, and like any chemical reaction, speed up when heated. There are optimal temperatures in which plants operate, above and below which there is a reduction in efficiency and at the extremes of which death occurs. It follows that arctic and antarctic plants have become adapted to endurance of temperatures very much lower than those to which temperate or equatorial plants are subject; such adaptations to temperature are to a greater or lesser degree fixed in plants. No amount of acclimatization is capable of altering the reaction of the plant to the temperature of its surroundings, short of hybridizing with a more tolerant type.

All flowering plants have tiny aeration pores, 'stomates', in the surfaces of the leaves, and while essential air can get into the leaf, water in the form of water-vapour can also leak out. High temperatures increase the amount of water lost from the leaves; hence plants growing in hot areas, like deserts, often have a leaf structure which helps to reduce water-loss.

Very low temperatures kill the tissues and growing points of plants by causing ice crystals to form in the delicate cells, rupturing the highly complicated membranes and interfering with the complex chemical reactions inside each cell. Buds situated below the ground are protected against temperature fluctuation and hence the proportion of stunted, bulb-, corm-bearing, and rhizomatous plants increases in floras of areas with extreme temperature conditions.

Water shortage is responsible for three basic types of shoot adaptation in plants which grow in arid areas. Some plants complete their life-cycle within the brief rainy season, and persist as seeds in the dry season, such as most annuals. These plants have no marked adaptation to dry conditions, for their growing phase effectively 'side-steps' the periods of desiccation. Other plants, such as cacti and euphorbias, develop succulent tissues. A third group of plants, with leathery leaves or woody tissues, are adapted to endure long periods of drought. Such plants often have remarkable powers of recovery following a shower of rain. The Creosote bush, *Larrea tridentata* (*Zygophyllaceae*), is such a drought-enduring plant.

Whatever the individual types of adaptation to aridity, when the rains appear the plants soon come into flower. Hundreds of acres may become carpeted in the blooms of single annual species or groups of annual species, as may be seen in tourist brochures and posters inviting the botanically inclined to holiday in South Africa.

The soil
The soil is the environment from which wild flowers derive their water and mineral salts, and in which the plant is usually anchored. All soils are derived from rock by weathering processes such as the chemical action of rain-water, or the fragmenting action of repeated freezing and thawing, or heating and cooling. The rate of weathering depends on the type of rock involved, and the type of climate, and these factors effect the type of soil produced. A great variety of soil types have come to exist, which differ in chemical composition, e.g. limy and volcanic, and physical structure, e.g. sandy and clayey. Certain plants grow best in soils derived from particular types of rock such as dolomite or serpentine: indeed the plants may have evolved into species on one particular type of rock substrate. It is precisely this sort of habitat information that is so valuable when a wild flower is being introduced into gardens.

The requirements of some plants limit their growth to only well developed soils; others may grow on freshly eroded rock debris, and may actually help to form soil. Some even grow on rock surfaces provided sufficient nutrients are washed over the rocks, or provided the rocks contain available nutrients.

A cyclic system develops as the soil gets older, in which the plants take minerals from the soil, but on their death replace the organic matter and salts extracted from it. Gardeners strive to attain and maintain this balanced system in aerating the soil by digging and laying drains, counteracting the tendencies toward acidity and alkalinity, fertilizing with animal and artificial manures and maintaining a good humus content with compost.

With poor aeration acidic conditions develop, and following the accumulation of water, iron and sulphur compounds and noxious gases may accumulate. With high temperatures, excessive breakdown of humus may occur to produce a highly mineral soil, as found in tropical areas, and typified by red lateritic soils. Excessive percolation through the soil may wash away essential salts from the areas penetrated by the roots. Thus, in nature optimal soil-forming conditions are not necessarily attained, and many soil conditions come to exist, discounting the differences based on parent-rock composition. This is the sort of diversity of soil type in which wild flowers must grow, reproduce, and evolve.

Just as an atmosphere of gases, mainly nitrogen, with lesser amounts of oxygen and carbon dioxide, surrounds the aerial shoots, so do gases held in the spaces between the soil particles surround the roots. The soil atmosphere around the roots of sand-dune plants is not dissimilar to that of the outside air, because shifting dunes are well aerated. At the other extreme, marshes and swamps are completely waterlogged and therefore poorly aerated. Plants successful in these habitats have roots adapted to operate in conditions of low oxygen content. In general terms, the amount of water in the soil governs the amount and quality of the soil atmosphere, which influences the root's capacity to absorb nutrients. While the soil should be continually moist, water should not occupy an excessive volume of air-space in the soil; the soil should be sufficiently porous to allow percolation with some retention, but not complete drainage. This is why the maintenance of an open crumb-structure in the soil, by digging and drainage, is so important in the garden.

Whatever the amount of water in the soil, there is never extensive water movement within the soil above the water-table. Once a plant exhausts the water in the immediate vicinity of its root system, it must extend its root system into untapped areas in the absence of prolonged rains. From the gardener's point of view, it is important to provide the roots with an adequate water supply, and this can only be done by really soaking the soil. A short period of irrigation, such as a short shower of rain, simply moistens the soil surface, stimulates rooting in the superficial layers of the soil, and may make the plants more vulnerable to the next dry spell. The evaporation of water from an acre completely covered with plants has been calculated to resemble that from an open surface of water of the same area, which indicates the need to provide an adequate water supply even in temperate areas.

Water is a liquid chemical peculiar in that it dissolves or partly dissolves so many different substances. It may be more than coincidence that water is the basis for life on Earth, as well as being the universal solvent. The soil water is in fact a dilute solution of various inorganic and organic substances, from which plants derive their essential minerals, such as nitrogen, phosphorous and calcium, as well as the water itself, which comprises about 90% of their weight. It is also peculiar that, while the plant is surrounded by abundant gaseous nitrogen, this is not directly available for its nutrition: nitrogen is obtained only when combined with other elements, the relatively small amounts of nitrate salts in the soil.

Mineral nutrients are held in the soil by complicated chemical phenomena which need not concern us here, but it should be noted that the condition or 'heart' of the soil can lock up otherwise abundant nutrients from the plants. The plant has to work to obtain these nutrients, for they do not simply diffuse into the roots. Chief among the factors controlling the availability of nutrients not already mentioned is the acidity-alkalinity state or pH of the soil. Some plants function better in acid, others in alkaline soils; hence one can predict the acidity of the soil by observing the plants that grow in it. Thus the Heather *Calluna*

vulgaris indicates that the soil is likely to be acidic while a mullein, such as *Verbascum thapsus*, that it is more likely to be alkaline in reaction.

The soil temperature also influences the process of absorption of nutrients. Freezing brings the activity in the soil to a standstill, locking up water and blocking the pore-spaces with ice crystals. High temperatures dry the soil and overactivate soilborne organisms, which deplete the humus content. As soil temperatures fluctuate less than air temperatures, and fluctuations cease about 2 feet (61 cm.) down, deep root systems are obviously advantageous. The colour of the soil determines the amount of heat absorbed and can influence germination rate, darker soils heating up more readily than light-coloured ones. The amount of water in the soil also determines how quickly it heats up. Aspect influences the rate at which soils heat up, by determining the angle, and therefore intensity, with which the rays of the sun strike the surface. Mulching has the effect of limiting the build up of temperature at the soil surface by day, and limiting the heat lost at night, thus having particular value for plants with superficial root systems. Small herbs growing in coarse turf are similarly buffered against sharp temperature fluctuations.

The millions of microscopic and sometimes visible plants and animals within the soil maintain a steady turnover of nutrients through the breakdown of dead plant and animal remains. Some of these microbes synthesize nitrogenous and other substances which wild flowers utilize; certain bacteria even live in nodules on the roots of leguminous plants. Many microscopic fungi are associated with the roots of orchids and heathers, without which the plants would not grow.

The ways in which wild flowers respond to the physical factors outlined above, and others not mentioned, have been intensively studied in the 20th century. Long before then it was already understood that certain types of vegetation characterize certain habitats. Thus the moorland of northern areas experiencing heavy rainfall, cool summers, and cold winters, is characterized by a flora of sedges, grasses, such as *Nardus stricta, Molinia caerulea* and *Eriophorum angustifolium*, rushes, Heather and species of the moss genus *Sphagnum* in damper parts. Until the late 1940's, botanists had tended simply to document the composition of different types of vegetation, the factors which brought together such combinations of plants being largely unknown. But in the last twenty-five years, statistical methods have been devised and used for the analysis of groups of wild flowers, or 'communities', as they are often called.

It has become statistically possible to distinguish between plants which grow together by chance, and others which grow together because of some shared factor or nearly similar requirement. Patterns of distribution in small areas of apparently homogeneous vegetation of one species, such as stands of the cottongrass *Eriophorum angustifolium*, can be detected, and these patterns can sometimes be correlated with environmental factors, or growth processes within the plants concerned. The occurrence of particular types of vegetation can sometimes be accurately correlated with climatic gradients over areas of hundreds of square miles, such as the hardwood forests of Wisconsin. Such quantitative description of vegetation often gives great precision to the botanist's work.

Wild flowers are not only influenced by the physical environment; they are also influenced by other plants and animals which surround them and live with them. The most conspicuous animal effects are those of man, where his use of herbicides, his agriculture, his warfare and cities have depauperated the wild flora. Even today the flora and fauna of the earth dwindles, for conservation contains no immediate financial reward or interest for men of western society. The mushrooming populations of Asia and Africa have even less interest, and certainly fewer facilities for conservation than the west, so there is little hope of preserving what remains of our natural habitat for more than one or two generations at the most.

The coexistence of plants and animals depends on a delicate balance of animal numbers, large, small, wild and domestic, that any particular vegetation can support. Any natural environment, be it woodland, seashore, pond or mountainside, contains a more or less balanced number of plants and animals, and any disturbance is expressed elsewhere in the system. For example, diminished numbers of rabbits in Britain following the spread of rabbit-disease in the 1950's, has led to the spread and establishment of tree seedlings and coarse turf in chalk grassland. This is because rabbits once maintained a short turf and destroyed tree seedlings by grazing. As a consequence, the habitats of a number of short-turf plant species are now threatened and the floristic composition of large areas of chalk grassland is changing.

The introduction of wild flowers into foreign floras has similar destructive effects, because there is usually no native plant or animal competition to keep numbers of the alien at a reasonable level. Only after great multiplication and spread of the alien, which demonstrates the great reproductive potential of organisms in the absence of natural checks, and only after the alien becomes regarded as a weed, do the numbers usually stabilize.

Domestic animals also upset floristic composition by grazing. Sheep grazed throughout the year on the Welsh uplands before the First World War and maintained high grade upland pasture, but an alteration of the domestic meat demand during the war brought about a change in the husbandry of the sheep, so that they were only allowed to graze during the summer. This allowed the spread of *Nardus stricta*, the Mat-grass, which went unchecked in the early spring months when its leaves are palatable, and which was uneaten in the summer when the foliage becomes coarse. In consequence there has been a deterioration of upland pastures and an alteration of the upland vegetation of Wales. Grazing by sheep and goats in the Mediterranean area has for centuries had the effect of restricting tree growth there and causing loss of soil through erosion.

While the effects of grazing are usually quite obvious, plants compete with each other in silent struggle, where cause and effect are not always easily defined. The leaf and root secretions of some plants inhibit or depress the vigour of surrounding plants. When Flax, *Linum usitatissimum*, is sown with a 10% mix of *Camelina alyssum* seed, leaf substances washed into the soil from the *Camelina* depress the yield of the Flax by nearly half, according to Grümmer and Beyer (1960). *Polygonum persicaria*, the Red Shank, is thought to release root substances capable of depressing the shoot yield of Potato or Flax by half, according to Martin and Rademacher (1960).

However, more usual forms of competition between plants are for light, where one casts excessive shade over another; for water where one has a more vigorous and extensive root system than another, or for space, where one species overwhelms another in terms of seedling numbers and general competition for nutrients. The speed and efficiency of this sort of competition is seen if a herbaceous border is left untended for a period of four or five years. The more aggressive species will dominate the bed, with the loss or poor representation of the less aggressive species. The gardener nullifies the competition between his garden plants by spacing, pruning, and dividing old plants.

Wild flowers, then, are continually subject to the influence of animals, each other, and, most important of all, a complex physical environment. The effects of these factors are twofold. Particular habitats become characterized by a particular vegetation, and also, the plants in the vegetation slowly change, or evolve, with the passage of time, in response to selection for survival in relation to the various sorts of interference experienced.

The geography

Just as there is a short term correlation between habitat and type of vegetation, so there is a more general and slowly produced correlation between geographical location, climate, and type of vegetation. Whereas silting of a lake may take a century to change the vegetation from that of open water, through marsh, to water-meadow, global vegetation changes, such as the migrations produced by the last Ice Ages in Europe and North America, take thousands of years to complete. The longer the time taken in vegetational change, the greater the likelihood for the component wild flowers also to have changed.

The global distribution of plants in relationship to latitude, longitude and altitude was first studied in the 19th century by men such as Humboldt (see p. 25) and Hooker (see p. 19). A broad pattern of vegetation types duplicate the climatic zones which encircle the land masses of the earth. As climatic zones are modified by altitude, proximity to the sea, and local topographical features, so these differences are reflected by modifications which appear in the vegetation. Some 6,146,000 square miles (15,918,000 sq. km.), or 12% of the land, are covered by arctic, antarctic or alpine vegetation; 12,020,000 square miles (31,131,700 sq. km.), or 23·5% of the land, are characterized by temperate vegetation; 17,418,000 square miles (45,112,400 sq. km.), or 34% of the land, by subtropical vegetation; and 15,715,000 square miles (40,721,600 sq. km.), or 30·5% of the land, by tropical vegetation, according to R. Good (1964), *The Geography of the Flowering Plants*.

Within these broad categories certain families occur more frequently in particular parts of the world. The *Caryophyllaceae*, *Cruciferae*, *Ranunculaceae*, *Rosaceae* and *Scrophulariaceae* occur more commonly in temperate parts of the world. The *Orchidaceae* and *Rubiaceae* are more common in the tropics. It is found that whereas the *Cruciferae* and *Umbelliferae* have predominantly temperate distribution, they are broadly equivalent and replaced in the tropics by the *Capparaceae* and *Araliaceae* respectively. Authors have also noted how common woody legumes, *Leguminosae*, are in equatorial forest, but how uncommonly scarce the *Compositae* and *Gramineae* are in the same habitat. The *Myrtaceae*, *Pittosporaceae* and *Proteaceae* are common in Australasia; the *Campanulaceae-Lobelioideae* are common in Hawaii. More detailed peculiarities of family distribution exist, such as the poor representation of *Theaceae* in Africa and Australia, or the poor representation of *Taccaceae* in tropical America. Families with species confined to fresh or salt-water habitats tend to have widespread distribution by virtue of their habitat requirements, such as *Alismataceae* and *Lemnaceae*.

Certain parts of the world, particularly tropical regions, support a richer flora than others. The 31,600 square miles (81,844 sq. km.) of Panama support seven thousand five hundred species, yet the 32,000 square miles (82,880 sq. km.) of Austria support only two thousand three hundred species; the 228,000 square miles (590,520 sq. km.) of Madagascar contain some six thousand species, while the 226,000 square miles (585,340 sq. km.) of Germany contain only two thousand six hundred species. Exhaustive botanical collecting over an area of 200 square miles (518 sq. km.) of rugged topography on Cape Peninsula in South Africa would involve finding about two thousand five hundred species, whereas the 150 gently undulating square miles (389 sq. km.) of the Isle of Wight, off the south coast of England, would yield only some eight hundred and fifty species. As a generalization it is true to say that tropical Africa is poorer in species than either tropical America or tropical Asia, and that tropical America is richer in ornamental and striking plants than tropical Asia.

Although the distribution of any particular group of plants is slowly changing, as indeed are geographical features on a geological time-scale, it is possible and convenient to recognize certain types of distribution into which most wild flowers fall. These types of distribution are as follows.

1. Cosmopolitan distribution.
Genera such as *Senecio* (*Compositae*) and *Drosera* (*Droseraceae*) extend over a wide range of temperate, subtropical and tropical areas, but as in most cosmopolitan groups, do not extend into the polar regions. Certain species including a number of weeds are nowadays also cosmopolitan, such as Shepherd's Purse, *Capsella bursa-pastoris* (*Cruciferae*); Broad-leaf Plantain, *Plantago major* (*Plantaginaceae*); and Bermuda Grass, *Cynodon dactylon* (*Gramineae*). Certain aquatic plants also have a cosmopolitan distribution, such as the Common Reed, *Phragmites australis* (syn. *P. communis*).

2. Tropical distribution.
Genera such as *Bauhinia* (*Leguminosae*), *Hibiscus* (*Malvaceae*), and *Phyllanthus* (*Euphorbiaceae*) occur throughout the tropical regions of the world, and are not usually found elsewhere. The palms, *Palmae*, are an essentially tropical family, but genera also extend into the subtropics and Mediterranean area. Map 1 shows the distribution of the *Palmae*.

3. Temperate distribution.
Genera such as *Iris* (*Iridaceae*), *Aquilegia* (*Ranunculaceae*) and *Ribes* (*Grossulariaceae*) occur mainly in the temperate parts of the world. The way in which altitudes modify climatic and vegetable zonation is illustrated in the distribution of *Ribes*, species of which extend as a distributional lobe along the Andean chain, cutting through tropical and subtropical climates alike, see Map 2. Some temperate groups, such as *Polemonium* (*Polemoniaceae*) and *Asarum* (*Aristolochiaceae*) are confined to temperate areas without extending at high altitudes into tropical areas.

4. Discontinuous distribution.
Genera such as *Meconopsis* (*Papaveraceae*), *Hibbertia* (*Dilleniaceae*), *Magnolia* (*Magnoliaceae*), *Nepenthes* (*Nepenthaceae*), *Fuchsia* (*Onagraceae*), and *Gunnera* (*Gunneraceae*) and *Eryngium* (*Umbelliferae*) occur in two or more widely separated geographical areas. Genera such as these pose the most difficult problems. How were their present distributions attained? *Meconopsis* species are mostly found in the Himalaya and China, but a single isolated species, *M. cambrica* (see plate 11) occurs in western Europe; *Hibbertia* is found in Australasia and Madagascar (see plate 128); magnolias occur in eastern Asia and northeast America (see plates 90 and 150) and are not the only plants to have this particular Old World, New World distribution. *Fuchsia* occurs in New Zealand and tropical America (see plates 133 and 173). Families as well as genera show discontinuous distribution, such as the *Liliaceae* (*Philesiaceae*) in South America, South Africa and Australasia, and *Eucryphiaceae* in Australasia and South America. Map 3 shows the distribution of the *Eucryphiaceae*.

The factors governing existing plant distributions must involve both the past geomorphological history of the Earth, and the past evolution of flowering plants. Present distributions are the outcome of an interplay between these two factors. In recent years, geophysical and geological information suggests that the continents have drifted apart from what was once a united and ancient land-mass. This notion is upheld by and partly explains some discontinuous distributions for if the edges of the continents of America, Africa and Australasia were fitted into each other, jig-saw fashion, the distribution becomes continuous! This can be said for the distributions of *Hibbertia*, *Gunnera* and *Symphonia* (*Guttiferae*) and the family *Proteaceae*.

5. Endemic distribution
Genera such as *Arctagrostis* (*Gramineae*), *Haberlea* (*Gesneriaceae*), *Sarracenia* (*Sarraceniaceae*), *Napoleonaea* (*Lecythidaceae*), *Gasteria* (*Liliaceae*), *Rafflesia* (*Rafflesiaceae*), *Sinningia* (*Gesneriaceae*), and *Eccremocarpus* (*Bignoniaceae*) all occur in one geographical area only, and often have a limited distribution in that area. *Arctagrostis* is confined to arctic regions, *Haberlea* to the mountains of the Balkan Peninsula, *Napoleonaea* to tropical Africa, *Gasteria* to South Africa and *Sinningia* to Brazil. Families such as *Tropaeolaceae*, map 4, and *Cephalotaceae*, map 4, are also endemic, being confined to South America and south-west Australia respectively.

Plant distributions in reality only represent a phase in a slowly changing patchwork of plant migration. Some groups will never become cosmopolitan. Some endemic genera such as *Delonix* (*Leguminosae*), confined in the natural state to a small area of Madagascar and to India, may be groups of great antiquity now on the decline, but others such as *Neocogniauxia* (*Orchidaceae*), confined to the West Indies, may simply be evolutionary products with very restricted ranges; they may not need or have the potential to occupy a wide distribution. It is anthropomorphic to assume that only widespread species and common species are successful.

Precisely how many plant seeds and other propagules move about is still unknown. Some seeds like those of the Seychelles Palm, *Lodoicea*, are washed up on shores all around the Indian Ocean, but how far can tiny orchid seeds blow? Birds most certainly carry some seeds across wide stretches of sea, such as the Atlantic Ocean, either in their stomachs or on plumage or feet. Other seeds are known to have been spread on drift wood or by flotation in ocean currents, still retaining their viability despite the surrounding brine; but we still know little about how plants travel about.

With so many different ways of potential dispersal, and because seeds differ in size and length of viability, it becomes obvious that rates of migration are not necessarily similar. 'Migration of genera' is an often discussed topic in plant geography, but is only a simplified descriptive term for the spread or contraction of the ranges of species, which are continually changing, evolving, and able to fit into new habitats in a continually changing environment. Some plants probably spread into new territory across tracts of land (land-bridges) now covered by sea, under past climatic conditions differently distributed from those of today, as is indicated by coal-measures found in parts of Antarctica. It is sobering to think that, as we fly to the Moon, we are still ignorant of the plants upon which we ultimately depend for our existence.

Learning about wild flowers.

The acquisition of knowledge about plants has been a long varied process involving many enthusiastic men, mainly European in the early days, who dedicated themselves to a study of plants, and dependent upon the interaction of many cultural, economic and 'political' factors. The political and colonial development of newly acquired territories led to the gathering of information about the floras of areas such as South Africa, India and South East Asia. Horticultural exploitation of new floras, such as those of North America and China, increased our knowledge of the native plants of these regions. Expeditions of scientific enquiry have been a major source of information on the plants of distant lands, some led and financed by individuals, others backed by various governments. In more recent years, the universities and botanical societies of particular countries have carried out research on their own flora in contrast to the international research which was largely centred in European institutions in previous

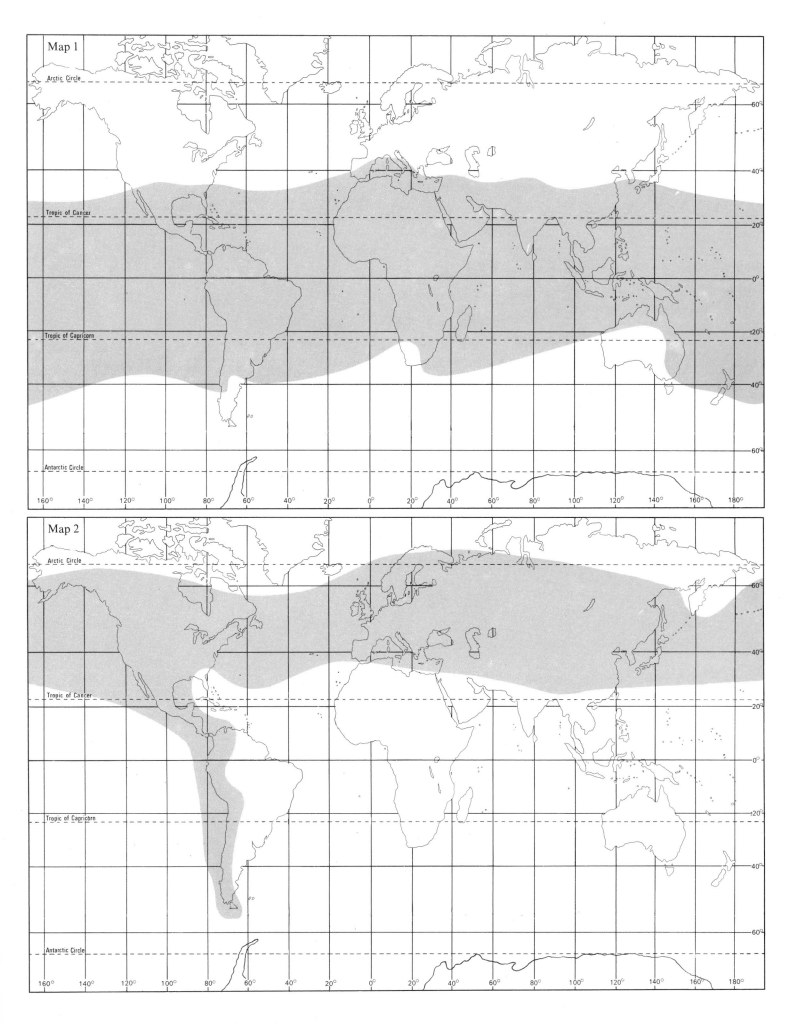

Map 1   Tropical and subtropical distribution: *Palmae*

Map 2   Temperate distribution: *Ribes*

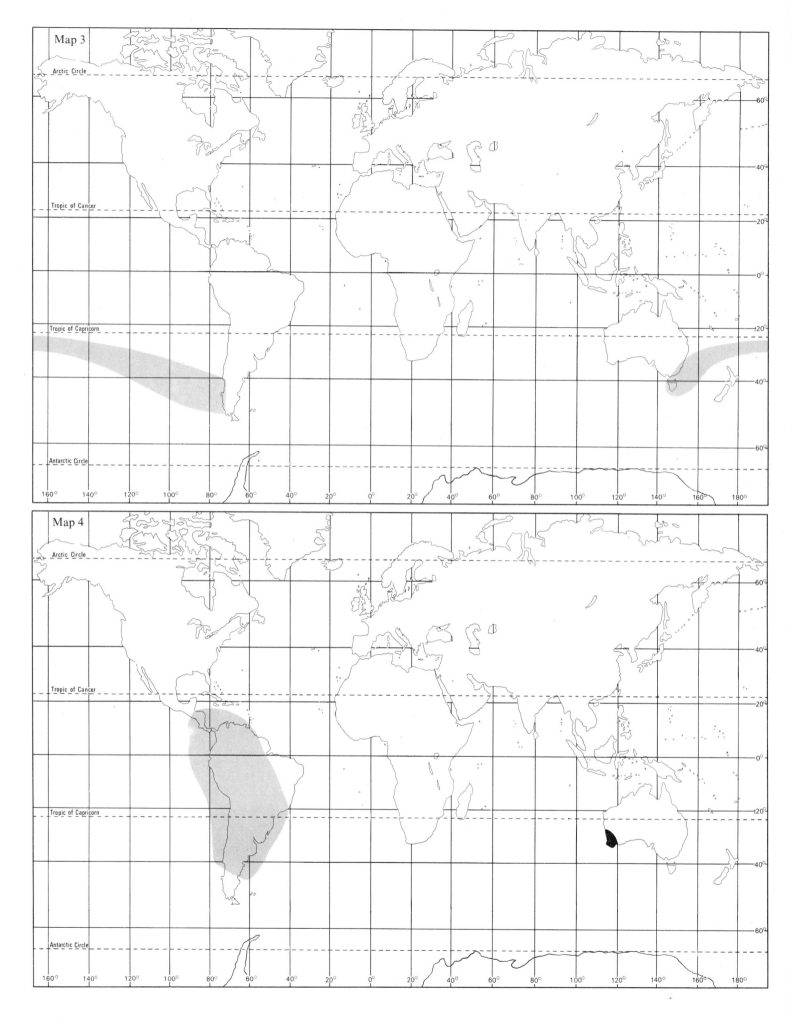

Map 3   Discontinuous distribution: *Eucryphia*

Map 4   Endemic distribution: *Tropaeolaceae* (Central and South America) *Cephalotaceae* (Australia)

centuries. But let us go back to the first botanists and see what they knew about wild flowers.

The beginnings in Europe.

In most parts of the western world, botanical exploration began in the 16th or 17th centuries and grew out of the search for medicinal plants or 'simples' by herb gatherers. Botany is organized knowledge about plants. The men influential during its formative years were mostly physicians often with a general interest in natural history, but their enquiries would have been restricted and of little avail but for technical improvement in the graphic arts and particularly the woodcut, and the spread of the use of paper and the printing press.

The Medieval world of the 13th century received from Arabic sources the classical teachings of the Greeks, Aristotle (384–322 B.C.) and his successor Theophrastus (*c.* 370–287 B.C.), who made an *Enquiry into Plants.* However, of greater fame in the Middle Ages was a book called in Latin *De Materia medica* by the Greek Dioscorides (1st century A.D.), which consisted of accounts of medicinal plants, mostly derived from earlier sources. Dioscorides was a widely travelled medical man, a contemporary of Nero and Vespasian. Even at the height of the Renaissance, Dioscorides' writings were still regarded as infallible and the absolute authority concerning wild plants.

It was the medieval scholastic attitude of reliance upon received authority rather than of continuous reference to nature which led to the deterioration of plant illustration as generation after generation of artists copied and contributed errors to the originals. Even Pliny, a contemporary of Dioscorides and who wrote an encyclopaedic natural history, complained of the deterioration of plant portraiture in his day. By the end of the 13th century, many illustrations had sunk to the level of ornamental shapes bearing little relation to any plant, and in no small way due to the contemporary artistic fashion for stylization. Indeed, the origins of the woodcut were in the decoration of textiles, which helps to explain the symbolic and bold style of the period. A few original minds such as Albertus Magnus and Rufinus wrote descriptions indicating firsthand observation but in general descriptions of plants by writers such as Dioscorides were simply copied without improvement.

The study of plants began to alter, like philosophy, sculpture and painting as sceptics questioned the authority of the Church, as Michelangelo provided an alternative to the classical nude, and Dürer's woodcut techniques revolutionized plant illustration. The need to understand and remedy universal problems such as plague, and the growing forces of witchcraft, spurred doctors and physicians to acquire a greater knowledge of simples and created a demand for herbals, or books of 'medicinal' herbal descriptions, the development of which we may briefly consider.

The transition from crude plant symbolism to attractive representations came suddenly with the publication of Otto von Brunfels' (1464–90?-1534) *Herbarum vivae Eicones* in 1530. The author, once a Carthusian monk, later a Lutheran, taught for some years in Strasbourg before becoming a physician in Berne shortly before his death. Hans Weiditz, one of the Dürer school, illustrated the herbal with drawings made direct from living, though sometimes limp and wilting, plants. Brunfels is commemorated in the solanaceous genera *Brunfelsia* and *Brunfelsiopsis.*

Nine years later Hieronymus Bock (1498–1554) provided his *New Kreutterbuch,* which was at first unillustrated, but contained descriptions far superior to those of Brunfels. Bock followed a classical scheme of arranging his plants under the headings trees, shrubs, and herbs, and this was better than the alphabetical arrangement which appeared in Leonhart Fuchs' (1501–1556) *De Historia Stirpium,* published in 1542. However, Fuchs' herbal contained excellent illustrations, perhaps the best produced in his era, and they continued to be used in works as late as those of Bauhin in 1650. Fuchs is commemorated in the genus *Fuchsia.*

Mathias de L'Obel was born in Lille in 1538, and studied at Montpelier under Guillaume Rondelet, after whom *Rondeletia* is named. In 1570 de L'Obel published with Pierre Pena the *Stirpium adversaria nova,* which represented a major advance of plant classification. The plants are arranged according to leaf characters, an arrangement that broadly anticipated the modern concept of monocotyledons (with parallel veined leaves) and dicotyledons (with net-veined leaves). De L'Obel died in 1616, and is commemorated by the genus *Lobelia.*

Pierandrea Mattioli was born in 1501, a native of Siena, and died at the age of 76 in 1577, a victim of the plague. His *Commentari,* first published in 1544, contains very elegant and characteristically well filled woodcuts, which showed that botanical illustration could be aesthetic as well as scientific. The crucifer genus *Matthiola* is named after this Italian botanist.

Another Italian, Andrea Cesalpino (1519–1603), produced a book called *De Plantis Libri* in 1583 which was the first theoretical botany book of the Renaissance. Cesalpino recognised the importance of reproductive structures in plants, but, as his classification was based solely on these characters, it was largely artificial and limited in its usefulness. Cesalpino is commemorated in the leguminous genus *Caesalpinia.*

Charles de L'Ecluse (1526–1609) was a close friend of de L'Obel, and in 1601 published his *Rariorum Plantarum Historia,* which included the first serious writings on fungi—mushrooms, moulds and toadstools, as well as numerous detailed descriptions of then little-known flowering-plants, remarkable for their clarity and accuracy. The illustrations in de L'Ecluse often feature fruits and other details of botanical value, and it seems that the author closely supervised the artist, Pierre van der Borcht. De L'Ecluse was a multilingual scholar of great erudition, and amongst other works, he translated Nicolas Monardes' Spanish writings on South American plants into Latin, and Garcia da Orta's writings on Indian plants from Portuguese into Latin. His botanical travels took him into the Iberian Peninsula, Austria and Hungary, and he is commemorated in the genus *Clusia* and *Clusiella.*

It is in the *Pinax Theatri botanici* of Kaspar Bauhin (1560–1624), published in 1623, that the affinities of plants as we now see them, began to fall into place. Kaspar, the brother of Johann Bauhin (1541–1612), recognized daisies, crucifers and poppies as discrete groups, but he largely failed to distinguish other plant groups which we now call families. Kaspar also listed about six thousand species with the names of their authors, so that the growing number of names was for once recorded in a single reference book. This list proved to be of use to botanists such as Linnaeus as late as 1730. Many of Bauhin's plants were given two names, binomials, consisting of the equivalents of genus and species, which is in accord with, and anticipated modern practice. While Bauhin served plant classification, the original illustrations that accompanied his works were of little artistic merit. The Bauhin brothers are commemorated in the genus *Bauhinia.*

The end of the 16th century saw the rise of metal engraving, and the decline of the woodcut, for the former allowed more detail. The 17th century saw many books illustrated by copper plates, though engravings were so much more expensive than woodcuts, and the text more difficult to relate to the pictures for technical reasons.

In summary we see the development of competence in illustrating and describing plants immediately follows the Renaissance, so that when K. Bauhin's *Pinax* was published, several thousand names existed. As even more material accumulated, a system of classification in which the data could be accommodated became urgently needed. There have indeed been many attempts since then to devise systems taking note of increasing knowledge but without any one becoming completely accepted.

The influence of individuals.

Without the enthusiasm and dedication of certain individuals, our knowledge of wild flowers would be infinitely smaller. One of many such men was Georg Everhard Rumpf (often latinized as Georgius Everhardus Rumphius). Born about 1627, he spent his youth in Hanau (near Frankfurt) on the river Main, and enlisted in the so-called 'Venetian Army' as a young man. In fact, the recruits were intended for trans-shipment from Texel in the Netherlands to Venice, and then would have been shipped to Brazil for service in the Dutch West Indies Company. However, the scheme misfired, for the ship in which Rumpf travelled was attacked by a Portuguese vessel, and the captives enlisted in the Portuguese Army. Such were international relations in the early 17th century.

Sometime in 1648 or 1649, Rumpf left Portugal and returned to Hanau where he stayed for a time, but late in 1652 he enlisted in the Dutch East Indies Company, and sailed from Texel on the Boxing Day of that year. Rumpf arrived at Batavia, in Java, in 1653, and in the November he travelled to the island of Amboina in the Moluccas, an island which he was to make famous. In 1657 he was transferred from maritime to civil duties, and by 1661 had earned a worthy position in the service. It was at this time, when nothing was known of the natural history of the Moluccas, or Indonesia in general, that he developed a great interest in botany and zoology which was to remain with him until he died.

He obtained books to further his studies through, and with the permission of, the Company. However, in 1670 Rumpf became blind, and his whole future was threatened. The Governor of Amboina, Jacob Cops, informed Rumpf that his services were no longer required, he was an encumbrance; but the Governor-General in Batavia, called Maetsuycker, was sympathetic towards Rumpf's studies, and over-ruled Cops. Owing to his long and satisfactory term of service, the Company retained Rumpf in an advisory capacity on a full salary, and allowed his studies to proceed unhindered, if this was possible with the naturalist's affliction. This partial solution to Rumpf's problems was only short-lived; some four years later in 1674 an earthquake shook Amboina and falling rubble tragically killed his wife and youngest daughter.

Slowly the blind man regained interest in natural history after the loss of most of his family, and in 1679 the Company provided Rumpf with a secretary, in 1680 an assistant, and in 1686 his son, Paul, was transferred from Batavia to Amboina, where he helped his father with the description and illustration of the natural history of the island. Rumpf had made his own illustrations when he had been able to see, and his written descriptions possess a clarity and vividness borne of delight in close observation of tropical plants. The information obtained from many years of work in Amboina filled twelve volumes, which were to serve as a foundation for later botanical investigation in the East Indies. When the text was ready and about half the illustrations prepared, a fire swept through the Dutch quarter of the island, and destroyed most of Rumpf's books, collections and manuscripts, together with the drawings Rumpf had done in his early years.

The government provided an artist called van Eyck, who together with Paul Rumpf and other helpers, made ready the first six volumes once more. The merit of the work so impressed the Governor-General of Batavia, Camphuys, that he ordered it to be copied, a most wise precaution. The first six volumes were sent by sea to Holland in 1692, but the French sunk the unfortunate vessel on its way home, with the entire loss of its cargo. Camphuys

now had the six volumes copied for the third time, and together with volumes 7, 8 and 9 they successfully reached Holland in 1696. Volumes 10, 11 and 12 also followed without mishap.

The Directors of the Company in Amsterdam were much impressed with Rumpf's work, but did not publish despite the requests of several printers in 1700, a time when botanical interest in South East Asian plants was on the increase in Europe. Yet some three months after the death of Rumpf in 1702, the Company made unsuccessful attempts to find publishers, and it was not until 1736 that Johann Burman (1706–1779) undertook to produce the *Amboinsche Kruidboek*. It was published in six volumes with nearly seven hundred plates between 1741 and 1755, and contains descriptions of some twelve hundred species, thus being the first botanical studies ever carried out in a tropical area.

Like Rumpf, Michel Adanson (1727–1806) was another pioneer of tropical plant study. Adanson studied botany in Paris under his fellow Frenchman Bernard de Jussieu (1699–1776) where he spent six years. Wishing to obtain first hand experience in the tropics, Adanson obtained a passage and post in the French East India Company in Senegal, in West Africa. At that time no naturalist had ventured into West Africa.

He left Paris on 20 December 1748, and sailed from Port de l'Orient on 3 March 1749, proceeding through stormy seas much to his discomfort for he suffered from chronic sea-sickness. The ship entered the mouth of the river Senegal, which he called river Niger, with some difficulty on 25 April, losing one man from the ship's boat before dropping anchor at nightfall.

Adanson was received by the Director-General, M. de la Brue, who subsequently provided him with guides, transport and interpreters. Adanson was intrigued by this new world, and in no small way by the African women, who he said were 'perfect beauties'. 'They have a great share of vivacity, and a vast deal of freedom and ease, which renders them extremely agreeable'. After familiarizing himself with the language and customs of the people, he began his wanderings on the deltaic island called Sor. The simple tribal dwellings, and the unaffected behaviour and manner of the Africans appealed to him, while his compliance with local custom made him acceptable to the local inhabitants. However, he never came to accept the dung-plastered walls of the village huts, which he remarks 'stunk abominably'.

Three days voyage up the river Senegal after 30 June brought him to Podor, where he witnessed Africans amusing themselves by riding on ostriches and the strength of the birds amazed him. No less interesting were the elephants, hippopotami and crocodiles found along and in the river. In August, he made another trip to the nearby island of Sor, where he found a tree with a greatly thickened trunk some 65 feet (19·8 m.) in circumference. This was the Baobab which was later named *Adansonia* after him (see plate 76).

Soon after, Adanson made a stormy voyage to the island of Goree, south of Cape Verde, and later accompanied a trading party to the mainland where he found the Silk-cotton tree, *Ceiba* species, the trunks of which are soft and utilized for the construction of canoes. After a dangerous canoe journey through the surf to the ship, Adanson returned to Goree. There followed a short excursion to the twin Magdalen Islands, only one of which was accessible. On the return voyage to Senegal, he caught four European Swallows, and concluded that they migrate from Europe to Africa in Autumn, after nesting in the north, for he says he found no nests in Senegal during his stay.

On a second trip to Podor, new plants, insects, birds and other animals constantly appeared before him. He often went ashore and continued along the bank while the canoe followed him upstream and he was much impressed with the forested banks of the Senegal, hung with flowers, but the oppressive heat and the often thorny bush wearied him. It was November, and the hottest part of the year, with mosquitoes and bees adding to the discomfort of the journey. He made observations on the 9–10 feet (2·7–3 m.) tall termite-mounds which dot the landscape around Podor, before returning to the coast.

In January 1750, Adanson set out on a trip to the river Gambia, to Albreda upstream on the north bank from what is now Bathurst. In Albreda he witnessed the ravages of locust-swarms, although on finding that the locals ate these insects, wryly said 'I should willingly resign whole clouds of locusts to the Negroes of Gambia, for the meanest of their fishes'. In his narrative, Adanson took great pains to correct misinterpretation and misappellation, and it is this hard-headed clarity for which he is remembered today. In March Adanson set sail for Goree, where he stayed for a time, before being driven from his dwelling, not to say severely bitten, by small ants which lived in the soil under his hut.

It seems that because Adanson exposed himself to the daily danger of crossing the surfy waters between Goree and the mainland in an open canoe, the Director of the island arranged for him to stay with the head of a tribe not far south of Cape Verde, in late April 1750. Here he saw *Kigelia*, with its sausage-like fruits (see plate 62), more Baobabs, and watched the locals tap palms for their sap. This juice ferments of its own accord to yield an intoxicating beverage, not unlike a wine. In early May, while walking along the beach from Ben to Rufik, he was unaccountably, but unsuccessfully, attacked by an African, a serious occurrence as he was alone in this then remote part of West Africa. On the same day he returned to Goree, no doubt ill at ease, and a month later returned to Senegal, where the ship had to stand off shore for four days owing to adverse winds. His discomfort aboard the vessel can be detected in his reflection that someone might study the causes of sea-sickness with a view to curing it. After this trip he resolved not to put to sea again until his return to France.

Between September 1750 and August 1753, he made short but intensive journeys in the estuarine region of the Senegal and as far inland as Podor. In March 1751, he canoed around Sor island. It is illuminating to find how often Adanson the naturalist used his gun, sometimes killing for the joy of it, while the 'uncivilized' natives more often resented his killing of inedible animals with the true spirit of the conservationists. Anyone reading Adanson's narrative should remember that he recorded temperatures in units Reaumur, not Fahrenheit or Centigrade. The 60·3° he noted amongst some sand-dunes was sufficient to cook the eggs that he buried, being equivalent to about 167°F. or 75°C.

Despite the adverse conditions in which Adanson worked, where mosquitoes and vicious flies swarmed about the explorer and his party, he still expressed rapture about the birds and new plants he saw. In November 1752, he made a most exhausting trip from the coast to Galel across scorching sands, and unlike his native companions could not bring himself to remedy his weariness by rubbing his forehead with a live toad! In July 1753, Adanson made his final trip to Podor in order to collect a last selection of woody plants to take back for cultivation in France. On this trip he was taken ill for the first time and he was still recouperating when he embarked on a ship bound for France in September.

Ill winds, calms, and the need to call at the Azores for water and provisions, followed by eight weeks of storms nearing the French coast, caused the voyage home to last until the beginning of January. He arrived in Paris during February 1754, where the bitter winter of that year killed the remaining live plants the voyage had failed to take.

As stated by Stearn in 1961, 'Adanson was a man of independent and original ideas, which did not commend themselves to his contemporaries, neither by their content nor presentation . . . he spent four years and four months in complete mental isolation from the small crude European trading community, eagerly studying plants, animals, customs, dialects etc., like A. R. Wallace later in Malaysia, and burning with ideas and observations that seemed to him new and important. The bewildering diversity of tropical vegetation made the systems of classification proposed by Tournefort and Linnaeus appear pitifully inadequate. . . . The new plants Adanson found at almost every step would not fit into the genera and classes founded on the corolla and stamens by [Joseph Pitton] Tournefort [(1656–1708)] and Linnaeus. He therefore made other systems . . . in all sixty-five systems, and he found them equally unsatisfactory . . . Adanson's rejection of Linnaean nomenclature was even less acceptable to his classically minded contemporaries than his rejection of Linnaean classification, and his attempt to make French spelling completely phonetic probably also displeased them. . . . That seventy or more generic names coined or adopted by Adanson ahead of other now better known names for the same groups are listed in the *International Code of Botanical Nomenclature* as names to be rejected, is both a tribute to his taxomonic judgment and originality in distinguishing the genera concerned and a condemnation of his linguistic unorthodoxy'. His *Familles des Plantes* published in 1763 is a pioneer work in 'natural classification', classification based on the maximum characters available for study, but his adoption of such uncouth names as *Katoutsjeroe* and *Tsjerucanitam* repelled other botanists and led to the neglect of his ideas and his nomenclature.

Rumpf and Adanson worked in solitude in the East Indies and West Africa respectively, where they were out of touch with botanical thought in Europe, but in contrast, Joseph Dalton Hooker became director of the Royal Botanic Gardens at Kew in his later years, and so occupied a focal position of European botanical activity. He was born in Halesworth, Suffolk, England, on 30 June 1817, the younger of two sons of William Jackson Hooker, one time Professor of Botany at Glasgow University, and Director of the Royal Botanic Gardens, Kew before his son.

By the time Joseph Hooker had come of age, he had proved himself to be a competent botanist and entomologist, and in 1839 when he graduated, his father's reputation helped the young man to be appointed Assistant Surgeon and Naturalist aboard the 'Erebus' on the Ross Expedition to Antarctica. The sister ship to the 'Erebus' was the 'Terror', and both set sail in September 1839, bound for Madeira. They also landed on Teneriffe, the Cape Verde Islands and St Helena, making magnetic recordings before arriving at the Cape. Unlike his close friend, Charles Darwin, who also made a long voyage as a young man, Hooker never suffered from sea-sickness. From the Cape the expedition proceeded to Kerguelen Island, where it remained for about two and a half months, during which time Hooker found about a hundred and fifty species, including the cabbage-like *Pringlea antiscorbutica* (see plate 1). Some of his collections seem to have been obtainable only by his sitting on them to thaw them from the ice, and it is recorded that gales were blowing for forty-five of the sixty-eight days spent at anchor off Kerguelen.

Then late in July they sailed across the South Indian Ocean, losing one crew-member overboard in those stormy seas, before landing in Tasmania. At this time Captain Dumont D'Urville aboard 'L'Astrolabe' and Captain Charles Wilkes aboard 'Porpoise' were exploring in antarctic waters for their respective governments, France and the United States. Disturbing reports that both foreign expeditions had already discovered land at about 67°S, were received by the Ross Expedition. When Ross left Tasmania some three months later, he struck south in a different direction from that which the French and American expeditions had taken.

Sailing via Auckland Island and Campbell Island, where

Hooker made important collections which formed the basis for his *Flora Antarctica*, the expedition penetrated to 78°3′S. While their main aim was to visit the south magnetic pole, they were frustrated in finding its location some hundred and sixty miles (258 km.) from the sea, and were unable to make the overland trip. They did however plot much of the coast of Victoria Land before meeting up with the Ross Ice Barrier which impeded further progress south. They unwittingly entered what is now called McMurdo Sound, and saw for the first time the 13,000 foot (4000 m.) antarctic volcano set in a snowy scene of pinks and golds with its column of smoke rising unbroken for miles into the blue sky. This they called Mount Erebus, and it was to become a familiar landmark for later antarctic explorers such as Scott and Fuchs.

They returned to Tasmania, then after a rainy stay in Sydney, on to New Zealand, where Hooker met the famous plant collector the Reverend W. Colenso. They made a second trip into antarctic waters in November 1841. From early December until February 1842 they were driven deep into pack-ice, and on New Year's Day a spirited party was held on the ice beside the ship to keep up morale. A storm in mid-January battered the tiny vessels, the ice rubble heaving and crashing against the trembling ships' timbers. They finally reached the impenetrable Ice Shelf, before heading north once more, rounding Cape Horn and landing in the Falkland Islands where the ships were repaired in April 1842. Hooker botanized in the area in an exhaustive way, including the Magellan Straits, and the nearby Hermite Island, and later incorporated his findings in his *Flora Antarctica*. After a third voyage in antarctic waters, the expedition turned for home via the Cape of Good Hope, and arrived in England in September 1843, after having spent four years away.

Hooker worked on his antarctic flora for a time, but then became employed in the Geological Survey, and worked with fossil plants. It was in this connection that he embarked on a trip to northern India in 1847, financed by the Treasury, and sent live and pressed plants to Kew, where his father was Director. He travelled via Lisbon, Gibraltar, Malta, Alexandria, Suez, before the canal was built, and on to desolate Aden, then Ceylon, Madras and Calcutta. After visiting the famous Calcutta Botanic Gardens, he explored the valley of the river Damuda, and Mount Parasnath—sacred to the Jains, before crossing the river Son to Mirzapur. From there he travelled down the river Ganges and arrived at Darjeeling in April 1848, where he spent the summer. His ascent to Darjeeling took him through tropical leech-infested forest, and gradually more temperate vegetation types as he got higher, on which he made observations and began to formulate his ideas on plant distribution.

Late in 1848 he made an expedition on foot to Kanchenjunga and the surrounding area, through Nepal into Sikkim. Wallanchoon in Nepal was a particularly profitable area in which he worked, before he crossed the Singalila Range in Sikkim, where trouble awaited him. The Sikkimese authorities, and the Prime Minister in particular, were uncooperative, but after Dr Archibald Campbell, British Political Agent to Sikkim, had consultation with the Raja, permission was given for Hooker to botanize the southern slope of Kanchenjunga down to the river Ratong. In May 1849 Hooker made another expedition to higher altitudes in eastern Sikkim and Tibet, proceeding from Darjeeling up the river Tista and its tributaries. At about 12,000 feet (about 3660 m.) in the river Zamu valley, he found *Rheum nobile*, illustrated on plate 96. After ascending to between 19,000 and 20,000 feet (5800–6100 m.), and in so doing becoming the holder of the world altitude record—18,130 feet (5526 m.)—until 1856, he descended to more comfortable heights at Yumtang where he met and continued with Campbell down to Tsungtang. Hooker and Campbell returned to climb Mount Pauhunri and

Mount Bhomtso before visiting the Raja's palace on their way to the Chola Pass.

It was in Chumanako in November that the travellers were arrested by about ninety armed Tibetans and imprisoned in the Raja's capital. Campbell, with whom the Sikkimese had a quarrel, was tortured and maltreated, but Hooker was unharmed during their seven weeks as hostages. Their capture aroused concern at home, when the news appeared in the European press and culminated in Sikkim being annexed to the British Crown.

During the early months of 1850, Hooker transported his not inconsiderable collections to Calcutta, where he joined forces with his old college friend Dr Thomas Thomson, on a trip into the Khasi Hills of Assam. They spent about seven months in the hills and collected more than two thousand five hundred species before Hooker returned to Calcutta in February 1851, and went home.

Apart from trips to Russia and Morocco, and one to western North America, the rest of Hooker's life was associated with the botanic gardens at Kew, and his publication of a number of great floristic works. He became Director of the Gardens in succession to his father in November 1865, a post which he held for twenty years. During this time the Cedar Avenue, Holly Walk, Berberis Dell, the Pinetum, the T-Range, including the *Victoria amazonica* house, the Rock Garden, the beautiful Marianne North picture gallery, Wing C of the Herbarium, and the old Jodrell Laboratory were added to the gardens. The water supply to the gardens was also improved during his administration.

Among Hooker's many contributions to botany was the distribution of South American rubber plants to Malaya and the East via Kew, which helped to initiate the rubber industry in South East Asia. He also made important contributions to the science of plant distribution, as well as publishing several floras including *Flora Antarctica, Flora Novae Zelandiae, Flora Tasmaniae,* the *Handbook of the New Zealand Flora.* Other publications were *Himalaya Journals, The Rhododendrons of Sikkim-Himalaya,* the *Flora of British India* with T. Thomson, *Genera Plantarum* with George Bentham, and he also revised Bentham's famous *Students' Flora of the British Isles.* Hooker died at Windlesham on 10 December 1911 at the age of 94, and his headstone can be found with that of his father in St Anne's Church on Kew Green, not very far from the Herbarium.

The influence of political development.

Knowledge of the vegetation of a newly discovered territory was of great importance before the advent of industrialization, when natural vegetable and mineral resources were the major part of the wealth of a country. This is seen in the importance placed on botanical work in the Dutch Empire of South East Asia, between the 1600's and 1900's and the colonial floras produced in the British Empire in the 1800's and 1900's, and with modified motives and title, continuing to be produced today. The development of botany under colonization in South East Asia included not only exploration by Dutch botanists, but botanists of many European nationalities attracted by the exotic flora of a territory administered with relative stability and by a botanically sympathetic nation. Later, British and American influences were felt.

Chinese sea-traders had shipped Malaysian vegetables such as cloves (*Eugenia caryophyllus*), and areca (*Areca catechu*) before the dawn of history for use as betel-quids, in which the chopped areca nuts mixed with lime are folded in a leaf of betel pepper (*Piper betle*), fastened with a clove, and chewed. Inhabitants of India had described the religious and economic properties of Malaysian plants with which they were familiar some twenty or thirty centuries ago. The notes of advisers accompanying Alexander's armies into the Punjab provided information on South East Asian plants some of which Theophratus later incorporated in his penetrating plant commentaries.

The pre-eminent trading position occupied by the Egyptians brought them into contact with the economic vegetable world of the East Indies. By the end of the 1st century A.D., regular trade was taking place between Malaysia and the Mediterranean cultures. The political supremacy of the Arabs between 700 and 1200 was accompanied by active trading between the Persian Gulf and Malaysia. Avicenna's writings of between 980 and 1037 contain some of the first descriptions of bananas and coconuts, both of which are Old World plants. Some fourteen hundred medicinal entries involving plants are enumerated in Ibn Baithar's *Medicinal Catalogue* which was derived mainly from Greek sources, but contained some original observations; he died in Damascus in 1248.

After the decline of the Arab World, the momentous travels of Marco Polo (1236–1324) provide us with the next descriptions of Asian plants, and a steady flow of merchants and missionaries began to travel to and from South East Asia. By the late 1400's Portuguese explorers were penetrating deep into Malaysia, and by 1526 New Guinea was reached. However, Portuguese discoveries were put to economic use and little scientific information resulted from their presence in South East Asia.

Not until the rise of the Dutch Empire in the 1600's was there an improvement in the state of botanical knowledge. Jan van Linschoten (1563–1611) was one of the first explorers to describe South East Asian plants such as the Mango, *Mangifera indica* (see plate 120), the Durian, *Durio zibethinus* (see plate 115), and the Jak Fruit, *Artocarpus heterophyllus*. The Dutch East India Company, chartered in 1602, showed its regard for botanical exploration in a recommendation made to all its employed apothecaries and surgeons that they should collect and preserve all plants whether economically valuable or not. Soon after, Malaysian plants began to appear in greater numbers in the hot-houses of Leyden and Amsterdam in Holland, and Hampton Court and Chelsea in England. However, the Dutch authorities were for a long time guarded in what they allowed to be published about the botanical wealth of their realms, for political and economic reasons. It was this policy that delayed the publication of Rumpf's work on the natural history of Amboina.

Notable for his presence amongst the ranks of early botanists in this area is the buccaneer William Dampier (1652–1715), who made several voyages to the East Indies and published a first account of the plants of New Holland (Australia). In Java, Jacobus Bontius (1592–1631) contributed to the botany of the island between 1627 and 1631, noting the preponderance of woody legumes in the tropics compared with herbaceous legumes in temperate areas. In 1687 Georg Meister transferred seed and living plants back to Europe. Georg Joseph Kamel, born in 1661 and a Jesuit missionary, made descriptions and drawings during his lifetime in Manila in the Philippines, where he died in 1706. His work was largely published by two English botanists of the period, John Ray (1628–1705) and James Petiver (1658–1718). Other 18th and early 19th century visitors included Pehr Osbeck, Anders Sparrman, Carl Peter Thunberg, Joseph Banks and Daniel Carl Solander, Pierre Poivre and L. A. Deschamps.

In 1820 the Dutch officially inaugurated the Board of Natural Sciences and followed this by the appointment of a number of collectors in a brave attempt to make known more of the Javan flora. However, the officials were frustrated by a fierce tropical climate, for H. Kuhl died only nine months after arriving, J. K. van Hasselt died three years after taking up his appointment, while A. Zipelius and H. Macklot had only five years active service before they too died. We should pay tribute to men who botanized in the tropics before the facilities of efficient medicine and speedy transport were available. One of the many dangers a botanist had to face was dying during the voyage to his destination, for many sailing vessels became insanitary while at sea, and were then swept by dysentery and fevers. Ports of call were often centres where disease lurked, particularly in the tropics.

H. Zollinger collected some twenty thousand specimens, in Java from 1842 to 1845, in south Sumatra in 1845, in Bali and Lombok in 1846, and in the Celebes and Sumbawa in 1847. After returning to Switzerland in 1848, he felt again the fascination of the tropics and settled in Java in 1855, where he died in 1859. Zollinger is remembered for demarcating the general limits of the Malesian flora. It was R. H. C. C. Scheffer's administration of the Buitenzorg Botanic Garden from 1868 until 1880 which laid the foundations for the progress made under the administrations of later Directors, like M. Treub. From small beginnings, Buitenzorg grew in importance until under Treub it was officially recognized by the Dutch Government as a self-contained Department within the Netherlands Indies Government. Buitenzorg, now Bogor, became an important centre for research in tropical botany, K. von Goebel, A. F. W. Schimper, G. Haberland, J. P. Lotsy and O. Warburg being but a few of the eminent visitors.

In the Philippines, pre-war botany was dominated by the American E. D. Merrill (1876–1956) who arrived in Manila in 1902 and who was Director of the Bureau of Agriculture from 1919 until 1923. The large herbarium and library which he gathered together were tragically lost during the Second World War, but parts of the herbarium were subsequently replaced from duplicates which had been distributed to various parts of the world. The commercial collector Adolph Daniel Elmer (1870–1941) was associated with Merrill's work on the Philippine flora.

Dutch interest has continued in South East Asia with the work of C. A. Backer, C. E. B. Bremekamp, B. H. Danser, H. J. Lam, W. M. D. van Leeuwen, R. Schlechter and C. G. G. J. van Steenis, and a mighty project called the *Flora Malesiana* is slowly being completed, volumes of which have already proved invaluable to students of South East Asian botany. Malaysian botany has also had some British influence, in more recent years being directed by the work of H. N. Ridley, I. H. Burkill, R. E. Holttum and E. J. H. Corner.

The influence of horticulture and gardening.

During the Middle Ages in western Europe gardens were mostly small, being usually enclosed within the walls of monasteries and castles, and the plants available for their decoration were relatively few and grown as much for their culinary and supposed medicinal virtues as for their beauty. Increased social stability at the end of the Middle Ages led to changes in house building and garden design and the introduction of more foreign plants: these have continued ever since, and in the 16th and 17th centuries made Europe the centre of botanical learning. The Renaissance in garden design originated in Italy at a time when fortified country houses were becoming redundant, and a nationalistic movement towards the antique and Romanesque was developing. The Florentine garden, a geometrical arrangement of low clipped hedges and flower beds interspersed with statuary, owed much to Roman influence. Terraces were later introduced, as were waterworks, which were Persian in origin. However, plants were subordinated to the formal garden lay-out which was all important, and this continued to be the case until the late 19th century.

At a later stage, Baroque influence crept into the ornamentation and plan of the garden, as did various national interpretations of the 'Italian garden scheme'. During the 16th, 17th and 18th centuries various fashions came and went, including the French garden in the expansive geometrical style of Le Nôtre, and a phase in which novelty water-works were the vogue. During the 18th century landscaped gardens became popular, in no small way determined by Italian landscape painting of the time, and the advocacy of landscaping by Alexander Pope and others. At the end of the 19th century there was a change from the still highly organized landscape garden to a more natural landscaped appearance, pioneered by men like William Robinson. Also by this time interest in gardens had spread wherever European influence was felt, in North America, Canada, South Africa, Australia and, in modified form, in many tropical territories. As interest in gardens spread, so did the international exchange of plants and exploration for them, and also our knowledge of these plants.

For centuries the Chinese had cultivated plants on a scale that now shows European efforts to have been immature in comparison. The Chinese garden was for some time isolated from developments in other parts of the world, due partly to the isolationism and conservatism that runs through the history of the Chinese people. However, various religious doctrines such as Mohammedanism and Buddhism penetrated these barriers and changed ideas, garden ideas among them. Taoism, with its naturalistic and individualistic outlook, promoted the development of gardening in Confucian China in the 3rd and 4th centuries A.D. The Chinese art of reproducing natural scenes in miniature (and here we include Japanese and Korean cultures which are derived from Chinese) stems from the garden requirements of a less wealthy section of the ancient Chinese community, who could not own the lakes, forests and mountains of their wealthy neighbours and so created replicas in miniature. The art of 'bonsai', or tree dwarfing, and pan-gardening are the products of the miniature garden. Gardening was sponsored by Chinese Emperors of the earlier dynasties, and helped to make gardening a national hobby. Zen Buddhism, with its ritual and symbolism, simplified the Japanese garden into a unique thing. The design remains a peculiar blend of naturalism brought about by the strict adherence to formal rules of construction, where even the number of stones, plants and nails used in the woodwork are specified. However, the formality of the Japanese garden bore little resemblance to that found in European gardens of the Renaissance; the former being naturalistic, the latter being consciously artificial.

The Chinese had an aesthetic and scientific love for flowers not shown by their European contemporaries. Symbolism was attached to different flowers and led to a greater interest in plants. For example, the Spring-orchid symbolizes spring and refinement, while the Lotus, summer and truth. This superstitious love of flowers gave way to exhaustive volumes devoted to particular plants, which made the Chinese early authorities on the Peony, Chrysanthemum, Peach and Rose. A large number of cultivated varieties and numerous monographs bear witness to the deep botanical interest that the Chinese must have had at this time; literary development in the 1100's was well in advance of that in western Europe. This was the heritage that European observers found when they explored China in the late 19th century.

The political attitudes of the Chinese rulers to the outside world long made it difficult for westerners to study Chinese flora, but the herbarium specimens collected in the 19th century by French missionaries, notably David and Delavay, at the turn of the present century indicated its richness, and popular interest in foreign plants led horticultural firms to send plant collectors into the interior. This situation was made possible by western aggressiveness and military superiority at a time when the traditional powers of the emperors were declining, and when China had yet to realize how outdated her military strength had become.

It was the Portuguese who 'discovered' the sea route to China in 1516, and who for the next century monopolized sea trade to the Far East from Euro   They produced no botanical findings of any merit if we discount the writings of Garcia da Orta, a refugee Jew. Catholic missionaries became established in Kwantung, Kiangsu, and Chekiang provinces, and provided much early information on Chinese economic plants. By 1610 the Dutch gained control of many parts of South East Asia, but the Portuguese remained in Macao and frustrated Dutch attempts at trading with China. The Dutch gained more influence in Japan. There had been English trading companies established in China throughout the 17th century, but none could be described as fruitful ventures because of Chinese foreign policy and restrictive legislation. However, James Cunningham in the 17th century and John Bradley Blake (1745–1773) were two of the first men to send plants to England from China, while Pierre Nicholas le Cheron d'Incarville (1706–1757) collected and dispatched plants to Paris, London and St Petersburg. William Kerr, a Kew gardener who went to China in 1803 and after whom *Kerria* is named, made introductions such as *Rosa banksiae* and *Lilium tigrinum*. By 1812 the latter had been so successfully propagated at Kew by Aiton (William Townsend) that more than ten thousand bulbs had been distributed. The great philanthropist Sir Joseph Banks also helped introduce Chinese plants at this time, as part of his policy for close collaboration between Kew and the British Empire. John Reeves (1774–1856), a tea inspector in the East India Company, did much to make shipments of plants from China more reliable and successful. He was a valued overseas correspondent with the Horticultural Society of London from 1817 when he began to send paintings and living plants of the Chinese flora as well as animals to England. Two of the plants which passed through his hands are *Camellia reticulata* (see plate 101) and *Wisteria chinensis*. His son, John Russell Reeves (1807–1877), was likewise an active naturalist and collector in China.

The reluctance of Chinese officials to enter into trading agreements with the West, and home troubles in England, caused British influence to develop only in the 1880's. After the Opium Wars of the early 1840's there followed an unsettled peace with the signing of the Treaty of Nanking, during which time Hong Kong and Chusan were explored, and Robert Fortune (1812–1880) was chosen by the Horticultural Society of London (founded in 1804 and becoming the Royal Horticultural Society in 1861) to collect in China in 1843. Never able to venture far from treaty ports without hazard, Fortune made introductions such as *Anemone hupehensis* var. *japonica*, *Jasminum nudiflorum*, *Dicentra spectabilis* and *Forsythia viridissima*. Botanical exploration slowly spread inland through the activity of men like Henry Fletcher Hance (1827–1886), who worked in southern China, and the Russian Karl Maximovicz (1827–1891), many of whose botanical collections come from Manchuria and Japan, and who later became a great authority on east Asian plants.

Between 1856 and 1860 further fighting occurred between the Chinese and the allied French and British, but with the signing of a second peace treaty travel into the interior of China was permitted. By 1868 Yunnan and the Tibetan and Burmese frontiers were being explored, and Veitch, a British horticultural firm, began to send plant collectors to China, which was proving to be unexpectedly rich in plants.

About this time Russian collectors and missionaries did much work on the Chinese flora and, although having no horticultural connections, deserve mention as certain of their discoveries are now garden plants. Russian exploration of China increased from the north, and characteristically successful semi-military expeditions, which were government-sponsored and highly organized, took home large collections of plants new to science. Nicolai Mikhailovich Przewalski (1839–1888) explored during a period between 1870 and 1888, visiting Inner Mongolia, Kansu, and Tsinghai Provinces, the Lop Nor area, and northern Tibet. In later trips he visited the Tien Shan Range south-east of Lake Balkhash, the Tarim river, and the Gobi Desert. These areas though full of interest were not botanically rich, but even so the explorer accumulated about fifteen thousand specimens. Grigori Potanin (1835–1920), after a time in which he had been sent to Siberia for political crimes, explored Mongolia, the Tsinghai-Kansu borders, and the Tsinling Shan Range in Shensi Province, and south to Chengtu in Szechuan Province, accumulating about twenty-two thousand specimens. Emil Bretschneider (1833–1901) is remembered as the great botanical historian of China, who from 1866 to 1883 was stationed in Pekin, and published his still valuable *History of European botanical Discoveries in China* in 1898.

French missionaries penetrated deep into rural China in order to spread Christian teaching and were confronted with a rich and often beautiful flora. Jean Pierre Armand David (1826–1900) was one of the most versatile of these naturalist-missionaries. His exploration of the Tibetan Marches yielded plants such as *Davidia involucrata, Stranvaesia davidiana,* and *Lilium davidii.* Jean Marie Delavay (1834–1895) was another French missionary who is remembered for his meticulous work on the flora of north-west Yunnan, and who introduced *Osmanthus delavayi,* and *Incarvillea delavayi* (see plate 103). He is said to have collected more than two hundred thousand specimens. Other remarkable missionaries whose lives are well worth reading about are Jean André Soulie (1858–1905) who worked in Tibet, and Urbain Faurie (1847–1915) who worked in Japan and Formosa.

The professional collector acting for the botanical institution and gardener alike came into his own with the close of the 19th century. Most Chinese plants were introduced by British or American collectors, although Augustine Henry (1857–1930), an Irishman, was an exception. Ernest Henry Wilson (1876–1930), sent to China by Messrs Veitch, specialized in collecting from Hupeh and Szechuan Provinces, on the borders of which is to be found one of the world's richest floras. The reason for this has sometimes been attributed to the lack of glaciation of the area. On his first trip of 1900–1902 he collected mainly in Hupeh, but on his second trip of 1903–1905 he travelled widely in Szechuan and made introductions like *Rosa moyesii* (see plate 92) and *Meconopsis integrifolia* (see plate 93). In Szechuan in 1901 Wilson was caught in a landslide and broke his leg, but four years later he was again collecting, this time in Japan. Between 1917 and 1918 he visited the Riu Kiu Archipelago, Formosa and Korea. After his dangerous expeditions in the East it is paradoxical that he should have been killed in 1930 in Massachusetts in a motor accident.

The first fifty years of this century are roughly circumscribed by the careers of George Forrest and Frank Kingdon Ward. George Forrest (1873–1932) was a Scot with training in the chemist's trade, but he made his contribution to science in the field of botany. After obtaining a post in the Royal Botanic Garden, Edinburgh, he was sent out to China by A. K. Bulley of Ness, Cheshire. On this first expedition to Yunnan, which lasted until 1907, he explored the Tseku area of the Mekong river, but became involved in a local quarrel between militant Tibetan monks from Batang in the north and the Chinese and missionary community of Tseku. Trouble spread, murdering occurred, and Forrest was searched for but not found in his woodland hiding place. After a week he escaped to a friendly village nearby and continued his botanizing with only the loss of his possessions and current collection. It was on his first expedition that he found *Gentiana sino-ornata* (see plate 97), but he did not introduce it until 1910.

During his third expedition of 1912 to 1915, prolonged rains in the Lichiang area lasted over forty days and ruined his seed harvest, but the fourth expedition of 1917 to 1920 was more successful. He covered a wide area and including that around Teng-yueh where large-leaved rhododendrons dominate the forest and dwarf bamboos form the undergrowth. The fifth expedition of 1921 to 1923 included the rich *Rhododendron* flora of the Salween-Kui-Kiang Divide. On his last, the seventh, expedition he died early in 1932, but had sent back to Britain a large seed harvest. Forrest wrote little about his experiences and impressions while collecting, but this deficiency is offset by the wealth of plant material, both living and dried, the explorer sent home. He collected thirty-one thousand and fifteen dried sheets during his career, nearly five thousand four hundred *Rhododendron* specimens including over three hundred new species, and introduced amongst other species *Iris chrysographes, Magnolia delavayi, Pieris forrestii, Primula nutans, Primula malacoides* and *Rhododendron giganteum.* His ability to understand and be trusted by local inhabitants made it possible for him to organize reliable native collectors, some of whom remained active while he was away in Europe. In this way, Forrest botanized over wide areas in a relatively intensive manner.

Frank Kingdon Ward (1885–1958) was born in Lancashire, and differed from Forrest in temperament and method of working. Kingdom Ward spent over forty years hunting plants and exploring, leaving numerous books as a tribute to the areas he visited, and obviously derived great artistic pleasure as well as satisfaction from his career. Where Forrest collected on a grand scale by means of hired servants, Kingdon Ward preferred to collect personally, and so was forced to work on a smaller scale. After reading Natural Science at Cambridge, where his father had been Professor of Botany, Kingdon Ward went to Shanghai in 1907 as a school teacher, but he broke his teaching contract to join the American zoologist Malcolm Anderson on a trip across China from 1909 to 1910. From 1911, he became a professional plant collector when he too was sponsored by A. K. Bulley. As Forrest was in Yunnan at the time and was a man who resented intruders upon his own 'property', Kingdon Ward turned his attention to the little visited frontiers of Assam, Burma and southeast Tibet.

All of Kingdon Ward's major expeditions were recorded by descriptions in books or scientific papers. During 1913 he discovered three ranges separating the four great rivers of Burma, Yunnan and Tibet, namely the Yangtze, Mekong, Salween and Irrawaddy. Exploring north to Pitu, he attempted to penetrate the upper reaches of the N'mai-hka river, but had to return to Pitu defeated in his aim. With trouble stirring between the Chinese and Tibetans, he returned to Atuntze. During 1914 he climbed the 13,370 foot (4085 m.) Imaw Bum, and crossing the Wulaw Pass, proceeded to Fort Hertz via the Shing rup-chet Pass. These considerable exertions in an unequable climate reduced him to sickness by the time he reached Fort Hertz. When the Great War had finished in Europe, during which he served in the Indian Army, he reclimbed Imaw Bum, and in 1921 he returned to Yunnan. A proposed crossing from Fort Hertz into Assam had to be postponed due to a serious attack of fever, but he later made this crossing in 1926, and was able to witness the striking climatic divide between rain-forest and dry Central Asian steppe produced by the ranges of mountains in that area. In 1924 the expedition to the Tsangpo Gorge in Bhutan and south Tibet was spectacular, and is described in *The Riddle of the Tsangpo Gorges.* During World War Two he served in Burma, and his knowledge of the area aided his escape into India when the Japanese invasion took place. After the war he was employed by the United States to search for wartime wreckage in the forests, and during such work he discovered and introduced *Lilium mackliniae,* named after his second wife. After locating *Cornus chinensis,* and awaiting its fruiting time, he and his wife escaped disaster during the earthquake in 1950. The tremors desolated parts of the forest in the vicinity by causing landslides, and these threw up an enormous dustcloud. Their experiences are vividly described in *Pilgrimage for Plants*, his last book. *C. chinensis* seed was finally obtained after the earthquake, and now grows in Windsor Great Park, England. When he died in London he was planning further trips to Vietnam, northern Iran and the Caucasus. He collected about twenty-three thousand sheets during his lifetime, and as well as being a capable field botanist, surveyed and mapped geographical features in his travels. Above all he was able to describe his experiences, and his books make readable and often amusing documents, with biographical value.

The influence of specialist exploration.

Organized exploration, purely botanical and otherwise, has been another major source of information about wild flowers, and the habitats in which they grow. Some such expeditions have been models of efficiency and of great value such as the privately financed Humboldt and Bonpland expedition; others have been less efficient, sometimes farcical, and for various reasons of less value, such as the state financed expedition of Ruiz, Pavon and Dombey. Hipolito Ruiz Lopez (1764–1815) and Jose Antonio Pavon (1754–1844) were employed by the Spanish Government to explore and botanize in Peru and Chile between 1777 and 1788. Anne Robert Jacques Turgot, chief minister to Louis XVI, first suggested an expedition to Peru, and this was found to be acceptable to the Spanish who were anxious to promote scientific enquiry in their realm at a time when Spanish natural history was little developed. The Spanish Government stipulated that two Spaniards were to accompany the Frenchman, and all collections were to be duplicated with half to be deposited in Spain when the expedition returned.

Joseph Dombey (1742–1796) was much the more experienced botanist compared with the outspoken, brusque and patriotic Ruiz, and the quieter, ingratiating Pavon. As the expedition progressed, Dombey became more and more estranged from his colleagues, partly due to certain injustices concerning his more meagre salary paid by the French Government, and later to Spanish suspicions concerning his integrity over properly splitting his collections. It seems Dombey was an impulsive and explosive person, with a broad streak of romanticism in his makeup. This quality may explain some of his more extreme statements such as when he quelled an epidemic which he said had taken over thirty-five thousand lives in Chile, when contemporary records fail to show such a disaster.

The three sailed for America from Cadiz in November 1777, and arrived in Lima in April 1778, where they spent nearly three months attending social functions in their honour. In late July they ventured to Arnedo, some forty miles (64 km.) north along sandy coastal plain, and on the second night, possibly because of widespread publicity in Lima, were attacked by bandits. Fortunately the expedition used its firearms and the bandits were repelled, chiefly by Dombey, says Dombey. In September they went a little further north, but by October were back in Lima. A short journey to the south of Lima in December, where they stayed until early March, and almost a year had passed without notable exploration having taken place. The travellers were less than intrepid, each with a bulky wardrobe which included items such as silk suits, numbers of velvet and plain breeches, pairs of silk stockings, silk hair nets, and sleeping caps.

In May 1779 they journeyed into the Andes bound for Tarma at 10,000 feet (3050 m.), losing as they ascended mules and stores which absconding guides stole. The explorers spent eight months in the area and made collections before they returned to the capital in January 1780. In late April they returned to Tarma, then moved north to Huanuco on the river Huallaga. By August they were at Cuchero about fifty miles (80 km.) north-east of Huanuco, and one evening, as a practical joke, a workman informed the explorers that they were surrounded by several hundred fierce Chuncho Indians. The Europeans fled, stumbling through the mud of the forest, so that when morning came, Pavon and Dombey were found in Casapillo, a nearby settlement, while Ruiz had been forced to remain in Cuchero after losing the other two in the darkness of the forest.

From August until October, Ruiz and two artists remained in Chinchao near Cuchero, while Pavon and Dombey went back to Huanuco, where they all came together late in March 1781. News reached them that the 'Buen Consejo' in which their first shipment of collections of plants had been sent in the April of 1779, had been captured by the English, so the expedition was required to recollect all materials for replacement. The expedition also received instructions to visit Chile; accordingly in December 1781 they set sail in the 'Nuestra Senora de Belen' from Callao bound for Talcahuano in Chile. After arriving they moved to Concepcion, where they were to stay for more than a year, collecting amongst other plants the Monkey-puzzle tree, *Araucaria araucana*, which is not an Angiosperm but a Gymnosperm. It was unsuccessfully shipped to Spain, where the plants were found to be dead, but was later introduced to Europe by Archibald Menzies in 1795.

By October 1783, Dombey, suffering from scurvy and complaining of deafness and blindness, had done all the useful botany he could or would do on the trip, and he sailed from Valparaiso for Lima. In April 1784 he was aboard 'El Peruano' bound for Cadiz, although a bad passage around Cape Horn, dysentery, and the breakage of the ship's steering-gear, nearly cost Dombey his life. Only after repairs in Rio de Janeiro, and a lapse of three months, could the voyage across the Atlantic be resumed in November 1784. By February 1785 he had arrived in Cadiz.

Meanwhile Ruiz and Pavon returned from Chile in November 1783, and, under the impression they were to return to Spain, sold all their stores as they were short of money. However, when in February 1784 they received orders to continue their work, they were overjoyed, and set about repurchasing their stores. They packed fifty-five cases with collections and saw them loaded aboard the 'San Pedro de Alcantara' by May, these representing five years' work in South America, before setting out on their next trip. Ruiz was a sick man on their return to Huanuco, and he slowed the party, but by early July he had recovered, and they reached Pozuzo where they did the most profitable two months work of their entire stay. Although this locality was remote, and the men were weary and suffering from the climate, the wealth of plant life intoxicated them. Between October 1784 and June 1785, the summer rains and the sickness of Ruiz, which had recurred, confined the party to Huanuco.

In mid-June they moved to Macora, to the north-east of Huanuco, where discontent amongst the artists finally caused them to desert the expedition on 6 August 1785. On the same day the house in which two months' collections, three years' notes and manuscripts and reference books were housed, as well as food, guns and clothing, was accidentally set alight and almost completely destroyed. With this tragedy in their minds the explorers returned to Huanuco a few days later. The conflagration at Macora was to involve a lengthy legal action, largely as the outcome of accusations made by Ruiz. By mid-October Ruiz was very depressed partly because of repeated attacks of fever, and no doubt the fire, and in late December he petitioned the Spanish King for their return to Spain.

About this time the 'San Pedro' had set sail from Rio de Janeiro after repairs had been made to the badly leaking hull. By February 1786, Europe was in sight, but unfortunately the vessel ran aground and foundered off the Portuguese coast, with the loss of all the collections of Ruiz and Pavon and considerable bullion. While the precious metals were salvaged from the wreck, the botanical collections were beyond recovery. The bad news reached Peru, and between August and September 1786, much activity enabled Ruiz to accompany seventy-three cases of collection replacements into Lima in January 1787. These were loaded aboard 'El Brillante', 'El Pinar', and 'La Fe', all of which voyaged safely back to Spain.

The last trip of Ruiz and Pavon was made to Pillao and Chaca-hussi to the north-west of Huanuco, on which they started in August 1787. These settlements were centres for the collection of 'quina', the material from which quinine is extracted. It depressed the explorers to see the local population reduced to a low level of subsistence so that they might collect quina for a small sum of money, with the neglect of their land and crops. The King's order for their return had been granted in March 1787, and by October the news reached them. By February they were again in Lima, and at the beginning of April, together with some three thousand descriptions which represented the results of their explorations, they sailed for Spain aboard 'El Dragon'.

There was much intrigue and scandalous behaviour concerning the publication of the results of the expedition. Ultimately shortage of money held up the production. In 1791, Charles IV asked the administrations of Spanish dominions in the Americas to make contributions to the cost of production of the flora, and in this way some 801,969 reales, about £20,000, were collected. Ruiz and Pavon were slow to begin the work, and insubordination by Pavon and the illustrators tells of the heavy-handed character of Ruiz.

By September 1794 a few copies of the introductory *Florae Peruvianae, et Chilensis, Prodromus* were obtainable, with a more general release taking place early in 1795. There was further delay, when Ruiz and Antonio José Cavanilles were employed in bitter professional rivalry around the year 1796. Volume I of the flora was published in 1798 after further quarrels between the artists who were making the illustrations. Volume II was published in 1799 with a rapid dwindling of the funds recently taken into the custody of the State, and poor sales of the volume already produced. Volume III was published in summer 1802, but because of outstanding debt for this volume, Volume IV was not printed when it was received in 1804, and only appeared in facsimile about a hundred and fifty years later. In 1807 Volume V was almost ready, but in March 1808, Charles IV abdicated and French forces entered Madrid soon after. Under occupation, the flora was allowed to continue, but money was scarce, and the final blow to the project came, when in 1815 Ruiz died. The flora came to a standstill and was never resumed. Pavon was said to have sold many of the collections for his own profit, and certainly did little to promote publication of the results. A small edition of Volume IV was published in 1957.

In contrast to the expedition of Ruiz, Pavon and Dombey, the no less memorable exploration of South and Central America by Humboldt and Bonpland was financed by Humboldt himself. Friedrich Heinrich Alexander von Humboldt (1769-1859) was left money by his mother in 1796 and his inheritance he freely used throughout his life to further the cause of science. In his later years he was obliged to accept employment with the King of Prussia, so serious had his financial position become.

It was in 1790, and in the company of Georg Forster (1754-1794) who sailed on Captain Cook's Second Voyage in the Pacific in the years 1772 to 1775, that Humboldt resolved to visit the tropics. Uncharacteristically for his day and age he began to make detailed preparations for his expedition and read widely. While Humboldt was staying in Madrid in 1799, and trying to find a Spanish ship that would take him and his friend and helper Aimé Jacques Alexandre Bonpland (1773-1858) to Smyrna, the Saxon Chargé d'Affaires obligingly made known Humboldt's zeal and desires to the liberally-minded Spanish minister Luis d'Urquijo. He obtained permission for the two men to travel throughout Spanish possessions in America. Two months later in June 1799, they sailed from Corunna.

By mid-July they were in eastern Venezuela at Cumaná, after stopping off at Teneriffe in the Canaries in mid-June. They stayed in Cumaná and the vicinity for about four months, before sailing along the coast to La Guaira, the port which serves Caracas. In February 1800 their first trip into the interior took them across the hot llanos (steppe) to San Fernando de Apure, the river Apure and tropical rain-forest. The two Europeans and five Indians comprising the party, proceeded downstream to the confluence with the river Orinoco, or Oroonoko as Humboldt called it, up which they then continued, through swarms of biting insects, against the current, and in worsening river conditions. There was little opportunity for botanizing in the humid conditions, or for storing collections in the single canoe they used. We might reflect on the difficulties facing any botanist in the tropics, when he tries to dry and press and store plant specimens in the field where a daily thunderstorm is a regular occurrence.

South of San Fernando de Atabapo, the Orinoco and the Amazon river systems are nearly confluent, but a stretch of land near Pimichin separates the Orinoco-derived river Atabapo, from the Amazon-derived river Negro. The tributary of the Orinoco, called the river Cassiquiare, actually links the Negro to the Orinoco system. Taking thirty-three days, the travellers journeyed south from the Orinoco to the Amazon system, then returned north down the Cassiquiare to the Orinoco. This was one of the hardest parts of their entire expedition; here the humidity never falls below the upper 80% level and here the large ants require vegetable crops to be grown in hanging-baskets by the missionaries of this remote area. The ants drove the explorers from several of the infrequent camping sites along the Cassiquiare, and the ferocious mosquitoes, quite the worst in the whole of South America, caused their hands and faces to swell alarmingly. Humboldt tells of the paucity of dry wood with which to make a fire for cooking their scanty provisions, and describes how they reduced their hunger by eating small amounts of ground sugar and cacao washed down with large amounts of river water. At Esmeralda they recorded the preparation of the poison 'curare', and learnt about the source of the Orinoco to the east, then in territory of hostile cannibalistic Indians, before continuing to Angostura where they arrived on 14 June 1800. Here their fever-ridden state forced them to stay for a while.

From Angostura they recrossed the llanos to the coast and Nueva Barcelona, where once more Humboldt fell ill with fever. The voyage from Nueva Barcelona to Cumaná was eventful. Hoping to avoid trouble, they sailed in a smugglers' ship instead of a Spanish vessel, for at that time England and Spain were at war and the English were blockading the Venezuelan coast. Unfortunately their ship was attacked by a Nova Scotian privateer, but an English warship called 'The Hawk' intervened, and the English captain, Captain Garnier, met Humboldt. After Humboldt explained the predicament, Garnier reacted sympathetically, and the explorers continued on their way. After staying briefly in Cumaná, they returned to Nueva Barcelona, and late in November 1800, they set sail for Cuba.

The four and a half months on the island produced little botanical material, even though Cuba is floristically rich, for Humboldt was chiefly concerned with geographical and sociological observations. At the beginning of March 1801, the men travelled overland from Havana to Batabano on the south coast, where they set sail for Cartagena in Colombia. Arriving in late March they spent three weeks in the area before moving to Barranquilla, from where they began a trip up the river Magdadalena, as far as Honda. Then they went overland to Bogota where they settled down for a three month stay, during which time they visited places of interest. From Bogota they proceeded to Popayan across the Quindio Mountains and along the river Cauca, arriving at their destination in November. The Christmas of 1801 was spent in Pasto, where they arrived after a journey through dense forest, swamp, and high above the tree line in the paramo (treeless alpine vegetation), taking a route via Almaguer. By January 1802 they reached Quito, journeying via Tulcan, and until July made excursions to the nearby volcanoes Cayambe, Antisana, Cotopaxi and, most noteworthy, climbed Pichincha three times! They also nearly scaled the summit of Chimborazo, then thought to be the world's highest point, and held the altitude record until it was broken by Hooker in the Himalaya.

Continuing south towards Loja, the remote but important centre of the quinine trade, they then spent about one month in Upper Amazonia, in the Jaen de Bracamoros area. On their return into the mountains they passed Caxamarca with its Inca Palace, and on descending saw for the first time the Pacific Ocean at Trujillo. Following the coast to Lima where they arrived late in October, they spent a month in the area before sailing for Guayaquil, in Ecuador, in December 1802. After spending about one month in Guayaquil they sailed for Acapulco in Mexico.

In April 1803 they travelled from the coast to Mexico City, and then made a series of short excursions to Actopan, Guanajuato, Valladolid, and the volcano Jorullo. Early in 1804 they visited the volcano Popacatepetl, and in February made their way to Vera Cruz where they caught a boat to Havana. After collecting material stored in Cuba from their Venezuelan trip, they sailed for Philadelphia in late April, and then at the beginning of July sailed from Philadelphia bound for Bordeaux. Some sixty thousand specimens had been accumulated, largely by the labours of Bonpland, and on arriving in Europe all that remained to be done was to publish their results for fellow botanists.

It was Humboldt who again financed the venture and published the seven illustrated volumes entitled *Nova Genera et Species Plantarum*. Bonpland was not a diligent writer, he was more of a field botanist, and the documentation of the collections was carried out by Carl Ludwig Willdenow (1765–1812) until his death. Then Carl Sigismund Kunth (1788–1850) took over, working in Paris, and after twenty-two years of toil completed the work. Production of the literature was steady and regular unlike that of the Ruiz and Pavon expedition; Volume I was published in 1816, Volume II in 1817–1818, Volume III in 1818–1820, Volume IV in 1820, Volume V in 1821–1823, Volume VI in 1823–1824, and Volume VII in 1824–1825. Shortly after the death of Willdenow, Bonpland emigrated to Argentina, where he farmed and became involved in local politics. So ended the expedition which furnished the world with so much fresh information on the wild flowers of South America.

ACKNOWLEDGEMENTS

Author's acknowledgements

The author wishes to thank Sir George Taylor, Mr J. P. M. Brenan and Dr C. R. Metcalfe for their hospitality and assistance during the work at Kew, and also the following members of Kew staff: Dr R. K. Brummitt, Mr R. G. C. Desmond and the Library staff, Mr L. L. Forman, Mr C. Grey-Wilson, Miss P. Halliday, Mr F. N. Hepper, Professor R. E. Holttum, Mr D. R. Hunt, Mr P. F. Hunt, Dr J. Hutchinson, Mr C. Jeffrey, Mr G. Ll. Lucas, Mr R. D. Meikle, Dr R. Melville, Mr E. Milne-Redhead, Mr E. G. H. Oliver, Mr R. M. Polhill, Mr J. R. Sealy, Mr P. Taylor, Mr C. C. Townsend, Dr P. Thomson, and Dr B. Verdcourt. Mr J. Lewis and Mr F. Ludlow and the Library staff at the British Museum (Natural History) Herbarium are also thanked, as are Mr F. P. Knight and Mr C. D. Brickell of the Royal Horticultural Society Garden at Wisley; Lord Talbot de Malahide; Dr C. D. Adams, Kingston, Jamaica; Dr H. G. Baker, Berkeley, California; Mr A. Brady, National Botanic Garden, Glasnevin; G. M. Chippendale of Northern Territory Administration, Australia; Dr O. Degener, Hawaii; Professor and Mrs O. Hedberg; Mr J. E. Lousley; Dr Palliwal, New Delhi, India; Mr O. Polunin; Mr and Mrs J. Sankey; Dr A. Takhtajan, Leningrad, U.S.S.R.; Professor D. A. Webb; Mr J. B. Williams, Armidale, Australia; and Dr P. Yeo.

Particular thanks are due to Dr W. T. Stearn and Mr P. S. Green, consultative editors; Mr T. Wellsted and Miss C. Lewis of the editorial staff of Rainbird Reference Books Ltd, Mrs B. Everard for her unflagging energy, and my wife for her active participation in the venture.

B. D. MORLEY

Artist's acknowledgements

How to express my thanks to the Director, Royal Botanic Gardens, Kew, I do not know. I doubt if this book, in this day and age, could ever have been made without the help of Kew. I am deeply grateful for the help and courtesy extended to me throughout these twenty months, whether sketching in the Houses or in the Garden, and particularly in the Herbarium to Mr R. D. Meikle, Mr Lucas, Mr and Mrs R. Polhill, Miss Mary Grierson, Miss Mulford, Miss Halliday and Mr P. S. Green.

I thank Dr H. R. Fletcher, Regius Keeper, Royal Botanic Garden, Edinburgh for the loan of herbarium material, The Royal Horticultural Society for several plants, and Mr Oleg Polunin for the loan of colour slides. For plants or the loan of photographs, Mrs Olive Lunn, Mr Ben Johnson, Mr I. K. Simpson, Mrs D. Head, Mrs Ian Bateman, Mr A. H. Venison, Miss Pemberton, and Mrs Wells. Lastly, I thank my husband, without whose help I could not have painted at all.

BARBARA EVERARD

SELECTED BIBLIOGRAPHY

ARCTIC AND ANTARCTIC

BÖCHER, T. W., et al., 1968, The Flora of Greenland, Copenhagen.
HOOKER, J. D., 1844–1847, Flora Antarctica (2 vols), London.
POLUNIN, N., 1959, Circumpolar Arctic Flora, Oxford.
VALLENTIN, E. F., 1921, Illustrations of the Flowering Plants and Ferns of the Falkland Islands, London.

EUROPE

COSTE, H., 1901–1906, Flore descriptive et illustrée de la France, de la Corse, et des Contrées limitrophes . . . (3 vols), Paris.
FIORI, A., and PAOLETTI, G., 1895–1904, Iconographia Florae Italicae . . . , Padova.
HEGI, G., 1906–1931, Illustrierte Flora von Mittel-Europa, ed. i, (17 vols), München.
MACKAY, J. T., 1836, Flora Hibernica . . . , Dublin.
TUTIN, T. G., HEYWOOD, V. H., et al., 1964– , Flora Europaea (2 vols and continuing), Cambridge.

MEDITERRANEAN AND MIDDLE EAST

BOISSIER, E., 1867–1884, Flora Orientalis (5 vols), Geneva, Basel and Lyon.
MOLDENKE, H. N., and A. L., 1952, Plants of the Bible, Waltham, Mass.
POLUNIN, O., and HUXLEY, A., 1965, Flowers of the Mediterranean, London.
SIBTHORP, J., and SMITH, J. E., 1806–1840, Flora Graeca . . . (10 vols), London.

TROPICAL AFRICA

ADANSON, M., 1759, Voyage to Senegal, (English translation), London.
ANDREWS, F. W., 1950–1956, The Flowering Plants of the Anglo-Egyptian Sudan (3 vols), Arbroath, Scotland.
EXELL, A. W., and WILD, H., et al., 1960– , Flora Zambesiaca . . . (continuing), London.
HUTCHINSON, J., and DALZIEL, J. M., 1954– , Flora of West Tropical Africa, ed. ii, (continuing), London.
PALISOT DE BEAUVOIS, A. M. F. J., 1805–1821, Flore d'Oware et de Benin en Afrique (2 vols), Paris.

SOUTH AFRICA

BATTEN, A., and BOKELMANN, H., 1966, Wild flowers of the eastern Cape Province, Cape Town.
HARVEY, W. H., and SONDER, O. W., 1859–1933, Flora Capensis: being a systematic Description of the plants of the Cape Colony, Caffraria and Port Natal (7 vols), Dublin.
HUTCHINSON, J., 1946, A Botanist in Southern Africa, London.
LETTY, C., et al., 1962, Wild flowers of the Transvaal, Johannesburg.
MARLOTH, R., 1913–1932, The Flora of South Africa (4 vols), Cape Town and London.
PALMER, E., and PITMAN, N., 1961, Trees of South Africa, Amsterdam and Cape Town.

HIMALAYA AND CHINA

BRETSCHNEIDER, E., 1898, History of European botanical Discoveries in China, London.
COX, E. H. M., 1961, Plant Hunting in China, London.
HARA, H., et al., 1963, Spring Flora of Sikkim Himalaya by Japanese Members of the Indo-Japanese Botanical Expedition to Sikkim and Darjeeling in 1960, Osaka.
HOOKER, J. D., 1855, Illustrations of Himalayan plants chiefly selected from drawings made for the late J. F. Cathcart Esq., of the Bengal Civil Service . . . , London.
HOOKER, J. D., et al., 1872–1897, The Flora of British India (7 vols), London.
LI, H. L., 1959, The garden Flowers of China, New York.
NAKAO, S., 1964, Living Himalayan flowers, Tokyo.

SARGENT, C. S., 1913–1917, Plantae Wilsonianae, an Enumeration of the woody plants collected in Western China for the Arnold Arboretum of Harvard University during the years 1907, 1908 and 1910 by E. H. Wilson (3 vols), Cambridge, Mass.

SOUTH EAST ASIA

BACKER, C. A., and BAKHUIZEN VAN DEN BRINK, R. C., 1963–1968, Flora of Java (3 vols), Groningen.
BENNETT, J. J., and BROWN, R., 1838–1852, Plantae Javanicae rariores, descriptae Iconibusque illustratae, quas in Insula Java Annis 1802–1818 legit et investigavit Thomas Horsfield, M. D. . . . , London.
BLATTER, E., and MILLARD, W. S., 1954, Revised by STEARN, W. T. Some beautiful Indian Trees, Bombay.
BLUME, C. L., 1828–1851, Flora Javae nec non Insularum adjacentium . . . (5 vols), Brussels.
BLUME, C. L., 1835–1848, *Rumphia*, sive Commentationes botanicae imprimis de Plantis Indiae orientalis, tum penitus incognitis tum quae in libris Rheedii, Rumphii, Roxburghii, Wallichii . . . (4 vols), Leiden.
CORNER, E. J. H., 1952, Wayside Trees of Malaya (2 vols), ed. ii, Singapore.
ROXBURGH, W., 1795–1820, Plants of the Coast of Coromandel, selected from drawings and descriptions presented to the Hon. Court of Directors of the East India Company . . . (3 vols), London.
WALLACE, A. H., 1869, The Malay Archipelago, London.
WALLICH, N., 1829–1832, Plantae Asiaticae rariores, or Descriptions and Figures of a select Number of unpublished East Indian Plants . . . (3 vols), London.
DE WIT, H. C. D., 1948–1954, Flora Malesiana, Series 1, vol. 4, pp. lxxi-clxi. History of Malaysian phytography, Groningen.

AUSTRALASIA

ALLAN, H. H., 1961, Flora of New Zealand, Vol. 1, Indigenous Tracheophyta, Wellington, N.Z.
BENTHAM, G., 1863–1878, Flora Australiensis: a Description of the Plants of the Australian territory (7 vols), London.
BLOMBERY, A. M., 1967, A guide to native Australian Plants, Sydney.
COCKAYNE, L., ed. GODLEY, E. J., 1967, New Zealand plants and their Story (ed. iv), Wellington, N.Z.
CURTIS, W., ill. by STONES, M., 1967, The endemic Flora of Tasmania (2 vols and continuing), London.
SALMON, J. T., 1963, New Zealand Flowers and Plants in Colour, Wellington N.Z. and Auckland.
SINCLAIR, D. W., 1963, New Zealand Birds and Flowers: a Selection of colour Plates, Wellington, N.Z.

OCEANA

DEGENER, O., 1946–1957, Flora Hawaiiensis or New illustrated Flora of the Hawaiian Islands.
HILLEBRAND, W., 1888, Flora of the Hawaiian Islands: a description of their phanerogams and vascular cryptogams, London.
SEEMANN, B. C., 1865–1873, Flora Vitiensis . . . , London.

NORTH AMERICA

MUNZ, P. A., and KECK, D. D., 1959, A California Flora, Berkeley and Los Angeles.
PURSH, F. T., 1814, Flora Americae Septentrionalis (2 vols), London.
RICKETT, H. W., 1966– , Wild Flowers of the United States, 1. the north-eastern States, 2. the south-eastern States (4 vols and continuing), New York.
SARGENT, C. S., 1891–1902, The Silva of North America (14 vols), Cambridge, Mass.
STEYERMARK, J. A., 1963, Flora of Missouri, Iowa.

CENTRAL AND SOUTH AMERICA

BERNARDI, L., and ROBERT, P. A., 1966, Fleurs tropicales; Amérique latine, Neuchatel, Switzerland.

FAWCETT, W., and RENDLE, A. B., 1910-   , Flora of Jamaica (continuing), London.
GOODING, E. G. B., LOVELESS, A. R., and PROCTOR, G. R., 1965, Flora of Barbados, London.
LITTLE, E. L., and WADSWORTH, F. H., 1964, Common Trees of Puerto Rico and the Virgin Islands, U.S. Department of Agriculture No 249, Washington.
PERTCHIK, B., and H., 1951, Flowering trees of the Caribbean, New York and Toronto.
PULLE, A., 1932-   , Flora of Surinam, (continuing), Amsterdam and Leiden.
RUIZ, H., and PAVON, J., 1798-1802, Flora Peruviana, et Chilensis, sive Descriptiones et Icones Plantarum Peruvianarum et Chilensium, secundum Systema Linnaeanum digestae . . . reformatis (4 vols), Madrid.
STEARN, W. T., ed., 1968, Humboldt, Bonpland, Kunth and tropical American botany, a miscellany on the 'Nova genera et species', Lehre.

GENERAL
ARBER, A., 1938, Herbals, their Origin and Evolution, a Chapter in the History of Botany, 1470-1670 ed.ii, Cambridge.
BAILEY, L. H., 1949, Manual of Cultivated Plants (revised edition), New York.
BAKER, H. A., and OLIVER, E. G. H., 1967, Ericas in southern Africa, Cape Town.
BEAN, W. J., 1950-1951, Trees and Shrubs hardy in the British Isles (3 vols) ed.ii, London.
BECK, C., 1953, Fritillaries - a Gardener's Introduction to the Genus *Fritillaria*, London.
BOWLES, E. A., 1952, A Handbook of *Crocus* and *Colchicum* for gardeners, ed.ii, London.
CHITTENDEN, F. J., et al., 1951-1956, The Royal Horticultural Society Dictionary of Gardening, a practical and scientific Encyclopaedia of Horticulture (4 vols and supplement), Oxford.
CLIFFORD, D., 1958, Pelargoniums including the popular Geranium, London.
COATS, A. M., 1963, Garden Shrubs and their Histories, London.
COATS, A. M., 1968, Flowers and their Histories, London.
CORNER, E. J. H., 1964, The Life of Plants, London.
CORNER, E. J. H., 1966, The Natural History of Palms, London.
DARWIN, C., 1882, The various Contrivances by which Orchids are fertilised by insects, London.
DYKES, W. R., 1913, The genus *Iris*, Cambridge.
ELWES, H. J., 1877-1880, A Monograph of the Genus *Lilium*, London.
ENGLER, A., and PRANTL, K., 1887-1915, Die natürlichen Pflanzenfamilien, Leipzig.
ENGLER, A., 1900-   , Das Pflanzenreich (continuing), Leipzig.
FLETCHER, H. R., 1969, The story of the Royal Horticultural Society, 1804-1968, Oxford.
FRYER, A., and EVANS, A. H., 1898-1915, The Potamogetons of the British Isles, London.
HEDBERG, O., 1957, Afroalpine vascular plants, a taxonomic revision. Symbolae Botanicae Upsaliensis 15 no 1. Uppsala.
HEDBERG, O., 1964, Features of Afroalpine plant ecology. Acta Phytogeographica Suecica 49, Uppsala.
HOLTTUM, R. E., 1964, A revised Flora of Malaya, Vol. 1, Orchids of Malaya, ed. iii, Singapore.
HOOKER, W. J., 1851, *Victoria regia* or illustrations of the Royal Waterlily, in a Series of Figures chiefly made from Specimens flowering at Syon and at Kew by Walter Fitch . . . , London.

HUTCHINSON, J., 1959, The Families of Flowering Plants (2 vols), ed. ii, Oxford.
KOORDERS, S. H., 1918, Botanisch, Overzicht der Rafflesiaceae van Nederlandsch-Indië, Batavia.
LEENHOUTS, P. W., 1963, Flora Malesiana, Series 1, vol. 6, part 2, 293-387, *Loganiaceae*.
MAIDEN, J. H., 1909-1933, A critical revision of the genus *Eucalyptus* (8 vols), Sydney.
MAW, G., 1886, The genus *Crocus*, London.
MOORE, H. E., 1957, African Violets, Gloxinias and their Relatives - a guide to the cultivated Gesneriads, New York.
NEL, G. C., 1947, *Lithops* - Plantae succulentae, rarissimae, in Terra obscuratae, e familia Aizoaceae, ex Africa australi, Cape Town.
PIERS, F., 1968, Orchids of East Africa, Lehre.
PRAEGER, R. Ll., 1920-1921, An Account of the Genus *Sedum* as found in cultivation (1967 reprint available), London.
PRAEGER, R Ll., 1932, An Account of the *Sempervivum* Group (1967 reprint available), London.
PURSEGLOVE, J. W., 1968, Tropical Crops - Dicotyledons (2 vols), London.
RAUH, W., 1961, Weitere Untersuschungen an Didiereaceen, Teil 1. Sitzungsberichte der Heidelberger Akademie der Wissenschaften, Math.-naturw. Klasse, 1960-1961 (Abhandlung 7): 185-300.
RAUH, W., and SCHÖLCH, H. F., 1965, Weitere Untersuchungen an Didiereaceen, Teil 2. Sitzungsberichte. [as above] 1965 (Abhandlung 3): 221-443.
SCHWANTES, G., 1957, Flowering Stones and Mid-day Flowers, London.
SEALY, J. R., 1958, A revision of the genus *Camellia*, London.
SMITH, L. B., 1955, The *Bromeliaceae* of Brazil, Smithsonian Miscellaneous Collection 126 no 1, (Publication 4148), Washington.
SMITH, L. B., 1957, The *Bromeliaceae* of Colombia, Contributions from the U.S. National Herbarium, 33, Washington D.C.
STEARN, W. T., 1966, Botanical Latin, London.
SUMMERHAYES, V. S., 1951, Wild Orchids of Britain, London.
TAYLOR, G., 1934, An account of the genus *Meconopsis*, London.
TURRILL, W. B., 1959, The Royal Botanic Gardens, past and present, Kew, London.
WHITE, A., and SLOANE, B. L., 1937, The *Stapelieae* (3 vols), Pasadena.
WILLIS, J. C., 1966, A dictionary of the Flowering plants and Ferns, ed. vii, revised H. K. Airy Shaw, Cambridge.
WOODCOCK, M. B. D., and STEARN, W. T., 1950, Lilies of the World, their Cultivation and Classification, London.
WRIGHT, R., 1963, The Story of Gardening, New York.

JOURNALS
Baileya
Bulletin: Jardin Botanique de Buitenzorg
Curtis's Botanical Magazine
Cactus and Succulent Journal
Gardeners Chronicle
Gentes Herbarum, Ithaca
Journal of the Royal Horticultural Society
Kew Bulletin
Mémoires: Académie Impériale des Sciences de St Pétersbourg
Notes from the Royal Botanic Garden, Edinburgh
The Garden
University of California Publications in Botany

GLOSSARY
and Abbreviations used in the text

Achene – small dry indehiscent single-seeded fruit, as in buttercup, formed from superior ovary. (see **Cypsela**)

Adpressed (**Appressed**) – lying close to, or pressed flat against, but not fused with another organ or that upon which it is growing.

Alien – not native to a given area but introduced from elsewhere.

Alternate – not opposite each other but arranged successively at approximately regular intervals at different heights on the stem, as evident in spiral insertion.

Amplexicaul – clasping the stem.

Annual – completing a life cycle, i.e. from germination of seed to production of mature fruits and death, within twelve months. (see **Biennial, Perennial**)

Androecium – the male parts of the flower, the stamens as a whole. (see **Gynoecium**)

Anther – pollen-containing part of the stamen.

Asymmetrical – not symmetrical, lop-sided.

Aril (adj. **Arillate**) – fleshy appendage to seed, in true aril arising from seed stalk or funicle, but in structures of similar function (called strophioles, caruncles, arillodes) arising from surface of the seed.

Autotrophic – neither parasitic nor saprophytic. but living as is usual for green plants: able to synthesize their own food from inorganic sources.

Axil (adj. **Axillary**) – upper angle between leaf or bract and stem.

Axis – (i) central part of plant, on and around which the organs are placed. (ii) elongated part of receptacle on which floral organs are placed.

Berry – fleshy several-seeded fruit without a stony layer around the seeds, which are embedded in pulp, e.g. gooseberry or tomato.

Biennial – completing a life cycle within twenty-four months from germination, not flowering in first year. (see **Annual, Perennial**)

Bilabiate – two-lipped.

Bisexual – having both sexes (i.e., androecium and gynoecium) on the same flower, inflorescence or individual plant.

Bract – any leafy appendage subtending flowers or belonging to an inflorescence, usually smaller, and differently shaped from a foliage leaf.

Bud – undeveloped branch, leaf or flower within protective scales.

Bulb – subterranean compacted stem surrounded by a number of swollen leaf-bases or scales, enclosing the bud for the next year's growth.

Bulbil – a small bulb, usually arising in a leaf axil or in inflorescence florets.

Calyx (pl. **Calyces**) – the outer perianth members, the sepals as a whole.

Campanulate – bell-shaped, i.e. cup-shaped with an outward-curving rim.

Capitate – head-shaped, i.e. gathered together into a dense cluster.

Capitulum (pl. **Capitula**) – condensed inflorescence as found in daisies, a telescoped raceme.

Capsule – dry dehiscent fruit composed of more than one carpel, splitting lengthwise when ripe.

Carpel – a unit of the gynoecium (= pistil), containing one or several ovules.

Catkin – an often pendulous spike or narrow raceme of unisexual flowers clothed in scale-like bracts and usually falling as a whole.

Chlorophyll – green pigment found in leaves and stems.

Chromosomes – small bodies found in all nuclei and observable at certain stages of cell development when suitably stained; bodies which carry most of the inherited characters of organisms.

Cladode – green leaf-like shoot, i.e. a branch functioning and looking like a leaf, as in Butcher's Broom (*Ruscus*).

Claw – narrowed lower part, or stalk, of some petals.

Compound – composed of several similar parts.

Corm – subterranean stem of one year's duration, with next year's arising on top of the older one; bulb-like in function and general form, but solid and not composed of several overlapping scales.

Corolla – inner perianth members, the petals as a whole.

Corona – a ring of appendages, or a ring-like appendage on the inside of the petals or perianth.

Corymb (adj. **Corymbose**) – a flat-topped inflorescence, usually a raceme with flower stalks becoming shorter near the top so that all the flowers occur at the same level.

Cotyledon – first leaf-like organ(s) of a plant, either remaining within the seed-coat (in hypogeal germination), or turning green and raised above the ground (in epigeal germination).

Culm – stalks of grasses or sedges.

Cyme (adj. **Cymose**) – inflorescence with growing point terminated by a flower, so further flowers must appear by new lateral growths; the central or terminal flowers opening first and the whole forming a usually broad, flattish cluster with buds at the outside.

Cypsela – small indehiscent single-seeded fruit, as in sunflower, formed from inferior ovary. (see **Achene**)

Deciduous – dropping off, usually with reference to leaf-fall at the end of the growing season, particularly of trees which remain bare of leaves for a season.

Decumbent – lying along the ground but with the free end or tip rising from it.

Decussate – with opposite insertion, successive pairs being placed at right-angles to each other.

Dehiscent – opening to shed spores or seeds along a definite slit or valve.

Dentate – with teeth, these generally pointing outwards.

Dimorphic – having two forms.

Disc – fleshy or nectar-secreting part of receptacle surrounding or on top of the ovary, or in *Compositae* the broadened end of the stem bearing tubular flowers.

Dominant – chief constituent, usually in terms of floristic composition, i.e. beech in beech-woods.

Drupe (adj. **Drupaceous**) – fleshy fruit with one or more seeds surrounded by a hard or stony layer, as in plum or cherry.

Endemic – restricted geographically to a single area, growing naturally only in one place, region or country.

Endosperm – a nutritive tissue or food reserve surrounding the embryo in flowering plants.

Entire – not cut nor toothed nor divided.

Epigynous – with stamens and perianth inserted around the top of the ovary, i.e. above the ovary and not below it. (from the Greek *epi* 'upon', *gyne* 'woman')

Epiphyte (adj. **Epiphytic**) – a plant perched on another plant, i.e. attached to it but not deriving nourishment from it as a parasite does.

Exserted – protruding beyond or sticking out from the surrounding parts.

Family – a group of genera resembling each other by a combination of characters more closely than they resemble other groups. In botany given a Latin name based on one of the genera in the family with the suffix *-aceae* or *ae*, e.g. *Rosaceae* and *Iridaceae*; *Compositae* and *Umbelliferae*.

Fascicle – bundle.

Filament – anther stalk.

Fimbriate – with margin divided so as to form a fringe.

Flora – (i) the kinds of plants making up the vegetation of an area. (ii) a book in which the families, genera and species of plants found in a given area are listed and may be described.

Follicle – dry dehiscent fruit formed of one carpel and opening lengthwise along one side only.

Free – separate from and not united with another organ or part.

Fruit – structure containing the seeds, whether comprising simply the ripened ovary and seeds, or also parts of the receptacle.

Funicle – stalk of an ovule or seed.

Genus (pl. **Genera**) – a group of species resembling each other by a combination of characters more closely than they resemble other groups. The generic name forms the first part of the two-word specific name, e.g. *Rosa* and *Iris*. (see **Species**)

Glabrous – without hairs.

Glaucous – with bluish appearance produced by a 'bloom' on the surface.

Glumes – chaffy scales enclosing groups of flowers of grasses and sedges.

Gynoecium – the female part of the flower, i.e. the ovary, style and stigma as a whole. (see **Androecium, Pistil**)

Herb (adj. **Herbaceous**) – (i) any non-woody plant, excluding mosses and algae. (ii) non-botanical name for medicinal and culinary plants, not always non-woody.

Hermaphrodite – with functional male and

female organs both in the same flower.

Heterostylous – with styles and stamens at different lengths in flowers on different individuals of the same species, e.g. in primrose, which has some individuals with long styles and short stamens, and others with short styles and longer or higher placed stamens.

Hood – organs fused together, or so positioned as to create a cowl or hood-shaped structure.

Hybrid – offspring resulting from fertilisation of a member of one subspecies, species or genus by another member; an intra-specific hybrid is one between different plants in the same species, an inter-specific hybrid is one between different species in the same genus, and an inter-generic hybrid is one between species of different genera.

Hypogynous – with stamens and perianth inserted around the base of the ovary. (see **Epigynous**)

Indehiscent – not opening at maturity to release spores or seeds.

Inferior Ovary – with perianth and stamens inserted above the ovary. (see **Epigynous**)

Inflorescence – flowering part of shoot, not usually leafy, and consisting of axis, flowers and bracts.

Internode – the portion of the stem between nodes.

Involucre – bracts forming a calyx-like collar beneath a condensed inflorescence, as in a capitulum.

Lamina – thin flat piece of tissue, the blade or expanded part of a leaf as distinct from its stalk (petiole), or of a petal as distinct from its narrowed lower part (claw).

Latex – milky juice.

Leaflet – a separate part (division) of a compound leaf.

Legume – capsule opening along one or two sutures, as in pods of *Leguminosae* (*Papilionaceae*, *Caesalpiniaceae* and *Mimosaceae*).

Lepidote – clothed with scales.

Liana – any tropical woody climbing or twining plant.

Lip – a united group of perianth segments clearly separated from the others, and forming an upper or lower division of the flower.

Monotypic – comprising only one species (in genus) or only one genus (in family).

Node – part of the stem, often marked by slight swelling which bears a leaf or bract. (see **Internode**)

Nut – simple dry indehiscent one-seeded fruit with bony shell.

Ochrea – sheathing tube formed from two stipules encircling the stem above a node in *Polygonaceae*.

Opposite – when two organs arise at the same level but on opposite sides of the stem.

Ovary – the part of the gynoecium enclosing the ovules; it may be formed of one or more carpels, and develops into the fruit.

Ovule – body containing the egg which develops into a seed on fertilisation.

Palmate – consisting of five or more leaflets arising from the same point as in a horse chestnut; a leaf with two leaflets is described as 'bifoliolate', with three as 'trifoliolate'.

Panicle (adj. **Paniculate**) – much-branched loose inflorescence.

Pappus – late maturing calyx which forms a crown on top of the fruit (cypsela) in daisies and other members of *Compositae*.

Parasite – any organism deriving its food from other living organisms on to, or in which, it is attached.

Pedicel – stalk of an individual flower.

Peduncle – stalk of an inflorescence.

Perennial – living longer than twenty-four months, usually flowering each year.

Perianth (Perigon) – sterile floral organs outside the stamens and ovary, i.e. the sepals and petals together, generally used when they are so alike as not to be conveniently distinguishable, as in lilies; one perianth segment is often called a 'tepal'.

Petal – one member of the inner perianth series (corolla) between sepals and stamens, often coloured.

Petiole (adj. **Petiolate**) – leaf stalk.

Pinnate – with leaflets or leaf divisions in two rows, one opposite the other along a common stalk; each division may be further divided.

Pistil – the female part of the flower. (see **Gynoecium**)

Pollen – the male spores of a flowering plant, i.e. the dust-like powder produced by anthers.

Pollinium – regularly shaped mass of cohering pollen which facilitates wholesale pollen-transfer in orchids and asclepiads.

Primitive – combinations of characters thought to be less highly evolved than others, and so reflecting an ancestral condition.

Propagule – any material in the form of a unit of dispersal capable of propagating a species, e.g. seeds, bulbils.

Procumbent – lying loosely along the ground without putting out roots.

Pubescent – covered with short hairs, usually soft and downy.

Raceme (adj. **Racemose**) – inflorescence of stalked flowers the growing point of which adds to the inflorescence and thus is theoretically of indefinite length, with the youngest buds at the top.

Receptacle – that part of the stem from which the flower parts of an individual flower, or the florets of a capitulum arise; it may be flat, concave, or convex to conical. (see **Axis**)

Rhachis (Rachis) – main stalk of a compound leaf or of any inflorescence on which the leaflets or flowers are placed.

Rhizome (adj. **Rhizomatous**) – subterranean stem lasting for more than one season.

Samara – dry indehiscent fruit, part of the wall of which is expanded into a flattened wing.

Saprophyte – plant deriving its food from dead organic matter.

Scabrid – with a rough or scurfy surface.

Scape (adj. **Scapose**) – leafless or bract-bearing flower stem of a plant with basal leaves.

Seed – reproductive body containing an embryo, often accompanied by food reserves and enclosed within a protective coat (testa).

Sepal – one member of the outer perianth series (calyx), often green.

Septum (pl. **Septa**) – a partition dividing an ovary into separate compartments.

Serrate – toothed like a saw, i.e. with teeth pointing forwards.

Sessile – stalkless.

Siliqua – dry dehiscent fruit which splits open by two valves and leaves a persistent partition called a replum.

Simple – not divided.

Spadix (pl. **Spadices**) – fleshy axis bearing stalkless flowers as in aroids.

Spathe – large, often coloured bract sheathing an inflorescence during its early growth as in amaryllids, aroids and palms.

Species – a group of individual plants resembling each other by a combination of constant characters; usually interfertile, but often not so with individuals of another species. In botany given a Latin name in two parts such as *Rosa rugosa* or *Iris graminea*. The basic unit in biological classification.

Spike (adj. **Spicate**) – simple inflorescence with stalkless or almost stalkless flowers, the axis elongated but not fleshy. (see **Spadix**)

Spur – hollow conical or tubular projection from base of perianth segment, usually containing nectar.

Stamen – a male reproductive organ in flowering plants, the essential part of which is the anther.

Staminode – a sterile, modified stamen.

Stem – the central support for leaves, branches and flowers. (see **Axis**)

Stigma – receptive surface for pollen capping the end of a style or ovary, or oblique down the side of an ovary, usually with minute projections or sticky.

Stipule (adj. **Stipulate**) – appendage at base of leaf.

Stolon (adj. **Stoloniferous**) – creeping leaf-bearing above-ground stem capable of forming a new plant at its tip.

Style – the part of the gynoecium between stigma and ovary.

Sucker – shoot arising from the root of a plant and appearing some distance from it.

Superior Ovary – with perianth and stamens inserted below the ovary. (see **Hypogynous**)

Suture – line of junction in a young fruit which often becomes a line of splitting in a mature fruit.

Symbiosis – the living together of dissimilar organisms with consequent benefit to one or both.

Symmetrical – all the parts in a given circle of floral organs, such as stamens and petals, being alike; having more than one plane of symmetry.

Tepal – one member of the perianth.

Terete – neither grooved nor angled.

Terminal – borne at the end of a shoot and limiting further growth.

Tube – fused portion of the corolla or calyx.

Tuber (adj. **Tuberous**) – swollen piece of stem or root of one year's duration not giving rise directly to subsequent tubers.

Tubercle – spherical or peg-like swelling.

Umbel (adj. **Umbellate**) – inflorescence in which the pedicels all arise from one point at the top of the stem.

Unisexual – having only one sex in a flower or inflorescence.

Viviparous – sprouting or germinating while still attached to the parent plant.

Whorl – a group of more than two similar organs arising at the same level, e.g. leaves or floral parts.

Zygomorphic – bilaterally symmetrical or having one vertical plane of symmetry. (see **Asymmetrical**)

ABBREVIATIONS USED IN THE TEXT

f. = forma   ssp. = subspecies
syn. = synonym(s)   var. = variety   × = hybrid

Plate 1 ARCTIC AND ANTARCTIC

The difference between the plants of the two polar regions is to a great extent one of size, the vegetation of the arctic being smaller and more stunted than that of the antarctic, as a comparison of the *Draba* genus (see G) of the former area with the *Pringlea* (see J) or *Ranunculus pinguis* (H) of the latter will show. The crucial factors responsible for this difference are, perhaps, the higher latitude in the arctic of land that will support plant life, and the greater and less isolated area of the arctic land mass.

A plant of the arctic of eastern Europe, western Asia and eastern Greenland, and also found in the higher mountains of western and central Europe, *Ranunculus glacialis* (A) is a perennial herb 2 to 10 inches (5–25 cm.) tall. As its name implies, it usually grows in damp, open ground near snow banks and glaciers. Characteristic of wet, open areas and mossy marshes, *R. sulphureus* (B), with its usually single, sulphur yellow flowers, inhabits the most severe of arctic environments. Like many of the region's plants, it is circumpolar in distribution.

Walpole's Poppy, *Papaver walpolei* (C) occurs in arctic eastern Asia, Alaska and Yukon. Its densely tufted rosettes of leaves which may measure no more than $1\frac{1}{2}$ inches (38 mm.) in height are overtopped by the $4\frac{1}{2}$ inch (11 cm.) flower stalk, bearing white, or more rarely, yellow, blooms. It is related to the Arctic Poppy (see below) but differs in the shape of the fruit and in having less hairy, and less deeply lobed, leaves.

One of the commonest, and perhaps the best known of all the arctic plants is *Papaver radicatum* (D), the Arctic Poppy, a circumpolar species found in drier, more open habitats. The plant is so variable throughout its range that botanists have reached no general agreement on how the varieties should be classified: numerous subspecies have been distinguished and certain variants have even been described as separate species.

With a distribution from Alaska and Yukon to eastern Greenland, *Draba crassifolia* (G) is a diminutive plant that rarely reaches a height of more than 4 inches (10 cm.) overall. In habit this plant resembles an annual, a type of plant not usually found in the arctic since the brief summer there would not allow enough time to complete a life cycle, and it has, mistakenly, been taken for such. However, the fact that it is generally found in sheltered ravines and similar areas that are covered in winter with deep drifts of late-melting snow and that, consequently, it only flowers late in summer, implies that it must reproduce itself vegetatively and therefore be a perennial.

Another diminutive member of the same family, *Cruciferae*, is *Braya thorild-wulffii*, which occurs from the Canadian arctic to eastern Greenland. The species forms very tiny, tufted plants with flowering stems no more than $2\frac{1}{2}$ inches (6·3 cm.) long and has a short annual cycle of quick flowering and fruiting during the brief season of milder weather. The genus, which comprises some twenty species of which four are arctic, commemorates the Franco-German diplomat and botanist Graf von Bray (1765–1832).

Caltha dionaeifolia (E) is common in Tierra del Fuego and on Hermite Island, where it covers the ground with shiny, deep green leaves, reminiscent at first glance of those of the North American Venus' Flytrap, *Dionaea*. The similarity is, however, quite fortuitous, as the leaves of *Caltha* do not catch flies and the two species are in no way related.

A native of boggy hillsides and rocky crevices on the Auckland Islands and Campbell Island, *Ranunculus pinguis* (H) is now, on Campbell Island at least, more or less restricted to inaccessible ledges because of grazing by sheep. The two populations are beginning to diverge morphologically and to show minor differences in the hairiness of the leaves, and in the number and size of the petals.

Also found in similar habitats on the same islands is *Cardamine depressa* var. *stellata* (F). The variety differs from the true New Zealand species in having coarse white hairs on leaves and stems, shorter leaves, and shorter fruits. It has yet to be determined whether these differences are genetically or environmentally induced.

Sir Joseph Hooker considered *Pringlea antiscorbutica* (J), the Kerguelen Cabbage, to be the most interesting plant to be found by him on his voyages to the antarctic with the 'Erebus' and 'Terror' (1839–1843). It bears some resemblance to a horseradish with a rosette of cabbage-like leaves from whose base, and slightly to one side, arise the inflorescences. The horizontal rhizomes extend for 4 feet (1·2 m.) or even further, and the heads of leaves measure about 18 inches (46 cm.) in diameter. The importance of the plant to sailors crossing the Roaring Forties on their way from the South Atlantic to Australia lay in the fact that not only is it edible, containing a pale yellow juice which, in Hooker's opinion, renders it easily digestible, but also in its value as an antidote to scurvy. Its very name, bestowed by the surgeon and naturalist William Anderson, who first discovered the plant during Cook's third voyage, honours a pioneer in the study of the disease, Sir John Pringle. It is possible that the species was only saved from extinction at the hands of vitamin starved sailors by the change in shipping routes that came about with the introduction of steam. *P. antiscorbutica* is the sole species in its genus and is restricted to Kerguelen and the Crozet Islands, growing from sea-level, where it is largest, to an altitude of about 2000 feet (610 m.). The flowers usually lack petals but an occasional one, or more rarely as many as 4, tinged with pink, may develop. Since there are no flying insects on these remote islands, it is presumed that the flowers are pollinated by the wind.

Arctic

RANUNCULACEAE

Ranunculus glacialis
A1 flowering plants $\times \frac{2}{3}$. A2 flower sectioned $\times 2$.

R. sulphureus
B1 flowering plant $\times \frac{2}{3}$. B2 fruiting head $\times 2\frac{2}{3}$.
B3 seed $\times 6$.

PAPAVERACEAE

Papaver walpolei, Walpole's Poppy
C1 flowering plant $\times \frac{2}{3}$. C2 leaf $\times 2$.

P. radicatum, Arctic Poppy
D1 flowering plant (flower stem cut) $\times \frac{2}{3}$.

CRUCIFERAE

Draba crassifolia
G1 flowering and fruiting plants $\times \frac{2}{3}$.
G2 flower $\times 4$. G3 immature fruit $\times 2$.
G4 mature fruit $\times 2$. G5 leaf $\times 2\frac{2}{3}$.

Antarctic

RANUNCULACEAE

Caltha dionaeifolia
E1 part of flowering plant $\times \frac{2}{3}$. E2 leaf $\times 2\frac{2}{3}$.

Ranunculus pinguis
H1 fruiting plant $\times \frac{2}{3}$. H2 flower $\times \frac{2}{3}$.
H3 seed $\times 4$.

CRUCIFERAE

Cardamine depressa var. *stellata*
F1 flowering plant $\times \frac{2}{3}$. F2 flower $\times 4$.

Pringlea antiscorbutica, Kerguelen Cabbage
J1 part of fruiting plant $\times \frac{2}{3}$.
J2 fruiting inflorescence $\times \frac{2}{3}$.
J3 immature fruit $\times 2$. J4 petal $\times 2$.

A1

A2

B1

B2

B3

C1

C2

D1

E1

E2

F1

F2

G1

G2

G3

G4

G5

H1

H3

J1

J2

J3

J4

Plate 2   ARCTIC AND ANTARCTIC

Only the most severe restrictions imposed by cold climates prevent the existence of plants like the two saxifrages illustrated opposite, both of which have a circumpolar distribution and occur on the most northern promontaries of land inside the Arctic Circle. In fact, *Saxifraga flagellaris* (E), the Flagellate Saxifrage, is one of the most northerly occurring of all flowering plants, often growing in damp chalky habitats or on exposed clay or gravel barrens, although it is also found on the high mountains of Asia. It is characterized by its long, 10–11 inch (25–27·5 cm.) reddish whip-like stolons, bearing plantlets at their tips which develop and flower as the parent plant dies.

One of the commonest arctic plants which will survive on some of the most exposed ridges where no other flowering plant exists, the Purple Saxifrage, *S. oppositifolia* (G) often grows in drier habitats than the previous species and may dominate the arctic barrens. It occurs throughout Greenland but is also found in alpine habitats in Europe and Asia and is sometimes successfully grown as a rock garden plant.

Inhabiting dry cliffs and south-facing slopes of Novaya Zemlya and Vaigach Island in the Arctic, *Potentilla sericea* (B) has a rosette of silky hairy leaves much divided and feathery in appearance. They are densely tufted around the stumpy stem which is invested with dead stipules during the winter months. Flowering shoots may be 16 inches (41 cm.) tall, clothed in a few divided leafy bracts and bearing 2 to 6 small terminal yellow flowers, each about $\frac{1}{2}$ inch (13 mm.) in diameter.

Although the Arctic Cinquefoil, *P. hyparctica* (A) is hardier with a fully circumpolar range, it needs a sheltered position where it grows amongst grasses and other herbs. Like many arctic plants, the Arctic Cinquefoil is covered with hairs which help protect it from a bright and sometimes hot sun, during summer months, and the cold nights of early spring.

Another genus in the rose family, *Dryas* has two species (although some botanists recognize more) confined to arctic and montane habitats in the northern hemisphere. Mountain Avens, *D. octopetala* (C) is a tussock- or mat-forming perennial found in arctic Eurasia (as well as the mountains of Europe), in Greenland, Alaska and Yukon, but apparently absent from the Canadian arctic. Here it is replaced by the Arctic Avens, *D. integrifolia*, recorded throughout arctic North America, including Greenland. This differs from the former in having elongate-triangular leaves, not elliptical, and the margins of the leaves lack the small lobes of the Mountain Avens. Where the range of the two species overlaps, intermediate hydrids are produced which have caused confusion in the recognition

of the species. When the attractive white flowers of the Mountain Avens have died and as the achenes ripen, the persistent elongated styles become silky and plumed which helps the wind distribution of the fruit. The diminutive beauty of the oak-like leaves of this plant inspired the generic name, from the Greek tree nymphs or dryads.

The Cloudberry, *Rubus chamaemorus* (D) is found throughout most of the arctic although apparently absent in eastern Greenland. It also occurs on the mountains of Britain, Scandinavia, central and eastern Europe, Canada and the northern United States. Growing on acidic bog and peat tundra, its herbaceous shoots arise from the rhizome which creeps through the wet peat and individual plants often spread over a wide area. The unisexual plants have single, terminal white flowers which often have only 4 petals, unlike most *Rubus* species. The edible fruits, which are yellowish when ripe, are said to taste like baked apples.

Growing in heathy or gravelly places in the Canadian arctic and the arctic of eastern Asia, *Oxytropis bellii* (H) forms a noticeably pale green, tufted plant. Its leaves, arising from a deep tap-root, measure up to 7 inches (17·5 cm.) long and are delicately dissected into numerous (rarely as few as 21) lateral leaflets. These are not always opposite, as would be the normal arrangement, and 2 or 3 often grow from the same point on the leaf stalk. In winter, the stem is thickly clustered with the remains of old stipules which afford some protection to the growing point during the cold months.

Found only on the Falkland Islands and discovered there by the young Joseph Dalton Hooker, *Hamadryas argentea* (F) is one of five perennial species in a genus belonging to the buttercup family and found in antarctic America. It grows near the sea, on grassy slopes and also on the mountains; although now a rare plant, it was probably more abundant before the introduction of sheep. These plants, covered with silver or golden hairs, are unisexual, and the flowers appear in November or December.

A most complex genus, *Coprosma* contains over ninety species, about half of which are native to New Zealand. *C. pumila* (J) is found in alpine pastures in New Zealand but also extends into the antarctic sea on Auckland, Campbell and Macquarie Islands, also being the only New Zealand species to be found in Australia (in Victoria) and Tasmania. Its habit is that of a prostrate creeping shrub which forms broad matted patches and, as in all species in the genus, the plants are unisexual with male and female flowers on separate individuals. The fertilized ovary matures into a globose red drupe, about $\frac{3}{8}$ inch (9·5 mm.) in diameter.

Arctic

ROSACEAE

Potentilla hyparctica, Arctic Cinquefoil
A1 flowering plant × $\frac{2}{3}$.

P. sericea
B1 part of flowering plant × $\frac{2}{3}$.

Dryas octopetala, Mountain Avens
C1 part of flowering plant × $\frac{2}{3}$.
C2 side view of flower × $\frac{2}{3}$.
C3 young fruiting head × $\frac{2}{3}$. C4 single fruit × 2.

Rubus chamaemorus, Cloudberry
D1 part of male flowering plant × $\frac{2}{3}$.
D2 part of fruiting plant × $\frac{2}{3}$.

SAXIFRAGACEAE

Saxifraga flagellaris, Flagellate Saxifrage
E1 flowering plant × $\frac{2}{3}$. E2 flower × $\frac{2}{3}$.

S. oppositifolia, Purple Saxifrage
G1 flowering plant × $\frac{2}{3}$. G2 petal × $5\frac{1}{3}$.
G3 ovary × $5\frac{1}{3}$. G4 stamens × $5\frac{2}{3}$. G5 node × 6.

LEGUMINOSAE

Oxytropis bellii
H1 part of flowering plant × $\frac{2}{3}$. H2 fruits × $\frac{2}{3}$.

Antarctic

RANUNCULACEAE

Hamadryas argentea
F1 flowering plant × $\frac{2}{3}$. F2 flower × $\frac{2}{3}$.
F3 petal × 2.

RUBIACEAE

Coprosma pumila
J1 part of male flowering shoot × $\frac{2}{3}$.
J2 male flower × $2\frac{2}{3}$. J3 female flower × $2\frac{2}{3}$.
J4 part of fruiting shoot × $\frac{2}{3}$.

A1

B1

C1
C2
C3
C4

D1
D2

E1
E2

F1
F2
F3

G1
G2
G3
G4
G5

H1
H2

J1
J2
J3
J4

Plate 3   ARCTIC AND ANTARCTIC

A most attractive plant with usually abundant purple-pink blossoms, the Moss Campion, *Silene acaulis* (A), is found throughout the arctic and on the higher mountains of western and central Europe. It forms small hummocks of leafy stems, woody at the base, up to 6 inches (15 cm.) tall, to which the persistence of the dead leaves adds density. In the northernmost areas of its range the flowers appear only on the south side of these hummocks.

The petals of *Lychnis apetala* (B) do, despite the implication of the plant's Latin name, exist, but are often entirely hidden by the inflated calyx within which they are enclosed. The nodding flowers grow one to a stem and in fruit the stalk below the calyx straightens and holds the capsule erect, thus allowing the small teeth at its mouth to project slightly beyond the calyx. *L. apetala* is a very familiar circumpolar plant capable of flourishing in a wide range of habitats.

Most of the twenty to thirty species of *Sagina* are found in northern temperate Eurasia but some occur in North America and at high altitudes in South America and New Guinea. The tiny cushions, about 1¼ inches (3 cm.) tall, formed by the perennial *S. caespitosa* (C) grow from the Canadian arctic, Greenland and Jan Mayen Island to Iceland and the mountains of Norway and Sweden. The abundant flowers, which scarcely protrude beyond the cushions, turn into pale brown capsules, each about ⅛ inch (3 mm.) long, before the snow covers them for the long winter. The closely related *S. intermedia* has longer flower stalks than *S. caespitosa* but shares the same low-lying, tufted habit—a form of growth peculiarly well suited to the windswept polar regions, since the smallness of the amount of foliage reduces the physiologically necessary water-loss while providing just enough stored nourishment for the flowers and fruit to come to maturity in the shortest possible time. *S. intermedia* is probably circumpolar in distribution and it also occurs in Scotland.

Also growing in tufts, or sometimes in extended tussocks and loose mats, is the Polar Chickweed, *Cerastium regelii* (F), probably one of the few plants unrecorded outside the Arctic Circle (its occurrence in north-westernmost America and north-eastern Siberia is dubious). Its yellowish green leaves are succulent, but not hairy like those of its close relative, the Alpine Chickweed, *C. alpinum*, a plant that is circumpolar but which also occurs on British mountains, the Pyrenees and the Alps.

Claytonia commemorates John Clayton, a celebrated 18th century American botanist (1694–1773) who helped produce the first *Flora Virginica*. The genus contains about twenty species, mostly American, and of which five occur in the arctic. A diminutive perennial found in arctic Siberia, Alaska and the Yukon, the Arctic Spring Beauty, *C. arctica* (D), has a

fleshy root-stock and broad basal leaves up to 1¼ inches (3 cm.) long and grows in wet grassy areas on peaty soils.

Only the blooms, which consist of 4 whitish, petal-like bracts subtending a terminal mass of 7 to 25 small purple flowers, betray the relationship between the beautiful tree *Cornus nuttallii* (shown on plate 155) and its dwarf relative the Dwarf Cornel, *C. suecica* (E), a shrubby perennial found in dry or rocky habitats throughout the arctic of Eurasia, America and Greenland and south into the northern parts of Britain, Germany and Japan. Its stems, which grow from an underground rhizome, rarely exceed 12 inches (30 cm.) in height and bear 3 to 6 pairs of pale green rounded leaves. The flowers of the species, which is also known as *Chamaepericlymenum suecicum*, are succeeded by clusters of red fruits.

The fifty or so species of the genus *Gunnera* are confined almost entirely to the southern hemisphere, reaching the tropics of Malaysia at one extreme of their range and Juan Fernandez and the Falkland Islands at the other. One of the commonest American antarctic plants, *G. magellanica* (G) is abundant, except where it has suffered from grazing livestock, throughout the Andes, in southern Chile, Tierra del Fuego and the Falklands. In November, the southern spring, the flowers appear, male and female on separate plants. The male inflorescences are larger than the female and exceed the leaves in height. No petals exist and sepals are found only in the female flowers, which also have feathery styles—an indication that they are wind pollinated.

Once found blanketing whole cliff-tops during the Falkland Island spring but now restricted by the depredations of sheep, *Oxalis enneaphylla* (H) is the most southerly species of its large genus and is mainly found near the sea in the above-mentioned islands and round the Straits of Magellan. Most plants are white-flowered but a pink-flowered form is also known; both make excellent subjects for cultivation in northern temperate regions.

Rated by Sir Joseph Hooker as second only to *Pringlea* (see plate 1) in interest among the plants found on his voyages to the Antarctic, *Lyallia kerguelensis* (J) is rare even on Kerguelen Island, its only home. The species, which forms large, low tufts of vegetation in exposed habitats, was originally placed by Hooker in the *Caryophyllaceae* family but recent assessments of the microscopic characteristics of its pollen have led to its being placed with another antarctic perennial, *Hectorella*, in the family *Hectorellaceae*. *Hectorella*, like *Lyallia* a genus of only one species, is confined to southern New Zealand. The name of the genus illustrated commemorates Dr David Lyall, surgeon on board H.M.S. 'Terror' during Ross's antarctic voyage of 1839–1842.

Arctic

CARYOPHYLLACEAE

Silene acaulis, Moss Campion
A1 flowering plant × ⅔.

Lychnis apetala
B1 flowering plant × ⅔. B2 flower × 1⅓.

Sagina caespitosa
C1 flowering plant × ⅔. C2 flower × 2⅔.
C3 sepal × 4. C4 node × 4.

Cerastium regelii, Polar Chickweed
F1 flowering plant × ⅔. F2 flower × 1⅓.

PORTULACACEAE

Claytonia arctica, Arctic Spring Beauty
D1 flowering plant × ⅔.

CORNACEAE

Cornus suecica (syn. *Chamaepericlymenum suecicum*), Dwarf Cornel
E1 flowering plant × ⅔. E2 flower × 6.
E3 part of fruiting stem × ⅔. E4 fruit × 2⅔.

Antarctic

GUNNERACEAE

Gunnera magellanica
G1 male flowering plant × ⅔.
G2 male flowers × 4.
G3 female flowering plant × ⅔. G4 ovary × 4.

OXALIDACEAE

Oxalis enneaphylla
H1 part of flowering plant × ⅔.
H2 stamens, styles and ovary × 2.

HECTORELLACEAE

Lyallia kerguelensis
J1 flowering plant × ⅔.
J2 flower (enlarged after Hooker).
J3 branch system × 1⅓.
J4 leaves on part of stem × 1⅓. J5 leaf × 6.

A1

B1

B2

C1

C2

C3

C4

D1

E1

E2

E3

E4

F1

F2

G1

G2

G3

G4

H1

H2

J1

J2

J3

J4

J5

Plate 4   ARCTIC AND ANTARCTIC

The genera illustrated on this plate exemplify various possible patterns of distribution among plants found on both ice-caps. *Epilobium*, *Gentiana* and *Androsace* all have representatives in the Arctic and Antarctic but these appear as dwarfed and much modified versions of a larger number of temperate species. A less common type of distribution is demonstrated by *Primula stricta* of the Arctic and its southern counterpart *P. magellanica*: the two are very closely related but no intervening primulas directly link their respective ranges.

Primula stricta (A) is a delicate, erect little primrose that grows in damp or marshy grassland throughout the northern region though it might be more accurate to classify it as subarctic rather than arctic. It has, at times, been treated as a variety or subspecies of the closely related European *P. farinosa* but, because of slight yet distinct differences in appearance, a separate distribution and, above all, a quite different number of chromosomes, it is now generally regarded as a separate species.

Native in Alaska, Yukon, the Aleutian Islands and north-eastern Asia, *Primula cuneifolia* (D) occurs in damp turf and flushes of melt-water from snow-fields. The somewhat fleshy leaves and pinkish purple, yellow-eyed flowers, of which up to 9 are produced, are borne on stems that often show the 'farina' or mealiness characteristic of many primulas.

A small, densely tufted plant of the gravelly tundra and shoreline of Novaya Zemlya and the central arctic regions of Asia, *Androsace triflora* (B) rarely exceeds $\frac{3}{4}$ inch (19 mm.) in height or 2 inches (5 cm.) in the diameter of the tuft. The specific epithet refers to the three terminal yellow flowers carried on short stems.

About two hundred and fifteen species from both the northern and southern temperate zones belong to the genus *Epilobium* in addition to those representatives in both the polar regions mentioned above. The arctic *E. davuricum* (C) typifies the weak, herbaceous type of willow-herb; others may be taller, semi-woody and much more robust. A small individual of the species may be only $\frac{3}{4}$ inch (19 mm.) high, though in favourable situations it sometimes reaches a height of 16 inches (41 cm.). The few, whitish flowers appear to stand at the end of long stalks but these are in fact conspicuously elongated ovaries. The fruit capsules, like those of all but one, Tasmanian, species of willowherb, contain plumed seeds. *E. davuricum* grows in damp, sheltered situations on open patches of soil, and would be circumpolar in distribution were it not absent from certain parts of the Eurasian arctic.

The Fireweed or Great Willowherb, *Epilobium angustifolium* (F), is a robust weed that became an ubiquitous element in the townscapes of Britain and other parts of Europe during the Second World War, when it colonized bomb-sites, often in pure stands. Were it not for its weedy tendency, it would also have become a familiar and ornamental garden plant. In the Arctic, the species never reaches the 6 to 7 feet (1·8–2·1 m.) it attains under good conditions in temperate areas, and may be as little as 4 inches (10 cm.) in height. Self-pollination in individual flowers is almost excluded, and cross-pollination enforced, by the cycle in which the reproductive

organs grow: the stamens mature as soon as the flower opens and while the style, with its 4 stigmas closed, is bent down out of the way; later the position is reversed, the stamens withering and drooping as the style, its stigmas open, stands erect. A group of ten species of *Epilobium* centred around that illustrated is sometimes split off into a separate genus, *Chamaenerion*, on the grounds that their flowers are not radially but bilaterally symmetrical; under this classification *E. angustifolium* becomes *Chamaenerion angustifolium*.

A native of the Arctic from Greenland to Eurasia but also found in western Europe and south to the Azores and to Morocco and in America south to the mountains of New England and Washington, the Marsh Violet, *Viola palustris* (E) has a system of reproduction that is the inverse of that found in the previous species. Although it may produce seed from its showy flowers by cross-pollination with another plant, as much, or usually more, seed is produced by small, self-pollinated flowers which never open and are generally hidden amongst the leaves on shorter stalks. The phenomenon of self-pollination is shared by many species of *Viola* and other, unrelated northern plants, since it acts as an insurance against sterility in an adverse climate where insects may not appear at the appropriate moment or where normal flowering may be impossible. In the Arctic, the Marsh Violet most often occurs in damp, marshy turf, mossy places or, in exposed situations, in the shelter of drainage channels.

An annual gentian rarely as much as 10 inches (25 cm.) and usually not more than 5 inches (12·5 cm.) tall, *Gentiana tenella* (G) occurs in most arctic areas either as a shoreline plant in sand or turf, or inland on damp slopes. Like many arctic plants it also grows on the higher mountains in the northern hemisphere.

Lending a welcome touch of colour to an otherwise barren landscape, *Gentiana concinna* (H) flowers in abundance from November to December in exposed positions on the hills of Auckland Island, to the south of New Zealand. White with red or purplish streaks, or pinkish all over, the flowers may at first appear atypical in view of the better known blue Himalayan gentians (see plate 97), but the colour is in fact characteristic of the twenty-four or so species found in New Zealand and the adjacent islands.

Primula magellanica (J) grows to a height of about 7 inches (17·5 cm.) and is fairly common on hillsides and in other exposed habitats in the Falkland Islands, Cape Horn, the Magellan Straits region and the southernmost Andes. It differs from *P. farinosa*, of which it is regarded as a variety by some, only in having white or pale lavender flowers in tighter heads, each with a yellow 'eye'. *P. farinosa*, as was mentioned before, is found with other species of the same complex in the northern temperate areas and a considerable geographical gap divides it from *P. magellanica*. This pattern of distribution, found in a number of plant groups, presumably reflects the fact that during the Ice Age some temperate plants were able to migrate along the continuous chain of mountains that consists of the Rockies and the Andes but later, with the return of a warmer climate, became restricted to its two extremes.

Arctic

PRIMULACEAE

Primula stricta
A1 flowering plant (stem cut) $\times \frac{2}{3}$.
A2 opened out corolla $\times 3\frac{1}{3}$.

Androsace triflora
B1 flowering plant $\times 1\frac{1}{3}$. B2 leaf $\times 2$.
B3 opened capsules $\times 2$.

Primula cuneifolia
D1 flowering plant $\times \frac{2}{3}$. D2 flower $\times 1\frac{1}{3}$.

ONAGRACEAE

Epilobium davuricum
C1 flowering plant $\times \frac{2}{3}$. C2 fruiting stem $\times \frac{2}{3}$.
C3 seed $\times 5\frac{1}{3}$.

E. angustifolium (syn. *Chamaenerion angustifolium*), Fireweed, Great Willowherb
F1 part of flowering stem $\times \frac{2}{3}$. F2 flower $\times 2$.
F3 anthers $\times 6$.

VIOLACEAE

Viola palustris, Marsh Violet
E1 flowering plant $\times \frac{2}{3}$. E2 flower $\times 2$.

GENTIANACEAE

Gentiana tenella
G1 flowering plant $\times \frac{2}{3}$.

Antarctic

GENTIANACEAE

Gentiana concinna
H1 flowering plant $\times \frac{2}{3}$.
H2 opened out corolla $\times 2$.

PRIMULACEAE

Primula magellanica
J1 flowering plant $\times \frac{2}{3}$. J2 flower $\times 2$.

A2

B3

A1

B1

B2

E2

E1

D2

F2

F3

D1

C2

C1

C3

F1

J2

G1

H1

H2

J1

Plate 5   ARCTIC AND ANTARCTIC

Among the Antarctic representatives of the genera *Ourisia, Myosotidium* and *Calceolaria* are several species worthy of cultivation. The Arctic members of their families, however, are usually less ornamental in comparison.

Small bulbils characteristic of Alpine Bistort or *Polygonum viviparum* (A) replace the flowers along the lower part of the inflorescence and become detached to form new plants. This method of propagation allows the species to reproduce itself even during seasons when normal procreation by flower production is not practicable. Coupled with the general hardiness of the species, this facility has helped to give the plant a circumpolar distribution. It is commonly found in turfy habitats throughout the Arctic and it also occurs on the higher mountains in Europe, Asia and America.

The prostrate mats formed by *Thymus arcticus* (B) have stems rooting at the nodes. Also known as *T. praecox* ssp. *arcticus*, the plant, a native of Greenland, grows in dry, sunny situations. Its small elliptical leaves, up to about $\frac{3}{8}$ inch (9·5 mm.) long, last for 2 to 3 years and have a leathery texture. *T. drucei*, a very common plant in north and west Britain, is closely related.

Many *Pedicularis* species inhabit the montane regions of central and eastern Asia. Hairy Lousewort, *P. hirsuta* (C), one of about five hundred species in the genus, has an almost circumpolar distribution but is apparently absent from Alaska, Yukon and the most north-eastern parts of Asia. Tolerant of great variety in such ecological factors as exposure, moisture, soil and competition, the species occurs in a wide range of heath or grassland habitats.

Some botanists have split off segregate species from the complex *Myosotis alpestris* (D), the Alpine Forget-me-not. This species occurs in the high mountainous areas of the northern hemisphere, especially from eastern arctic Eurasia into Alaska and the Yukon. Bright blue flowers with yellow eyes make it a most attractive plant. The Alpine Forget-me-not is the floral emblem of the State of Alaska and it was from this species that the forget-me-nots of herbaceous gardens were bred.

Popularly known as the Chatham Island Lily or, more appropriately, as the Giant Forget-me-not, *Myosotidium hortensia* (E) is an endemic species on Chatham Island. It was described from wild material in 1846 and introduced into cultivation by a Mr Watson of St Albans, who exhibited flowering specimens at the Horticultural Society in London in 1858. The following year it was redescribed and illustrated in the *Botanical Magazine* (t. 5137) from a plant erroneously said to have been cultivated in 1829 by Standish, but this was a misprint for 1859. *M. hortensia* grows wild in rocky and sandy coastal habitats; in cultivation it requires a cool, moist atmosphere and is said to appreciate a mulch of seaweed and rotting fish. In recent years grazing animals have made it a rare plant, now found only in inaccessible places out of their reach.

Unlike *Myosotis* and *Gentiana*, the genus *Ourisia* has no representative in the northern hemisphere. It is composed of some twenty species from New Zealand, Tasmania and South America. *O. breviflora* (F), a native of the area around the Magellan Straits, was collected from southern parts of Tierra del Fuego by Charles Darwin and from Hermite Island by Joseph Hooker. Only a few inches tall, the locally common plant bears 2 to 4 flowers.

A native of Auckland Island and Campbell Island, to the south of New Zealand, *Myosotis capitata* (H) is often found close to the high water mark. Further inland it occurs up to an altitude of about 1800 feet (550 m.). Dense heads of deep blue flowers help to distinguish it from most other southern forget-me-nots.

Charles Darwin was the first to discover *Calceolaria darwinii* (G). He collected it on Elizabeth Island during his visit to the Magellan Straits area as a crew member of the 'Beagle'. This uncommon plant grows along the shoreline and flowers during November and December. Together with *C. fothergillii* it is one of the most attractive plants in antarctic America, but the latter—unlike *C. darwinii*—is hairy and has a corolla blotched with rich dark red. It too is a coastal plant which occurs in the Falkland Islands, where it is quite rare now.

Arctic

POLYGONACEAE

Polygonum viviparum, Alpine Bistort
A1 flowering stem × $\frac{2}{3}$. A2 bulbil × 6.
A3 flower and bulbils × 4.

LABIATAE

Thymus arcticus (syn. *T. praecox* ssp. *arcticus*)
B1 flowering plant × $\frac{2}{3}$.

SCROPHULARIACEAE

Pedicularis hirsuta, Hairy Lousewort
C1 part of flowering plant × $\frac{2}{3}$.
C2 portion of leaf × 2.
C3 fruit and subtending bract × $1\frac{1}{3}$.

BORAGINACEAE

Myosotis alpestris, Alpine Forget-me-not
D1 flowering plant × $\frac{2}{3}$. D2 flower × 2.

Antarctic

BORAGINACEAE

Myosotidium hortensia, Chatham Island Lily, Giant Forget-me-not
E1 flowering stem × $\frac{2}{3}$. E2 leaf × $\frac{2}{3}$.
E3 corolla opened out × 2.

Myosotis capitata
H1 flowering plant × $\frac{2}{3}$. H2 flower × $2\frac{2}{3}$.

SCROPHULARIACEAE

Ourisia breviflora
F1 flowering plant × $\frac{2}{3}$. F2 flower × 2.
F3 fruit × 2.

Calceolaria darwinii
G1 flowering and budding plants × $\frac{2}{3}$.

A2

A3

A1

B1

C3

C2

C1

D2

D1

F2

F3

F1

E3

E1

E2

G1

H1

H2

Plate 6   ARCTIC AND ANTARCTIC

Despite its specific epithet, *Diapensia lapponica* (A) is not confined to Lapland, though it was first described from there, but is found throughout almost the entire Arctic. The plant forms tufted hummocks with many branched, crowded stems and tough, curved, spoon-shaped leaves about $\frac{5}{8}$ inch (16 mm.) long. The cream-coloured flowers only last for a short time but, while they are open, make the species most attractive in its windswept and desolate surroundings. The other three species of *Diapensia* are natives of the Sino-Himalayan mountains.

The many branched, low-lying, woody stems and small, hard, leathery leaves make the Alpine Azalea, *Loiseleuria procumbens* (B), a plant ideally suited to arctic conditions. The species, the only one in its genus, occurs in relatively dry, peaty or gravelly places in most parts of the region as well as in the Alps, the Pyrenees and the mountains of central Europe. The genus takes its name from J. L. A. Loiseleur-Deslongchamps (1774–1849), a French botanist and physician.

Another almost circumpolar species, absent only from the western European arctic, *Pyrola grandiflora* (C), the Arctic Wintergreen, grows in colonies on well-drained heathy soils. The height of the flowering stalks, which spring from a rhizomatous stem, and the number of the flowers vary according to the degree of exposure the plant must withstand: there may be as many as 9 flowers on a stalk $5\frac{1}{2}$ inches (14 cm.) long or as few as 2, projecting a mere 2 inches (5 cm.) beyond the rosette of leaves.

Though the Alpine or Black Bearberry, *Arctous alpina* (D), has been frequently placed in the larger evergreen, genus *Arctostaphylos*, it is better classified, with three or four other polar and northern temperate mountain species, under the name given here. *A. alpina* grows in sandy, heathy and rocky habitats over the greater part of the arctic region and in alpine environments. Its prostrate woody twigs, covered with peeling bark and entangled with the trapped remains of dead leaves, form mats of vegetation 3 feet (90 cm.) in diameter. The tufts of deciduous leaves, bright green in spring, take on autumnal

tints at the end of the summer. Both the common and generic names (*Arctous* means 'of a bear') allude to the fact that the berries, black when ripe, are edible and favoured by bears.

The flowers of most Wormwoods, or Sagebrushes, as many species are called, are dingy and unappealing, though the silvery foliage of some has a graceful charm. The majority of the four hundred or so species in the genus *Artemisia* are typical prairie or steppe plants, well adapted to life in semi-arid environments, but a few, among them the Northern Wormwood, *A. borealis* (F), are found in the Arctic. *A. borealis* is a variable species that grows in colonies on sandy or gravelly banks and produces rosettes of deeply divided silky or hairless leaves. It occurs in all arctic areas with the exception of those of western Europe and those of eastern Greenland.

It is, no doubt, the oceanic climate in which they live and their proximity to the rich floras of New Zealand, Australia and South America that accounts for the contrast between the splendid *Pleurophyllum speciosum* (E) of the Antarctic and the nondescript northern Wormwoods of the same family, a contrast that is not confined to these two members of the *Compositae*. The three species of *Pleurophyllum* are found only on the Auckland, Campbell, Antipodes and Macquarie Islands to the south of New Zealand. All are robust herbs, closely related to *Celmisia*. The two more attractive species are the one illustrated, which is restricted in distribution to the Auckland and Campbell Islands, and *P. hookeri*, also found on the Macquarie Islands. The third, *P. criniferum*, though it may reach 6 feet (1·8 m.) in height in contrast to the 2 or 3 feet (61–91 cm.) reached by the others, has outer, or ray, florets that are inconspicuous.

Perezia recurvata (G) is known as 'lavender' on the Falkland Islands, where it grows amongst rocks and on sandy shores. The species, which also occurs at the southern tip of South America, in Tierra del Fuego and Patagonia, forms a perennial with stems clothed in numerous spiny and transversely wrinkled leaves and bearing sweetly fragrant blue, lilac, or white flowers.

Arctic

DIAPENSIACEAE

Diapensia lapponica
A1 flowering plant in situ × $\frac{2}{3}$.
A2 part of flowering shoot × $\frac{2}{3}$. A3 flower × 2.

ERICACEAE

Loiseleuria procumbens, Alpine Azalea
B1 flowering plant × $\frac{2}{3}$. B2 flower × 4.

Arctous alpina, Alpine or Black Bearberry
D1 part of flowering shoot × $\frac{2}{3}$.
D2 flowers × $1\frac{1}{3}$. D3 ovary × $1\frac{1}{3}$. D4 leaf × $1\frac{1}{3}$.

PYROLACEAE

Pyrola grandiflora, Arctic Wintergreen
C1 part of flowering plant × $\frac{2}{3}$.

COMPOSITAE

Artemisia borealis, Northern Wormwood
F1 part of flowering plant × $\frac{2}{3}$.

Antarctic

COMPOSITAE

Pleurophyllum speciosum
E1 part of flowering stem × $\frac{2}{3}$.
E2 ray-floret × 2. E3 disc-floret × $2\frac{2}{3}$.
E4 stigmatic arms × $5\frac{1}{3}$. E5 leaf × $\frac{2}{3}$.

Perezia recurvata
G1 part of flowering shoot × $\frac{2}{3}$.
G2 ray-floret × $2\frac{2}{3}$. G3 leaf × 2.

A3

A2

A1

B1

B2

C1

E4

E3

D3

D2

D1

D4

F1

E2

E1

E5

G2

G1

G3

Plate 7 ARCTIC AND ANTARCTIC

Tussocks of grass and sedge are a characteristic element of the flora of the antarctic islands in particular and of both polar regions in general—proof of the great climatic adaptability of these plants. Lilies and orchids are also found in both areas, but those of the Antarctic are far larger and much more beautiful than their northern counterparts.

The branched, fleshy rhizomes common to its fifteen or so saprophytic species have, by their resemblance to certain kinds of coral, given the northern temperate *Corallorhiza*, the Coralroot genus, its name. *C. trifida* (A), the only one that occurs in the area, grows in bogs or heathland from the arctic of Eurasia and America to western Greenland, but is also found in western, central and eastern Europe, including Britain, the Caucasus, Siberia and North America, usually in peaty or mossy woods. It has neither roots nor true leaves but lives in symbiotic association with a fungus and through it, derives its food from decaying organic matter in the manner of all saprophytes. The flowering stem bears 2 to 10 blooms which at first are held erect but soon droop; they persist in that position while the fruit develops.

About twenty species, with a distribution in North America, the Andes and the mountains of Venezuela and Guyana, belong to the genus *Tofieldia*. The Scottish Asphodel, *T. pusilla* (C) is circumpolar and a member of the group of species within the genus that have a 3-lobed involucre of bracts beneath the calyx. It differs from the only other arctic *Tofieldia*, *T. coccinea* of Siberia, North America and Greenland, in having a leafless flower stem and greenish white, instead of purplish, flowers. The Scottish Asphodel grows from a short rhizome in marshes and other wet habitats.

Edward Lloyd or Lhuyd (1660–1709), the Welsh naturalist who was at one time Keeper of the Ashmolean Museum, Oxford, and a friend and correspondent of John Ray, is commemorated in the dainty lily genus *Lloydia*, which contains about twenty northern temperate species. Despite its delicate appearance, *L. serotina* (D) flourishes over a wide area of the Eurasian arctic, Alaska and the Yukon, as well as in the great mountain ranges of Eurasia and western North America. The small bulb with a grey, fibrous skin produces slender stems bearing grass-like leaves and pretty white flowers, purple-veined and sometimes tinged with pink.

Like so many of the flowers in the area, *Festuca brachyphylla* (B), the Short-leaved Fescue, has a circumpolar range but is also found on the mountains further to the south. It is closely related to the better-known and more southerly Sheep's Fescue, *F. ovina* and to the Baffin Fescue, *F. baffinensis*, found at the highest latitudes at which the land can support life in arctic America and Greenland.

One of the hardiest of all flowering plants, *Pleuropogon sabinii* (E) is almost circumpolar in distribution and belongs to a genus of six grasses, the rest of which are natives of the western United States. It grows in pools or on wet, muddy slopes, and its creeping rhizomatous stems send up, at intervals across the ground, leafy flowering shoots with what have been described as 'long tassel-like spikelets dancing in the breeze or, in a stronger blast, held out like tiers of flags'. This latter phenomenon has given the species of this genus the common name of Semaphore Grasses.

A very small arctic sedge inhabiting well drained places, *Carex nardina* (F) ranges from eastern arctic Asia across arctic America to Greenland and Spitsbergen. The inflorescence, about $\frac{5}{8}$ inch (16 mm.) long, carry a few male flowers at the top and a larger number of female flowers surrounded by dark brown glumes below. *C. rupestris* (H), the Rock Sedge, found on barren and sandy heaths, has a completely circumpolar distribution and also occurs in Scotland, the Pyrenees, Alps and Carpathians, Corsica, the Urals and Siberia. The solitary dark brown inflorescences are divided between male and female flowers in much the same way as those of the preceding species. The Black Alpine Sedge, *C. atrata* (M) is a handsome plant that grows, usually in the sheltered grassy spots, in parts of the central Eurasian arctic and Greenland, in the higher mountains of Europe, and the northern area of the Rocky Mountains.

Juncus antarcticus (G) was first described from Campbell Island where it is a rare plant growing on the tops of mountains. It also occurs all over New Zealand and on Stewart Island, usually at high altitudes but sometimes as low as sea-level. It is generally no more than 1 to 4 inches (2·5–10 cm.) in height and the inflorescences consist of only a few flowers grouped in small heads.

A diminutive relative of the *Astelia* shown on plate 141, *Astelia pumila* (J) occurs in the south of Chile from Chiloe to Cape Horn and is common in the Falkland Islands where its compact carpets cover quite large areas of wet ground and, decayed, constitute a large proportion of the local peat. Its inconspicuous flowers, immersed amongst the foliage, are faintly fragrant.

Oreobolus is a small sedge genus of ten species found from Malaya and the East Indies to Australasia, Polynesia and the Andes, often in montane habitats. *O. pectinatus* (K), a native of Auckland and Campbell Island, as well as New Zealand, forms dense tussocks on exposed mountain sides or, on southern islands, on hills. The species is characterized by its curved leaves, strictly arranged in 2 ranks.

The name of Captain Sir James Clark Ross, commander of H.M.S. 'Erebus' and 'Terror' on their antarctic voyage of 1839–1843, was given to *Chrysobactron rossii* (L) by Sir Joseph Hooker in gratitude for the gift of a particularly fine specimen, some 3½ feet (105 cm.) tall with 7 inflorescences, of the species which is found only on Auckland and Campbell Islands. As a genus *Chrysobactron* is closely related to the South African *Bulbinella* and the species illustrated is in fact placed in that genus by certain botanists. The generic name means 'golden staff', an allusion to its magnificent stalks of yellow flowers.

Arctic

ORCHIDACEAE

Corallorhiza trifida
A1 flowering plant × $\frac{2}{3}$. A2 flower × 6.

GRAMINEAE

Festuca brachyphylla, Short-leaved Fescue
B1 flowering plant × $\frac{2}{3}$. B2 spikelet × $6\frac{2}{3}$.

Pleuropogon sabinii
E1 flowering plant × $\frac{2}{3}$. E2 spikelet × 4.

LILIACEAE

Tofieldia pusilla, Scottish Asphodel
C1 flowering plant × $\frac{2}{3}$. C2 flower × 6.
C3 fruiting head × $\frac{2}{3}$. C4 fruit × $4\frac{2}{3}$.

Lloydia serotina
D1 flowering plant × $\frac{2}{3}$. D2 flower × $\frac{2}{3}$.
D3 petal and stamen × 2.

CYPERACEAE

Carex nardina
F1 flowering and fruiting plant × $\frac{2}{3}$.
F2 fruit × 6. F3 glume × 6.

C. rupestris, Rock Sedge
H1 flowering plant × $\frac{2}{3}$. H2 inflorescence × $\frac{2}{3}$.
H3 fruit × $6\frac{2}{3}$.

C. atrata, Black Alpine Sedge
M1 flowering spike × $\frac{2}{3}$. M2 male flower × $6\frac{2}{3}$.
M3 female flower × $6\frac{2}{3}$. M4 fruiting plant × $\frac{2}{3}$.
M5 fruit and glume × $6\frac{2}{3}$.

Antarctic

JUNCACEAE

Juncus antarcticus
G1 fruiting plant × $\frac{2}{3}$. G2 fruiting head × $2\frac{2}{3}$.
G3 seed × $5\frac{1}{3}$.

LILIACEAE

Astelia pumila
J1 flowering plant × $\frac{2}{3}$. J2 leaf × $1\frac{1}{3}$.

Chrysobactron rossii
L1 part of flowering plant × $\frac{2}{3}$.
L2 flower and bract × $3\frac{1}{3}$.

CYPERACEAE

Oreobolus pectinatus
K1 flowering plant × $\frac{2}{3}$.

A1

A2

B1

B2

C1

C2

C3

C4

D1

D2

D3

E1

E2

F1

F2

F3

G1

G2

G3

H1

H2

H3

J1

J2

K1

L1

L2

M1

M2

M3

M4

M5

Plate 8   EUROPE

Buttercups and their allies vary enormously in habit and floral details but they preserve features usually regarded as primitive, such as numerous spirally arranged stamens. They are divided into two subfamilies: true buttercups, *Ranunculoideae*, with carpels containing only 1 seed, as in *Ranunculus, Anemone* and *Myosurus*; and hellebores, *Helleboroideae* (treated by some as a separate family) with carpels containing more than 1 seed, as in *Trollius, Helleborus* and *Aquilegia*. Hellebores should not be confused with helleborines, which are orchids of the genus *Epipactis*.

The twelve or so species of the genus *Trollius* are found in north temperate and arctic areas. The large 'petals' curve round the central flower parts in most species, giving the flower a globular shape and its common name of Globe Flower. *T. asiaticus* (C), a native of Siberia, has attractive orange flowers and nectaries longer than the stamens, whereas the Globe Flower usually found in western Europe, *T. europaeus*, has greenish yellow flowers and nectaries and stamens of equal length. Found beside rivers and streams and in wet meadows, it extends north into Norway and into arctic America.

The Mousetail, *Myosurus minimus* (G) is one of the ten species in the genus found throughout the north temperate zone and in Chile and New Zealand. Although it is rather an insignificant looking plant, it has been included in this plate to emphasize the variety of habit to be found in the buttercup family. As its small greenish flowers age, the receptacles become elongated so that the numerous ripe achenes are borne on a spike. This dwarf, hairless annual, found throughout Europe, though it also occurs in North Africa and south-west Asia, usually grows in damp, arable fields and along tracks. Plants found in North America and Australia are thought to have been introduced.

Aquilegia vulgaris (F) occurs from southern Scandinavia into western Russia and throughout Austria, Serbia, Italy and Spain to the British Isles. It is a variable species, and Philip A. Munz separated the group into twenty-four varieties in his review of the genus in 1946. It has stems between 12 and 24 inches (30–61 cm.) high, branched above, bearing two or more nodding violet (sometimes pink or white) flowers with the nectar-bearing spurs strongly hooked. Commonly known as Columbine, *A. vulgaris* was the first species to be cultivated, probably sometime in the 13th century, and by the 16th century many colours and varieties existed. In the 1860's, the introduction to Britain of *A. caerulea* from the Rocky Mountains led to the production of numerous hybrids with long spurs,

for the European species all have short-spurred flowers like *A. vulgaris*. Modern garden hybrids are mostly derived from crosses involving *A. caerulea* and *A. chrysantha* from Arizona and New Mexico.

The erect purple-blue flowers which appear with the expanding leaves covered with silky hairs make the Pasque Flower, *Pulsatilla vulgaris* (E) an attractive plant and worthy of cultivation. It is one of about thirty species which occur throughout Eurasia—this particular plant being fairly local in distribution in Europe as well as western Asia; it varies in colour and white-flowered forms are known. Although similar to *Anemone*, the *Pulsatilla* species differ in having fruit with long, graceful, feathery styles and nectar-secreting staminodes.

Anemone is a cosmopolitan genus of about one hundred and twenty species. The fruits are never plumed and a 3-leaved whorl is borne some distance below the flowers. *A. blanda* (D) is a native of south-east Europe and Turkey, where it grows among rocks and in woodland. It is not as widespread as *A. nemorosa*, commonly known as the Wood Anemone, which occurs throughout the temperate zone of central Europe and west Asia in drifts of white flowers spread out in woodlands and bracken in early spring.

Ranunculus, with its three hundred or more species, is also cosmopolitan. Some species—such as the trio of cosmopolitan weedy buttercups: *R. acris*, Meadow Buttercup, *R. repens*, Creeping Buttercup and *R. bulbosus*, Bulbous Buttercup—are meadow or wasteland herbs with yellow petals. Others, the crowfoots, such as *R. circinatus* (A), are aquatics with white flowers. This species, distributed throughout Europe as far north as Finland and as far east as the Balkans, grows in the mineral-rich waters of lakes, canals, ditches and similar water-courses.

The hellebores, *Helleborus* species, are notable for flowering early, even in December. Most of the twenty species grow on chalk in Europe and west Asia. Some have rather woody leaf-bearing stems, as in *H. foetidus* and *H. lividus*, whereas others are almost stemless with a crowd of basal leaves. These include the Christmas Rose, *H. niger, H. dumetorum* and the Lenten Rose, *H. orientalis. H. dumetorum* subspecies *atrorubens* (B), a native of Yugoslavia, differs from pure *dumetorum* in having larger purplish (not green) flowers. The Christmas Rose has white flowers, which turn green after fertilization. True *H. niger* is a low-growing plant with 5-lobed leaves and white or pink tinged flowers and should be distinguished from 'Lent Roses' of hybrid origin, which are taller, flower later and have white, cream or purple flowers.

RANUNCULACEAE

Ranunculus circinatus
A1 flowering and fruiting plant $\times \frac{2}{3}$.
A2 petal showing nectary $\times 4$.
A3 fruiting head $\times 6\frac{2}{3}$. A4 achene $\times 7\frac{1}{2}$.
A5 leaf $\times 1\frac{1}{3}$.

Helleborus dumetorum ssp. *atrorubens*
B1 plant with leaf and buds $\times \frac{2}{3}$.
B2 part of flowering stem $\times \frac{2}{3}$.
B3 flower nectary $\times 4\frac{2}{3}$.

Trollius asiaticus
C1 part of flowering stem $\times \frac{2}{3}$.
C2 radical leaf $\times \frac{2}{3}$. C3 stamen $\times 2\frac{2}{3}$.
C4 flower nectary $\times 2$.

Anemone blanda
D1 flowering plant $\times \frac{2}{3}$.
D2 side view of flower $\times \frac{2}{3}$. D3 petal $\times 2\frac{2}{3}$.
D4 stem with fruiting head $\times \frac{2}{3}$. D5 achene $\times 8$.

Pulsatilla vulgaris (syn. *Anemone pulsatilla*),
Pasque Flower
E1 flowering plant (stem cut) $\times \frac{2}{3}$.
E2 section through ovary, stamens and style $\times 2$. E3 stamen $\times 6$.
E4 part of fruiting stem $\times \frac{2}{3}$.
E5 immature fruit $\times 4$. E6 achene $\times 2$.

Aquilegia vulgaris, Columbine
F1 part of flowering stem $\times \frac{2}{3}$.
F2 radical leaf $\times \frac{2}{3}$. F3 flower $\times 1\frac{1}{3}$.

Myosurus minimus, Mousetail
G1 young and mature flowering plants $\times \frac{2}{3}$.
G2 flower $\times 2\frac{2}{3}$. G3 petal $\times 4$.

Plate 9   EUROPE

The brambles form a group so puzzling to the non-specialist, differing among themselves in combinations of minute and overlapping characters and hence difficult to separate into entities distinguishable by readily evident ones, that they are usually grouped today under the general name 'Rubus fruticosus aggregate', although some two thousand 'species' have been described at one time or another. Most of them are apomictic, that is, they produce fruit without fertilization, but they may hybridize as well, and so new types may frequently arise and 'breed true' by apomixis. One of the few that is not apomictic and therefore reasonably easy to identify because of its greater constancy of character expression, although it does hybridize too, is R. ulmifolius (B) of west, south and central Europe, north-western Africa and the Canaries. Other species of Rubus, not contained in the R. fruticosus aggregate, are of world-wide distribution and include the Raspberry, R. idaeus and the Loganberry, a cultivated hybrid which originated in the garden of Judge J. H. Logan of Santa Cruz, California, in 1881; but not cultivated Blackberries, which, as the variations in their shape and colour imply, are part of the larger group. The hairy leaves, conspicuous flowers and large, bright fruits, make some species, such as R. jamaicensis and R. deliciosus very decorative plants. However, the speed with which their creeping, root-bearing stems spread, tends to transform them into weeds, and this has prevented them from becoming popular as garden plants. When one wishes to try and identify a bramble, it is important to have a portion of the old, woody part of the stem still bearing a leaf or two, the inflorescence with its leaves, and, sometimes, the fruits, in order to be able to consider the full range of characters.

Another genus which presents difficulties in the identification of individual species, caused, as in the brambles, by the phenomenon of apomixis, is Alchemilla, with a distribution in the temperate north and the mountains of tropical Africa; over three hundred so-called species have been described from Europe alone. All species of Alchemilla are notable for having an ovary with a basal style and no petals. The majority are generally referable to 'A. vulgaris aggregate', but an exception is A. conjuncta (E), a native of the Alps of Savoy and Dauphine, the Jura and western Switzerland. It has been recorded from two localities in Scotland, but it is doubtful if it is truly native there.

The ten species of Filipendula occur mainly in the northern temperate zone, though some range as far as Turkey and North Africa. One such is F. vulgaris (D), commonly known as Dropwort, which extends from the Mediterranean area to France, Britain and Scandinavia in the west, the Caucasus and northern Russia in the east. An even hardier species, F. ulmaria, Meadow-sweet, is found in arctic Russia and Mongolia, and is naturalized in North America. The two species may be distinguished by counting the number of pairs of the larger leaflets arranged along the midrib of the leaf (a maximum of 5 in the case of F. ulmaria, 8 or more shorter ones in F. vulgaris), and by comparing the size of the inflorescences, which are smaller and more slender in Dropwort. F. vulgaris likes dry places, F. ulmaria moist ones.

Bogs, marshes, and similar habitats, in a belt from western Europe, central Spain to Iceland, through arctic Russia and central Asia to Japan are the habitats of Potentilla palustris (C), the Marsh Cinquefoil. This species is also found in Canada and northern states of the U.S.A. from northern California in the west to New Jersey in the east. The deep purple petals, which are shorter than the sepals, contrast richly with the still deeper purple of the stamens. The well-developed epicalyx, that is the series of bracts resembling a second calyx below the sepals, is a feature that Potentilla shares with a number of genera in the Rosaceae, Alchemilla among them.

Lime-rich soils and dry stony places in Europe, from the southern Baltic and the Mediterranean (except for Spain) and eastward to western Russia and Turkey form the habitat of Rosa rubiginosa, the Sweet Briar (often referred to as R. eglanteria) (A). The species occurs in Britain, too, though its relative, the Dog Rose, R. canina, is better known, at least in England. The Sweet Briar has long been a favourite, with its bright pink scented flowers and foliage which emits a characteristic and delicious fragrance in the hot sun or when lightly bruised.

ROSACEAE

Rosa rubiginosa (syn. *R. eglanteria*), Sweet Briar
A1 portion of main stem with part of flowering and budding shoot × $\frac{2}{3}$.
A2 long section of flower × $1\frac{1}{3}$. A3 petal × $1\frac{1}{3}$.
A4 fruiting twig × $\frac{2}{3}$.

Rubus ulmifolius
B1 flowering shoot × $\frac{2}{3}$.
B2 long section of flower × 2.
B3 style and ovary × 6. B4 stamen × 6.
B5 part of mature stem with leaf × $\frac{2}{3}$.
B6 new shoot × $\frac{2}{3}$. B7 fruiting twig × $\frac{2}{3}$.

Potentilla palustris, Marsh Cinquefoil
C1 part of flowering stem × $\frac{2}{3}$. C2 flower × $1\frac{1}{3}$.
C3 long section of flower × $1\frac{1}{3}$.
C4 style and ovary × $2\frac{2}{3}$.

Filipendula vulgaris (syn. *F. hexapetala*), Dropwort
D1 part of flowering stem × $\frac{2}{3}$. D2 flower × $2\frac{2}{3}$.
D3 radical leaf × $\frac{2}{3}$.

Alchemilla conjuncta
E1 flowering plant × $\frac{2}{3}$. E2 flower × 6.
E3 portion of back of leaf showing adpressed hairs × 2. E4 calyx and fruit × 6. E5 fruit × 6.

A1

A4

A2

A3

B1

B5

B6

B2

B3

B4

B7

C2

C4

C3

C1

D2

D1

D3

E1

E3

E5

E2

E4

Plate 10   EUROPE

The family *Leguminosae* is made up of major groups which may be roughly typified by the mimosas, the bauhinias and the peas. Because of overall similarities, these divisions are best treated as subfamilies although, by some botanists, they are given family status with the names *Mimosaceae, Caesalpiniaceae* and *Papilionaceae*; the genera represented opposite belong to this last subdivision which, at subfamilial rank, has the name *Papilionoideae*. One characteristic which marks the whole family as economically important is the presence, on their roots, of nodules containing colonies of the bacteria *Rhizobium*. These are able to combine the gaseous nitrogen of the air into nitrogenous substances within their cells, and, as such substances are vital to the healthy growth of green plants, and the leguminous host plant can then obtain them from the nodules, the association of the bacteria and flowering plant, called symbiosis, is of marked mutual benefit. It is because of this that leguminous crops, such as peas and beans, are so important in crop rotation, for when they die down or are ploughed under as green manure, they increase the nitrogen content of the soil.

Related to the garden pea genus, *Pisum, Lathyrus* differs in having stems which are angular or winged and not circular in cross-section, narrower not leaf-like sepals and a flattened style which is not reflexed at the margins. The Black Bitter Vetch or Black Pea, *L. niger* (B), grows throughout Europe, north into Norway and east into the Caucasus and has the curious but attractive habit of turning black when it dies. It lacks the leaf tendrils of many members of the genus, but possesses leaflets in the adult condition while most other species only have normal leaves during the seedling stages. *L. aphaca*, with yellow flowers, has leaf tendrils but no leaflets, whereas, in the crimson-flowered *L. nissolia*, the leaves lack tendrils and are reduced to grass-like blades by a flattening of the midrib and absence of leaflets.

The Black Medick, *Medicago lupulina* (D), is a widespread component of grassland and roadside verges throughout Europe, also growing in North America, west Asia and the islands of the Atlantic. The fruits of this species differ from those of most medicks; they contain only 1 seed, lack a spiny decoration and, instead of being spirally coiled, scarcely complete one turn, having a kidney-shaped outline (see fruits of *M. murex*, plate 29).

The Broom, *Cytisus scoparius* (F), otherwise known as *Sarothamnus scoparius*, ranges from southern Sweden and Denmark to Spain and east from the British Isles into Hungary and Poland. It forms a much-branched shrub up to 6 feet (1·8 m.) high, with pliable, angled green shoots, differing from the gorse genus, *Ulex*, and the whin or greenweed genus, *Genista*, in lacking spines. (The spines of *Ulex* are branched; those of *Genista* single). However, the pods of Broom are like those of gorse, and disperse the seeds by exploding violently. Whereas the Broom is widespread, most of the other ten species of *Cytisus*, section *Sarothamnus*, are confined to the Iberian Peninsula.

The genus *Trifolium* contains some three hundred temperate and subtropical species, the majority being found in north temperate areas. They include a number of valuable fodder plants, some of which have been selected and improved agriculturally, the best known being the White Clover, *T. repens*; Alsike Clover, *T. hybridum*; Red Clover, *T. pratense*; and, in warmer regions, Subterranean Clover, *T. subterraneum*. The annual or biennial species illustrated, *T. arvense* (C), the Hare's-foot Clover, is found throughout Europe and into northern and western Asia and North Africa; it is naturalized in North America. As in all clovers, the fruits are small and enclosed in the persistent sepals and, occasionally, petals; the fruiting heads of this species are much longer than the flowering heads.

Sometimes called the Purple-beaked Milk Vetch, *Oxytropis halleri* (E) is one of about three hundred species found throughout north temperate regions and into the Arctic. The genus is closely related to *Astragalus*, but the keel of the flower ends in a fine point and the septum of the pod develops from a suture on the 'standard' side of the flower. The range of this species includes Scotland, the Pyrenees, the Alps, the Carpathians and the Balkans.

Found in northern temperate and South American regions, most of the hundred and fifty or so species of the vetch genus, *Vicia*, are herbs, climbing by means of tendrils. The Broad Bean, *V. faba*, cultivated before the dawn of history, is thought to have originated in the Mediterranean area. Close to the Tufted Vetch, *V. cracca*, the illustrated *V. villosa* (A) differs in having racemes of flowers longer than the subtending leaves and the claw of the 'standard' petal twice as long as the upper expanded portion. It is a variable species growing in central and south Europe, into western Asia. The specimen which was used for the plate opposite was collected from a rubbish tip near Southampton, England.

LEGUMINOSAE

Vicia villosa
A1 part of flowering stem × ⅔. A2 flower × 2⅔.
A3 stipule × 2⅔.

Lathyrus niger, Black Bitter Vetch, Black Pea
B1 part of flowering stem × ⅔. B2 flower × 2.
B3 side view of older flower × 2.
B4 lower part of plant showing root nodules × ⅔. B5 part of fruiting stem × ⅔.
B6 pods, one open showing seeds in position × 1⅓. B7 seed × 2⅔.

Trifolium arvense, Hare's-foot Clover
C1 flowering plant × ⅔. C2 flower head × 1⅓.
C3 flower × 5⅓. C4 stipule × 2⅔.
C5 fruiting plant × ⅔. C6 fruiting head × 2.
C7 fruit × 6.

Medicago lupulina, Black Medick
D1 part of flowering and fruiting stem × ⅔.
D2 flower × 7⅓. D3 fruit × 6⅔.

Oxytropis halleri (syn. *O. sericea, O. uralensis*), Purple-beaked Milk Vetch
E1 part of flowering plant × ⅔.
E2 part of fruiting stem × ⅔.

Cytisus scoparius (syn. *Sarothamnus scoparius*), Broom
F1 part of flowering stem and old twig with new buds and old pods × ⅔.
F2 male and female parts × 2. F3 fruit × 1⅓.

A1

2

4
C1
C2
C3
C5
C6
C7

B1
B2
B3
B4
B5
B6
B7

D1
D2
D3

E1
E2

F1
F2
F3

Plate 11   EUROPE

The crucifers, *Cruciferae* family, are mainly herbs, chiefly north temperate in distribution, but also abundant in the Mediterranean region. Cabbage, brussels-sprout, cauliflower and kale, radish and turnip are all members of this family but, as can be seen opposite, it includes many attractive flowering plants, a number of which are cultivated and improved to provide a wider colour selection.

Honesty, *Lunaria annua* (B), is a native of south-east Europe but it is often found as an escape and sometimes as a weed, in areas where it has been introduced. There are three species in the genus, all European, with characteristic thin-walled, translucent silicula fruits, divided inside by a glossy white septum or partition. *L. rediviva*, a central European species of shady woodland habitats, has scented flowers, more elliptical fruits and stalked upper leaves, unlike the illustrated plant.

Erysimum is a genus of some eighty to a hundred species with a Mediterranean and Eurasian distribution. The yellow-flowered Treacle Mustard, *E. cheiranthoides*, is a wide-spread European plant and, like all species in this genus, it differs from the apparently similar *Cheiranthus* species (the Wallflower genus), in having nectaries at the base of both inner and outer series of stamens; the latter have nectaries only at the base of the 2 outer stamens. *E. perofskianum* (A) is a native of Afghanistan and was originally found near Kabul, but it now occurs as a casual plant in some parts of Europe, including Britain. Friedrich Ernst Fischer (1782–1854) sent seeds to the Royal Botanic Garden, Edinburgh in 1838.

The drabas are tufted little plants with hairy shoots and rosettes of small leaves. The diminutive flowers are white or yellow but their appearance is a memorable event, when discovered on some ledge high in the mountains where all around is grey and brown. The three hundred or so species are found in arctic and alpine habitats throughout the northern hemisphere and also in Central and South America; some make excellent rock garden plants. The Yellow Whitlow Grass, *Draba aizoides* (E) is a native of mountains in central and south-eastern Europe from the Pyrenees to the Carpathians and the Balkan Peninsula.

Wild Mignonette, *Reseda lutea* (D), is a native of south and central Europe, north to Sweden, into Turkey and in North Africa. It is introduced in North America, as is the related *R. luteola* or Weld from which a yellow dye is obtained. The illustrated plant differs from *R. luteola* in having pinnately lobed, not entire leaves, 6 petals and sepals, not 4, and longer capsules.

A native of shady places amongst rocks in Wales, south-west England, west Ireland, west France, Portugal and north Spain, the Welsh Poppy, *Meconopsis cambrica* (F), is the sole European representative of an essentially Himalayan and Chinese genus (see plate 93). The tufted plants with their delicate yellow flowers are particularly attractive when scattered along footpaths, with box or yew hedging as a background, as can be seen in the garden of Chateau Rhianva in Anglesey.

The genus *Corydalis* is some three hundred species strong, reaching its greatest density in the Sino-Himalaya region, and differs from *Fumaria* in having a capsular fruit containing many seeds, not 1-seeded nutlets. Both these genera have zygomorphic flowers, that is, flowers with one plane of symmetry, and some botanists place them in a separate family, the *Fumariaceae*. The illustrated plant, *C. solida* (C), is a native of central and southern Europe and extends into north and west Asia. Unlike many species with pale yellow or cream flowers, *C. solida* has dull purple flowers. It differs from *C. bulbosa*, also with purple flowers, in having a solid instead of hollow tuber, a conspicuous scale on the stem below the lowest leaf and lobed bracts.

A1

A2

A3

A4

A5

A6

A7

B1

B2

B3

B4

B5

C1

C2

C3

D1

D2

D3

E1

E2

E3

E4

E5

F1

F2

F3

F4

F5

F6

Plate 12   EUROPE

The members of these families are all woody plants, ranging in habit from lofty forest trees such as oak and beech, down to low creeping shrubs such as arctic and alpine willows. Their flowers are small and inconspicuous, either lacking both sepals and petals or with only a minute calyx, and are usually grouped in a simple spike or spike-like inflorescence called a 'catkin'; the names *Apetalae* (without petals) and *Amentiferae* (catkin-bearing) for this group of families refer to these features, which can be variously interpreted as to origin. Some botanists regard their flowers as representing the primitive state of flowering plants, the ancestors of which are believed to have been wind-pollinated and to have lacked sepals or petals. A more generally accepted view is that they are highly evolved and their apparent simplicity is the outcome of adaptation to wind-pollination by the loss or reduction of 'unnecessary' floral organs, such as coloured sepals or petals and nectar-producing parts attractive to insects, birds and bats. When members of a group adapted to wind-pollination change to insect-pollination, they usually attract insects by the development of a distinct scent and more brightly coloured stamens, and some members of these families exemplify this transition.

The beech family is almost world-wide in distribution, though absent from tropical South America, tropical and South Africa. The species number about nine hundred and belong to eight genera, of which *Fagus* (Beech), *Nothofagus* (Southern Beech), *Quercus* (Oak) and *Castanea* (Sweet Chestnut) are the best known.

The beech genus comprises ten species found in north temperate areas and also in Mexico. In Europe *Fagus sylvatica* (A) forms pure beech-woods in some areas, and these have a characteristic but meagre ground flora associated with them. Beech casts a dense shade and allows the growth of few other plants; two of these are the White Helleborine, plate 26, and Sweet Wood-ruff. The Common Beech is found from Norway to central Spain, Greece and the Crimea, being replaced eastwards by *F. orientalis*, with 8–12 instead of 5–8 lateral veins to the leaves. Beech is easily identified by the massive smooth trunk, the winter shoots with slender buds and the spring shoots covered with shiny emerald expanding leaves, fringed with silken hairs. Beech timber, being hard, strong and readily bent by steaming, is much used for making furniture and tool handles. The beech, some say, was introduced by the Romans to Britain, but pollen grains preserved in peat dating from before disproves this.

The oak has played a large role in the fortunes of the British Isles, and the tree is often regarded as symbolic of England. Oak timbers founded the distinctive architecture of Elizabethan and Tudor times; the durability and strength of the wood made its use in sailing ships an obvious choice.

The oak genus, *Quercus*, has some five hundred species which are found in North America and parts of South America, temperate and subtropical Eurasia, and North Africa. Some are evergreen, such as *Q. ilex*, the Holm Oak, and a number are important timber trees, such as the North American *Q. alba*, the White Oak; *Q. robur*, the Common Oak of Europe; and the closely allied *Q. petraea*, the Durmast. Indeed, the Common Oak was of great economic impor-

tance as its timber was the basis for all large scale structural work before the advent of metal girders and prestressed concrete units. *Q. suber*, the Cork Oak, has a thick spongy bark which yields cork. The berry-like, female coccid insects infesting such Mediterranean species as *Q. coccifera, Q. ilex* and *Q. suber* were once an important source of red dye (see plate 31).

The illustrated Turkey Oak, *Q. cerris* (B), is a native of Austria, Romania and throughout Turkey. It is introduced and naturalized in France and Britain. The persistent linear stipules surrounding the bud provide a means of identification. The male and female flowers occur in separate inflorescences. The fruits ripen the second year after flowering and are characterized by a cupule with long curving appendages, the involucral scales.

The Filbert, *Corylus maxima* (C), native to the Balkan Peninsula has been introduced into most European countries for its large nuts, and sometimes become naturalized. A larger shrub than the Common Hazel, *C. avellana*, it has a tubular involucre about twice as long as the nutshell. The edible nuts are rich in oil and were an important article of food for prehistoric man. Another thirteen or so species are found in north temperate areas.

A few species of birch are low shrubs, but most are trees of graceful habit, with conspicuous whitish or grey papery bark. The Common Birch, *Betula pubescens* (D), has hairy, not pendent, twigs which lack resin glands and the coarsely serrated leaves are often pubescent. The Silver Birch, *B. pendula*, has pendent twigs with resin glands but no hairs and leaves with marginal teeth of two sizes. Identification may be difficult as hybrids occur between them. The drooping male catkins are borne at the ends of new shoots with the erect female catkins borne further back. The catkins are clothed in bracts, each containing 3 flowers as shown. The fruits are flattened nuts with wings, which in early autumn are released in multitudes on the wind, often finding their way indoors. The seed readily germinates and often makes birch a rapid colonist of abandoned or cleared land and it may become a serious but lovely weed. Many uses have been found for the bark, timber and twigs of birch, in furniture, plywood, kitchen utensils, bobbins, reels and clogs from the wood; besoms, birches for chastising schoolboys, baskets and bedding from the twigs; and roofing from the bark, which is impervious to water. In Scandinavia, birch-woods create an atmosphere and setting which must have been common in many parts of Europe after the retreat of the last Ice Age.

As a whole, willows are not economically useful, but some species are used for making cricket-bats, baskets, trugs and poles, while others are grown simply for ornament. The species *Salix cinerea* (E), the Sallow, is separated into a widespread subspecies, *cinerea*, occurring over most of Europe and extending into Scandinavia and northern U.S.S.R., and the Grey Willow, a more western subspecies, *atrocinerea*, with a range from Morocco, north through Spain and Portugal, into Britain. *Cinerea*, with the previous year's twigs hairy, and *atrocinerea*, with them glabrous, are sometimes treated as separate species connected by hybrid intermediates.

FAGACEAE

Fagus sylvatica, Beech
A1 part of flowering branch $\times \frac{2}{3}$.
A2 male and female flowers $\times 5\frac{1}{3}$.
A3 fruit and seed $\times \frac{2}{3}$.
A4 part of branch showing autumn colour of foliage $\times \frac{2}{3}$. A5 budding twig $\times \frac{2}{3}$.

Quercus cerris, Turkey Oak
B1 part of flowering branch $\times \frac{2}{3}$.
B2 female flowers $\times 3\frac{1}{3}$ and male flowers $\times 4$.
B3 fruiting twig $\times \frac{2}{3}$.

CORYLACEAE

Corylus maxima, Filbert
C1 part of flowering branch $\times \frac{2}{3}$.
C2 male flower and female inflorescence $\times 5\frac{1}{3}$.
C3 part of branch showing leaves and ripening nuts $\times \frac{2}{3}$. C4 nuts $\times \frac{2}{3}$.

BETULACEAE

Betula pubescens, Birch
D1 part of flowering branch $\times \frac{2}{3}$.
D2 female flowers $\times 8$ and male flowers $\times 6\frac{2}{3}$.
D3 part of branch showing ripening female catkins $\times \frac{2}{3}$.
D4 fruits within bract $\times 5\frac{2}{3}$ and fruit showing wings $\times 8$.

SALICACEAE

Salix cinerea, Sallow
E1 part of the flowering branches $\times \frac{2}{3}$.
E2 male and female flowers $\times 6$.
E3 part of branch showing leaves and ripening fruits $\times \frac{2}{3}$.
E4 fruit containing plumed seeds $\times 4\frac{2}{3}$.

♂ male and ♀ female symbols are used on this plate

4

A3

A5

A1 ♀ ♂

B2 ♀ ♂

B3

C

B1 ♂

C1 ♂ ♀

C2 ♂ ♀

C3

C4

D3 ♀

D2 ♂

D1

D4 ♀

E1 ♂

E2 ♂ ♀

E3 ♀

E4

Plate 13   EUROPE

The family which contains the pinks is a mainly herbaceous one common throughout Britain and Europe (where, after four hundred years of study, a considerable refinement in botanical classification has been reached, well exemplified by the technical characters used to distinguish the genera in this family). It is also common in North Africa and the Middle East and frequent in south temperate regions.

An attractive representative, and a frequent sight in hedgerows and at the edge of woods in spring, is the Greater Stitchwort, *Stellaria holostea* (B), one of a genus of a hundred and twenty species. Unlike some of its common sister species, which will readily fertilize themselves if not visited by insects, *S. holostea* has stamens which tend to ripen before the stigmas are receptive and so favours cross-fertilization; indeed, in the absence of insects, very little seed is produced.

The *Arenaria* genus belongs to that side of the family which is characterized by its members having free, rather than fused, sepals (as in *Dianthus, Silene* and others below), and shallow flowers whose nectar, secreted at the base of the stamens, is attainable by a number of different types of insect with short tongues. *A. procera* (F) (syn. *A. graminifolia*), is a native of central and eastern Europe and a very variable species. As its synonym suggests, it is difficult to spot amongst grass, except when in flower.

Petrorhagia saxifraga (A), the Tunic Flower, is a perennial found throughout southern and central Europe to west Siberia and northern Iran, a range which, with the inclusion of Mediterranean region, covers that for the whole genus of about twenty species. Its flowers, like those of its close relatives, are surrounded by an involucre of somewhat chaffy bracts (see A2).

Though once recommended by herbalists as antidotes for 'putrid fevers' and 'trembling limbs', the three hundred or so species of *Dianthus* owe their present popularity with gardeners to their scented and colourful flowers. Among the best known are the Sweet William, *D. barbatus*, a native of the Mediterranean area, the Balkans and southern Russia, and the Clove Pink or Gilly Flower, *D. caryophyllus*, also a native of southern Europe, where Pliny recorded it in Spain, and of North Africa. The Common Pink, *D. plumarius* (D) comes from east central Europe, from the Italian Alps to the Tatra Mountains, although naturalized elsewhere. Hybridized with *D. caryophyllus* it has produced the cultivated carnation whose name is said to be derived from 'qaranful', the Arabic for cloves, the product of an unrelated tropical plant named *Eugenia caryophyllus*, with which *D. caryophyllus* has only a spicy scent in common.

Found amongst rock-debris or in open, sandy country, *Lychnis viscaria* (E) the Red German Catchfly, has a distribution from western Europe east as far as western Asia; it is, however, rare in Britain. The leafy shoots, which grow to a height of 2 feet (61 cm.), bear flowers between June and August. A Russian species, *L. chalcedonica*, introduced to Europe via Byzantium at the time of the Crusades and popular in England by the end of the 16th century, is a more common garden plant.

The genus *Silene* is a large one closely related to *Lychnis*. There are perhaps five hundred species with about one hundred and sixty in Europe alone. *Silene nutans* (C), known in Britain as the Nottingham Catchfly, is notable for the staggered flowering mechanism by which its nocturnal blooms pass through three stages, on three successive nights, during which period they remain fragrant and attractive to night-flying moths. On the first night the petals are held horizontally and the first whorl of 5 stamens are mature (see C2); on the second, the petals are reflexed and the first series of stamens have withered to be replaced by 5 new stamens (see C3); finally, on the third night, these too wilt and the styles become receptive and protrude.

A2

A3

A1

B1

B2

C2

C5

C3

C4

C6

C1

D7

D2

D8

D3

D5

D4

D6

D1

E5

E4

E1

E2

E3

F1

F2

Plate 14 EUROPE

Members of the chenopodium family, which includes spinach, beet and glasswort, frequently grow on soils with a high salt content. Generally, these plants have little decorative value, but *Chenopodium amaranticolor* with its attractive green and violet-red bicoloured foliage, is an exception. *Geranium*, on the other hand, has numerous decorative species—among them the Caucasian *G. psilostemon*, with black and vivid magenta flowers and the purple-pink flowered species *G. macrorrhizum* from Europe. Several *Oxalis* species are now grown as temperate garden perennials and cultivated *Polemonium* plants have larger, more gaily coloured flowers than the wild species shown opposite.

The *Chenopodiaceae* family is classified into two units: those like spinach and beet with a horseshoe or ring-shaped embryo in the seed, and those which have spirally twisted embryos like the Seablite, *Suaeda maritima*. Further subdivision into tribes of the one hundred and two genera is based on flower, fruit and inflorescence characteristics.

Most of the one hundred and twenty or so species of *Chenopodium*, natives of temperate areas, are weeds with no economic value. *C. quinoa*, however, is used like spinach, while the Peruvians boil and eat its seeds as well; and *C. anthelminticum*, as its name implies, is used for de-worming the alimentary canal. The All-seed, *C. polyspermum* (E), originates in temperate Eurasia, but has been introduced into North America where it is often found as a weed on waste ground.

Its root storage organ gives the European and Mediterranean genus *Beta* its importance. Swede, sugar-beet, beetroot and mangold are all derived from *B. vulgaris*. Sugar-beet in particular has become an important commercial crop, providing good yields of sugar from the root tissues. The cultivation of mangolds for farm livestock has declined for two reasons: the drift away from rotation to intensive farming, and the switch from bulk to concentrate feeding.

About four hundred species of *Geranium* occur throughout the world. As mentioned on plate 74, the species have symmetrical, often attractive flowers, which lack a spurred calyx. The Dusky Cranesbill or Mourning Widow, *G. phaeum* (D), is a native of central and southern Europe, although it has become naturalized in northern areas. Nectaries are situated at the base of each blackish purple petal. The way in which the fruit splits open is illustrated opposite: compare the unsplit fruit of *G. pratense* (B6) with that of the partly splitting fruit of *G. phaeum* (D5). The Meadow Cranesbill, *G. pratense* (B), is found from Europe through central Asia as far as Japan. This perennial has a rhizomatous root-stock and rich violet-blue flowers.

Wood Sorrel, *Oxalis acetosella* (A), grows in woods and shady places throughout Europe and across north and central Asia to Japan. Sometimes the dominant component of ground flora in oak woods, it has a low, stemless habit and, as in many *Oxalis* species, 3-lobed leaves and different stamen lengths. The leaves are occasionally used in salads but excessive consumption can result in poisoning.

A rather uncommon British native, Jacob's Ladder, *Polemonium caeruleum* (C), has long been cultivated in gardens. It occurs throughout northern and central Europe and eastwards into Siberia and also in North America where most of the fifty species in the genus are found. All of the stamens, which curve downward, are inserted at the same height in the corolla. The pale to dark blue flowers borne in shortly branched clusters on stems up to 3 feet (90 cm.) tall are clothed with divided leaves of 20 or more leaflets. The sepals enlarge during fruit maturation to enclose the fruit.

OXALIDACEAE

Oxalis acetosella, Wood Sorrel
A1 flowering plant × $\frac{2}{3}$.
A2 stamens, style and ovary × $2\frac{2}{3}$.
A3 petal × $2\frac{2}{3}$.

GERANIACEAE

Geranium pratense, Meadow Cranesbill
B1 part of flowering stem × $\frac{2}{3}$. B2 petal × 2.
B3 base of plant with radical leaf × $\frac{2}{3}$.
B4 part of fruiting stem × $\frac{2}{3}$. B5 fruit × 6.
B6 seed × 6.

G. phaeum, Dusky Cranesbill, Mourning Widow
D1 part of flowering stem × $\frac{2}{3}$. D2 flower × 2.
D3 part of fruiting stem × $\frac{2}{3}$. D4 fruit × 2.
D5 seed × $2\frac{2}{3}$.

POLEMONIACEAE

Polemonium caeruleum, Jacob's Ladder
C1 part of flowering stem × $\frac{2}{3}$. C2 flower × $1\frac{1}{3}$.
C3 petal with stamen in position × 2.
C4 style and ovary × 2.

CHENOPODIACEAE

Chenopodium polyspermum, All-seed
E1 part of flowering and fruiting stem × $\frac{2}{3}$.
E2 flower and fruit × 17. E3 fruit × 23.
E4 portion of decumbent root stock × $\frac{2}{3}$.

A1 A2 A3

B1 B2 B3 B4 B5 B6

C1 C2 C3 C4

D1 D2 D3 D4 D5

E1 E2 E3 E4

Plate 15 EUROPE

The fresh delicate colours of European wild flowers, as they appear massed together in fields and woodlands are a sight to be appreciated by all. Some of the more typical wayside and mountain species are illustrated opposite, though the limited space available, prevents the inclusion of many lovely and familiar plants.

The Bogbean or Buckbean, *Menyanthes trifoliata* (A) is an unusual member of the *Menyanthaceae* in that its leaves are divided into 3 leaflets and the leaf stalks sheath each other. It creeps from an often submerged rhizome and may form dense platforms of vegetation over the surface of ponds. The thick spreading lobes of the corolla are covered on the inside with erect long, fine hairs, giving the flower its exquisite appearance. As in the Primrose, there are two forms of flower, pin- or thrum-eyed, corresponding to the long and short styles. The five genera in the family, including *Menyanthes* and *Nymphoides* (the fringed, yellow-flowered water lily), are all marsh plants found in north and south temperate areas and tropical South East Asia.

The Bellflower family, *Campanulaceae*, has about two thousand species growing in north temperate, Mediterranean and some tropical mountain areas. Many of the three hundred species of *Campanula* are popular garden plants which can be divided into the small creeping types such as *C. rotundifolia*, and the erect and larger flowered types such as *C. trachelium*. The popular names of Canterbury Bells and Coventry Bells (both for *C. medium*) are descriptive of the shape of the flowers. At an early stage in the flowering of *Campanula* species, the anthers release pollen, which is deposited on hairs on the style. For a short while, these hairs present pollen to visiting insects, usually bees, but when the flower is older and the stamens have withered, the several stigma lobes separate and curl back into the stylar hairs, bringing about self-pollination as an insurance against earlier failure of cross-pollination by insects. A characteristic of the genus is that the pollen is frequently shed while the flower is in bud. *C. saxifraga* (D) is a small Causcasian rock plant, sometimes confused with *C. tridentata*. The Yellow Bellflower, *C. thyrsoides* (F), is a variable biennial species which grows on the mountains of central Europe between 5000 and 8500 feet (1520–2630 m.). Its dense clubs of greenish flowers are produced only once in the life of the plant; it then sets seed and dies.

The Devil's Claw, *Phyteuma comosum* (B) is so unlike the thirty other species in the genus that it can be placed in a genus by itself as *Physoplexis comosa*. It is an alpine species found only on limestone and dolomite in Austria, where it is legally protected, and northern Italy, between 3300 and 5500 feet (1000–1670 m.). The petals of each flower are elongated and tapering, and cohere at the tips, enclosing the anthers. The style pushes through them as it grows, driving the purple pollen out of the end of the flowers, where some is picked up by visiting insects and the rest is scattered over the leaves of the plant. Only later do the stigmatic lobes expand as shown in the illustration. The Devil's Claw is noted for its large umbellate, short-stalked flowers whereas the species of *Phyteuma* proper have sessile flowers in dense heads or spikes.

Blackstonia is a gentian genus, and *B. perfoliata* (E), the Yellow-wort, is one of the six European and Mediterranean species. An erect annual, varying in height from 4 to 16 inches (10–41 cm.), it is found in most of Europe and North Africa, growing in chalk grassland. The bluish green colour of the leaves, which are joined together at base, and the yellow corolla, make it a beautiful and easily recognized plant.

An equally widespread and common plant is *Primula vulgaris* (G), the Primrose, the flowers appearing singly among the leaves, and enabling one to distinguish it easily from *P. elatior*, the Oxlip, and *P. veris*, the Cowslip. (The Cowslip has uniformly pale green sepals and fruits enclosed by the calyx; the Oxlip has a dark green sepal midrib and fruits which protrude beyond the tips of the sepals, its corolla being larger and paler than that of the Cowslip.) Certain Primrose flowers have stamens inserted near the mouth of the corolla tube (thrum-eyed) and others have them inserted deep inside the tube (pin-eyed); the latter type is illustrated.

The multicoloured 'polyanthus' (*Primula* × *polyantha*) is the product of a cross which probably first occurred in about 1660 between coloured forms of primroses and cowslips and which were improved by artisan amateur gardeners in the late 19th century. Another popular plant of the 19th century was the 'auricula' descended from *P. hirsuta* and *P. auricula*, which hybridize in the Alps where their areas meet. In the 16th century peasants used to bring plants from the mountains to sell them in Vienna and among these was apparently a vigorous hybrid which provided the starting stock.

P. halleri (C), the Long-flowered Primrose, is a mountain plant from the Alps, the Carpathian mountains and the north Balkans; it grows at altitudes of 3000 to 9000 feet (910–2740 m.). A thrum-eyed flower of this species is illustrated.

Cyclamen, which grows throughout the Mediterranean as far east as Iran, is the only member of the *Primulaceae* with corms. As in *Dodecatheon*, the flowers are nodding and the petal lobes reflex upwards. After fertilization the flower stalk spirals up in all species except *C. persicum*. The seeds themselves are distributed by ants. The edible corms contain starch and because pigs consume them they have been called 'Sowbread'. Common Sowbread, the corms of *C. repandum*, was reputed to have the most excellent properties: it stopped balding, assisted childbirth and made the shy more amorous—something for all the family. *C. alpinum* (H) is a Turkish species, probably confined to the south west of the country. It is sometimes regarded as a subspecies of *C. coum*, but its larger flowers have a different shape. It was cultivated in the 1890's, but its habitat was not recorded and it was lost to cultivation until recently.

Plantago is the largest of the three genera which constitute the *Plantaginaceae* and it contains all but five of the two hundred and seventy species in the family. Three of the commonest are European natives. *P. major*, the Great Plantain, and *P. lanceolata*, the Ribwort Plantain, are wind-pollinated and have inconspicuous flowers, whereas *P. media* (J), the Hoary Plantain, is insect-pollinated and has delightfully scented flowers with conspicuous pink stamens. There are a large number of endemic species found in other parts of the world, particularly the Hawaiian Islands and islands of the southern seas.

MENYANTHACEAE

Menyanthes trifoliata, Bogbean, Buckbean
A1 part of flowering plant × ⅔.
A2 detail of corolla × 2.

CAMPANULACEAE

Phyteuma comosum, Devil's Claw
B1 part of flowering stem × ⅔. B2 flower × 2.

Campanula saxifraga
D1 part of flowering plant with buds × ⅔.
D2 detail of flower × 2.

C. thyrsoides, Yellow Bellflower
F1 part of flowering stem × ⅔.
F2 male and female parts × 2.

PRIMULACEAE

Primula halleri, Long-flowered Primrose
C1 flowering plant × ⅔.
C2 detail of flower × 1⅓.

P. vulgaris, Primrose
G1 flowering plant × ⅔. G2 female part × 2.
G3 section of corolla × 2.

Cyclamen alpinum
H1 flowering plant × ⅔.

GENTIANACEAE

Blackstonia perfoliata, Yellow-wort
E1 flowering plant × ⅔. E2 detail of flower × 2.

PLANTAGINACEAE

Plantago media, Hoary Plantain
J1 flowering and fruiting plant × ⅔.
J2 flower × 6. J3 fruit × 6.

A1

A2

B1

B2

C1

C2

D1

D2

E1

E2

F1

F2

G1

G2

G3

H1

J1

J2

J3

Plate 16   EUROPE

Most of the plants illustrated opposite are found in damp or boggy places in Europe.

Moschatel, *Adoxa moschatellina* (A), is also known by the quaint name Town-Hall Clock, a reference to the inflorescence with its flowers resembling the faces of a clock tower. It grows in woods, under hedges and amongst rocks throughout Europe and even into the mountains of Morocco, eastward to Kamchatka and across northern Asia into North America.

The Great Sundew, *Drosera anglica* (F), is one of the hundred or so species found throughout the world but mainly in South Africa and Australasia. When mature all the species possess densely glandular leaves. The first leaves of seedlings are glandless but the number of glands increases on successive leaves. These vary in shape from almost circular to spoon shaped in European species; they may be linear or even several times divided and forked in Australasian species. In mature plants the leaves form rosettes which often survive the cold season as tight winter-buds, only expanding their leaves when growing conditions become favourable. The upper leaf surface bears stalked, mucilage-secreting glands which trap small insects attracted by the shining, dewy leaf-surfaces. By arching over the prey, the glands cover it in mucilage and it is possible that the insect may become incapacitated by the high surface-tension of the plant secretion. Given sufficient stimulus, the leaf also may bend around the insect's body. The secretion from the glands appears to contain digestive substances which reduce the insect to a state in which it can be absorbed by the plant, thus providing a source of nitrogenous material which is particularly valuable as the boggy habitat of *Drosera* often lacks these substances. Like the other species illustrated, the Great Sundew is found in suitable habitats throughout Europe, including Great Britain, and extending into northern Asia and North America. It grows amongst *Sphagnum* mosses in the wet parts of bogs and at the edges of pools.

The leaves of the Common Sundew, *D. rotundifolia* (E), differ from those of the Great Sundew in that they are almost as broad as they are long, and the two plants have much the same distribution. Hybrids between the species are called *D. × obovata*. Superficially they resemble the Love-nest Sundew, *D. intermedia,* but have inflorescence stalks twice to three times as long as the leaf while those of the Love-nest Sundew are not quite the length of one leaf.

Comprising about forty species native to Europe, North Africa, Turkey and eastward to the Caucasus, the genus *Sempervivum* differs from *Sedum* in several characteristics; it has a basal rosette of leaves and flowers with more than 8 sepals whereas *Sedum* species have leaves arranged on a long stem and flowers with less than 5 sepals. The Houseleek, *Sempervivum tectorum* (B), is referred to by Greek and Roman writers and has long been grown as a charm to prevent lightning from striking the roofs of dwellings; the Emperor Charlemagne, for example, directed it to be planted on the houses of his gardeners. Ranging from the Pyrenees across the Alpine system to the Apennines and the northern Balkan region, Houseleek may be found as far north as Ireland and Scandinavia and as far east as Iran. The populations of the species in the Alps are variable and authors have recognized some groups, such as *S. rupestre* and *S. arvernense,* as separate species.

Grass of Parnassus, *Parnassia palustris* (C), a native of Europe ranging into Morocco and temperate Asia, is a marsh plant which also grows on wet moorland. Its name is derived from Mount Parnassus, the home of the mythological Muses. Conspicuously veined white petals and elegantly fringed staminodes make it one of the most beautiful and distinct of British native plants.

The genus *Ludwigia* consists of some twenty species, mostly aquatic, which bear small flowers with minute petals—or none at all. *L. palustris* (G) has a wide range in Europe, western Asia, North Africa and North America and grows under acid conditions in shallow pools, such as those found in the New Forest in England, the only remaining location of this species on mainland Britain.

About forty perennial species of *Geum* are found in both north and south temperate areas and the Arctic. The style of flowers in this genus has a kink in it and when this forms an awn on the fruit, the upper part may break off. Water Avens, *G. rivale* (D), does not extend into the Arctic but is found as far north as Iceland and in northern U.S.S.R. It reaches southward as far as Spain and its eastern limit is the Caucasus and Turkey. In the New World, Water Avens is found in an area from Newfoundland and New Jersey to Colorado and British Columbia. A marsh and streamside plant, it may also grow in shade in moist woods or on rock ledges. *G. rivale* is interfertile with *G. urbanum* but the two rarely form hybrids because the latter species does not usually grow near the wet habitats of *G. rivale.* The hybrids, called *G. × intermedium,* are exceedingly variable when they do occur.

ADOXACEAE

Adoxa moschatellina, Moschatel, Town-hall Clock
A1 flowering plant × $\frac{2}{3}$. A2 lateral flower × 4. A3 style and ovary × 4. A4 inflorescence × 2.

CRASSULACEAE

Sempervivum tectorum, Houseleek
B1 flowering plant with new shoots (stem cut) × $\frac{2}{3}$.
B2 rosette to flower the following year × $\frac{2}{3}$.
B3 flower × 2. B4 sterile stamen × 6.
B5 fertile stamen × 6. B6 carpel × 6.

PARNASSIACEAE

Parnassia palustris, Grass of Parnassus
C1 flowering and budding plant × $\frac{2}{3}$.
C2 flower × $1\frac{1}{3}$. C3 staminode × $3\frac{1}{3}$.

ROSACEAE

Geum rivale, Water Avens
D1 flowering and fruiting plant × $\frac{2}{3}$.
D2 petal × $2\frac{2}{3}$. D3 style and ovary × $2\frac{2}{3}$.
D4 seed × $2\frac{2}{3}$.

DROSERACEAE

Drosera rotundifolia, Common Sundew
E1 flowering plant × $\frac{2}{3}$. E2 leaf glands × $6\frac{2}{3}$.

D. anglica, Great Sundew
F1 flowering plant × $\frac{2}{3}$. F2 leaf × 2.

ONAGRACEAE

Ludwigia palustris
G1 part of flowering and fruiting plant × $\frac{2}{3}$.
G2 flower × $4\frac{2}{3}$. G3 fruit × $4\frac{2}{3}$.

A1 A2 A3 A4 B1 B2 B3 B5 B6 C1 C2 C3 D1 D2 D3 D4 E1 E2 F1 F2 G1 G2 G3

Plate 17   E U R O P E

The *Umbelliferae* was one of the first natural groups to be recognized by early botanists groping as they were for systems of classifying plants. Many species have an umbellate inflorescence (as in Fennel, illustration C opposite) and this conspicuous feature attracted their attention; but of course there are exceptions—for example, *Astrantia* and *Eryngium*, both lack the characteristic inflorescence—whereas the inflorescence of the Teasel (B) superficially resembles those of some *Eryngium* species although it belongs to a completely different family, the *Dipsacaceae*.

A cosmopolitan family, the *Umbelliferae*, with some two hundred and seventy genera, is basically north temperate in distribution. Nearly all the species are herbs, often with hollow stems, sheathing leaf bases and usually, much divided leaves, although there are a few species which are shrubby in habit or climbers. In some members of the family the outermost of the small flowers in the umbel have enlarged petals, similar to the ray-florets of the daisy, which make them more conspicuous to flies, beetles and bees, their principal pollinators. The family also includes plants of economic importance, the carrot, parsnip and celery and such culinary herbs as caraway, coriander, cumin and anise.

The genus *Foeniculum*, consisting of four or five species, is found in Europe and the Mediterranean area. Fennel, *F. vulgare* (C), probably originated in south Europe, but it is now naturalized in many temperate areas as a result of its cultivation for culinary purposes; the aromatic oils of its leaves and fruit are used for flavouring and its swollen leaf bases are eaten like celery.

Found in Europe and western Asia, the genus *Astrantia*, with some ten species, is easily distinguished from *Eryngium* as its leaves are not spiny. The *Astrantia* inflorescence consists of a dense head of flowers, surrounded beneath by an involucre of cream, greenish or purple-tinged bracts. In the Great Masterwort or Mountain Sanicle, *A. major* (E), the flowers are usually hermaphrodite, though those produced later in the year are often functionally male and therefore do not produce fruit. This species is found in most parts of Europe and into the Caucasus, but growing in the higher mountains from the southern Alps to north-west Spain is var. *carinthiaca*. This variety can be distinguished by its bracteoles which are twice as long as the umbels and not of the same length as is found in the illustrated species.

Characterized by their spiny, rigid glaucous leaves and often electric blue flowering heads, the two hundred species of the genus *Eryngium* are found in most temperate and subtropical areas, but particularly in the Mediterranean region and Central and South America. The sepals are frequently longer than the petals and, as in *Astrantia*, bracts surround the base of the dense heads of small flowers. *E. alpinum* (D), which grows in the mountains of Provence in France and in Italy, Austria, Switzerland, east into Bosnia, is a variable species, both in its height and in the size and colour of its flowerheads. The specimen illustrated was grown at Kew and is pale in colour, compared with the intense blue of some wild plants growing at high altitudes and in bright sunlight.

The valerians, family *Valerianaceae*, are herbs with opposite leaves and flowers borne in more open inflorescences, called in this case, cymose panicles. The family is distributed in Europe, Asia, Africa and the Americas. The illustrated Red Valerian, *Centranthus ruber* (A), is one of the twelve species of this genus which is found in Europe and the Mediterranean region and has only a single stamen in each flower. The flowers may vary in colour from white, pink to deep crimson; the pink form seems to have the largest clusters of flowers. In the British Isles, the Red Valerian is an introduced plant but it is now locally common and can be most attractive, growing on old walls or massed on sunny banks.

The Teasel, *Dipsacus fullonum* (B), belongs to the same family as the scabious, the *Dipsacaceae*. The genus *Dipsacus* is easily distinguished from other European genera in the family for it is the only one with a spiny stem and involucral bracts which are spine tipped. Superficially it resembles a thistle, just as some species of scabious are daisy-like, but the *Dipsacaceae* have anthers which are free whereas in the *Compositae*, the thistle and daisy family, they are fused. The Teasel exists as two varieties: the 'Wild Teasel' and the cultivated 'Fuller's Teasel'. Both have spiny bracts between each flower, but in the Fuller's Teasel they are hooked. It is this feature which has led to the use of the fruiting heads for raising the nap on certain kinds of cloth, especially wool.

VALERIANACEAE

Centranthus ruber, Red Valerian
A1 part of flowering stem × ⅔.
A2 dissected flower × 3⅓. A3 flowers × 3⅓.

DIPSACACEAE

Dipsacus fullonum, Teasel
B1 part of flowering stem with bud × ⅔.
B2 flower × 2⅔.

UMBELLIFERAE

Foeniculum vulgare, Fennel
C1 flowers and buds on part of stem with radical leaf × ⅔. C2 flower × 8. C3 fruit × 5⅓.
C4 section of fruit × 5⅓.

Eryngium alpinum
D1 part of flowering stem with lateral leaf × ⅔.
D2 flower × 6. D3 petal × 6.

Astrantia major, Great Masterwort, Mountain Sanicle
E1 part of flowering stem with leaf × ⅔.
E2 hermaphrodite flower × 6.
E3 male flower × 6. E4 petal × 6.

A2

A1

3

B2

B1

C4
C3
C2

C1

D1

D2

D3

E1

E2

E3

E4

Plate 18   EUROPE

Austrian Flax, *Linum austriacum* (A), is related to another European species, *L. perenne,* but its flower stalks are flexuous and bent instead of straight and erect. Found throughout central and southern Europe, it grows to a height of about 2 feet (61 cm.). Flax, from which linen is spun, comes from the stem fibres of *L. usitatissimum*; linseed oil is pressed from its seeds and the remaining 'cake' is used as cattle fodder. This species is unknown in the wild but it may have arisen from *L. bienne* as a result of continued cultivation. *L. bienne* is biennial or perennial and usually has several stems and small capsular fruits while the annual *L. usitatissimum* has a single stem and a large capsular fruit.

About five hundred species of *Polygala* are found in all parts of the world except the Arctic, Oceana and New Zealand. The genus is characterized by zygomorphic flowers with 5 sepals, 2 of which are often coloured and larger than the others, and also 3 to 5 petals, the lower ones fused together and the upper ones minute or lacking. Common Milkwort, *P. serpyllifolia* (D), occurs on acid soils throughout Europe from southern Norway to the Pyrenees and eastward into Czechoslovakia. The common name dates from the time when the plant was reputed to induce the flow of milk of nursing mothers. The plant has also been known as the Cross Flower because it blooms during Cross or Rogation Week, when it was made into a garland and worn by young girls.

North temperate species of *Viola*, generally known as violets or pansies, are herbs, but elsewhere may occur as shrubby plants. The five hundred species in the genus are characterized by stalked flowers of bilateral construction where the lower petal develops into a spur; the sepals have outgrowths at their point of insertion and the stamens are fused in a ring around the ovary. Violets have long been considered a romantic or sentimental symbol, yet they are among the most wayward and dissolute of flowers, perplexing botanists by their readiness to interbreed with other species, making their identification difficult. Hybrids frequently occur in the wild, especially between the North American species, while the Garden Pansy, *V. × wittrockiana*, is apparently derived from hybridization between *V. tricolor* and *V. lutea* which took place in British gardens at the beginning of the 19th century. Seed raising and selection on a large scale led to the development of some four hundred named pansies by 1835.

Frequently confused with the Pale Wood Violet, *V. reichenbachiana*, the Common Violet, *V. riviniana* (E), has large sepal appendages and a notched, light coloured corolla spur, rather than smaller appendages and an unnotched spur. The Common Violet extends as far east as Greece, while *V. reichenbachiana* reaches into Kashmir. Both species are distributed from Scandinavia into the Atlas Mountains of Morocco. The Long-spurred Pansy, *Viola calcarata* (F), grows to about 5 inches (12·5 cm.) in height and the large, solitary, mauve-violet flowers appear in June and July. The species occurs in an area from the Alps and Jura through the Apennines into Sardinia and further east to the Caucasus. The plants are so numerous that they form carpets of blossoms in alpine pastures at an altitude of around 7000 feet (2130 m.).

A north temperate genus of about forty species, *Malva* differs from *Lavatera* (shown on Mediterranean plate 35) in having 3 bracts below the calyx which are not fused together at the bases. The Common Mallow, *Malva sylvestris* (B), is found on wasteland and roadsides throughout Europe. It tends to be less common in the north and is absent, for example, from the Orkney Islands. The petals soon drop when the flowers are picked and it is altogether a rather weedy species with little value, although its leaves have been used in decoctions for soothing upset stomachs.

If Bindweed were a rare plant, the gardener would no doubt value this species for the abundance of clear white or pink flowers it produces between July and September each year. However, despite its attractive flowers it should be shunned as a garden plant. The Greater Bindweed, *Calystegia silvatica* (C), which is very similar to the native British Bindweed *C. sepium* but indigenous to southern Europe, has become widespread through an early piece of horticultural sales promotion. About the turn of the last century it was sold widely as a 'New American Bell-bine' but gardeners soon discovered its aggressive, weedy tendencies and threw it out onto wasteland and roadsides where it is found in abundance today.

Large bracts which enclose the sepals and basal portions of the corolla tube distinguish the genus *Calystegia* from *Convolvulus*. The pollen grains, moreover, have many scattered, rounded pores but no furrows. *Convolvulus* has small bracts beneath the calyx and the pollen grains are 3-furrowed. Altogether, about twenty-five species of *Calystegia* and two hundred and fifty species of *Convolvulus* are found in both temperate and tropical areas. The root of Bindweed contains a vigorous purgative, so effective it seems, that its use can be dangerous. We are told that in Gerard's time only 'runnagat physick-monger, quack salver, old women Leaches, and such like abusers of physic' stooped to the use of Bindweed.

The genus *Daphne* recalls the tragic metamorphosis of Perseus' daughter into a Laurel so that she might be spared the attentions of Apollo. There are upwards of seventy *Daphne* species widely distributed in the northern hemisphere of the Old World and as far east as Japan, Java and the Phillipines. Cultivated in Britain before 1561, the Mezereon, *Daphne mezereum* (G) was found 'wild' about 1759, but its status as a native species in Britain remains questionable. It is found mainly on calcareous soil from Scandinavia into central Spain and east into the Apennines, Greece and the Atlas Mountains. Its white, pink, or purple-red flowers, borne early in March or April, before the leaves appear, are sweetly fragrant and profuse on well established plants. The scarlet berries, which appear in September, also make the small shrub decorative and prove attractive to birds, yet all parts are poisonous to man if taken in any quantity.

LINACEAE

Linum austriacum, Austrian Flax
A1 part of flowering stem × ⅔.
A2 stamens, style and ovary × 4. A3 petal × 2.

MALVACEAE

Malva sylvestris, Common Mallow
B1 portion of main stem with flowering shoot × ⅔. B2 flower × 1⅓.
B3 bracts at base of calyx × 2.

CONVOLVULACEAE

Calystegia silvatica, Greater Bindweed
C1 part of flowering tendril twining on species of Bent Grass × ⅔. C2 calyx and ovary × ⅔.

POLYGALACEAE

Polygala serpyllifolia, Common Milkwort, Cross Flower
D1 part of flowering stem × ⅔.
D2 flower showing 3 green and 2 blue sepals with fused lower petals protruding × 4.
D3 sepals enclosing fruit × 4.
D4 fruit with sepals removed × 4.

VIOLACEAE

Viola riviniana, Common Violet
E1 part of flowering plant × ⅔.
E2 fruit × 2. E3 stipule × 1⅓.

V. calcarata, Long-spurred Pansy
F1 flowering plant × ⅔.

THYMELAEACEAE

Daphne mezereum, Mezereon
G1 part of flowering stem × ⅔.
G2 opened corolla showing stamens × 4.
G3 fruiting stem and mature leaves × ⅔.
G4 fruit × 3⅓.

A2

A3

A1

B3

B2

B1

C2

C1

D3

D4

D2

D1

E1

E3

F1

G1

G2

G3

G4

Plate 19   E U R O P E

The family *Aceraceae* consists of about two hundred species, two of which belong to the Chinese genus *Dipteronia*, the others to the maple genus, *Acer*. A group of about eight species under the name *Negundo* is sometimes separated from this latter genus; these bear leaves divided into 3 to 7 leaflets. Commercial and decorative uses for many maple species are numerous. The Sycamore Maple, *A. pseudoplatanus* (C), is one of several species which provide valuable timber. All maples have sugar in their spring sap but that of the Sugar Maple, *A. saccharum*, of eastern North America, is the sweetest and most copious. It is harvested in quantity by boring a hole about half an inch deep in the trunk, when the sap begins to flow in the spring, and inserting a spout from which the sticky sap drips into buckets. Some Chinese and Japanese species, such as *A. palmatum*, have wonderfully ornamental foliage and are valued as garden plants.

A native of central and southern Europe but now naturalized in the British Isles, the Sycamore or Sycamore Maple appears to have been introduced into Britain in the Middle Ages although, since the Romans used its wood, it may have arrived earlier. Its pendulous clusters of green flowers are conspicuous in spring, as are the clusters of fruits in summer and autumn. Several garden varieties include specimens with pink, purple, yellow, white-blotched and yellow-blotched leaves, known respectively as 'Leopoldii', 'Purpureum', 'Worleei', 'Variegatum' and 'Flavovariegatum'. Some plants, it appears, do not bear hermaphrodite flowers but have only functional male flowers. In others only the lower flowers in the inflorescence are functionally hermaphrodite, as the upper flowers are male. Sycamore timber, pale and long-wearing even when repeatedly moistened, is popular for kitchen utensils and ornamental carvings.

A native of Europe from southern Scandinavia east to the Urals and northern Iran, then southward into Spain and Greece, the Norway Maple, *Acer platanoides* (B), is similar to the Sycamore. Both form spreading trees up to 100 feet (30 m.) high, but the Norway Maple flowers almost a month earlier, in March or April, when its bright greenish yellow flowers provide a welcome splash of colour in the spring woodland. Like the Sycamore, the Norway Maple has produced several varieties of horticultural interest; the most common of these include those which have yellow marginal variegations, white speckles, white variegations or purplish leaves.

The Horse Chestnut, *Aesculus hippocastanum* (A), originated in the central Balkans, but it has been planted and sometimes become naturalized in many parts of Europe. It was first described in 1557 from a fruiting twig brought to Vienna from Istanbul. The flowers were then unknown and Clusius, the celebrated botanist who recorded it, did not see them until 1603. Seeds were brought from Istanbul to France, and probably to England, in 1615. During the 17th century it began to be cultivated in the major cities of northern Europe. Trees may reach a height of 80 feet (24 m.) and a fine row of them flanks the eastern wall of Kew Gardens, overlooking the herbaceous beds. When in flower, their fallen petals swathe the pathways; when in fruit the seeds, often called 'conkers'—a name probably derived from the game of conquerors—are much sought after by children. The Pink-flowered Horse Chestnut, a smaller tree than *A. hippocastanum*, is called *A. carnea*. It arose in cultivation from a cross between *A. hippocastanum* and the North American *A. pavia* which belongs to a different section of the genus, but whereas both the species have 40 chromosomes, *A. carnea* has 80 and is now a true-breeding species. The Sweet Chestnut, *Castanea*, belongs to the Beech family, *Fagaceae*, and is completely different from the chestnuts mentioned above.

HIPPOCASTANACEAE

Aesculus hippocastanum, Horse Chestnut
A1 part of flowering stem and leaf × $\frac{2}{3}$.
A2 stamen × $3\frac{1}{3}$. A3 petal × $3\frac{1}{3}$.
A4 part of fruiting stem with winter bud × $\frac{2}{3}$.
A5 open fruit showing seed × $\frac{2}{3}$.
A6 leaf showing autumn colour × $\frac{2}{3}$.

ACERACEAE

Acer platanoides, Norway Maple
B1 part of flowering stem × $\frac{2}{3}$.
B2 flower (functionally male) × $2\frac{2}{3}$.
B3 part of fruiting stem × $\frac{2}{3}$. B4 fruit × $\frac{2}{3}$.

A. pseudoplatanus, Sycamore Maple
C1 part of flowering stem and leaf × $\frac{2}{3}$.
C2 flower × $2\frac{2}{3}$. C3 part of fruiting stem × $\frac{2}{3}$.
C4 fruit (samara) × $\frac{2}{3}$.

A4

B4

B1

B3

B2

C2

A3

A2

C1

C4

C3

1

A6

A5

Plate 20   EUROPE

There are about one hundred genera in the *Boraginaceae*, occurring in tropical and temperate areas, especially those in the northern hemisphere with a Mediterranean climate.

A jumble of herbalists' lore surrounds the Bugloss, *Anchusa officinalis*: the leaves were recommended as a specific against melancholia and epilepsy; the roots were said to promote the onset of smallpox. In view of this one can only admire the perseverance of those less scientifically-minded members of the community who continued to use the boiled leaves as a substitute for cabbage (or mixed them with water, lemon, sugar and wine to brew 'cool tankard') and made a conserve out of the flowers. In the modern context, the plant is best employed in herbaceous borders. Though closely related to the genus *Anchusa*, *Pentaglottis*, a genus with one species, *P. sempervirens* (A), commonly known as Alkanet, differs from the former in having stalked nutlets (A4 & A5) and net-veined leaves.

The legend that *Myosotis scorpioides* (B), or in other versions *Veronica chamaedrys* (plate 21), Forget-me-not, keeps lovers' memories fresh, dates from the early 15th century, though, with the Gothic revival of the early 19th, more romantic etymologies, concerning the last words of a drowning knight who stepped too close to the water's edge while gathering his lady a posy, were invented. At an earlier date the medieval doctrine of signatures gave rise to the idea that, because of their shape, the curled inflorescences of this and other forget-me-nots could cure the stings of scorpions, whose tails they were thought to resemble.

The thirty species of *Echium* occur in Europe and the Mediterranean with an outpost in the Azores, the Canaries and Madeira where a number of large and striking species grow (see plate 44). Viper's Bugloss, *E. vulgare* (F), is found from Scandinavia to Spain and east to the Urals and Turkey.

The family *Labiatae* is not too distantly related to the *Boraginaceae*, although it has flowers which are bilaterally symmetrical. As well as the Dead-nettles, it includes many culinary herbs such as Sage, Mint, Rosemary, Marjoram and Thyme. The Garden or Common Thyme, *Thymus vulgaris*, is a small, erect perennial of southern Europe, which has been grown in England since the 15th century, at first, according to some, for its supposed medicinal qualities. It owed its wide popularity, however, to the effectiveness of its aromatic leaves in disguising the taste of putrid meat in days before adequate refrigeration. Oil of thyme, an early specific against colds and the like, is a distillation of the entire plant, made in early summer when the flowers are open. In the impure state it is a heavy, reddish-brown oil that clears on redistillation. The aromatic thymol, in which it is rich, gives the liquid a burning taste. The genus *Thymus* itself contains between three and four hundred species, all from temperate Eurasian areas. Specific differentiation is often very difficult, hence the doubtful number of species. *T. doerfleri* (G) is known only from Mount Koritnik on the Jugoslavian-Albanian border, where it was first collected by J. Döerfler. The plant illustrated comes from the Vienna Botanic Garden where the species was subsequently grown and is probably derived from the material originally described there by Ronniger. The illustrated plant has flowers with abortive stamens, being functionally female; hermaphrodite flowers are known on other specimens.

Balm-leaved Archangel, *Lamium orvala* (E), one of a genus of some forty species found in temperate Eurasia and North Africa, is an attractive native of the area from northern Italy to Hungary. Despite attempts to cultivate the species in Britain, the risk to the flowers of damage by late frost has prevented it from becoming popular. *L. album*, the White Deadnettle (D), so called, as every country child knows, because its leaves resemble those of the Stinging Nettle, is found right across from western Europe through the Himalaya mountains to Japan. The related *L. maculatum*, the Spotted Dead-nettle, which has whitish leaf markings and purple-pink flowers, is often found in British gardens, both under cultivation and as a weed.

About forty-five species of *Ajuga*, with corollas characterized by short upper and pronounced, 3-lobed lower lips, are to be found throughout the temperate parts of the Old World. *A. genevensis* (C), sometimes called Blue Bugle, occurs from Sweden to Italy, and east into south-western Asia. Unlike *A. reptans*, the Common Bugle, an attractive native of Britain, *A. genevensis* is an introduction.

A number of valuable aromatic herbs come within the genus *Mentha*: Peppermint, *M. × piperita*, was intensively cultivated in the suburbs of London for use as a flavouring as early as the late 17th century; and Spearmint, *M. spicata*, so easily and widely grown for making mint-sauce. With a range extending further to the south into North Africa and Turkey, *M. pulegium*, Pennyroyal, has an aroma less pleasant than that of either Peppermint or Spearmint. It was, however, considered by the ancient Greeks to have medicinal value, and by the Roman and medieval herbalists to be an effective flea killer, hence the Latin name based on the Latin for 'flea', *pulex*. This name *Pulegium* was in time corrupted into the dog Latin 'puleium regium' which in time became the common name, 'pennyroyal'.

A5

A4

B1

B2

B3

A2 A1 A3

D3

E1

E2 E3

F2

C3

C2

C1

D2

D1

G1

G2 G3

F1

Plate 21   EUROPE

All the families and genera represented here, with the possible exception of *Vinca* (*Apocynaceae*), are members of a group whose flowers have the same number of parts and basic construction. The apparent floral diversity rests upon variations in the shape of the corolla, the main technical differences upon the characters of the ovaries.

Most of the three hundred species of the genus *Verbascum*, native to Eurasia but introduced to and often naturalized in other temperate areas, have bright yellow flowers. *V. phoeniceum*, the Purple Mullein (A) is an exception. The species occurs in southern, central and eastern Europe, Turkey, and adjacent Russia and Iran, but was introduced into cultivation in western Europe before 1597. The best known yellow-flowered species is, perhaps, the Great Mullein, *V. thapsus*, which is found from western Europe to the Himalaya. Apart from the common name given above, Aaron's Rod, Hag's Taper, Bullock's Lungwort and Candlewick are also used colloquially in Britain. Folk lore recommends the plant for a number of purposes, from the burning of warts with its juice to the lining of shoes with its woolly leaves, which are particularly well developed when most needed, in autumn and winter.

The name 'foxglove', it has been suggested, refers to the likeness of the flower arrangement to an early musical instrument, consisting of a string of variously sized bells on an arched support—'glove' being derived from *gleow*, the Anglo-Saxon word for music; the entire name meaning 'foxes music'. Others have suggested a derivation from 'folks glove', meaning 'gloves for fairy-folk', but this seems less likely. The eighteen species of the foxglove genus, *Digitalis*, occur in Europe, the Mediterranean area and the Canary Islands. A particularly splendid plant, when grown in groups, the Yellow Foxglove, *D. grandiflora* (B), also known as *D. ambigua*, comes from France, Belgium and the Balkans. The hardier Common Foxglove, *D. purpurea*, is the source of the drug and poison digitalin, widely used in the treatment of heart complaints. Its introduction into legitimate medicine around 1780, following the investigations of Dr William Withering, is a classic example of the incorporation of a folk cure into the official pharmacopoeia.

If one excludes the hundred or so southern species now usually placed in the genus *Hebe*, some three hundred northern and southern

temperate, alpine and tropical mountain species still remain within the genus *Veronica*. All are immediately identifiable at the right season by their apparently 4-petalled flowers (there are in fact 5 petals, the upper 2 being fused) and the 2 stamens that jut out on either side of the single style. The fly-pollinated Germander Speedwell, *V. chamaedrys* (E) is common in grassland and hedgerows from Scandinavia to Portugal and east to northern and western Asia. The name 'germander' is a corruption of the originally Greek *chamaedrys* meaning ground-oak, an allusion to the supposed similarity between the leaves of the two plants.

The flowers of the Lesser Periwinkle, *Vinca minor* (C), are, as the name implies, smaller than those of *V. major* but both species are widely grown and hardy, often being the last survivors in overgrown and uncared-for gardens. The fact that both rarely produce fruit in Britain supports the view that neither is native to the country. In the Middle Ages, *V. minor* was traditionally associated with death and garlands were made of the flowers to adorn corpses and condemned criminals. About five other species belong to this Eurasian genus.

All thirty-five or so species of the butterwort genus *Pinguicula*, found in northern temperate areas and south along the Andes to antarctic South America, are insectivorous and have a basal rosette of leaves armed with glands that secrete a sticky fluid with which to trap their prey; digestive juices are secreted by other leaf-glands. As Darwin was the first to observe, the edges of the leaf also curve over towards the trapped insect but whether this plays any part in the catching or digesting of the animal is uncertain. The Large-flowered Butterwort, *P. grandiflora* (D), is a native of the French Alps, the Pyrenees and the other mountains of northern Spain; it also occurs in bogs and on wet rocks in southern Ireland.

The motif which characterizes the Corinthian capital is derived from the foliage of either *Acanthus mollis* or the more spiny leaved *A. spinosus*, the Spiny Bear's Breech (F), both of which are southern European examples of a genus of fifty or so species that also occurs in tropical or subtropical Africa and Asia. The former, commonly called Bear's Breech, is said by some to have been introduced into Britain as early as the 13th century, though others contend that it did not arrive until the middle of the 16th.

4

3

A5

A2

A1

B3

B2

B1

C1

C3

C2

D2

D3

D4

D5

D1

E1

E2

F2

F3

F4

F5

F1

Plate 22   EUROPE

Europe is richly endowed with many graceful and colourful daisies, family *Compositae*, from the ubiquitous white *Bellis* flowers to the rich blue flowers of the *Cicerbita* and *Cichorium* species or the yellow-headed species of *Hieracium, Sonchus* and *Crepis*. While European species are predominantly herbs, tropical species include arborescent types (see plate 56) in a family distinguished for diversity of vegetative form and variety of flower and fruit structure.

Found in western Asia, Europe and the Canary Islands, *Carlina* comprises some twenty species. *C. vulgaris* (B), the Carline Thistle, grows mainly in chalk or limestone grassland from southern Europe to south Norway, east to Siberia, Turkey and Caucasia. Long bracts, brownish outside but straw-yellow inside, surround the inflorescence or capitulum and simulate ray-florets. In winter, the withered spiny shoots persist in the short turf and are a conspicuous feature when other plants have died. Related thistles, the Silver Thistle, *C. acaulis*, with purple disc-florets, and the Acanthus-leaved Thistle, *C. acanthifolia*, with yellow disc-florets, have such short stems that the large capitula rest on the ground. The bracts surrounding the capitulum of these species close up in wet weather, but re-open in drier conditions.

About fifteen species of *Bellis* are found in Europe and the Mediterranean regions. The Daisy, *B. perennis* (C), native throughout Europe and into western Asia, is abundant in short grassland, such as lawns, where it may almost replace the grass as it spreads by short rhizomes and seeds freely. Cultivation of the numerous double forms, some red, some white, that it has produced, goes back at least to the 15th century. The Daisy, which belongs to the same group as *Aster* and *Erigeron*, generally flowers between March and October, although it may also be found in mid-winter.

Of the nine *Cichorium* species, one is found in northern Europe, another in Ethiopia, but the majority occur in the Mediterranean region. The root of one form of Chicory, *C. intybus* (D), is dried and ground before being incorporated into coffee; another form known as 'Witloef' (white leaf) is grown for salad purposes, the leaves being blanched by forcing the plants in darkness during the winter months. Its natural distribution is from North Africa and southern Europe to central Scandinavia, central Russia and western Asia. This plant has been introduced to many parts of the world and is one of the few commercially important food plants which is also very attractive.

Also a member of the chicory group, the genus *Cicerbita* has eighteen species, of which four are American, but the majority are European, Asian or North African. The Blue Sowthistle, *C. alpina* (F), also known as *Sonchus alpinus* and *Lactuca alpina*, is found in montane Europe from the Pyrenees to the Carpathians and also in Scotland and Scandinavia. A perennial herb, up to 6 feet (1·8 m.) tall, it may grow at altitudes of 7000 feet (2100 m.) in the Swiss Alps. In gardens, the genus *Cicerbita* is usually represented by *C. bourgaei*, a species from Turkey, which grows to the same height.

The montane genus *Homogyne* is exclusively European and consists of three dwarf perennial species which belong to the *Senecio* group of the *Compositae*. The Alpine Coltsfoot, *H. alpina* (G), ranges from the Pyrenees through the Alps into the northern Balkans at altitudes from 1500–9800 feet (460–2980 m.). The central flowers of the inflorescence are hermaphrodite while the marginal flowers are female; the former have 5 equal corolla lobes instead of the single lobe of the marginal flowers. This condition is intermediate to that of daisies with well developed central (disc) and marginal (ray) flowers. The related *H. discolor* has white hair beneath the leaves while the leaves of *H. sylvestris* are green beneath and deeply toothed.

The hawkweed genus, *Hieracium*, is made up of an indeterminate number of taxonomic groups, chiefly because seeds can be produced independently of fertilization and therefore minute differences are constantly perpetuated by seed without the intermingling of characters produced by outbreeding. Such asexual reproduction means that each individual can be regarded as a 'microspecies' and it is estimated that between ten and twenty thousand exist in north temperate and arctic areas, South America, South Africa and southern India. A group of these species, with pappus hairs almost equal, instead of variable, in length, is sometimes separated as the genus *Pilosella*; to this group *H. brunneocroceum* (E) belongs. Alternatively known as *Pilosella aurantiaca* ssp. *brunneocrocea*, it is similar to Foxes and Cubs, *H. aurantiacum*. Both species are natives of central Europe but, because of efficient stoloniferous propagation and profuse seed-production, they appear as garden escapes in many parts of western Europe. They are now widespread in Britain but differ slightly in leaf-shape and flower colour. The Mouse-ear Hawkweed, *H. pilosella* (A), occurs throughout temperate and subarctic Europe into western Asia. The leaves have stiff white hairs on both sides and combine with pale lemon flowers to produce a delicate and pretty plant.

A1   A2   A3   A4

B1   B2

C1   C2   C3   C4

D1   D2   D3   D4   D5

E1   E2   E3   E4   E5

F1   F2

G1   G2   G3   G4

Plate 23   EUROPE

A plant not commonly seen in gardens, but one in which well-grown specimens respond to cultivation by producing fine heads of flowers, is the Flowering Rush, *Butomus umbellatus* (D), the sole species of its genus. It is found growing in shallow water in ditches and ponds and along the edges of rivers and canals throughout temperate Eurasia. There is no division in the leaves between stalk and blade, and the flowers are borne in umbels.

Another fresh-water species from Eurasia is the Frogbit, *Hydrocharis morsus-ranae* (C). The male and female flowers are generally borne on different parts of the same plant or form separate plants of their own. If the canal from which the illustrated specimens were collected is a typical habitat, it would seem that the female plants, or parts of plants, prefer stretches of water shaded by trees and bushes, while the male favour open water. The female flowers are easily identified by a swelling formed by the ovary beneath the petals.

The tall, luxuriant leaves and compact cylindrical flower heads of *Typha latifolia*, the Great Reed-mace (A), (not, correctly, the Bullrush, as it is often called) dominate the swamps in which it grows from the Arctic to areas as far south as the Mediterranean. Each highly reduced flower of the furry spike is surrounded by a number of hairs or scales, believed by some botanists to be vestiges of a form of petal. The upper part of the inflorescence is male and turns yellow as the pollen is released, while the lower, the female part, becomes dark brown when in fruit;

dispersal of seed by the wind is facilitated by the hairs attached to each. In fact, if an inflorescence (they are often used in flower arrangements) is collected when fully mature, it quickly and easily breaks up to produce a remarkable amount of fine fluff, to one's ready annoyance if this happens indoors.

Potamogeton lucens, Shining Pondweed (B), belongs to a family with world-wide distribution, all members of which inhabit lakes, ponds, canals and other stretches of slow-flowing or still water. This particular species occurs throughout Europe and into western Asia. It is characterized by the shortness of the leaf stalks, the size of the leaves and the thick fruiting spike that curves upwards from them. Perfoliate Pondweed, *P. perfoliatus* (F), is so called because the stem appears to pass through the middle of the leaf. The species is found in all northern temperate areas, and in Australia.

The Sharp-leaved Pondweed, *P. acutifolius* (E), grows in the ditches, streams and ponds of chalk and limestone areas in Europe, and is found as a rare plant in south-eastern England. Its fruit appears in the form of a sharp-toothed nut. In all there are about one hundred species of Pondweed, many of them noted for the numerous hybrids they form with one another; in fact it has been suggested that the extensive hybridization that occurs in the wild in *Potamogeton* is directly attributable to the breakdown of isolation that occurred when rivers and lakes were linked together with the construction of canals in the 18th and 19th centuries.

TYPHACEAE

Typha latifolia, Great Reed-mace
A1 part of flowering stem × $\frac{2}{3}$.
A2 female flower × $13\frac{1}{3}$. A3 male flower × $13\frac{1}{3}$.

POTAMOGETONACEAE

Potamogeton lucens, Shining Pondweed
B1 part of flowering plant × $\frac{2}{3}$.
B2 flower × 8. B3 fruiting head × $\frac{2}{3}$.
B4 fruiting flower × $7\frac{1}{3}$. B5 fruit × 8.

P. acutifolius, Sharp-leaved Pondweed
E1 part of flowering and fruiting plant × $\frac{2}{3}$.
E2 flower × $5\frac{1}{4}$. E3 fruiting head × 2.
E4 fruit × $2\frac{2}{3}$. E5 leaf tip × 2.

P. perfoliatus, Perfoliate Pondweed
F1 part of flowering plant × $\frac{2}{3}$. F2 flower × $4\frac{2}{3}$.
F3 fruiting flower × 4. F4 fruit × 6.

HYDROCHARITACEAE

Hydrocharis morsus-ranae, Frogbit
C1 flowering female plant × $\frac{2}{3}$.
C2 female flower × 1. C3 style × 6.
C4 flowering male plant × $\frac{2}{3}$.
C5 male flower × 1. C6 stamen × $2\frac{2}{3}$.

BUTOMACEAE

Butomus umbellatus, Flowering Rush
D1 flowering plant (stem cut) × $\frac{2}{3}$.
D2 flower × 2.

A1

A2

A3

B1

B2

B3

B4

B5

C1

C2

C3

C4

C5

C6

D1

D2

E1

E2

E3

E4

E5

F1

F2

F3

F4

Plate 24   EUROPE

The family *Liliaceae* includes many spectacular plants among its north temperate members, notably the true lilies (*Lilium* and *Cardiocrinum*), and many with comparatively small flowers which are nevertheless attractive.

The Bog Asphodel, *Narthecium ossifragum* (A) is one of eight north temperate species which closely resemble each other in character while being widely separated geographically and mostly very restricted in range; one in Corsica, another in the Balkan Peninsula, a third in the Caucasus and the illustrated plant further west in Europe from Portugal to the Faroes and Norway. Two grow in eastern North America, one in western North America and one occurs in Japan. They form little tufts of iris-like leaves and have starry yellow flowers which are notable for the dense and attractive hairs on the stamen filaments. Although they lack honey, these plants apparently supply enough pollen to ensure insect pollination. The Bog Asphodel is a moorland plant, typical of moist acid soils, but its local appearance is restricted by the increasing disappearance of suitable habitats; its general distribution closely corresponds to the Atlantic (as distinct from the Continental) climatic region. Its fruiting heads are most attractive and conspicuous in September and October.

Found only in the Old World, the Star of Bethlehem genus, *Ornithogalum*, contains some hundred species growing throughout Europe, western Asia and Africa. The name should not be confused with *Ornithoglossum* which is a related but endemic South African genus of some three species. Of the European species, perhaps *O. umbellatum*, the Star of Bethlehem, is the best known and is recognizable for its corymbose inflorescence instead of one where the flower stalks are of equal length. It attracted the attention of Leonardo da Vinci and is illustrated in an often-reproduced pen and ink drawing done by him about 1505 or 1508, which is now in the Royal Library, Windsor Castle (number 12,424). *O. montanum* (B) grows in southern Europe, in Italy and the Balkan Peninsula. In some plants, for example the specimen illustrated opposite, the inflorescence stalks are not well developed.

Fritillaria nigra (C) occurs in France, Italy, the Tyrol, Hungary, the Balkan Peninsula and western U.S.S.R. It is about 9 to 12 inches (23–30 cm.) high; the flowers vary in intensity of colour and, despite the name *nigra* 'black', are mostly a deep reddy brown. A native of Siberia, *F. pallidiflora* (G) ascends to 9000 feet (2740 m.) and its stems, about 18 inches (46 cm.) high, bear 3 to 12 pale greenish flowers. In nature many species of fritillary grow in stony soil, so that for the purposes of cultivation, good drainage is essential; most will grow in a well-drained loam. Different species thrive in different habitats and therefore *F. acmopetala*, *F. imperialis*, plate 41, *F. meleagris*, plate 41, and *F. pyrenaica* thrive in a sunny position while *F. camschatcensis*, *F. pallidiflora*, *F. lanceolata* and *F. obliqua* grow best in the shade. Bulbs can be moved when the leaves are withering and it is advisable periodically to split mature groups as overcrowding can inhibit flowering. Contrary to the belief of many people, these plants are not difficult to grow; they are quite hardy towards frost but will not tolerate excessive damp. *F. sewerzowii*, with a bulb formed of a single thick scale instead of several scales, is now put in a genus by itself under the name of *Korolkowia sewerzowii*.

The Bluebell, *Endymion non-scriptus* (D), belongs to a small genus of three to four west European and North African species. It is common in woods and along hedges throughout western Europe, but is probably not native in northern Germany, northern Spain, Portugal and Italy. The flowers are gathered in arm-fulls in many parts of Europe and while they do not last as cut flowers, this practice causes little harm provided the bulbs are left intact in the ground.

Although similar in appearance to the bluebell genus, *Scilla* lacks its tubular bulb scales and has free, not partially fused petals. Also the filaments of the stamens are inserted on the base of the perianth, not partly along the petal as in *Endymion* (see D2). There are about eighty species of *Scilla* found in temperate Eurasia and parts of Africa. The Spring Squill, *S. verna*, grows in western Europe from the Faroes and Norway to central Spain and Portugal and flowers in April and May. *S. autumnalis* flowers from July to September and is distinguishable from *S. verna* because it lacks inflorescence bracts. A native of the Mediterranean, *S. peruviana* is a far nobler species than the above-mentioned plant, producing pyramids of dense blue flower heads in early spring. The illustrated species, *S. bifolia* (F), the Two-leaved Squill, is found in parts of France and Germany, the Balkan Peninsula and into the U.S.S.R.

Allium is a north temperate genus of at least five hundred species, including the cultivated onions, ranging across Europe, North Africa, Asia and North America. It reaches its southern limits in Ethiopia, Ceylon and Mexico. All species have a distinctive, usually pungent flavour and wild plants are often gathered by native peoples to season their food. As culinary plants, some have been in cultivation for many centuries and have diverged much from their ancestral stocks. Among these are Garlic, *A. sativum*; Leek, *A. porrum*—derived from *A. ampeloprasum*; Onion, *A. cepa*, of which the Shallots are variants; Chives, *A. schoenoprasum*; the Welsh Onion, *A. fistulosum*; Chinese Chives or Cuchay, *A. tuberosum*. A number of species are cultivated simply as ornamental plants. The range of flower colour displayed by the genus is truly remarkable—white, yellow, greenish, pink, purple, blue and red—as is the range of habit; the bulbs provide important characters for classification. In some species the flowers of the umbel may be replaced partly or entirely by bulbils, a habit which has enabled Crow Garlic, *A. vineale*, to become a widespread and pernicious weed, very difficult to eradicate as bulbils may lie dormant in the soil for some years. Ramsons, *A. ursinum*, which sometimes carpets woods with its broad leaves and starry white flowers, is a widespread European species with peculiar biological features: for example, owing to a twist in the stalk, what would normally be the lower side of the leaf is turned uppermost. The illustrated *A. moly* (E) is a south-western European species notable for its clear yellow flowers.

A1

A2

A3

A4

B1

B2

C1

D1

D2

D3

E1

E2

F1

F2

F3

G1

G2

G3

Plate 25   EUROPE

Economically the grass family, *Gramineae*, is the most important group of plants for the well being of mankind. Long before the dawn of history, men were gathering the seeds of wild grasses to supplement their often meagre and precarious supplies of food and out of such gathering, followed by accidental growth and later deliberate cultivation of such grasses near dwellings, developed the basic groups of neolithic times; wheat (*Triticum*) and barley (*Hordeum*), followed by rye (*Secale*) and oats (*Avena*) in the Near East and Europe; maize (*Zea*) in tropical America; rice (*Oryza*) in eastern Asia; and grain sorghum (*Sorghum*) in Africa. The illustrations opposite show the relationship between the rushes *Juncaceae*, sedges *Cyperaceae*, and grasses. Rushes are thought to be derived from a liliaceous stock, as the detail of the flower (A2) shows, while sedges and grasses, with their reduced scale-like petals, appear to be derived from rush-like ancestors.

One of eighty cosmopolitan species found in cold temperate regions of the northern hemisphere, the Greater Woodrush, *Luzula sylvatica* (A), grows in acid soils in woods or on rocky ground near streams throughout Europe, as far east as the Caucasus and Turkey. The genus belongs to the rush family but differs from *Juncus* in having flat, sparsely hairy leaves.

Sedges, *Carex* species, are distinguishable from grasses in having a stem triangular in cross-section, leaf blades not jointed at the junction with the leaf-sheath and flowers which are unisexual instead of bisexual. The thousand or so species are often found growing in moorland and bog areas of cold temperate regions. The Great Pond Sedge, *C. riparia* (F), grows close to water, in ditches and near ponds throughout Europe, though rarely in the north, to North Africa and into western Asia. One can see from the fruiting stem illustrated opposite (F4) that the upper inflorescences are male and the lower ones female. The British species are more fully described in the book *British Sedges* by A. C. Jermy and T. G. Tutin (1968).

A member of the grass family, the genus *Milium* has about six species growing in temperate Eurasia and North America. *M. scabrum* (E) is an annual found in coastal areas from the Netherlands to Spain, occurring also in Guernsey and the Mediterranean area. Usually about 6 inches (15 cm.) tall, it is a much smaller plant than the perennial Wood Millet, *M. effusum*, which grows up to 4 feet (1·2 m.).

The Yellow Oat Grass, *Trisetum flavescens* (D), is one of about sixty species growing in north temperate and tropical montane areas. This species is usually found on calcareous soils throughout Europe, into Algeria and western Asia; in North America it has been introduced as a pasture grass and become naturalized. The shiny parts of the spikelets make this plant most attractive when the glistening inflorescence is blown about in the wind.

The hundred or so species of the genus *Bromus* are found in temperate areas and mountainous regions of the tropics. The Drooping Brome, *B. tectorum* (B), is sometimes classified as *Anisantha*, but the difference between this genus and *Bromus* are very slight and perhaps not worth consideration. A native of the Mediterranean area, it grows throughout Europe, but like most bromes, has little fodder value. Its characteristic brome-like spikelets are pendulous and very decorative when in flower.

Mainly cosmopolitan in distribution, the three hundred or so *Festuca* species are important pasture grasses known collectively as 'fescues'. *F. vivipara* (C) is very similar in habit to the Sheep's Fescue, *F. ovina*, but as its specific name suggests, it is viviparous and produces young plants from its spikelets.

A1 A2 A3 A4 A5 A6 A7

B1 B2 B3 B4

C1 C2

D1 D2 D3

E1 E2 E3

F1 F2 F3 F4 F5

Plate 26   EUROPE

All temperate orchids are terrestrial plants, unlike their tropical cousins which are more often found growing on the bark or on the branches of trees. However, all orchids, tropical and temperate, are noted for growing in intimate association with fungi, in and about their roots. They should never be collected from the wild for those which are popular are too easily depleted and may be obtained through a reputable grower who will propagate them himself and not threaten the diminishing wild populations.

The genus *Orchis* as now defined, contains about thirty-five species which occur from Madeira, throughout temperate Eurasia, into India and south-west China. *Orchis ustulata* (A), commonly known as the Burnt-tip Orchid, is so called because, from a distance, the colour of the unopened flowers gives the top of the inflorescence a charred appearance. When the seed of *O. ustulata*, like those of all terrestial species, germinates, it grows underground for two to four years or more as a cylindrical seedling or protocorm before the first leaves appear and, during this period, obtains its food from an associated fungus growing in its tissues. Fungi do not possess chlorophyll and so do not require light for growth, but live on plant and animal tissues; in the case of soil fungi, usually dead and rotting wood, leaves and animal remains. After about five to seven years, a fully recognizable orchid plant with flowers will develop. Each time *O. ustulata*, or any orchid, becomes established from seed, the plant undergoes this prolonged development and is dependent on the fungus before it begins the more usual process of food manufacture from light, water and carbon dioxide in its green leaves. The Burnt-tip Orchid has a wide range from north-western Europe and the Mediterranean to western U.S.S.R. *O. laxiflora* (J) is becoming rare in Europe, for, with the encroachment of agriculture, its marshy habitats are being progressively drained. It grows to a height of 12 to 20 inches (30–51 cm.) and its inflorescence consists of 10 to 20 loosely borne red-purple or sometimes violet flowers.

The genus *Anacamptis* has only one species, *A. pyramidalis*, the Pyramidal Orchid (D) with a distribution from south Sweden to parts of North Africa and east into Iran. While a common plant in the Mediterranean region, in Britain it is usually confined to chalklands. The name Pyramidal Orchid is derived from the shape of the delicately scented pale pink to red flower spike. One of the notable characteristics of most orchids, other than the Lady's Slipper Orchids, is the fact that the pollen is held together in waxy masses called pollinia. There may be 2 or more pollinia per flower, borne in pockets on a special structure in the centre of the flower, the highly modified stamens and style, called the column. The pollinia are usually attached to a sticky gland which, when it comes into contact with the head or other part of an insect, sticks tight, so that the pollinia are carried off when the insect flies away, all ready to touch against the stigmatic surface of another flower. Pollination in the Pyramidal Orchid is almost certainly by butterflies and moths; Charles Darwin observed a moth with no less than eleven pairs of pollinia attached to its proboscis.

The Little Bog Orchid, *Malaxis paludosa* (C)

grows only in acidic soils; it is one of about three hundred cosmopolitan species but, not being typical of the genus, is sometimes classified by itself under the name *Hammarbya paludosa*. Its size and inconspicuous colouring make it difficult to find amongst the *Sphagnum* moss in which it often grows. The base of the stem is swollen into 2 bulbils and the 2 to 4 leaves sometimes produce buds which form new plants when detached. The roots are much less developed than in many species and the plant is even more dependent than usual upon associated fungi for its source of food.

The twenty-five species of the genus *Spiranthes* have a widespread distribution, although they do not occur in tropical Africa and America. Autumn Lady's Tresses, *S. spiralis* (H), with its dainty spirals of white flowers, is peculiar in having flowering shoots with withered leaves; the next year's vegetative growth being made by a new shoot beside it at the base. This process eventually gives rise to the characteristic clumps in which this species grows. It is found in west and central Europe, and is common around the Mediterranean.

The Common Twayblade, *Listera ovata* (B) is one of a genus of about fourteen species found in Europe north to the Arctic Circle and east to Siberia and the west Himalaya; some also occur in Turkey and Iran. This plant spends about four years in the seedling or protocorm stage and takes another ten years to reach flowering, when its easily overlooked green inflorescence may reach a length of about 12 inches (30 cm.). It is pollinated by insects who, on visiting the flower, trigger off a micro-explosive mechanism whereby the release of a sticky fluid instantly cements the two pollinia to the head of the visiting beetle or fly. Vegetative propagation also occurs from root-buds, by-passing the lengthy process of establishment from seed. The Common Twayblade appears to be a most successful species for it is widespread in a great variety of woody or grassland habitats where the soil is not too acid.

The genus *Ophrys* contains some thirty species, found in Europe, North Africa and western Asia and is characterized by the large and often bulbous lip and spurless flowers. The Early Spider Orchid, *O. sphegodes* (K), occurs in west and central Europe, south to the Mediterranean. The flower, which bears a resemblance to the body of a spider, differs from the Late Spider Orchid, *O. fuciflora*, in having green instead of pink sepals. Another species, the Brown Bee Orchid, *O. fusca* (E), has a more Mediterranean range, and narrower petals, like those found in *O. insectifera* (see E3) where they are thought to resemble the antennae of a fly. The insect-like form of the lip, and the scent of the flowers in *Ophrys*, attract the males of certain insects and stimulate them into abortive attempts at copulation. During this pseudocopulation the insects pick up pollinia or transfer pollen to the stigmas. Some tropical orchids have likewise been shown to possess particular scents which excite insects sexually: the attraction of flowers for insects is not always in terms of food.

The flowers of the single species of *Aceras* differ from those of *Orchis* in having no spur, but otherwise the Man Orchid, *A. anthropophorum* (G) has a lip similar in shape to that of the Military and Monkey Orchids; for all of these species have a lip shaped like a body with

two arms and legs. The Man Orchid grows from western Europe and Morocco across to western Asia.

Cephalanthera damasonium, the White Helleborine (F), has a similar distribution and is one of fourteen species in the genus, all confined to northern temperate regions. In *C. damasonium* the fully expanded flowers do not open completely and are often self-pollinated. The erect rootstock, which often penetrates deep in the soil, produces flowering spikes up to 18 inches (46 cm.) tall. In Britain, at the western limit of its distribution, it is confined to the south-eastern half of the country on lime-rich soils, often in Beech woods, but in Europe it is not so restricted and grows on a variety of soils.

ORCHIDACEAE

Orchis ustulata, Burnt-tip Orchid
A1 part of flowering stem × ⅔.

Listera ovata, Common Twayblade
B1 flowering plant × ⅔. B2 flower × 3⅓.

Malaxis paludosa (syn. *Hammarbya paludosa*),
Little Bog Orchid
C1 flowering plant × ⅔. C2 flower × 8.

Anacamptis pyramidalis, Pyramidal Orchid
D1 part of flowering stem × ⅔.
D2 front view of flower × ⅔.
D3 side view of flower × ⅔.

Ophrys fusca, Brown Bee Orchid
E1 part of flowering stem × ⅔.
E2 detail of flower lip × 2.
E3 flower of *O. insectifera* × 1⅓.

Cephalanthera damasonium, White Helleborine
F1 flowering plant × ⅔.

Aceras anthropophorum, Man Orchid
G1 part of flowering stem × ⅔. G2 flower × 2.

Spiranthes spiralis (syn. *S. autumnalis*),
Autumn Lady's Tresses
H1 flowering plant × ⅔. H2 flower × 2⅔.

Orchis laxiflora
J1 part of flowering stem × ⅔. J2 flower × 2.

Ophrys sphegodes, Early Spider Orchid
K1 flowering stem × ⅔. K2 flower × 2.
K3 pollinia on column × 5⅓. K4 pollinium × 5⅓.

A1

C1

C2

B2

B1

D2

D3

D1

E1

E2

E3

F1

G2

G1

H1

H2

J2

J1

K1

K2

K3

K4

Plate 27   MEDITERRANEAN

Attractive foliage and gaily coloured flowers characterize a number of Mediterranean species in the *Ranunculaceae*. The mention of Love-in-a-mist, *Nigella*, Winter Aconite, *Eranthis*, *Anemone* and Pheasant's Eye, *Adonis*, is enough to suggest a list of lovely plants which provide colour at different times for much of the year.

Because of the simple flower structure of some species, the *Ranunculaceae* is regarded as somewhat primitive, but even so, it manifests evidence of specialization. The various floral contrivances for attracting insects show a progressively complicated series from the Marsh Marigold, *Caltha*, where special tubular nectaries secrete nectar to *Ranunculus* and *Nigella*, where the nectary is situated at the base of the petal. All of these genera have symmetrical flowers. Specialization in the family is most marked in genera such as *Aconitum*, Monkshood, and *Delphinium*, where the nectar is contained in long spurs in flowers which are asymmetrical. A wide range of animals can readily obtain nectar from any angle above the petals of the Marsh Marigold, but in delphiniums, only long-tongued or deeply probing animals can reach the nectar from an angle determined by the shape of the flower.

One of about seven species confined to temperate parts of the Old World, the Winter Aconite, *Eranthis hyemalis* (A) is found from south-east France, throughout southern Europe into Bulgaria and also as a naturalized species in central and western Europe. Growing no taller than 6 inches (15 cm.) but usually only half that height, the yellow flowers appear in February and March, providing a brief splash of colour in those severe months. *Eranthis* species quickly lose their foliage and remain for much of the year in a dormant state, as the large tuberous root-stock testifies. Often grown in gardens, the hybrid *E.* × *tubergenii*, derived from the parents *E. hyemalis* and *E. cilicicus*, has larger flowers than the Winter Aconite.

Commonly cultivated as Love-in-a-mist, *Nigella damascena* (B) is found throughout southern Europe, from Spain to Turkey, and also in North Africa and the Middle East. It flowers in May and June, usually along roadsides, in dunes or wasteground. This species is characterized by the involucre of much-dissected bracts which closely surround the flowers. The follicular fruit can also be most attractive, for, as they mature, they become inflated and globular and sometimes tinged with purple.

Nigella ciliata (C) is an east Mediterranean species, found especially in Cyprus, Syria and Israel. This plant also grows on wasteground but is cultivated in some temperate gardens for its curiously constructed and hairy flowers which are a contrast to those of many *Nigella*

species. The aromatic seeds of *N. sativa* are used for culinary purposes and, according to Gerard, 'seed parched or dried at the fire, brought into pouder,' then 'laid on mixed with vinegar' will remove freckles. This plant, thought to be a native of south-east Europe, is widely cultivated.

There are about two hundred and fifty species in the north temperate genus *Delphinium*. The Violet Larkspur, *D. peregrinum* (D), found in fields, wasteland and vineyards throughout the Mediterranean region, especially in central and eastern areas, is an annual plant which flowers in May and June. This species tends to be variable, particularly along the southern coast of Turkey. The majestic spires of blue flowers so often associated with cottage gardens belong to *D. elatum*, a variable species from central and northern Europe and U.S.S.R., which has been much 'improved' by horticulturists. Other garden delphiniums include *Consolida ambigua*, the Rocket Larkspur, which is extensively naturalized in the U.S.A. but is a native of the Mediterranean area; *D. cheilanthum*, the Garland Larkspur, from Siberia and China; and *Consolida regalis*, the Forking Larkspur from Europe.

The flowers of *Anemone coronaria* (F) are among the first to appear in spring. They are up to 3 inches (7·5 cm.) across and vary in colour from red to lavender, purple and blue, the red and purple ones being most commonly found. This species is much cultivated and marketed under such names as the 'St Brigid' or 'de Caen' anemone. Although similar to the illustrated species, *A. pavonina*, with pink, scarlet or purple flowers is distinguished by its less divided leaves and undivided or only apically 3-toothed bracts forming the leafy involucre beneath the flowers. It is one of about eighty species which are mostly natives of cool temperate areas. The *Hepatica*, *Pulsatilla* and *Anemone* genera are all very similar but *Hepatica* has an involucre of sepal-like bracts immediately beneath the flower, while the other two have an involucre of leafy bracts well separated from the flower. Presumably the brightly coloured petals serve to attract pollinators to *Anemone* species, as there are usually no floral nectaries, but the flowers offer abundant pollen to bees.

The Pheasant's Eye genus, *Adonis*, consists of twenty temperate herbs which are found only in the Old World. The illustrated species, *A. annua* (E), although a native of southern Europe, is sometimes naturalized further north and west. The flowers are borne in May and June, amid a cloud of finely dissected green leaves and, being bright scarlet with blackish purple anthers, are very ornamental in the fields, wastelands and along the roadsides where the plant usually grows.

RANUNCULACEAE

Eranthis hyemalis, Winter Aconite
A1 flowering plant × ⅔. A2 petal × 4⅔.
A3 fruit × ⅔.

Nigella damascena, Love-in-a-mist
B1 part of fruiting stem × ⅔.
B2 mature fruit × ⅔. B3 seed × 6.
B4 part of flowering stems × ⅔. B5 petal × 2.
B6 ovary × 1⅓.
B7 lower part of stem with root and leaves × ⅔.

N. ciliata
C1 part of flowering stem with bud × ⅔.
C2 flower × 2. C3 petal showing nectary × 2⅔.
C4 stamen × 4. C5 fruit × ⅔.

Delphinium peregrinum, Violet Larkspur
D1 flowering spike × ⅔. D2 flower × 1⅓.
D3 leaf × ⅔.

Adonis annua (syn. *A. autumnalis*), Pheasant's Eye
E1 part of flowering stem with fruit × ⅔.
E2 flower × 2. E3 petal × 4. E4 fruit × 1⅓.
E5 seed × 4⅔.

Anemone coronaria
F1 flowering plant (stem cut) × ⅔.
F2 flower bud × ⅔.

A1 A3 B1 B2 B3 B4 B5 B6 B7 C1 C2 C3 C4 C5 D1 D2 D3 E1 E2 E3 E4 E5 F1 F2

Plate 28   MEDITERRANEAN

Only two species are contained in the genus *Punica*, one an obscure plant entirely restricted to the island of Socotra, the other the Pomegranate, *P. granatum* (B), known since the days of the ancient Egyptians and Babylonians and intimately involved with the life and myths of the Mediterranean world, to which it was brought at an early date from further east. The fruit grows on a bush or small tree with sometimes spiny branches and, beneath its leathery rind, contains numerous seeds, each surrounded by an envelope of pink pulp that is either eaten raw or used as an ingredient in the cold drinks and sherbets of the area. Roots, rinds and seeds are a source of astringents and antihelminthics, and the unripe rind yields a red dye used in the tanning of Morocco leather. Because, presumably, of the large number of seeds it produces, the Pomegranate has long been regarded as a symbol of fertility. In Turkey, a newly wed woman may predict the number of her offspring, it is said, by throwing a Pomegranate on the ground and counting the scattered seeds. The fruit and flowers appear frequently as a motif in ancient Middle Eastern art, especially embroidery, and the shape of the persistent sepals is believed to have inspired that of King Solomon's crown, the ancestor of those of many western monarchs. Evidence of the antiquity of the plant's divine associations is provided by the fact that it is thought to have symbolized the Babylonian and Syrian god of thunder and storms, Ramman; indeed, its Arabic name is still 'rummān'. In western Europe, the Pomegranate has been cultivated for many hundreds of years and in Britain, where in particularly fine summers reasonable crops have been recorded since at least the middle of the 16th century.

The Judas Tree is, traditionally, the tree upon which Judas hanged himself, the flowers having blushed with shame and retained their purple-rose colour ever since. A native of the eastern Mediterranean, but much grown throughout the area, *Cercis siliquastrum* (C) is one of seven northern temperate species in its genus and forms a tree about 27 feet (8·2 m.) tall. In habit it more closely resembles tropical than temperate trees, since it often bears its pea-like flowers in clusters on the old branches or trunk; the genera related to *Cercis* are in fact tropical. The smooth, kidney-shaped leaves, which often appear after the flowers, are purplish at first but soon change to a pale green. The Judas Tree has been cultivated in Britain since the 16th century. There is also a white-flowered, presumably shameless, form.

Geum coccineum (A), a member of a genus of some forty species found in northern and southern temperate areas and in the Arctic, is a native of the Balkan mountains and Turkey and grows in damp meadows or beside streams. In its remarkable likeness to the Chilean and Argentinian *G. chilense* (also known as *G. chiloense* and *G. quellyon*) it provides an excellent example of parallel evolution in two widely separated parts of the world. Forms and hybrids of the two species are often found as colourful perennials in herbaceous borders.

The rose species of the Mediterranean area tend to become more stunted and spiny the further east one goes. *Rosa glutinosa* (D), a native of south-eastern Europe, Turkey and Iran, is outstanding for its glandular, hairy limbs and sometimes gnarled habit, and forms a shrub that is rarely more than 3 feet (91 cm.) in height and may be as little as 1 foot (30 cm.). Its leaves are pine-scented. The species, introduced into western Europe in 1821, is closely related to the Sweet Briar (see plate 9).

The first climbing rose of any merit to reach western Europe, where it arrived about 1629, *Rosa sempervirens* (E) is native to southern Europe and the north-west coast of Africa. In these areas it can ascend through other vegetation by means of its hooked prickles to heights of 20 or 30 feet (6–9 m.). *R. sempervirens* is an evergreen with firm, glossy leaves and slightly scented white flowers.

ROSACEAE

Geum coccineum
A1 part of flowering stem × ⅔.
A2 basal rosette × ⅔.

Rosa glutinosa
D1 part of flowering shoot × ⅔. D2 fruit × 1⅓.

R. sempervirens
E1 part of flowering shoot × ⅔.

PUNICACEAE

Punica granatum, Pomegranate
B1 part of flowering shoot × ⅔. B2 flower × ⅔.
B3 flower sectioned × 1⅓. B4 fruit on twig × ⅔.

LEGUMINOSAE

Cercis siliquastrum, Judas Tree
C1 part of flowering shoot × ⅔.
C2 leafy fruiting shoot × ⅔.

A1

A2

B2

B3

B4

B1

C2

C1

D1

D2

E1

Plate 29   MEDITERRANEAN

All the genera represented opposite belong to a subfamily of the *Leguminosae* known as the *Papilionoideae*, a group containing a number of important edible plants—peas, beans, ground nuts, soya beans, lentils and liquorice root—and some that have commercial value in other fields —tonka beans, indigo and gum tragacanth.

About one hundred species of *Medicago*, commonly called medicks, grow in temperate Eurasia, the Mediterranean and parts of South Africa and are characterized by interesting, spiralled pods which, in some species, are spiny and become entangled in the coats of passing animals, thus dispersing the seeds. Lucerne or Alfalfa, *M. sativa*, is an important fodder plant now grown throughout the world. The illustrated *M. murex* (A), a native of the Mediterranean region, is a variable species whose several forms are classified according to the size and shape of the fruit. Another attractive species, sometimes cultivated in Britain, where it is also native, is the Spotted Medick, *M. arabica* (syn. *M. maculata*) with purple-spotted leaflets and spiny fruit, which is found mainly around the Mediterranean and western Asia.

Ornithopus, a genus of some ten species distributed from the Mediterranean region and western Asia to tropical Africa and subtropical South America, derives its name from its clusters of fruit, which resemble birds' feet (Greek *ornis*, *ornithos* 'bird', *pous* 'foot'). *O. sativus* (C) is a native of south-west Europe but is widely cultivated elsewhere as a fodder plant.

The six or so *Tetragonolobus* species, all from the Mediterranean area, are sometimes placed in the genus *Lotus* but differ from the latter in having 3, not 5, leaflets, large green, instead of small brown, stipules, and pods with 4 membranous wings; the walls of *Lotus* pods are smooth. *T. purpureus*, the Asparagus Pea (F), native around the Mediterranean, is sometimes grown for its edible pods which are used like peas, the entire pod being boiled and eaten.

One of the two members of the genus *Scorpiurus*, *S. muricatus* is a variable species. Those plants whose fruits have long, slender appendages on the curled pods are classified in variety *subvillosus* (E); those with short, warty appendages on the fruits are placed in variety *muricatus*.

Vicia species are described more fully on plate 10. The Yellow Vetch, *V. lutea* (D), occurs around the Mediterranean basin and occasionally, on cliffs and seaside shingle in Britain, though it is doubtful whether the plant is native there.

The Sweet Pea, *Lathyrus odoratus* (B), has its origin in southern Italy and Sicily, but the genus as a whole is found throughout northern temperate areas and in the mountains of tropical Africa and South America. *L. odoratus* was introduced into Britain when Father Francesco Cupani sent seed to an English schoolmaster, Dr Uvedale, in 1699. Albeit the flowers were relatively small and only borne in pairs, seed was generally available on the market by 1730, the fragrance no doubt contributing much to the plant's quickly achieved popularity. By 1837 only six colour varieties had been produced but after 1870, when Henry Eckford began to select seedlings, the shape and number of the flowers were 'improved' and numerous new colour varieties produced; the Spencer type, with large flowers having waved standard petals, arose as a mutation about 1900 and contributed much to the subsequent popularity of the Sweet Pea. The height of the Sweet Pea vogue came, perhaps, with the Edwardian era, when it was a favourite for the house and button-hole alike.

Gum tragacanth is secreted from the stems of a number of *Astragalus* species, such as *A. adscendens* from south-western Iran, many of which have a spiny, domed, cushion-like habit. Tragacanth has long been used in medicine (it was, indeed, known to Theophrastus and Dioscorides) as a matrix to bind ingredients in pills and lozenges. The substance, which in its purest form is dull white, translucent, odourless and plastic to the touch, with a very slightly bitter taste, consists in part of broken-down stem tissue; as Daniel Hanbury, the notable Victorian pharmacist, remarked in 1874, when the stem is cut across 'there immediately exudes from the centre a stream of soft, solid tragacanth, pushing itself out like a worm, to the length of $\frac{3}{4}$ of an inch (19 mm.), sometimes in the course of half an hour'.

Liquorice is obtained from the root system of *Glycyrrhiza glabra*, a native of the region around the Mediterranean and east to southern Russia and Afghanistan but also, at times, much cultivated elsewhere. Although mentioned by the earliest Greek writers, the plants were not introduced into western Europe until about 1300. The English name 'liquorice' comes from the medieval name 'gliquiricia', a corruption of *Glycyrrhiza*. Its chief use is as an ingredient of confectionery and medicines.

LEGUMINOSAE

Medicago murex
A1 part of flowering and fruiting stem × $\frac{2}{3}$.
A2 stipules × $2\frac{2}{3}$. A3 seed pods × $3\frac{1}{3}$.
A4 ripe seed pod × 2.

Lathyrus odoratus, Sweet Pea
B1 part of flowering stem × $\frac{2}{3}$.
B2 stamens, style and ovary × 1. B3 keel × 1.
B4 wing × 1.
B5 young seed pods on stem × $\frac{2}{3}$.

Ornithopus sativus
C1 part of flowering and fruiting stem × $\frac{2}{3}$.
C2 flower × 2. C3 pod × 2.

Vicia lutea, Yellow Vetch
D1 part of flowering and fruiting stem × $\frac{2}{3}$.
D2 flower × $1\frac{1}{3}$. D3 stipule × $3\frac{1}{3}$.

Scorpiurus muricatus var. *subvillosus*
E1 part of flowering stem with immature pods × $\frac{2}{3}$. E2 ripe fruits on penduncle × $\frac{2}{3}$.
E3 pod × $1\frac{1}{3}$.

Tetragonolobus purpureus, Asparagus Pea
F1 part of flowering stem with immature pods × $\frac{2}{3}$. F2 flower and calyx × $1\frac{1}{3}$.
F3 fruit on part of stem × $\frac{2}{3}$.
F4 part of fruit opened to show seeds in position × $\frac{2}{3}$. F5 seed × 2.

A4

A3

A2 A1

B5

B2

B3

B4

B1

C3

C2

C1

D2

D3 D1

E2

E3

E1

F2

F3

F1

F5

F4

Plate 30   MEDITERRANEAN

Spring and early summer in the Mediterranean are dominated by the poppy, a clear majority of whose hundred or so species grow there, or in south-west Asia. The former is also the main centre of diversity of the *Cruciferae*, the other family illustrated on this plate.

Unlike most true poppies, *Papaver pilosum* (G) is a perennial, found wild, among rocks high in the mountains, only in the classical Bithynia, a small area in north-western Turkey. The species is characterized by orange to orange-red petals and hairy leaves; it may be distinguished from the similar and closely related *P. spicatum* by the shape of its capsular fruit. Both plants are occasionally grown in gardens.

Also perennial, or sometimes biennial, *Glaucium flavum* (D) is a native of coastal areas from Oslo to the Black Sea and the shores of North Africa, occasionally penetrating the interior along river estuaries. The plant springs from a thick, deep-growing tap-root and produces attractive shiny yellow petals and the distinctive curved and slender fruits, 8 inches (20 cm.) or more long, to which it owes its popular name of Yellow Horned Poppy. The *Glaucium* genus contains about twenty-five species, some of which are found throughout Europe and in south-western and central Asia, though most are Mediterranean. The splendid *G. grandiflorum*, a perennial with crimson flowers up to $4\frac{1}{2}$ inches (11 cm.) in diameter, is a native of the eastern Mediterranean and Iran. The smaller-flowered Violet Horned Poppy, *Roemeria hybrida*, is a typical plant of the wastelands and vineyards of south and west Europe and also occurs in North Africa and south-west Asia. *Glaucium*, *Roemeria* and *Chelidonium* (the Greater Celandine genus), all differ from *Papaver* in having stalked stigmas: true poppies have unstalked stigmas, borne at the top of the ovary.

Most of the stocks grown in gardens are derived from some of the fifty-five species of the genus *Matthiola* which extends from the Atlantic islands through western Europe to central Asia. Brompton Stocks and Ten-week Stocks, for instance, have their origin in *M. incana* (F), a species that occurs from the northern Mediterranean to Egypt and Arabia, and were selected for their tendency to produce double

flowers. Doubling of the flower consists of repeated production of petals and sepals at the expense of stamens and carpels, with the result that the most desirable double forms do not yield seed. Selection is, therefore, usually made at the seedling stage, from material known to be prone to a high percentage of doubling; in good strains, some 70% of selected seedlings may produce double flowers. The Sea Stock, *M. sinuata* (C), has a slightly more westerly range than *M. incana* and is occasionally found as a native in southern England, Wales and Ireland. Its mature flattened fruits, 'siliquae', have stalked, blackish or yellow glands, a feature that is absent from the eastern species. The Night-scented Stock, *Matthiola longipetala* subspecies *bicornis*, and the Virginian Stock, *Malcolmia maritima*, are both Mediterranean species too, despite the latter's common name.

Sometimes called the Purple Cabbage, *Moricandia arvensis* (E) is one of about eight species with a distribution from the Mediterranean into central Asia. This particular species grows on calcium-rich soils in fields and wasteland and by roadsides, in the western part of the generic range. In spring and summer its violet flowers contrast handsomely with the clasping, greyish leaves.

So widely cultivated for use in salads is *Eruca sativa* (A) that it would be difficult now to say what is its true native distribution; at present it is to be found in field margins, olive groves, waysides and the like throughout the Mediterranean Basin. A highly variable plant with whitish or pale yellow petals veined with purple, it is sometimes treated as a subspecies of *E. vesicaria*. With the other four species in its genus, all confined to the Mediterranean area, it differs from the otherwise similar Charlock, *Sinapis arvensis*, in having erect instead of spreading sepals. Oil is extracted from the seeds of both.

About twelve subspecies of the very variable Buckler Mustard, *Biscutella laevigata* (B), are recognized, according to distribution, hairiness and leaf-form. Its early-blooming yellow flowers are valued in many gardens. The forty species belonging to the *Biscutella* genus are found in the Mediterranean region and in mountainous parts of central Europe and south-west Asia.

CRUCIFERAE

Eruca sativa
A1 part of flowering stem and lateral leaf $\times \frac{2}{3}$.
A2 flower $\times$ 2. A3 pod $\times 1\frac{1}{3}$.

Biscutella laevigata, Buckler Mustard
B1 part of flowering stem and lower part of stem with leaves $\times \frac{2}{3}$.
B2 part of fruiting inflorescence $\times \frac{2}{3}$.

Matthiola sinuata, Sea Stock
C1 part of flowering stem and lower leaf $\times \frac{2}{3}$.
C2 flower $\times 2\frac{2}{3}$.

Moricandia arvensis, Purple Cabbage
E1 flowers, buds and young fruits on part of stem with lower leaf $\times \frac{2}{3}$. E2 petal $\times 2\frac{2}{3}$.

Matthiola incana
F1 part of flowering stem with buds $\times \frac{2}{3}$.
F2 petal $\times 1\frac{1}{3}$. F3 stamens, style and ovary $\times$ 2.

PAPAVERACEAE

Glaucium flavum, Yellow Horned Poppy
D1 part of flowering stem with developing fruit $\times \frac{2}{3}$. D2 opening bud $\times \frac{2}{3}$.

Papaver pilosum
G1 flower, buds and immature seed pods on part of stem with radical leaf $\times \frac{2}{3}$.

A2

A3

B2

B1

A1

C2

C1

D2

D1

E2

E1

F1

F2

F3

G1

Plate 31   MEDITERRANEAN

The trees illustrated opposite, characteristic if not unduly showy inhabitants of the Mediterranean, help to create the flora of this often arid region. Tropical elements may also be found in the Mediterranean flora, for example, the rafflesiaceous genus *Cytinus* as well as a number of *Aristolochia* species.

Often found in dry calcareous habitats, the Box, *Buxus sempervirens* (A), belongs to a genus of about seventy species; it often grows gregariously and forms shrubs or small trees up to 20 feet (6 m.) in height. Its evergreen foliage, glossy green or yellowing, is dense; the leaves are elliptical in shape with recurved margins. Small inflorescences bear separate male and female flowers, the latter producing $\frac{1}{3}$ inch (8·5 mm.) capsules filled with glossy black seeds. Sometimes columnar, sometimes straggling and bushy, occasionally almost prostrate, Box has a variable habit and after centuries of cultivation, some of the extreme forms are maintained in gardens. Valued for its firm, close grain, the wood, which makes fine turned objects, is also excellent for engraving and woodcuts.

The hundred and thirty or so species of *Styrax* grow in the warmer parts of Europe, in Asia as far as Malaysia and in the Americas. *S. officinalis* (B), sometimes spelt *S. officinale* as Linnaeus originally published it, is the source of 'storax', a gum used in perfumery and the manufacture of incense, which is obtained by making cuts on the branches and collecting the exudate. An irregularly branched, deciduous tree up to about 20 feet (6 m.) tall, it has pale green foliage. Young shoots are woolly, as are the undersides of the leaves. Pure white flowers occur during April and May in small clusters of 3 to 6 and resemble orange or lemon blossom; green fruit the size of cherries and covered with white felt take their place, the seeds of which are sometimes used for making rosaries. *S. officinalis* may be found from France, through Italy to Palestine.

The Mastic Tree, *Pistacia lentiscus* (C), grows to a height of about 25 feet (7·5 m.). Its leathery, evergreen leaves on winged leaf stalks are dark, shiny green above, with 3–6 leaflets on either side of a central rib. Between April and June, dense yellowish or purplish spikes of small flowers with red anthers bloom in the axils of the leaves; later the fruits appear, pea-sized and red, becoming black. The whole tree has a strong resinous smell, and 'mastic' exudes from wounded stems. This resin, useful in varnish making and medicine, has been chewed from earliest times to strengthen teeth and gums and deodorize the breath; the best form, yellowish white and translucent, comes from the island of Chios. Native throughout the Mediterranean area, the Mastic tree also occurs in Portugal and is common in arid habitats and maquis vegetation.

Occurring in stony places and at the edges of fields throughout the Mediterranean area, *Aristolochia rotunda* (D) springs from a tuberous root with stems up to 2 feet (61 cm.) high and clasped by the rounded leaves which vary in width from $\frac{3}{4}$ to $3\frac{1}{2}$ inches (2–9 cm.) and are virtually stalkless. The purplish yellow flowers, narrow and funnel shaped with long brownish lips bent over the openings, appear from the leaf axils between April and June, later being replaced by the globose capsules, $\frac{3}{4}$ inch (2 cm.) in dia-

meter. Most temperate members of the genus have small flowers, not unlike those of *A. rotunda* and *A. clematitis*—both natives of southern Europe as far as the Caucasus—the latter producing clusters of 4–8 yellowish flowers from its leaf axils was once widely grown as an aid to childbirth and known as 'Birthwort'; however, in the tropics, some species have gargantuan flowers as can be seen on plate 170.

The Holm or Evergreen Oak, *Quercus ilex* (F), forms a shrub or a tree up to 90 feet (27 m.) tall with a trunk girth of about 20 feet (6 m.). The dense crown of foliage consists of small, leathery leaves, variable in shape and length ($1\frac{1}{4}$–$2\frac{3}{4}$ inches, 3–7 cm.) with shiny upper surfaces, hairy grey undersurfaces and, sometimes, spiny, toothed margins; young shoots particularly, are covered with felt but the foliage of sucker shoots is often atypical. Flowering occurs between April and May, the male catkins being long and pendulous; later, the fruit cupules have closely adpressed scales. At one time, the tough wood of the Holm Oak was much used in construction work, also producing a high quality charcoal, and the acorns fed to pigs. Often stunted and shrub-like, *Q. ilex* is a characteristic element in the Mediterranean flora, widespread on limestone hills and in maquis. It is hardy enough to persist in southern and western parts of Britain and has been cultivated in England since the 16th century.

The equally characteristic *Q. coccifera* (E), the Kermes Oak or Grain tree, forms a low shrub, rarely exceeding 12 feet (3·7 m.) in height, with evergreen holly-like leaves distinguishable from those of the Holm Oak as they are usually smaller and are shiny on both upper and lower surfaces; also the Kermes Oak has shorter male catkins and the cupule scales are sharper and less adpressed. The popular names for *Q. coccifera* date from ancient times when the Cochineal insect (*Coccus ilicis*), which fed on the tree, was gathered for its dye; the Arabic name for the bug was 'kermes', while Latin sources referred to the insects as 'grana tinctorum', 'grain' in English; through the centuries these names became associated with the tree. Widespread use of the pigment dates from Biblical times and early in the 15th century, a coat of arms granted to the Worshipful Company of Dyers consisted of 'a wreath of the colours, three sprigs of the grain tree, erect vert, fructed, gules'. In this instance, the insect was interpreted as a fruit of the tree and until about 1910 the red bodies and spiny-leaved twigs were thought to represent holly; only after some study were they identified as those of *Q. coccifera* and the fruit as cochineal insects. The European cochineal was prepared from the female insect, often having been pickled previously in vinegar, and later, heated. Mexican cochineal was discovered in 1518 and is obtained from insects which live on cacti species of the genus *Opuntia*. Today, synthetic dyes have largely replaced cochineal although the older dye is still regarded as more penetrating and durable.

Found throughout the Mediterranean area, *Cytinus hypocistis* (G) parasitises the roots of rockroses (*Cistus* species); it is a complete parasite, without any chlorophyll, and only the flowering heads are conspicuous as they emerge from the soil beneath the host bush. Borne on stems $1\frac{1}{4}$ to 3 inches (3–7·5 cm.) tall, a tight,

bright yellow and globular cluster of 5–10 flowers is surrounded by numerous overlapping yellow, orange or red leaf-like scales. Each small tubular flower, consisting of 4 fused sepals, is subtended by 2 small, inconspicuous bracts; the upper part of the inflorescence bears male, the lower part, female flowers. Later in the year, the latter mature into sweet, pulpy berries.

BUXACEAE

Buxus sempervirens, Box
A1 flowering twig × $\frac{2}{3}$. A2 female flower × 6.
A3 male flower × 6.

STYRACACEAE

Styrax officinalis (syn. *S. officinale*)
B1 flowering twig × $\frac{2}{3}$. B2 fruiting twig × $\frac{2}{3}$.
B3 calyx × 2.

ANACARDIACEAE

Pistacia lentiscus, Mastic Tree
C1 part of flowering branch × $\frac{2}{3}$.
C2 part of fruiting branch × $\frac{2}{3}$. C3 fruit × $2\frac{2}{3}$.

ARISTOLOCHIACEAE

Aristolochia rotunda
D1 flowering plant × $\frac{2}{3}$. D2 flower × $1\frac{1}{3}$.

FAGACEAE

Quercus coccifera, Kermes Oak, Grain tree
E1 flowering twig × $\frac{2}{3}$. E2 fruiting twig × $\frac{2}{3}$.
E3 fruit and cupule × $\frac{2}{3}$.

Q. ilex, Holm Oak, Evergreen Oak
F1 male and female catkins and young leaves × $\frac{2}{3}$. F2 female catkin × $3\frac{1}{3}$.
F3 male catkins on part of pedicel × 2.
F4 mature leaves and acorns × $\frac{2}{3}$.

RAFFLESIACEAE

Cytinus hypocistis
G1 flowering plant × $\frac{2}{3}$.

A3

B3   B1

B2

C2

C3   C1

D2

E1

E2

E3

F2

F3

D1

F1

G1   F4

Plate 32   MEDITERRANEAN

Both pinks and geraniums are members of cosmopolitan families well represented in the Mediterranean.

A delightful miniature pink, *Dianthus subacaulis* ssp. *brachyanthus* (A), with its greyish foliage and many small white or pale pink flowers, provides excellent ground cover for rock gardens. The leaves, borne on a ramifying system of woody branches, measure about $\frac{3}{8}$ inch (9·5 mm.) in length, and there are 4 epicalyx scales at the base of the calyx, $\frac{1}{3}$ as long as the calyx. *D. subacaulis* and its subspecies are natives of France, Portugal and Spain.

The eastern Mediterranean also contains a number of attractive species, among them *Dianthus pendulus*, which grows in cracks on limestone cliffs in Lebanon, Syria and adjacent countries. Stems reach a height of 2 feet (61 cm.), with narrow leaves up to $2\frac{3}{4}$ inches (7 cm.) long. The flowers, which appear between April and September, are borne singly or in clusters of 2 or 3 and have pink petals 2 inches (5 cm.) long, deeply toothed at the edge and surrounded by a calyx about $1\frac{1}{4}$ inches (3 cm.) in length.

The Rose Campion, *Lychnis coronaria* (E) is a native of south-eastern Europe often cultivated as an ornamental, particularly in those forms in which the undivided petals are of a rich purple-red that contrasts splendidly with the thick covering of soft, white, woolly hairs on the leaves and stems: forms with pink and/or white flowers are less striking. The only other species of *Lychnis* likely to be confused with *L. coronaria*, since they both have densely haired white leaves, is *L. flos-jovis*, the Flower of Jove; the latter, however, has a dense head of flowers and less richly coloured, bilobed petals.

Flowering from April to June, *Silene colorata* (B and C) is a characteristic element in fields and sandy places along the Mediterranean coasts. Its pubescent stems, often less than a foot (30 cm.) but sometimes as much as 20 inches (51 cm.) in height, are erect or spreading, with linear to spoon-shaped leaves $\frac{3}{8}$ to $1\frac{1}{4}$ inches (9·5–32 mm.) long. Each flower has a cylindrical calyx tube marked with 10 reddish veins and becomes club-shaped when in fruit and surrounds the capsule. The latter is about $\frac{3}{8}$ inch (9·5 mm.) long and contains numerous winged seeds with wavy edges. The blunt teeth of the calyx are fringed with hair and the pink or white petals, about the same as the calyx in length, are bilobed at the tip. As a comparison between plants B and C will show, the species is variable. Found in the Levant and east of Turkey is *S. aegyptiaca*,

whose clouds of pink blossom transform fields and olive groves in winter and early spring. Flowers about $\frac{3}{4}$ inch (19 mm.) in diameter, a red calyx, and stalked, rounded leaves distinguish it from *S. colorata*.

Erodium comprises about ninety Eurasian, South American and Australasian species, *E. macradenum*, or *E. petraeum* as it is called in the recent *Flora Europaea*, is a variable plant with four subspecies centred in different parts of the Pyrenees, another in south-eastern Spain, and the possibility of a sixth in Morocco. In ssp. *glandulosum* (D), the 2 upper petals are a little larger than the 3 lower, and are blotched with intense purple at their bases. The violet, pink or white flowers, borne in umbels of 1 to 5, dance above stemless rosettes of much divided leaves, which may be silvered with minute hairs or almost hairless. Each leaf measures up to $2\frac{3}{4}$ inches (7 cm.) in length. When the flowers die, their place is taken by equally interesting fruits, each of which has a beak up to $1\frac{3}{8}$ inches (3·5 cm.) long from which has arisen the common generic name of Storksbill. This *Erodium* makes a hardy and attractive rock garden plant.

The Long-beaked Storksbill, *Erodium gruinum* (G), has larger fruits and a beak up to $4\frac{1}{4}$ inches (10·8 cm.) long. The plant forms stems 20 inches (51 cm.) tall, armed with erect or deflexed hairs, and grows in sandy places near the coast, in dry grassland, and on rocky slopes in Sicily, North Africa, the Aegean area and east as far as Iran. The 2 to 6 flowers are clustered together on single stalks and have short-lived, violet petals.

Geranium tuberosum (F), the Tuberous Cranesbill, is so called because of the spherical tuber from which springs its branched stem. This, covered with fine hairs, grows to a height of about 16 inches (40·5 cm.) and has basal leaves some 3 inches (7·5 cm.) wide, divided into about 6 deeply cut lobes. The purple-pink petals are $\frac{1}{2}$ inch (12·7 mm.) long, veined in a deeper purple, and notched at the apex. The species flowers between March and June and is found in south-east France and from North Africa to Iran.

In the Mediterranean area, the genus *Pelargonium* (the gardeners' Geraniums) is represented by one Turkish species, *P. endlicherianum*. Another species, *P. quercetorum*, was described from northern Iraq in 1967, but most species, including those from which the majority of garden hybrids has been raised, are found in South Africa (see plate 74).

CARYOPHYLLACEAE

Dianthus subacaulis ssp. *brachyanthus* (syn. *D. brachyanthus*)
A1 part of flowering plant × $\frac{2}{3}$.
A2 part of fruiting stem × $\frac{2}{3}$. A3 fruit × $1\frac{1}{3}$.

Silene colorata
B1 fruiting and flowering stem × $\frac{2}{3}$ (grown at Kew). B2 petal × $4\frac{2}{3}$. B3 calyx × 2.
C1 part of flowering stem × $\frac{2}{3}$ (plant from Mediterranean area). C2 petal × 2.

Lychnis coronaria, Rose Campion
E1 part of flowering stem × $\frac{2}{3}$.
E2 petal and stamen × 2.
E3 lower leaves and rootstock × $\frac{2}{3}$.

GERANIACEAE

Erodium petraeum ssp. *glandulosum* (syn. *E. macradenum*)
D1 flowering plant × $\frac{2}{3}$. D2 petal × $2\frac{2}{3}$.
D3 part of fruiting inflorescence × $2\frac{2}{3}$.

Geranium tuberosum, Tuberous Cranesbill
F1 part of flowering stem and tuber × $\frac{2}{3}$.

Erodium gruinum, Long-beaked Storksbill
G1 part of flowering stem with bud × $\frac{2}{3}$.
G2 petal × $2\frac{2}{3}$. G3 mature fruit × $\frac{2}{3}$. G4 seed × $\frac{2}{3}$

A1 A2 A3

B1 B2 B3

C1 C2

D1 D2 D3

E1 E2 E3

F1

G1 G2 G3 G4

Plate 33   MEDITERRANEAN

Despite the monopoly of flamboyance and exoticism attributed to tropical plants by the public imagination, a number of the Mediterranean species depicted on this plate rival them in brilliance and variety of colouring.

With flowers of a uniquely intense blue and leaves that often take on a reddish tint, *Sedum caeruleum* (A) makes a valuable garden plant, particularly as it is self-seeding in favourable situations. The species, a native of Morocco and Algeria, Corsica, Sardinia and Sicily, never grows more than a few inches tall but has a bushy habit with smooth, rounded stems. *Sedum hispanicum* (F), despite its specific epithet, does not occur in Spain but has a distribution that ranges from Switzerland and Italy to the Caucasus and northern Iran. The species is annual or biennial and reaches a height of between 2 and 6 inches (5–15 cm.). The related *S. bithynicum*, sometimes called *S. hispanicum* var. *minus*, or, in gardens, *S. glaucum*, is a perennial, smaller in all its parts and commonly used as a carpet bedder.

The pinkish-purple, or occasionally whitish flowers of *Cyclamen repandum* (D), found from France to Greece via Crete and Algeria, are slightly perfumed and, like those of most cyclamens, are replaced by fruits borne on spiral stalks. Its bright green triangular to heart-shaped, somewhat angular leaves rise from a tuber, $\frac{3}{8}$ to $1\frac{1}{4}$ inches (9·5–32 mm.) in diameter, flattened at the top and the bottom and from the base of which emerge the roots.

The genus *Anagallis* contains some twenty-eight species most of which occur in Europe, the Mediterranean and Africa, though there are also some South American representatives and one that is pantropic. The Blue Pimpernel, *A. arvensis* subspecies *foemina* (B), grows by roadsides, and in wasteland and fields, all over the Mediterranean area. The fruiting stalks are generally no longer than the leaf and the petals have few glands on their edges. The Scarlet Pimpernel, *A. arvensis* ssp. *arvensis*, although typically scarlet-flowered, produces, however, two blue-flowered varieties, the small-leaved var. *caerulea* and the larger-leaved var. *latifolia*, both of which may be distinguished from *foemina* by having fruiting stalks much longer than the leaf as well as numerous glands on the edges of petals.

Discovered by the Danish Consul for Morocco and introduced to Europe in 1802 by the French Consul, *Anagallis monellii* subspecies *collina* (C), is a perennial, not entirely restricted to North Africa, also occurring as a rare plant in Sardinia and southern Spain. Like the type species *A. monellii*, which has large blue flowers and is the commoner plant in Spain, it makes a useful rock-plant.

According to Reginald Farrer in his fine book *The English Rock Garden*, '*Symphyandra* suffers like *Adenophora* from coming so close beneath the tyrannous shadow of *Campanula*, which obliterates all rivals, or rather, forbids all approach.' *Symphyandra* is a genus of ten species, mostly Mediterranean but extending into north Iran and, in one case, into Korea. It differs from *Campanula* in the one technical respect that the anthers are joined into a tube round the style, hence the generic name, from the Greek *symphyo* 'growing together' and *aner, andros* 'anther'. *S. cretica* (E) is a native of Crete well worth cultivating and sometimes found in rock gardens. The related *S. asiatica*, the Korean species, was first described in 1909 and was introduced into Britain and America in 1918 from seed collected by E. H. Wilson.

More representative of the rest of its genus than the rather atypical *Phyteuma comosum*, shown on plate 15, *P. scheuchzeri* (G), the Horned Rampion, is a perennial found in the Apennines, Alps and Carpathians that grows to a height of between $4\frac{3}{4}$ and 12 inches (12–30 cm.) and bears slender, delicate stalks with spherical heads of blue flowers. Of the two sorts of leaves produced, the basal are triangular and the upper linear in shape. In a semi-shaded spot, the heads persist for about a week, improving any rock garden with their wealth of blue flowers.

A plant of the rocks and cliffs of Greece and the Aegean Islands, *Campanula rupestris* (J) is said to have been introduced into England in 1788 and has been grown there ever since on walls and in rock gardens. Despite the fact that it is monocarpic—that is to say that it flowers and fruits only once and then dies—its rosette of soft, grey leaves and handsome, bell-shaped, lilac-blue flowers make it a fine garden plant.

Also from the same family, but rather different in appearance, is *Diosphaera asperuloides* (K), otherwise known as *Trachelium asperuloides*, a diminutive species rarely more than 1 to $1\frac{1}{2}$ inches (2·5–3·8 cm.) in height with a highly localized distribution by the River Styx in the Peloponnese. Its lilac flowers, only $\frac{1}{4}$ inch (5 mm.) long, have rarely been illustrated. Like the two other members of *Diosphaera*, it is a native of the eastern Mediterranean.

The Sea Lavender, *Limonium sinuatum* (H), sometimes called *Statice sinuata*, is a circum-Mediterranean species that flowers between March and July amongst rocks or in waste places near the coast. It is often grown for its conspicuous bluish-mauve calyces, which retain their colour many months after being picked and dried, and may be used as an 'everlasting' in floral decorations. The specific epithet refers to the fact that the leaves of the basal rosettes have wavy edges.

CRASSULACEAE

Sedum caeruleum
A1 flowering plant × $\frac{2}{3}$. A2 flowers × 4.

S. hispanicum
F1 part of flowering plant × $\frac{2}{3}$. F2 flower × 4.
F3 fruit × 4. F4 leaf × $2\frac{2}{3}$.

PRIMULACEAE

Anagallis arvensis ssp. *foemina*, Blue Pimpernel
B1 flowering plant × $\frac{2}{3}$.
B2 two petals and stamens × $3\frac{1}{3}$.

A. monellii ssp. *collina*
C1 part of flowering plant × $\frac{2}{3}$. C2 flower × $2\frac{2}{3}$.
C3 petal and stamen × $5\frac{1}{3}$.

Cyclamen repandum
D1 part of flowering plant × $\frac{2}{3}$.

CAMPANULACEAE

Symphyandra cretica
E1 part of flowering stem and leaf × $\frac{2}{3}$.
E2 stamens, style and ovary × $1\frac{1}{3}$.

Phyteuma scheuchzeri, Horned Rampion
G1 flowering plant (stem cut) × $\frac{2}{3}$.
G2 flower × 8.
G3 flower opened to show construction × 8.

Campanula rupestris
J1 part of flowering shoot × $\frac{2}{3}$. J2 leaf × $\frac{2}{3}$.

Diosphaera asperuloides (syn. *Trachelium asperuloides*)
K1 part of flowering plant × $\frac{2}{3}$. K2 flower × $1\frac{1}{3}$.
K3 leaf × 2.

PLUMBAGINACEAE

Limonium sinuatum (syn. *Statice sinuata*), Sea Lavender
H1 part of flowering plant × $\frac{2}{3}$.
H2 flower × $2\frac{2}{3}$.

A1

A2

B1

B2

C1

C2

C3

D1

E1

F1

F2

F3

F4

G1

G2

G3

H1

H2

J1

J2

K1

K2

K3

Plate 34 MEDITERRANEAN

The family *Cistaceae* is centred in the Mediterranean area, but also occurs in other northern temperate areas and has a few species in South America. Its members, despite their common name of Rockroses, are unrelated to the true roses, family *Rosaceae*. *Cistus albidus* (C) is a western Mediterranean species belonging to a genus found throughout the Mediterranean and in the Canary Islands. A compact shrub about 3 feet (91 cm.) tall with downy, greyish foliage and clusters of 2 to 7 pink or magenta flowers borne at the ends of the twigs, it is a conspicuous inhabitant of the dry limestone tracts of the sort found in the French 'garigue' in the western half of the Mediterranean region.

A slightly larger species with highly aromatic, glandular, sticky shoots and leaves, and flowers that grow singly at the ends of the stems, is *C. ladanifer* (B), the Gum Cistus. The plant occurs on dry hillsides and in woodland in France, Spain, Algeria and Morocco. This and *C. creticus* (D) (also known as *C. incanus* ssp. *creticus* and *C. villosus* var. *creticus*) which is found in 'maquis' further to the east, are thought to have been the source of 'ladanum', a fragrant, bitter resin used in making perfume and medicine and referred to as myrrh in the Authorised Version of Genesis (37:25 and 43:11). The gum, secreted by the glands, is traditionally collected by pulling strips of cloth or leather through the shrubs during the heat of the day. The gum adheres to the strips as readily, in fact, as it does to the beards of browsing goats, which are combed in the evening to provide another source. Owing to a mistranslation from the Hebrew, 'ladanum' has been confused with myrrh, a quite different substance yielded by *Commiphora myrrha*, an unrelated tree of Arabia, Ethiopia and Somalia. True myrrh was, in fact, unknown in Palestine at the time of Joseph (i.e. the time of the references in Genesis above, circa 1700 B.C.).

Another Biblical plant, common in the eastern Mediterranean and in western Asia, is the Colocynth, *Citrullus colocynthis* which probably represents the 'Vine of Sodom', the 'Wild Gourd' and 'gall'. The fruits resemble oranges in form and colouring but have a hard rind and soft, bitter pulp which is poisonous in large quantities and purgative in small. It grows in semi-desert and individual plants straggle over wide areas producing great quantities of fruits.

The Squirting Cucumber, *Ecballium elaterium* (E) belongs to the same family as *Citrullus*, the *Cucurbitaceae*, and according to John Sims, editor, from 1800 to 1826, of the well-known and still published *Botanical Magazine*, 'few plants have a viler aspect'. The popular name refers to the way in which the seeds are shot out in a jet by water pressure, through the hole created as the mature fruit breaks from the stalk. So great is the pressure that the seeds are often shot for several yards. In nature the plant grows on wasteland and rubbish tips. Its coarse, cucumber-like foliage and small yellowish flowers, which appear from March to September, make it of no more value in gardens than as a curiosity. In the wild it is restricted to the Mediterranean Basin.

A native of the meadows of the Pyrenees, *Viola cornuta* (A) has been a popular and hardy garden violet since its introduction into western Europe in 1776. It grows to a height of about 8 inches (20 cm.) and has a creeping rhizome from which it may be easily propagated. Its specific epithet refers to the conspicuously long corolla spur resembling a horn. Abundant flowers are produced from March until August.

VIOLACEAE

Viola cornuta
A1 part of flowering stem × ⅔.

CISTACEAE

Cistus ladanifer, Gum Cistus
B1 flowering shoot × ⅔.

C. albidus
C1 part of flowering branch × ⅔.
C2 stamens, style and ovary × 1⅓.

C. creticus (syn. *C. incanus* ssp. *creticus,* *C. villosus* var. *creticus*)
D1 flowering shoot × ⅔.
D2 fruit with sepals × ⅔. D3 fruit × ⅔.

CUCURBITACEAE

Ecballium elaterium, Squirting Cucumber
E1 flowering shoot and immature fruit × ⅔.
E2 male flower, sectioned × ⅔. E3 stigma × 2⅔.
E4 fruit discharging seeds × ⅔. E5 seed × 2.

A1

B1

C1

C2

D1

D2

D3

E1

E2

E3

E4

E5

Plate 35   MEDITERRANEAN

The members of the mallow family, *Malvaceae*, are frequently found in the Mediterranean region, and like *Malope trifida*, illustrated opposite, many are now familiar garden plants.

One of about four species characterized by three large bracts beneath the calyx and many carpels arranged in vertical rows, *M. trifida* (E) is a native of the Guadalquivir region of southern Spain, adjacent Portugal, Morocco and Algeria. The related *M. malacoides* with smaller, paler flowers, is more widespread in the Mediterranean region, reaching Turkey, and was introduced into gardens in 1710, almost a century before the plant illustrated.

Belonging to the same family, the twenty-five or so *Lavatera* species are found from the Canaries across to the Himalaya and eastern Siberia, in California and Australia. *L. trimestris* (F) is native in fields and amongst rocks from Portugal east through the Mediterranean region to Greece, and has been cultivated for centuries, having been introduced to Britain as early as 1633. During its long period in cultivation several varieties have been selected.

Most members of the *Rutaceae*, the family which contains the genus *Citrus*, the oranges and lemons, are shrubs or trees, the leaves of which often have an aromatic scent when crushed, owing to the oil glands they contain. However, the genus *Ruta* consists of about sixty species of herbs, most somewhat woody towards the base, found in the Mediterranean region and temperate Asia. *R. graveolens* (B), Common Rue or Herb of Grace, is a native of the Balkan peninsula, Turkey and the Crimea, but has been cultivated for a long time and, in western Europe, for at least four centuries. It was better known perhaps in earlier times, for it was a famous medicinal and magical herb, said to be good for eyesight, as well as being a potent antidote against the forces of evil and witchcraft, and such desirable qualities must have favoured its spread amongst the householders of western Europe in the late Middle Ages. It is still grown occasionally and makes an attractive bushy herb with its glaucous foliage and curiously constructed flowers. The central or terminal flower opens first and has its flower parts in fives instead of fours, as shown in the plate opposite, where only a lateral portion of the inflorescence is depicted.

Belonging to the same family as *Ruta*, the genus *Dictamnus* contains five or six species spread over temperate Eurasia. *Dictamnus albus* (D), commonly called Dittany or Burning Bush, native from south and south-central Europe into and across eastern Asia, is a variable species. It was a popular garden plant with the Elizabethans, who regarded it as a relative of Marjoram (*Origanum*, family *Labiatae*), probably because of its aromatic properties. The pungent smell, pleasing to some people, has been likened to that of balsam or lemon peel, having an element of both. The vapours produced by the oil glands are so copious that on a sunny, hot and com-

pletely windless day it is possible to ignite them if a flame is placed near the leaves and, although the phenomenon lasts only for a moment, one can appreciate the origin of the name Burning Bush. It does not grow in Arabia and Egypt and so could hardly have been, as some commentators have suggested, the burning bush of the Bible which arrested Moses' attention.

Charles de l'Ecluse, after whom the genus *Clusia* (plate 177) was named, discovered *Viscum cruciatum* (A) on one of his exploratory trips in Iberia near Grenada, and in 1576 he published the first description of the species. It has since been found in western North Africa, and has a disjunct distribution, reappearing in Syria and Israel, where it has been recorded from the Garden of Gethsemene, amongst other places. Like the Common Mistletoe, *V. album*, it is a semiparasite; the leaves and female flowers are similar in both species, but the male flowers and fruits of the species illustrated are larger and more distinctive. The sixty or seventy species in the genus are mostly found in the warmer parts of the Old World, although a few, including Mistletoe, grow in temperate Eurasia. In northern Europe the Celts and Goths paid great attention to Mistletoe, as its fruiting coincided with their winter solstice festivals when they used it as decoration during their rituals. With the spread of Christianity the Church found the old pagan rites difficult to suppress, and although the Mistletoe was widely banned, because of its heathen associations, its decorative use was transferred to the home at Christmas time.

Euphorbia robbiae (C) commemorates its discoverer, Mrs Robb, of Liphook, Hampshire, who introduced it into Britain in the 1890's. It was grown in England under other names for several decades before being properly described or named scientifically. The name 'Mrs Robb's Bonnet' arises from the story recorded on the authority of E. A. Bowles who knew Mrs Robb herself, that she came across this plant when near the end of her travels in Asia Minor, presumably before crossing to Istanbul, and having nothing but her hatbox available in which to transport a plant back to England, she sacrificed the hat she used to wear in order to impress Turkish officials and brought the plant home instead of this bonnet. The plant received an Award of Merit from the Royal Horticultural Society in May 1968. It closely resembles the Wood Spurge, *E. amygdaloides*, although it lacks the hairs of that species. Each apparent 'flower' sits at the base of two partially fused bracts and represents a highly specialized inflorescence called a 'cyathium'. The male and female flowers are highly reduced and in each cyathium there is just one central female flower, reduced to nothing more than an ovary on a stalk, surrounded by a number of male flowers, simplified to a single, stalked stamen, on the inside of the cup-shaped involucre, which bears 4 crescent-shaped nectarial bracts to attract insects.

LORANTHACEAE

Viscum cruciatum
A1 twig with male flowers × $\frac{2}{3}$.
A2 male flower × $2\frac{2}{3}$. A3 fruiting twig × $\frac{2}{3}$.
A4 fruit × $2\frac{2}{3}$.

RUTACEAE

Ruta graveolens, Common Rue, Herb of Grace
B1 part of flowering stem × $\frac{2}{3}$. B2 flower × $3\frac{1}{3}$.

Dictamnus albus, Dittany, Burning Bush
D1 part of flowering stem × $\frac{2}{3}$.
D2 stamen × $1\frac{1}{3}$. D3 fruiting stem × $\frac{2}{3}$.

EUPHORBIACEAE

Euphorbia robbiae, Mrs Robb's Bonnet
C1 part of flowering stem with leaves × $\frac{2}{3}$.
C2 individual inflorescence or cyathium × $2\frac{2}{3}$.
C3 female flower (style and ovary) × $2\frac{2}{3}$.

MALVACEAE

Malope trifida
E1 part of flowering stem with buds and leaves × $\frac{2}{3}$. E2 stamens × 2.
E3 anthers, one open to show pollen × 6.

Lavatera trimestris
F1 part of flowering stem with buds and immature fruit × $\frac{2}{3}$. F2 petal × 1.

A1

A2

A3

A4

B2

B1

C2

C1

D2

D3

D1

E3

E2

E1

F2

F1

Plate 36 MEDITERRANEAN

Normally a foetid little shrub not more than 12 inches (30 cm.) tall but transformed between April and September by its masses of pink flowers, into an elegant wayside ornament, *Putoria calabrica* (C) is one of a genus of three Mediterranean species and inhabits rocky limestone and gravel sites in all parts of the region except France. The members of the *Rubiaceae* family in the temperate areas are nearly all herbaceous and appear quite different from their woody tropical counterparts, but *Putoria*, although growing in a warm temperate region, is allied to more tropical genera. The herbaceous members are mostly various Bedstraws (*Galium*) or Madders (*Rubia*, *Sherardia*) which usually have whorls of 4 or more leaves at each node, often covered in minute spines or hooks.

Convolvulus, with two hundred and fifty, mainly temperate, species, differs from the large, related but tropical genus *Ipomoea* (see plates 79 and 180) in having a bilobed stigma, and from *Calystegia* (see plate 18) in lacking the conspicuous bracteoles in which the calyx of the latter is enclosed. Botanically the most important differences between them are to be found in their pollen which is spiny in *Ipomoea*, smooth and 3-furrowed in *Convolvulus*, smooth and many-pored but not furrowed in *Calystegia*. *Convolvulus tricolor* (E) is native to both shores of the western Mediterranean where it is often found naturalized near settlements. It may be distinguished from the related *C. siculus* by its oblong leaves which narrow into a leaf-stalk towards the stem, and bigger flowers. The beauty of the three-coloured blooms has led to its being cultivated both in its native area and in other temperate regions. Given a sunny situation, it can be expected to flower throughout the summer. *C. althaeoides* (D) is a climber, reaching a height of about 3 feet (91 cm.) in favourable habitats, found in bush-covered areas on the coast, in cultivated ground and by hilly waysides all over the region. It is sometimes known as the Mallow-leaved Bindweed.

The Rose Bay or Oleander, *Nerium oleander* (B), is found right round the Mediterranean and is particularly common in the valley watercourses, or 'wadis', of the Holy Land. It is widely cultivated, though under glass in colder areas, for its often double, fragrant pink, or occasionally white, flowers. The paired fruits, typical of the *Apocynaceae* family, open when ripe (see B2) to release a large quantity of seeds, which the wind disperses. All parts of the plant contain a poisonous white 'milk' or latex, used in medicine for its glucosides. The Oleander, so named because of the resemblance of its foliage to that of the olive, is, probably, the 'rose growing by the brook of the field' referred to in Ecclesiasticus (39:13). It has been cultivated in western Europe for at least three hundred and fifty years. The genus *Nerium* contains three species, with a range that extends from the Mediterranean and Arabia to India; one of them has, in addition, been cultivated for centuries in China and Japan.

Unlike other genera of *Asclepiadaceae*, *Periploca* has stamens that are free, not fused, and pollen that is granular and not held together in waxy pollinia. For this reason the ten species, which occur from the western Mediterranean and tropical Africa to eastern Asia, have been placed by some in a family of their own, the *Periplocaceae*. *P. graeca* (A) is a vigorous twiner native to western and south-eastern Asia. Although it is ideal for training against walls and may reach a height of 30 feet (9 m.), it has been neglected by gardeners because of its short, July to August flowering season, inconspicuous flowers and the poisonous latex contained in its tissues. However, to those with an eye for hidden beauty, the unusual flowers provide ample reward for any trouble taken. The fruits, which frequently fail to form in western Europe, where the species has been cultivated since the 16th century, are paired and, like those of the Oleander, contain plumed seeds with silky hairs—hence the plant's common name, Silk Vine. The species grows best in a sunny position.

ASCLEPIADACEAE

Periploca graeca, Silk Vine
A1 part of flowering stem × ⅔. A2 flower × 2.
A3 petal, stamen and appendage × 4.

APOCYNACEAE

Nerium oleander, Rose Bay, Oleander
B1 flowering shoot × ⅔.
B2 part of fruiting stem × ⅔.

RUBIACEAE

Putoria calabrica
C1 flowering shoot × ⅔.

CONVOLVULACEAE

Convolvulus althaeoides, Mallow-leaved Bindweed
D1 part of flowering stem × ⅔.

C. tricolor
E1 part of flowering stem × ⅔.

A1

A2

A3

B1

B2

C1

D1

E1

Plate 37 MEDITERRANEAN

Aromatic herbs and shrubs, abundant in dry areas of the Mediterranean, often permeate the air with their fragrance. Characteristic of the area are *Rosmarinus. Lavandula, Salvia, Satureja* and *Thymus*, some species of which are popular food seasoning while the oil obtained from Rosemary, *Rosmarinus officinalis,* is an ingredient of Eau de Cologne. This plant was once regarded as a symbol of fidelity and remembrance.

A handsome plant when in flower, *Lavandula stoechas* (G) bears deep purple bracts which terminate the inflorescence of small flowers and contrast pleasantly with the greyish leaves. All parts of the plant possess the characteristic odour of lavender, once so popular for perfuming linen. Small bags of lavender may still be purchased from market stalls in France, where this use continues. The more widely known *L. officinalis,* a less handsome plant but more hardy than many lavenders, is grown in many parts of western Europe. Altogether, there are twenty-eight species of *Lavandula* with a distribution centred on the Mediterranean Basin but extending as far east as India.

The genus *Horminum*, comprised of the single species *H. pyrenaicum* (A), is found only in the mountains of southern Europe, including the Pyrenees, and as far east as the Tyrol. Its chief value is as a rosette rock-plant; its deep purple-blue inflorescences look very attractive in groups and a type with rose coloured flowers is sometimes seen in cultivation.

About one hundred species of *Phlomis* are found in the temperate regions of the Old World, perhaps the best known and most widely cultivated being the Jerusalem Sage, *P. fruticosa* (B), which is hardy in western Europe and parts of North America. Woolly, whitish leaves and whorls of yellow flowers make this small shrub very desirable when it flowers between April and June. In nature it inhabits dry rocky places throughout the Mediterranean Basin, and is often so numerous that it colours whole hillsides a bright golden yellow. Other species have purple, pinkish or white flowers.

Teucrium aroanium (C) grows wild on the mountain massif of Aroania in the Peloponnese of Greece, formerly called Mount Chalmos, out of which the River Styx flows. Its diminutive size and its pink-purple flowers, which appear enlarged out of proportion, make it a useful creeping rockery plant. Its long exserted stamens also draw attention to the flowers. Other more shrubby species in this genus of about three hundred are *T. fruticans* and *T. chamaedrys*, both from Europe. The former has whitish woolly leaves and small blue flowers borne on stems up to 3 feet (91 cm.) tall, while the stems of the latter are about 2 feet (61 cm.) tall with leaves about ¾ inch (2 cm.) long, and reddish purple flowers with red and white spots. *Teucrium* is named after Teucer, the first king of Troy, and many of its species are natives of the Mediterranean.

The *Boraginaceae* is another family well represented in the Mediterranean region. *Borago officinalis*, or Borage, with its clear blue flowers and purple anthers, grows about 2 feet (61 cm.) tall and is found throughout the Mediterranean Basin, including Turkey and North Africa. It has long been cultivated for culinary and doubtful medicinal purposes, but is perhaps best used as a decorative annual which blooms from July to September.

Alkanna contains about thirty species, all hairy perennial herbs with yellow, blue or white flowers borne in racemes or cymes and found throughout the Mediterranean, as far east as Iran. A wasteland plant, sometimes found near the coast, Alkanet, *A. tinctoria* (D), has bright blue flowers borne on shoots springing from a woody base, which appear between April and June. Its dried roots turn reddish-purple and contain the ancient red dye 'alkannin'.

About ten species of *Cerinthe* are found in damp situations from Spain into Israel and North Africa. Although an annual, *C. major* (F), with its somewhat glaucous foliage and bracts which envelop the yellow and brownish-red flowers, is worth growing in gardens and will bloom well during a good western European summer. It is a variable species and the bracts of some plants, instead of being green, may be suffused with purple.

Commonly called Purple Viper's Bugloss, *Echium lycopsis* (E) is another plant of the stony wayside. Found throughout the Mediterranean, it also is a variable species with spreading or erect shoots, softly hairy leaves and large blue or red-violet flowers with projecting stamens; these appear from March to June. When introduced into Australia, it spread widely and rapidly on arable and pastoral land, becoming a noxious weed and collecting the Australian name Paterson's Curse. *E. judaicum* has blue and pink or violet and purple flowers which occur during the spring rains in Lebanon and Israel. *E. pomponium*, found in Spain, Morocco and Algeria, blossoms from April to July, bearing spikes of pink flowers about ⅜ inch (1 cm.) in diameter. The foliage is covered with white hairs and, although tender, the plant is most attractive for cultivation.

LABIATAE

Horminum pyrenaicum
A1 flowering stem and radical leaf × ⅔.
A2 side view of flower × 4.
A3 top view of flower × 4.
A4 fruit, calyx removed × 8.
A5 fruit with calyx × 4.

Phlomis fruticosa, Jerusalem Sage
B1 flowering stem × ⅔.
B2 stamens and style × 2. B3 anther × 2.
B4 new shoot × ⅔.

Teucrium aroanium
C1 flowering and budding stem × ⅔.
C2 side view of flower × 2. C3 anther × 8.

Lavandula stoechas
G1 flowering and budding stem × ⅔.

BORAGINACEAE

Alkanna tinctoria, Alkanet
D1 flowering and budding stem × ⅔.
D2 corolla × 1⅓.

Echium lycopsis, Purple Viper's Bugloss, Paterson's Curse
E1 flowering stem × ⅔.
E2 opened out corolla × 2⅔.

Cerinthe major
F1 flowering stem × ⅔. F2 anther × 6.
F3 opened corolla × 2.

A2

A3

A4

A5

A1

B2

B3

B1

B4

C2

C3

C1

D2

D1

E1

F3

F1

F2

G1

Plate 38 MEDITERRANEAN

Because botany had its origins in classical Greece and Italy with its first written works those of Theophrastus, Dioscorides and Pliny, it is no surprise that Mediterranean plants were the first to be described and illustrated. The Mandrake is one such plant. The family *Solanaceae*, to which it belongs is famous for its medicinal and poisonous plants, among them the Henbane, Woody and Deadly Nightshade and Thornapple as well as the potato, tomato and tobacco. The family *Scrophulariaceae* is closely related botanically and so is the *Orobanchaceae*, containing the broomrapes, all members of which are complete parasites. An allied family, with most of its members native to the tropics, is the *Gesneriaceae*, noted as containing the popular house plants, the gloxinias and African violets, *Saintpaulia*. In the mountainous region of southern Europe, bordering the Mediterranean, are a few very interesting members of this family, relics of the wider distribution and warmer European flora before the Ice Age. This group of genera, *Ramonda*, *Haberlea* and *Jankaea* contain one or very few species and are now found in very limited scattered areas.

Mandrake, *Mandragora officinarum* (D), provided the most important anaesthetic drug known to the Ancients, and the *rhizotomoi* or herb-gatherers probably perpetuated the story that it could only be uprooted at midnight and with great risk, in order to protect the stock from excessive exploitation by the uninitiated. It is one of the herbs described in the 4th or 5th century catalogue and recipe book of medicinal herbs of Apuleius Platonicus. Mandrake, famed as an aphrodisiac, was sometimes regarded as a bewitching and elusive plant, liable to run away on its leg-like forked tap root. Its 'capture' was not without ritual as a translation of the Anglo-Saxon version of the *Herbarium* says: 'When first thou seest its head, then inscribe thou it instantly with iron, lest it fly from thee ... touch it not with iron, but thou shalt earnestly with an ivory staff delve the earth. And when thou seest its hands and its feet, then tie thou it up. Then take the other end and tie it to a dog's neck, ... next cast meat before him, so that he may not reach it, except he jerk up the wort [plant] with him. ... Therefore, as soon as thou see that it be jerked up, and have possession of it, take it immediately in hand, and twist it, and wring the ooze out of its leaves into a glass ampulla.' In this account, no mention is made of the shriek which the plant makes on being pulled up, a shriek which was supposed to kill its up-rooter. Hence, the use of the dog for 'jerking up the wort'. In reality *M. officinarum* is one of six species of stemless perennials with a long, sometimes forked tap-root which supposedly resembled the body and legs of a man, and a rosette of dark green corrugated leaves up to 12 inches (30 cm.) long. A series of single stalked flowers arise from the centre of this rosette early in the year, and have greenish, blue, or purple petals. Later, in May, the plum-like, yellow berry fruits lie in the middle of the rosette. They are sweet and edible but with a smell offensive to some and were known as Devil's Apples by the Arabs, who believed they induced voluptuousness. Mandrake occurs on wasteland, in stony places throughout the Mediterranean, Levant, and southern Europe,

and is still grown in more rural communities for whatever magical value it might have.

Also members of the *Solanaceae* like *Mandragora* are the Henbanes, *Hyoscyamus*. There are twenty species with a range through Europe, the Mediterranean, and North Africa, into southwestern and central Asia. *H. niger*, the common Henbane, with softly downy and foetid leaves and one-sided leafy inflorescences of dingy yellow flowers, veined with dark purple, is famous for the narcotic substances in its tissues; sufficient to have once made the plant a minor industry in Mitcham market gardens, south of London. Boswell Syme tells of the effects on some monks who ate Henbane roots for supper by mistake; 'One rang the bell for matins at 12 o'clock at night; of those who attended to the summons, some could read, others fancied the letters were running about like ants, and some read what they did not find in their books.'

The Yellow Henbane, *H. aureus* (A), occurs in the eastern Mediterranean, where it grows on cliffs and walls, reaching a height of 2 feet (61 cm.). The flowers are larger, but they are not long lived. *H. albus*, the White Henbane, is a more widespread Mediterranean plant, with greenish flowers having a purple or green centre.

There are about one hundred and fifty species of Toadflax, *Linaria*, found especially in the Mediterranean area. *L. triornithophora* (B), a native of Spain and Portugal, was introduced to Britain about 1710. It grows to about 3 feet (91 cm.) high and its showy rose-purple flowers, which appear from May, are often borne in 3's and resemble perched birds with long tails, hence the epithet *triornithophora*—bearing three birds. *L. triphylla* (E), an annual which flowers from February to June, occurs from Spain, through Greece to Israel, in vineyards, wasteland near the coast and the headlands of fields; it is also found in North Africa. The plant grows about 18 inches (46 cm.) tall and is easily identified in having leaves borne in 3's at each stem-joint, hence the common name of Three-leaved Toadflax.

Ramonda, of the *Gesneriaceae*, with three species, commemorates Baron L. F. E. Ramond de Carbonnières (1753–1827), a French natural historian. *R. myconi* (C) is a native of the Pyrenees, has leaf rosettes up to 8 inches (20 cm.) diameter, 3–5 flowers on a stalk about 6 inches (15 cm.) tall and yellow anthers in the centre of a pale mauve corolla. It is said to have been cultivated since 1640 and grown by Philip Miller at Chelsea in 1731. *R. serbica* comes from Albania and Serbia, and is smaller in its parts than *R. myconi* and the less numerous flowers have blue anthers. The third species, *R. nathaliae*, is a closely related native of Serbia and northern Macedonia.

In Bulgaria, on limestone cliffs and in damp ravines, the two species of the genus *Haberlea* may be found. They differ from ramondas in having a more tubular corolla. Further east, in Greece, in the vicinity of and on Mount Olympus, lives the single species of the genus *Jankaea*. *J. heldreichii* compared to a *Ramonda* has smaller rosettes with leaves silky hairy above and 4 to 5 lobed lavender flowers with a longer corolla tube.

Broomrapes are complete root parasites and have no chlorophyll in their scale-like leaves and

stems. While some species will parasitize a range of plants, others may often be associated with a particular plant host or host family. For example the Branched Broomrape, *Orobanche ramosa* (F), is often a parasite of members of the *Solanaceae*, while the Ivy Broomrape, *O. hederae*, as its name suggests grows on *Hedera helix*, the Ivy. *O. ramosa* occurs throughout the Mediterranean region in cultivated places, and unlike most broomrapes, the flowering spikes are normally branched.

SOLANACEAE

Hyoscyamus aureus, Yellow Henbane
A1 part of stem with flowers, buds and immature fruit $\times \frac{2}{3}$. A2 sectioned flower $\times 1\frac{1}{3}$. A3 anther $\times 4$.

Mandragora officinarum, Mandrake
D1 part of flowering and fruiting plant $\times \frac{2}{3}$.
D2 root-stock $\times \frac{2}{3}$.

SCROPHULARIACEAE

Linaria triornithophora
B1 part of flowering stem $\times \frac{2}{3}$.
B2 unopened flower $\times 1\frac{1}{3}$.
B3 part of fruiting stem $\times \frac{2}{3}$. B4 fruit $\times 1\frac{1}{3}$.

L. triphylla, Three-leaved Toadflax
E1 part of flowering plant $\times \frac{2}{3}$.

GESNERIACEAE

Ramonda myconi
C1 part of flowering and fruiting plant $\times \frac{2}{3}$.
C2 stamens, style and ovary $\times 1\frac{1}{3}$. C3 fruit $\times 2$.

OROBANCHACEAE

Orobanche ramosa, Branched Broomrape
F1 flowering plant $\times \frac{2}{3}$. F2 flower $\times 2$.

A2

A3

A1

B3

B4

B2

B1

C2

C3

C1

D2

D1

E1

F1

F2

Plate 39   MEDITERRANEAN

The easily recognized daisy family consists of about nine hundred genera, and is one of the largest wild flower groupings. Members are found in most parts of the world, with the exception of equatorial rain forests, where they occur only as weeds in clearings.

The daisy 'flower' is in fact an inflorescence, a compact head of small flowers or florets, surrounded underneath by whorls of bracts called an 'involucre', which have the function of a calyx. The similarity to a true flower is further enhanced by the fact that, in many cases, the florets are of two sorts, the first—in the outer whorl—usually strap-shaped and petal-like (ray-floret), the second less conspicuous and often tubular (disc-floret) (see B3 and D3), comprising an inner mass that stands where the stamens and ovaries would be found. Sometimes all the florets are tubular (see A1 and F1 and 2), or all strap-shaped, as in a dandelion, and they may be functionally hermaphrodite or female.

In the centre of the florets the anthers are characteristically fused into a tube around the style, the latter armed with a ring of hairs, or 'brush' of some kind, which, as the style elongates, sweeps the pollen out of the tube formed by the anthers and places it in a position where it can be picked up by any insect crawling over the surface of the flower head. Immediate self-pollination is prevented by the 2 stigmatic surfaces being held together, face to face, at the tip of the style; after the pollen has been shed, the 2 stigmatic arms, which form the tip of the style, bend out and back, to reveal the receptive stigmas on their upper surface. In some species the arms eventually curl right over and back so that they come into contact with any pollen which may still remain attached to the lower part of the style and effect a second self-pollination. In species of *Centaurea* a certain resistance and tension is built up in the floret and when the style is touched the pollen is visibly jerked out of the anther-tube. The calyx of the individual floret has become greatly modified and adapted for fruit dispersal, commonly taking the form of a ring or plume of fine hairs which make a parachute (as in a dandelion, *Taraxacum*) or thistle-down (as in *Cirsium* and some others). In other genera, such as *Bidens,* it takes the form of hooks, which help the fruits to adhere to the fur of passing animals.

The family is not outstandingly important economically, but includes the Jerusalem Artichoke, *Helianthus tuberosus*; Chicory, *Cichorium intybus*; Lettuce, *Lactuca saliva,* and the Safflower, *Carthamnus tinctorius*. From the latter a red dye and rouge—basically the treated and powdered flowers mixed with talc—are obtained. *Othonnopsis,* or *Hertia* as perhaps the genus ought to be called, contains about twelve species. *O. cheirifolia* (C), introduced into Britain in 1752, is an Algerian and Tunisian species. Somewhat similar, but with smaller flowers and smaller, narrower leaves, is *O. marocana,* which grows in the Middle and High Atlas, and on the Saharan side of that range. Both species have thick leaves, suitable for the hot and dry, rocky habitats in which they live.

In the strict sense, *Chrysanthemum* is a small genus confined to Eurasia and the Mediterranean area, but by some, especially in the past, it has been construed to include another two hundred species which extend into Africa and America. *Chrysanthemum catananche* (D) is widespread on the Atlas Mountains at altitudes of between 7000 and 10,000 feet (2130–3050 m.), where, on the northern slopes, it forms mats of vegetation only a very few inches tall, though in favourable sites it can grow up to 8 inches (20 cm.) in height. *C. segetum* (B), the Corn Marigold, is a common Mediterranean plant, and, like its also common relative *C. coronarium,* is an inhabitant of arable and waste land. The Corn Marigold, although probably introduced centuries ago, behaves like a native in Britain and much of Europe, where it has been a bad weed on ploughed fields of light soil.

Garden chrysanthemums, *Chrysanthemum morifolium,* have a very different origin, being complex hybrids whose exact source is somewhat obscure. The dominant ancestor of many appears to be the yellow-flowered *C. indicum.* Subsequent selection over a long period has produced the many varieties which now exist. Chrysanthemums have been grown in Japan, where many hybrids were raised, since about 800 A.D., and were cultivated in China centuries before that (see plate 106).

Carduncellus is a Mediterranean genus of about twenty species. *C. rhaponticoides* (E) is found in the mountains of Algeria and Morocco and resembles the Stemless Thistle, *Cirsium acaulon,* in the way the flower head is borne at ground level, surrounded by a ruff of leaves.

Centaurea is one of the largest genera in the family, with some six hundred species found mainly in temperate and warm temperate Eurasia; some also occur in temperate parts of the New World, and there is one Australian species. The florets in this genus are all tubular, not strap-shaped like those of the typical daisy. However, in many species the outer florets are enlarged and serve to make the flowers more prominent. *C. cyanus,* the Cornflower, is a European species, once common in the weedy arable fields of Britain, but, like the poppies, now scarce. It was a popular plant in Tudor gardens, and its blue petals yield a pigment once used by artists. Another species well known in gardens is *C. moschata,* the Sweet Sultan or Blackamoor's Beauty, which came from Iran in the early 17th century. *C. hypoleuca* (A) is a native of Asia Minor and Caucasia. It is similar to the better known *C. dealbata,* but has less dissected leaves and broader lobes than that species. It normally grows between 9 and 12 inches (23 and 30 cm.) tall; the specimen illustrated is rather luxuriant, having been produced in cultivation. *C. salonitana* (F) occurs in the Balkans and on the Aegean Islands. Sometimes called the Yellow Knapweed, it has spine-tipped involucral bracts which vary in length of the spine.

COMPOSITAE

Centaurea hypoleuca
A1 part of flowering and budding stem × $\frac{2}{3}$.
A2 radical leaf × $\frac{2}{3}$. A3 involucral bract × $3\frac{1}{4}$.

Chrysanthemum segetum, Corn Marigold
B1 part of flowering and budding stem × $\frac{2}{3}$.
B2 ray-floret × $2\frac{2}{3}$. B3 disc-floret × $2\frac{2}{3}$.

Othonnopsis cheirifolia (syn. *Hertia cheirifolia*)
C1 part of flowering stem × $\frac{2}{3}$.
C2 part of budding stem × $\frac{2}{3}$.

Chrysanthemum catananche
D1 part of flowering and budding stem × $\frac{2}{3}$.
D2 ray-floret × $2\frac{2}{3}$. D3 disc-floret × $2\frac{2}{3}$.

Carduncellus rhaponticoides
E1 flowering plant × $\frac{2}{3}$.
E2 portion of leaf showing spiny and fine hairs × 2.

Centaurea salonitana, Yellow Knapweed
F1 part of flowering and budding stem × $\frac{2}{3}$.
F2 floret × 2. F3 involucral bract × $2\frac{2}{3}$.
F4 radical leaf × $\frac{2}{3}$.

A1

A2

A3

B1

B2

B3

C1

C2

D1

D2

D3

E1

E2

F1

F2

F3

F4

Plate 40   MEDITERRANEAN

The best known members of a genus of fourteen species that range from the Mediterranean area east into Kurdistan, the Cardoon, *Cynara cardunculus* and the Globe Artichoke, *C. scolymus* (A), have become familiar plants in both the kitchen garden and the herbaceous bed, and the former now also grows as a weed over large tracts of the South American pampas. The Cardoon, a native of Mediterranean Europe, is a massive perennial that attains a height of 5 feet (1·5 m.) when mature and bears splendid, arching, greyish-green leaves, pinnately divided and spiny, that measure up to 2 feet (61 cm.) in length; the plant reaches its most magnificent stage in August and September when the violet-purple inflorescences, borne on erect, individual stems, appear. The Globe Artichoke is unknown in the wild state and seems to be a cultivated derivative of the Cardoon. The vegetable, which has been cultivated and eaten since classical times, consists of the capitulum, clothed in less sharply pointed bracts than those of the Cardoon, their fleshy bases, and the 'heart' or receptacle of the young flower heads. In the Cardoon, it is the young leaves and stalks that are eaten, after being blanched in the same way as celery or chicory. Both make attractive garden flowers and when dried are useful as winter decoration, though the flower heads of the Globe Artichoke are larger, measuring up to 6 inches (15 cm.) in diameter, and bluer than those of the Cardoon.

Usually found in dry fields and stony places near the coast in Italy, Greece and the Levant, *Cardopatium corymbosum* (B) is one of a small genus with three Mediterranean and one central Asian species. The sturdy tap-root produces a rosette of decorative, spiny and much divided leaves whose fibrous remains are often found at the base of the plant, and an erect stalk bearing a compound head of blue inflorescences. Each capitulum is invested with slender, spiny involucral bracts.

The two hundred or so species of the camomile genus, *Anthemis*, range from Europe and the Mediterranean region east into Iran. Confined to Cyprus, where it grows in dry, open places

throughout the island, *A. tricolor* (C) is a grey-leaved, tufted herb with spreading grey side-stems that end in flower heads with white ray- and disc-florets. Like those of all species in the genus, the small, much divided leaves have a fern-like appearance. Though it would make a charming addition to rock gardens in milder climates, the plant is not often seen in the temperate world. The true Camomile (or Chamomile), *A. nobilis* (syn. *Chamaemelum nobile*), is a native of western Europe and western North Africa and has a much branched, creeping stem with fragrant, downy, divided leaves. The solitary flower heads with their white ray- and yellow disc-florets used to be dried and used medicinally, as a tonic and febrifuge. Considerable quantities of the plant used to be grown for this purpose in the late 19th century at Mitcham in Surrey, one acre yielding 4 cwt (203 kg.) of flower heads with a market value of between £4–£9 sterling per cwt (50·8 kg.). Although double-flowered plants were grown, those with single flowers were considered to have the greatest medicinal value. Camomile has also been used for lawns, especially in the past, as an alternative to grass, since it is both resistant to drought and emits a pleasant smell when trodden or sat upon but it does not, however, wear as well.

A native of Greece, *Crepis incana* (D) grows in rocky alpine habitats at altitudes of between 4800–6000 feet (1460–1830 m.). Its irregularly lobed and divided, loosely woolly leaves surround the branched and woolly inflorescence stem, which has clasping, leaf-like bracts and a terminal, carmine-pink flower head. There is no distinction between ray- and disc-florets, all being strap-shaped and merely diminishing in size towards the centre of the capitulum. An allied species, *C. rubra*, native from Italy to Turkey, is sometimes to be seen in gardens. The plant grows to a height of between 6 and 12 inches (15–30 cm.) and has almost leafless inflorescence stalks and usually solitary, autumnal, reddish-flowered capitula. It was one of the few species in this genus to be recommended for cultivation by Reginald Farrer, who considered most of the rest completely unsuitable.

COMPOSITAE

Cynara scolymus, Globe Artichoke
A1 young inflorescence and leaf on part of stem × $\frac{2}{3}$. A2 mature flowering head × $\frac{2}{3}$. A3 floret × $1\frac{1}{3}$. A4 leaf × $\frac{2}{3}$.

Cardopatium corymbosum
B1 part of flowering stem × $\frac{2}{3}$. B2 flower × 2. B3 base of plant with leaf × $\frac{2}{3}$.

Anthemis tricolor
C1 part of flowering plant × $\frac{2}{3}$.
C2 ray-floret × $2\frac{2}{3}$.

Crepis incana
D1 flowering plant × $\frac{2}{3}$.

A1

A2

A3

A4

B1

B2

B3

C1

C2

D1

Plate 41   MEDITERRANEAN

This plate illustrates some plants of the lily family to be found in the Mediterranean area, although they are perhaps more familiar as cultivated plants to people living in temperate regions.

There are about eighty species in the fritillary genus, *Fritillaria*. The Crown Imperial, *F. imperialis*, is a plant of the Middle East and grows wild in Iran and Afghanistan. It has been grown in limited numbers in English gardens since its introduction to Europe from Turkey in the 1600's. Introduced to Britain from France later in the same century, the Snake's-head Fritillary, *F. meleagris*, is native over much of Europe. It was, however, found wild in Britain in the 1700's. Its chequered flowers were popular in Stuart and Elizabethan gardens, although their shape and colour also gave rise to the more sinister name of Leper's Lily, the bell-shaped flower representing the leper's bell once carried by the diseased and the colouring representing the disease itself. The illustrated *F. citrina* (A), a native of Turkey, is closely allied to *F. dasyphylla*, likewise of Turkey and possessing greenish yellow flowers. Fritillaries grow in Asia, Europe, North Africa, the western U.S.A. and Canada, in a variety of habitats but mostly at high altitudes, each area having particular groups of species which are sometimes difficult to identify (see plates 24, 51 and 108).

The Madonna Lily, *Lilium candidum* (B), is represented in the middle Minoan art of Crete and so has an association with man going back to at least 1700 B.C. Growing from 2–4 feet (61–122 cm.) tall, it is found in the eastern Mediterranean area from Macedonia in the Balkan Peninsula, over western Turkey to Palestine, occurring now only in a few widely separated localities. It was much cultivated in the Roman Empire and preserved in medieval monastic gardens for its utility as a medicinal plant as well as its beauty. The association of this flower with the Virgin Mary is attributed to the Venerable Bede and it appears as her symbol in a number of works of art, but it was not until the 19th century, when other white lilies began to be introduced from China and elsewhere, that it received the name Madonna Lily. The broad-petalled form of *L. candidum*, illustrated here, flowers in June and July and represents the old cultivated stock. The narrow-petalled var. *cernuum* is also known as *L. peregrinum* or as the 'starry' variety of *L. candidum*. *L. candidum* var. *salonikae* flowers some two weeks before the Madonna Lily, has more open flowers and, unlike the type form, produces seed in cultivation without the necessity of hand-pollination with pollen from a different clone.

Cultivated in France prior to 1598, the Yellow Turk's-cap Lily, *L. pyrenaicum* (C), grows in woods and fields of Cantabria, the eastern Pyrenees and the Tarn area of southern France. Being fairly hardy, it also occurs in a naturalized state in southern England. The variety *rubrum*, with orange-red maroon-spotted flowers, should be distinguished from *L. pomponium* with red, black-spotted flowers, the latter being a smaller plant with narrower leaves, native in the Alpes Maritimes.

The Yellow Asphodel, *Asphodeline lutea* (D), is also known as King's Spear and Baton de Jacob. It is one of fifteen members of this essentially Mediterranean genus which differs from *Asphodelus* in having leaf-bearing, instead of leafless, flower stems which may, in this species, reach about 3 feet (91 cm.) high. This plant is recorded in the writings of Apuleius and Pliny; its roots once were used as food by the Greeks. It is not a common garden plant in western Europe where it is often too cold and damp for successful growth.

Grape-hyacinths, in the genus *Muscari*, are amongst the least demanding of bulbous ornamentals although the species illustrated, *M. neglectum* (E), with a native distribution around the Mediterranean, is not often seen in cultivation. More commonly grown species are the central and southern European, *M. botryoides*, the Grape-hyacinth, with white and pale blue varieties; *M. comosum*, which has purplish, erect, sterile flowers in the upper part of its inflorescence contrasting with the brownish fertile flowers below and, in recent years, *M. armeniacum*, a native of Turkey and the Caucasus, and especially its cultivar 'Heavenly Blue'.

Butcher's Broom, *Ruscus aculeatus* (F), is one of five species from Madeira, the Mediterranean, central and western Europe and the Near East. These plants are given a family of their own, the *Ruscaceae*, by some botanists, characterized by being shrubs with the leaves reduced to insignificant, scaly structures and their function taken over by flattened, leaf-like stems known botanically as 'cladodes'. The flowers, which are often unisexual, are borne in *R. aculeatus* on the surface of these cladodes and are followed by attractive, bright red berries, about $\frac{1}{4}$ inch (7 mm.) in diameter.

LILIACEAE

Fritillaria citrina
A1 part of flowering and budding stems × $\frac{2}{3}$.
A2 stamen × $3\frac{1}{3}$.

Lilium candidum, Madonna Lily
B1 flowers and buds on part of stem and radical winter leaf × $\frac{2}{3}$.
B2 ovary and stamens × $\frac{2}{3}$.
B3 anther × $1\frac{1}{3}$.

L. pyrenaicum, Yellow Turk's-cap Lily, Pyrenean Lily
C1 part of flowering stem with bulb × $\frac{2}{3}$.
C2 ovary and stamens × $1\frac{1}{3}$.
C3 fruiting heads × $\frac{2}{3}$.

Asphodeline lutea, Yellow Asphodel, King's Spear, Baton de Jacob
D1 part of flowering stem × $\frac{2}{3}$.
D2 part of fruiting stem × $\frac{2}{3}$.

Muscari neglectum
E1 part of flowering plants × $\frac{2}{3}$.
E2 flower × $2\frac{2}{3}$. E3 maturing fruit × $2\frac{2}{3}$.

Ruscus aculeatus, Butcher's Broom
F1 part of flowering and fruiting stem × $\frac{2}{3}$.
F2 male flower × 8. F3 female flower × 6.

A2

B2

B3

A1

C2

C3

E3

C1

E2

E1

F1

F3

D1

B1

F2

Plate 42   MEDITERRANEAN

The Mediterranean climate, with its hot, arid summers and moist, cool winters, has favoured the development of bulbous plants which produce leaves and flowers during the winter and spring, and survive the unfavourable summer below ground. Another adaptation to this climate is the development of hard, leathery leaves and woody stems but this is unusual in Mediterranean monocotyledons.

The genus *Crocus* is a member of the iris family and should not be confused with *Colchicum* in the *Liliaceae* and *Sternbergia* in the *Amaryllidaceae*, plants with a superficial crocus-like habit. There are about seventy-five *Crocus* species and they are often hard to identify; perhaps the best way is to refer to *The Genus Crocus*, a classic monograph written by George Maw in 1886, where the presence or absence of a spathe-like bract at the base of the flower and the nature of the corm-skin are used as distinguishing features.

Crocus niveus (H) was first described by Theodor von Heldreich (1822-1902) in 1876 as *C. marathonisius*, but his description and specimens were confused and included *C. boryi* which had already been described. In 1900, in the *Gardener's Chronicle*, Edward A. Bowles (1865-1954) described it as a new species from cultivated material of unknown provenance and firmly established the name *C. niveus*. The attractive clear white flowers with an orange throat and scarlet stigmas are about 2 inches (5 cm.) long and appear in the autumn, so care should be taken to protect them from possible frost. *C. boryi*, with white anthers and *C. longiflorus* with purplish, sweetly scented flowers are similar to *C. niveus*. *C. niveus* is now known to grow wild in the Mani region of the Peloponnese, southern Greece, near Kalamata.

The Saffron, *C. sativus*, was once widely cultivated for its stigmas, the source of saffron, used for flavouring, in medicine and as a dye. One ounce of saffron is said to require the stigmas from over 4300 flowers so that it has always been an expensive product and a valuable crop. Its cultivation in England is reflected in the name of the village of Saffron Walden. Adulteration of saffron was a constant temptation in commerce due to the increased profits which might be obtained and in medieval Germany, in 1444, Jobst Findeker of Nuremburg is said to have been burnt to death for the crime, along with his adulterated saffron. Some saffron is still grown in Spain, but the more economical ways of making synthetic colouring matter, and the delicate constitution of the crocus crop, have largely killed the industry.

The Hoop-petticoat Narcissus, *N. bulbocodium* (D), is one of about sixty species found in Europe, the Mediterranean area and Asia, and grows from the Iberian Peninsula, through southern France and into parts of North Africa. It is a very variable species with a number of cultivated varieties—var. *citrinus* with lemon flowers and about 6 inches (15 cm.) tall; and var. *nivalis*, only about 3 inches (7·5 cm.) tall with orange and yellow flowers.

Another small but easily distinguishable species is *N. cyclamineus* with reflexed perianth segments, reminiscent of those of a cyclamen. The narrow, bright yellow corona is borne on a stalk 4-8 inches (10-20 cm.) above the ground and was perfectly described by Bowles as a 'neat living bloom with its wide-awake expression'. It may be found in Spain and Portugal in February and March.

The species of *Narcissus* with the widest range is *N. tazetta*, which grows throughout the Mediterranean Basin, across Asia and as far as Japan. On stems about 18 inches (46 cm.) tall, it has clusters of strongly scented white and gold flowers which appear between November and April. It thrives wherever the soil is slightly damp, in garrigue, fields and beneath walls.

The basic difference between Snowdrops (*Galanthus* species) and Snowflakes (*Leucojum* species) is that the former have 3 long and 3 short perianth segments, or petals as they are sometimes, but loosely, called, while the latter have six equally long segments. Many Snowdrops also have a single flower on each stalk, but in Snowflakes there are a number of flowers in the inflorescence. Apparently, 'Snowdrop' is a 16th century word derived from the German 'Schneetropfen', a reference to the pendant ear-rings of that time.

Galanthus elwesii (E) is one of the twenty species of *Galanthus* which are found in Europe, the Mediterranean and Caucasia. It was discovered by B. Balansa in 1854, and grows in Turkey, Greece and the Aegean Islands. H. J. Elwes (1846-1922), whose name is commemorated in the specific epithet, and who was co-author with Augustine Henry of the fine *Trees of Great Britain and Ireland*, introduced the species to Britain from the mountains near Smyrna in 1874 and it was from his garden at Cirencester, England, that the plant was described. It is easily distinguished from the other species by its broad and erect glaucous leaves, and large rounded outer petals. Plants from Bulgaria, and southern Macedonia may be found to differ from *G. elwesii* in having twisted leaves and these have been called var. *maximus*.

The Sea Lily, *Pancratium maritimum* (C), is a characteristic seaside plant throughout the Mediterranean, flowering between July and October. The heads of 4 to 12 fragrant flowers are borne on stalks 12-16 inches (30-41 cm.) long and its leaves are bluish tinged and glaucous. The fifteen species of *Pancratium* are distinguished botanically from those of the similar New World genus *Hymenocallis* in having numerous ovules, instead of 2, in each of the 3 cells of the ovary.

A weak stemmed herb about 12 inches (30 cm.) tall, the Snake's-head Iris, *Hermodactylus tuberosus* (A), bears its purple-black and yellow flowers between April and May. Its sombre colouring is unusual for an iris and it differs further in having only 1 ovary chamber instead of 3. It is the only species in the genus and, in distribution, a typical Mediterranean plant.

Altogether there are about three hundred species of true *Iris*, the majority of which occur in northern temperate areas. *I. pumila* (G), ranging from Spain to Greece and into Turkey, is a variable plant but is characterized by the almost complete absence of a stem and of over-wintering leaves. At the time of flowering, the leaves are about 4 inches (10 cm.) long but may eventually grow to 8 inches (20 cm.). Very closely related and by some regarded only as a subspecies, *I. pumila* ssp. *attica*—*I. attica* (F) has smaller yellow and violet flowers and narrower leaves than *I. pumila* and grows on rocky hillsides in Greece and Caucasia.

A native of southern France and the north-western coast of Italy, *I. chamaeiris* (B) has a well defined stem and longer leaves than *I. pumila* but the colour of its flowers is equally variable. It is often mistakenly grown as '*I. pumila*' in gardens but, because of early growth made in the winter, it is more tender when grown in western Europe.

Plate 43   MEDITERRANEAN (Atlantic Islands)

The Atlantic Islands—the Canaries, the Azores, the Cape Verdes, and the islands of Madeira, St Helena and Ascension—have had, until recent times, little botanical communication with the neighbouring landmasses, and their floras, predictably, have evolved along lines that diverge from those followed by their continental relatives. The flora of each island contains an extraordinarily large proportion (97% in the case of St Helena) of species that are endemic, that is to say, species found nowhere else. There are even some endemic genera, such as the Cabbage-tree Daisies of St Helena. In their favourable environment, isolated from related mainland plants with which they might breed, the floras of these oceanic islands have become greatly diversified, often with the production of extreme forms. The same applies to animals and it is tragic that organisms of such value and fascination should frequently find themselves threatened or, too often, already destroyed by uncontrolled human activity in general and the grazing of goats in particular. The flora of the Azores, Madeira and the Canaries have a strong affinity with that of the Mediterranean, many of the plants representing isolated relics from past geological ages.

Closely related to the foxglove genus *Digitalis*, *Isoplexis* contains three species found only on Madeira and the Canaries. From the latter group of islands comes the Canary Foxglove, *I. canariensis* (C), a vividly-flowered plant that grows in stands, its stems up to 6 feet (1·8 m.) in height, the leaves, whose undersides in some individuals are downy, crowded at their bases. The blooms, which appear between May and June, are borne on spikes up to 12 inches (30 cm.) long. *I. canariensis* and its smaller-flowered relative from Madeira, *I. sceptrum*, can be grown successfully out of doors as bushy evergreen perennials in such places as the Scilly Isles, but require cool glasshouse conditions elsewhere in Britain. First mention of the Canary Foxglove's cultivation in Britain occurs in 1698 when the species was to be found in one of the collections of Mary Somerset, first Duchess of Beaufort (1630–1714), an early and enthusiastic patron of botany, now commemorated in the Australian myrtle genus *Beaufortia*.

A twelve volume herbarium bequeathed by the Duchess to Sir Hans Sloane is now housed at the British Museum.

A highly decorative species, *Campanula vidalii* (A) is endemic to certain islands in the Azores, where it was discovered in 1842 by its eponym, Captain Vidal, R.N. So characteristic is it of the island's flora that the Swiss botanist Heinrich Feer (1857–1892) placed it in a genus of its own, as *Azorina vidalii*, though this has not been maintained. The thick stems, spotted with scars that mark the positions of fallen leaves, contain a milky juice and bear flowers that are white in one form and pink in another. The species has been popular in Britain since its introduction in 1850 but is sensitive to frost and needs a cool glasshouse.

When the genus *Canarina* was first described in 1771, *C. canariensis* (B) was the only species known. It had first been called *Campanula canariensis* and the new generic name was coined as an allusion to its country of origin. Later, however, near the end of the 19th century and early in the 20th, two more, quite distinct, species were discovered and described from eastern tropical Africa and southern Ethiopia. This remarkable, disjunct distribution is paralleled in only a few other groups and presumably reflects an ancient distribution that existed before the Ice Age. *C. canariensis* is a somewhat fleshy, herbaceous climber that produces edible, black berries and grows in shady ravines and woodland. It has been cultivated in Europe since about 1695 but, like most plants from the Atlantic Islands, requires the protection of a cool glasshouse in such places as Britain.

Mato Blanco, *Senecio appendiculatus* (D), grows in the Canaries at altitudes of between 1600 and 3000 feet (490–910 m.), in moist, shady woods of Canary Laurel (*Laurus azorica*, itself a tree endemic to the Azores and Canaries). The plant is variable as far as the lobing of its leaves, its hairiness and the colour of its flowers are concerned: the central flowers of var. *lacteus* are yellow, while those of var. *appendiculatus*, shown here, are violet or deep purple-magenta. The leaves resemble those of the poplar and, like all the younger parts of the plant, have a dense, white felt underneath.

CAMPANULACEAE

Campanula vidalii
A1 part of flowering plant (stem cut) × $\frac{2}{3}$. A2 habit sketch × $\frac{1}{9}$.

Canarina canariensis
B1 part of flowering shoot × $\frac{2}{3}$.

SCROPHULARIACEAE

Isoplexis canariensis, Canary Foxglove
C1 part of flowering stem × $\frac{2}{3}$.
C2 flower, face-view × 2.

COMPOSITAE

Senecio appendiculatus var. *appendiculatus*, Mato Blanco
D1 part of flowering stem × $\frac{2}{3}$.

A2

A1

C1

C2

B1

D1

Plate 44   MEDITERRANEAN (Atlantic Islands)

In secluded and inaccessible places high in the mountains of the Canary Islands, and nowhere else, grow some of the more than twenty species of *Echium* endemic to those islands, a number of which grow to about 10 feet (3 m.) high and almost assume the proportions of trees. Many of them have a very limited distribution on particular islands, yet a few hybridize with one another; certainly identification and discrimination between several species is very difficult.

Known only from Teneriffe at heights above 6600 feet (2010 m.), *Echium wildpretii* (A) flowers from April until about August. It is a biennial species and forms a dense rosette of linear, greyish and softly hairy leaves in the first year and only flowers and reaches its full and magnificent height of 8 feet (2·4 m.) in the second. *E. wildpretii* (sometimes referred to by its synonym *E. bourgaeanum*) is named after H. Wildpret, Curator of the Orotava Botanic Garden, Teneriffe, in the late 19th century, who sent Kew the seed from which the first specimens to be formally described were raised. Similar to the species illustrated in its rose-coloured flowers, *E. perezii* has a branched inflorescence and appears to have been found only once and on La Palma. Plants were raised from seed at Kew and it was named in honour of Dr G. V. Perez, an ardent student of the genus. Another, more subalpine endemic, this time from Teneriffe, is *E. auberianum*. It differs from *E. wildpretii* and *E. perezii* in having blue flowers and leaves covered with coarse, instead of soft, hairs.

One of the largest species is *E. pininana* from La Palma, which forms tapering spires of soft, lavender-blue flowers up to about 10 feet (3 m.) high. Another unbranched, columnar type, between 8 and 12 feet (2·4-3·7 m.) tall, is *E. simplex*, found on the north-east cliffs of Tene-riffe. Several feet up the main stem a dense inflorescence of small white flowers is borne. When artificially hybridized with *E. candicans*, a native of nearby Madeira, *E. simplex* produces a columnar offspring with pale blue flowers. *E. candicans*, commonly called Pride of Madeira, is branched and grows 4 to 6 feet (1·2-1·8 m.) in height, in masses on the sea-cliffs. It produces inflorescences 20 to 30 inches (51–76 cm.) long, crowded with small azure flowers.

The first specimen of *E. coeleste* to flower under cultivation was reared at Kew in 1922 out of seed sent from La Palma by Dr Perez. The plant had a single stem about 30 inches (76 cm.) tall whose upper part bore silvery-grey, linear leaves to whose surface adhered a mat of coarse hairs. The pyramidal inflorescence was composed of a series of small, sky-blue flower clusters and measured about 12 by 3 inches (30 by 7·5 cm.). This plant, upon which the description of the species was based, had flowers which were all functionally female and, without a staminate plant beside it, died without setting seed. It appears that several at least of the species of *Echium* from the Canaries produce inflorescences that are either mostly male or mostly female. In the wild this increases the chances of cross-fertilization, but as many of these species are monocarpic, that is to say that they flower once and then die, they are often difficult to maintain in cultivation.

If seed can be obtained these remarkable and striking plants from the Canary Islands can be grown without much difficulty in the milder parts of Britain, such as Cornwall and the Scilly Isles, and in parts of France, or California, if given a sunny position and soil that is not too rich. In frosty areas they can be grown under glass.

BORAGINACEAE

Echium wildpretii (syn. *E. bourgaeanum*)
A1 lower part of plant × $\frac{2}{3}$.
A2 inflorescence × $\frac{2}{3}$. A3 flowers and bract × 4.
A4 flower and bracteole × $2\frac{2}{3}$.
A5 habit sketch × $\frac{1}{24}$.

Plate 45   MIDDLE EAST

With popular names like Rose of Sharon and Aaron's Beard, one would suspect *Hypericum calycinum* of being a plant of the Holy Land, whereas it actually comes from south-eastern Europe and western Turkey. The plate opposite also illustrates four members of the rose family, all of them attractive flowering species—the Apricot, in addition, being widely cultivated for its fruit.

The Apricot, *Prunus armeniaca* (A) is probably a native of China and adjacent central Asia, where wild and obviously uncultivated plants are found, but it must have been carried to south-western Asia at an early date by migrating traders, where, together with the Mediterranean region and southern Europe, it is widely cultivated. In nature, it forms a tree about 30 feet (9 m.) tall, with twisted reddish branches and deep green leaves. The white or pinkish flowers appear in March and April, often crowded together on short, spur-like branchlets. The fruits are variable, about $1\frac{1}{4}$ inches (3 cm.) in diameter, or larger on the best cultivated varieties. When ripe, they are yellow tinged with red and the flesh is firm and sweet. The stone has a thickened, furrowed margin.

Ranging from the Mediterranean region into China, the forty *Amygdalus* species are often included in the genus *Prunus*. A native of Turkey, into Kurdistan, and therefore adapted to life in arid conditions, *A. orientalis* (B) rarely exceeds 9 feet (2·7 m.) in height. The young shoots, together with their elliptic leaves, are densely covered with silvery down and even the small fruits, which are only $\frac{5}{8}$ inch (16 mm.) long, are covered with the same silvery hairs. The pink flowers occur singly or in pairs and are about 1 inch (2·5 cm.) in diameter. This plant was introduced into Europe in 1756 but is too tender to thrive in places like Britain.

The Almond, *A. communis*, although a native of central and south-west Asia, is now widespread as a cultivated plant, especially in the Mediterranean region, forming a tree about 25 feet (7·6 m.) tall. The large and decorative flowers precede the leaves which lengthen to about 4 inches (10 cm.). The firm, pubescent fruits are valued for the seeds, which in the best cultivated forms, have a relatively soft seed coat, surrounding the almond nut used in cooking and confectionary. Certain types of almond have kernels with a high yield of the poisonous prussic or hydrocyanic acid which is sometimes present in small quantities in the common Almond, giving it a bitter taste. When placed in the genus *Prunus*, the correct name for the species is *Prunus dulcis*, based on Miller's name, *Amygdalus dulcis*, for the Sweet as opposed to the Bitter Almond.

Austrian Briar, *Rosa foetida* (syn. *R. lutea*) (C) has been in cultivation for over four hundred years and, although a native of Armenia, northern Iran, Kurdistan and Afghanistan, has become naturalized in some of the sunnier parts of southern Europe. The leaves are borne on arching, brownish, sparsely-prickled stems, and the large, deep yellow flowers occur singly or in small clusters. The fruits are red and round and rarely seen in cultivation. The variety *bicolor*, the Austrian Copper Rose, has beautiful copper-coloured petals.

At one time included in *Rosa*, though with undivided leaves and no stipules to the leaf stalks, the one species of *Hulthemia* is a native of Iran, south central U.S.S.R. and Afghanistan. Once considered as two species, *Rosa persica* and *R. berberifolia*, *H. persica* (E) was discovered by Peter Simon Pallas (1741–1811) about 1760 and was introduced into England some thirty years later by Sir Joseph Banks. It has never become a popular garden plant because it is so difficult to grow, but is mentioned periodically in horticultural literature and appears occasionally in exhibitions, usually after being grown under glass. The fact that it is a plant of arid regions probably accounts for its failure to thrive in temperate western Europe. The small yellow- and red-blotched flowers appear from April to June and are borne on slender, prickly stems about 3 feet (91 cm.) tall. The undivided, greenish-blue leaves are oval and toothed near the tip, and the fruits, which are rarely seen, are prickly, green and globular.

The popular garden plant *Hypericum calycinum* (D) was first discovered by the Reverend Sir George Wheler in 1675 or 1676, growing in a village not far from Constantinople. He sent seed to Robert Morison, the first Professor of Botany at Oxford University, who later erroneously described the plant as coming from Mount Olympus. Later, in 1767, when Linnaeus gave it its botanical name he attributed it to North America, although with some doubts. The popular biblical-sounding names have no basis, for the 'Rose of Sharon' mentioned in the Bible probably refers to *Tulipa montana* or *T. sharonensis* and in the 18th century, in the time of Gilbert White of Selbourne, it was apparently known as 'Sir George Wheler's Tutsan'. Whatever the intricacies of its popular nomenclature, its merit as a garden plant is undoubted; it is easy to grow, forms an evergreen subshrub about 12 inches (30 cm.) tall with creeping or ascending stems, leathery leaves and splendid large yellow flowers. These are borne singly at the end of the shoots and appear over a long period from June to September.

ROSACEAE

Prunus armeniaca, Apricot
A1 part of flowering branch × $\frac{2}{3}$.
A2 fruiting twig with leaves × $\frac{2}{3}$.

Amygdalus orientalis (syn. *Prunus argentea*, *P. orientalis*)
B1 flowering twig × $\frac{2}{3}$.
B2 young fruits and leaves on twig × $\frac{2}{3}$.
B3 fruit × $\frac{2}{3}$.

Rosa foetida (syn. *R. lutea*), Austrian Briar
C1 flowering twig with leaves and buds × $\frac{2}{3}$.
C2 petal × $1\frac{1}{3}$.

Hulthemia persica (syn. *Rosa berberifolia*, *R. persica*)
E1 part of flowering branch with leaves and buds × $\frac{2}{3}$. E2 flower × $1\frac{1}{3}$.

HYPERICACEAE

Hypericum calycinum, Rose of Sharon, Aaron's Beard
D1 flowering plant with bud × $\frac{2}{3}$.
D2 ovary × $1\frac{1}{3}$. D3 stamen × $2\frac{2}{3}$.

A1

A2

B1

B2

B3

C1

C2

D1

D2

D3

E1

E2

Plate 46   MIDDLE EAST

The Middle East is an area rich in poppy species, including the large decorative Oriental Poppy. There is also a bewildering array of mustards and other crucifers and some genera are found only in the deserts and semideserts of that area, where, dictated by the rains and droughts, most of the herbs have a well marked seasonal pattern for growth, flowering and then dormancy in the form of seed.

The Oriental Poppy, *Papaver orientale* (A), is a native of eastern Turkey, Caucasia, Armenia and northern Iran. Together with the related *P. bracteatum*, which has more robust stems, broader petals and flowers surrounded by bracts, *P. orientale* and its cultivars are the familiar perennial poppies of gardens, growing from 2–4 feet (61–122 cm.) tall. *P. bracteatum* has a very similar wild distribution but in cultivation every kind of intergradation occurs between the two species.

The Opium Poppy, *P. somniferum*, with its white, lilac, purple or red tinged flowers, borne on stems to 4 feet (1·2 m.) tall, is of doubtful origin but is generally thought to have come originally from a region of the eastern Mediterranean or the Middle East. It was known to the ancient Greeks but the Arabs and Persians monopolized early trade in the small cakes of dried raw opium latex. The latex is obtained from incisions made on the unripened capsule and contains 20% alkaloids. The most important of these are morphine, codeine and heroin, which make opium a useful sedative and pain killer. India and China received opium from the west by 800 A.D. and the people soon acquired the habit of opium eating and smoking in efforts to sustain and repeat the pleasurable hallucinations and dreams produced by the drugs. Continued use of opium destroys the physical and mental coordination of the body and finally results in death. The seeds, extensively used in baking to ornament bread and cakes and, on account of their oil content, in the manufacture of paints and varnishes, contain no alkaloid.

Closely related to and looking much like poppies, the seven species of *Roemeria* are native to the Mediterranean region and Middle East. They differ from true poppies in having stalked stigmas and seed capsules which open by slits instead of pores. *R. refracta* (C) has also been known as *R. rhoeadifolia* and is native from Transcaucasia and northern Iran to western Pakistan. It is a slender, much branched herb of about 2 feet (61 cm.) with feathery foliage. The nodding hairy buds open into erect flowers in which purple-black stamens and blotches at the base of the petals contrast well with the bright red petals and yellow pollen. The black blotches are sometimes edged with white and the com-bination of these features makes *R. refracta* a pretty annual for the garden. The violet-flowered *R. hybrida* also occurs in the Middle East but with a more western distribution as it is also found in south and west Europe and north-west Africa.

Count Pierre de Tchihatcheff (1812–1890), who travelled widely and wrote, amongst other works, an eight volume work on the natural history of Asia Minor, discovered *Tchihatchewia isatidea* (B). This plant is the only species of its genus but is related to *Peltaria*, a Mediterranean and Middle East genus of seven species. *T. isatidea* was discovered near the sources of the River Euphrates at Erzinghan at about 5500 feet (1680 m.) and seed sent to Kew from St Petersburg in 1896 flowered, for the first time in Britain, in 1898. The whole plant, except the flowers and fruit, is clothed in long, simple whitish hairs and the stem, 10 inches (25 cm.) long, is much branched at the top and densely clothed below with narrow, somewhat bristly leaves. The fragrant red-purple flowers are clustered into dome-shaped heads and are very attractive, yet the plant, distinctive though it is, is seldom grown in cultivation.

Another genus with only one species but perhaps more famous, though again little cultivated, comprises the Rose of Jericho, *Anastatica hierochuntica* (D), native of Mediterranean north Africa and parts of the Middle East. It has a stout tap-root, spreading aerial branches and inconspicuous white flowers. The notable feature is the way in which the whole plant, in the dry conditions after flowering and setting fruit, turns into a skeletonized hollow ball—the branches curve in and the stem snaps off at ground level, leaving the plant free to be blown about by the wind on the surface of the ground. Many hundreds of these vegetable balls may be seen tumbling across dry plains, often startling animals with their blind aeolian progress. They roll until they reach a muddy spot or until the rains come again and then, even more strange, the stems quickly reabsorb moisture and regain their original spreading habit and the seeds are shed. Should the mud dry up, they curl up again and continue to roll before the wind. This curious process and the legend that, at the birth of Christ, all the plants of this species expanded, became green again and flowered, gave rise to the common names Mary's Flower and Rose of Jericho. The development of such tumbling weeds is found in open and seasonally arid areas such as in the Middle East, the prairies of North America and the steppes of central Asia. Here dissemination of the plants by wind, until they come to stop in favourable conditions for growth, is a distinct advantage.

PAPAVERACEAE

Papaver orientale, Oriental Poppy
A1 part of flowering stem and leaf × ⅔.
A2 part of budding stem × ⅔. A3 stamen × 4.
A4 immature fruit on part of stem × ⅔.
A5 fruit in transverse section × 1⅓.

Roemeria refracta (syn. *R. rhoeadifolia*)
C1 part of flowering stem with leaf, fruit and buds × ⅔. C2 flower with petals removed × 1⅓.

CRUCIFERAE

Tchihatchewia isatidea
B1 flowering plant × ⅔.
B2 part of fruiting stem × ⅔.
B3 leaf hairs × 4.

Anastatica hierochuntica, Rose of Jericho, Mary's Flower
D1 plant with flowers and young fruit × ⅔.
D2 flower × 5⅓. D3 old fruiting plant × ⅔.
D4 fruit × 4.

A2

A1

A5

A3

A4

B2

B3

B1

C1

C2

D1

D3

D2

D4

Plate 47   MIDDLE EAST

Although usually associated in one's mind with the Arctic, or the moist woodlands of North America and Europe, a number of willow species, among them such ornamental plants as *Salix aegyptiaca*, are to be found by watercourses in the arid parts of the Middle East and central Asia. The same region also possesses two of the world's most majestic campanulaceous genera, *Michauxia* and *Ostrowskia*, the former remarkable for its spires of ornately constructed flowers, the latter for the sheer size of its pale lilac blooms.

Despite its name, *Salix aegyptiaca* (C) (syn. *S. medemii*) is no native of Egypt, but of south-western Asiatic Russia, eastern Turkey and northern Iran. This quickly developing shrub or small tree, up to 12 feet (3·7 m.) in height, is notable for its large, decorative catkins, which emerge in January, February or March, before the leaves appear, the males with their bright yellow anthers being particularly attractive. The branches, which are grey and downy when young, reddish or brown when old, bear prominently ridged twigs and elliptical leaves up to 4 inches (10 cm.) or more in length, with crinkled edges. Both leaf-surfaces, at the start of the season, are hairy, but the upper later becomes smooth. The species seems to have been cultivated in Europe since 1874, and at Kew, from where the material depicted opposite came, it has been grown since 1879.

Ostrowskia is a monotypic genus consisting only of *O. magnifica* (A), a native of Turkistan. It was discovered at an altitude of 7000 feet (2130 m.) on Chanat Darwas in eastern Bukhara by Albert von Regel. His father, Eduard August von Regel, sometime Director of the Imperial Botanic Gardens of St Petersburg and founder

of the journal *Gartenflora*, named the plant in honour of Michael Nicolajewitsch von Ostrowsky, a Russian patron of botany. The genus differs from *Campanula* in having whorled leaves, more numerous flower parts and dissimilar fruits. When *Ostrowskia* first flowered in cultivation, about 1887, the gardening journals of the day prophesied a great future for this ornamental plant with its enormous flowers. The promise, however, was never fulfilled, mainly because the seedlings take four to five years to mature and require protection in spring. The stems grow to a height of 4 or 5 feet (1·2–1·5 m.) from a tuberous rootstock.

Michauxia tchihatcheffii (B) commemorates, in its generic name, André Michaux (1746–1803), a French botanist who did much work on North American plants during a ten year stay in the New World, and, in its specific epithet, P. de Tchihatcheff (see plate 46), who discovered the species in 1849 at altitudes between 2800 and 5000 feet (850–1520 m.) in the Anti-Taurus Mountains of Turkey. Seed was introduced by Walter Siehe to Germany and from there some was bought by Kew, where the first flowers were seen in 1899. It forms a most striking plant, with an unbranched stem that may attain a height of 7 feet (2 m.) and ends in a spike of flowers up to 2 feet (61 cm.) long and 5 to 6 inches (12·5–15 cm.) across. A very beautiful biennial, *M. campanuloides* was an earlier introduction made about 1787 from the mountains of Cilicia. The plant is hardy in Britain and grows to a height of about 4 feet (1·2 m.), with pyramidal, branched inflorescences about 12 inches (30 cm.) long. The flowers may be as much as 5 inches (12·5 cm.) across, but are usually about 3 inches (7·5 cm.) and have creamy white, reflexed lobes.

CAMPANULACEAE

Ostrowskia magnifica
A1 part of flowering stem (cut) $\times \frac{2}{3}$.
A2 habit sketch $\times \frac{1}{12}$.

Michauxia tchihatcheffii
B1 part of flowering plant (cut) $\times \frac{2}{3}$.
B2 habit sketch $\times \frac{1}{24}$.

SALICACEAE

Salix aegyptiaca (syn. *S. medemii*)
C1 part of male flowering shoot $\times \frac{2}{3}$.
C2 male flower $\times 8$.
C3 part of female flowering shoot $\times \frac{2}{3}$.
C4 female flower $\times 8$. C5 leafy shoot $\times \frac{2}{3}$.

A1

A2

B1

B2

C1

C2

C3

C4

C5

Plate 48 MIDDLE EAST

Many parts of the Near and Middle East and central Asia present an arid and sometimes saline environment and the genera *Acantholimon*, *Limonium* and *Dionysia* represented opposite, have evolved to fit into such habitats.

Campanula propinqua is a variable species, the corolla exhibiting a complete gradation in dimensions from as large as that in the illustrated variety, var. *grandiflora* (A), down to others with a diameter only half the size. The species, ranging from Kurdistan and Armenia to Amasia in Turkey, was first collected in Azerbaijan and described from plants grown in the St Petersburg Botanic Garden in 1835. In 1930 R. W. E. Cecil collected material, from the Rowanduz district of Iraq, which was subsequently raised in cultivation by his mother Lady Rockley, in Dorset. The plants were considered to be varietally distinct and so, in 1934, they were described as var. *grandiflora*, which, in flower size and colouration is superior to var. *propinqua*; it is restricted to Armenia and Kurdistan at altitudes between 600 and 1600 feet (180–490 m.) where it is found growing as a weed. It received an Award of Merit from the Royal Horticultural Society in 1931 and, being a half hardy annual, is easy to grow in sandy soil. The plants grow to about 12 inches (30 cm.) tall and the numerous branches are terminated by the flowers, which, in order to set seed, must be artificially pollinated.

Belonging to a large and complex genus, the hundred and fifty or so species of *Acantholimon* form a conspicuous part of the vegetation in parts of Turkey, Iran, Turkestan and Afghanistan, and, as these plants often grow in somewhat saline soils, they may become encrusted with a mineral deposit. A variable species in shape and hairiness of the leaves, colour of the flowers and proportions of the inflorescence, the Prickly Thrift, *A. venustum* (D) is a native of Turkey, Iraq and Iran where it grows at altitudes between about 4000 and 7000 feet (1220–2130 m.). If grown in a climate like that of Britain, it requires good drainage and plenty of sun.

Allied to *Acantholimon*, the genus *Limonium* has about three hundred species with some representation in most continents but especially found in the eastern Mediterranean region and central Asia, particularly in salt marshes and steppes. *L. tartaricum* (C), or *Goniolimon tartaricum* as it is often called, is a native of saline soils in Dalmatia and Hungary, eastward to the Crimea and north Caucasus. It was introduced into Britain about 1731 by Philip Miller, and has since been grown for its corymbs of tiny red flowers produced in June and July. The cultivated heads may be 3 feet (91 cm.) across with ruby coloured flowers surrounded by chaffy sepals.

First discovered by Albert von Regel near Leninabad in north-west Tadzhikistan (part of Turkestan), *L. suworowii* (B) commemorates Ivan Petrowitsch Suworow, the Inspector of Military Hospitals in that area at the time. Plants may grow to 5 feet (1·5 m.) tall and the purple-lilac inflorescences remain in flower for as long as eight weeks. Each individual flower only measures a few millimetres and 2 or 3 are clustered together in a cup of chaffy bracts, each cluster placed close together to form a continuous cylinder of flowers. *L. suworowii*, or *Psylliostachys suworowii* if one recognizes the segregate genus, was described and first illustrated in 1882 in *Gartenflora* with a figure that did not really do justice to the attractive long sinuous inflorescence. Plants were first raised at Kew from seed sent from Germany, first flowering there in 1886.

The sole parent of the well known house and glasshouse 'cyclamen' with its many colour forms, *Cyclamen persicum* (G) as a wild plant, is native in the eastern Mediterranean and, being taller and more erect than many cyclamens, it is probably the most beautiful of all the wild species. The white, pale pink or pale carmine flowers have a charm which has often disappeared in the more flashy products of 'improvement'. Furthermore the flowers are sweetly fragrant, a character that has been lost in the larger cultivated varieties. Old tubers produce numerous flowers and in western Europe and similar places, the plants should spend the winter in a cool glasshouse where they should flower in March and April and then spend the summer plunged in soil out of doors.

Closely related to *Primula*, the thirty-five species of the genus *Dionysia* are native of Iran and the surrounding areas and are characterized by a dense cushion habit made up of numerous small erect stems bearing small overlapping leaves. This arrangement permits the minimum water loss in very arid and rocky habitats; these plants usually grow in cracks on limestone cliffs. The single or few-clustered flowers are usually small, with the corolla tube sometimes 4–6 times as long as the calyx. Like the species of *Primula*, *Dionysia* has capsular fruits, but these contain only 1–4 seeds. They are a challenging subject for the alpine gardener and resent overwatering.

Growing in rock crevices in western Iran and eastern Anatolia, *D. odora* (E) has glandular hairy leaves and scented, stalkless flowers which are yellow and appear in July. Flowering in May and found in similar habitats in south-western Iran, *D. bryoides* is another species with densely tufted branches, about $1\frac{1}{4}$ inches (3 cm.) long and their resemblance to moss plants gave rise to the specific epithet from *Bryum*, a genus of mosses. *D. curviflora* (F) is also an Iranian species with cushion habit which flowers in April. Its tiny hard leaves have fringed leathery tips which contrast well with the yellow flowers and their slender corolla tubes.

Species of *Dionysia* only appeared in cultivation in 1932 and the story of their introduction is related by W. E. Th. Ingwersen who tells how Dr P. L. Giuseppi hunted for these diminutive plants in Iran and how disappointed he was at seemingly being unable to secure fresh seed or living plants. Yet with perseverance and by pounding up the withered remains of the cushions with rolling pins and then using flour sieves, seeds from old capsules of previous years were obtained. These germinated to produce the first dionysias ever seen in cultivation.

CAMPANULACEAE

Campanula propinqua var. *grandiflora*
A1 part of flowering stem × $\frac{2}{3}$.
A2 flower, face on × $\frac{2}{3}$.
A3 flower sectioned × $1\frac{1}{3}$.

PLUMBAGINACEAE

Limonium suworowii (syn. *Psylliostachys suworowii*)
B1 inflorescence on part of stem × $\frac{2}{3}$.
B2 flower × $6\frac{2}{3}$.
B3 rosette of leaves with roots × $\frac{2}{3}$.

L. tartaricum (syn. *Goniolimon tartaricum*)
C1 part of flowering plant × $\frac{2}{3}$.
C2 flower × 2.

Acantholimon venustum, Prickly Thrift
D1 part of flowering plant × $\frac{2}{3}$.

PRIMULACEAE

Dionysia odora (syn. *D. aucheri*)
E1 part of flowering plant. E2 leaf × 4.

D. curviflora
F1 part of flowering plant × $\frac{2}{3}$.
F2 flowering branchlet × $1\frac{1}{3}$.

Cyclamen persicum
G1 flowering plant × $\frac{2}{3}$.

A2

A1

A3

B2

B1

B3

C2

C1

D1

E2

E1

F1

F2

G1

Plate 49   MIDDLE EAST

There has been increased botanical exploration in the Middle East in recent years, but there is still much to be done. Even collection on a month's vacational trip can reap scientific reward, and plant identification in the area is becoming easier with the publication, volume by volume, of the *Flora of Iraq*, the *Flora Iranica* and the *Flora of Turkey*. There is always the chance, too, of finding new, undescribed material, by the collector who visits places off the usual tourist-routes and out of the tourist season. But just as important as finding new species is the collecting of inadequately and poorly known species and the recording of community structure in the vegetation. The organizer of any trip which might provide botanical information should make a point of contacting a botanical institution or a professional botanist with knowledge of the area, who is likely to be able to help in a number of ways, both scientific and practical.

Aipyanthus echioides (D) is popularly called the Prophet Flower because the brownish spots which mark the petals of young flowers are supposed to represent the finger prints of Mahomet but they fade and disappear as the flower ages. It is native in Asia Minor, Iran and the Caucasus and illustrates some of the complexities of nomenclature and the way in which the correct botanical name for a plant can vary according to the genus in which it is classified. This species was first described by Linnaeus in 1762 as *Lycopsis echioides* but differs in so many characters from the typical species of *Lycopsis* that it was transferred to the genus *Arnebia* and was known as *Arnebia echioides*. However, according to the last authority to specialize in the *Boraginaceae*, Dr I. M. Johnston, its unique but somewhat technical characters are such that in his opinion it should be put in a genus of its own, and in 1954 he called it *Echioides longiflorum*. Tautonyms like *Echioides echioides* are not permitted in botanical nomenclature, although they are acceptable for animals. However, the prior use of the name *Echioides* for *Lycopsis* proper prohibits its later use, so yet another has to be adopted and that given by the Finnish botanist, C. Steven, in 1851, and the correct name when placed in a segregate genus on its own is *Aipyanthus echioides*. It has also been included in *Macrotomia* and *Lithospermum* by other authorities. Although it has been cultivated in Britain for more than a century and was figured in the *Botanical Magazine* in 1848, *A. echioides* is still rarely seen in gardens. This is a pity because the clear yellow flowers persist until the first severe frosts of the winter, some-times being the last garden flowers to die, and because of the curious disappearing petal marks.

Verbascum is a perplexing genus when it comes to the recognition of species. They are often so close as to be almost identical and interspecific hybridization is no doubt responsible for the way in which some of the characters are shared. *V. dumulosum* (A) was introduced and discovered by Dr Peter H. Davis, author of the notable *Flora of Turkey and the East Aegean Islands* which is still being written, with two volumes so far published (1969). He first collected it with withered flowers in August 1947, when he found it growing on the walls of ruined temples at Termessus in Antalya Province, Turkey, where it formed a rounded shrub about 12 inches (30 cm.) tall. It was found with flowers in June 1948 by J. Renz at the same locality and in 1949 Davis again collected the species, this time in fruit, from which seed was obtained for the introduction into cultivation. Termessus was an ancient city which resisted capture by Alexander the Great, and the presence of this species on ruined walls, an artificial habitat, poses the question of its true native habitat, for so far, apparently, it has not been found elsewhere. If it is cultivated where there is a danger of cold winter frosts, it requires the protection of a greenhouse but its neat shrubby habit makes it a bright and gay subject, easily propagated from seed. It is related to *V. pestalozzae* which has a similar appearance but larger flowers and sepals. The specific epithet *dumulosum* is a diminutive of *dumosus* meaning 'bushy'.

Salvia indica (B), formerly known as *S. brachycalyx*, is a native of rocky places in Israel, Syria, Lebanon and Kurdistan. It is a large herb, notable for its decorative flowers, and although cultivated by Philip Miller in his Chelsea garden in 1731, is one of those plants which have never become popular garden subjects. It grows to about 5 feet (1·5 m.) and requires staking if its June and July blooms are to look their best.

Another tall labiate native from the same general area is *Eremostachys laciniata* (C), which was also first grown in Britain by Philip Miller, at about the same time in the remarkable garden, the Chelsea Physic Garden. It is one of the westernmost representatives of the genus, which is mainly found in western and central Asia, and contains five or fifty species, according to how fine one draws the lines of distinction between them. The botanist is classifying and naming evolving organisms, not made by man, and here, as so often, it is a matter of opinion where one species starts and another ends.

SCROPHULARIACEAE

Verbascum dumulosum
A1 part of flowering and fruiting plant × $\frac{2}{3}$.
A2 petal × 4. A3 stamen × 4.

LABIATAE

Salvia indica (syn. *S. brachycalyx*)
B1 inflorescence and leaf × $\frac{2}{3}$.
B2 part of corolla × 2. B3 stamen × 4.

Eremostachys laciniata
C1 inflorescence and leaf × $\frac{2}{3}$.

BORAGINACEAE

Aipyanthus echioides (syn. *Arnebia echioides*, *Macrotomia echioides*), Prophet Flower
D1 part of flowering stem × $\frac{2}{3}$.
D2 corolla × 2.
D3 calyx and developing nutlets × $2\frac{2}{3}$.
D4 leaves and root × $\frac{2}{3}$.

A1

A2

A3

B1

B2

B3

B4

B5

B6

Plate 51   MIDDLE EAST

Particularly conspicuous in the flora of the central Asian steppes, the genus *Tulipa* consists of about one hundred species. *T. polychroma* (A), which belongs to the *Biflores* section of the genus characterized by plants with 2 or more flowers borne on a branched inflorescence, is found in Iran and, possibly, Baluchistan and Turkistan. Closely related to it is *T. turkestanica*, which has purple or chocolate anthers and half the number of chromosomes, being what is known as a diploid, whereas *T. polychroma* is a tetraploid. *T. linifolia* (E), distinguished in May by its glossy scarlet flowers blotched with purple-black, is native to eastern Bukhara. The flower may be borne against the upper leaf of the stalk, which has a maximum length of 6 inches (15 cm.). The narrow leaves measure $4\frac{3}{4}$ inches (12 cm.) in length.

Puschkinia scilloides (B) is one of two species in its genus, both of which are restricted to western Asia and differ from the related genera *Scilla* and *Chionodoxa* in possessing fused perianth segments and a corona-like structure around the stamens and style. An intense blue stripe set against the delicate blue background of the rest of the petal has earned the plant the popular name Striped Squill. In the wild, the species is native to the Caucasus, Turkey and the Lebanon, but it is also frequently cultivated in rock gardens and alpine-houses.

One of the earliest fritillaries to be introduced to European gardens, to which it was brought by merchants from Iran or Syria via Constantinople, *Fritillaria persica* (D) presents an imposing appearance, with greenish mauve to greenish violet flowers carried on stems up to 3 feet (91 cm.) in height.

Turkestan and north-eastern Afghanistan are the home of the delightfully coloured *Crocus korolkowii* (F), discovered by General Korolkov between Tashkent and Karak-Ati in 1882 and distributed to growers later in the same year. The freely borne yellow flowers, veined with mahogany or purple outside and varnished inside, appear at Christmas or early in the New Year and are surrounded by many grooved, narrow leaves. In the genus *Crocus*, the ovary is situated initially right at the base of the floral tube, not much above the flat corm itself, and below ground level; when the fruit is ripe, it is carried upwards on a stalk until the capsule is above ground level when it dehisces and releases its seeds. *C. korolkowii*, however, is an exception as the ripe capsule remains below the soil.

Perhaps the most beautiful of all irises are contained in the *Oncocyclus* section of the genus *Iris*, many of them with highly restricted local distributions dotted over an area roughly bounded by the Mediterranean, central Turkey, the Caucasus, the mountains of northern Iran, western Iran and Israel. *Oncocyclus* irises caught the eye of man as early as the second millenium before Christ, when they were depicted on Egyptian murals, and Thothmes III is said to have cultivated them; nevertheless, it was not until the 19th century that species were to be found in western European gardens. *Iris lortetii* (C) is one of a group of such tall, less hardy oncocyclus irises from the region of Israel, Syria and northern Iraq as *I. bismarckiana*, *I. atrofusca* and *I. gatesii*, all closely related and often only clearly distinguishable from one another by variation in flower colour. Discovered by Dr Lortet on Mount Lebanon in thickets of *Quercus coccifera*, the wavy pinkish-violet standards and crimson-dotted, darker lilac, sharply reflexed falls make *I. lortetii* supreme even among the oncocycli. It is, however, a difficult plant to grow, the short rainy season and prolonged drought to which it is adapted making survival through a western European winter a most uncertain prospect.

Iris paradoxa (G) is a more hardy oncocyclus species with shorter habit and more distinctive characters than *I. lortetii* and its immediate allies; in this it resembles *I. iberica* and *I. acutiloba*. The species, a native of northern Iran, Armenia and Transcaucasia, produces leaves some 6 inches (15 cm.) long and curious, yet attractive, single flowers, for which it is well worth growing, on slightly shorter stems. The variety *choschab*, which has almost white standards with faint veining, is sometimes referred to as *I. medwedewi*.

Like all members of the *Reticulata* section of *Iris*, *I. histrio* (H), from Syria and Turkey, is a bulbous plant. At flowering time it produces 1 or 2 leaves about 8 inches (20 cm.) long and square in cross section. Also in section *Reticulata* is *I. bakeriana* (J), named after J. G. Baker, a botanist at Kew for thirty-three years and a leading authority on bulbous plants. The species was first introduced into England by means of bulbs sent from Armenia in 1887 by the Reverend G. F. Gates to Sir Michael Foster; its native range extends through Turkey into northern Iraq. Each bulb produces 2 leaves about 6 inches (15 cm.) long simultaneously with the flowers, but these later grow to be twice that length. It is the leaves, which are cylindrical and octagonal in cross-section, and the smaller flowers that distinguish *I. bakeriana* from the better known and related *I. reticulata*. The flowers appear in January and February and are sometimes beautifully scented but require protection from damage by rain and frost.

LILIACEAE

Tulipa polychroma
A1 flowering plant × $\frac{2}{3}$.
A2 part of flowering stem × $\frac{2}{3}$.

Puschkinia scilloides, Striped Squill
B1 flowering plant × $\frac{2}{3}$.

Fritillaria persica
D1 part of flowering stem × $\frac{2}{3}$.

Tulipa linifolia
E1 part of flowering and budding stems × $\frac{2}{3}$.
E2 ovary × 2.

IRIDACEAE

Iris lortetii
C1 part of flowering stem and leaves × $\frac{2}{3}$.
C2 style branch × $\frac{2}{3}$.

Crocus korolkowii
F1 two flowering plants × $\frac{2}{3}$.
F2 style and stigmas × $2\frac{2}{3}$.

Iris paradoxa
G1 flowering plant × $\frac{2}{3}$.
G2 part of flowering stem × $\frac{2}{3}$.

I. histrio
H1 flowering plant × $\frac{2}{3}$. H2 fall petal × $1\frac{1}{3}$.

I. bakeriana
J1 two flowering plants × $\frac{2}{3}$.

A2

A1

C2

B1

C1

D1

E2

E1

F2 F1

G1 G2

H2

H1

J1

Plate 52 TROPICAL AND CENTRAL AFRICA

Delphiniums are usually found in the temperate north, but the higher altitudes of the East African highlands provide habitats cool enough to suit certain species. One such is *D. macrocentron* (A), found in the Kenya Highlands, and on Mount Elgon in Uganda, at altitudes of between 6000 and 12,700 feet (1830–3870 m.) in moist bamboo thickets and grassland. The herb grows to a height of about 6 feet (1·8 m.) with a stem covered in soft hairs and leaves that manifest a number of shapes similar to that shown. The bluish-green flowers have a thick, erect spur that holds nectar, and are borne on curved flower stalks which straighten out as the fruits develop and so hold the capsules erect, only allowing the seeds to spill when violently agitated by the wind. The species was discovered in 1884 by Joseph Thomson, an early traveller in tropical Africa, near Laikipia.

The wooded grasslands of the southern Tanzanian highlands are the home of *Clematopsis uhehensis* (D), discovered by Walter Goetze near Kissinga in 1899. As its name implies, the genus is related to *Clematis*, but the species are perennial herbs with erect stems, not climbers. In *Clematopsis uhehensis* the flowers are solitary on each stem and up to 5 inches (12·5 cm.) in diameter. There are no true petals but showy, cream coloured sepals, tinged with purple-pink and hairy along the midrib, while the central boss consists of an outer ring of greenish yellow stamens and an inner 'eye' of carpels, each of which ends in a purplish, hairy style. In fruit the flower stalk, which has been curved, straightens out, and the plumed seeds break off and are dispersed by wind.

About one hundred and fifty subtropical and tropical species of the genus *Cleome* exist. *C. angustifolia* (or *C. diandra*, as it was known until recently) (B) is a sometimes prickly-stemmed annual that grows to a height of up to about 30 inches (76 cm.) and has a distribution that ranges throughout eastern Africa at low altitudes, from southern Arabia southwards and from Angola to South Africa, where it was discovered by William Burchell (1781–1863). It is usually found in low rainfall areas in scrub, savannah or semi-desert, and has a tendency to become a weed in cultivation. In the flower only 2 stamens, of exaggerated length, are fertile, and, as in all members of this family, the ovary is borne on a stalk within the flower. It matures into a capsule up to about 4 inches (10 cm.) long.

One of the most attractive species of the tropical African genus *Ritchiea* (not to be confused with the Australasian genus *Richea*, see plate 136) is *R. polypetala* (C), with its 50–60 delicate stamens and numerous crisped petals radiating from the base of the long-stalked ovary. The 4 sepals are often tinged with purple. The plant was discovered by Charles Barter, who died of dysentery while on the Baikie Niger expedition in 1859, but was introduced to cultivation at Kew by Gustav Mann, probably from the island of Fernando Po, which lies off the west coast of Africa, its main area of occurrence.

The flowers of *Euadenia eminens* (E), one of possibly three species in an African genus of small trees or shrubs, are remarkable for the way in which the 2 upper and enlarged petals stand up like a pair of burning gas jets. In addition there are only 4–7 fertile stamens and the remainder form a group which are reduced, infertile and fused together. The fruits which develop from the stalked ovary may exceed 7 inches (18 cm.) in length when mature. The species occurs in rain forests from Uganda across to Sierra Leone.

RANUNCULACEAE

Delphinium macrocentron
A1 part of flowering shoots and leaf × $\frac{2}{3}$.
A2 part of fruiting inflorescence × $\frac{2}{3}$.

Clematopsis uhehensis
D1 part of flowering stem × $\frac{2}{3}$.
D2 stamen × 2. D3 ovary × 2.
D4 part of fruiting stem × $\frac{2}{3}$. D5 fruit × $3\frac{1}{3}$.

CAPPARACEAE

Cleome angustifolia (syn. *C. diandra*)
B1 part of flowering and fruiting stem and leaf × $\frac{2}{3}$. B2 seed × 4.

Ritchiea polypetala
C1 flowering shoot × $\frac{2}{3}$.

Euadenia eminens
E1 part of flowering stem × $\frac{2}{3}$.
E2 flower (only the bases of the two larger petals shown) × $\frac{2}{3}$.

A1

A2

B1

B2

C1

D1

D2

D3

D4

D5

E1

E2

Plate 53   TROPICAL AFRICA

There are perhaps no species of the *Annonaceae* family more attractive than those in the genus *Monodora*, found only in tropical Africa, while *Hydnora* may safely be included amongst the most ugly of flowering plants: indeed, one might be excused for passing it over as a fungus. Another curious genus, widely distributed in all tropical areas, is *Dorstenia*, immediately recognizable wherever it occurs because of its flat, fleshy inflorescence of minute, unisexual flowers. Examples of more conventional plants shown opposite are members of the genera *Clitoria* and *Crotalaria*.

Monodora consists of fifteen or twenty species having large woody fruits which hang from the branches like the equally distinctive pendulous flowers. *M. myristica* (B), the Calabash Nutmeg, is found in West Africa, Uganda and Angola, but when first described by Gaertner it was thought to be an introduced South American plant found on Jamaica and other West Indian islands. However, Robert Brown wisely thought it probable the plant had been introduced from the Old World, as at that time an active slave trade operated between Africa and Jamaica. Not until the Kew collector Gustav Mann found and introduced another *Monodora* from the Bight of Benin, in what is now Nigeria, about 1860, was it established that the genus was Old World in origin. Mann's collection was successfully grown and flowered in the Palm House at Kew and named *M. grandiflora*, although it is now realized that it only represents a large-flowered form of the variable *M. myristica*. The large, smooth, shiny leaves are purplish when they first expand, but soon become pale green, and solitary long-stalked flowers appear at the tips of branches and in the axils of leaves. The large, globular and furrowed fruits contain many tightly packed seeds which are surrounded by pulp, and contain an oil which smells of nutmeg and is discernible even in the dried state, hence the name Calabash Nutmeg. In fact, the seeds and their oil are widely used as a condiment and in medicine throughout West Africa. When mature *M. myristica* forms a tree up to 60 feet (18 m.) tall, and the graceful fragrant flowers have made the species deservedly popular in tropical parks and gardens; because of this, it is now widely distributed about the tropical world.

One of twelve African and Madagascan species, *Hydnora africana* (C), like its fellows, is a root parasite, in this case on *Euphorbia* species. It forms horizontal, 5- or 6-angled, warty rhizomes just below the soil surface, and from these arise flesh-coloured flowers, measuring up to 6 inches (15 cm.) long, rough and warty outside but smooth within. The 3 or 4 erect fleshy lobes which project from the flower represent the perianth and are covered on their inner face with a whitish, spongy substance, or

'bait body', which generates a carrion smell and attracts carrion beetles as pollinators. At the base of the perianth there is a ring-like series of stamens and below this a short cushion-like stigma terminates an ovary sunk in the 'stem' of the flower, therefore underground. The globular fleshy fruit matures underground and, as its pulp is attractive to porcupines, baboons and other animals, the fruits are sought out and dug up, and the seeds disseminated. The *Hydnoraceae* has been included in the *Rafflesiaceae* by some botanists, and is closely related in its parasitic way of life and general structure, but rafflesiaceous flowers are unisexual.

Dorstenia crispa (A), one of one hundred and seventy species generally found in moist rain forest habitats, is adapted to life in arid conditions. It grows in dry places from the mountains of Somaliland, south into Kenya in the Mombasa region, and develops a fat stem up to 15 inches (38 cm.) tall, decorated with protective tubercular leaf-scars, and sometimes branched. The leaves, which are borne at the top of the stem, have a scattering of short hairs, are crinkled and crisped at the margin, and tend to be narrow and acutely pointed. Inflorescences arise singly from leaf axils and immediately proclaim the identity of the genus, with their flat disc-shaped receptacle and many unisexual flowers distributed over the surface. The female flowers are sunk into little pits and from these the small fruits are shot when ripe by the contraction of the surrounding tissue of the receptacle.

A climbing pea with stems as long as 15 feet (4·5 m.), *Clitoria ternatea* (E) has been cultivated in western Europe since at least 1739, apparently from seed introduced from the island of Ternate, one of the Moluccas in the East Indies. The species has a distribution stretching from West Africa into tropical Asia and the East Indies, but is often naturalized elsewhere. The clear blue and delightful flowers (a white form also exists) are interesting in that they are inverted and the petal, called the standard, appears on the underside, not the top, and the pollinating insects are dusted with pollen from above onto their backs instead of their bellies, as is more usual with pea-flowers.

The genus *Crotalaria* is a complex one containing six hundred or more species and distributed in all tropical and subtropical areas. The African ones have recently been revised and sorted into some semblance of order by R. M. Polhill (1968) who recognizes four hundred and thirty-eight species from the continent. *C. agatiflora* (D) is a variable species which, with five subspecies, has a distribution from Ethiopia to Tanzania and the Congo; ssp. *agatiflora* which is illustrated here comes from the mountains of Kenya and Tanzania and has actually been introduced to cultivation in Britain, where it has been grown under glass.

MORACEAE

Dorstenia crispa
A1 flowering plant × $\frac{2}{3}$.

ANNONACEAE

Monodora myristica, Calabash Nutmeg
B1 part of flowering shoot × $\frac{2}{3}$. B2 fruit × $\frac{2}{3}$.

HYDNORACEAE

Hydnora africana
C1 closed flower and rhizome × $\frac{2}{3}$ (N.B. soil level). C2 mouth of perianth from above × $\frac{2}{3}$. C3 bud sectioned × $\frac{2}{3}$.

LEGUMINOSAE

Crotalaria agatiflora ssp. *agatiflora*
D1 part of flowering stem × $\frac{2}{3}$. D2 fruit × $\frac{2}{3}$.

Clitoria ternatea
E1 part of flowering shoot × $\frac{2}{3}$.

A1

B1

B2

C1

C2

C3

D1

D2

E1

Plate 54 TROPICAL AND CENTRAL AFRICA

A characteristic tree genus of some six African species, *Calpurnia* is cultivated in India as a decorative tree. *C. aurea* (D), found from Eritrea and Sudan throughout East Africa into Natal, and west into Angola, has inflorescences not unlike the temperate *Laburnum*, a small European and western Asian genus of some four species. In Africa *C. aurea* has been planted as a shade tree in coffee plantations, and is frequently used as an ornamental. The bright or pale yellow flowers are variously clustered in lax or dense racemes and after the flowers have withered the dry pods develop and persist on the tree for long periods.

It was Friedrich Martin Josef Welwitsch (1806–1872) who discovered *Afzelia quanzensis* (C), the Mahogany Bean, between Sansamanda and Quisonde in Angola and who named it after the nearby river Cuanza. A number of botanists have held that '*A. cuanzensis*' is the correct spelling for the species name but as Welwitsch intentionally and consistently used *'quanzensis'* this must be retained. One of thirteen tropical species, six in Malaysia and the remainder in Africa, *A. quanzensis* grows into a tree up to 115 feet (35 m.) tall with flaky, pale brown bark. The fragrant flowers are borne erect, and although there are 4 sepals (the outer pair being smaller than the inner) there is, curiously enough, only one red petal, tinged with green on the outside, the others being greatly reduced or wanting. The massive, woody fruits, up to 9 inches (23 cm.) long, contain a number of black seeds, each embedded in an orange or red aril attractive to birds. A woodland tree, the Mahogany Bean is found among thickets in dry evergreen forests and occurs in most areas of eastern and southern tropical Africa. A reddish timber, resembling mahogany, is obtained from the tree and used in the manufacture of boats and furniture.

The genus *Baikiaea*, in comparison with *Afzelia quanzensis*, possesses a full complement of 5 petals and 10 stamens; only 1 of the petals is slightly reduced in size and different in colour. *B. insignis* (A) is one of ten species all confined to tropical Africa and can grow to a height of about 112 feet (34 m.). It has smooth grey bark and somewhat leathery leaves composed of 3 to 8 (rarely 10) leaflets about 10–12 inches (25–30 cm.) long. (Three such leaflets are shown opposite.) The large flowers have 4 sepals up to 6 inches (15 cm.) long, covered with a felty, chocolate-coloured layer of hairs, and petals 8 inches (20 cm.) long, creamy-white with a densely hairy midrib. The fruits, covered by the same chocolate felt which is found on the sepals, develop into pods which can be up to as much as 2 feet (61 cm.) long, and each contains a number of ellipsoidal dark red seeds. Botanists have separated *B. insignis* into two subspecies; ssp. *insignis*, found in rain forest areas of western Africa, and ssp. *minor* which has all its organs on a smaller scale and which grows in similar habitats in eastern Africa and to the south of ssp. *insignis*.

The genus *Bauhinia* was so named by Linnaeus because of its characteristic bilobed leaves which he said symbolized the two famous early Swiss botanists and brothers Johann (1541–1613) and Kaspar (1560–1624) Bauhin. The genus contains some three hundred species of climbers, shrubs or trees, all of which show a diversity of flower structure, and many of which are popular garden plants throughout the tropics. *B. petersiana* (B) forms a tree up to about 30 feet (9 m.) tall in woods and savannahs at altitudes of 400 to 6000 feet (122–1830 m.) in Tanzania, Zambia, Malawi, Mozambique and the Congo. It was discovered by Wilhelm Carl Hartwig Peters (1815–1883) near Sena in Mozambique between 1842 and 1848 and was named after him.

LEGUMINOSAE

Baikiaea insignis
A1 part of flowering shoot × $\frac{2}{3}$. A2 fruit × $\frac{2}{3}$.

Bauhinia petersiana
B1 part of flowering stem × $\frac{2}{3}$.
B2 open fruit × $\frac{2}{3}$.

Afzelia quanzensis, Mahogany Bean
C1 part of flowering stem × $\frac{2}{3}$.
C2 open fruit × $\frac{2}{3}$.

Calpurnia aurea
D1 part of flowering shoot × $\frac{2}{3}$.
D2 seed pods × $\frac{2}{3}$.

A1

A2

B2

B1

C1

C2

D1

D2

Plate 55 TROPICAL AND CENTRAL AFRICA

The high, volcanic mountains that dot the East African plateau provide a particularly harsh climate for their flora: though the average temperature hardly varies from year to year, or from season to season, each day is summery and warm (54°F, 12°C) and each night wintery and cold (21°F, −6°C). At night it often snows or hails, the topsoil freezes and the ground is broken up by frost. By day, the heat of the sun is intense and, as the morning temperatures rise rapidly (often by as much as 18°F, 10°C in an hour), the plants have to be particularly well adapted to the difficult physiological conditions.

The mass of the flora is alpine in character but, among the tussock grass, cushion plants and other small species, grow a number of spectacular giants. The lobelias are one such group that have adapted to this severe environment. The leaves of *Lobelia telekii* (B), for instance, protect the growing point at night, insulating it at a temperature of about 34°F (1°C), while that of the outside air is as much as 13°F (7°C) lower. Later, when the inflorescence has reached its full height (2–6 feet (0·6–1·8 m.)) the 9 inch (23 cm.) elongated leaves are no longer sufficient, and the long, silver haired bracts amongst which the flowers are immersed, take over the protection which, though it may not amount to more than 1° or 2°, is enough to maintain the delicate balance between organism and environment. The species is named after Count Samuel Teleki who led the big-game hunting expedition of 1887–1888 which led to the discovery of Lake Rudolf. The species was found growing in a valley on Mount Kenya, now called Teleki Valley and grows in its greatest numbers at altitudes between 10,700 and 13,800 feet (3260–4210 m.).

The genus *Canarina* of the *Campanulaceae* has, as was mentioned on plate 43, a particularly disjunct distribution in the Canary Islands and the highlands of eastern Africa. *C. abyssinica* (A), a climbing herb with a large bulbous root, grows amongst moist rocks or in moist grassland and although first discovered in southern Ethiopia at the turn of this century is now known on high ground south to Tanzania. The attractive elongated corollas are a pinkish orange streaked with red, and sometimes lighter in colour within. The fruit is almost spherical and yellow or tomato-coloured.

The commonest of the three species of *Clappertonia*, all of them African, is *C. ficifolia* (C) which is found in moist spots from Guinea and Sierra Leone east to central Africa and south to Angola. The flowers are composed of 4 narrow sepals of the same colour as the broader petals, 10 stamens, and a mass of short, infertile stamens, or staminodes, that surround the ovary. This latter grows ever more spiny and woody as it develops into the purplish fruit, which turns reddish-brown before opening.

CAMPANULACEAE

Canarina abyssinica
A1 part of flowering shoot × ⅔.

Lobelia telekii
B1 part of flowering plant and leaf × ⅔.
B2 flower subtended by bract × ⅔.
B3 opened corolla × 1⅓. B4 habit sketch × 1/13.

TILIACEAE

Clappertonia ficifolia (syn. *Honckenya ficifolia*)
C1 part of flowering and fruiting stem × ⅔.
C2 leaf × ⅔. C3 fruit (open) × ⅔.

A1

B2

B3

B1

C3

C1

C2

B4

Plate 56   TROPICAL AND CENTRAL AFRICA

The East African mountains are famous for their unique and remarkable giant lobelias and tree senecios. *Lobelia deckenii* (A) is very similar to a number of closely related plants found on other high mountains in the region. These, with the mountains to which they are restricted include *L. bequaertii* on Ruwenzori; *L. burttii* on Mounts Hanang, Loolmalassin and Meru; *L. elgonensis* on Mount Elgon; *L. keniensis* on Mount Kenya; and *L. sattimae* in the Aberdares. These allied species differ in such minor characters as the shape and hairiness of the floral bracts and degree of splitting of the corolla, and in some ways it might be more realistic to treat them as sub-species or varieties of *L. deckenii*. What is certain is that each mountain area has its own particular type of lobelia. It seems fanciful to speak of senecio-woodlands, especially if one is familiar with Groundsel *Senecio vulgaris*, the common garden weed in temperate regions; yet in East Africa some species of the subgenus *Dendrosenecio* do attain the stature of small trees.

Lobelia deckenii grows only on Kilimanjaro in Tanzania in wet moorland at altitudes between about 9000 and 13,500 feet (2740–4110 m.). Its name commemorates one of the collectors who first found it, Baron Carl Claus von der Decken (1833–1865). The flowers, as in several other species of tree-lobelias, are buried amongst the bracts of the inflorescence which are held out rigidly and reflexed at the tips. On these tips the sunbirds, such as *Nectarinia* species, find a perch and often tear them with their frequent visits. In feeding from the flowers the birds act as polli-nators and, when different species occur close to one another, occasional hybrid plants may appear. Flowering specimens of *L. deckenii* may reach a height of 12 feet (3·7 m.), with leaves about 10 inches (25 cm.) long arranged around the hollow stem. Sometimes the old leaves drop off, as indicated on one of the plants in the habit sketch, or they wither and form a protection for the stem. On Kilimanjaro, *L. deckenii* is asso-ciated with the tree-daisies *Senecio cottonii* and *S. kilimanjari*.

The stem in *S. brassica* (B) is prostrate but the companion species on Mount Kenya, *S. kenio-dendron*, forms trees up to about 18 feet (5·5 m.) tall with heads of leaves, before they flower, resembling cabbages on the end of stalks clothed in dead leaves. *S. keniodendron* tends to occur on drier slopes at altitudes between 12,000 and 14,000 feet (3660 and 4270 m.), while *S. brassica*

seems to prefer moister habitats between about 10,000 and 13,000 feet (3050 and 3960 m.); *Lobelia telekii* and *L. keniensis* are both asso-ciated with the tree-daisies on Mount Kenya.

The giant *Senecio* species show no dormancy, unlike the arctic-alpine species found in northerly and southerly latitudes, for with Mount Kenya almost on the equator, there are virtually no seasons. There are, however, great fluctuations in temperature and during the day the large leaves of *S. keniodendron* are spread open round the stem, while at night they close up so that only the backs of the outer leaves are exposed. Temperature measurements show that the folding of the woolly leaves keeps the temperature in the centre of the shoot at about 35°F (1·7°C) while it is 25°F (−3·9°C) outside. Similarly, the dead leaves surrounding the stem maintain the temperature of the stem tissues at about 37°F (2·8°C) while the outside temperature is a killing 23°F (−5°C). Instead of protective leaves, the stems of *S. barbatipes*, from Mount Elgon, are covered in a thick fissured bark like conventional trees. *S. barbatipes* is found only on Mount Elgon, where it has as companion species *S. elgonensis, Lobelia telekii* and *L. elgonensis*.

The Aberdare mountains have an open tree-daisy woodland where the ravines and cliffs support *S. battiscombei*, while the gentler slopes carry *S. brassiciformis*. In this area two further species of giant *Lobelia* occur.

Senecio brassica derives its name from its cabbage-like appearance, (*Brassica oleracea* is the Cabbage), and the pale undersides of the leaves, which although woolly, together resemble a cabbage-head from a distance. The species was described from a locality on Mount Kenya between the Teleki and Höhnel Valleys at about 10,000 feet (3050 m.), where it was found by the brothers R. E. Fries and Th. C. E. Fries in 1922; but the leaves had been collected in 1893 by Dr J. W. Gregory and, due to a mix-up arising from the similarity of habit, had become asso-ciated with the inflorescence of a *Lobelia* and described in 1894 as *L. gregoriana* (correctly known as *L. keniensis*). In flower, *S. brassica* grows to a maximum of about 6 or 7 feet (1·8 or 2·1 m.), after which the shoot dies, but lateral crowns normally develop in the axils of old basal leaves and continue the growth. Found only on Mount Kenya, it is thought to hybridize with *S. keniodendron* on occasion and is reported to flower almost throughout the year.

CAMPANULACEAE

Lobelia deckenii
A1 inflorescence × $\frac{2}{3}$. A2 flower × $1\frac{1}{3}$.
A3 anthers showing tuft of hair × $2\frac{2}{3}$.
A4 habit sketch × $\frac{1}{15}$.

COMPOSITAE

Senecio brassica
B1 inflorescence × $\frac{2}{3}$. B2 disc-floret × $3\frac{1}{3}$.
B3 ray-floret × $3\frac{1}{3}$. B4 involucral bract × $2\frac{2}{3}$.
B5 habit sketch × $\frac{1}{22}$.

A4

A3

A2

A1

B4

B3

B2

B5

B1

Plate 57 TROPICAL AND CENTRAL AFRICA

Many of the three hundred or so species of *Hibiscus* are found in tropical Africa, although others occur in all tropical parts of the world. *H. schizopetalus* (B) is a native of East Africa where it grows to a height of about 15 feet (4·6 m.) in coastal woodland and scrub around Mombasa (where John Kirk discovered it in 1874) and Kwale. As in all members of this family, the stamens are clustered at the end of a tubular sheath which envelops the long style, and which is fused to the petals as an integral unit. The elegantly cut petals, which are quite natural and not induced by cultivation, and their bright colour, have made this species popular in gardens and glasshouses.

Perhaps the best known *Hibiscus* is *H. rosa-sinensis*, which is grown throughout the tropics, often escaping from the gardens in which it is initially planted. Sometimes called the Shoe Flower, because the mucilaginous flowers were used for polishing shoes in the West Indies, it is a native of China, where it has been cultivated for centuries for its large, bright red blooms. Three other species, originally from the Far East, are cultivated. The Cotton Rose, *H. mutabilis*, has white morning-flowers which change to a deep pink colour by evening. *H. syriacus*, a native of China, Korea and Indo-China, has pink, purple, bluish or white flowers and, as its numerous cultivars suggest, has a long history of cultivation. It is the hardiest species and can stand a considerable amount of frost.

Bombax costatum (C) may grow to a height of 50 feet (15 m.) in its savannah habitat in West Africa from Senegal to Nigeria. Its bark is rough and spiny and the twigs are densely hairy, with star-shaped hairs when young. A closely related West African species, *B. buonopozense*, has deep pink to red flowers. In both species the flowers appear when the leaves have been shed in January or February, and the crowded blossoms open in a burst of colour. Shortly after flowering the cylindrical or globose fruits fill with seeds and down and lengthen to 6 inches (15 cm.).

The Kapok, or Silk-cotton Tree, *Ceiba pentandra* is thought by some to be a native of Africa, and by others to be an ancient introduction from South America. Whatever its true history, it is a characteristic West African tree with a thick buttressed trunk, covered in prickles and growing to a height of over 160 feet (49 m.). The tree is often found scattered around settlements and also occurs in secondary forest—that is, forest which has regenerated after the disturbance or destruction of completely 'natural' forest by man. The main branches tend to be horizontal, thus giving the crown a pyramidal appearance, and a mature tree may carry between 1000 and 4000 fruits. Like the *Bombax* species shown on plate 115, these fruits contain grey or white seed-wool, or

Kapok, which is harvested for use in pillows, quilts, saddles and similar articles. The seeds are used in soups and the seed-oil serves as a lighting fuel. In addition, the trunks of *C. pentandra*, when felled and burnt out, make lightweight canoes; so, although this species tends to become a weed-tree, it has many uses.

There are over two hundred species of *Dombeya* distributed in Africa, Madagascar, and the islands of the Indian Ocean. Species such as the rose-pink flowered *D. calantha* from tropical Africa, the white and pink flowered *D. burgessiae*, and the pink flowered *D. acutangula* from Mauritius all have flowers 1 inch (2·5 cm.) in diameter, massed into round and occasionally pendulous heads of 20 or more. Each individual flower resembles that of a small hollyhock and the flowering heads, often fragrant, attract swarms of insects. These shrubs, between 10 and 15 feet (3–4·6 m.) tall make splendid garden plants in the tropics; hybrids have been raised in cultivation. The genus commemorates the French medical man, botanist and traveller, Joseph Dombey (1742–1794), who made extensive botanical collections in Peru and Chile with the Spaniards Ruiz Lopez and Pavon. He was not the most fortunate of men: the Spanish government prevented him from publishing his work, the living plants he brought to Spain rotted in the customs house, his collections were never properly studied and published, and he himself died in prison. *D. mastersii* (A) comes from the Sudan, Eritrea and Ethiopia. Early in 1867 the species first flowered at Kew Gardens and this event was reported on 26 January in the *Gardeners Chronicle* by Maxwell T. Masters, whom the specific epithet, given to the plant shortly afterwards, commemorates. Masters noted that the movements of the long stamens in the flower may transfer pollen from the short stamens to the stigma-lobes, should cross-pollination not occur.

Not strictly native to tropical Africa, the Lowveld Chestnut, *Sterculia murex* (D) from the eastern Transvaal occurs in rocky habitats. It is a quick-growing tree and in good conditions rises to a height of 30 feet (9 m.). With dark green leaves of 5–7 leaflets, it has unspectacular greenish yellow flowers tinged with red. What is remarkable, however, is the way in which the tiny 5-lobed ovary expands into a massive woody and warted fruit. Comparison with the sterculiaceous fruits of *Firmiana* and *Pterocymbium* on plate 116, shows the great variation found in the family. Each of the 5 pods eventually splits into a boat-shaped structure with the seeds 'moored' along one side. The inside of the pod is covered with small hairs irritating to the skin, so care must be taken in removing the grape-sized edible seeds, which taste like Sweet Chestnuts.

STERCULIACEAE

Dombeya mastersii
A1 part of flowering branch × ⅔.

Sterculia murex, Lowveld Chestnut
D1 part of flowering branch × ⅔.
D2 part of fruiting branch × ⅔.
D3 mature leaf × ⅔.

MALVACEAE

Hibiscus schizopetalus
B1 part of flowering branch with buds × ⅔.

BOMBACACEAE

Bombax costatum
C1 part of flowering branch × ⅔. C2 leaf × ⅔.

Plate 58   TROPICAL AND CENTRAL AFRICA

The genus *Euphorbia,* which includes the spurges, exhibits a fascinating range in habit, with one extreme found in the succulent species which, in response to arid environmental factors, have often become almost indistinguishable from cacti. *E. meloformis,* for example, closely resembles the Mexican *Echinocactus ornatus,* a compact bun-shaped plant. Tree and bush euphorbias exist as well as erect or creeping herbs, and they may or may not possess leaves. Some species have spiny stems, in others the stems are fleshy and rod-like, angled, tubercular, broadly winged or warty. But for all this vegetative diversity the inflorescence structure, the cyathium (see plate 35), is a constant feature throughout the genus. The unrelated *Thonningia* is a curious red parasite, often found on euphorbias and confined to tropical Africa, while *Cissus* is found in all tropical areas and belongs to the grape family (*Vitaceae*).

Euphorbia bupleurifolia (E) was originally described from cultivated material in 1797, probably collected by the Viennese gardeners Franz Boos and Georg Scholl during expeditions they made between 1786 and 1798 for the Royal Gardens at Schoenbrunn. Francis Masson also introduced it to Kew in 1791. The species grows in cool places south from Natal, into the eastern Cape region. Even for a euphorbia its bulbous stem, up to about 8 inches (20 cm.) tall, covered with the crowded, protruding remains of leaf-bases, is unusual.

Euphorbia stolonifera (C) has well developed, spineless branches up to about 2 feet (61 cm.) high arising from an underground and much reduced main stem from which spreading rhizomes arise to produce a diffuse plant. A central, shortly-stalked male cyathium is surrounded by 5 to 8 branches, each terminating in a bisexual cyathium. Unlike *E. bupleurifolia* there are no persistent leaves, but for a short time on new growth tiny juvenile ones $\frac{1}{5}$ inch (5 mm.) long appear. *E. stolonifera* was discovered in 1920 by Rudolf Marloth, and is restricted to Laingsburg District of Cape Province.

A large spiny tree up to 30 feet (9 m.) tall, *E. ingens* (B), the Naboom, has straight erect 4 to 7 winged branches regularly constricted into segments about 6 inches (15 cm.) long. Rudimentary leaves appear on new growth but these soon drop off and it is the green stem which has taken over the photosynthetic role, each wing being 2 inches (5 cm.) or more broad. Flowers and spines arise from 'eyes' situated along the narrow ridge of the wings, each 'eye' producing 3-stalked clusters each composed of 2 to 5 inflorescences, the whole measuring about 1 inch (2·5 cm.) long. The inflorescence (or cyathium) consists of a cuplike involucre provided with 5 lobes and 5 glands. In this species the sexes seem to be

separated on different individuals and the cyathia contain either all male or all female flowers. It grows in the Kalahari area and into Natal and the Transvaal, and was discovered in 1831 by Jean François or Johann Franz Drege on one of his numerous early collecting trips in South Africa between 1826 and 1834.

The African peoples have sometimes endowed euphorbias with supernatural powers: the Xhosa tribesmen, for instance, on rearing twins, collect and plant a pair of tree euphorbias near the entrance of their hut to ward away evil spirits. These plants persist long after the dwellings have fallen into decay. The Zulu chief, Dingaan, is said to have had his throne built beneath a particularly fine *E. ingens* specimen in Zululand, near the site where Piet Retief and his Boer followers were slaughtered on 6 February 1838.

A variable species, *Euphorbia milii* (A), is native in Madagascar and is widely cultivated under the name of *E. splendens,* which is really a different but closely related plant and possibly only a variety of *E. milii.* It makes a fine glasshouse plant with its large red inflorescence bracts. The flowers appear spasmodically throughout the year but the leaves are borne only on the young growth.

The genus *Cissus* contains some three hundred and fifty mainly tropical species, with *C. adenopodus* (D) occurring through much of tropical Africa. It was first found by M. T. Dawe in 1905 growing in the Mufukamata Forest of Uganda, and thinking it to be a decorative vine, he sent a root to Kew where it grew vigorously under glass and from there it has since been distributed to other growers. The flowers are inconspicuous, and there is nothing special about the globose black fruits about $\frac{2}{3}$ inch (17 mm.) in diameter, but the vigorous trailing stems and highly ornamental foliage of the leaves, with red hairs scattered over both surfaces, make it useful as a hot-house plant.

The genus *Thonningia* consists of two species, one in Madagascar and the other *T. sanguinea* (F), a variable species with a distribution in West Africa, Congo, Sudan, East Africa and Angola. It parasitises the roots of a wide range of forest trees from many different families and is particularly common in regenerating forest; all that one sees of the plant above ground is the inflorescence. The horizontal underground stem or rhizome gives rise at flowering time to groups of stalked inflorescences invested in rigid crimson or pink bracts, which later turn brown. Each inflorescence contains many greatly reduced and simplified flowers which are either all male or all female in any one head. Plants of *Thonningia* would seem to be long-lived and probably spread by means of their branching rhizome for seed is rarely found.

EUPHORBIACEAE

Euphorbia milii
A1 part of flowering shoot × $\frac{2}{3}$.

E. ingens, Naboom
B1 part of flowering stem × $\frac{2}{3}$.
B2 habit sketch × $\frac{1}{50}$.

E. stolonifera
C1 flowering plant × $\frac{2}{3}$. C2 cyathium × $2\frac{2}{3}$.

E. bupleurifolia
E1 flowering plant × $\frac{2}{3}$.

VITACEAE

Cissus adenopodus
D1 inflorescence × $\frac{2}{3}$. D2 leafy shoot × $\frac{2}{3}$.

BALANOPHORACEAE

Thonningia sanguinea
F1 flowering plant with bud and underground rhizome × $\frac{2}{3}$ (N.B. soil level)
F2 male flower sectioned × $\frac{2}{3}$.
F3 part of rhizome with female flower × $\frac{2}{3}$.

A1

B1

B2

C1

C2

D1

D2

E1

F1

F2

F3

Plate 59   TROPICAL AND CENTRAL AFRICA

A many-branched, spiny shrub or tree growing to about 40 feet (12 m.) tall, *Oncoba spinosa* (D) was discovered in Arabia in 1775 (its generic name is merely a latinization of the Arabic word for the plant), but it is now known to be widespread throughout West, East and South Africa. A number of uses have been found for the various parts of the plant in its native countries; the yellow pulp of the fruit contains an oil, although because of the number of seeds it is difficult to extract; the roots and leaves are used in medical decoctions; and rattles, snuff-boxes and ankle-decorations are made out of the globular fruits. The attractive, fragrant flowers, which are terminal or borne on short axillary shoots, measure about 3½ inches (9 cm.) in diameter. The fruits, whose edible pulp was mentioned above, are yellowish and woody.

The one hundred or more species of *Dissotis*, all African, contain both small-flowered creepers and erect, larger-flowered shrubs. *D. princeps* (B) belongs to the second group, being a shrub up to about 8 feet (2·5 m.) tall with handsome large flowers very reminiscent of the better-known South American plant of the same family, *Tibouchina semidecandra*, much cultivated in subtropical and warm temperate countries. The remarkable stamens, 5 of them short and 5 of them long, with their extraordinary shape and poral dehiscence, are very characteristic of the family.

A weedy plant, though one with a useful ability to stabilize dunes in the dry, sandy coastal regions in which it grows, *Calotropis procera* (A) grows to a maximum height of about 15 feet (4·6 m.) and has finely woolly young shoots and inflorescences. The flowers are followed by large inflated ovoid fruits 4 inches (10 cm.) or more in length and packed with a mass of hairs attached to the seeds and which provides an inferior substitute for kapok. The inner bark yields 'mudar' or 'yercum' fibre which makes strong rope but is difficult to extract; the milky juice or latex from the stem is used, mixed with salt, to remove the hair from hides and for many native medicinal purposes. Being extremely nicely adapted to the meagre water supply of its arid environment, *C. procera* usually succumbs in cultivation to overwatering. The species is one of six in a tropical African and Asian genus.

One of about twenty tropical and South African species in its genus, and widely cultivated in the tropics for its profusion of dramatically coloured, trumpet-shaped flowers, *Rothmannia longiflora* (C) is a shrub or small tree about 15 feet (4·6 m.) tall with many branched stems and shiny foliage. Its specific epithet refers to the length of the flowers, which may exceed 10 inches (25 cm.) and are held more or less erect. These are later replaced with globose fruits about 2 inches (5 cm.) in diameter and crowned with the remains of the calyx. In the natural state this plant (which has also been known as *Randia maculata* and *Gardenia speciosa*) grows in secondary forest in West Africa, the Congo, Angola and East Africa. With a similar range, *R. whitfieldii* is a larger species capable of forming a tree up to 40 feet (12 m.) in height and notable for its pendulous flowers, velvety brown on the outside and white inside, which are fragrant and even larger than those of *R. longiflora*.

ASCLEPIADACEAE

Calotropis procera
A1 part of flowering shoot × ⅔. A2 flower × 2.

MELASTOMATACEAE

Dissotis princeps
B1 part of flowering stem × ⅔.
B2 stamen × 1⅓.

RUBIACEAE

Rothmannia longiflora (syn. *Randia maculata, Gardenia speciosa*)
C1 part of flowering stem × ⅔.
C2 flower opened up × ⅔.

FLACOURTIACEAE

Oncoba spinosa
D1 flowering shoot × ⅔.
D2 fruit on part of stem × ⅔.

A2

A1

B1

B2

C2

C1

D2

D1

Plate 60 TROPICAL AND CENTRAL AFRICA

Several economically important plants belong to the families *Rubiaceae* and *Verbenaceae*, members of which are illustrated on the plate opposite. Among those worth mentioning, though not depicted, are *Cinchona*, whose bark produces the drug quinine; *Rubia tinctorum*, or Madder, from whose roots comes the red dye alizarin; *Uncaria gambir*, which provides the astringent 'gambier' used in Malaysia; and the Indian *Tectona grandis*, better known as Teak, yielding a timber valued for its rich grain, hardness, durability and colour.

Its deep red flowers have made *Clerodendrum splendens* (A) a popular cultivated climber both in the gardens of its native West Africa and in European hot-houses. In the wild, it inhabits forests from Senegal through the Congo to Angola and appears to be commonest in the north-west part of that area. *C. thomsonae* is another widely grown West African species, and has the added attraction of a white calyx.

Also a favourite in hot-houses and tropical gardens, but found in both western and eastern tropical Africa, *Clerodendrum capitatum* (C) is a small, thorny shrub or tree adapted to forest or savannah habitats, with heavily scented flowers. The hollow twigs are used to make pipe-stems and for tapping palm wine. The genus *Clerodendrum* (sometimes also spelt *Clerodendron*) as a whole occurs throughout the tropics and subtropics and contains about four hundred species.

Named after Peter Bally, who, with F. A. Bruce, first described the plant (unfortunately using the name *C. helicoides*, which had already been used), *Ceropegia ballyana* (B) was first collected, in Kenya, by Mrs Joy Adamson, author of *Born Free*. Mrs Adamson discovered the plant in the Mathews Range in 1945, and it has since been found growing in Teita and the Kitui District, and in the Mbulu District of Tanzania. The long, twisted corolla tubes are a good example of the bizarre features common in many members of the genus.

Only three of the forty or so species in the genus *Coffea* are grown in any quantity for commercial purposes, and of those the most widely cultivated is *C. arabica* (D), Arabian Coffee, a native of the Ethiopian Highlands from which it was introduced into Arabia at an early date, and thence taken to the East Indies, by the Dutch, late in the 17th century. Only later, however, did material suitable for cultivation reach Amsterdam, and, via Holland, the Dutch territory of Surinam, and Brazil, which now produces over half the world's coffee crop. At about the same time, the French introduced the plant into the West Indies.

The 'bourbon' variety of coffee differs somewhat in its origins from the 'typica' variety described above, having been brought to the island of Réunion (formerly called Bourbon) off the coast of Madagascar, from Arabia, and then spread throughout the world. 'Robusta' coffee, *C. canephora*, native from Guinea to the Congo and Uganda, is grown mainly in Africa and Asia but was introduced from Brussels into the East Indies. 'Liberian' coffee, *C. liberica*, has much the same distribution but produces inferior fruits. 'Peaberry' refers to abnormal coffee fruits, regarded as superior to regular types, in which only one of the two seeds develops. Such commercial names as 'Costa Rican', 'Kenya' and 'Blue Mountain' emphasize the importance of a type's origin, in determining its flavour. Although the plant is cultivated primarily for its fruits, its wood is also used to make furniture.

To prepare coffee for consumption, the ripe fruits are stripped from the stems, the fleshy coat is removed and the seeds are dried and bagged. Seeds should be roasted only just before they are sold, and only ground just before use. Boiling water should never be used to prepare the drink, as the flavour and aroma are driven off at this temperature; very hot water is sufficient. Coffee is valued, of course, not only for its pleasant flavour, but also for the stimulant caffeine that it contains.

The two hundred or so species in the genus *Mussaenda* are characterised by certain of the flowers having a colourful, enlarged sepal. Although sometimes shrubby, Ashanti Blood, *M. erythrophylla* (E), found from Guinea west and south through much of tropical Africa, is normally a tall climbing plant. The flowers turn pink when old, and the fruits are composed of numerous seed capsules covered with hair. The species, which is cultivated in many parts of the world, is best propagated by seed, since, as the shoots are hollow, cuttings are difficult to root.

Though said to include among its medicinal properties the ability to cure constipation, caries, stomach upsets, fevers and venereal disease, *Nauclea latifolia* (F) is a plant to be treated with care, since it may also induce abortion and is used in the preparation of arrow poison. In one area of its distribution, which ranges from Senegal to Angola in the west and south to Uganda in the east, it bears the slightly sinister yet stoical common name 'Tsoja-Tsuru', which means 'If father dead, eat half; if orphaned, eat all'. A small tree or shrub found in savannah woodland, it bears fragrant flowers and juicy, pitted red fruit that are spherical and edible, and give the species its common English name of Guinea or African Peach. The genus *Nauclea*, whose thirty-five or so tropical species occur in Africa, Asia and Oceana, differs from the related genera *Mitragyna*, *Uncaria* and *Adina* in having flowers fused together, instead of free, at the ovaries and calyx-tubes.

A1

A2

B1

C1

C2

D1

D2

D3

D4

E1

F1

F2

F3

Plate 61   TROPICAL AND CENTRAL AFRICA

The most remarkable of the characteristics of the stout creeping shrub *Strophanthus preussii* (A) and the majority of the other species in its genus, is the trailing tip that extends from each petal. In this species they hang down for from 5 to 12 inches (12·5–30 cm.) and entangle themselves in the surrounding foliage as the flower falls. The corollas, from which these purple trailers dangle, are white on their first opening, their throats streaked with purple, but gradually turn, through cream, to a dirty orange. The species is found, growing to a height of about 10 feet (3 m.), in scrub and secondary woodland (woodland that has regrown after having been cleared by man or fire) in Central and West Africa; the wood is used locally in the making of bows and the sap as a constituent in arrow poison. A sister species, *S. gratus* (E), which has a more limited range within the same area, lacks the extended petal-tips but compensates by having exaggerated appendages around the mouth of the corolla. This evergreen climber has flowers that vary in colour from white to rose, the outside, the appendages and the throat being darker in colour. As is the case with many tropical plants, the flowers are particularly fragrant in the evening, perhaps correlated with a decreasing volatilisation of the perfume and an increased sensitivity of the nostrils as they recover from the heat of the day. The plumed, sharp-edged seeds contain a high yield of the drug strophanthin.

Another poisonous species, from a genus in the same family as the above, occurring in the drier parts of northern tropical Africa, right across from the west to the east and in Arabia, is *Adenium obesum* (D). In form, it resembles a miniature Baobab (plate 76) while the action of the poison it contains, which interferes with the nervous action of the heart, is similar to that of digitalin, a Foxglove extract. It grows to a height of about 10 feet (3 m.) and its thick succulent tissues are filled with copious milky sap. Since it normally flowers on bare branches, only after the leaves have been shed, it would appear that the specimen used for the illustration opposite had its flowering rhythm upset by having been cultivated under glasshouse conditions in a temperate region.

A particularly attractive denizen of the evergreen forests of West Africa from Gambia to Ghana is *Combretum grandiflorum* (B), a climber usually found on the edges of clearings, which reaches heights of up to 20 feet (6 m.). Among its pleasant attributes are the richness in nectar of its flowers, which children suck. In fact, the shape of the flowers with their abundant nectar, the way in which they are borne and, above all, their colour points to the probability that they are pollinated by nectar-seeking birds. The fruits are characteristic of the genus, being 1-seeded, dry and winged.

The discovery of *Napoleonaea imperialis* (C) or *Napoleona* as it is commonly but incorrectly spelt, was one of the results of a saga nearly as extended and eventful as that of the Emperor's campaigns. Ambroise Marie François Joseph Palisot de Beauvois (1752–1820) set off in 1786 with Captain Landolphe for the Gulf of Guinea to establish a trading colony, a pretext that, on Beauvois' part concealed an ambition to botanise in Africa. From November 1786 to the end of 1787, while two hundred and fifty of the company of three hundred died of fever, Beauvois, himself sick, explored the delta between Benin and Warri, sending his collections to A. L. de Jussieu in Paris. By February 1788, Beauvois was so ill that Captain Landolphe put him on a slave-ship bound for Haiti, a dubious gesture of concern, but perhaps the only one possible. On arrival in Haiti, Beauvois, who had recovered very slowly on a journey that had proved fatal to a number of the other passengers, indefatigably continued his botanical studies, despite continued and involved crises, only returning to France, after further explorations in North America, in 1798. Not until J. Heudelot and Thomas Whitfield found, in the 1840's, another species which was independently given the names *N. heudelotii* (1844) and *N. whitfieldii* (1848), and at first mistaken for *N. imperialis*, was the genus rediscovered. *N. imperialis* forms a tree about 20 feet (6 m.) tall and is found in rain forest from Nigeria, through the Cameroons, into the Congo and Angola. The dissection of the flower in the plate opposite (C2) shows 4 of the stamens with the filaments bent over towards the style, under the rim of which the anthers are held.

APOCYNACEAE

Strophanthus preussii
A1 part of flowering shoot × ⅔.
A2 corolla opened out × 1⅓.

Adenium obesum
D1 flowering shoot × ⅔.

Strophanthus gratus
E1 part of flowering stem × ⅔. E2 fruit × ⅔.
E3 seeds × ⅔.

COMBRETACEAE

Combretum grandiflorum
B1 part of flowering and fruiting stems × ⅔.

LECYTHIDACEAE

Napoleonaea imperialis
C1 part of flowering shoot × ⅔.
C2 section of flower showing (from centre) stigma, a row of fertile stamens, a row of coronal staminodes, 2 filiform staminodes and a portion of the corolla with 1 lobe × 1⅓.
C3 fruit × ⅔.

A2

A1

B1

D1

C3

C2

C1

E3

E2

E1

Plate 62   TROPICAL AND CENTRAL AFRICA

The exotic 20 to 70 foot (6–21 m.) Sausage Tree takes its name from the fruits, 1 to 2 feet (30–61 cm.) in length, that hang down from the branches, sometimes even touching the ground. *Kigelia africana* (A) (the name of the genus is derived from the vernacular word used for the tree in Mozambique) is a member of a family of tropical and subtropical shrubs, and, especially, woody climbers. Many of them have large attractive flowers but those which flower by night, *Kigelia* among them, are pervaded by odours reminiscent of fermentation and are pollinated by bats. Almost as notable as the fruit are the often even longer pendulous inflorescences that precede them. The plant illustrated, drawn from a pressed specimen, does not show fully the convoluted and crumpled nature of the petals, nor the normal position of the stamens, which are usually hidden behind the two upper lobes of the variously coloured and sized corolla. *K. africana* is a variable species with a range throughout tropical Africa. It is a good example of how, in a widespread and variable plant, the different variations have, at first, been described as separate species from different areas, but gradually, with increased explorations and collections, it has been realized that they really belong to one diverse species. No less than ten species have been recognized in what is today called *K. africana*.

The wide cultivation of the African Tulip Tree, *Spathodea campanulata* (B), is due to its fine scarlet flowers and to its reputation as an attractor of sun-birds which are the natural pollinators. It is possible, however, that its employment for the latter purpose may conceal mildly sadistic impulses on the part of the planter, since the inflated calices of the unopened buds, borne high in the dark green crown of the tree, have the unpleasant property of squirting sharp-beaked and probing birds, with an evil-smelling and tasting liquid which is secreted in the cavity between the calyx and corolla. The flowers of this 20 to 70 foot (6–21 m.) tree, which occurs in savannah on the fringes of secondary woodland, open in the early morning, and last for about 3 days. The fruits, shaped like spear heads pointing upwards from the ends of the branches, are 5 to 10 inches (12·5–25 cm.) long. The roots are shallow and sometimes give rise to suckers. Despite its most popular name, *S. campanulata* is in no way related to the Tulip Tree of China and North America. Other common names are Scarlet Bell Tree and Fountain Tree.

BIGNONIACEAE

Kigelia africana, Sausage Tree
A1 inflorescence × ⅔. A2 leaf × ⅔.
A3 fruit × ⅔.
A4 habit sketch of young fruiting tree.

Spathodea campanulata, African Tulip Tree, Scarlet Bell Tree, Fountain Tree
B1 flowering and budding shoot × ⅔.

A1

A2

A3

A4

B1

Plate 63 TROPICAL AND CENTRAL AFRICA

Although the chief centre for the family *Labiatae* is the Mediterranean, the African flora nevertheless includes a large number of genera and species, many of which are tall and shrubby in comparison with their more temperate counterparts.

The beautiful variegated and multicoloured leaves of some of the one hundred and fifty Old World *Coleus* species give them value as glasshouse plants. Dr Friedrich Welwitsch discovered *C. frederici* (A) during his travels through the Pungo Andongo province of Angola in April 1857, although the species did not become popular in European glasshouses until the 1930's. It first flowered at Kew in December 1931 from seed sent there by the well known field botanist and specialist in the Angola flora, J. Gossweiler. Intensely blue, cymose clusters of flowers borne terminally on inflorescences up to 10 inches (25 cm.) long in the winter are the plant's chief hothouse attraction. Although totally unrelated, the corolla has parts which resemble in some ways those of members of the Sweet Pea alliance; a small 'standard' and a larger, somewhat inflated 'keel', in which the stamens and style nestle. In detail, a tongue-like appendage projects from one side of the ovary above the 4 compressed fruits or nutlets.

Wild Dagga, *Leonotis leonurus* (B), was amongst the first South African species to be grown in Europe, having been recorded in cultivation as early as 1663 in the Netherlands. Although readily propagated from offsets, cuttings or seeds and resistant to mild frost, it has never become a popular garden plant, which is surprising because its 2 to 7 whorls of vivid orange flowers are very ornamental. It grows up to 8 feet (2·3 m.) tall and occurs from the Transvaal through Natal into Cape Province and Cape Peninsula. Its 4-angled stems bear pairs of unstalked, narrow leaves 4 inches (10 cm.) long. Each whorl of flowers really consists of 2 rows, the upper of which opens first.

The rather similar *L. nepetifolia* occurs as a weed in Africa and many other tropical areas. Its orange whorls of flowers, borne on shoots 4 to 8 feet (1·2–2·4 m.) tall, make it, however, a charming weed and almost welcome. There is a variety *africana*, which, in contrast, bears cream coloured flowers.

Alexandrine P. F. Tinne, who, with her mother and aunt made a journey in central Africa from 1856–1858, and discovered *Tinnea aethiopica* (D), gave their family name to this genus of thirty tropical African species. This species ranges from Mali and Nigeria to the Sudan, East Africa and Malawi and forms a twiggy shrub 4 to 10 feet (1·2–3 m.) tall. The flowers occur in terminal elongated spikes and have a 2-lipped inflated calyx flattened transversely; the broad corolla tubes, also transversely compressed, have projecting 3-lobed lower lips. Although the plant had been previously discovered by Captain James Grant in the Umyoso Forest during explorations of the Upper Nile with Speke, it was Alexandrine Tinne who sent seeds to her brother in Liverpool after finding the species. When the plant flowered it delighted growers with its profusion of rich, fragrant maroon-purple blossoms. In fruit the hairy club-shaped nutlets with a structure like a miniature parachute are interesting and unusual for this family.

Pendulous bell-shaped flowers borne on large inflorescences make *Trichodesma physaloides* (C) one of the more conspicuous spring veld flowers. It grows in the vicinity of Pretoria and Johannesburg, but has a distribution northwards into Rhodesia. Its reddish, hairless stems may reach 2 feet (61 cm.) in height and mature leaves, 1½ inches (38 mm.) long and covered with small white tubercles, appear only after the flowers have gone. The flattened ovary, curiously, has a thin transparent roof through which the ovules inside can be seen. Another plant in this genus of about thirty-five species is *T. africanum*, a hardy scabrid herb 2 to 3 feet (61–91 cm.) tall, which bears small yellow flowers with brown spotted throats. It is found in West Africa, Mauritania, and the Cape Verde Islands, eastward to the Red Sea and southward to South Africa.

The genera *Cordia*, with sometimes decorative white, yellow or bright orange flowers in cymes, and *Heliotropium*, with characteristic curled and unfurling cymes of small white flowers, are other borages well represented in Africa.

LABIATAE

Coleus frederici
A1 part of flowering stem × ⅔.

Leonotis leonurus, Wild Dagga
B1 part of flowering stem × ⅔.

Tinnea aethiopica
D1 part of flowering shoot × ⅔.
D2 fruits × ⅔. D3 fruiting ovary × ⅔.
D4 nutlet × 4.

BORAGINACEAE

Trichodesma physaloides
C1 part of flowering stem × ⅔.

A1

B1

C1

D1

D2

D3

D4

Plate 64 TROPICAL AND CENTRAL AFRICA

Like most of the fifty or so *Crossandra* species, *C. nilotica* ssp. *massaica* (A) tends to have a short flowering season in cultivation. Its large 5-lobed brick- to orange-red corollas, massed to form an inflorescence 2 inches (5 cm.) long, contrast elegantly with its shiny, deep green leaves, making it a most attractive plant. The plant illustrated is very similar to subspecies *nilotica* and also to an African subspecies of the essentially Asian *C. infundibuliformis*. The plant illustrated grows in Ghana, the Congo and eastward to Tanzania and Kenya at altitudes between 3450–7200 feet (1050–2200 m.), and was painted from material grown at Kew.

William Henry Harvey (1811–1866) must have named *Ruttya* in honour of Dr John Rutty purely as a token of esteem, for—although this physician wrote a natural history of Dublin (1772)—he apparently had nothing to do with the six species in this tropical African genus. An elegant shrub which occasionally suffers from a paucity of flowers in cultivation, *R. fruticosa* (B) grows in open, arid, scrubby habitats in the wild. Distributed from southern Arabia, through Somaliland, to Tanzania, it sometimes attains a height of 15 feet (4·6 m.). As many as 40 flowers may be clustered along a single slender branch, but often only 5 to 10 are found. Each of the striking corollas has a warty, shiny black throat, which glistens with nectar, in contrast to the orange-red corolla tube and corolla lobes. A form with yellow flowers sometimes occurs. *R. fruticosa* was first discovered in Somaliland, and only later found to extend further south into East Africa. It has been cultivated at Kew for some years—certainly since the mid-1950's—and produces flowers there every year.

Especially diverse in Madagascar, the genus *Hypoestes* comprises one hundred and fifty species found in the Old World tropics. Wooded monsoon forest in northern Madagascar is the only known habitat of *H. taeniata* (C) where it was discovered and the material first described and named in 1927. A woody herb which reaches about 2 to 3 feet (61–91 cm.) in height, its diffuse, sizeable inflorescence contains many characteristically slender magenta-purple flowers with long, curling corolla lobes. These have a rather worm-like appearance, referred to in the specific epithet: *Taenia* is a genus of tapeworm. *H. taeniata* has been successfully grown at Kew for a number of years, making a fine display in pots on a hothouse staging. Propagation may be accomplished by rooting cuttings.

Its richly decorative purple-veined leaf-rosette crowned by several spikes of small lilac flowers, make *Stenandriopsis guineensis* (E) valuable in the hothouse, particularly in shady corners, as the species is a herb of the forest floor in nature. One of fifteen or so *Stenandriopsis* species, this species extends from Sierra Leone in West Africa to the Congo, Sudan and Uganda. It was first described in 1847 from material from coastal Guinea, without a more specific location; then Gustav Mann collected it in 1859 and 1862 from the island of Fernando Po at a height of 2000 feet (610 m.). Until recently it has been classified as a *Crossandra* species. It was first introduced into cultivation by the famous, but now disbanded, firm of Veitch as a house plant or for growing under glass.

Sir John Kirk, who accompanied David Livingstone on the Zambesi expedition, introduced *Streptocarpus kirkii* (D) into Europe as seedlings. In a Wardian-case in which he was sending some Tanzanian ferns to Kew 'he had', to use Hooker's words, 'with characteristic foresight, sowed seeds of plants of which he had no herbarium specimens worth sending.' The plants thrived and flowered in 1884. *S. kirkii* is allied to *S. caulescens* which can be distinguished from the former by its more reddish-violet flowers having less open mouths. Both are among several closely related species called the 'caulescens' group, all natives of dry, rocky habitats in East Africa. Another interesting species, although not illustrated, *S. saxorum* has conspicuously succulent stems. It was first described in 1893 from material found on rocks by C. Holst in the Usambara Mountains near Lutindi. Very hairy leaves and large lilac flowers distinguish *S. hirsutissimus* from *S. saxorum*; it is found only in the Morogoro district. *S. stomandra*, from the Nguru Mountains of Tanzania, was first described as recently as 1958. Its unequal corolla lobes bear exaggerated, scooped-out lips.

ACANTHACEAE

Crossandra nilotica ssp. *massaica*
A1 part of flowering stem × $\frac{2}{3}$.
A2 corolla tube opened to show stamens × $1\frac{1}{3}$.
A3 flower and calyx × 1.

Ruttya fruticosa
B1 flowering twig × $\frac{2}{3}$.
B2 side view of corolla × $1\frac{1}{3}$.
B3 front view of corolla × $1\frac{1}{3}$.
B4 stigma, style, ovary and calyx × $1\frac{1}{3}$.

Hypoestes taeniata
C1 part of flowering stem × $\frac{2}{3}$.
C2 flower × $1\frac{1}{3}$. C3 calyx and bud × 2.

Stenandriopsis guineensis
E1 flowers and leaves × $\frac{2}{3}$. E2 flower × $1\frac{1}{3}$.

GESNERIACEAE

Streptocarpus kirkii
D1 part of plant with flowers, buds and fruits × $\frac{2}{3}$. D2 flower × 2. D3 fruit × $1\frac{1}{3}$.

A1

A3

B1

B2

B3

B4

C1

C2

C3

D1

D2

D3

E1

E2

Plate 65   TROPICAL AND CENTRAL AFRICA

Wherever the giant lobelias and senecios occur (see plate 56) on the upper slopes of the East African Highlands, there is, in addition, a characteristic scrub composed of certain species of *Helichrysum. H. meyeri-johannis* (A), a perennial, stoloniferous herb is found on Mounts Elgon, Kenya and Kilimanjaro where on occasions it hybridizes with related species. The tiny florets appear inconspicuous beside the soft pink bracts of the involucre which surround them.

A relatively small member of the genus whose giants play *diva* to *Helichrysum's* chorus on the mountains of this area is *Senecio adnivalis* (B), which grows to a height of up to 26 feet (8 m.) at about an altitude of 12,000 feet (3660 m.) on Ruwenzori in Uganda where it was discovered by Morely Thomas Dawe (1880-1943). Like the lobelias mentioned on plate 55, it has developed ingenious mechanisms with which to withstand the harsh conditions of its environment. The upper sides of the leaves are shiny, so that they reflect a great amount of the light and heat, and have a thickly waxed, impermeable surface. In addition, the sides of the leaves droop during the day, thus presenting themselves to the sun's rays at an acute angle. The undersurface is covered with silvery, woolly hairs that cut down water loss and, again, help to reflect the heat. The yellow flowers are surrounded by, and contrast with, the purplish bracts. Five varieties of *S. adnivalis,* all displaying differences in the hairiness of the leaf, and the shape and dimensions of the leaf stalk, have been recognized.

One of a genus of thirty Old World daisies, and a weed, though attractive, *Emilia coccinea* (C) probably originated in tropical Africa but is now established from the New World, including Jamaica where it bears the name Cupid's Paintbrush, to the tropics of Asia. The flowers range in colour from yellow through orange to scarlet and crimson. The species rarely exceeds 12 inches (30 cm.) in height.

COMPOSITAE

Helichrysum meyeri-johannis
A1 flowering plant × $\frac{1}{24}$.
A2 involucral bract × $4\frac{2}{3}$.

Senecio adnivalis
B1 top of flowering shoot × $\frac{2}{3}$.
B2 disc-floret × $3\frac{1}{3}$. B3 ray-floret × $3\frac{1}{3}$.
B4 leaf × $\frac{2}{3}$. B5 habit sketch × $\frac{1}{22}$.

Emilia coccinea, Cupid's Paintbrush
C1 part of flowering stem × $\frac{2}{3}$.
C2 young leafy shoot × $\frac{2}{3}$.
C3 part of fruiting stem × $\frac{2}{3}$.
C4 fruiting head × 2. C5 seed × 6.

A1

B1

B2

B3

B4

B5

C1

C2

C3

C4

C5

Plate 66 TROPICAL AND CENTRAL AFRICA

Although South Africa is notable for its rich flora of bulbous plants, the forests and savannah of the rest of Africa also contain a number of intriguing monocotyledons. There are many species of *Asparagus, Dracaena, Aloe, Anthericum, Chlorophytum* (Spider Plant) and *Sansevieria* (Mother-in-law's Tongue). *Crinum* and *Hypoxis* have representatives in both parts but *Gloriosa* is essentially a tropical African genus.

Crinum, which occurs through tropical and subtropical regions of the world, comprises about one hundred species of bulbous herbs, often large and with clusters of showy flowers. The genus differs from the South African *Amaryllis* in having a fairly well developed floral tube in which the stamens are inserted, instead of an inconspicuous or absent tube with stamens inserted on the base of the petals. Like many plants that grow in areas having a marked dry season, most crinums pass the unfavourable period in a dormant state.

Crinum ornatum (C) is a West African species, found in moist habitats in such states as Sierra Leone, Ghana, Togo, Nigeria and the Cameroons. It is an attractive and gregarious plant with a flowering stalk which may be 1 to 3 feet (30–91 cm.) tall, bearing 6 to 8 unscented, pendulous flowers striped pink, purple or red. They appear from April to July, only opening in the evening and lasting for a mere twenty-four hours. The bulb is often large, up to 3 inches (7·5 cm.) in diameter and from it a number of leaves arise, each with an undulate margin. *C. ornatum* is a variable species and recent research indicates that this is reflected in the variability of the chromosomes.

The five species of *Gloriosa*, or possibly only one in the opinion of some, are found in tropical Africa and Asia. They have large, brightly-coloured flowers and are peculiar lilies in that they are herbaceous climbers, ascending by means of the leaves which have twining tendril tips. Three species of *Gloriosa*, or Glory-lilies, are commonly cultivated in glasshouse collections in temperate areas: *G. simplex* and *G. superba* with red and yellow petals which in the latter have a crisped margin and in the former are merely somewhat wavy, and *G. rothschildiana*, with broad undulate crimson and yellow petals. In all three there are some varieties in which the petals are entirely yellow.

Gloriosa simplex (B), with pendulous flowers, is found from West Africa to Uganda and south into Madagascar, Natal and Angola, growing from 4 to 5 feet (1·2–1·5 m.) tall. As in all Glory-lilies, the style is sharply reflexed to one side from its point of insertion on top of the ovary and around it the 6 stamens radiate symmetrically.

The *Hypoxidaceae* is related to the *Haemodoraceae* (Kangaroo-paws, plates 143 and 144) and the *Velloziaceae*, but unlike *Haemodoraceae*, they have an inferior ovary and lack the plumed hairs which so often characterize this last family. On the other hand, unlike the *Velloziaceae*, they have clusters of leaves emerging from the base of the plants instead of in tufts from the apices of the woody shoots. There are about one hundred species of *Hypoxis* (A): the illustration is possibly *H. goetzei* but the genus is in need of revision and until this is done it is difficult to name many collections with confidence. The plant illustrated was collected by A. Bullock in Tanzania in 1949, and again by E. Milne-Redhead and P. Taylor in 1956. It grows in dry open country in the Songea and Ufipa districts and the numerous charred leaf-bases surrounding the shoot-base indicate its resistance to bush-fires. The broad and very hairy leaves of this species are characteristic, as are the many-flowered inflorescences, which nod when in fruit.

HYPOXIDACEAE

Hypoxis species
A1 flowering plant × ⅔.

LILIACEAE

Gloriosa simplex
B1 part of flowering stem with leaves × ⅔.

AMARYLLIDACEAE

Crinum ornatum
C1 part of flowering stem and leaf × ⅔.
C2 habit sketch of plant × 1/15.

A1

B1

C1

C2

Plate 67 TROPICAL AND CENTRAL AFRICA

Aroids are found in both temperate and tropical regions, in the former as terrestrial herbs ranging in size from the large-leaved Skunk-cabbage, *Symplocarpus foetidus*, to the smaller species of *Arum*; in the latter, as epiphytic, marsh or floating plants. Many, from both regions, have been or still are of economic value: the pounded tubers of the European Cuckoo-pint, *Arum maculatum*, for instance, provide Portland Arrowroot, an easily digestible form of starch; species of *Colocasia* have starchy, edible rhizomes, those of *C. esculenta* give us taro; and *Zantedeschia aethiopica*, the Arum Lily, is much used in floristry.

Amorphophallus abyssinicus (A), one of a genus of some hundred species, is a highly variable plant that occurs in different forms from Ghana to Ethiopia and south into Rhodesia and Zambia. So distinct indeed are some of these variants that a number have been described as separate species, for instance, *A. schweinfurthii* and *A. barteri*. Plants from north-west Africa may have shorter, thinner clubs at the end of the spadix, but this is by no means a predictable feature. The inflorescence arises, unaccompanied by any leaves, from a flattened somewhat globose tuber about 10 inches (25 cm.) in diameter. The spathe, when fully developed, measures about 8 inches (20 cm.) in height and is supported by a stalk almost as long again. The spadix, whose resemblance to a penis gave the genus its name, is of a rather attractive livid purple colour with a conspicuous bloom on its surface. It is usually shorter than the spathe, with only the club of sterile tissue exposed, the hidden part bearing small, reduced and crowded flowers; female at the base and male above. The whole has a particularly pungent smell and lasts for 3 to 7 days, depending on the weather. After its death the tissues partly gelatinize. Later, each tuber produces a single ornamental and much divided umbrella-like leaf.

The largest of all the many species of *Amorphophallus* is the almost legendary *A. titanum* of Sumatra. Odoardo Beccari (1843–1920) who discovered the plant in Padang Province in 1878 described the difficulties of collection thus, 'the single flower . . . with the tuber . . . form together so ponderous a mass that for the purpose of transporting it, it had to be lashed to a long pole, the ends of which were placed on the shoulders of two men'. This is hardly surprising in view of the fact that the tubers measure up to 20 inches (51 cm.) in diameter, the leaf stalks about 15 feet (4·6 m.) in height, and the leaf blades, which are of the same form as those of *A. abyssinicus*, 15 feet (4·6 m) across. The spathe alone may attain a height of 8 feet (2·4 m.) and a diameter of 4 feet (1·2 m.), and have a spadix 42 inches (106·7 cm.) long and 6 inches (15 cm.) thick. When *A. titanum* flowered in the Orchid House at Kew in 1881, the smell, akin to rotting fish and burnt sugar, that in nature attracts the flies by which the plant is pollinated, is said to have made a visit to the house unendurable. In 1889, when the plant again flowered at Kew, the young inflorescence was seen to grow in height at a rate of 3 inches (7·5 cm.) a day, though it lasted only 6 hours in the fully expanded state. Not surprisingly, the tubers may lose up to 9 lb. (4 kg.) in weight after such mammoth activity during the flowering period. The upper, sterile and also the male parts of the spadix rot away as the fruit ripen, to leave a mass of carmine berries, the size of cherries, clustered around its base.

Nephthytis afzelii (B) is a native of Sierra Leone and Liberia, whence its synonym *N. liberica*. It was discovered by the Swede Adam Afzelius (1750–1837), who, with H. Smeathman, was one of the first botanists to study the flora of Sierra Leone. Unlike species of *Amorphophallus*, *Nephthytis* grows from a stout creeping rhizome that terminates in two or three leaves produced slowly and periodically throughout the year. Twice as much of the spadix is covered by male flowers as by female. The species was introduced to cultivation in 1881 by William Bull (1828–1902), the celebrated Victorian nurseryman; the combination of the dark and pale greens of the leaves and inflorescences with the orange colour of the fruits makes it an interesting stove plant.

The sole species in its genus, *Pistia stratiotes* the Water Lettuce, is regarded by botanists as a link between the aroids and the simpler Duckweed genus, *Lemna*. The plant consists of a stemless rosette of bright green cabbage-like leaves, each about 1 to 5 inches (2·5–7·5 cm.) long, that float on the surface of rivers and lakes in all tropical and subtropical areas. The inflorescence is typically aroid, a small spathe subtending a short spadix, the upper portion of which bears 3 to 8 male flowers, the lower, a single female flower partly fused to the spathe. The fruit consists of a many-seeded berry with a thin, fleshy covering and propagation takes place extensively by means of stolons. Since the fibrous roots rarely anchor the plant, it is effectively distributed by floods and by wind on the surface of the water.

ARACEAE

Amorphophallus abyssinicus
A1 flower and leaf × $\frac{2}{3}$.
A2 habit sketch of plant in the vegetative state × $\frac{1}{6}$.
A3 habit sketch of flowering plant × $\frac{1}{6}$.

Nephthytis afzelii (syn. *N. liberica*)
B1 flowering and fruiting plant and leaf (stem cut) × $\frac{2}{3}$.
B2 fruit × $1\frac{1}{3}$.
B3 cross section of fruit × $1\frac{1}{3}$.

A2 A3

B2

B3

A1

B1

Plate 68 TROPICAL AND CENTRAL AFRICA

Dr Selmar Schönland and Dr J. B. Greathead discovered *Aloe greatheadii* (C) (syn. *A. pallidiflora*) during an expedition to Botswana in 1903. It has since been found further north in Rhodesia, Zambia, Mozambique and north-west into the Congo. The fresh pink buds and white striped flowers were sufficiently attractive to catch the eye of German naturalists, who introduced it to their homeland sometime prior to 1903. This German material was distributed and Sir Thomas Hanbury (1832–1907) grew it in his famous garden at La Mortola, Ventimiglia, Italy, where it flowered for the first time in 1904. A catalogue of the plants at La Mortola, founded in 1867, was compiled in 1897 by Kurt Dinter, later to become an authority on South African succulents, and in 1912 another enlarged edition was written by Alwin Berger, who also became an authority on succulents and cacti. In 1892, Hanbury founded the Botanical Institute of the University of Genoa and his garden is still visited and consulted by many botanists and visitors.

The decorative, reddish brown to deep green upper leaf surface of *A. greatheadii* is marbled with white, while the underside is pale green and the margins armed with reddish teeth. The thick leaves are frequently about 16 inches (41 cm.) long. Sometimes 2 or 3 inflorescences arise from a single rosette on a stalk about $4\frac{1}{2}$ feet (1·4 m.) tall, which branches and terminates in racemes 8 inches (20 cm.) long. The plants from Rhodesia are mostly smaller but have taller, more branched inflorescences, in contrast to plants from the Congo, which tend to have larger leaves and, because of suckering, grow in groups.

Some one hundred and fifty *Costus* species, found in all tropical parts of the world, are distinguished from other gingers by their enlarged lip and projecting, petal-like stamen. *C. spectabilis* (B) a plant of rocky habitats in grassland vegetation with scattered tree cover, has a wide distribution from Senegal throughout West Africa into tropical East Africa, and Angola. It consists of a rosette of usually 4, sometimes 6, rounded, somewhat fleshy leaves 2 to 9 inches (5–23 cm.) long. These are often tinged purple with hairs at the margin and spread flat against the ground. Stalkless, bright orange or yellow flowers appear from the crown of the rosette, almost simultaneously with the leaves, and are followed by fruits which are membranous capsules. The rosette habit of *C. spectabilis* is in marked contrast to the majority of *Costus* species.

One of fifty *Aframomum* species, a genus confined to Africa, *A. sceptrum* (A) was discovered in 1861 along the Gabon River by Gustav Mann and it flowered at Clapham in London during 1869, in the garden of Daniel Hanbury, brother to Sir Thomas Hanbury mentioned above, although it had also been introduced to Britain by E. J. L. Simmonds in 1863. *A. sceptrum*, unlike the preceding species, grows in deep forest habitats. Its 12 inch (30 cm.) inflorescences arise at the base of the leafy shoots or independently some distance away from these shoots which themselves are 5 or 6 feet (1·5–1·8 m.) tall and clothed in 10 inch (25 cm.) long leaves, with a sheathing base. *A. sceptrum* occurs in many parts of West Africa and also extends eastward into the Congo and southward to Angola.

ZINGIBERACEAE

Aframomum sceptrum
A1 part of flowering plant × $\frac{2}{3}$.
A2 side view of flower × $\frac{2}{3}$.
A3 new leafy shoot × $\frac{2}{3}$.

Costus spectabilis
B1 flowering plant × $\frac{2}{3}$.

LILIACEAE

Aloe greatheadii (syn. *A. pallidiflora*)
C1 part of inflorescence × $\frac{2}{3}$.
C2 portion of leaf × $\frac{2}{3}$.
C3 habit sketch × $\frac{1}{15}$.

A1

A2

A3

B1

C1

C2

C3

Plate 69   TROPICAL AND CENTRAL AFRICA

Though less rich in orchids than America or Asia, tropical Africa has its complement of beautiful species. The savannahs and lightly wooded areas are the home of a large number of ground orchids, while certain epiphytic types inhabit the more densely forested areas.

An easy and rewarding plant to grow, and therefore a favourite among gardeners since its introduction into Europe in about 1895, *Eulophia quartiniana* (C) is a native of Central and East Africa, Sudan, and Ethiopia, where it was discovered by its eponym, the French botanist and explorer Richard Quartin-Dillon, who died in Abyssinia in 1841. In the savannahs the plant ceases active life during the cool season, thus protecting itself from damage when the temperatures may drop to as low as 60°F (16°C). The inflorescence emerges in spring, just before the leaves, as soon as a plentiful supply of water is available. The species illustrated is often confused with *E. guineensis,* and their distribution overlaps in parts of central and west Africa and the Congo. At one time the two were regarded as con-specific, but the fact that the leaves of *E. quartiniana* never precede the flowers as in *E. guineensis* serves to distinguish the species.

The majority of the African species of the pantropical genus *Habenaria* are dry grassland orchids with inconspicuous, greenish or yellowish flowers. One species, however, though not illustrated, is worthy of notice—the East African *H. egregia*. Its 4 greenish, white and cream flowers, easily the largest to be found on any African *Habenaria*, consist of a spur about 7½ inches (19 cm.) in length and a lip 2 inches (5 cm.) long, and divided into 3 lobes, each of which is subdivided into spidery fingers. The plant grows to a height of about 3 feet (91 cm.) and was discovered in 1936 in the French Cameroons. It was formally described ten years later on the arrival of more specimens from Kenya, but since it is a species that has only recently been recognized, information on its distribution between Kenya and the Cameroons is scanty.

The genus *Angraecum* contains two hundred and fifty species found throughout Africa, in Madagascar, on the islands of the Indian Ocean

and in the Philippines. One of the largest-flowered species is *A. infundibulare* (B), which is found among rocks or climbing small trees in an area from Uganda to the Congo Basin and Nigeria, including the islands of the Gulf of Guinea. It produces stems up to 2 feet (61 cm.) tall with the flowers borne directly opposite a leaf or below the insertion of an aerial root. The waxy blooms last for about ten days and have an attractive perfume. *A. infundibulare* is not difficult to cultivate, provided it is supplied with considerable warmth and humidity and the flowers adequately protected, for even the slightest damage results in their discoloration.

Named in commemoration of John Ansell, an early 19th century botanist who was the first to come across species of this genus, *Ansellia* is easily recognised by the dense upward-growing masses of roots which arise from a hidden rhizome and by which they cling to their high perches in the trees. Elongated, spindle-shaped, green or yellowish pseudobulbs give rise to 6 to 15 tough, lanceolate leaves, and shoots with many flowered inflorescences. Insects are attracted to the flowers, which may or may not be scented, by a sticky liquid secreted by the buds. Although such plants grow on the branches of trees they are not parasites as is commonly believed. They merely use the tree as a perch and are known as epiphytes.

The genus *Ansellia* contains two variable species found in East and West Africa. *A. gigantea* (A), known as the Leopard Orchid, is a native of coastal areas in Kenya and Tanzania, and is often found growing on the trunks of the Doum Palm (*Hyphaene* species, plate 191). The flowers of what has been called variety *azanica* (A) are the largest and most colourful. They appear between March and September and last for about a month. Further inland, with a range chiefly in eastern and south-eastern Africa but also west in Nigeria, is found another variety, var. *nilotica,* having fewer, more widely spaced flowers with finer markings, and favouring moister habitats. The second species, *A. africana* is mainly West African but has a purple-brown flowered eastern form found around Lake Victoria and to the west of the Great Rift Valley.

ORCHIDACEAE

Ansellia gigantea var. *azanica*, Leopard Orchid
A1 inflorescence × ⅔.
A2 leafy base of plant with roots × ⅔.
A3 habit sketch × 1/10.

Angraecum infundibulare
B1 part of flowering stem × ⅔.

Eulophia quartiniana
C1 part of flowering plant (stem cut) × ⅔.
C2 old pseudobulb × ⅔.
C3 column from above × 2.
C4 head of column showing anther sacs × 2⅔.
C5 pollinia × 2⅔.

Plate 70 TROPICAL AND CENTRAL AFRICA

Madagascar, it has been estimated, has about six thousand endemic species, approximately 80% of the total flora—a remarkable number for an island of its size—and six whole families of flowering plants, including the *Sarcolaenaceae*, *Geosiridaceae*, *Humbertiaceae* and *Didiereaceae* (the last represented here by the genus *Didierea*), that are found nowhere else in the world. It is, therefore, a major disaster for science, and one that we hope will not reach greater proportions, that a flora in so many ways unique should have suffered so greatly from deafforestation and the disturbance of natural vegetation. Incidentally, although it is illustrated under South East Asia (plate 113) for reasons given in the relevant caption, *Delonix regia* is native to Madagascar.

The southern and south-western coastal districts of Madagascar are semi-desert, supporting a drought-resistant flora with a high proportion of succulents. This area is the home of the *Didiereaceae*, a family of branched or unbranched, often cactus-like, spiny trees, without any close relatives, that contains the genera *Didierea* (two species), *Decaryia* (one species), *Alluaudia* (six species), and *Alluaudiopsis* (two species). Perhaps the strangest member of this odd family is *Alluaudia procera*, which resembles a thorny and slightly curved telegraph-pole with a number of tall, almost erect branches near the base and often surmounted by diffuse inflorescences in an incongruous tuft. Adding to the oddity of its already bizarre appearance are small, fat, fleshy leaves that arise from all parts of the trunk, even the oldest, giving it a geometrical decoration most unusual among plants.

The two species of *Didierea* are *D. madagascariensis* (syn. *D. mirabilis*) (B), found in the southern part of the western coastal area, and *D. trollii*, which occurs around the southern end of the island. In part, they are distinguishable by habit, *D. trollii* having smaller leaves and stems that tend to bend into a horizontal position. The mature stems of *D. madagascariensis* are divided internally by transverse diaphragms of pith into a series of horizontal chambers which give them a lightweight but rigid construction.

The stems are covered with clusters of spines, each cluster being a highly modified shoot. From the apex of each spine cluster, a series of elongated leaves and, later, male or female flowers arise. As the stems age, the spines become shorter and stouter in appearance (see B5). The flowers, male and female borne on different plants, appear during the rainy season, in October or November, and are so numerous that the stem may be completely hidden. Male flowers consist of 2 small sepals and 4 larger petals surrounding the 8 stamens (see B3). Female flowers also possess 2 sepals and 4 petals, and an ovary terminated by a stigma with 3 to 4 irregular lobes (see B4).

The genus *Kalanchoë* contains about two hundred species distributed throughout tropical Africa into South Africa and Madagascar, and east into Java and China; there is also one South American species. Most possess fleshy leaves and stems, and are easily reproduced vegetatively. *K. tomentosa* (A) is a native of south-west Madagascar, where it grows to a height of 30 inches (76 cm.) amongst semi-desert scrub. The woody mature stems are covered with dark brown to fox-red hairs which also spread to the inflorescence, including the outer surface of the petals, often obscuring their pale yellow colour. The plant's decorative value lies in the trimming of similar reddish-brown hairs about the marginal tips of the fat, fleshy leaves and for this *K. tomentosa* is frequently included in glasshouse collections of succulents; unfortunately however, it rarely flowers under cultivation. The thick, hairy leaves of *K. beharensis* (C) are borne in a cabbage-like cluster at the top of a woody leafless stem about 9 feet (2·7 m.) tall and have a maximum length of 12 inches (30 cm.). Inflorescences grow to about 2 feet (61 cm.), but are rare. The specific name derives from Behara in southern Madagascar, whence the species originated. Always a valuable addition to glasshouse collections of succulents because of its short-haired coloured leaves and yellowish inflorescences on long stalks, *Kalanchoë velutina* (D) is native from Angola, through the Congo, Malawi and Tanzania, to Zanzibar.

CRASSULACEAE

Kalanchoë tomentosa
A1 part of flowering plant × $\frac{2}{3}$.

K. beharensis
C1 part of inflorescence × $\frac{2}{3}$. C2 leaf × $\frac{2}{3}$.
C3 habit sketch × $\frac{1}{24}$.

K. velutina
D1 part of flowering stem × $\frac{2}{3}$.
D2 flower × 2.

DIDIEREACEAE

Didierea madagascariensis (syn.
D. mirabilis)
B1 stem tip in leaf × $\frac{2}{3}$.
B2 part of male flowering shoot × $\frac{2}{3}$.
B3 male flower × $2\frac{2}{3}$. B4 female flower × $2\frac{2}{3}$.
B5 spine from the lower stem × $\frac{2}{3}$.
B6 habit sketch.

A1

B1

B2

B3

B4

B5

B6

C1

C2

C3

D1

D2

Plate 71   TROPICAL AND CENTRAL AFRICA (Madagascar)

The purpose of this plate is not only to show some of the well known decorative species with which Madagascar has provided horticulture in the past, but also some of the more rarely illustrated plants found on this enormous island. The Madagascar Periwinkle is a familiar glasshouse plant throughout the world and has become naturalized among the native flora in the West Indies and other tropical areas. In contrast, *Rhodolaena* and *Uncarina* have never before been illustrated in a popular publication. The species of *Mascarenhasia* illustrated opposite was figured in both the *Botanical Magazine* and *The Garden* in 1882.

There has been some uncertainty about the country of origin of the Madagascar Periwinkle. *Catharanthus roseus* (A), now found wild throughout the tropics but recent authorities confirm that it is native to Madagascar. It was brought to Paris by the French possibly about 1750 and from France it soon found its way into the capable hands of Philip Miller, who grew it at Chelsea in 1757. The species forms a bushy plant up to 2 feet (61 cm.) in height, with clear, rose-coloured flowers that are borne near the ends of the shoots; a white-flowered form also exists. It is, moreover, not merely a colourful and ornamental plant, but an important source of drugs as well; sixty alkaloids, some of which have been found to have potential value in the treatment of cancer, are reported to have been extracted from it. Though the botanical name (taken from the Greek *katharos* 'pure', *anthos* 'flower') given above is the correct one, the species is often cultivated under the names *Vinca rosea* and *Lochnera rosea*, despite the fact that the genus *Vinca* differs from *Catharanthus* (syn. *Lochnera*) in a number of botanic details.

Likewise a member of the Periwinkle family, *Mascarenhasia curnowiana* (B) is one of ten species in a genus found in tropical Africa and Madagascar and commemorates the early 16th century Portuguese navigator Pedro Mascarenhas, who discovered the island now known as Réunion, but once called Ile Mascaraigne; Mascarenhas is also commemorated in the name of the Mascarenes, a group of islands in the Indian Ocean to the east of Madagascar. *M. curnowiana* was introduced to Europe about 1880 by Richard Curnow and first described in 1882 after being given an Award of Merit by the Royal Horticultural Society in August 1881. Though the flowers are abundant and long-lasting, very high temperatures are required for their successful cultivation, so they are rarely seen in collections. Another species, *M. elastica*, is a tall, slender tree from Mozambique and Malawi and contains in its tissues a latex that yields an inferior type of rubber.

One of a small Madagascan genus of five species belonging to the *Pedaliaceae*, a family some of whose members have been called 'grapple-plants' because of the extraordinary hooks of different types borne on the characteristic fruits, *Uncarina grandidieri* (C), despite its striking appearance, has been but rarely illustrated. Indeed, as far as the author knows, the painting opposite is the only coloured figure of the flowers in existence. The plant grows to a height of about 12 feet (3·6 m.) and in spring, before the leaves appear, produces dense, domed heads of golden flowers at the tips of the few, stout branches. Inside, the throat and tube of the flower are a rich, deep purple. The sharply beaked capsular fruits that follow are armed with barbed spines. The long-stalked, bright green, lobed leaves emerge in summer and fall in the autumn. The 'winter', in Madagascar the dry season, is spent in a dormant state during which the sparsely branched trunk with its papery bark looks pale and dead.

Rhodolaena bakeriana (D) is one of five species in a genus belonging to the small, endemic Madagascan family *Sarcolaenaceae*, which contains eight genera in all. Possibly related to the camellias, *Theaceae*, it forms a beautiful shrub or small tree with very pale pink flowers, with 5 or 6 petals and 3 leafy sepals, that resemble those of *Eucryphia*. *Rhodolaena* lacks the conspicuous involucre of bracts beneath the flower that is a feature of other genera in the family. An equally attractive species from southern Madagascar, *R. altivola*, has large, white flowers borne in pairs.

APOCYNACEAE

Catharanthus roseus, Madagascar Periwinkle
A1 flowering shoot × $\frac{2}{3}$. A2 flower × $\frac{2}{3}$.
A3 flower in longitudinal section × $1\frac{1}{2}$.
A4 fruit × $1\frac{1}{3}$. A5 seed × 8.

Mascarenhasia curnowiana
B1 flowering shoot × $\frac{2}{3}$.

PEDALIACEAE

Uncarina grandidieri
C1 inflorescence and leaf × $\frac{2}{3}$.
C2 base of opened corolla × $1\frac{1}{4}$.
C3 fruit × $\frac{2}{3}$. C4 tip of barbed spine × 2.
C5 habit sketch × $\frac{1}{36}$.

SARCOLAENACEAE

Rhodolaena bakeriana
D1 flowering shoot × $\frac{2}{3}$.

A1

A2

A3

A4

A5

B1

C1

C2

C3

C4

C5

D1

Plate 72   SOUTH AFRICA

Several colourful legume genera, such as *Liparia* and *Sutherlandia*, which form part of the rich endemic flora of the region, are unique to South Africa. A member of the small family *Bruniaceae*, the species in the decorative genus *Brunia*, also grow only in South Africa and are typical of its native vegetation. Others such as *Schotia* and *Erythrina* are more widespread African genera.

The genus *Schotia* commemorates Richard van der Schot (d. 1790), at one time head gardener of the Imperial Garden at Schönbrunn and companion to the famous botanist, Baron Nikolaus von Jacquin (1727–1817) during his travels in the West Indies. The Tree Fuchsia, *Schotia brachypetala* (A), usually reaches a height of 25 to 35 feet (7·6–10·7 m.). It is sometimes found on river banks and termites seem to build their mounds nearby. Flowers appear in October, after the leaves have fallen, and are borne in congested masses up to about 5 inches (12·5 cm.) in diameter. Each flower consists of 4 leathery red sepals fused to one another at the base, 10 stamens with red filaments also fused at the base, and reduced or absent petals; plants in the Zoutpansberg and Blauwberg areas have 2 to 4 exserted red petals, while others in Natal and eastern Cape, like the one illustrated, have no petals at all. The name *S. rogersii* has been given to a plant that is really only a form of *S. brachypetala* with visible petals. The fruits are woody pods up to 4½ inches (11 cm.) long, each containing 1 or more seeds with a basal yellowish aril. The pod is constructed with a thickened peripheral rim to which the seeds often remain attached when the 2 valves of the pod have fallen away. This plant may be found in an area from Rhodesia and Mozambique to South Africa.

A well known species in southern Africa, *Erythrina caffra* has become associated with the Republic as a national emblem, having been used, for example, on stamps. The illustrated species, *E. lysistemon* (C), is a close relative of *E. caffra* but tends to occur in drier habitats. Its longer, thinner flowers are more scarlet than those of *E. caffra* and it rarely exceeds 35 feet (10·7 m.) in height. In addition, the sepals of *E. caffra* are relatively longer in proportion to the petals and, an interesting distinction in seedling habit, the seed leaves (cotyledons) are always carried about ¾ inch (19 mm.) above the soil but those of *E. lysistemon* at soil level.

Spikes of flowers appear on thorny branches after the leaves have been shed, and the fruits are extremely attractive with their black exteriors and red seeds which become visible as the pods open. *E. lysistemon* is found in Rhodesia, Zambia, Malawi and Mozambique, through South Africa and into Angola.

The genus *Liparia* contains two species, both found only in the south-west part of Cape Province. (Until recent revision in the classification of this genus there were thought to be four species.) The larger species, *L. sphaerica* (D) occurs in the mountains of the Cape Peninsula where it grows into a shrub between 1 and 8 feet (0·3–2·4 m.) tall. Large, showy inflorescences appear throughout the year but May to November are the best months for flowering. The warm colours of the flower heads are partly produced by the petals and partly by the subtending bracts.

Among the early colonists the Kankerbos or Cancer-bush, *Sutherlandia frutescens* (B) was reputed to cure cancerous growths. Though widespread on dry hillsides in the coastal and inland areas throughout the provinces of South Africa, it is not a common plant. The bushes reach about 6 feet (1·8 m.) in height and the scarlet flowers, which sometimes have a background streaking of white, are very attractive set against the silvery foliage. After the flowers have fallen, the unusual fruits, resembling those of the Mediterranean shrub *Colutea arborescens*, the Bladder Senna, begin to develop. These inflated papery fruits contain several seeds and the wind blows them long distances before the walls rot to release the seeds. Easily raised from seed, the Cancer-bush has been cultivated in Europe since about 1683 and is grown in the Temperate House at Kew. James Sutherland (1639–1719), the Scottish botanist and the first Regius Keeper of the Royal Botanic Garden at Edinburgh, is commemorated in this genus of six South African species.

The South African family *Bruniaceae* comprises twelve genera and about seventy-five species. The plants are somewhat heather-like in habit, but some botanists believe that the flowers suggest a closer affinity with the witch-hazel family, the *Hamamelidaceae*. Of the seven species of *Brunia*, *B. stokoei* (E), is the most attractive. It was discovered in 1922 when T. P. Stokoe collected it near Hang Klip in the Hottentots Holland Mountains and was formally described later that year by Edwin Percy Phillips. A shrubby plant, it grows to a height of about 3 to 16 feet (0·9–5 m.). Its ½ inch (12·7 mm.) leaves are triangular in cross-section and have a tiny black prominence at the tip. Clustered into stalked heads, the flowers terminate shoots of the current year's growth, and overtop the inflorescences of the previous year. Two old inflorescences are illustrated opposite. Each flower is subtended by a spoon-shaped bract covered on the outside with hairs and having longer hairs at the base. A view of the inside of one such bract is shown in E3. There are 4 sepals covered with hair, 5 red petals, and 5 stamens, also red, which alternate with the petals. The ovary is terminated by a forked style with 2 stigmas. As may be seen from the illustration, the inflorescence develops from the base upward, each reddish ring of massed flowers opening in unison.

LEGUMINOSAE

Schotia brachypetala, Tree Fuchsia
A1 part of flower and leaf shoots × ⅔.
A2 fruit × ⅔. A3 seed with aril × ⅔.

Sutherlandia frutescens, Kankerbos, Cancer-bush
B1 part of flowering stem × ⅔.
B2 fruiting shoot × ⅔.

Erythrina lysistemon
C1 part of stems with leaves and flowers × ⅔.
C2 fruit × ⅔. C3 seed × 1.

Liparia sphaerica
D1 part of flowering stem × ⅔.

BRUNIACEAE

Brunia stokoei
E1 part of flowering stem × ⅔. E2 leaf × 4⅔.
E3 bract × 4.

A1

A2

A3

B2

B1

C3

C1

D1

E2

E1

E3

Plate 73   SOUTH AFRICA

The strange way in which South African members of the family *Aizoaceae* mimic their surroundings has long been a source of controversy. The numerous *Lithops* and *Conophytum* species, tiny spherical objects growing among stones, are often indistinguishable from the surrounding pebbles until a flower pushes its way out of the apex, when the disguise becomes immediately apparent. Can this resemblance be attributed to a specific biological cause or is it merely fortuitous? There is probably some truth in thinking that the plants have evolved an excellent camouflage. Whatever the answer, the crusty and white blotched leaves of *Titanopsis calcarea* are incontrovertably similar to the limestone substrates on which the plants grow and *Pleiospilos bolusii* has pitted, coarse leaves very like bits of stone.

The name *Lithops* means 'stone-like' and plants in this genus of about fifty species confined to South and South-west Africa do closely resemble stones. The 2 leaves are more or less fused together and the new shoots arise between them. As a pair of new leaves develops there is a corresponding shrinkage in the old pair and the new growth effectively 'sucks dry' the older one, which remains, however, as a protective sheath around the bare leaves. The upper surface of the 2 leaves is devoid of chlorophyll; only the 'undersurface', that is the sides of the plant, contains photosynthetic tissue. The upper surface acts as a window through which light is transmitted, passing through transparent water-storage tissue to the chlorophyll-containing tissue around the sides of the plant. In general, light cannot reach the sides from without because in nature the plants are buried to the level of the top of the leaf in stones and sand. The plants are very drought resistant and periods without water may exceed eighteen or nineteen months.

The majority of *Lithops* species occur in South-west Africa, though a few are found south of the Orange River. Quaintly known as Hottentots' Backsides, the plants possess so few characters that their identification is often based on leaf colour. *L. terricolor* (A), the most widely distributed species in Cape Province, is variable and often found in clumps of 6-10 plants growing in areas with as little as 2 inches (5 cm.) of rain a year. The leaves are greenish pink to greenish yellow and the upper surface is decorated with more or less brownish green spots. *L. optica* (B) has a more restricted range in the coastal desert of Prince of Wales Bay. It grows on quartz hills and screes and is said to extend inland for only 2 or 3 miles (3·2-4·8 km.). A variety or form with reddish leaves, var. *rubra*, grows scattered amongst the true species.

L. lesliei (C), discovered by T. N. Leslie in the Transvaal, also occurs in western Griqualand, the Orange Free State and Cape Province. Its unscented flower opens in the late afternoon. The species is said to withstand 20°F (−11°C), of frost on occasion, but at such times the plants are in their resting phase and well dried out.

Bright, succulent, yellow-green leaves which resemble a cluster of tongues characterize *Glottiphyllum fragrans* (D), one of about fifty species in this South African genus, the name of which means 'tongue leaf'. The scented, yellow flowers are up to 4 inches (10 cm.) across and the plants are easy to cultivate but, unless pollen is obtained from another individual raised from different seed, it will not set fruit, for the species is self-sterile.

The unequal length of the leaves and a tendency to form a humped habit gives *Gibbaeum*, a genus of some thirty species found in South Africa, its name, derived from the Latin *gibba*, 'a hump'. One of the first species in the genus to be described was *G. gibbosum* (G) and like most of the species it is confined to the Little Karoo. *G. album* appears to be restricted to whitish quartz outcrops, the greyish-white clumps of firmly adpressed leaves covering many acres and being an excellent example of mimicry.

Named after Dr Louise Bolus (née Kensit) who first described this species in the genus *Mesembryanthemum*, the genus *Kensitia* consists of the single species *K. pillansii* (M). Curious spoon-shaped 'petals' characterize this species which is unlike any other stone-flower. The plants reach 12 to 18 inches (30-46 cm.) high and the flowers do not close at night. As can be seen in illustration M2, a series of staminodes enclose the inward bent stamens around the 8 to 10 stigmas, but the staminodes later part to allow pollination.

Probably the first stone-flower introduced into Europe, in about 1660, *Carpanthea pomeridiana* (L), an annual which occurs in Cape Province, is variable in hairiness and leaf size with slender petalled yellow flowers about 2½ inches (6·4 cm.) across. The delicately sculptured fruits are particularly attractive when open. Two or three of the sepals are peculiar, being narrower and having chaffy wings at the base.

The majority of the two hundred and fifty *Conophytum* species are found in Little Namaqualand as far north as the Orange River and Karas Mountains of South Africa; to the south they grow quite near to Cape Town, and in the east as far as Uniondale. The generic name means 'cone-plant', for, as the leaves are almost completely fused, in contrast to *Lithops*, they resemble small inverted cones growing in the soil. Some species are little bigger than a pea and similar in shape, while in others the 2 leaves are more clearly perceptible. Remains of the previous seasons' growth sheathe the plant, and in this way it is sometimes possible to determine the age of older clumps. *C. minusculum* (K), a native of the Clanwilliam district, was discovered there by Mr N. S. Pillans and is an excellent plant to cultivate. The flower, large in proportion to the leaves, lasts for about two weeks. *C. minutum* (J) which grows in the Van Rhynsdorp area near Bakhuis, was first introduced into cultivation by Francis Masson in 1795. Its flowers are smaller and less frequently produced than *C. minusculum*. Plants of this genus dry up to almost nothing during the resting period and prove very difficult to find at that time. They must be plumped-up and preferably flowering if they are to be seen in the wild. Species may well await discovery in the many areas still requiring botanical exploration.

Found only in South Africa, the seventy or so species of the genus *Drosanthemum* are related to the genus *Lampranthus* which contains species which play an important role in the make-up of the flora of Cape Province and the Karoo, and form one of the tourist attractions of the country. *D. splendens* (H) was discovered in 1932 by R. Pickard and is restricted to the Montague district of South Africa.

Possibly the most spectacular species of the genus *Faucaria*, which comprises about thirty-five species confined to South Africa, is *F. tigrina* (E). Commonly called Tiger's Jaws (in fact the generic name means a collection of jaws), its pairs of leaves have soft but fierce-looking teeth, while the rows of white dots down the sides of the leaf remind one of the striping of a tiger. It was introduced to Europe in 1790 by Francis Masson and is found in the veld around Albany and Grahamstown.

Trichodiadema means 'hairy crown', an allusion to the curious tuft of bristles found on each leaf tip in species of this genus. *T. stellatum* (F) comes close to looking like a cactus in its superficial appearance but whereas cactus stems are succulent and bear spiny leaves it is the leaves in *Trichodiadema* which are succulent. Apart from the bristly leaves and plumed stigmas there is little to distinguish the genus from *Drosanthemum*.

AIZOACEAE

Lithops terricolor
A1 four plants × ⅔.
A2 pair of new leaves emerging × ⅔.

L. optica
B1 two plants × ⅔.

L. lesliei
C1 flowering plant × ⅔.
C2 budding plant × ⅔.
C3 vegetative plant × ⅔.

Glottiphyllum fragrans
D1 flowering plant × ⅔.

Faucaria tigrina, Tiger's Jaws
E1 flowering plant × ⅔.

Trichodiadema stellatum
F1 flowering plant × ⅔.
F2 leaf × 2.

Gibbaeum gibbosum (syn. *G. perviride*)
G1 flowering plant × ⅔.

Drosanthemum splendens
H1 flowering stem × ⅔.
H2 petal and staminode × 1⅓.

Conophytum minutum
J1 flowering plant × ⅔.

C. minusculum
K1 flowering plant × ⅔.

Carpanthea pomeridiana
L1 flowering plant × ⅔.
L2 sepal × 2.
L3 fruiting heads on part of stem × ⅔.

Kensitia pillansii (syn. *Piquetia pillansii*)
M1 part of flowering stem × ⅔.
M2 stamens and staminodes × 2⅔.
M3 petal × 2⅔.

A2 A1 C3 C2 C1 D1 B1 E1 F2 F1 G1 H2 H1 J1 K1 L1 L2 L3 M2 M1 M3

Plate 74   SOUTH AFRICA

Geranium species occur throughout the world, but most species of *Pelargonium*, commonly called 'geraniums', grow only in South Africa. The bizarre, fleshy and woody habit of some, such as *P. gibbosum* and *P. ferulaceum* found in north-western districts, exemplifies adaptation to arid conditions in nature; Rudolf Marloth reported that dried Herbarium specimens of *P. moniliforme* started sprouting after having been on a sheet of herbarium paper for seven months. The divided leaves of some species help to reduce water loss from their surfaces and the hairy or shiny leaves of others help to minimize the harmful effects of intense insolation. Aromatic oils contained in the tissues of many pelargoniums tend to prevent animals eating the leaves and these oils, known collectively as geranol, have commercial value in the perfumery trade; *P. odoratissimum*, *P. graveolens* and *P. karooense* being cultivated for their oils in southern France, Algeria and the island of Réunion. Pelargoniums have been popularly called 'geraniums' for very many years (the genus *Pelargonium* having earlier been part of *Geranium*) despite the repeated attention drawn to this error. *Geranium* proper has no spurred calyx, and has rounded symmetrical flowers, while *Pelargonium* has a calyx spur fused to the flower stalk, and asymmetrical flowers; however, through selection among cultivated hybrids, these have now come near to those of the true *Geranium* in form. The presence of the end of the spur is indicated as a lump near the base of the calyx, see A2. The flower has 5 carpels united at the top, to produce an elongated style. When ripe each carpel separates into a 1-seeded unit which frees itself from the stylar column, springing up and becoming twisted above the column, and this movement may be so violent as to catapult the seed from the opening fruit. Self-planting of the seeds often occurs, for a bristle-like awn at one end of the seed drawn to the moisture in the soil, coils and uncoils, and so effectively works the seed into the ground.

Named after Colonel James Henry Bowker (d. 1900), who collected it in South Africa between 1853 and 1883, *P. bowkeri* (C), has a characteristic tuberous and thickened rootstock and umbels of flowers with fringed petals. A native of Transvaal and Natal, where it grows at altitudes of 5000–6000 feet (1520–1830 m.), it was first introduced to Europe in 1863.

A much earlier introduction, around 1794, *P. echinatum* (B) grows in the shade of shrubs in the hills of its native Namaqualand, in western South Africa. It has persistent spiny stipules on the stems, although in younger plants these are completely herbaceous. The leaves may be kidney-shaped, palmate or, occasionally, finely divided and have long stalks and a hairy undersurface. The flowers, with 6–7 stamens, vary in colour from white through pink to purple, and in some cases the upper petals have blotches of deeper colour in the centre.

Also introduced around 1794, *P. acetosum* (F) is a much rarer plant which grows near rivers in the Cape region. It has fleshy branches and its leaves, which are very rarely divided, are said to taste like those of sorrel. The upper petals are smaller than the others and 2 of the 7 stamens are shorter than the rest. Related to *P. acetosum*, *P. stenopetalum* (A) is a native of Zululand, introduced into Europe in 1710. It has been called *P. zonale* var. *stenopetalum* but this is an error based on species misidentified as *P. stenopetalum* by Harvey. *P. hirsutum* (E) with tuberous roots and a small stem, is another species with very variable leaves growing on long stalks, and flowers which vary in colour from pale pink to blackish purple. Introduced into Europe in 1724, *P. papillionaceum* (D) is a native of wet shady habitats in the area east of Cape Town. These plants are not fleshy and are much branched, with a paniculate inflorescence and flowers which are distinctive in having 2 large upper petals.

Although the wild species of *Pelargonium* are not well known, there are numerous hybrid types which have become popular garden plants and are briefly described below. Zonal Pelargoniums of horticulture have leaves with semicircular bands of deeper, and sometimes brightly coloured pigmentation. These hybrids are usually called *P. × hortorum* and although their ancestry is uncertain, they were probably derived from such parents as *P. inquinans, P. zonale, P. hybridum* and *P. frutetorum*.

Regal Pelargoniums have flowers with usually more than 5 large, ruffled petals and are again hybrid in origin. Their parents probably include *P. cucullatum*, a species grown in Europe as early as 1690, but a native of the Capetown area and the west, where it forms dense masses about 5 feet (1·5 m.) tall, *P. grandiflorum, P. fulgidum* and *P. angulosum*. Two early hybrids, *P. × macranthon* and *P. × pavoninum*, probably formed the progenitors of the first Regals, which were raised at Sandringham in Norfolk, England, in 1877.

Ivy-leaved Pelargoniums are also hybrids, probably derived from *P. peltatum, P. zonale, P. inquinans* and *P. hybridum*. Pelargoniums cultivated for their especially scented leaves include the species *P. abrotanifolium, P. tomentosum, P. crispum* as well as those already mentioned.

Most plants have a diploid number of chromosomes—that is duplicate sets of rod-like bodies which reside in the cells and transmit inherited characters . Duplicate sets are normally present, for during sexual reproduction the gametes contain single sets of chromosomes (haploid numbers) and when gametes fuse, as they must in sexual reproduction, the diploid number is restored. Only with this sort of mechanism can a gradual and deleterious accumulation of chromosomes in the cells be avoided. It is therefore remarkable that the bedding cultivar called 'Kleine Liebling' never has more than a haploid or unduplicated set of chromosomes in its cells. It is virtually unique in this characteristic. Because these plants are regularly propagated by cuttings, it seems that they have lost the faculty of sexual reproduction.

GERANIACEAE

Pelargonium stenopetalum
A1 part of flowering stem with leaves × ⅔.
A2 flower showing spurred calyx × 2.

P. echinatum (syn. *P. reniforme*)
B1 part of flowering stem × ⅔.
B2 stamens, style, ovary and calyx × 6.
B3 leaves and lower part of stem × ⅔.

P. bowkeri
C1 flowering plant with leaves × ⅔.
C2 flower × 2.

P. papillionaceum
D1 part of flowering stem × ⅔.
D2 flower × 2⅔. D3 style and ovary × 2⅔.

P. hirsutum (syn. *P. atrum*)
E1 part of flowering stem × ⅔. E2 petal × 2⅔.
E3 stamens, style and ovary × 4.

P. acetosum
F1 part of flowering stem × ⅔. F2 petal × 2⅔.
F3 calyx with stamens, style and ovary × 2⅔.

A1

A2

B1

B2

B3

C1

C2

D1

D2

D3

E1

E2

E3

F1

F2

F3

Plate 75   SOUTH AFRICA

The sixteen or so species of *Mimetes*, all confined to South Africa, are more or less similar in appearance to *M. hottentotica* (A). Like several other members of this family they are easily recognized by the compact clusters of often brightly coloured flowers arranged in a sessile flower-head around which the subtending bracts are also occasionally coloured. This bizarre plant has softly hairy silver leaves, withered, reflexed perianth segments of a yellow hue, and red and yellow styles which contrast with an almost black stigma. Its anthers are situated in the spoon-shaped tips of the perianth lobes illustrated in A2. The plant, discovered relatively recently—in 1922—by T. P. Stokoe, grows on the steep, moist slopes of the Hottentot Hollands Mountains—hence its specific epithet.

Another of T. P. Stokoe's discoveries, *M. stokoei*, has bright yellow styles tinged with red, nearly black stigmas, pinkish bracts subtending the flower clusters and satiny leaves. Another isolated species, this plant too is found only in the Hottentot Hollands Mountains. Mr Stokoe, who has revisited the original locations of the species, reports that their numbers are un-accountably diminishing, notwithstanding the apparent absence of animal grazing and over-enthusiastic plant collectors. Many members of the *Proteaceae* appear to suffer from a tendency to become rare, perhaps connected with their slow rate of growth and low annual production of fertile seeds.

The floral bracts of *Protea obtusifolia* (D), one of about one hundred and thirty species in the genus, are smooth, shiny and have a brittle, chaffy texture. In the figure opposite the boss of central flowers within the confines of the red bracts has not yet opened, but the arrange-ment is essentially that shown for *P. amplexi-caulis* (E). *P. obtusifolia* grows on white sandy soils in the coastal region of southern Cape Province. A variety with white bracts is said to occur in the Albertinia district.

Another *Protea* species which is confined to South Africa is *P. amplexicaulis* (E). This is a characteristically small shrub with inflores-cences having bracts which are strikingly col-oured—unlike the faintly coloured and leaflike bracts of *Mimetes*. This species is peculiar in that the main stem is situated underground while only the side branches protrude above the sur-face. These aerial branches, usually untidy and irregular in arrangement, struggle to a height of about 2 feet (61 cm.). *P. amplexicaulis* is so named because the leaves clasp the stem from which they arise, or, to use the technical term, are amplexicaul. Its red-brown inflorescences do not show to the best advantage, placed as they are near the ground on one of the aerial branches;

nevertheless they are remarkably coloured, with bracts which are velvety outside and paler inside. *P. amplexicaulis*, also from southern Cape Province, occurs at altitudes between 1000 and 2000 feet (300–610 m.).

Former localities of *Protea grandiceps* (F) in the mountains of the Cape Peninsula are now occupied by other vegetation and *P. grandiceps* is extinct there. This rare species has been found on Table Mountain, Devil's Peak (near Cape Division), Langeberg (near Swellendam), the Jonkershoek Mountains (near Stellenbosch), and the Cockscomb Mountains (near Port Elizabeth). The plant produces only a few seeds from each inflorescence and has a very slow rate of growth. These, coupled with its tendency to flower only when quite old, may account for the precarious existence of the species. Excessive numbers of bush fires are thought to account for the death of many *P. grandiceps* plants. The bearded tops of the terminal inflorescence bracts may be pure white (as shown), grey, or brownish, and, unlike those of *P. amplexicaulis* and *P. obtusifolia*, its bracts never open any further than the illustration opposite indicates. Only those leaves near the inflorescence are edged with red, those occurring lower on the 5 foot (1·5 m.) tall bush are entirely green.

A genus of only two species, *Endonema* is one of five genera which comprise the family *Penaeaceae*, itself restricted to South and South-west Africa. A brightly coloured species when in flower, *E. retzioides* (B) displays a yellow receptacle tube with 4 equally conspicuous fleshy red sepals and anthers. The plants grow to about 24 inches (61 cm.) tall and have yellowish green foliage. Leaves, not unlike those of ericas, are equally tolerant to dry conditions. It is found only in the Caledon and Swellendam Divisions of Cape Province, where *E. latiflora* (syn. *E. thunbergii*), the other species, also occurs but has broader, shorter leaves which crowd the stem and somewhat obscure the small flowers from view.

In the opinion of many, *Drosera cistiflora* (C) is the loveliest of all sundews. This native of South and South-west Africa grows in the vicinity of Cape Town in damp habitats from a small, subterranean tuber which enables the plant to die down during the dry season and await more favourable conditions. Its flowers, characteristically pale rose with a dark eye (C2), may occasionally be scarlet (C1), white, or yellow. The plant grows 5 to 10 inches (12·5–25 cm.) tall and bears 1 to 4 flowers 2 inches (5 cm.) in diameter. Each flower lasts about two weeks and a small colony of these plants with their heads following the sun round, makes an attractive picture.

PROTEACEAE

Mimetes hottentotica
A1 part of flowering stem × $\frac{2}{3}$.
A2 tip of perianth lobe with sessile anther × $2\frac{2}{3}$.
A3 single flower showing perianth lobes and style × $1\frac{1}{3}$.

Protea obtusifolia
D1 part of flowering stem × $\frac{2}{3}$.

P. amplexicaulis
E1 part of flowering stem × $\frac{2}{3}$.

P. grandiceps
F1 part of flowering stem × $\frac{2}{3}$.

PENAEACEAE

Endonema retzioides
B1 flowering twig × $\frac{2}{3}$.
B2 portion of leaf × 2.

DROSERACEAE

Drosera cistiflora
C1 flowering plant × $\frac{2}{3}$.
C2 pale rose flower × $\frac{2}{3}$.
C3 portion of leaf showing glands × 2.

A1

A3

B1

B2

C1

C2

C3

D1

E1

F1

Plate 76   SOUTH AFRICA

Perhaps the most remarkable of all vegetable curiosities to the traveller in Africa is the Baobab tree, *Adansonia digitata* (B): so familiar is it indeed that no precise records of its overall distribution have been made. As far as South Africa is concerned, however, it is true to say that the occurrence of the tree diminishes rapidly south of a line joining the Olifants river and the Zoutpansberg, on whose northern slopes grow the most southerly dense stands that remain. The Baobab inhabits arid, sandy environments throughout tropical and southern Africa. It reaches heights of between 45 and 70 feet (14–21 m.), the massive bole, 85 to 140 feet (25–43 m.) in circumference, appearing disproportionately large in comparison to the small crown, an imbalance that is exaggerated in the dormant season, after the leaves have fallen. The habit sketch illustrates a fairly young tree, for in older specimens the trunk, with its smooth grey or red-brown bark, becomes extensively convoluted and buttressed. Seedlings differ from adult plants in having entire and simple, rather than palmate leaves. The saplings are prone to damage by grazing and bush fires, whereas the mature trees are virtually indestructible, suffering only from the ravages of elephants. Old trees do not, as some romantics claim, ignite spontaneously and consume themselves, but, with the loss of water from the wood, collapse relatively rapidly and spectacularly into a pile of bleached fibrous material.

The tree yields few materials of any great economic value, but plays an important part in the economy and life of many African tribes. The fruit pulp, when dried to a powder and mixed with water, makes a drink rich in citric and tartaric acid, while a fibrous material can be obtained, after long pounding, from the wood, which is spongy and difficult to chop. The fruits, which measure up to about 12 inches (30 cm.) in length, are woody when ripe and covered with an at first greenish velvet that later becomes variously coloured in yellowish-browns. The white pulp, in which numerous black seeds are embedded, also provides food for baboons,

which crack open the fruit to obtain it. Otherwise the tree, when hollow or hollowed out, may be used to catch and store water, or, in one recorded case, as a jail.

The flowers, which have a waxy texture, appear soon after the leaves; authorities differ over whether they are scented or odourless when growing, but it is certain that if picked they soon begin to smell unpleasantly, and discolour. Pollinators may include bats and bush-babies, the latter having been observed to eat the petals and toy with the powder-puff stamens.

Because of their unusual bulk, estimates of the age of Baobabs by annual-ring counting is difficult. However, dating of wood by means of the radiocarbon method has shown an age of approximately a thousand years. The Baobab has been a protected tree under the South African Forestry Act since 1941.

The genus *Sparmannia*, named in honour of Andreas Sparrman, who botanized in the Cape from 1772 to 1776 (during which period he joined Captain Cook on his second voyage when he called there en route to New Zealand) contains about seven species. *S. africana* (A) is a showy shrub that grows to about 20 feet (6 m.) in height near rivers and in other damp spots. The flowers, which are very delicate and only last about a day, are held erect when open, though the buds droop. The peculiar thickening of their filaments (see A2 and A3) is in some way connected with the way in which they move when touched, presumably to aid pollination.

One of a genus of some fifty species found throughout Africa and in Madagascar and Arabia, *Acridocarpus natalitius* (C) is, as its name implies, a native of Natal, but also occurs in Transvaal, Zambia and Mozambique. The plant, found on forest edges or in clearings, varies in size but is often to be seen in the form of a straggling bush up to 8 feet (2·4 m.) tall. A number of varieties, classified according to the size and shape of the leaf, are also recognized in different parts of its range, that shown being the type variety, var. *natalitius*), with long, broad leaves pointed at the tip.

TILIACEAE

Sparmannia africana
A1 part of flowering stem × $\frac{2}{3}$.
A2 stamen × $3\frac{1}{3}$.
A3 staminode × $3\frac{1}{3}$.

BOMBACACEAE

Adansonia digitata Baobab
B1 flowering shoot × $\frac{2}{3}$.
B2 bud × $\frac{2}{3}$.
B3 fruit × $\frac{2}{3}$.
B4 seedling × $\frac{2}{3}$.
B5 habit sketch of a young tree × $\frac{1}{50}$.

MALPIGHIACEAE

Acridocarpus natalitius
C1 flowering and fruiting shoot × $\frac{2}{3}$.
C2 petal × 2.

A1

A2 A3

B1

B5

B3

B4

C2

C1

B2

Plate 77 SOUTH AFRICA

The heather or heath genus, *Erica*, though common through much of Europe, the Mediterranean, the islands of the Atlantic, and tropical Africa, has its highest concentration of species in southern Africa: six hundred and fifty species occur south of the Limpopo River, five hundred and eighty of them in southern Cape Province alone. Bridal or Albertinia Heath, *E. bauera* (A), takes its specific epithet from Francis Bauer (1758–1840), sometime botanical artist at Kew. This white or pink flowered species is restricted in the wild state to two areas in Cape Province but is widely cultivated, favouring poor, sandy soils. Its characteristic, slightly bent, tubular flowers are typical of the *Syringodia* section of *Erica*. The stamens shed their pollen through apical pores and appendages on the anthers (see A3) facilitate the deposition of pollen by ensuring that the stamens which hang down within the corolla are shaken by visiting insects. A very rare, and outstandingly superb *Erica*, first described by the famous South African botanist H. Bolus (1834–1911) and aptly named by him in honour of the Queen of the Gods, is *E. junonia* (C). The larger flowered of its two varieties is confined to a single mountain in Cape Province. The smaller flowered variety, illustrated here, has a slightly wider distribution. The 'star' formed by the outspread lobes of the corolla is characteristic of species of the *Stellanthe* section.

E. atrovinosa (D) is easily recognizable because of its curious dark, wine-coloured flowers, whose corollas, suitably enough, have a flush of grape-like bloom, and because of its densely clustered, soft leaves. Such a lovely species obviously suggests itself for cultivation, but its rarity (only two or three populations are known) and the consequent need for protection, prevents this, unless seed is carefully employed. Though first discovered in 1942 the species was not described until 1967. The flowers of *E. urnaviridis* (G) take the form, as the name implies, of green urns. This is yet another rare species found only on the Muizenberg Mountains from Steenberg to Kalk Bay in Cape Peninsula, where it usually flowers between December and July.

Yellow flowers, coloured calyces and unfused carpels mounted on a receptacle that swells and becomes fleshy during fruiting characterize the eighty-five African and tropical Asian species of the genus *Ochna*. One example, occurring in many eastern districts of South Africa, is *O.*

atropurpurea (B), a shrub about 8 feet (2.4 m.) tall that grows in scrub, often near rivers or the sea. The mode of growth, and size of leaf and flower, are variable. The striking effect of the splashes of colour made by the massed calyces of *O. macrocalyx* (H) against the tawny background of the savannah is borne witness to by the number of early explorers in southern and central Africa whose attention it attracted. It was one of the species collected by Dr Livingstone on his expedition to the Zambesi River in 1861, and again by Speke and Grant on their 1860–1863 expedition to the sources of the Nile. In dry areas, it forms a mass of woody roots underground and its aerial parts are limited to a height of between 4 and 24 inches (10–61 cm.). However, in more favourable habitats—in thickets or near rivers—it may reach 7 feet (2·1 m.). The splendid yellow flowers soon drop their petals, but the sepals persist even after the fruits have fallen off or been eaten.

Sir George Grey (1812–1898), Governor-General of the Cape Colony from 1853 to 1861, is commemorated in the genus *Greyia*, which comprises three species, found only in south-eastern South Africa. *G. sutherlandii* (F) is a native of the Drakensberg in Natal, the Transvaal, Orange Free State and Swaziland. It has hairless leaves, densely clustered inflorescences with oblong petals, and copious nectar.

The Wild or Cape Chestnut, *Calodendrum capense* (E), owes its common name to the resemblance of the leaves and fruit to the Sweet Chestnut; the trees grow to a height of about 60 feet (18 m.) and are covered, between October and December, with scented, lilac-pink blossom. The overall colour of the variously sized flowers is made up from the 5 large pink petals, sometimes spotted with purple, and the 5 spotted staminodes. The stalked ovary (see E2) matures into a warty, woody capsule, about $2\frac{1}{2}$ inches (6·3 cm.) in diameter, containing shiny black, angular, bitter-flavoured seeds which yield an oil that is used in the manufacture of soap. The empty capsules, left on the tree in winter, are a characteristic sight. The tree has shiny foliage, a spreading crown and smooth, grey bark. *C. capense* is found from the Southwest Cape north-east to Natal and north from there to Kenya. Near the coast it generally behaves as an evergreen, but inland it is deciduous, the leaves colouring to a variety of yellowish shades in autumn.

ERICACEAE

Erica bauera, Bridal Heath, Albertinia Heath
A1 part of flowering stem × $\frac{2}{3}$.
A2 calyx, stamens, style and ovary × $2\frac{2}{3}$.
A3 stamen × $5\frac{1}{3}$.

E. junonia
C1 part of flowering stem × $\frac{2}{3}$.

E. atrovinosa
D1 part of flowering stem × $\frac{2}{3}$.
D2 flower × 2.

E. urna-viridis
G1 part of flowering branch × $\frac{2}{3}$.

OCHNACEAE

Ochna atropurpurea
B1 flower and young fruit on part of stem × $\frac{2}{3}$.
B2 stamen × $8\frac{2}{3}$.
B3 fruiting twig × $\frac{2}{3}$.

O. macrocalyx
H1 flowering and budding shoot × $\frac{2}{3}$.
H2 part of fruiting stem × $\frac{2}{3}$.

RUTACEAE

Calodendrum capense, Cape Chestnut, Wild Chestnut
E1 part of flowering twig × $\frac{2}{3}$.
E2 flower × $\frac{2}{3}$.

MELIANTHACEAE

Greyia sutherlandii
F1 part of flowering stem and leaf × $\frac{2}{3}$.
F2 flower × 2.

A1
A2
A3
B1
B2
B3
C1
D1
D2
E1
E2
F1
F2
G1
H1
H2

Plate 78   SOUTH AFRICA

Tropical and subtropical Africa is the home of a number of curious genera belonging to a division of the family *Asclepiadaceae* and generally referred to as stapeliads after the best-known genus *Stapelia*. This genus contains seventy species and occurs throughout South and tropical Africa, one member, *S. gigantea*, bearing the largest flowers in the family; corollas with a diameter of 18 inches (46 cm.) have been recorded. *S. nobilis* (B) resembles this species, but has smaller flowers, a deeper throat and more compact stems. The flowers of both are clothed with dense and shaggy purple hairs that give their surfaces an almost velvety appearance. Both give off a smell of carrion that serves to attract the flies by which the flowers are pollinated; as a result, old flowers are usually found to be crawling with maggots.

The thirty species of *Huernia* extend from South and tropical Africa into southern Arabia. One of the more peculiar is *H. hystrix* (A), with its fleshy and spiny petals, dull yellow, banded with red (see A1), found in the eastern regions of South Africa, and north into Rhodesia and Mozambique. The flowers of this, the Porcupine Huernia, vary in size and in the colouring of the corolla. The species was introduced into cultivation at Kew in 1869, from material sent by M. J. McKen of Durban. Among other interesting huernias are *H. barbata*, which derives its specific epithet from the beard of conspicuous, long purple hairs at the throats of the yellowish, red-spotted flowers; *H. oculata*, whose abruptly contrasting white throats and purplish black petals give the impression of eyes, peering from the base of the stem; and *H. confusa*, which has a fleshy, shiny ring, yellow-crimson in colour, around the throat of the flower that contrasts bizarrely with the greenish, red-patched petals. All three species are native to South Africa.

Caralluma retrospiciens (F), one of a genus of a hundred species found throughout Africa, in parts of the Mediterranean region, and east through the arid areas of India to Burma, is not a South African species but has been included so that its strange structure may be used to provide a comparison with other stapeliads. The plant is conspicuous for its stature—it grows to a height of 4 feet (1·2 m.)—and its globular heads of stinking flowers. It usually occurs in arid areas and is difficult to cultivate. The variety illustrated comes from the Witu area of Kenya and, since it lacks the hairs found on the flowers of the true species, is known by some botanists as var. *glabra* ('glabrous' means 'without hairs'). The original plant, and type variety, discovered on Dahlak Island in the Red Sea by Christian Gottfried Ehrenberg (1795-1876) in 1820, extends, in various forms, south into Kenya and

four thousand miles west across northern Africa. The habit sketch shows how the stems cluster together and also shows the forked fruit which follows the fly-pollinated flower.

Arid conditions similar to those that prevail in cactus-producing areas of the world, have given rise to vegetative organs in this group of genera that greatly resemble those of cacti. Such a development is known as 'parallel evolution', the adoption of a similar trait in unrelated organisms in response to similar conditions. Particularly striking is this resemblance in *Decabelone grandiflora* (D) which was discovered about 1886 in South-west Africa by Hans Schinz, and described in 1895. It has since been found to extend into Botswana, Cape Province, the Transvaal and Rhodesia. Easterly specimens have straight-tubed corollas; those from the west slightly curved tubes.

Another solution to the problems posed by an arid environment is exemplified by *Brachystelma barberiae* (E). As can be seen from the illustration this species is neither spiny nor succulent, but the short stalk and hairy leaves are dominated by the relatively massive tuber from which they rise. This tough tuber is the form adopted by the plant for the greater part of the year, the leaves and flowers only lasting for a brief period, in spring, though when they are present the flowers are a remarkable sight, since the tips of the petals continue to adhere to one another even after the blooms have opened, and form curious structures resembling bird cages. This species, which was discovered in the Transkei by James Henry Bowker (1822-1900), and named by him in honour of his sister, Mrs Mary Barber, is found from the eastern Cape to Rhodesia, but is commonest in the high veld of the Transvaal.

Thomas Bain, son of Andrew Geddes Bain, engineer and father of South African geology, discovered *Hoodia bainii* (C), a species native to South-west Africa, with pale yellow- or buff-coloured flowers often tinged with pale pink or purple. The illustration of this species in the *Botanical Magazine* marks an heroic moment in the history of that remarkable journal: the famous botanical artist Walter Hood Fitch, finding himself in disagreement over his salary with the editor, Joseph Dalton Hooker, withheld a number of his drawings, that of *Hoodia bainii* among them. The threat to the continued appearance of the magazine was only averted by the efforts of the editor's daughter, Harriet, who nobly provided a series of drawings that enabled the issue to go forward. Shortly before Harriet had married William Turner Thiselton-Dyer, who described this species, and who succeeded his father-in-law as Director of Kew Gardens and was later knighted.

ASCLEPIADACEAE

Huernia hystrix, Porcupine Huernia
A1 part of flowering plant × $\frac{2}{3}$.
A2 spines on portion of corolla × $5\frac{1}{3}$.

Stapelia nobilis
B1 part of flowering plant with bud × $\frac{2}{3}$.

Hoodia bainii
C1 flowering plant × $\frac{2}{3}$.

Decabelone grandiflora (syn. *Tavaresia grandiflora*)
D1 flowering plant × $\frac{2}{3}$.
D2 spines × $3\frac{1}{3}$.

Brachystelma barberiae
E1 flowering plant × $\frac{2}{3}$.

Caralluma retrospiciens var. *glabra*
F1 part of flowering stem × $\frac{2}{3}$.
F2 fruit × $\frac{2}{3}$.
F3 habit sketch in flower and fruit × $\frac{1}{10}$.

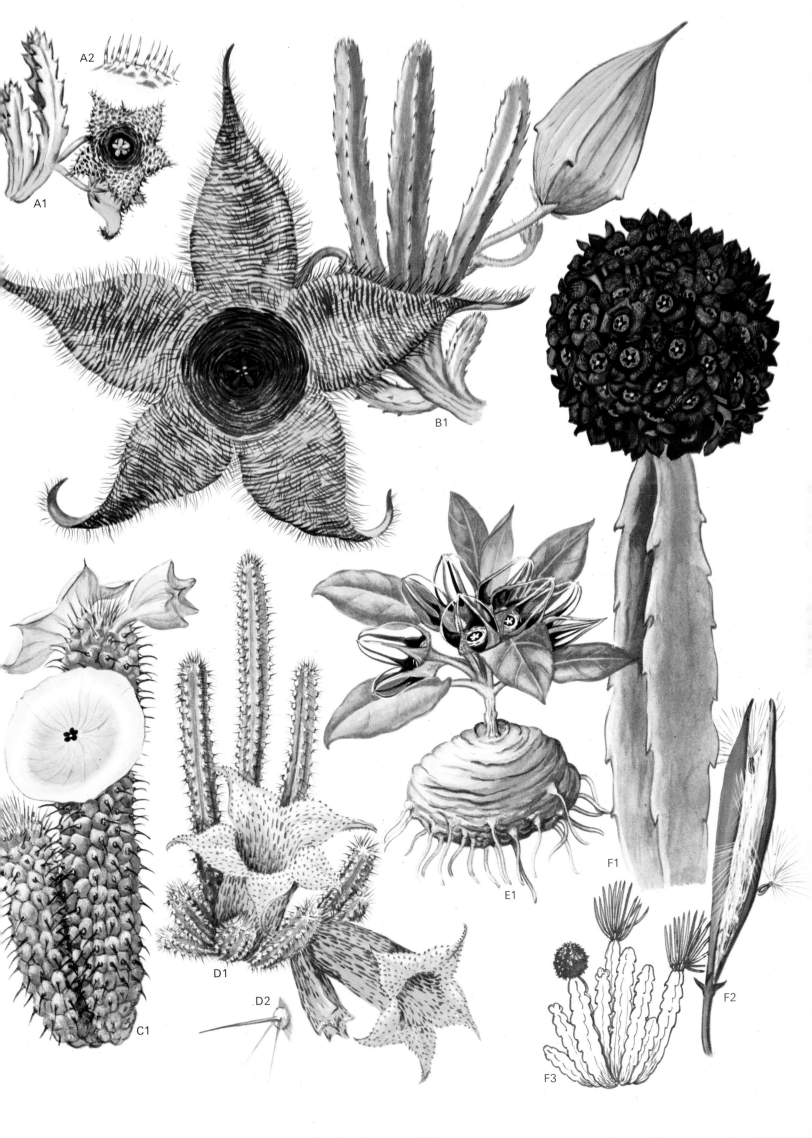

A2

A1

B1

D1

D2

C1

E1

F1

F2

F3

Plate 79   SOUTH AFRICA

On the grassland north of the Orange river are found the extensive trailing stems of *Harpagophytum procumbens* (A), member of a genus of about eight species, all of which are natives of South Africa or Madagascar. It bears single, red to purplish flowers that spring from the axils of the variously-shaped leaves. It is, however, only when the fruits ripen that the species comes to play that dramatic role in the life of the local fauna that has given it the popular name of Grapple Plant. As the fruit grows it develops peculiar outgrowths on the wall of the capsule which when fully mature are armed with sharply pointed and recurved spines that attach themselves to the bodies or feet of antelope and similar animals. After a time the capsule, having been carried some distance from the parent plant, opens to release the small, corrugated, oblong seeds. They have also been known to hook themselves onto the jaws of grazing cattle and so painful are the embedded spines that they may seriously incapacitate the beast, by interfering with its ability to eat or walk, and so cause it eventually to die.

Albertus Magnus (1193–1280), theologian, scholar and author of, among other works, *De Vegetabilibus Libri*, is commemorated by the plant name *Alberta magna* (B), the South African representative of a genus, the other two species of which come from Madagascar. Unfortunately the name *Alberta* is pre-empted as it had already been proposed and used for another plant a year earlier and so the correct but little known, name for the plant illustrated opposite is *Ernestimeyera magna*. It is a plant known to most people as a cultivated shrub but in the wild it forms a large tree up to 30 feet (9 m.) high. It was first discovered by Johann Franze Drège (1794–1881) in 1832 and introduced to cultivation through Kew, where it is still cultivated, by John Medley-Wood in 1889.

Found in woodland from Swellendam to Zululand and northern Transvaal, *Burchellia bubalina* (E) is an evergreen shrub about 15 feet (4·6 m.) tall. It is attractive when in flower, for the flowers often change colour from orange to red as they age, and also when in fruit with sepals which enlarge, turn orange and envelope the berries. The toughness of its wood has given the plant the popular name of Buffeldoorn (buffalo-horn); it is also known as Wild Granaat (wild pomegranate). The genus, which contains only one species is named after the explorer William Burchell (1782?–1863).

The *Gardenia* so well liked by florists is gener-

ally a double-flowered cultivar of Chinese or Japanese origin. There are, however, two hundred and fifty species in the genus, distributed throughout the warmer parts of the Old World; ten of them are native to South Africa and the surrounding areas. *G. thunbergia*, the Stompdoorn, for example, is a particularly fragrant, night-flowering species with leathery fruits that remain on the bush, to be eaten by large antelope, via whose intestines the hard seeds are dispersed. *G. spatulifolia* (G), an untidy bush with twiggy stems and grey bark found in savannah and other dry scrub, has a range that extends from eastern South Africa into Rhodesia, Malawi and Angola. The flowers turn creamy yellow when old. Species of the related genus *Rothmannia* are also found in South Africa.

The seeds of the coastal-bush climber *Coccinia quinqueloba* (F) depend in part for their dispersal on the somewhat devious medical lore of the Xhosa peoples, who tie the stems around the ankles of nursing mothers to prevent their babies from getting diarrhoea. The species is a perennial, occurring from Bathurst to East London, with bright red fruits that bear thin, waxy outer coats when ripe. About thirty Old World species of *Coccinia* exist, the majority of them in tropical Africa.

Ipomoea crassipes (D) is a twining plant found in coastal areas from Bathurst to Natal. Its silkily hairy leaves, sometimes tinged with purple, contrast attractively with the short-lived flowers. Another decorative South African convolvulus is *Merremia verecunda*, which has yellow flowers with bright crimson centres, and inflated purple-striped calyces.

Cape or Kaffir Honeysuckle is a misleading name in that it implies a spurious relationship between *Tecomaria capensis*, one of two species in a genus of the *Bignoniaceae*, and the true honeysuckles, *Lonicera*, in the *Caprifoliaceae*. *T. capensis* (C) does, however, bear a superficial resemblence to a honeysuckle in certain respects; it is a popular garden shrub in warm regions, is valued for its contrasting bright orange flowers and green foliage, and makes loosely grown but flowering hedges. Its popularity is also attributable to the ease with which it may be propagated by layering. When transplanted to tropical America, it attracts hummingbirds as readily as it does their Old World equivalents, the Sunbirds, in Africa. The species is found in eastern South Africa and was introduced into Europe about 1820 from seed collected by William Burchell in the Bathurst district.

B1

B2

A2

A1

A3

C1

D1

E1

E3

E2

F2

F1

G1

G2

Plate 80   SOUTH AFRICA

The labiates of tropical and subtropical Africa are sometimes very striking, with vivid orange or blue flowers, but sometimes rather dull, with innumerable tiny flowers, and, unlike their temperate equivalents, some of them may grow to a height of many feet and form thickets.

A native of the Transvaal, where it is commonly called Blue Boys, *Pycnostachys urticifolia* (B) grows in moist localities and, depending on conditions, may reach 8 or even 10 feet (2·4–3 m.) in height. The dense heads of flowers attract numerous insects. The genus comprises about thirty-seven species, found in tropical and South Africa and Madagascar.

Plectranthus is a large and widespread genus of some two hundred and fifty species and extends from Africa through Malaysia, into the Pacific area. *P. behrii* (F), named to commemorate Charles Behr, who collected the species in the Lusikisiki area of Pondoland in 1931, is a most desirable glasshouse species with fine inflorescences that make an imposing sight when grown en masse. The plant flourishes in both sunny and shaded habitats and is usually about 3½ feet (1·6 m.) tall.

Salvia aurea (D), originally named *S. africana-lutea*, inhabits the coastal areas of Namaqualand and the Cape Peninsula and is often found in sand dunes. The leaves of this, one of the smaller African labiates, measure ⅜ to 1 inch (10–25 mm.) in length; the plants themselves may be as much as 6 feet (1·8 m.) tall but are commonly less. Even after the corollas have withered, the persistent calyx, which sometimes turns a reddish brown, continues to give the species colour.

The best known *Plumbago*, frequently used in western conservatories and glasshouses, and employed as a flowering hedge-plant throughout Africa, is *P. auriculata* (E), better known, perhaps by the synonym *P. capensis*. It was intro-

duced to Europe from its native South Africa about 1818 and grows to height of approximately 8 feet (2·4 m.). Although it has a tendency to spread and climb, it can be kept in hand easily by trimming. In season, it is smothered with pale blue flowers. Another of the twelve species of *Plumbago*, which are found in the warmer parts of both the Old and New Worlds, may be seen on plate 114.

Almost as curious as their name (which commemorates the Danish botanist Theodor Holmskjold (1732–1794)), the flowers of the genus *Holmskioldia* have scooped corollas with a pronounced lower lip surrounded by a coloured, papery calyx shaped like a shallow dish. A native of East Africa, *H. tettensis* (C) is a very conspicuous plant when in flower, growing to height of about 20 feet (6 m.) and well worthy of stove cultivation in temperate regions. Although all the eleven species in the genus are native of the Old World, certain species such as *H. sanguinea*, the Chinese Hat Plant, from the Indian Himalaya, with brick red calyces and darker red or orange corollas, are commonly cultivated in the New World tropics.

Selago serrata (A) is one of the more colourful species of this fairly large genus of heathy plants found especially in South Africa. The species was introduced to western Europe by the Kew collector Andrew Masson, but was temporarily lost in cultivation after the 1830's, when the interest in South African plants faltered and the flora of the tropics became the vogue. Cultivation has since been revived but it is still a rare glasshouse plant, though its heads of blue flowers and heather-like habit make it distinctive. The genera which comprise the family *Selaginaceae* are often classified as a group within the speedwell family, the *Scrophulariaceae* (see plate 81), but there is no unanimity amongst authorities on the matter.

A2

A1

B1

C1

D1

D2

E1

F1

F2

F3

Plate 81   SOUTH AFRICA

The Cape Figwort, *Phygelius capensis* (A), has become a well known temperate garden plant although shunned by some gardeners as it tends to form an untidy bush. One of the difficulties is that the long flowering heads often flop over so that the graceful curve of the more or less pendant red flowers cannot be seen to advantage. In nature it is a perennial, growing in south-eastern Cape Province, Natal and Lesotho. There is only one other species in the genus.

In contrast to the Cape Figwort, *Harveya capensis* (B) is rarely seen outside South Africa. The genus, with about forty species, is confined to southern Africa and the Mascarene Islands in the south-western Indian Ocean; several of the species, including the one illustrated, are root parasites and lack chlorophyll in their organs. The genus contains many attractive species: *H. huttonii* with smaller rose-coloured flowers, *H. purpurea* with large yellow and pink flowers and *H. speciosa* with flowers similar to *H. capensis* but pale blue or white in colour. The stamens of all species have only 1 fertile anther-cell, the other being modified into a spur which protrudes into the throat of the corolla to insure that insect visitors disturb the stamens and so become showered with pollen. Like many parasites and semi-parasites, these plants when dried make unattractive specimens as they always turn black. This is caused by the oxidization of the sap which, when the tissues are bruised, is exposed to the air, but it can be avoided to a certain extent by coating the plants in acid solution of sodium bisulphite before pressing.

The sole representative of the South African genus *Ixianthes*, *I. retzioides* (E) is named from its resemblance to *Retzia capensis*. It is a very rare plant of the south-western Cape Province, but has been found growing near the small village of Porterville and also beside the stream above the Tulbagh waterfall. It forms a beautiful shrub about 10 feet (3 m.) tall, with leaves arranged in a dense spiral from which the foxglove-like flowers emerge in an unbroken mass as much as 2 feet (61 cm.) long, giving the shrub a spectacular appearance. These delicately coloured sulphur and primrose flowers gradually turn brown as they age.

The common name of Witchweed was given to *Striga elegans* (F) because the plant has a surprising, seemingly magical, way of establishing itself from seed. It is a parasite which forms absorptive connections on the roots of certain grasses found in most parts of tropical and South Africa. The species is very variable in stature, some plants producing stems up to 2 feet (61 cm.) high, with widely spaced leaves and flowers, often consisting of a single unbranched stem. The flowers have unusual colouring—scarlet on the upper surface and apricot underneath. The related *S. asiatica* (syn. *S. lutea*), usually with red flowers too, despite its synonym, is a parasite of maize and, as the abundant and tiny seeds of *Striga* species are wind dispersed, is a threat to agriculture as a serious weed.

The genus *Nemesia*, with about fifty species all confined to southern Africa, has become well known because the brightly coloured flowers have made several species and particularly the cultivars derived from *N. strumosa* (C) and *N. versicolor*, popular as summer annuals in temperate gardens. The public's attention was first drawn to these plants in 1892 and 1893 when they were exhibited by Sutton and Sons at the Royal Horticultural Society and where their fantastic range of colours—cream, pink, scarlet, brick red, orange, yellow, bronze, as well as those with mottled petals—was a constant source of amazement. These plants are unusual in that the petals frequently retain their true colours when pressed and dried. In nature, the species illustrated has a restricted distribution, only being found in the south-west of Cape Province.

The Polish botanist Adam Zaluziansky von Zaluzian (1558–1613) is commemorated by *Zaluzianskya* a genus of about thirty-five species confined to South Africa. They are night-flowering annuals and perennials with fragrant flowers, characterized by a pale, often cream or white upper surface and dark purple or reddish under surface to the petals. The similarity of its flowers to those of *Lychnis* species gave the illustrated plant, *Z. lychnidea* (D), its name. Growing in western South Africa, it is usually found as a roadside plant on stony ground or, at higher altitudes, as a rather lanky plant in swampy areas, varying in height from 5–18 inches (13–46 cm.). The undersides of the petals are said to vary from pink, through yellow-orange, to a purplish black colour.

SCROPHULARIACEAE

Phygelius capensis, Cape Figwort
A1 part of flowering stem with buds × ⅔.
A2 flower × 2.

Harveya capensis
B1 flowering shoot × ⅔.

Nemesia strumosa
C1 part of flowering stem × ⅔.
C2 fruit × 1⅓.

Zaluzianskya lychnidea
D1 part of flowering plant × ⅔.

Ixianthes retzioides
E1 part of flowering stem × ⅔.

Striga elegans, Witchweed
F1 flowering plant × ⅔.

A1

A2

B1

C1

C2

D1

E1

F1

Plate 82   SOUTH AFRICA

The most curious and beautiful plants within the African gesneriads belong to the genus *Streptocarpus*. Unlike the majority of dicotyledons, whose young shoots end in 2 seed-leaves, followed by others that gradually come to resemble adult leaves, a number of streptocarps, though strictly 2-leaved, develop one at the expense of the other, and this single enlarged seed-leaf, when mature, sometimes exceeds 30 inches (76 cm.) in length. Three of the four species illustrated are like this, with a single leaf. At a later stage, buds give rise to one or more inflorescences and, in some cases, a number of new leaves may begin to appear.

Although discovered by William Tyrer Gerrard in the Biggars Berg, Buffalo river area of Natal about 1865, *Streptocarpus cooksonii* (A) was not described until 1955, and named after Clive Cookson who had donated material to the Royal Botanic Garden, Edinburgh. The unique colouring and patterning of the corolla, and the dense array of the flowers, make the species worthy of cultivation. Leaves as much as 3 feet (91 cm.) in length and 18 inches (46 cm.) in width have been recorded.

The only species illustrated opposite with more than one leaf, and resembling in this respect such species as *S. rexii*, of which it was once thought to be a variety, *S. primulifolius* (B) has relatively large flowers characterized by fingers of pink running from the throat out onto the corolla lobes. *S. rexii* is the parent of many attractive hybrid cultivars found all over the world.

Streptocarpus dunnii (D), remarkable for its brick red flowers in a group of normally violet- or blue-flowered plants, was discovered by E. J. Dunn (1844–1937) in the Goldfields area of the Transvaal at altitudes of between 3600 and 6000 feet (1100–1830 m.). Two years later, in 1886, seed sent by Dunn flowered at Kew. Like many other streptocarps, it grows in rock crevices and amongst granite and sandstone boulders. In the wild, the most notable feature of *S. dunnii* is its leaf, which may reach as much as 3 feet (91 cm.) in length. Streptocarps, as is shown in D2 and D3, have 2 fertile stamens, the other 3 being inconspicuous and sterile. The fertile anthers tend to adhere to one another, with the stigma arching over them in the roof of the corolla tube.

The graceful and colourful species with long inflorescence stalks, lax clusters of flowers and a solitary leaf coloured deep red on the underside, *S. saundersii* (C) occurs in woodland at altitudes of 2000 to 2300 feet (610–700 m.) in Natal and southern Zululand. The flowers vary in colour from almost pure white to pale violet and all have a yellow stripe over the floor of the corolla tube. Leaves may be 30 inches (76 cm.) long and 25 inches (64 cm.) broad.

Though South Africa is the stronghold of the streptocarps, they extend into other parts of Africa as far as Ethiopia, where the most northerly species, *S. phaeotrichus* is found.

GESNERIACEAE

Streptocarpus cooksonii
A1 flowering plant × $\frac{2}{3}$.

S. primulifolius
B1 flowering plant × $\frac{2}{3}$.

S. saundersii
C1 flowering plant × $\frac{2}{3}$.

S. dunnii
D1 part of flowering plant × $\frac{2}{3}$.
D2 mouth of corolla × $3\frac{1}{3}$.
D3 corolla sectioned to show stamens and style × $3\frac{1}{3}$.

A1

B1

C1

D1

D2

D3

Plate 83   SOUTH AFRICA

A member of the largest and perhaps most cosmopolitan genus, *Senecio tamoides* (A), the Canary Creeper, is a climber found among bushes and at the edges of woodland, along the coast and in other moist spots, from Cape Province to the Transvaal and Rhodesia. A warm glasshouse is needed if the plant is to be cultivated in temperate Europe. The genus *Kleinia*, which is very closely related to *Senecio* and considered to be part of that genus by some, commemorates the German naturalist Jacob Theodor Klein (1685-1759) and consists of about fifty species of succulents found in Africa and Arabia. *K. fulgens* (or *Senecio fulgens*) (C) resists desiccation during dry spells in the rocky areas of the Transvaal and Natal, where it is native, by means of thick, woody stems and succulent leaves, the latter contrasting conspicuously with the bright red shaggy heads of flowers.

After the start of the rainy season, whole valleys may be found covered with masses of Gousblom or African Daisy, *Arctotis venusta* (B), often, but incorrectly, known as *A. stoechadifolia*. Found throughout much of South Africa, except the southern parts of Cape Province, the blooms, in the manner of many daisies, face the sun and follow its course through the sky, bending towards the east during the night, ready for the rising sun at dawn. The name *Arctotis*, translated from the Greek, means 'bear's ear', a fanciful allusion to the shape of the scales on the top of the individual achenes which, in this genus, take the place of the usual pappus of hairs to be found in this family. In all there are about sixty-five species found in South Africa and Australia.

The most notable attribute of the genus *Helipterum*, which also comes from South Africa and Australia, but contains about ninety species, is the involucre of scaly bracts that surrounds the flowers and renders them 'everlasting' when dried. In the case of *H. canescens* (D), refraction of light inside the cellular air spaces of the bracts gives the flower heads a silvery sheen. The pigment situated inside the walls of the cells that comprise the bracts sometimes gives rise to white or yellow involucres. The species is widely distributed in the Cape Peninsula and in western and north-western districts.

Cenia turbinata (E), one of a genus of ten South African species, is a weed, widespread in its native country and occasionally found in Europe, where it is brought as seed entangled in wool; after all the cleaning processes to which wool is subjected have been completed, the remaining waste or 'shoddy' is used as a manure, especially in market gardening on light soil, thus giving the seeds a chance to germinate. The plant can form quite pretty clumps, attractive for their curious, button-like flower-heads; it never grows taller than 15 inches (38 cm.) and sometimes as little as 2 inches (5 cm.).

Like *Helipterum canescens*, *Phaenocoma prolifera* (F) depends for its colour—in this case usually bright red or rose—on the involucral bracts that surround the capitula. However, *P. prolifera* is a robust shrub, usually about 1 or 2 feet (30-61 cm.) high, with twigs which somewhat resemble those of the cypress, having small leaves that adhere closely to the hairy stem (especially during dry spells), and this coarse and aromatic foliage protects the plant from grazing. It is the sole species in its genus and is found in extensive stands in parts of the south-western Cape Province, to which it is restricted.

One of the earliest South African plants to be cultivated was *Gazania rigens*, with bright orange ray-florets with black and white markings which attracted the attention of gardeners as early as 1755, and possibly even before. In fact, *G. rigens* var. *rigens* (G), the variety illustrated, is not known in the wild and appears to have developed in cultivation from the smaller flowered *G. rigens* var. *uniflora*, which occurs along the shores of the south-east coast, north to Mozambique. Another wild variety, var. *leucolaena*, has been recognized from approximately the same area.

COMPOSITAE

Senecio tamoides, Canary Creeper
A1 part of flowering shoot × ⅔.
A2 disc-floret × 4.
A3 ray-floret × 4.

Arctotis venusta, African Daisy, Gousblom
B1 part of flowering stems × ⅔.
B2 ray-floret × 2. B3 disc-floret × 3⅓.
B4 lower leaf × ⅔.

Kleinia fulgens (syn. *Senecio fulgens*)
C1 flowering plant × ⅔. C2 floret × 4.

Helipterum canescens
D1 part of flowering plant × ⅔. D2 floret × 4.

Cenia turbinata
E1 part of flowering stem × ⅔.
E2 ray-floret × 4⅔. E3 disc-floret × 4⅔.
E4 section through capitulum × 2.

Phaenocoma prolifera
F1 part of flowering stem × ⅔.
F2 involucral bract × 2.
F3 stem with leaves × 4. F4 leaf × 8.

Gazania rigens var. *rigens*
G1 part of flowering stem × ⅔.
G2 corolla of ray-floret, showing markings × 2.
G3 closed capitulum × ⅔.

A1

A2

A3

E2

E3

E4

E1

B1

B2

B3

B4

C1

C2

D2

D1

F2

F1

F3

F4

G1

G2

G3

Plate 84   SOUTH AFRICA

In recent years, strelitzias have become popular in floristry because of their exotic and strikingly coloured flowers. To those who are unfamiliar with strange forms of plant life, the elaborate flowers seem almost incomprehensible. What possible force can have created structures so different from the typical lily-like monocotyledon floral plan and with a complexity only exceeded in gingers and orchids? In *Aponogeton*, evolution has produced yet another bizarre flowering plant in which parts of the flower have become peculiarly reduced and in which the inflorescence is thrust out of water during a life-cycle otherwise confined to an aquatic environment.

The Bird of Paradise genus, *Strelitzia*, and its type-species *S. reginae* (A) with brilliant orange and blue flowers of extraordinary structure, were thus named, rather inappropriately, in compliment to the dull and undistinguished, but certainly dutiful, Queen Charlotte Sophia (1744–1818), a daughter of the Duke of Mecklenburg-Strelitz in north Germany, wife of King George III and mother of fifteen children. The five species are all native to South Africa, the best known, *S. reginae*, is widely cultivated. It grows naturally along river banks and in clearings among scrub in coastal areas of Cape Province, where it may reach a height of about 4 feet (1·2 m.). The condensed spike of flowers is enclosed in a stiff horizontal green and pink sheath, out of which the flowers rise in slow succession, one after another at intervals of about a week. Each flower consists of 3 orange-coloured 'sepals' of which only 2 have emerged in the recently opened flower illustrated here, and 3 blue 'petals'. Two of these 'petals' are united into an arrowhead-like structure resembling a large blue anther, but in fact enclosing the 5 thread-like anthers. The third much reduced 'petal' forms a small nectar-producing pouch at its base. These strange, complicated and conspicuous flowers are pollinated, it is thought, by sunbirds and sugarbirds. When a bird perches on the 2 fused 'petals' in order to reach the nectar below, these act as a lever and force the anthers out of their sheath so that they brush against its breast, depositing pollen. The anthers mature before the stigma which ultimately protrudes from the tip of the sheath, thus ensuring cross-pollination. The capsular fruit contains many black seeds, each provided with an orange aril or oil-body said to be attractive to birds. *Strelitzia parvifolia* has equally brilliant orange and blue flowers but is smaller in stature and has much narrower leaves. The other three species, however, are larger and *S. alba* with white petals, which is found in Cape Province, may grow to a height of 33 feet (10 m.) but is frequently less. *S. nicolai* of Natal and Cape Province, with its mauve and white petals,

may also grow as tall; its specific name commemorates the Emperor Nicolas of Russia. The third arborescent species is *S. caudata* of Transvaal and Swaziland. These are often called 'wild banana' (wilde pisang) in South Africa.

The thirty or so species of *Aponogeton* are natives of warm regions; they occur in ponds and lakes throughout tropical Africa, South Africa and India and extend into southern China, Malaya and north-east Australia. Some species have both submerged and floating leaves. Often grown as an aquarium plant, *A. fenestralis* has leaves which lack a solid blade, only the skeleton of nerve veins being evident, hence the common names of Lace- or Lattice-leaf. The Cape Pondweed, *A. distachyos* (B), a native of South Africa, which is more or less hardy out of doors in southern England, has only floating leaves. Its forked inflorescence which flowers in spring and summer, projects above the surface of the water and the numerous stamens and 3–6 carpels nestle at the base of the fleshy, white bract-like perianth segments. The flowers are scented rather like a hawthorn and this gives rise to the plant's alternative name of Water Hawthorn. Later, the white flowers turn green and the whole inflorescence bends back into the water where the fruit ripens. When mature, the individual fruits rise to the surface and release their seeds which float for a short time, thus ensuring their dispersal; they then sink and germinate soon afterwards. The rootstock and young inflorescences of the Cape Pondweed are said to be eaten by Africans. The name *Aponogeton*, from *Aponos*, now Abano, North Italy, *getōn* or *geitōn*, 'neighbour', was originally coined for an Italian water-plant and later transferred, inappropriately but irrevocably, to the present genus.

Xyris is a genus of about two hundred and fifty tropical and subtropical species. They are rush-like plants, usually dwarf, with narrow basal leaves in tufts and yellow flowers in tight bracteate heads terminating leafless stalks and giving rise to the common name of the genus, in North America, of Yellow-eyed Grass. Throughout the world the genus is easily distinguishable, being as botanists say, a 'natural group', distinct from any other group of plants. But the evolutionary origins of the *Xyridaceae* are more obscure. One can see something of the tradescantia or Wandering Jew family (plate 187) in the flowers, but the habit is closer to the little known family, *Rapateaceae*, found only in South America and West Africa. *X. capensis* (C) is one of eight species found in South Africa and, like most members of the genus, grows in marshy places. The characters separating even geographically wide apart species are few and slight, which adds to the difficulty of their identification.

MUSACEAE

Strelitzia reginae, Bird of Paradise Flower, Crane Flower
A1 habit sketch × $\frac{1}{6}$.
A2 flowering head and leaf × $\frac{2}{3}$.
A3 detail of base of flower × $\frac{2}{3}$.
A4 stamen and style × $\frac{2}{3}$.

APONOGETONACEAE

Aponogeton distachyos, Cape Pondweed, Water Hawthorn
B1 flowering plant × $\frac{2}{3}$.
B2 detail of inflorescence × 2. B3 stamen × 8.
B4 stamens, style and ovary × 4.
B5 fruiting inflorescence × $\frac{2}{3}$.
B6 fruiting flower and fruit × $1\frac{1}{3}$.

XYRIDACEAE

Xyris capensis, Yellow-eyed Grass
C1 flowering plant × $\frac{2}{3}$.
C2 detail of 3 inner perianth segments × 8, showing 3 stamens, 3 feathery staminodes and 3 style-arms.

A1

A2

A3

A4

B1

B2

B3

B4

B5

B6

C1

C2

Plate 85   SOUTH AFRICA

The species of *Aloe*, about three hundred and thirty in all, are characteristically succulent shrubs or tree-like plants with sharp-tipped, lance-shaped leaves arranged in rosettes at the ends of shoots which produce racemes of usually yellow or red flowers. They are mainly found in warm and tropical parts of Africa, including Madagascar, but also extend into Arabia. The great variation in size between the different species can be seen by comparing *A. saundersiae* which has a few stiff grass-like leaves and an inflorescence about 6 inches (15 cm.) tall, with *A. bainesii* which forms a tree up to 50 feet (15·2 m.) high, or more, crowned with many handsome racemes of rose-pink flowers. The illustrated *A. thraskii* (A) grows in sand at the very edge of shore vegetation, apparently never extending inland more than a few hundred yards, between Durban and Port Shepstone in Natal. It has deeply channelled, recurved leaves and a habit similar to that of *A. recurvifolia* from eastern Transvaal, but when in flower, the illustrated plant has a multiple inflorescence whereas the other has only a single one. In nature the stem, about 10 feet (3 m.) long, is clothed with persistent dead leaves, unlike the cultivated specimen shown in the habit sketch. Bees are attracted to the flowers with their yellowish petals and exerted orange stamens, giving the dense racemes a golden glow when the sun shines. The most widespread South African species are *A. arborescens* with scarlet racemes, a shrubby habit and leaves with conspicuously jagged edges, and *A. ferox*, with reddish-orange racemes and more erect leaves than *A. thraskii*. It is from *A. ferox* that the drug 'cape aloes' is prepared. The exuded juice from cut leaves is collected and allowed to evaporate and, when the residue has solidified, it is ready for use as an efficient purgative. For a fuller appreciation of these striking plants, the reader cannot do better than refer to *The Aloes of South Africa* by G. W. Reynolds (1950).

Growing in the southern parts of Africa, the fifteen or so species of *Eucomis* are unusual in that the inflorescence is crowned with a leafy 'coma', a tuft of bracts. The first to be introduced to Europe, in about 1760, was *E. autumnalis*, or as it has been previously but incorrectly known, *E. undulata*, called the Pineapple Flower because of the appearance of its inflorescence and leafy head. It grows throughout much of South Africa and has green flowers and leaves with an undulating margin. In *E. comosa* (syn. *E. punctata*) the inflorescence stalk, the ovary of the flowers and the base of the leaves are all purple-spotted, the leaves also having purple-edged undulating margins. Christopher Mudd, son of the one-time Curator of the Cambridge Botanic Garden, William Mudd (1830–1879), discovered *E. bicolor* (B) in Natal between 1876 and 1877 and sent it to Messrs Veitch in Britain where it flowered in 1878. In October of the same year it was featured in the *Gardeners Chronicle* as an attractive new garden plant. About five years later John Medley-Wood (1827–1915) sent more plants to Britain, this time to Kew where they flowered under glass during the winter of 1883–1884. It is now grown at Kew in an open border during the summer, under the walls of the Palm House, where it is protected from the occasional cold spell. The purple colour of the petal margins and stamen filaments varies from plant to plant but seems to distinguish the illustrated species from the two described earlier. When cut, the flowers will last for a long time but some people complain of their smell.

At one time *Gasteria*, *Haworthia* and *Aloe* were all thought to belong to the *Aloe* genus as they have many features in common. The seventy or so *Gasteria* species, all from South Africa, are characterized by two-ranked or compacted clusters of succulent leaves—often with white marbled markings—and petals which are often fused except for a small portion at the tip of each, forming a gently curving perianth tube. The flowers of *Aloe* species are similar but with a cylindrical or bell-shaped perianth tube and those of *Haworthia* species, smaller, frequently white with pink or green stripes. Henrik Bernard Oldenland and Carl Peter Thunberg were probably the first to collect *Gasteria* species towards the end of the 17th century. Later James Bowie sent plants to Adrian Hardy Haworth (1768–1833) who, between 1819 and 1826, described a number of species. The species opposite, *G. candicans* (C), is one of those described by Haworth during this period; it was also illustrated in a book produced by Joseph Franz Maria Anton Hubert Ignaz zu Salm-Reifferscheid-Dyck (1773–1861) between 1836 and 1863, called *Monographia Generum Aloes et Mesembryanthemi*. The ease with which these succulents could be shipped back to Europe and there survive, coupled with their inherent variability, led to the description of many species, notably by Karl von Poellnitz, so that the taxonomy of these plants has become very confused and it is probable that many of the so-called species are no more than varieties when considered in relation to specific delimitation in other groups.

LILIACEAE

Aloe thraskii
A1 part of leaves and inflorescence × $\frac{2}{3}$.
A2 flower × $2\frac{2}{3}$. A3 habit sketch × $\frac{1}{18}$.

Eucomis bicolor
B1 flowering stem with leaf × $\frac{2}{3}$.
B2 flower × $2\frac{2}{3}$.

Gasteria candicans
C1 part of flowering plant (stem cut) × $\frac{2}{3}$.
C2 flower × 2.

A3

A2

A1

B1

B2

C2

C1

Plate 86   SOUTH AFRICA

Though a native of South Africa, the Belladonna Lily, *Amaryllis bella-donna* (C), has long been cultivated in Europe and other parts of the world (and is often confused with *Hippeastrum*, a genus found only in the warmer parts of the Americas). The plants, which are particularly fragrant in the evening and much visited by moths, grow near coasts and rivers, sometimes amongst scrub. The flowers are usually produced some weeks before the leaves and are not unlike those of the *Nerine* species also illustrated (see A), albeit they are longer and broader. Artificial hybrids have in fact been raised between the two species and named × *Amarine tubergenii*. The flowers are larger than *Nerine* and have leaves at flowering time unlike the *Amaryllis*.

A species sufficiently hardy to grow and flower each year in such temperate areas as Britain, and one that can be raised from seed, *Nerine bowdenii* (A) is one of about thirty southern tropical African species in its genus. The plant, which is itself a native of eastern districts of South Africa, was named in commemoration of Mr Athelstan Bowden who sent bulbs from the Cape to his mother in Devon at the end of the 19th century. After flowering them for three years she presented bulbs to Kew. The related Guernsey Lily, *N. sarniensis*, is neither a native of Guernsey, where it was found in the 17th century, nor of Japan, as the botanists of the period hazarded; the mystery of its origin was solved at the end of the 18th century when Francis Masson (1741–1805), the first collector sent out from Kew, discovered the plant growing wild on Table Mountain. Later it was found in a number of other parts of South Africa. It seems likely that the Channel Island plants owed their appearance there to bulbs from the Cape taken on board a ship from Japan which was wrecked

on the island. From the ship they were washed ashore where they grew in the sand and were discovered, taken into their gardens and propagated by the islanders.

Occurring in all provinces of South Africa and in Angola, *Boöphone disticha* (B), popularly known as Cape Poison, or Sore Eye Flower, is a plant of dry grassland. It grows from a large bulb, sometimes up to 1 foot (30 cm.) in diameter but mostly consisting of dry scales, and bears dense, rather flattened heads of flowers in early spring, the pedicels lengthening from 2 to 9 inches (5–23 cm.) as the fruits develop and ripen. The leaves, which appear after the flowers, are arranged in two ranks and, when fully expanded, give the plant a curious fan-shaped habit (see B4). The bulbs contain a strong alkaloid poison called haemanthine, and have been used as remedies for a number of ailments; moreover the scent of the flowers and pollen is said to cause headaches, soreness of the eyes and, sometimes, sleepiness. Bulbs were introduced to Europe in the 18th century and all five species in the genus are confined to southern and eastern Africa.

Haemanthus albiflos (D) belongs to a genus of fifty species that occur in tropical Africa from Sierra Leone east to the island of Socotra off the Somali coast, and south to the Cape Peninsula in South Africa. This species, native to the areas around East London, bears, in addition to the tight head of flowers subtended by bracts, 3 to 4 fleshy broad leaves that lie more or less horizontally along the ground. It was introduced into Europe about two hundred years ago. Other species with larger heads of attractive red flowers are more spectacular and gave rise to the botanical name *Haemanthus*, meaning 'blood-red flowers'.

AMARYLLIDACEAE

Nerine bowdenii
A1 flowering plant and leaf × $\frac{2}{3}$.
A2 flower, with perianth removed × $\frac{2}{3}$.
A3 anther × 2.
A4 fruits on portion of stem × $\frac{2}{3}$.

Boöphone disticha, Cape Poison, Sore Eye Flower
B1 part of stem with inflorescence × $\frac{2}{3}$.
B2 anther × 4. B3 leaf × $\frac{2}{3}$. B4 habit sketch × $\frac{1}{12}$.

Amaryllis bella-donna, Belladonna Lily
C1 part of flowering stem × $\frac{2}{3}$.
C2 petal tip × 2.

Haemanthus albiflos
D1 part of fruiting plant × $\frac{2}{3}$.
D2 inflorescence on portion of stem × $\frac{2}{3}$.
D3 flower × $1\frac{1}{3}$.

A1

A2

A3

A4

B1

B2

B3

B4

C1

C2

D1

D2

D3

Plate 87   SOUTH AFRICA

Although the *Iris* genus itself is non-existent in South Africa, a most spectacular array of other iridaceous plants is to be found there. One of the most exotic is *Antholyza ringens* (A), with its 'bird-perch'—a leafless termination of the flower shoot with a dense spike of flowers springing at a wide angle from its base—on which the sun-birds by which the plant is pollinated alight: the bird, resting on the stem, probes deep into the scarlet flower-tube until its breast becomes dusted by the stamens with pollen, later to be pressed against the stigmas of a female flower. Similar 'perches' are to be found on certain South American species of *Puya*. The spike usually produces 4 to 8 closely grouped, ascending flowers, all on the upper side. The generic name, which means 'flower in a rage', refers to the two-lipped bloom, gaping as if about to bite, formed of a single segment above rolled into a tube around the style and filaments, and 5 shorter segments of unequal length below. The plant grows to about 10 inches (25 cm.) and has palm-like leaves; it favours dry, sandy habitats.

Named by Miller in 1758 in honour of Robert More, of Shrewsbury, a skilled botanist, *Moraea* contains about a hundred species found in Africa, expecially to the south. One of the most beautiful is the literally iridescent *M. villosa* (C) (syn. *M. pavonia*), known as the Peacock Flower after the sheen on the eye of the 3 inch (7·5 cm.) flower. The effect is thought to be produced by the blue sap and yellow bodies in the tissues of the outer perianth segments. The species, a native of the hilly areas of south-west Africa, is sparsely branched and grows to a height of about 18 inches (46 cm.).

A number of large-flowered and delicately coloured species of *Gladiolus* occur in South Africa. Now rare in nature owing to excessive collecting, and difficult to cultivate, *G. cardinalis* (D) is limited to remote mountain areas, where it inhabits moist ledges and the like. The flowers have the ability to adapt to strange situations, such as arise when the plant is found hanging upside down from a ledge, by changing their position in relation to the stem, so that the large red petal always remains uppermost.

Another plant whose numbers have been severely depleted by the depredations of collectors, doubly misguided since the bulbs they send to Europe can never flourish in such an unfavourable climate, is *Ixia viridiflora* (E), whose flowers have the colour, unusual in plants, of greenish-blue, of a shade resembling certain types of verdigris, and dramatized by a deep indigo eye. The species grows on dry hillsides and blooms in the spring.

Aristea contains fifty species occurring from southern and Central Africa, north to Ethiopia, west to the Cameroons, and east to Madagascar, the majority of them with deep blue flowers that open in the morning and are withered by the late afternoon. *A. ensifolia* (F) grows in forests and near streams from an altitude of 3000 feet (900 m.) down to nearly sea level.

Popular names seldom so accurately mirror what they describe as Wine Cups does the flowers of *Geissorhiza rochensis* (B): not only is their shape that of a wine-glass, and their colour that of claret, but there is even a white line of meniscus to be seen. Unfortunately, the white flecks opposite each of the perianth lobes suggest a floating sediment. *G. rochensis* rarely exceed 1 foot (30 cm.) in height.

IRIDACEAE

Antholyza ringens
A1 flowering plant (stem cut) $\times \frac{2}{3}$.

Geissorhiza rochensis, Wine Cups
B1 flowering plant $\times \frac{2}{3}$.

Moraea villosa, Peacock Flower
C1 flowering plant $\times \frac{2}{3}$. C2 inner petal $\times 2\frac{2}{3}$.

Gladiolus cardinalis
D1 part of flowering stem and leaf $\times \frac{2}{3}$.
D2 anther $\times 2\frac{2}{3}$. D3 style and stigmas $\times 2$.

Ixia viridiflora
E1 flowering plant (stem cut) $\times \frac{2}{3}$.

Aristea ensifolia
F1 flowering stem (cut) $\times \frac{2}{3}$.
F2 flower $\times 1\frac{1}{3}$.

A1

B1

C1

C2

D1

D2

D3

E1

F1

F2

Plate 88   SOUTH AFRICA

Zantedeschia is a genus of about nine species that occurs in many parts of tropical Africa. The name commemorates the physician and botanist Giovanni Zantedeschi (1773–1846) and is correct for these aroids, though *Richardia*, which properly refers to a genus of ten South American species in the coffee family *Rubiaceae*, was used at one time.

The Arum Lily, *Z. aethiopica* (D), is a characteristic and beautiful species from coastal and montane parts of South Africa, not Ethiopia, as its name suggests: the epithet *aethiopica* was given it in the 18th century when little of Africa was known and the name Ethiopia was applied indiscriminately to most parts of the continent. It occurs in swampy areas and is found especially in the region around the Cape. In temperate areas it has become a popular exotic cut-flower, but in those parts of Australia where it is naturalized it is now becoming an agricultural weed. The large dark green leaves appear late in the autumn and the flowers in the ensuing spring. As in all aroids, a leafy spathe, in this case white, encloses the small and tightly massed simple flowers that constitute the phallomorphic spadix. The male flowers are reduced to a number of stamens only, while the female consist of an ovary with 3 cavities, often surrounded by staminodes. If flowers are fertilized and mature successfully, the base of the spadix will bear a number of yellow berries that are attractive to birds. The large rhizomes contain a lot of starch and have been used as food for domestic animals.

A cousin of the Arum Lily, the Pink Arum, *Z. rehmannii* (E), is altogether smaller in stature, but its pink spathe makes it very decorative. The leaves are more elliptic in shape than those of the other species and about 15 inches (38 cm.) long. The arrangement of the flowers, which appear in summer, is like that of *Z. aethiopica*—the male above the female (see E2). The Pink Arum occurs in Natal in the Newcastle area and in Swaziland.

Other attractive Zantedeschias are *Z. pentlandii*, which has yellow spathes and short white streaks or spots on the leaves, and *Z. oculata*, with a purplish-black eye in the base of the yellow or creamy-white spathe.

The *Velloziaceae*, a family of two genera and about one hundred and seventy species, occur in Arabia, Madagascar, tropical Africa and the American tropics, especially on the arid campos of South America, and are adapted to life in an arid environment in a different way from the better-known cacti. *Vellozia retinervis* (B) grows to about 3 feet (91 cm.) in height with false 'stems' composed of innumerable leaf bases (see B2). New leaves and flowers, which emerge from areas at the top or sides of this 'stem', in fact grow from the ends of the real stem and branches, which are relatively thin, and hidden from view in the leaf bases. The lower portion of the stem above ground is covered with adventitious roots that arise near the points of insertion of the green leaves and ramify between the real stem and the dead leaf bases before growing into the soil. Each root has a spongy outer layer, and when the 'stem' becomes sodden with water during rain, or when water condenses on it in the form of dew, it is easily and readily absorbed by the root. Thus water is obtained both from the soil and from the false stem. The leaves are arranged in the tufts of 3 or 4, those at the apex of the 'stem' being longer and broader than the others. The dark brown leaf bases are sometimes charred at the tips in bush fires but, thanks to the protection they afford, the rest of the plant normally recovers. Flowers arise on single stalks in the axils of the leaves, 1 to 3 on each tuft. The petals vary in colour from blue to mauve and may even be white on occasion. The fruits are woody capsules containing many tiny seeds easily dispersed by the wind. Thus *V. retinervis*, which is a common plant in the Transvaal, is admirably adapted to the conditions of a habitat where bush fires occur, where a short rainy period must be exploited to the full, and where the wind may transport its seeds to any newly bared patch of ground.

The *Restionaceae*, to which belongs *Elegia juncea* (A), have a distribution centred on South Africa and Australia, with a few outlying species in New Zealand, Chile and South East Asia. Plants of this family resemble grasses and sedges but are in fact allied to the rushes, *Juncaceae*. They have cylindrical stems which bear sheathing leaves with little, if any, free leaf blade. The shoots, which may be branched, arise from a creeping rhizome and the male and female flowers are usually borne separately in terminal, bract-subtended clusters on different plants. The genus *Elegia*, with its thirty or so species, is confined to South Africa. *E. juncea* is quite a common plant and grows to a height of about 3 feet (91 cm.). Female flowering heads are used for decoration but the males are unsuitable for this purpose as the blooms have a habit of dropping when dried. As may be seen, the female flowers themselves are rendered inconspicuous by the brown sheathing bracts. *E. juncea* is found in the western and southern parts of Cape Province.

Elegia capensis closely resembles a horsetail, *Equisetum* species, with its terminal inflorescences and dense whorls of shoots with reduced bract-like leaves borne at successive nodes. In fact, this species (which has until recently been called *E. verticillaris*) was at first mistaken for a horsetail and given the name *Equisetum capensis* by the younger Burman in 1768. The epithet *capensis* thus antedates that of *verticillaris* given by the younger Linnaeus thirteen years later and, by the International Code of Nomenclature, takes precedence. *E. capensis* is found in wet places in many districts of southern and south-western Cape Province. *E. equisetacea*, a similar but smaller species also resembling a horsetail, has a more limited distribution in southern parts of Cape Province.

Restio comprises about one hundred and twenty species, eighty-nine of which are found in South Africa, the others in Madagascar and Australia. In these plants the green stems have taken over the role of food manufacturer and the sheathing leaves become vestigial. *R. compressus* (F) is a common swamp plant in south-western Africa. The male inflorescences, which are 3 to 4 inches (7·5–10 cm.) long, are composed of a series of 5- to 10-flowered clusters, while the female inflorescences, which are borne on separate plants, are clustered at the ends of shoots. Unlike those of the male flowers, the bracts subtending the female flowers hardly ever open. The plant is found in the southern coastal districts of Cape Province.

The sedge genus *Ficinia* contains some sixty species, all African. *F. radiata* (C) is native to the damp plains and mountains of the Capetown and Clanwilliam areas of south-western Cape Province and is notable for the ornamental bracts with bright, glossy yellow bases which surround the inflorescence. Despite this conspicuous coloration, which in most plants would serve to attract birds and insects, the small flowers, borne in a cluster at base of the bracts, are wind pollinated.

RESTIONACEAE

Elegia juncea
A1 lower part of plant and roots $\times \frac{2}{3}$.
A2 female inflorescence $\times \frac{2}{3}$.
A3 male inflorescence $\times \frac{2}{3}$.

Restio compressus
F1 female flowering shoot $\times \frac{2}{3}$.
F2 male flowering shoot $\times \frac{2}{3}$.

VELLOZIACEAE

Vellozia retinervis
B1 flowering plant $\times \frac{2}{3}$.
B2 portion of leaf base $\times 1\frac{1}{3}$.

CYPERACEAE

Ficinia radiata
C1 flowering plant $\times \frac{2}{3}$.

ARACEAE

Zantedeschia aethiopica, Arum Lily
D1 flower, bud and leaves $\times \frac{2}{3}$.
D2 habit sketch $\times \frac{1}{18}$.

Z. rehmannii, Pink Arum
E1 flower and leaves $\times \frac{2}{3}$.
E2 spadix $\times \frac{2}{3}$.

A2

A3

C1

E2

E1

D2

B2

B1

A1

D1

F1   F2

Plate 89   SOUTH AFRICA

The arid climate of many parts of South Africa favours the existence of terrestrial orchids, perhaps the most famous one being *Disa uniflora* (B) although, as can be seen opposite, some of the other species are equally intriguing. *Disa* is an essentially African genus, but is also found in Madagascar and the Mascarene Islands. There is still controversy over the generic limits of *Disa*, some authorities including *Herschelia* and *Penthea*, others treating these genera as distinct. The generic name is that of Queen Disa of Swedish mythology, who, being commanded to come before the Swedish king neither naked nor dressed, appeared draped in a fishing net. *D. uniflora* first flowered at Kew in 1843, but even at that time it was realized there was little hope of providing a second home for this species in the houses at Kew, so demanding were its requirements.

Disa uniflora grows near pools and streams where the temperatures may drop to below freezing on occasions, or rise to above 90°F (32°C) and during the dry season it is exposed to considerable drying. In Cape Province it is found on Table Mountain where, according to William Harvey (1811–1866), it borders almost every mountain stream. It grows to 2–2½ feet (61–75 cm.) tall, with 5 to 7 leaves and 1 to 3 flowers on each stalk. The species is also found near Tulbagh and in the Clanwilliam, Paarl, Worcester and Ceres districts of South Africa.

Satyrium princeps (E) is one of one hundred and fifteen species found in all the warmer parts of Africa, and into India and China in the east. This robust species has two fleshy leaves pressed close to the soil and from these the inflorescence grows to a height of about 2¾ feet (85 cm.) including the spike which is about 10 inches (25 cm.) long. The plants have densely clustered carmine flowers and are found growing in the Port Elizabeth, Humansdorp areas of South Africa, sometimes in dunes near the coast.

Of the three species of *Bartholina*, *B. burmanniana* (F) is as typically South African as *Disa uniflora*. This species, with its delicate little fringed flowers and small flat leaf, is found—often in large numbers—on wet sandy flats near Stellenbosch, Caledon, Capetown and Tulbagh. The plant is hairy all over and the horizontally held flower has a fringed appearance because the lobes of the lip are much dissected. The related *B. ethelae*, found in the Cape, Tulbagh and Knysna districts, has swollen tips to each of the slender sections of the lip. It was named after Ethel Bolus by her father Harry Bolus and is found in open veld, on dry banks and sandy places near the sea.

Most of the twenty or so species of *Herschelia* are native to South Africa. *H. charpentieriana* (H), which grows in the Tulbagh, Stellenbosch, Caledon and Prince Albert districts, is characterized by the elongated lip, some 1¾–2½ inches (6–6·5 cm.) long. This peculiar development may be a means of attracting pollinators for the wind sways these curious flowers when it catches the lip. Flowering occurs in November, but as the plant is rare, the 2–6 flowers, borne on slender stems about 18 inches (46 cm.) tall, are not often seen. *H. graminifolia* (C) grows in heathy habitats, often in the company of members of the *Restionaceae*. As its name suggests, the leaves are grass-like, but it is the flower which is the glory of this species, being a bright and intense blue. Between 2 and 7 flowers are borne at the top of an inflorescence stalk up to 24 inches (61 cm.) long during the months of February and March. The plant is sometimes very abundant on Table Mountain and in the Swellendam area, at altitudes of between 1800–3000 feet (540–900 m.). On one of the sheets in the Kew herbarium a painting of an *H. graminifolia* flower can be found on one of the silvery hairy leaves of *Leucadendron argentum*, the Silver Leaf Tree—the protea leaf being enclosed in a 1903 Christmas card. This must surely be one of the quaintest herbarium specimens in existence!

The attractive pink and purple flowers of *Penthea filicornis* (D) appear in October to December. This species, which does not exceed 10 inches (25 cm.) in height, is found fairly extensively in South Africa. The related *P. patens* has yellow flowers and both grow in moist places in the mountains.

Disperis comprises seventy-five African species which also extend into the Mascarene Islands and Indomalaysia. *D. capensis* (A) grows to about 18 inches (46 cm.) and is normally single flowered, rarely 2-flowered. Found in the Capetown and Table Mountain areas, *D. capensis* may also occur in Knysna, Port Elizabeth, and Albany districts and the Transkei. It is a variable species and yellow-flowered plants are sometimes found in the flowering period of August.

Huttonaea pulchra (G) is found in Stockenstrom district, the Kalahari region, the Transkei and Natal. It usually occurs in the mountains and often in grassy scrub. Growing to 18 inches (46 cm.) tall, the stout stems bear 1 or 2 leaves and are terminated by a more or less well developed raceme of pale greenish yellow flowers. The petals and lip of these curious orchids are deeply fimbriate or fringed. There are only five species in the genus, all of which are natives of South Africa.

ORCHIDACEAE

Disperis capensis
A1 flowering stem × ⅔.
A2 pollinia × 4.

Disa uniflora
B1 flowering plant × ⅔. B2 column × 1⅓.

Herschelia graminifolia
C1 flowering plant (stem cut) × ⅔.
C2 pollinia × 2.
C3 ovary of withered flower × ⅔.

Penthea filicornis
D1 part of flowering stem × ⅔.

Satyrium princeps
E1 flowering stem (cut) × ⅔.

Bartholina burmanniana
F1 flowering stem with leaf × ⅔.

Huttonaea pulchra
G1 flowering stem with leaves × ⅔.
G2 flower × 2⅔.

Herschelia charpentieriana
H1 flowering plant (stem cut) × ⅔.
H2 end of lip × 2.

Plate 90   HIMALAYA AND CHINA

Plant distribution becomes a key factor in discussing the hypothesis that western North America and eastern Asia were once a more or less continuous land mass. Two genera, *Magnolia* and *Mahonia* have disjunct distributions in eastern Asia and in North and Central America, while the *Lardizabalaceae* family is found in both eastern Asia and Chile. The Peony genus, too, has a more widespread distribution in temperate Eurasia and western North America. When affinity between the floras of two continents so widely separated can be proved, it is just a short step to the belief that they might once have been joined.

Although Magnolia flowers bear some resemblance to tulips, they should be distinguished from the Tulip Trees (*Liriodendron* species, see plate 150); magnolias have anthers which shed pollen towards the centre of the flower, and an aril-like seed coat in which the outer part of the ripening seed becomes fleshy and forms a coloured structure in which the seed lies. Tulip trees have stamens which shed their pollen facing outwards from the flower and the seeds lack any aril-like structure.

Some eighty *Magnolia* species are found in the Himalaya, China, Japan, parts of Malaysia, eastern North America and into Venezuela. The Frenchman, Pierre Magnol, a professor of medicine and botany who died in 1715, is commemorated by the genus. Its flowers are frequently showy; some of the loveliest trees are included in the American species, whose heavily scented flowers tend to appear while the trees are still in leaf. East Asian species, on the other hand, bear their flowers on leafless twigs. Other flower characteristics, common to both the eastern and western species, are a petaloid perianth, and stamens and carpels mounted on an elongated cone of tissue. When in fruit, each of the several follicles splits open, allowing one or both of the seeds to dangle out attached to a long, fine thread of the consistency of chewing gum. *M. stellata* (B), a native of Japan, forms a deciduous, compact shrub up to 10 feet (3 m.) tall which produces hundreds of small scented flowers before the leaves have expanded. Other *Magnolia* species are trees with large flowers, but these are often produced in smaller numbers. Hybridization among the north temperate species of eastern Asia has produced some superbly beautiful flowering trees, among them *M. × soulangeana*, a popular hybrid derived from *M. denudata* and *M. liliflora*. Often grown in American and European gardens, it commemorates Chevalier Soulange-Bodin, a French Army officer who raised the plant in his garden at Fromont near Paris in 1820. Old, gnarled specimens of *M. denudata*, a species commonly called the Yulan which has been cultivated at least since the T'ang dynasty (between 618 and 906 A.D.), were once to be found throughout China and this may still be so. The blooms of *M. campbellii*, a native of western China and the eastern Himalaya, are quite sturdy and last for a week or more. Fragrant, cup-shaped, and up

to 10 inches (25 cm.) in diameter, these white, rose or crimson flowers are spectacularly borne on a magnificent tree 30 to 35 feet (9–10·5 m.) tall. Many other *Magnolia* species doubtless merit mention here. Unfortunately, however, limited space prevents their inclusion.

Ranging throughout temperate Eurasia and into north-west America, the thirty species in the genus *Paeonia* have been represented in cultivation, until recently, by only a few species and hybrids with, however, many garden forms. A relatively recent discovery is *P. lutea*, a native of Yunnan, Tibet, and Bhutan, which was first found by the Abbé Delavay in 1882. The variety illustrated, var. *ludlowii* (A), which forms a bush up to 6 feet (1·8 m.) tall in Kew Gardens, is named after Frank Ludlow, the ornithologist and botanist, who collected with George Sherriff in Bhutan and Tibet. It is more handsome for garden use and was introduced in 1936.

The Moutan, *P. suffruticosa* (C), wild in Shensi, Kansu and Szechuan provinces of China, was introduced into central and south-eastern China in about 750 A.D., when it created an unrivalled floral craze. The summer palace of Emperor Ming Huang, it is said, was planted with ten thousand Moutan bushes of various colours. Ouyang Hsiu (1007–1072) recorded over ninety cultivars and wrote of sophisticated graft and cultivation techniques. The Loyang area was the centre of Moutan culture for centuries, but after 1700 this was moved to Ts'aochow and Fahuahsiang near Shanghai. *P. suffruticosa* reached Europe after 1787 and Robert Fortune introduced some forty varieties in 1842; over a hundred cultivars are now grown.

P. lactiflora, the Shaoyao, has an even longer history of cultivation—records mention it as early as 900 B.C.—and it was another popular garden plant during the Moutan craze in China. Yangchow was the centre of Shaoyao culture until 1600 and the gardens of the Chu family are said to have contained sixty thousand plants of one variety or another. Liu Pin wrote a monograph on the species and the roots of cultivars commanded high prices.

One of the five species in the *Akebia* genus, *A quinata* (D) is a native of Japan, Korea and China. The generic name is a latinized form of the Japanese vernacular name 'Akebi'. Though its fruits are edible it is usually grown as an ornamental climber, flowering in spring.

Bernard McMahon (1775–1816), an American horticulturalist born in Ireland, gives his name to the *Mahonia* genus which comprises some seventy species ranging from the Himalaya through China into North and Central America. One of these, *M. nepaulensis* (E), a native of Nepal, grows to a height of about 20 feet (6·1 m.) in wet oak and rhododendron forest. Its racemes with long, usually persistent inflorescence bracts are very imposing when they bloom. The American species, however, have the same clusters of fasciculate inflorescences but with short, deciduous bracts or else loosely paniculate, racemose inflorescences with few flowers.

PAEONIACEAE

Paeonia lutea var. *ludlowii*
A1 part of flowering stem with leaves and buds and faded flower showing ovary and styles × $\frac{2}{3}$. A2 stamen × $2\frac{2}{3}$.

P. suffruticosa, Moutan
C1 part of flowering stem × $\frac{2}{3}$.
C2 stamens, style and ovary and disc × $\frac{2}{3}$.

MAGNOLIACEAE

Magnolia stellata
B1 twigs with flowers, buds and leaves × $\frac{2}{3}$.
B2 stamens, style and ovary × $1\frac{1}{3}$.
B3 stamen × $2\frac{2}{3}$.

LARDIZABALACEAE

Akebia quinata
D1 flowers and buds on part of climbing stem × $\frac{2}{3}$.
D2 male flower × $2\frac{2}{3}$. D3 stamen × $5\frac{1}{3}$.
D4 female flower × $1\frac{1}{3}$.

BERBERIDACEAE

Mahonia nepaulensis
E1 part of flowering stem with leaves × $\frac{2}{3}$.
E2 flower × $2\frac{2}{3}$. E3 petal and stamen × $3\frac{1}{3}$.
E4 fruit on part of stem × $\frac{2}{3}$.

A1

B1

B2

B3

C1

C2

D1

D2

D3

D4

E1

E2

E3

E4

Plate 91   HIMALAYA AND CHINA

The Himalaya is rich in members of the buttercup family, including some lovely *Adonis* and *Delphinium* species that have found a place in temperate gardens. Among the delphiniums are a number of species suitable for the rock garden: *D. brunonianum* from Tibet which has pale blue flowers in a loose corymb and usually stands about 1 foot (30 cm.) tall, for instance; *D. glaciale* from Sikkim with its musky scented parts and few large, hairy flowers borne on a stem about 6 inches (15 cm.) tall; and the quietly attractive *D. lacostei* (A) from the western end of the Himalayan Range. However, charming as these species are, they cannot compare with the 'man-made' plants, grown in herbaceous borders and produced by hybridization from the Eurasian species *D. elatum*. These perennial cultivars are characterized by a conspicuous central column of dense blossom and exist in both single and double flowered varieties in a range of colours that is focused chiefly at the blue end of the spectrum. Annual larkspurs, which also exist in single and double flowered forms with a wide variety of flower colours, are derived from the south-west Asian and Mediterranean species *Consolida regalis*, *C. orientalis* and *C. ambigua*.

A native of Kashmir and Tibet, *Adonis chrysocyanthus* (E), sometimes called Golden Cup, has flowering stems about 9 inches (23 cm.) tall that extend to a height of 15 inches (38 cm.) after the golden flowers have developed into a dense head of fruits about $\frac{2}{3}$ inch (16 mm.) in diameter. The plant closely resembles *A. pyrenaica*, a restricted Pyrenean species with fewer, larger fruits or achenes.

Corydalis rutifolia (B) has a wide distribution stretching from Crete and Turkey to the western Himalaya in the east, where it is found at altitudes of between 6000 and 10,000 feet (1830–3050 m.). A similar European species with fewer-flowered racemes and longer spurs to the corolla is *C. uniflora*. There is also a large, decorative Chinese species, *C. saxicola* (syn. *C. thalictrifolia*) which is sometimes grown in gardens, with pale green leaves about 6 inches (15 cm.) long that contrast well with the golden racemes of the same length. The leaves are shaped something like those of Meadow Rue, *Thalictrum*, hence the specific epithet of its synonym—the epithet *saxicola* means growing in rocks.

Discovered by Nathaniel Wallich in 1824, *Podophyllum hexandrum* (C) is one of the Himalaya's earliest flowering plants. Two shiny leaves expand from the bud and are at first deflexed (C2) but later, when fully expanded, come to be held horizontally, by which time the large ovary in the single flower has matured into a most ornamental ellipsoidal fruit, said to be edible. *Podophyllum* contains ten east Asian species and one North American. The latter, *P. peltatum*, the American Mandrake or May Apple, was the first species to be discovered and was introduced into England as early as 1616. It differs from *P. hexandrum* in having leaves with more lobes, larger flowers and twice as many stamens as petals. *P. pleianthum*, discovered on Formosa by T. Walter in 1881 and introduced to Kew from the Hong Kong Botanic Gardens in 1885, has 6 to 12 deep purple flowers that give off an offensive smell.

Euryale ferox (D), the sole species in its genus, is a curious but little cultivated plant from India, east Pakistan and China that was introduced into Europe in 1809 by the Director of the Calcutta Botanic Garden, William Roxburgh. The flat circular leaves which float on the surface of the water reach up to about 4 feet (1·2 m.) in diameter and are spiny all over the undersides. The deep violet flowers give rise to fruits 2 to 4 inches (5–10 cm.) in diameter which contain pea-sized, farinaceous seeds that may be roasted and eaten. The South American *Victoria amazonica* (see plate 169), which being larger, is even more spectacular, closely resembles *E. ferox* and was, when first discovered, placed in the genus *Euryale*; since then some botanists, while recognizing that the two plants belong to separate genera, have created a new family, the *Euryalaceae*, for them. Others, however, keep them with the water-lilies, in the *Nymphaeaceae*.

RANUNCULACEAE

Delphinium lacostei
A1 flowering plant × $\frac{2}{3}$.

Adonis chrysocyanthus, Golden Cup
E1 flowering stems × $\frac{2}{3}$.

PAPAVERACEAE

Corydalis rutifolia
B1 part of flowering plant × $\frac{2}{3}$.

BERBERIDACEAE

Podophyllum hexandrum (syn. *P. emodi*)
C1 flowering plant × $\frac{2}{3}$.
C2 side view of flower × $\frac{2}{3}$. C3 fruit × $\frac{2}{3}$.

NYMPHAEACEAE

Euryale ferox
D1 part of flowering and budding stems and leaves × $\frac{2}{3}$.
D2 fruit × $\frac{2}{3}$. D3 seed × $\frac{2}{3}$.

A1

B1

C2

C3

C1

E1

D3   D2   D1

Plate 92   HIMALAYA AND CHINA

A conspicuous element in north temperate vegetation, some of the two hundred and fifty species of *Rosa* are also known on mountains in tropical regions. Many of these species have been cultivated and hybridized for years. Prized for its white flowers in ancient China, Korea and Japan, *R. multiflora* featured in more modern times as the ancestor of the Rambling Roses while what we now know as the Polyanthus Roses were very probably produced by hybridization of *R. multiflora* and *R. chinensis*. Our popular Hybrid Tea Roses are derived from ancestors which include the tea-scented roses. A common wild Chinese rose, *R. laevigata*, is now found naturalized in the south-eastern United States, where it arrived after being sent to Europe through the East India Company in the 18th century. Some botanists have suggested, however, that it spread to the American continent prior to the last Ice Age and, believing the species to be native, point to it as another example of the affinity between the floras of North America and eastern Asia. Attar of roses is distilled from the petals of *R. damascena*, which may be a native of Turkey, although there is some doubt about its place of origin. The Greeks wrote about its medicinal qualities as early as 650 B.C. and it was probably introduced to western Europe by monks in the 1100's and soldiers returning from crusades in the 1200's.

A popular garden species, *Rosa moyesii* (E) has deep red flowers, attractive foliage and curiously shaped red hips. The bushes reach 10 feet (3 m.) in height and are found amongst other shrubs in the mountainous areas of south-west China and adjacent Tibet between altitudes of 7000 and 13,000 feet (2130-3960 m.). It was introduced into cultivation in the West from seed collected by E. H. Wilson, possibly his 1903 collection, although it appears this may represent a closely allied species. Wilson named the species after the Reverend J. Moyes, a missionary stationed at Tachien-lu in western Szechuan, who was host to him and accompanied him on a plant collecting foray into eastern Tibet.

If the genus *Prunus* is taken in a broad sense to include apricots, peaches, almonds, cherries and plums, then it is a truly cosmopolitan genus with some four hundred to four hundred and thirty species. The blossoms and fruit of *P. persica*, the Peach, were symbolic of longevity in prehistoric China and were traditionally given as presents on birthdays. This delicate fruit is a native of China which reached southern Europe about 100 A.D. via Persia and the Silk Route, spreading into western Europe only after the Renaissance. *P. davidiana* of northern China is, if one regards it as distinct from *P. persica*, closer to the cultivated form than any other native peach.

The Japanese Apricot, *P. mume*, another species with a long history of cultivation in China and Japan, is a native of the former country. As early as the 14th and 15th centuries, the flowers provided a subject for decorative patterns on domestic items in China; the 5 petals denoted good luck. Painting the Japanese Apricot is a specialist branch of the highly calligraphic Chinese art and the plant is popular amongst bonsai fanciers.

Authors have recently begun to suspect that the Yoshino or Tokyo Cherry, *P. yedoensis* (B), is a hybrid which has the Japanese *P. lannesiana* and *P. pendula* as its parents. It is also possible that it is a natural hybrid, for it was unknown prior to the 1880's which is strange in a nation with such a long horticultural tradition as the Japanese. Western European gardeners first grew the plant between 1907 and 1910 and it is appreciated for its early pale pink blooms.

One of the species of *Prunus* discovered by E. H. Wilson is *P. conradinae* (D) or Conradine's Cherry, a native of western Hupeh and Szechuan and so named after the author's wife Frau Conradine Koehne. It forms a tree about 40 feet (12 m.) tall and, given the right conditions, is exceptionally early to flower: February and March are normal. Introduced to western Europe in 1907, it bears $\frac{3}{8}$ inch (1 cm.) long, oval red fruits in the autumn.

The genus *Chaenomeles* contains three species which are confined to eastern Asia. *C. speciosa* (A), the illustrated species, was introduced to Kew by Sir Joseph Banks in 1796 when it gained immediate popularity as it produces its flowers between January and June. This and the other species have given rise to a great number of cultivars with single or double flowers in many colours, among them scarlet, salmon, orange and white, sometimes even yellowish. The common name of Japanese Quince was given to the plant because its globose yellowish green fruits resemble quinces.

Some five hundred variable species of *Potentilla* have a chiefly north temperate and arctic distribution and material from the Himalaya, such as that illustrated, is often called *P. arbuscula* (F), which is part of the aggregate species *P. fruticosa*. Many cultivated types exist, conveniently divided into bright yellow, pale yellow or cream flowered forms. In the broad sense, *P. fruticosa* has a wide distribution: from Britain and Sweden to the Pyrenees, through the Urals and Caucasus, into north and central Asia, the Himalaya and Japan, and then from the American north-west, across the continent to New Jersey, with many names for the geographical segregates.

Like other members of the *Calycanthaceae*, most parts of Wintersweet, *Chimonanthus praecox* (C), are aromatic. The Japanese put bundles of the fragrant twigs in cupboards and drawers to scent clothing, in much the same way as Westerners use lavender. Grown for centuries in the Far East, it was introduced to England in 1760 but has never become as widespread as some other eastern introductions, such as *Forsythia* or *Syringa*, perhaps because it is not quite so hardy. The strongly scented flowers appear in late winter, while the branches are still devoid of leaves and are said to be pollinated by beetles. If a few flowers are taken into a warm room, they soon fill it with a sweet fragrance. The illustrated species is one of four in the genus.

ROSACEAE

Chaenomeles speciosa, Japanese Quince
A1 flowering twig with new leaves $\times \frac{2}{3}$.
A2 twig with mature leaves $\times \frac{2}{3}$.
A3 section of flower $\times 2$.

Prunus yedoensis, Yoshino or Tokyo Cherry
B1 flowering twig $\times \frac{2}{3}$.
B2 twig with mature leaves $\times \frac{2}{3}$.

P. conradinae, Conradine's Cherry
D1 flowering twig $\times \frac{2}{3}$.
D2 shoot with mature leaves $\times \frac{2}{3}$.
D3 base of leaf showing glands $\times 2$.

Rosa moyesii
E1 flowering branch $\times \frac{2}{3}$.
E2 sectioned flower, showing stamens, styles and ovary $\times 1\frac{1}{3}$.
E3 anther $\times 5\frac{1}{3}$. E4 twig with hips $\times \frac{2}{3}$.
E5 sectioned hip $\times 1\frac{1}{3}$.

Potentilla arbuscula
F1 part of flowering branch $\times \frac{2}{3}$.
F2 sectioned flower $\times 2\frac{2}{3}$.
F3 fruiting twig $\times \frac{2}{3}$. F4 fruit $\times 2\frac{2}{3}$.

CALYCANTHACEAE

Chimonanthus praecox, Wintersweet
C1 flowering twig $\times \frac{2}{3}$.
C2 twig with mature leaves $\times \frac{2}{3}$. C3 flower $\times 1\frac{1}{3}$.

A1

A2

A3

B1

B2

C1

C2

C3

D1

D2

D3

E1

E2

E3

E4

E5

F1

F2

F3

F4

Plate 93   HIMALAYA AND CHINA

The family *Papaveraceae* is mainly temperate in distribution and provides many ornamental plants for gardens. A few have had some economic use besides the Opium Poppy, described on plate 46; the rhizome of Bloodroot, *Sanguinaria canadensis* being used medicinally in a dried state as an emetic, the latex of *Bocconia frutescens* for treatment of warts.

Meconopsis, so named from the Greek *mēkōn* 'poppy', *opsis* 'resemblance', has its centre of distribution in the Himalaya and western China, with about forty species mostly having blue, purplish or yellow flowers. However, the type species is the European *M. cambrica*, the Welsh Poppy (plate 11), the only one not found in the Far East. Perhaps the most famous of the Blue or Himalayan Poppies is *M. betonicifolia*, of which a variety with a hairy ovary was named *M. baileyi*; this last plant created a horticultural sensation after its introduction by F. Kingdon Ward in 1924. *M. nepaulensis* was the first Asian species described botanically, being published in 1824. By 1896 botanical exploration had provided another twenty-two different species.

The popular horticultural plants are the blue-flowered species such as the Himalayan Poppy, *M. betonicifolia* and *M. grandis* but purity and intensity of colour often depend on soil and climate. The yellow-flowered *M. dhwojii*, *M. integrifolia*, *M. paniculata* and *M. regia* are also not without beauty. Perhaps the most serious disadvantage about *Meconopsis* as garden plants is that most species are monocarpic and so die after flowering and fruiting only once.

Ranging from central Nepal, east through upper Burma and into China, *M. horridula* (A) grows at altitudes between 10,000 and 19,000 feet (3050–5790 m.) with its uppermost recorded limit high on Mount Everest. It was so named in 1855 on account of its bristly nature, after being collected in Sikkim. *M. horridula* is a variable plant and at various times some of these varieties have erroneously been given specific names by botanists. It was introduced in 1904 and continues to show extreme variation even under the relatively uniform conditions of gardens, luxuriant and dwarf plants sometimes growing side by side.

Discovered by N. Przewalski in Kansu in 1872, *M. integrifolia* (B) was intially placed in the genus *Cathcartia* by Maximowicz, in commemoration of James W. Cathcart (1802–1851), an amateur botanist and student of Himalayan flora. The species is found in alpine meadows and on screes in western China, upper Burma and Tibet, where it sometimes grows to 3 feet (91 cm.) tall and may bear 15 or more flowers, although at its highest limit of growth, about 16,000 feet (4900 m.), the rosette of leaves may only have a solitary, stalkless flower in its midst. The leaves may be up to 15 inches (38 cm.) long and 2 inches (5 cm.) broad with an attractive covering of golden or brownish hairs. As well as the yellow flowered form, white and pink flowered forms are known, the latter collected by Joseph Rock in 1932. The plant was originally introduced to cultivation in France in 1896 by Abbé Farges, while British gardens received seed from E. H. Wilson and Koslov in 1904. It has since been hybridised with *M. betonicifolia*, *M. grandis* and *M. simplicifolia*.

Found in Kashmir and the north-western Himalaya to Kumaon, at altitudes between 8000 and 14,000 feet (2440–4270 m.), *M. aculeata* (C) grows amongst rocks and beside streams. Hugh Francis Clarke Cleghorn (1820–1895) sent seed to Kew from north-west India and in 1864 it flowered for the first time in cultivation. It is not so widely grown as the larger and more intensely coloured species, such as *M. betonicifolia*.

PAPAVERACEAE

Meconopsis horridula
A1 flowering stem with leaves and buds × $\frac{2}{3}$.
A2 flower showing colour variation × $\frac{2}{3}$.
A3 stamens, style and ovary × 2.
A4 stamen × $3\frac{1}{3}$.

M. integrifolia
B1 part of flowering plant × $\frac{2}{3}$. B2 stamen × $1\frac{1}{3}$.
B3 style and ovary × $1\frac{1}{3}$.

M. aculeata
C1 inflorescence × $\frac{2}{3}$.
C2 style and ovary × 2. C3 stamen × 2.
C4 part of fruiting stem × $\frac{2}{3}$.

A2

A3

A4

B1

B2 B3

C1

C2 C3

C4

A1

Plate 94   HIMALAYA AND CHINA

The six species of witch hazel belong to the genus *Hamamelis* and occur in China, Japan and eastern North America. Bearing a profusion of small, scented, yellow or red flowers on leafless twigs in early spring or late autumn, they make particularly useful garden shrubs. The Chinese Witch Hazel, *H. mollis* (A), did not reach England until 1879 when it was introduced by Charles Maries. The first species to arrive, *H. virginiana*, was brought to Europe in 1736, by Peter Collinson, philanthropist, horticulturist and correspondent of John Bartram, but because it flowers as the leaves are falling in the autumn it is not such a prized plant for the garden. Its inner bark contains substances used to soothe inflammations and bruises, a remedy known to the North American Indians long before it became popular in Europe.

The twenty Himalayan and east Asian species of *Corylopsis* are, like those of *Hamamelis*, early flowering shrubs, their delicately petalled catkins of yellow flowers appearing before the leaves have emerged. *Corylopsis sinensis* (F), closely related to *C. veitchiana* and *C. henryi*, is found from central and southern China to Szechuan in the west.

Stachyurus is a little cultivated genus of ten Himalayan to east Asian species; it has the advantage over *Corylopsis*, which rarely fruits in Britain, of producing attractive dull red berries late in summer. The characters that divide several of the species are very slight. *S. chinensis* (B) from central China was the second to be discovered.

The sole species of its genus, *Kolkwitzia amabilis* (D), the Beauty Bush, is a native of China and was first collected by Père Giraldi in Shensi Province between 1890 and 1895. Its flowers, however, were unknown until 1910, when seed sent by E. H. Wilson some ten years earlier first blossomed in England. When he collected the seed he had no idea what the plant that he had collected was, nor how beautiful it would prove. The small blooms, which cover the entire plant, often hiding the leaves, are enhanced by a silver-haired calyx and stalk. Unlike those of the related genus *Abelia* they are fused in pairs in the region of the ovary (D2).

Named in honour of Clarke Abel (1780–1826), who accompanied Lord Amherst's embassy to Peking, in 1816, and based at first on a specimen of *A. chinensis* that was one of the few to survive the destruction of Abel's collection in a shipwreck, the genus *Abelia* is now known to consist of thirty species. *A. triflora* (H) was discovered in Kumaon by R. Blinkworth and introduced in 1847 as seed to the Glasnevin Botanic Gardens, Dublin, where the original live material still persists. It is found, often in dense thickets, in the western Himalaya at altitudes of between 4000 and 9000 feet (1220–2740 m.). In the mountains of north-eastern Afghanistan, its leaves and sepals are notably smaller.

Dipelta floribunda (E), one of a genus of three or four Chinese species, is remarkable for its striking combination of handsome flowers and interesting fruits with paired bracts and sepals. The plant was first discovered by the Russian naturalist, painter and army surgeon, P. J. Piasetski, in Shensi Province on Captain Sosnovski's expedition to China in 1874–1875, and was introduced by E. H. Wilson, from Hupeh, in 1904.

The twelve eastern Asian species of *Weigela* are notable for the change in colour that their flowers undergo after pollination. The species are sometimes combined with the two or three very similar North American members of the genus *Diervilla*, but are generally kept apart today. This affinity demonstrates once again the strong link between certain elements of the floras of both regions. *W. venusta* (G) occurs in Korean woodland, where it was first found by J. G. Jack (1861–1949) near Seoul in 1905. The plant is very close to *W. florida* and is probably no more than a variety of it; the number of hybrids and selections commonly planted in gardens offer a possible clue as to why the species in the genus are difficult to identify in nature.

Though confined to southern and central Kashmir and Chitral in the western Himalaya, *Viburnum foetens* (C) differs from *V. grandiflorum*, found further to the east, only in having less silkily hairy bracts around the flowers and less downy undersides to the leaves. The pink flowers of the species appear very early, before the emergence of the leaves, and are scented. Both species are allied to *V. farreri* (syn. *V. fragrans*), widely grown in the West as well as in China and wild in north-western China.

HAMAMELIDACEAE

Hamamelis mollis, Chinese Witch Hazel
A1 flowering twig × $\frac{2}{3}$. A2 flower × 4.
A3 leafy twig with flower buds × $\frac{2}{3}$.
A4 leaf and vegetative bud × $\frac{2}{3}$.

Corylopsis sinensis
F1 flowering and leafy twigs × $\frac{2}{3}$.
F2 flower × $4\frac{2}{3}$.

STACHYURACEAE

Stachyurus chinensis
B1 flowering twig × $\frac{2}{3}$. B2 flower × 4.
B3 fruiting twig × $\frac{2}{3}$. B4 fruit × 2.
B5 fruit sectioned × 2.

CAPRIFOLIACEAE

Viburnum foetens
C1 flowering twig × $\frac{2}{3}$.
C2 calyx, ovary and bract × $6\frac{2}{3}$.
C3 leaf × $\frac{2}{3}$.

Kolkwitzia amabilis. Beauty Bush
D1 flowering twig × $\frac{2}{3}$.
D2 ovaries of two flowers with calyx × 2.

Dipelta floribunda
E1 flowering twig × $\frac{2}{3}$.
E2 ovary, calyx and one of the two paired bracts × 2.

Weigela venusta
G1 flowering twig × $\frac{2}{3}$.
G2 corolla opened out × $1\frac{1}{3}$.

Abelia triflora
H1 flowering twig × $\frac{2}{3}$. H2 flower × 2.

A1

A2

A3

A4

B1

B2

B3

B4

B5

C1

C2

C3

D1

D2

E1

E2

F1

F2

G1

G2

H1

H2

Plate 95   HIMALAYA AND CHINA

Alexander Andrejewitsch von Bunge (1803–1890), a famous Russian botanist, discovered *Xanthoceras sorbifolia* (B) near Peking when accompanying a political mission from St Petersburg in 1830–1831. There are two species in the genus, both from northern China and allied to the Horse Chestnut. *X. sorbifolia* forms a tree about 20 feet (6·1 m.) tall with 8 inch (20 cm.) compound leaves divided into 9 to 15 leaflets, and edible, quince-like fruits. Following von Bunge's discovery, the Abbé David sent the first seed to the famous Jardin des Plantes in Paris, where the species flowered in 1872. However, despite its great beauty when in flower, the plant is not popular in western gardens.

An attractive flowered plant sometimes found naturalized in London's waste-ground, the legacy of windborne seeds that spread from gardens to bomb-sites during the Second World War, is the Chinese *Buddleja davidii*, commonly known, because butterflies find its flowers alluring, as the Butterfly Bush. *B. crispa* (A) is an allied species, less commonly seen in gardens but growing to the same 15 feet (4·6 m.) in height. Like *B. davidii*, it bears clusters of pale lilac flowers but is covered with an even more densely woolly coat of hairs. It is native to the Indian Himalaya, where it was discovered by Nathaniel Wallich, and introduced to Britain in about 1850 by Edward Madden.

The largest of all buddlejas capable of being grown in temperate areas, *B. colvilei* (C) grows in scrub and at the edges of woods at altitudes of between 10,000 and 12,000 feet (3050–3660 m.) in the Sikkim Himalaya. In its natural setting, the species reaches about 40 feet (12 m.) in height, with arching shoots bearing leaves up to 10 inches (25 cm.) long and a profusion of pale or deep red flowers in 8 inch (20 cm.) clusters. Under cultivation in Britain, however, it is less impressive and somewhat shy to flower. The genus *Buddleja*, which contains about one hundred species with a centre of diversity in eastern Asia, commemorates the Reverend Adam Buddle (1660–1715), Essex parson and author, in 1708, of an unpublished English Flora.

The genus *Lonicera*, named after the German naturalist Adam Lonitzer (1528–1586), includes a number of the more elegant east Asian members of the *Caprifoliaceae*. *L. hildebrandiana* (F), for instance, has the honour of being the world's largest-flowered honeysuckle, though, it must be admitted, prettier and more sweetly scented species exist. On opening, the flowers are a pale yellow but later deepen to an orange which, about the time the corollas drop from the plant, assumes reddish tints. The species was first described from a collection made by

Brigadier-General Sir Henry Collet (1836–1901) at a height of about 5000 feet (1520 m.) in the Shan Hills of Burma, and first flowered in Britain in the last years of the 19th century. It is also known from Manipur and Yunnan.

The Lilac genus *Syringa* (not to be confused with *Philadelphus*, often popularly referred to as 'Syringa') is cultivated throughout Europe in a bewildering variety of differently coloured, single- and double-flowered cultivars, most of them derived from the eastern European native, *S. vulgaris*, the Common Lilac, which was introduced into western Europe in the 16th century. About a hundred years later, *S. × persica*, the Persian Lilac, arrived from the Orient, where it had long been cultivated. Until recently it was considered to be a species but it is now realized that it must be a hybrid of ancient origin. This idea is supported by the fact that, unlike a good species, it is quite sterile. Its probable parentage is thought to be *S. laciniata* (E) crossed with *S. afghanica*. *S. laciniata*, often known as the Cut-leaved Persian Lilac, was introduced to the west at about the same time as *S. × persica*. It is native to south-west China but has probably been in cultivation in Afghanistan and Iran for centuries, and even today is found in gardens in Kabul. It forms a small but handsome bush of considerable character, remarkable among lilacs for its dissected leaves, and merits a more frequent inclusion in collections. *S. afghanica*, the other putative parent, is a somewhat rare and little known plant from easternmost Afghanistan and westernmost Pakistan and is the only species of lilac not yet introduced to cultivation. When it is, we may hope that an attempt will be made to cross it with *S. laciniata* and prove, or disprove, the hypothetical origin of *S. × persica*.

Another early import from the Orient was the jasmine, the white-flowered *Jasminum officinale* being mentioned in western Europe as early as the middle of the 16th century, spread there by trade from its native Iran and northern India. A closely related species introduced from China in 1891 is *J. polyanthum* (D), which, as its name suggests, produces a profusion of flowers. Perhaps not quite so hardy as *J. officinale*, it will nevertheless grow out of doors in mild spots in south and south-west England and does very well in parts of southern U.S.A., Australia and New Zealand. Elsewhere it may be grown under glass, where in spring, its cascades of fragrant flowers will hang down from the roof support. However, when subjected to the cooler temperatures of growth in the open, the blossoms have more colour, with the outsides of the buds wine-red, in contrast to the pure white of the insides of the open flowers.

LOGANIACEAE

Buddleja crispa
A1 part of flowering shoot × ⅔.
A2 flower and buds × 2.

B. colvilei
C1 part of flowering shoot × ⅔.
C2 ovary and calyx × 2.
C3 fruiting cluster × ⅔.
C4 fruit and calyx × 2.

SAPINDACEAE

Xanthoceras sorbifolia
B1 part of flowering branch × ⅔.
B2 stamens and glands × 2⅔.

OLEACEAE

Jasminum polyanthum
D1 part of flowering shoot × ⅔.
D2 fruit × ⅔.

Syringa laciniata, Cut-leaved Persian Lilac
E1 part of branch with flowering shoot × ⅔.
E2 flower × 2. E3 fruiting twig × ⅔.
E4 fruit × 2.

CAPRIFOLIACEAE

Lonicera hildebrandiana
F1 flowering shoot × ⅔.

A1

A2

B1

B2

C3

C1

C4

C2

E2

D1

E4

E1

E3

D2

F1

Plate 96   HIMALAYA AND CHINA

Although many plants belonging to the knot-grass family or *Polygonaceae* are large, un-attractive and weed-like, their massed flowers, autumnal leaf colours, rapid growth and some-times peculiar appearance have won a few species favour as garden plants.

Polygonum comprises about three hundred species growing mostly in temperate climates with great diversity of habit. They usually com-pensate for the smallness of their flowers by the profusion with which they produce them. A perennial herb, *P. campanulatum* (A), which is found along the Himalaya from Kumaon to Nepal and from southern Tibet into western China between the altitudes of 6500 and 12,000 feet (1980–3650 m.) grows to 1–2 feet (30–61 cm.) tall. Its neatly veined leaves are covered on the underside by a whitish or pale brown cobwebby down as illustrated here by var. *campanulatum*, but this is lacking in var. *oblongum*. The in-florescence of rose-tinted, bell-shaped flowers is branched and paniculate in contrast to the spicate inflorescence of many *Polygonum* species.

Dense, unbranched spikes of pink flowers arise from thick mats of foliage which creep along the ground in *P. affine* (C), found high in the Himalaya from north-west Pakistan to eastern Nepal, between 9000 and 18,000 feet (2750–5500 m.). In autumn, when the shoots become frosted, its leaves turn a rich red colour, as can be seen in the illustration opposite. The western forms, such as var. *brunonis*, are dis-tinguished from the eastern forms, var. *affine*, by their more slender inflorescences.

Valued for the swiftness with which it covers unsightly fences or walls, the woody climber, *P. baldschuanicum* comes from Balzhuan, Tad-zhik S.S.R. adjoining Afghanistan. Though its masses of small white flowers are attractive it can easily become a nuisance if not controlled. The closely related *P. aubertii* grows in China.

Another member of the knotgrass family is *Fagopyrum esculentum* (syn. *F. sagittatum*) or Buckwheat, a native of central Asia introduced into Europe as a food plant in medieval times. The seeds yield a type of flour which is some-times fed to livestock. It has been extensively cultivated in the U.S.S.R.

Approximately fifty temperate and subtropical species of *Rheum* are known, including *R. rhaponticum*, the garden Rhubarb which is a native of eastern Asia. The illustrated *R. nobile* (B) is indeed a noble rhubarb, thriving rooted amongst rocks at altitudes between 13,000 and 15,000 feet (3950–4550 m.) in the eastern Himalaya. 'Chuka', as it is called by the local inhabitants, grows to a height of 3 feet (91 cm) and its rhubarb-like stem is eaten. When in flower, a pyramid of creamy bracts hides the blossoms and a rosette of green leaves surrounds the base of the inflorescence. After flowering the bracts wither and fall away to expose a tattered series of brown fruiting spikes which resemble those of the dock or *Rumex*.

POLYGONACEAE

Polygonum campanulatum var. *campanulatum*
(syn. *Aconogonum campanulatum*)
A1 part of flowering stem × $\frac{2}{3}$. A2 flower × $6\frac{2}{3}$.

Rheum nobile
B1 part of flowering stem and lower leaf × $\frac{2}{3}$.
B2 fruits on part of stem × $\frac{2}{3}$. B3 fruit × 4.
B4 habit sketch × $\frac{1}{18}$.

Polygonum affine
C1 part of fruiting and flowering stems with leaves × $\frac{2}{3}$. C2 part of autumn stem × $\frac{2}{3}$.

Plate 97   HIMALAYA AND CHINA

The Himalaya and China are the home of many beautiful genera: lovely gentians, such decorative bellflowers as *Codonopsis,* and the daisies of *Saussurea,* which in miniature strangely mimic the giant tree-daisies of Hawaii and East Africa. The introduction of these plants to our gardens was the result of the labours of a few collectors who, in some cases, devoted the major part of their lives to giving the West a better understanding of the richness of eastern flora. The names of Delavay, Forrest and Sharma, in particular, are intimately connected with the plants shown opposite.

Member of a genus of about thirty-five species found in eastern Asia as far as New Guinea, *Codonopsis ovata* (F) favours grassy spots with sandy or stony soil in the Indian and southern Kashmiri Himalaya, at altitudes of between 10,000 and 14,000 feet (3050–4270 m.). Beneath the earth, a fleshy root produces a scaly stem from which arise branching shoots bearing the small leaves and nodding flowers. The latter, which appear between June and July, are sky blue veined with purple. The species was introduced into Europe in 1856.

A related species well worth cultivation, being a hardy perennial with an unusually striking combination of colours, is *C. meleagris* from Yunnan, discovered by George Forrest in 1916. It grows in grassy clearings in pine forests and reaches a height of about 14 inches (36 cm.). The nodding bell-shaped flowers, which number between 1 and 3 and measure up to $1\frac{1}{2}$ inches (38 mm.) in length, are bluish- or greenish-white veined with chocolate. The closely related *Leptocodon gracilis* (A), the sole species in its genus, differs from *Codonopsis* in being a slender climber with a delicate, inflated, tubular flower. It was first discovered by J. D. Hooker in 1849 and is a native of Sikkim, at altitudes of between 6000 and 9000 feet (1830–2740 m.).

The four hundred, mostly alpine, species of gentians are to be found in all suitable parts of the world, including the mountains of South America and New Guinea, with the exception of Africa. *Gentiana cachemirica* (B) grows on exposed slopes in Kashmir and western Himalaya. Its rosettes of leaves produce side-shoots with purplish stems, each more or less upward-pointing and bearing 1 to 3 flowers. It can be seen from the illustration that, in gentians, there are small lobes known as the plicae situated in between the larger lobes of the corolla; these are often useful for differentiating between related species. *G. cachemirica* is allied to, and has, at times, been confused with, the similar *G. loderi.* The former, however, has sepal lobes that are linear (not spoon-shaped), stamens inserted near the base of the corolla tube (not near the middle) and stalked ovaries.

Exhibiting a quite different mode of growth is the erect *G. cephalantha* (C), which was discovered by Père Delavay in 1887 in north-western Yunnan, where it inhabits dry pine forests at altitudes of up to 11,000 feet (3350 m.). It was not, however, until George Forrest, on his

expedition of 1930–1932, sent back seed that the plant was first grown in Britain. The species reaches a height of about 12 inches (30 cm.), with a basal rosette of lanceolate leaves up to $4\frac{3}{4}$ inches (12 cm.) long.

At about the same time that the above was belatedly introduced by Forrest, Professor K. N. Sharma did the same for another neglected species, *G. depressa* (E), which was first found by Nathaniel Wallich, or one of his collectors, on the Gossain Than, Nepal, in 1821. It is now known to inhabit Sikkim, Tibet and Bhutan as well. Although vigorous, forming dense, mat-like cushions, the species can be shy to flower, especially in Britain: flowers formed late in the season occasionally fail to open before winter and remain in the bud until the following spring.

A gentian of European origin, but quite as attractive as any Himalayan species, *G. excisa* (G) is, nevertheless and unfortunately, fickle under cultivation as regards flowering. No reason for this sterility has yet been deduced, though a number of extreme remedies, which include jumping on the plant and the annual tearing apart of clumps, have been attempted.

G. sino-ornata (H) is regarded by some as the finest plant to have been introduced this century. In the wild, it appears to be confined to moist alpine meadows between 12,000 and 16,000 feet (3660–4880 m.) in north-western Yunnan, where it was discovered by George Forrest in 1904. With *G. farreri, G. veitchiorum* and *G. ornata,* with which it was at first confused, it forms a group of outstanding garden plants. The species flowers from September to November.

Of the Himalayan alpine daisies, none are more intriguing than those in *Saussurea,* a genus of over four hundred species, most of them found in the mountains of temperate Asia. In altitude, these daisies extend to the upper limits at which plant life is found. They vary in height from 1 inch (2·5 cm.) to 4 feet (1·2 m.).

In the words of its collector George Forrest, *S. gossypiphora* (D) resembles 'a teased out pyramid of glistening pinkish- or yellowish-tinged cotton'. Only the lower leaves are visible, a dense mass of hair, in whose cavities the flower-heads are situated, obscuring all other foliage. Plants reach a height of between 6 and 18 inches (15–46 cm.), growing on exposed patches of limestone at altitudes of 16,000 to 17,000 feet (4880–5180 m.), from Kumaon in India to Bhutan and Tibet. The hairy coating is said to protect the plant from the long winter cold and brief summer heat in much the same way as similar hairs do the arborescent East African *Senecio* (plate 56) or Hawaiian *Argyroxiphium* (plate 149). A related Chinese species is *S. leucoma* which grows at high altitudes on the massive limestone screes of the Lichiang Range in Yunnan. Its white leaves are more finely dissected than those of *S. gossypiphora,* and woolly, while the flower-heads are borne above the vestiture, not in amongst it. The flowers themselves are bluish crimson, scented and 2 to 3 inches (5–7·5 cm.) broad.

CAMPANULACEAE

Leptocodon gracilis
A1 part of flowering shoot × $\frac{2}{3}$.

Codonopsis ovata
F1 part of flowering plant × $\frac{2}{3}$.
F2 withered flower × $\frac{2}{3}$.
F3 stamens, style and ovary × 2.
F4 immature fruit × 2.

GENTIANACEAE

Gentiana cachemirica
B1 part of flowering shoot × $\frac{2}{3}$.

G. cephalantha
C1 part of flowering shoot × $\frac{2}{3}$.
C2 petal tip × $1\frac{1}{3}$.

G. depressa
E1 flowering plant × $\frac{2}{3}$.

G. excisa (syn. *G. acaulis*)
G1 part of flowering plant × $\frac{2}{3}$.

G. sino-ornata
H1 flowering plant × $\frac{2}{3}$.

COMPOSITAE

Saussurea gossypiphora
D1 part of flowering plant × $\frac{2}{3}$.

A1

B1

C1

C2

D1

E1

F1

F2

F3

F4

G1

H1

Plate 98   HIMALAYA AND CHINA

Most garden species of *Primula* have their origin high in the mountains of the Sino-Himalayan region, an area in which the genus is particularly well represented. Although certain species retain characteristics that enable even the layman to recognize them as 'primroses', other members of *Primula* show a fascinating array of modifications in appearance and habit, a few of which can be seen opposite. However, before discussing individual species of *Primula*, it would be as well to turn to the single example depicted here of the closely related genus *Androsace*.

Androsace is a smaller-flowered, but no less appealing, northern temperate genus, many of whose hundred or so species inhabit the mountain area mentioned above. It differs from *Primula* in having a corolla tube that is shorter than the calyx and constricted at the throat. *A. strigillosa* (A), a native of Sikkim, Bhutan and adjacent Tibet, is typical in form of many members of the genus. Its small flowers are white, pink or red and the leaves, arranged in rosettes, are clothed in a dense mat of stiff hairs. The entire plant frequently measures no more than 6 inches (15 cm.) in height. A possibly better known relative, often found under cultivation, is *A. sarmentosa*, which ranges from the Himalaya to Szechuan. Both species are hardy and easily grown in Britain.

To return to *Primula*, one of the most imposing sights provided by any of the five hundred species in the genus is that of a bed of *P. vialii* (F) coming into full flower: red or pink buds crown the erect inflorescences above, while below the violet-blue petals of the opened flowers curve gently backwards. The buds derive their colour from the red sepals, which, like the 2 foot (61 cm.) naked stalk, are covered with a powdery meal. The leaves, which have a cobwebby undersurface, may reach 8 inches (20 cm.) in length. Père Delavay discovered *P. vialii*, which is native to south-western China, in 1888, and named it after his colleague Père Vial; later, however, George Forrest, unaware of the earlier finding, came across the plant, and renamed it *P. littoniana*. The earlier name has priority.

According to its discoverer, J. D. Hooker, thick carpets of the profusely blooming yellow *P. sikkimensis* (B) are to be found between May and June in moist and boggy habitats in Sikkim at altitudes of 12,000 to 17,000 feet (3650–5200 m.). Hooker sent seeds to his father, Sir William Hooker, Director at Kew, in 1850, and the first plants flowered there a year later. It is a large species with a scape that attains a height of 2 feet (61 cm.) and leaves with pale undersides and strongly toothed edges that may grow up to 12 inches (30 cm.) in length. Both in habit and colouring it bears some resemblance to *P. prolifera* of Java and Sumatra (see plate 114).

Though a somewhat smaller species than those so far considered, the purple to lilac flowers and mealy undersides of the leaves, flower-stalks and calyces of *P. macrophylla* (C) make it most

attractive. A native of Nepal and the north-western Himalaya, it was brought to Britain in 1820. Popular for its long, March to August, flowering season ever since it was introduced into Europe in 1879, and now familiar in many gardens, *P. rosea* (E) is found in the natural state from the north-western Himalaya to Kashmir.

Primula cawdoriana (D) was discovered by Frank Kingdon Ward during his 1928 expedition to the Tsang-po and named by that well known explorer after his companion, Lord Cawdor. It grows among dwarf *Rhododendron* scrub on steep slopes at altitudes of between 10,800 and 13,500 feet (3300–4150 m.)—an environment in which dry winters alternate with wet summers to produce a rich alpine flora. The species is too delicate to survive long in a man-made environment: although a number of flowering plants were obtained in Britain in 1926, by 1928 they had been lost to cultivation.

Equally distinct and even more diminutive, *P. reidii* (G) was discovered in 1884 by J. F. Duthie, sometime Superintendent of the Saharunpur Botanic Garden, and his companion, a Mr Reid, while visiting a valley high in Kumaon. Finding the flower again the following year, in neighbouring Garhwal, Duthie introduced seed to Britain where it was successfully flowered.

A species less easily introduced to cultivation was *P. sonchifolia* (H) whose seed, unlike that of most primulas, loses viability in ordinary storage. Though the plant, a native of south-western China, Tibet and north-western Burma, was discovered by Père Delavay in Yunnan in 1884, it was not until 1921 that the first seed was successfully brought to Britain, in a vacuum flask. Another attempt, which started with a dangerous journey by Forest Ranger Sukve in northern Burma in November 1930, resulted in the presentation of live plants to King George V: Sukve dug dormant plants out of the icy ground and managed to get them down, stored in ice-packed bamboo stems, to lower altitudes, just before the arrival of the first heavy snows. They were then despatched in the refrigerated hold of a steamer and, by February 1931, were in full flower at the Royal Horticultural Society. *P. sonchifolia* grows amongst scrub in alpine meadows or moist stony tracts and has a peculiar, dormant, scale-enveloped rootstock somewhat resembling a bulb, which, in big plants, may measure as much as 6 inches (15 cm.) in circumference. In spring, the inflorescence emerges from the resting structure to be followed shortly after by the expanding leaves. These, when mature, resemble those of the Sow Thistle, *Sonchus*—hence the specific epithet.

As the name implies, the flowers of *P. capitata* (J) are held in a tightly clustered head which is borne at the end of a mealy scape some 12 inches (30 cm.) long. The plant was discovered by J. D. Hooker in the Sikkim Himalaya, where it grows at altitudes of between 12,000 and 19,000 feet (3650–5800 m.).

PRIMULACEAE

Androsace strigillosa
A1 part of flowering plant (stem cut) × ⅔.
A2 side view of flower × 2⅔.
A3 face on view of flower × 2⅔.

Primula sikkimensis
B1 flowering plant × ⅔.

P. macrophylla
C1 flowering plant × ⅔.

P. cawdoriana
D1 flowering plant × ⅔. D2 flower × 2.

P. rosea
E1 flowering plant × ⅔.

P. vialii (syn. *P. littoniana*)
F1 part of flowering plant (stem cut) × ⅔.
F2 bud × 4⅔. F3 corolla × 4⅔.

P. reidii
G1 part of flowering plant × ⅔.

P. sonchifolia
H1 part of flowering plant × ⅔.

P. capitata
J1 flowering plant × ⅔. J2 flower × 2.

A2

A3

A1

B1

C1

D2

D1

E1

F2

F3

F1

G1

H1

J1

J2

Plate 99   HIMALAYA AND CHINA

Carl Peter Thunberg (1743–1828), a Swedish doctor in 1775–1776 at the Dutch trading post on an island in Nagasaki harbour, southern Japan, was the first European to make known the Asiatic shrubs now commonly grown under the name *Hydrangea*, although, misled by the form of the inflorescence, he described them as species of *Viburnum*. The severe restrictions then imposed upon Europeans in Japan limited his botanical studies largely to specimens brought by Japanese servants, specimens which were often inadequate or of garden origin, and consequently he made many mistakes. His *Viburnum macrophyllum* is now called *Hydrangea macrophylla* ssp. *macrophylla*, his *V. serratum* now *H. macrophylla* ssp. *serrata*.

From China in 1789, by order of Sir Joseph Banks, Kew received its first Asiatic *Hydrangea*: a tender, coarse form with greenish flower heads of the same species as that first encountered by Thunberg and still to be found under cultivation in some places. Part of the material introduced by Banks was sent to France, to which, in 1796 and 1830, further shipments of Japanese plants were made. To these beginnings may be traced many of the numerous and distinctive cultivars —the three hundred different mop-headed 'hortensias' and the eleven flat-headed 'lace-caps'— that are grown today. In eastern Asia itself, the genus had been cultivated for so many years prior to the arrival of European botanists that it was impossible to distinguish the natural from the induced, with the result that the classification of the cultivated hydrangeas of the area has remained confused.

The hydrangea illustrated opposite, *H. aspera* ssp. *aspera* (B), was introduced from Szechuan in 1908 by E. H. Wilson, and first flowered at Kew in 1915. It is found over a wide area of southern and eastern China and extends into Tibet, Bhutan, northern India, Burma and Sumatra. The richly coloured fertile blooms, with their purple stamens, contrast well with the pink of the sterile flowers, while the dark green leaves act as a foil for both. It provides an example of the often observed phenomenon of the true species surpassing the hybrid and cultivar in both beauty and proportion.

In 1867, Maximowicz discovered in Japan one of the two species of *Deinanthe*, a genus in the same family as *Hydrangea* but herbaceous with the leaves often 2-lobed. This, the Japanese species, has creamy white flowers and was named by Maximowicz *D. bifida*. The Chinese species, *D. caerulea* (A), was discovered in Hupeh by A. Henry, introduced to England as seed by E. H. Wilson and grown for the first time in 1909 by Henry John Elwes (1846–1922) at Colesborne, Cheltenham. Like the *Hydrangea*, *Deinanthe* species have both nodding fertile, and chaffy sterile, flowers. The blooms of *D. caerulea* are borne in a lax cluster at the end of an 18 inch (46 cm.) stalk. The leaves may grow to be three times the size of the one illustrated.

A genus, many of whose fifty species were introduced to Britain from China and Japan in the 19th century, is *Deutzia*, named after Johann van der Deutz (1743–1784), a lawyer of Amsterdam and keen amateur botanist. The centre of diversity of the genus lies in the Himalaya and eastern Asia. One of the hardiest species is *D. scabra* (syn. *D. crenata*) which grows to about 10 feet (3 m.) in height and bears white or rose coloured, sometimes double, flowers. Introduced

about twenty years later, in 1840, *D. gracilis* has a height of about 4 feet (1·2 m.) and is sometimes found with variegated yellow and green leaves. The discovery of *D. longifolia* (E) in Szechuan was one of Abbé David's numerous contributions to the 19th century's knowledge of the flora and fauna of the area. It was not, however, introduced into Europe until 1901 and 1905 by E. H. Wilson, and was then erroneously named from the cultivated plant as a separate species, *D. veitchii*; this is now considered to be a mere form of *D. longifolia*.

The herbaceous genus *Saxifraga* is a large one with about three hundred and seventy species. Most of them are alpine plants and show considerable diversity (see also plate 2). The leaves of some species become encrusted with lime by glands on their edges which secrete a fluid rich in dissolved calcium; this is left as a deposit on the leaves as the water evaporates. *S. fortunei* (C) belongs to a group in which one or more petals in each flower are longer than the others. It was discovered in Japan by Robert Fortune in 1862 and is sometimes found in British gardens where it will grow hardily, if given a little protection, and produce dancing white blooms late in the summer. It prefers a moist humus-rich soil and in its native Japan frequents such damp habitats as rocks at the edges of mountain streams. Japanese botanists have distinguished a number of varieties, according to the consistency and lobing of the leaves.

The German botanist, Karl August von Bergen (1704–1759), is commemorated in *Bergenia*, a genus of some six species, and numerous hybrids, that comes from the Central Asian Plateau and mountains. Being hardy, it is familiar in British gardens and provides an attractive display of blooms in spring and early summer. *B. purpurascens* (D) is from the Sino-Himalayan mountain area, where it ranges from Yunnan and south Szechuan in China, through northern Burma, south-east Tibet, Bhutan, Sikkim and Assam, to eastern Nepal, growing amongst moist rocks or under light scrub at altitudes of between 6000 and 15,000 feet (1830–4570 m.). The beauty of the purple-red to pink flowers has made the species popular as a garden plant since its discovery and introduction by Joseph Hooker in 1849. In the mid-1950's, V. Pavlov discovered a species in the Tashkent province of the U.S.S.R. which he named *B. ugamica*. However, Dr P. Yeo, in a recent revision of the genus, suggests that the plant may be *B. purpurascens*, spread into Tashkent over 1400 miles (2250 km.) of ancient trade routes.

The seventeen species of the genus *Morina*, all of which bear a close resemblance to one another, are placed by some botanists in a family of their own, the *Morinaceae*, related to the *Dipsacaceae*, but with the flowers arranged in a way similar to those of the *Labiatae*. *M. longifolia* (F) is a prickly herb some 18 inches (46 cm.) tall found amongst grassland and scrub in slightly varying forms across much of the Himalaya, at altitudes of between 7000 and 12,000 feet (2133–3660 m.). It is supposed, by certain Kashmiri hill folk, to restrict the breathing at such high altitudes. Several of the species, from the spineless leafed *M. kokanica* of Tien Shan onwards, exhibit such varying degrees of spininess and luxuriance as to suggest that they are merely local variations selected in response to the prevailing climate of their area.

HYDRANGEACEAE

Deinanthe caerulea
A1 part of flowering stem with leaf × $\frac{2}{3}$.

Hydrangea aspera ssp. *aspera*
B1 flowering shoot × $\frac{2}{3}$. B2 sterile flower × 2.
B3 fertile flowers × $2\frac{2}{3}$. B4 anther × $12\frac{2}{3}$.

Deutzia longifolia
E1 part of flowering shoot × $\frac{2}{3}$.
E2 stamen × 2.
E3 portion of stem showing hairs × 27.

SAXIFRAGACEAE

Saxifraga fortunei
C1 part of flowering stem and leaves × $\frac{2}{3}$.
C2 flower × 2.

Bergenia purpurascens
D1 flowering plant × $\frac{2}{3}$.
D2 fruit × $1\frac{1}{3}$.

DIPSACACEAE

Morina longifolia
F1 part of flowering stem × $\frac{2}{3}$.
F2 flower, face view × 4.
F3 flower, showing base of corolla tube, calyx and ovary × 4.
F4 ripened fruit with persistent calyx × 2.

A1

B1 B2 B3 B4

C1 C2

D1 D2

E1 E2 E3

F1 F2 F3 F4

Plate 100   HIMALAYA AND CHINA

Had Hieronymous Bosch created an outlandish and weirdly beautiful climbing plant for one of his suffering landscapes or visions of hell, it might well have resembled *Hodgsonia hetero-clita* (A), a strange Asian cucurbit. The cucurbits —tropical and subtropical plants with few representatives in cooler climates—have been divided into the *Cucurbitoideae*, with flowers possessing 1 style, and the 3-styled *Zanonioideae*. The squashes and pumpkins (*Cucurbita*), the loofahs or vegetable sponges (*Luffa*), the colocynth (*Citrullus*), the Squirting Cucumber (see plate 34) and *Hodgsonia* all belong to the *Cucurbitoideae*, while there are no commonly known cucurbit groups in the *Zanonioideae*.

Trichosanthes cucumerina, the Snake Gourd from South East Asia, may have greenish white fruits, coiled like snakes and some 6 feet (1·8 m.) in length. The white flowers and fringed petals resemble those of *Hodgsonia* but in *Trichosanthes* the flowers are smaller. The immature fruits are boiled and eaten in Malaysia and the ends of the ripening fruits are often weighted in an effort to keep them straight.

The dried tissues of the Loofah fruit provide an alternative to the true sponge, but this function has been displaced by the increasing use of polyurethane foam sponges. According to Purseglove (1968), the loofah was also once used as a filter in steam and diesel marine engines. *Luffa cylindrica* yields the best loofah and although the plant was probably first domesticated in India, the highest quality now comes from Japan where the species is much cultivated.

The Cucumber, *Cucumis sativus*, is probably a native of northern India, where the related *C. hardwickii* still grows. The yellow flowers and pendulous fruits have become known throughout the world as the salad plant. In Malaysia the young leaves are cooked and eaten like spinach.

Hodgsonia comprises the single species *H. heteroclita*, placed in the *Trichosanthes* section of Jeffrey's 1962 cucurbit classification. Its fruits are quite unlike those of other *Trichosantheae* as they contain ovules in pairs, one of which always develops at the expense of the other. For this reason *Hodgsonia* has been put in a subtribe of its own, the *Hodgsoniinae*. The species grows in east Bengal, Assam, Chittagong, Burma, Sumatra and Java, and occurs from sea level to 5000 feet (1500 m.) in the Himalaya.

The stems of *H. heteroclita* may be as long as 100 feet (30 m.). They climb trees so that the foliage, entwined in the tree canopy high above, is invisible from the ground. At flowering time, however, the flowers can be found strewn on the ground below. These extraordinary flowers, which perish very quickly, are borne on separate male and female plants; as the latter bear only a few flowers, they are less conspicuous than the males. At fertilization the fruit is watery inside, but it later hardens to a green viscid inedible pulp. The Sikkimese, however, who call the fruit 'Kai Hior Pot', eat the insides of the seeds. The genus commemorates Bryan Houghton Hodgson (1800–1894), who was British Resident at Katmandu until 1843 and was later stationed in Darjeeling, Sikkim. He was a keen amateur naturalist, chiefly interested in Himalayan and Tibetan mammals and birds.

CUCURBITACEAE

Hodgsonia heteroclita
A1 male flowers, buds and leaves on stem × ⅔.
A2 female flower × ⅔. A3 young tendril × ⅔.
A4 fruit and leaf × ⅔. A5 seed × ⅔.

A1

A2

A3

A4

A5

Plate 101   HIMALAYA AND CHINA

Camellias in general, *Camellia reticulata* (C) in particular, have been so long and intensively cultivated by the Chinese and Japanese that there are numerous asiatic cultivars, including many with semi-double flowers, such as that illustrated, as well as double-flowered forms. Specimens similar to that on the plate were sent to England in 1824 by John Damper Parks from one of the trading ports of south or east China. In Yunnan the species has been cultivated for centuries, while in the west of that province the truly natural species, totally untouched by the effects of cultivation, grows in scrub and pine woodland at altitudes of between 6000 and 9000 feet (1830–2740 m.). This wild plant with only 5 or 6 (rarely 7) petals has been named *C. reticulata* f. *simplex*. A startling example of how a totally new species may turn up in an area already well botanized is provided by *C. granthamiana* (F) discovered as recently as 1955 in a remote, wooded valley on mainland Hong Kong by C. P. Lau, a forester, and subsequently named in honour of Sir Alexander Grantham, at that time Governor of Hong Kong. Plants now flower in the Temperate House at Kew.

In the opinion of some the Tea plant *Camellia sinensis* possibly originated not in the traditional tea-growing areas of China and Assam but around the headwaters of the Irrawaddy in northern Burma. However, the plant has been cultivated as a beverage crop in China for at least three thousand years and the local varieties, slow-growing dwarf shrubs with solitary flowers and leaves that produce a tea with a somewhat tarry taste, differ sufficiently from the taller, faster-growing, sweeter tasting and less hardy tea plants of Assam for some botanists to regard the two as distinct species. In *A revision of the Genus Camellia* by J. R. Sealy (1958), the standard monograph on the genus, they are treated as two varieties, the one known to be wild in Yunnan and the other in Assam. In ancient China, tea was at first considered a nobleman's drink, but had become widespread by 200 B.C. In England the drink followed a similar course, being introduced in the 16th century and overtaking coffee in popularity, until at the end of the 18th century the younger Pitt lowered the high tax on tea and thus allowed the market to expand considerably.

'Green' teas are produced by steaming and drying the leaves soon after they have been picked, a process that prevents the polyphenols contained in them from turning into the astringent compounds that characterize 'black' tea. The latter is only made after the leaves have been allowed to wither, crushed so that their enzymes may digest the polyphenols by a process of fermentation, and then dried. It is these 'black' teas that dominate the world market.

The related genus *Stewartia* contains about ten species, found in east Asia and south-eastern North America. The illustrated *S. serrata* (E) is a native of Japan, where it was discovered in 1863 by Maximowicz. It forms a tree about 30 feet (9 m.) tall and is very similar to a Chinese species, *S. sinensis*, which was discovered by Augustine Henry and brought to the West by E. H. Wilson in 1901. The latter differs from the Japanese species mainly in having a hairy ovary and lacking hairs in the angles of the veins on the undersides of the leaves. *S. malacodendron*, one of the two American species, was the first *Stewartia* to be grown in Britain, being found in London gardens as early as 1742.

A small evergreen shrub growing in the Naga and Khasia hills of Assam, *Agapetes odontocera* (D) is chiefly admired for the beauty of its clusters of flowers, borne on the old wood, with their waxy dull pink or red corollas, striped transversely with red or purple. According to some, *A. odontocera* is not a separate species but one of several varieties of the very similar *A. variegata*. The genus as a whole comprises about eighty South East Asian and eastern Himalayan species.

Enkianthus campanulatus (B), one of ten Far Eastern species in the genus, is a native of Japan, from where it was brought to England in 1880 by Charles Maries (1851–1902), one of the Veitches' collectors. It resembles the slightly larger-flowered Chinese *E. chinensis*, introduced in 1900.

Noted for its brightly coloured autumnal leaves and equally decorative fruit, *Euonymus sachalinensis* (A) is also a native of Japan, but found in Manchuria and Kansu, in China, as well. The species was originally, and wrongly, thought to be a variety of the European *E. latifolius*.

CELASTRACEAE

Euonymus sachalinensis
A1 fruiting twig × $\frac{2}{3}$.
A2 fruit × $1\frac{1}{3}$. A3 seed × 2.

ERICACEAE

Enkianthus campanulatus
B1 flowering shoot × $\frac{2}{3}$.
B2 flower × 2. B3 stamen × 4.
B4 fruiting twig × $\frac{2}{3}$. B5 fruit × $2\frac{2}{3}$.

Agapetes odontocera
D1 flowering shoot × $\frac{2}{3}$. D2 anthers × $1\frac{1}{3}$.

THEACEAE

Camellia reticulata
C1 part of flowering stems × $\frac{2}{3}$.
C2 group of stamens × 2. C3 anther × 4.

Stewartia serrata
E1 flowering shoot × $\frac{2}{3}$.
E2 fruit on twig × $\frac{2}{3}$. E3 seed × $\frac{2}{3}$.

Camellia granthamiana
F1 flowering shoot with bud × $\frac{2}{3}$.
F2 bud scales and ovary × $\frac{2}{3}$.
F3 stamen × 4.

A2

A3

A2

B1

B2

B3

B5

B4

C1

C3

C2

D2

F3

F2

D1

E2

E3

E1

F1

Plate 102   HIMALAYA AND CHINA

The genus *Rhododendron* contains between five and six hundred species in northern temperate areas, a number in North America, fewer in Europe but with concentrations in the Himalaya, China and Japan, while Malaysia, the East Indies and New Guinea are the home of about two hundred and fifty further species. They form trees or shrubs with leathery leaves, sometimes downy on the undersurfaces, and with shoots tipped, in winter, with scaly buds. In fact, because the flower buds are terminal on the shoots and tend to open before the leaf buds, the whole surface of the plant may be covered in blossom, a characteristic that has contributed greatly to the popularity of the genus. Azaleas, one of the best known groups within the genus, are usually to be distinguished from 'true' rhododendrons by the fact that they lose their leaves each year: rhododendrons keep their leaves for several seasons. But this division is not strictly botanical and all azaleas are classified within the genus *Rhododendron*.

A remarkable feature is the way in which rhododendrons will readily hybridize in cultivation, even species from different continents which must have been separated geographically for a very long time and yet appear to have developed few or no genetic barriers. However, one major group of species which have scales on their leaves, stems and flower parts, the lepidote species (see for example B3, C4 and D2 opposite), are never known to hybridize with those without these scales, the elepidote rhododendrons (for example note A3 and E2 opposite), despite numerous attempts, except on one occasion when *R. griersonianum* was successfully crossed with *R. dalhousiae*.

Most of the many hybrids and cultivated varieties now found in our gardens were developed as a result of the 'rhododendron mania' of the late 19th and early 20th centuries when so many new species were introduced from southwest China by such collectors as E. H. Wilson, J. F. Rock, F. Kingdon Ward and, in particular, George Forrest. This enthusiastic interest is spreading even today in such countries as the U.S.A., Australia and New Zealand.

A native of Yunnan and Szechuan where it grows at altitudes of between 10,000 and 13,000 feet (3050–3960 m.), *R. fictolacteum* (A) is an example of those species with beautiful leaves, in this case covered with a brown felt beneath which contrasts with the dark green upper surface. Seeds of this species were first collected by Abbé Delavay and grown at the Jardin des Plantes in Paris. The material illustrated is from the collection at Wisley, where the species attains a height of about 12 feet (3·7 m.) although it may grow nearly four times as tall in the natural state.

Rhododendron fastigiatum (B) grows to a maximum height of 3 feet (91 cm.) in its natural habitat at 11,000 to 13,000 feet (3350–3960 m.) in Yunnan. The flowers vary in colour from pale to intense purple-blue and, with its compact habit, it makes a fine plant for the rock garden. At altitudes of about 7500 to 11,000 feet (2280–3350 m.) in Szechuan, *R. ambiguum* (C) forms a shrub 5–6 feet (1·5–1·8 m.) tall. The species is related to *R. lutescens* in what is known as the *Triflorum* series. Also in the same series and introduced by Wilson and others, *R. augustinii* (D) is named after its original discoverer, Augustine Henry, who, as Assistant Inspector of Customs, spent several years from 1882 in south-west China and made a great many botanical collections; later he became Professor of Forestry at Dublin. This species is native of western Hupeh and Szechuan at altitudes up to about 9300 feet (2840 m.). The shrubs grow to a height of about 10 feet (3 m.) and the colour of the flowers varies from rose, through lavender to violet, some of the forms being particularly attractive.

Named after Thomas Thomson (1817–1878), surgeon, college friend and travelling companion of J. D. Hooker on his trip to the eastern Himalaya, Dr Thomson's Rhododendron, *R. thomsonii* (E), is a bush or small tree growing to about 15 feet (4·6 m.) tall, with beautiful, almost waxy but scentless flowers which is found in abundance in Sikkim Himalaya, Nepal, Bhutan and Tibet. It grows at altitudes of 10,000 to 14,000 feet (3050–4270 m.) and flowers in May or June.

ERICACEAE

Rhododendron fictolacteum
A1 part of flowering stem × $\frac{2}{3}$. A2 stamen × 2.
A3 ovary with style and stigma × 1$\frac{1}{3}$.

R. fastigiatum
B1 flowering twig × $\frac{2}{3}$. B2 stamen × 2$\frac{2}{3}$.
B3 leaf × 2.

R. ambiguum
C1 flowering shoot × $\frac{2}{3}$.
C2 flower × 1$\frac{1}{3}$. C3 stamen × 2.
C4 portion of stem showing minute scales × 2.

R. augustinii
D1 flowering twig × $\frac{2}{3}$.
D2 style and ovary showing glands × 1$\frac{1}{3}$.

R. thomsonii, Dr Thomson's Rhododendron
E1 flowering shoot × $\frac{2}{3}$.
E2 calyx and ovary, with style and stigma × 1$\frac{1}{3}$.

Plate 103   HIMALAYA AND CHINA

The superb flowering trees of the genus *Paulownia*, named in 1835 in honour of Anna Paulowna (1795–1865), daughter of Czar Paul I of Russia and at that time married to the Crown Prince of the Netherlands, are a splendid memorial even for royalty; yet, with the others illustrated on this plate, they provide examples of the endless numbers of beautiful garden-plants native to the eastern Himalaya and western China, 'the garden of the world'. The seventeen species in the genus *Paulownia*, although they are trees, belong to the mainly herbaceous family *Scrophulariaceae*. They are confined to eastern Asia and are only distinguished from the remarkably similar genus *Catalpa* (in the *Bignoniaceae*, see plate 162) by certain characters of the ovary, generally considered basic in classification. *P. tomentosa* (B) is a native of Japan and China or, according to some, it is not native in China but an early and long cultivated introduction. From Japan it was brought to the Netherlands in 1834. It is a deciduous tree which grows up to 50 feet (15 m.) and has thick, spreading branches with more or less downy vegetative parts. The leaves are often differently shaped according to their size, the smaller ones are oval but the larger triply or quintuply lobed, and usually 10 inches (25 cm.) long, though sometimes up to as much as 3 feet (91 cm.). Flowers are formed in the autumn, and spend the winters as naked buds, ready to open in the spring. *P. tomentosa* makes a fine park tree in continental Europe but, presumably because of the climate, only flowers irregularly in the British Isles.

Somewhat the reverse of the systematic situation with *Paulownia*, the genus *Incarvillea* provides the exception of herbaceous plants in the otherwise woody family *Bignoniaceae*. The fourteen species are restricted in range to the Himalaya and China, and commemorate the French Jesuit missionary Pierre d'Incarville (1706–1757).

A dwarf species, adapted to the windswept Tibetan mountain slopes, *I. younghusbandii* (C) is named after Sir Francis Edward Younghusband, whose remarkable journeys as a young soldier across the Central Asian Plateau and over the Karakoram Range led to his being given the command of the British Mission to Lhasa that resulted in the Anglo-Tibetan treaty of 1904, and Younghusband's knighthood. It was collected in Tibet in 1903 by Younghusband himself while on the mission.

Another lovely species, discovered by the French missionary Père Jean-Marie Delavay in 1889 in the mountains at the source of the Lankiung river in Yunnan, *I. lutea* bears corollas with a pale yellow to apricot tinge above contrasting dark green, glossy leaves. The difficulty of getting the plant to flower, however, has been overcome only once or twice in Britain, causing Reginald Farrer to chide it for 'saving our nerves the shock of such splendour by never revealing it . . . though it grows like any cabbage'.

Much easier to grow, *I. delavayi* (D) produces an abundance of carmine and yellow-tinged blossoms in well-drained, sunny, temperate gardens. This species was also discovered by Delavay in Yunnan and introduced by him into Europe in 1893. It was subsequently lost to cultivation but reintroduced by George Forrest. Flowering stalks, 1 to 3 feet (0·3–0·9 m.) tall, with a number of large, trumpet-shaped corollas, ascend from the centres of clumps of radiating almost over-abundant leaves. Though always a curious and attractive plant when well grown, it tends to be too small for the herbaceous bed and, with its excess of basal foliage, too large for the rockery.

Strophanthus divergens (A) is an erect shrub about 4 feet (1·2 m.) in height and a native of China, from where it was introduced to Europe as a conservatory plant in about 1816. The species is easily confused with the tropical Asian *S. dichotomus*, which has longer leaves and corolla lobes.

Cultivated in China almost since pre-historic times as a medicinal and ornamental climber (its Chinese common name means 'sky-approaching flower'), *Campsis grandiflora* (E) differs from the allied North American *C. radicans* (see plate 162) in having smooth, hairless leaves and producing, during August and September, the largest flowers to be found in its genus. In Britain, unfortunately, it will only flower if sited in the sunniest of positions, and even then only in the best of summers. The species was discovered by Engelbert Kaempfer (1651–1716) in Japan in 1691, but did not reach Europe until the beginning of the last century.

APOCYNACEAE

Strophanthus divergens
A1 flowering twig × $\frac{2}{3}$.
A2 dissected corolla × $1\frac{1}{3}$.
A3 fruit × $\frac{2}{3}$. A4 seed × $\frac{2}{3}$.

SCROPHULARIACEAE

Paulownia tomentosa (syn. *P. imperialis*)
B1 flowering shoot × $\frac{2}{3}$.

BIGNONIACEAE

Incarvillea younghusbandii
C1 flowering plant showing rootstock × $\frac{2}{3}$.
C2 flowering plant in situ × $\frac{2}{3}$.

I. delavayi
D1 flowering shoot and leaf × $\frac{2}{3}$.

Campsis grandiflora (syn. *C. chinensis*)
E1 flowering shoot × $\frac{2}{3}$.

A1

A2

A3

A4

B1

C1

C2

D1

E1

Plate 104   HIMALAYA AND CHINA

The outstanding decorative feature of *Callicarpa rubella* (A) is its long-lived, deep purple berries. They only caught the interest of the gardening press and public on their reintroduction by Robert Fortune in 1857, about thirty years after they had first been brought to Britain from Canton by John Potts, a collector working for the Royal Horticultural Society. The foliage is attractive too, with gracefully arching woolly stems up to 9 feet (2·7 m.) tall, but the flowers, which appear in July and August, are tiny and insignificant. The species, which has a wide distribution that ranges from southern China to eastern India, is one of about one hundred and forty in the genus, most of them from the tropics and subtropics. A closely related species is said to extend into Malaysia, but, in fact, may not be specifically distinct. In places such as Britain *C. rubella* needs to be grown under glass but there are hardy species such as *C. dichotoma*, *C. japonica* and *C. giraldii*.

As well as the familiar stove-plants, plate 60, used to decorate glasshouses *Clerodendrum* includes a number of woody shrubs such as *C. bungei* (F), which was discovered by Alexander von Bunge in northern China and introduced by Robert Fortune about 1844. Although it can develop into a tree, in Britain it is not completely hardy and is usually cut back by frost. Nevertheless it will send up shoots which form a bush 3 to 4 feet (0·9–1·2 m.) tall with, in August and September, a profusion of fragrant flowers. The synonymous specific epithet *foetidum* probably refers to the unpleasant smell given off when the leaves are crushed.

In the same large family as the coffee plant, the *Rubiaceae*, the five species of *Luculia* (the name is derived from the native designation), occur in the Himalaya and south-western China. The first to be introduced to Europe, *L. gratissima*, brought from Nepal in about 1816, created a stir of admiration in horticultural circles for its large trusses of fragrant pink flowers, but was eclipsed in the middle of the century by the arrival of another, yet lovelier

Nepalese species, *L. pinceana* (B). The latter forms a shrub about 6 feet (1·8 m.) tall and differs from *L. gratissima* in having larger, white flowers and, less conspicuously, two flaps of tissue situated at the base of the sinus between each of the corolla lobes.

Ten large-flowered, hairy, glandular species of herbs comprise the genus *Rehmannia*, which commemorates the St Petersburg physician Joseph Rehmann (1799–1831). The genus lies more or less intermediate between two families and although it is now classified in the *Scrophulariaceae* today, it has often been placed in the *Gesneriaceae*. *R. henryi* (C), named after Augustine Henry, who discovered the plant about 1885 near Ichang in south-western China, consists of an erect, single or branched stem with basal leaves about 7 inches (18 cm.) long and $2\frac{1}{2}$ inches (7 cm.) wide. Seed was sent to the Arnold Arboretum, 'America's greatest garden', by E. H. Wilson and from there was forwarded to Kew, where it flowered in 1909; however, it is only hardy in the warmest parts of Britain. *R. glutinosa* (E) is a somewhat taller plant and also a native of China where it was discovered near Peking by von Bunge. The purplish suffusion on the dull yellow flowers is sometimes restricted to the throat, sometimes wider spread. Other decorative species from China include the 3 foot (91 cm.) *R. angulata*, and the even larger *R. elata* with which it is often confused.

At first placed in the genus *Rehmannia*, but actually quite different, the Formosan *Titanotrichum oldhamii* (D), the only species in its genus as it is now constituted, has a curiously greater affinity with such New World genera as *Kohleria*, *Sinningia* and *Smithiantha* than with the more closely related Old World gesneriads, none of which have its scaly rhizome. Being a herbaceous perennial with 1 to 3 erect stems and colourful flowers borne in terminal racemes, it does bear a superficial resemblence to *Digitalis* and *Rehmannia* but may always be identified by its woody rootstock with numerous, horizontally spreading rhizomes.

A1

A2

B

B1

C1

D1

E1

F1

F2

Plate 105   HIMALAYA AND CHINA

Though few hybrids, natural or otherwise, have been illustrated in these plates, they cannot be ignored completely. The spectacular *Lychnis × haageana* (F) is a hybrid between the Siberian *L. fulgens* and *L. grandiflora* (probably the same as the earlier *L. coronata* of Japan and China) and combines the attractive points of both parent species. The hybridization was first performed by Ernest Benary of Erfürt in Germany, who named the progeny after his friend F. A. Haage. The hybrid is hardy in Britain and grows to about 2 feet (61 cm.) in height, its 7 or more scarlet flowers contrast with the purple-flushed leaves.

The eight species of *Ceratostigma* range in distribution from East Africa, through the Himalaya and Burma to Thailand and China. The late-flowering, gentian-blue petals of *C. plumbaginoides* (B), discovered in northern China and described in 1833, and the final reddish hue of the foliage, make it a valuable addition to an autumn garden. It is closely related to the western Chinese *C. willmottianum* introduced by E. H. Wilson, the specific epithet of which commemorates Miss Ellen Ann Willmott (1858–1934), of Warley Place, Essex, who raised it from seed given to her by the Arnold Arboretum. It differs from *C. plumbaginoides* being a much branched, taller shrub with paler blue flowers, hairier leaves and lateral buds protected by chaffy scales (unlike those of its companion species, which are naked).

Of wider generic distribution are the six species of *Macrotomia*, found from the Mediterranean to the Himalaya, a group now included in the genus *Arnebia*, which then has about twenty species. In Kumaon, Robert Blinkworth, Nathaniel Wallich's correspondent, discovered *A. benthamii* (E), a species that also occurs at altitudes of between 9000 and 13,000 feet (2740–3960 m.) in Kashmir, where it is called 'Khou Ka Zaban' or 'Goazaban'. In 1884, F. J. Duthie introduced the species to Kew, where flowers were first obtained in 1887. The plant is unusual in appearance, thick stemmed, covered in hair and with huge, plantain-like leaves at the base of the plant capable of reaching a length of 10 inches (25·4 cm.). The 3 foot (91 cm.) stem bears, on its top 9–12 inches (23–30 cm.), a cylindrical cluster of hairy flowers with maroon, funnel-shaped corollas from which protrude hairy green sepals. The subtending floral bracts further exceed the sepals and emerge from the inflorescence in characteristic manner.

A German patron of botany from Darmstadt, Friedrich von Lindelof, is commemorated in another boraginaceous genus, *Lindelofia*, which contains ten species extending from Afghanistan into the Himalaya. *L. longiflora* (G), which appears between May and August, grows to a height of 24 inches (61 cm.), is sparsely flowered and lacks bracts. The cylindrical blooms (which resemble those of the genus *Cynoglossum*, to which *Lindelofia* is closely allied) measure $\frac{5}{8}$ of an inch (16 mm.) in length, though in some areas larger flowered wild plants are to be found. This perennial, rarely found in gardens, is propagated from offsets, and was introduced from Kashmir by J. F. Royle in 1839.

An aromatic genus of labiates, usually with strongly scented leaves, *Nepeta*, is represented by two hundred and fifty species occurring from the mountains of tropical and North Africa throughout temperate Eurasia. Of these, *N. longibracteata* (A) is found in the western Himalaya and Tibet at altitudes of between 14,000 and 17,000 feet (4270–5180 m.). It rarely exceeds 6 inches (15 cm.) in height, has woolly, fan-shaped leaves, and congested spikes of blossom about 1 inch (2·5 cm.) in length.

At a lower altitude—8000 to 11,000 feet (2440–3350 m.)—is found *Salvia hians* (D), another characteristic labiate of the Himalaya, and one which occasionally finds its way into European gardens. It is a tall perennial, sticky and hairy, with long-stalked, toothed leaves, oval or halberd-shaped in outline. Attractive, large blue flowers 1½ inches (3·5 cm.) long are borne in 2 or 3 distinct whorls.

The genus *Colquhounia* is named after Sir Robert Colquhoun, who died in 1838 and was one time Resident in Nepal, patron of the Calcutta Botanic Garden, and a correspondent of Nathaniel Wallich. Its six species are found only in the mountainous Sino-Himalayan region. One of the most ornamental is *C. coccinea* (C), which was introduced into Britain as seed by Wallich from Nepal. Although it has been cultivated in Britain for more than a century it has never become a popular garden shrub in western Europe because of its tenderness and lanky growth. In the wild it occurs in thickets or scattered on grassy slopes from the western Himalaya to northern Thailand and Yunnan at altitudes of 6000–9000 feet (1830–2740 m.). It forms a shrub about 13 feet (3·9 m.) high, with fuzzy, hairy branches and buddleja-like leaves up to 5½ inches (14 cm.) long, and has been used for hedging in parts of Bhutan, where the colour of the flowers has significance for those of Buddhist faith.

LABIATAE

Nepeta longibracteata
A1 flowering plant × ⅔. A2 flower × 2.

Colquhounia coccinea
C1 flowering shoot × ⅔. C2 flower × 2.

Salvia hians
D1 part of flowering stem × ⅔.
D2 basal leaf × ⅔.

PLUMBAGINACEAE

Ceratostigma plumbaginoides
B1 part of flowering stem × ⅔.
B2 flower × 1⅓.

BORAGINACEAE

Arnebia benthamii (syn. *Macrotomia benthamii*)
E1 flowering shoot × ⅔.

Lindelofia longiflora
G1 flowering stem × ⅔.
G2 lower stem with basal leaves × ⅔.

CARYOPHYLLACEAE

Lychnis × haageana
F1 flowering stem × ⅔.
F2 petal and stamen × 1⅓.

A2

A1

B1

B2

C1   C2

D1   D2

E1

F2   F1

G1   G2

Plate 106   HIMALAYA AND CHINA

When Roman civilization had brought a superior, if somewhat alien and temporary, way of life to Europe, the Chinese were already compiling authoritative horticultural texts and had devised sophisticated plant care techniques. Ancient Chinese books, stated to have been compiled originally before 500 B.C., mention yellow-flowered chrysanthemums, probably not very different from the small-flowered wild Chinese species inappropriately named *Chrysanthemum indicum* by Linnaeus in 1753. During the T'ang dynasty in China, white and purple chrysanthemums became known. By natural crossing between these variants and by subsequent careful selection, the Chinese evolved a number of cultivars, particularly during the 10th to the 13th centuries A.D. In the 8th century, Chinese chrysanthemums were introduced to Japan and here again, being highly esteemed as garden plants, were evidently raised from seed in quantity and subjected to further selection. The result has been the evolution of a complex garden group, to the variability of which possibly seven wild species of *Chrysanthemum* native to China and Japan have contributed. About 1688, six cultivars with white, yellowish, pink, reddish, purple-red and purple flowers had been introduced from Japan to Holland, but were rather surprisingly then lost to cultivation in Europe. The first effective introduction was that of a purplish crimson Chinese cultivar into France in 1789; this received the name *Chrysanthemum morifolium* in 1792. By 1808, eight more cultivars had been introduced direct from China to England. Thereafter, the florist's chrysanthemum steadily rose in popularity as a garden plant, both in Europe and America. The massy bronze heads of the 'show chrysanth', and the smaller multicoloured heads of various chrysanthemum types such as 'pompon', are the product of centuries of cultivation initiated by long-forgotten plant lovers in China. Ancient Chinese tradition has it that dew collected from the flowers of chrysanthemums preserves and restores vitality in man and certain individuals even hoped to become immortal by eating chrysanthemum petals regularly. Some European species of *Chrysanthemum* are illustrated on plate 39.

As well as cultivars, China and the surrounding areas have produced noble wild daisy species which now grace western gardens. No amount of conceivable 'improvement' could better species like the ligularias shown opposite.

The herbaceous perennial, *Ligularia przewalskii* (A), is a native of Kansu, Shensi and Szechuan provinces in China, where it grows at high altitudes of between 7000 and 9000 feet (2100-2700 m.), and also in Mongolia, where the celebrated Russian explorer, Nicolai M. Przewalski (1839-1888) collected it on the banks of rivers.

Named after its discoverer, Christopher Pemberton Hodgson (1821-1865), *L. hodgsonii* (B) is a native of Japan. Hodgson, who was Consul in Japan between 1859 and 1861, found this plant on Hokkaido and introduced it into cultivation in England. (It was later named *Senecio yesoensis*.) Although very similar to *L. dentata*, *L. hodgsonii* has dense clusters of flowerheads, with 2 small bracts beneath each and smaller, more numerous ray-florets. *L. dentata*, on the other hand, has loose clusters of flowerheads with no bracts. It was introduced from western Hupeh by E. H. Wilson in 1900 and has since become a popular plant for water gardens as it thrives in moist soil. This species occurs throughout west and central China and into Japan and grows to a height of 5 feet (1·5 m.). It is often incorrectly known as *Senecio clivorum*.

The Chinese Aster, *Callistephus chinensis* (C), a native of Japan and China, is the parent of the annual garden aster. These plants, which represent double forms and colour varieties of the variable parental species should not be confused with *Aster* species (plate 165) and cultivars. The Chinese Aster was first introduced into France in 1728, and thence into England and the Chelsea Physic Garden under the direction of Philip Miller in 1731. By the 1770's a number of single and double cultivars were becoming popular and later the Victorians favoured them as bedding plants.

The genus *Echinops* is some one hundred species strong, and is found in southern and eastern Europe, parts of Africa and Asia. The spherical heads are composed of flowers inserted at a common point, each flower rising from its own whorl of bracts. In other words, every flower represents a much simplified inflorescence, the spherical head being a compound inflorescence. The Dahurian Globe Thistle, *E. dahurica* (D) is a native of north China, Korea, Manchuria and Mongolia, where it grows at altitudes between 3000 and 4800 feet (900-1400 m.). Other globe thistles include a blue-flowered species, *E. ritro*, from southern Europe and *E. giganteus*, an Ethiopian plant which will grow to a height of 15 feet (4·6 m.) in some habitats.

COMPOSITAE

Ligularia przewalskii
A1 part of flowering stem with lateral leaf × ⅔.
A2 disc-floret × 4. A3 ray-floret × 4.

L. hodgsonii (syn. *Senecio yesoensis*)
B1 part of flowering stem × ⅔.
B2 disc-floret × 3⅓. B3 ray-floret × 3⅓.

Callistephus chinensis, Chinese Aster
C1 part of flowering stem × ⅔. C2 ray-floret × 2.
C3 disc-floret × 3⅓.

Echinops dahurica, Dahurian Globe Thistle
D1 part of flowering stem × ⅔. D2 flower × 3⅓.

A2

A3

A1

B2 B1 B3

C3 C2 C1

D2 D1

Plate 107   HIMALAYA AND CHINA

In China and Japan, certain lilies have long been cultivated for food rather than aesthetic purposes, species with white bulbs, especially the Tiger Lily, *Lilium tigrinum*, usually being preferred. The fleshy bulb-scales, peeled and cooked with sugar-water, are thought to act as a tonic and purifier. The Tiger Lily, also popular in the east as a garden plant with a history of cultivation going back over a thousand years, was introduced to the west by the East India Company in 1804. Two later introductions from China which are now widely grown in western gardens, are *L. henryi*, with orange flowers spotted brown, sent as bulbs from the Ichang Gorge by Augustine Henry in about 1888, and the Regal Lily, *L. regale*, with white flowers shaded purple, which E. H. Wilson introduced in 1903–1904. Kaempfer and Thunberg were two of the first Europeans to see and study east Asian lilies although neither of them appears to have introduced any species. More popular garden plants in the west come from the east where many lovely *Iris* species originated, two favourites being *I. chrysographes* with deep violet and golden striped flowers and the rich purple flowered species, *I. kaempferi*.

Although *Lilium speciosum* (A) was seen by Kaempfer in its native Japan in 1691, it was first introduced by von Siebold in 1830, flowering for the first time in Europe at Ghent in 1832. Now a rarity in the wild on the islands of Shikoku and Kyushu, it has long been cultivated in Japan as well as being a favourite subject of Japanese silk artists. Numerous horticultural varieties continue to be grown there, as well as in China and Formosa, where most plants belong to the variety *gloriosoides*, initially brought to the west by Charles Maries in 1878. The popularity of *L. speciosum* is partly due to the ease with which it can be grown, although its stature, up to 4 feet (1·2 m.), and inflorescences bearing as many as 40 scented flowers in August and September have undoubtedly had an influence. Propagation is usually by bulblets or bulb-scales, as seedlings take four years to flower from germination.

As its name suggests, *L. nepalense* (E) was first collected in Nepal but it is now known to exist further to the east. The first trustworthy evidence of its introduction into cultivation is not until 1927 but, in the past, it has been much confused with *L. primulinum*, especially var. *ochraceum*. The latter, a closely related species, comes from south-west China, Upper Burma to northern Thailand. The tender *L. nepalense*, which in most of Britain is grown in a cool greenhouse, does better where it may be planted out for the plant spreads and 'wanders' by the production of subterranean stems which arise from the bulb and creep horizontally through the soil up to 2 feet (61 cm.) before producing bulblets. These then grow vertically to form aerial shoots and 1–3 nodding, trumpet-shaped flowers, each about 5 inches (12 cm.) long, are produced between June and July.

Sometimes known as Toad Lilies, the ten *Tricyrtis* species occur in the Himalaya and eastern Asia. *T. stolonifera* (B) is a Formosan plant closely allied to *T. formosana*, but has a stoloniferous habit and spotted purplish petals. Growing to about 2 feet (61 cm.) high, it has a quiet but attractive appearance and, providing autumn frosts do not spoil the September flowers, it is fairly hardy. Discovered by R. Oldham in 1864, it was introduced to Kew by H. J. Elwes and W. R. Price, from Karaping in Formosa, in 1912 and deserves more widespread cultivation.

Iris kumaonensis (D) is a native of the western Himalaya in Kumaon, at altitudes between 8000 and 18,000 feet (2380–5490 m.). When mature, the leaves are a full 18 inches (46 cm.) long and $\frac{1}{2}$ inch (12 mm.) broad, but at flowering time in spring, they are only 4–6 inches (10–15 cm.) long.

Perhaps the most unusual of *Iris* species is *I. wattii* (C) discovered by George Watt in Manipur in 1882, and later in Assam and Yunnan. It was introduced to cultivation in 1931 by Major Lawrence Johnston who, with George Forrest, found it near Tengyueh, Yunnan and collected rhizomes which he planted in his garden at Mentone in France. The species was subsequently introduced into Britain and received an Award of Merit from the Royal Horticultural Society when plants from Bodnant Gardens in North Wales were shown by Lord Aberconway in 1938. Its habit distinguishes *I. wattii* from all other irises except *I. confusa*, which has smaller, whiter flowers. Seeds of the latter were sent to W. R. Dykes, a well-known authority on *Iris*, from Yunnan in 1911 by Père Ducloux. At first, it was misidentified and wrongly called *I. wattii*, hence the epithet *confusa* which was given to it when the mistake was discovered. *I. wattii* often has stems measuring more than 3 feet (91 cm.), the inflorescence adding another 2–3 feet (61–91 cm.) to the height of the plant. Prior to flowering, the stem is short and the leaves crowded together near the ground. Then the stem elongates rapidly, carrying a cluster of leaves aloft in the year before flowering and in this state the plant spends the winter. Then in spring, an inflorescence rapidly develops and flowers may be borne a full 6 feet (1·8 m.) above the ground, although in the wild, the plants may only reach a total height of 3 feet (91 cm.). When the flowers have gone and the fruits have ripened, the shoot dies.

LILIACEAE

Lilium speciosum
A1 part of flowering stem × $\frac{2}{3}$. A2 anther × $1\frac{1}{3}$.

Tricyrtis stolonifera
B1 part of flowering stem × $\frac{2}{3}$.
B2 stamens, style and ovary × $1\frac{1}{3}$.
B3 stigma × 4.

Lilium nepalense
E1 part of flowering stem × $\frac{2}{3}$. E2 anther × $1\frac{1}{3}$.

IRIDACEAE

Iris wattii
C1 part of flowering stem (cut) × $\frac{2}{3}$.
C2 stamen × $1\frac{1}{3}$. C3 habit sketch × $\frac{1}{8}$.

I. kumaonensis
D1 part of flowering plant × $\frac{2}{3}$.
D2 stamen × $1\frac{1}{3}$.

A2

A1

B2

B3

B1

E2

E1

C3

C2

C1

D2

D1

Plate 108　HIMALAYA AND CHINA

Both the lilies and the aroids of this area include a number of outstandingly impressive species. Nothing, perhaps, can compare with the majesty of the mammoth, 12 foot (3·5 m.) lily, *Cardiocrinum giganteum,* whose every blossom measures between 6 and 12 inches (15–30 cm.); but a number of aroids, with their diversity of shapes and colours, are almost as striking.

An aroid that has the unusual property of producing only one leaf each year is *Arisaema candidissimum* (A), discovered by George Forrest in 1914 on rocky slopes and slate ledges at an altitude of between 8000 and 9000 feet (2440–2740 m.) in Yunnan. The species grows from a flattish tuber about 1½ inches (38 mm.) in diameter and puts forth shoots which, when fully developed, attain a height of 18 inches (46 cm.). The long-lasting, slightly scented flowers, which are either male or female, appear between May and June. The plant is reasonably hardy in places such as Britain.

Conspicuous among arisaemas for the white-tipped spike (spadix) at the centre of the flower, *A. sikokianum* (E) is a Japanese species native to the islands of Honshu, Shikoku and Kyushu. As with the above species, the flowers, which last for several weeks, bloom between May and June. The two leaves, one inserted higher than the other, are divided into 3, 4 or 5 leaflets whose blades may or may not be mottled in different shades of green. Under cultivation, small glossy orange or red berries about ¼ inch (6 mm.) in diameter, are sometimes produced.

Taken pounded and boiled with orange peel and sugar, the flattish, ¾ inch (19 mm.) thick bulbs of *Fritillaria roylei* (D) and the closely related *F. cirrhosa* are reputed to relieve chest ailments. The former species commemorates J. F. Royle, a pioneer of Himalayan botany, and is found on grassy slopes in forest glades and between rocks at altitudes of up to about 12,000 feet (3660 m.) in Kumaon, adjacent Tibet, Kashmir and northern Punjab. From the bulbs spring stems 2 feet (61 cm.) tall, naked below, clothed with linear leaves further up and ending in 1 to 3 nodding, bell-shaped flowers. Unlike the upper leaves of *F. cirrhosa* (from Nepal and China) and *F. verticillata* (from Siberia, China and Japan), those of the species depicted are not tipped with tendrils.

A membraneous coating to the bulb, and a stigma with 3 branches instead of 3 lobes are the characteristics that distinguish *Notholirion,* a genus of 6 species extending from Persia to China, from the superficially similar *Lilium.* The genus was established, and distinguished from *Lilium,* by Boissier in 1884, when he gave the plant illustrated opposite, *N. macrophyllum* (B), its present name. It had previously been recorded both as *Fritillaria* and as *Lilium hookeri.* The first examples to reach England were seen in Hyde Park in 1929 as the result of a gift of live bulbs sent to King George V by the Prime Minister of Nepal. The racemes of 2 to 6 flowers borne by *N. macrophyllum* are carried on slender, shiny green stems, up to 18 inches (46 cm.) in height, clothed with stalkless sheathing and spreading leaves. Mature fruits contain wingless seeds about ¾ inch (19 mm.) long.

Lilium taliense (C) takes its name from the Tali Range, one of two mountain ranges in Yunnan from which the first seed to be flowered in Europe was collected by George Forrest in the mid-1930's, though the species had been discovered by Père Delavay in 1883. It is said to grow to between 3 and 10 feet (0·9–3 m.) in height and bears numerous narrow leaves irregularly spaced up the stem, each with three faint veins. Each inflorescence comprises 1 to 10 nodding, scented, purple-spotted white flowers.

ARACEAE

Arisaema candidissimum
A1 two inflorescences and leaf × ⅔.
A2 spadix × ⅔.

A. sikokianum
E1 part of flowering plant × ⅔.

LILIACEAE

Notholirion macrophyllum
B1 part of flowering stem × ⅔.

Lilium taliense
C1 flowering shoot × ⅔.
C2 petal × 1⅓.
C3 bulb and stem roots × ⅔.

Fritillaria roylei
D1 part of flowering stems × ⅔.

A1

A2

B1

C1

C2

C3

D1

E1

Plate 109   HIMALAYA AND CHINA

Other orchids have certainly warranted equal praise yet few have produced a craze to rival that created by *Vanda caerulea* when it was introduced into western Europe in 1849. We in the west are captivated by the exuberance of *Dendrobium densiflorum* or the fragile beauty of *Dendrobium aphyllum*, but it all seems to be a matter of taste, for who in Europe would esteem *Cymbidium ensifolium* with the high regard accorded to it by the Chinese?

Dr W. Griffith discovered the Blue Vanda, *Vanda caerulea* (B), in Assam in 1837. Its pure blue flowers were remarkable at that time, although many blue orchids are known today. At the peak of the craze which followed its introduction individual plants cost £4 . 10. 0. each at a time when this sum represented a great deal of money (though nothing compared to the 1000 guineas paid about that time for plants of *Odontoglossum crispum*). Trade became so extensive that the collection of the plant from the wild had to be prohibited. It flowers mainly in autumn and winter, and the pale blue blossoms, up to 5 inches (12·5 cm.) across on large flowered forms, are mottled and veined with deeper blue. From 7 to 20 long-lived flowers are borne on erect leafy stems up to 4 feet (1·2 m.) long. The yellowish-green leaves measure up to about 12 inches (30 cm.).

Cymbidium ensifolium (D) known as Chien Lan or Fukien Orchid, with a range from China south through Indo-China into Sumatra and Java, has been a popular pot-plant in China for centuries. The flowers, which last for a month or more, have become a favourite subject for painters and many varieties with variegated leaves, and more fragrant and colourful flowers have been developed. Spikes of 3 to 7 flowers, 12 inches (30 cm.) tall, appear in summer from among the grassy leaves of the same length. Veined and spotted purple on a greenish-yellow background, the flowers are 2 inches (5 cm.) in width. The plant is one of several terrestrial cymbidiums which are favourites in China and are usually grown in pots there.

Dendrobium densiflorum (C) was introduced to Europe about 1829 from the tropical parts of the Himalaya. Its 4-angled pseudobulbs, 15 to 18 inches (38–46 cm.) long, produce leathery leaves measuring up to about 6 inches (15 cm.) in length and pendant racemes of flowers. It grows as an epiphyte in trees and the pendulous flowers fill the air with their scent. When the flowers have died they are replaced by seed capsules about 3 inches (7·5 cm.) long. In cultivation *D. densiflorum* never fails to produce a splendid show if properly cared for. One of its colour forms, var. *albolutea*, is often grown under the name *D. thyrsiflorum*.

Another easily cultivated species, *D. aphyllum* (A) was introduced to the Liverpool Botanic Garden in 1819 and thence to Glasgow Botanic Garden where W. J. Hooker illustrated and described it for his *Exotic Flora* in 1823. A native of India, Burma, Thailand, the Malay peninsula and China, its long, narrow, stem-like pseudobulbs, 2 to 8 feet (0·6 to 2·4 m.) long bear numerous fragile flowers in 2's and 3's where the leaves have fallen; hence the epithet *aphyllum* 'without leaves'. This species was introduced to the Calcutta Botanic Garden by M. Pierard, whose name is commemorated in the synonym *D. pierardii*.

In 1916 *Cypripedium himalaicum* (F) was sent from Sikkim by G. H. Cave (*c.* 1870–1965) of the Lloyd Botanic Garden, Darjeeling, to the famous horticulturist H. J. Elwes. The roots of the orchid and those of a liliaceous plant, *Smilacina oleracea,* were sent growing together and it flowered in June 1921, enabling the material to be illustrated in the *Botanical Magazine* of 1923. Found from Gharwal, along the Himalaya, to Szechuan in western China at altitudes of from 8000 to 13,000 feet (2400–3900 m.), it is a perennial herb about 18 inches (46 cm.) tall with leaves which sheath the stem. Solitary flowers subtended by a boat-shaped greenish bract terminate the flower stalk which is $2\frac{3}{4}$–$4\frac{3}{4}$ inches (7–12 cm.) long. *C. himalaicum* is related to *C. macranthos*, a plant distributed through the Soviet Union eastward into northern China and Kamchatka, while its other relative, *C. tibeticum*, has darker flowers and a shorter habit.

About fifty tropical Asian species are contained in *Paphiopedilum*, a genus closely related to *Cypripedium*. *P. venustum* (E), a quietly coloured native of Nepal, was introduced into cultivation between 1816 and 1819 from the Calcutta Botanic Garden, having been earlier discovered by Nathaniel Wallich. The leaves, up to 6 inches (15 cm.) long, are deep green, marbled with grey-green above and mottled with dull purple below. The scapes measure 9 inches (23 cm.) and terminate with a single flower charmingly coloured in harmony with the foliage and composing a most handsome plant. It is not a difficult orchid to cultivate and blooms in winter and spring.

ORCHIDACEAE

Dendrobium aphyllum (syn. *D. pierardii*)
A1 part of flowering stem × $\frac{2}{3}$.
A2 pollinia and column × 6.
A3 pollen mass × 6.

D. densiflorum
C1 flowering plant × $\frac{2}{3}$. C2 fruit × $\frac{2}{3}$.

Vanda caerulea, Blue Vanda
B1 flowering scape in position on plant showing aerial roots × $\frac{2}{3}$.

Cymbidium ensifolium, Chien Lan or Fukien Orchid
D1 part of flowering plant × $\frac{2}{3}$.

Paphiopedilum venustum
E1 part of flowering plant × $\frac{2}{3}$.
E2 side view of flower × $\frac{2}{3}$.

Cypripedium himalaicum
F1 flowering stem × $\frac{2}{3}$.
F2 side view of flower × $\frac{2}{3}$.

A3

A2

A1

A3

A2

D1

E2

E1

C2

C1

B1

F2

F1

Plate 110   SOUTH EAST ASIA

The well known tropical fruits, the Soursop, *Annona muricata,* the Sweetsop, *A. squamosa,* and the Custard Apple, *A. reticulata,* although often grown in South East Asia, are all natives of the American tropics and members of the family *Annonaceae,* which also has numerous species in the Old World.

The genus *Cananga* contains two species ranging through tropical Asia into Australia. A native of Malaysia, *C. odorata* (C), which yields the perfume known as Ylang-ylang or Macassar oil, is now cultivated in many tropical areas, in some of which it has become a commercial crop. This evergreen tree may grow up to 90 feet (27 m.) tall and the flowers are borne on the older wood of the drooping branches. Ten year old trees are said to produce about 23 lbs (10·4 kg.) of flowers each year, of which only about 2% of the weight is obtained in oil. The flowers must be picked very early in the day, even before the sun has risen, for the sun's heat volatilizes the oil which produces the perfume. Much of the production of Macassar oil takes place in Réunion, also famous for its production of geranium oil, but there is native production in the Philippines and Java. Ylang-ylang flowers are a favourite for personal adornment amongst the women of some parts of Malaysia.

A genus of some one hundred and twenty species, *Polyalthia* has a centre of concentration in South East Asia. *P. lateriflora* (A), sometimes called 'Pisang-pisang', occurs in the Malay Peninsula and several of the islands of Indonesia. A beautiful plant with greenish flowers tinged with yellow and red, it forms a tree from 40 to 90 feet (12–27 m.) tall. The fragrant flowers, borne, as illustrated, only on the stems of larger branches, are followed by fruits which change colour from green, through red to reddish black as they ripen. Heartwood is yellowish in colour while sapwood is whitish and the leaves, though shaped like those illustrated, are often much larger, sometimes reaching a foot (30 cm.) or more in length. As with a number of annonaceous species, the carpels situated in the centre of the flower are at first very small and inconspicuous. Later, those which have been fertilized enlarge greatly, each on the end of a stalk, to produce the characteristic fruiting heads. *P. lateriflora* often grows in association with dipterocarps, described on plate 119.

Belonging to the same family as *Magnolia,* *Michelia* differs in having its flowers in the axils of the leaves, whereas those of *Magnolia* are borne at the ends of the shoots. The forty-five species of this genus, which commemorates the early Italian botanist, P. A. Micheli (1679–1737), are found in tropical Asia and into China. *M. champaca* (B), its specific epithet derived from its Hindi common name, has fragrant golden to pale yellow blossoms which have made the tree popular as an ornamental plant in many parts of Asia, West and East Africa, the West Indies, the southern United States and parts of South America. It forms a tree from 40 to 70 feet (12–21 m.) tall and its fruits, which are usually greenish yellow, contain pink seeds when freshly opened. *M. champaca* is native to India and used there to ornament the grounds of Hindu and Jain temples: the fresh flowers yield a fragrant oil; the timber, which contains a very bitter substance, is very durable. These virtues and its association with Hinduism led, many years ago, to its introduction into Malaya and Indonesia, together with the Sanskrit name 'Champaka', in Malay, now 'Chempaka' or 'Jampaka'.

Described by Nathaniel Wallich and illustrated for him in his splendid *Plantae Asiaticae Rariores,* volume 2, *Aristolochia saccata* (D) was introduced into the Calcutta Botanic Garden in 1815 and in 1829 was sent to the Edinburgh Botanic Garden, where it thrived. In nature it is a climber up to 20 feet (6 m.) in length with narrow leaves up to 15 inches (38 cm.) long. Its yellow-throated, purple-red flowers are densely hairy and possess an offensive smell; they are followed by capsular fruits about 4 inches (10 cm.) long. Sir William Jackson Hooker, in the *Botanical Magazine* of 1839, describes how he examined the flowers and found them to be full of small flies, apparently unable to escape until he inclined the flowers from the vertical to the horizontal. Some of these insects had been captive so long that they had laid eggs from which grubs had hatched. Hooker mentions Pitcher-plants, *Nepenthes* (see plate 111), and likens the mechanism of insect capture in *A. saccata* to these plants, but the similarity is probably only superficial. It would seem the stink of the flowers initially lures the insects, while in *Nepenthes* the prey is attracted by shiny glands, and the smell is a secondary consequence of decaying matter in the pitchers. *Nepenthes* is an insectivorous genus and there is undoubted digestion of the insects caught in the pitcher, but it would seem that in *Aristolochia,* as in some members of the *Araceae,* the flies, usually trapped for a time only, are the agents of pollination. *A. saccata* ranges from the Khasia Hills of Assam to Nepal, where the plants have leaves which tend to be silky-hairy and broader. Both types frequently bear their flowers on older parts of the stem, that is near to the ground, where the heavy odour of the flowers is less likely to be blown away than it would be in the upper canopy of the trees.

ANNONACEAE

Polyalthia lateriflora, Pisang-pisang
A1 part of branch with flowers × ⅔.
A2 fruit of one flower on part of branch × ⅔.

Cananga odorata, Ylang-ylang
C1 flowering shoot × ⅔.
C2 part of fruiting stem × ⅔.

MAGNOLIACEAE

Michelia champaca
B1 flowering shoot × ⅔.
B2 twig with fruit of one flower × ⅔.

ARISTOLOCHIACEAE

Aristolochia saccata
D1 part of flowering branch and twining leafy stem × ⅔.

A1

A2

B1

B2

C1

C2

D1

Plate 111　SOUTH EAST ASIA

Pitcher-plants are perhaps the nearest thing in reality to those figments of the imagination, man-eating plants—although their 'prey' is seldom larger than a cockroach or beetle. While most green plants derive their nitrogen from the soil as solutes conducted through the root system, a few others such as *Nepenthes, Drosera* and *Utricularia* obtain nitrogen from captured animal prey. Carnivorous plants do not live solely on the captured animals, for the chlorophyll in leaves and stems, and the foods manufactured in conjunction with the chlorophyll, are quite as important as the captured prey. But, as a balance between photosynthesis and carnivorism is essential, it is true to say that such plants do not thrive in the absence of prey. It is interesting that quite similar yet complicated mechanisms for animal capture have arisen separately in different and unrelated groups of plants during the course of evolution.

There are some sixty-seven species of *Nepenthes,* a genus with its centre of distribution in Borneo, but extending to Madagascar in the west and New Caledonia in the east. Of the sixty or so species reviewed by Danser in 1928, almost one-third were known only as isolated species and found on solitary mountains; this signifies a high degree of 'localism' or 'endemism' which may be connected with recent evolution in the genus.

These curious plants occur from sea-level to an altitude of 11,000 feet (3350 m.) and favour nutrient deficient soils with high acidity, such as peat swamps. They may fail to develop if the soil is too rich or the air too dry. *N. northiana,* however, is found in a dry habitat—on limestone in Sarawak, and *N. phyllamphora* of Ceylon occurs in a type of dry scrub vegetation. Pitcher-plants are rarely found in the south-east Asian dipterocarp forest—characteristic in this area (see plate 119) possibly because the deep shade cast by this vegetation inhibits their flowering.

The plants are usually vines or epiphytes and the climbing shoots can ascend 60 feet (18 m.) into trees, while leaf tendrils support the plant. On the ground they form rosettes of pitcher-bearing leaves. The pitchers on climbing parts often differ in shape from those borne at ground level, and some species have up to three different shapes of pitcher. *N. rafflesiana* (B) has broad based pitchers near the ground while the bases

of the upper pitchers are more tapered. A suggested explanation of this difference is that aerial pitchers have less wind-resistance and are less bulky when full of liquid. Depending on the species, pitchers may grow to about 1 foot (30 cm.) in length, but more often they are about 5–7 inches (12·5–18 cm.) long.

Until the lid of the pitcher opens on completion of development, the contents are sterile, i.e. free from bacteria and other airborne bodies such as spores, pollen and dust. The lid, which is not moveable, is inclined away from the mouth; between each tooth on the inside of the curved edge of the pitcher is a nectar secreting gland. These and other nectaries distributed on the surfaces of leaves and tendrils serve to attract insects toward the pitchers. Attempts by flies to stride along the rim of the pitcher usually result in downfall, and the same fate awaits ants which try to walk on the waxy inner wall. Cockroaches probably fall into pitchers by sheer clumsiness, and crawling insects tend to be caught more frequently than flying ones. A group of digestive and absorptive glands is situated below the waxy zone inside the upper part of the pitcher; juices secreted by these glands aid the digestion of the drowned insects. The scant remains of a cockroach were found inside the pitcher of the *N. rafflesiana* illustrated opposite.

Ants are associated with some *Nepenthes* plants, living inside the tendrils at the base of the pitcher and feeding from the nectaries. Other inhabitants of the pitcher include certain spiders, insects and aquatic micro-organisms which are found nowhere else in the world.

Nepenthes hookerana (A) is thought to be one of the few natural hybrids in the genus; on the basis of shared characters and geographical distribution, it is probably the result of a cross between *N. rafflesiana* and *N. ampullaria.* It occurs as a solitary plant and is rarely found. In cultivation, *Nepenthes* species hybridize easily, which sometimes makes the identification of old botanical garden collections difficult.

Rumpf recorded that Malays used to pour the contents of the pitchers over the heads of the incontinent. The efficacy of the cure is hard to estimate, but since the odour of a soup of partly digested insects is thoroughly disagreeable, the cure was probably more objectionable than the disability.

NEPENTHACEAE

Nepenthes hookerana
A1 mature pitcher on leaf $\times \frac{2}{3}$.
A2 immature pitcher on leaf $\times \frac{2}{3}$.

N. rafflesiana
B1 male flowers on part of upper stem, with leaves and immature pitcher $\times \frac{2}{3}$.
B2 mature pitcher on leaf $\times \frac{2}{3}$.
B3 young pitcher $\times \frac{2}{3}$.
B4 unopened stamens $\times 5\frac{1}{3}$.
B5 male flower $\times 2\frac{2}{3}$. B6 female flower $\times 2\frac{2}{3}$.
B7 habit sketch $\times \frac{1}{10}$.

A1

A2

B1

B2

B3

B4

B5

B6

B7

Plate 112   SOUTH EAST ASIA

Though a great number of species in the genus *Cassia* have leaves which may be described as feathery, those of *C. fistula* (A) are large and simply pinnate. Commonly known as Indian Laburnum, this species is found throughout monsoon forest in India, Burma and Ceylon. It has dangling racemes of fragrant flowers, borne in early summer when the new leaves are expanding, which may reach 2 feet (61 cm.) in length; the immature leaves are bright green or sometimes copper-coloured. Unlike *Delonix* and *Amherstia* (see plate 113) which belong to the same subfamily, the flower parts of *Cassia* show little reduction or modification. There are 5 green sepals, 5 petals of nearly equal size and 10 unfused stamens; however, the 3 shortest stamens do not contain pollen. As with *Delonix*, the long cylindrical, almost black pods, green until ripe, are most conspicuous when the leaves have fallen. The fruits contain about 80 yellowish seeds embedded in a sweet-tasting pulp, palatable to monkeys, bears and other forest animals—the chief form of natural dispersal. This pulp is reputedly useful as a laxative while a decoction consisting of the ground shell of the fruit with saffron, rose-water and sugar, is said to aid childbirth.

Its pea-like flowers indicate that *Mucuna* is a member of one of the other subfamilies, the *Papilionoideae*. Some one hundred and twenty species of this genus are found throughout the tropics and subtropics of the world. *M. atropurpurea* (B), found from Ceylon and Madras to the western Himalaya, bears glorious trusses of purple flowers. Its ornamental fruits are covered with reddish hairs when young, which are later shed to expose an intricately sculptured pod-wall. These hairs, if they get on one's skin, especially where it is soft, can cause great irritation. The fruit may grow to a length of 9 or 10 inches (23–25 cm.).

With some sixty species in the genus, *Dillenia* gives its name to the family *Dilleniaceae*. The genus is distributed throughout South East Asia, and as far as Fiji and northern Australia; it also occurs in the Mascarene Islands, the other side of the Indian Ocean. The Burma Simpoh, *D. obovata* (C), is a typical monsoon forest tree which may grow to 90 feet (27 m.) tall in Burma, Thailand, Malaya, Indo-China, and Indonesia. Its rosettes of deep green and conspicuously veined leaves, shed early in the year, reach up to 1 foot (30 cm.) in length; the young leaves are a purplish brown before they have fully expanded. Flowers, normally about 6 inches (15 cm.) in diameter, appear in March or April, before the new leaves have matured. E. J. H. Corner describes the tree thus: 'The big blossoms are displayed along the gaunt twigs and the golden petals flap in the wind'. However, the flowers last only one day and are later followed by oval, orange fruits, 1–2 inches (2·5–5 cm.) across, with brown seeds embedded in a clear mucilage. The closely related *D. aurea* is native of India, Burma and Thailand.

The even larger flowers of *D. indica*, up to 8 inches (20 cm.) across, are white and never yellow. They are amongst the largest flowers borne by any plant and Linnaeus, who is responsible for the name *Dillenia*, by which he commemorated John James Dillenius (1684–1747), first Sherardian Professor of Botany at Oxford, said in 1737 that '*Dillenia*, of all plants, has the showiest flower and fruit, even as Dillenius made a brilliant show among Botanists'. Often found along the edges of streams in India, Thailand and Malaya, this species tends to be smaller in stature than *D. aurea*. Its glossy leaves are enhanced by the pattern produced by the numerous veins coursing along the leaf surface. Its greenish yellow fruits, up to 7 inches (18 cm.) in diameter, are heavy and very tough and are eaten, appropriately, by elephants.

Another common Malaysian member of this family, *Dillenia suffruticosa*, better known as *Wormia suffruticosa*, is a large evergreen shrub which frequently grows in swamps, where it forms thickets. Its yellow flowers, about 5 inches (13 cm.) across, are arranged in a raceme, set off by cabbage-like leaves up to about 15 or 18 inches (38–46 cm.) long. In suitable habitats, the plant may attain a height of 20 feet (6 m.). It is cultivated, and sometimes has become naturalized, in many tropical countries.

LEGUMINOSAE

Cassia fistula, Indian Laburnum
A1 flowering twig × $\frac{2}{3}$. A2 fruit × $\frac{2}{3}$.

Mucuna atropurpurea
B1 flowering stem × $\frac{2}{3}$. B2 fruit × $\frac{2}{3}$.

DILLENIACEAE

Dillenia obovata, Burma Simpoh
C1 flowering twig × $\frac{2}{3}$. C2 leaf × $\frac{2}{3}$.
C3 shoot with young leaves × $\frac{2}{3}$.

A2   A1

B1

B2

C1

C2   C3

Plate 113   SOUTH EAST ASIA

The tropics set fire to the imagination of some people, who furnish these areas with gorgeously coloured flowering plants, luxuriantly fern- and palm-clad dells, and scintillating birds which flit from tree to tree. In fact tropical forest has a varied assortment of green and brown hues, and, depending on the type of forest, may have an impenetrable undergrowth or virtually naked forest floor, composed of sand or swamp with all vegetation many tens of feet above one's head. Innumerable mosquitoes often make it difficult to derive any pleasure from the occasional flowering specimen encountered, but certain species do fulfil the dreams of the romantic: *Amherstia* is one of the world's loveliest flowering trees while *Delonix* is one of the most floriferous and gaudy. In contrast, *Moghania* has diminutive flowers which are so hidden amongst their chaffy bracts that one wonders how pollinators ever know of their existence.

The genus *Delonix* consists of two species, *D. regia* (B) and *D. elata,* the latter being a tree of Ethiopia, Arabia and India with white flowers which gradually turn yellow. Although often planted in India, it is not so widespread in the tropics and nothing like so spectacular as *D. regia* – the Flamboyant or Gul Mohur. The Flamboyant is not a native of South East Asia but has been included because it certainly occurs more commonly here than in its original home, Madagascar. Indeed, for many years the Flamboyant was unknown in a wild state. An Austrian botanist, Wenzel Bojer (1797–1856), found it in 1828 at Foul Point on the east coast of Madagascar, where it was evidently an introduced tree, probably brought there by Arab settlers, and apparently the thousands of trees of the Flamboyant now scattered over both the Old and the New World tropics are all descended from material collected by Bojer. He introduced it to Mauritius and thence it passed to India and elsewhere. Madagascar has been so devastated by forest fires and clearance that its extinction as a wild plant seemed probable until, in 1932, J. Leandri found it in an obviously native state near the west coast of Madagascar, south of Maintirano where it grew on steep rocks in the Antsengy forest reserve. The Flamboyant in full bloom is undoubtedly among the showiest of all tropical trees and may reach a height of 50 feet (15 m.). It usually sheds all its leaves and, apart from the persistent long, flattened seed-pods of previous years, stands bare for a short time before becoming completely covered with its large red or orange flowers and unfolding bright green leaves. A mature leaf may have from 800 to 1000 leaflets. The petals are abruptly narrowed from a broad upper part into a long slender stalk or claw and this feature led Rafinesque to coin the name *Delonix* from Greek *delos,* 'conspicuous', *onyx* 'claw'. The pods are green and pliable when young but reddish brown, woody and sometimes more than 2 feet (61 cm.) long when mature; their ripening takes about two years and then, blown by the wind, they crash to the ground. The heat of the sun causes the walls of the pod to warp and so makes it open to release the oblong seeds. This species was formerly placed in the genus *Poinciana* (as *P. regia*), hence its Jamaican name 'Fancy-Anna'.

The only species of *Amherstia* is a native of the Tenasserim region of southern Burma and, like *Delonix regia,* is apparently very rare in a wild state. *A. nobilis* (A) was refound near the Yoonzalin River, a tributary of the lower Salween River, in 1865, some forty-one years after its discovery, by Nathaniel Wallich, in a monastery garden near Martaban. It was not seen wild again until 1927 when R. N. Parker found it in the Mergui district. The fallen flowers are used as an offering at Buddhist shrines. Wallich named the genus after Sarah, Countess Amherst (d. 1838), the wife of William Pitt Amherst, and their daughter, Lady Sarah Elizabeth Amherst (d. 1876), who travelled and collected extensively in India between 1823 and 1828. A plant sent to Mrs (later Lady) Lawrence by the Governor General of India, Lord Hardinge, in 1847, now grows at Kew where it has flowered almost every year since it was given in 1854.

Amherstia nobilis may reach 30 feet (9 m.) or so in height but does not grow as tall as the Flamboyant and lacks the delicate feathery foliage of that plant. In common with a number of tropical trees, *Amherstia* has reddish-purple young foliage; the pinnate leaves are shiny and hang in a limp cluster before they expand. The dangling racemes of 20 to 30 pale red flowers arise in the axils of the leaves and may be as much as 3 feet (91 cm.) long. The 2 red bracts beneath the red calyx persist after the withered flower has dropped. There are 3 conspicuous petals, 1 being broader than the others, with a splash of yellow on the tip, while a further 2 are very small and hidden under the tube formed by the fused filaments of 9 of the 10 stamens, there being 5 long stamens and 4 very short ones situated between the sinuses of the longer stamens. The 10th stamen is the shortest of all and is free, see A3. The ovary matures into a flat, broad, reddish brown pod. This species has a reputation of being difficult to grow, particularly when young, but there is considerable literature on cultivation techniques. It is grown in a number of gardens in the tropics, including ones in the New World such as Castleton Botanic Garden, Jamaica.

Moghania or *Maughania,* better known under the later name *Flemingia,* is a genus of about thirty species native to tropical Asia and Australia, two of which, *M. strobilifera* (C) and *M. stricta* have become naturalized in the West Indies. They are either shrubs or herbs, with leaves consisting of 1 or 3 leaflets, small flowers and short swollen 1- or 2-seeded pods. The name *Moghania* is possibly a latinized form of an obscure oriental vernacular name. *M. strobilifera* forms a bush up to 6 feet (1·8 m.) high. It is widespread in India and extends to Ceylon, Malaya, Indonesia and the Philippines; it is naturalized elsewhere. The persistent yellowish membranous bracts, which give the inflorescence a hop-like appearance, enclose the flowers and later the fruits, so that the small reproductive structures are never clearly visible. As the fruit ripens, the bracts turn brown and chaffy.

LEGUMINOSAE

Amherstia nobilis
A1 flowering shoot × $\frac{2}{3}$.
A2 seed pod × $\frac{2}{3}$. A3 stamens × $1\frac{1}{4}$.

Delonix regia, Flamboyant, Gul Mohur
B1 flowering branch × $\frac{2}{3}$.
B2 seed pod × $\frac{2}{3}$. B3 seed × $\frac{2}{3}$.

Moghania strobilifera
C1 flowering branch × $\frac{2}{3}$.
C2 flower × 4. C3 fruiting inflorescence × $\frac{2}{3}$.
C4 seed pod and bract × 2.

A2   A1   B1

                                        B2

                                                              B3

A3

                                          C3

                              C4   C2   C1

Plate 114   SOUTH EAST ASIA

The bright red flowers of *Plumbago rosea* (A) make it a favourite conservatory plant, though it requires more heat than the blue-flowered *P. auriculata* from South Africa (see plate 80). One of the twelve species of *Plumbago*, it is possibly native in India and Sikkim, yet is widely cultivated throughout South Eastern Asia. It seems to have been introduced into Europe in 1777 and grows to a height of about 3 feet (91 cm.), when its long inflorescences may require staking.

Some of the fifty-three *Lagerstroemia* species, like the one illustrated here, are trees; others are smaller shrubs. *L. speciosa* (B), the Queen of Flowers, is a deciduous tree which attains a height of up to about 50 feet (15 m.), or occasionally up to 80 feet (24 m.) or more in the forest. Its dense crown is rounded and its bark a pale brown colour. Pinkish, mauve, or purple-lilac flowers reach 2½ inches (6 cm.) across, making a fine show of colour when arranged in their terminal, erect clusters, which open from below upwards. The fruits, 1 inch (2·5 cm.) long, are woody capsules which split lengthways into 6 woody portions. *L. speciosa* extends from Burma, Thailand and Malaya to Indonesia and the Philippines, and in the Malay Peninsula tends to be found in open country. The generic name commemorates a Swedish patron of science, Magnus Lagerstroem (1691–1759).

The genus *Primula* is essentially north temperate in distribution and it may be a surprise for some to learn that one species is found on the equator in Sumatra. But *P. prolifera* (C) most definitely does grow there, and also in Java, albeit at altitudes high above sea level. The occurrence of this species and also the more diminutive *P. umbellata* in the Philippines and New Guinea is more understandable when we recognize that they occur there only in mountainous areas and that they mark the most southerly limits of this genus, which has its highest density in the Himalaya and China areas.

The only other part of the world where *Primula*

crosses the equator is in South America, where *P. magellanica* is found in southern Chile and the Falkland Islands (see plate 4).

Primula prolifera forms a stout plant up to 40 inches (1 m.) tall, with inflorescence stalks bearing from 1 to 7 whorls of pale golden yellow flowers, set off by mealy sepals. Its natural habitats, damp and often exposed, are at altitudes of about 6300 to 9700 feet (2000–3000 m.) on the higher mountains of Sumatra and Java. Elsewhere it is found in Assam, Upper Burma and southern Yunnan.

Growing only to about 5 inches (13 cm.), *P. umbellata* is a much smaller plant, with an appearance something like that of the allied genus *Androsace*; with an inflorescence of 2 to 6 stalks, each with small white flowers, borne in an umbel. It is found from India and East Pakistan to China, Japan, Korea and Formosa; also in the Philippines and eastern New Guinea.

First found at Doi Chieng Dao, Thailand, in limestone crevices at an altitude of about 6000 feet (1800 m.) by A. F. G. Kerr (1877–1942) on 4 June 1921, *Primula siamensis* (E) is allied to the Chinese *P. nutans*. It appears to be a biennial species which is self-sterile when pollinated; pollen must come from another individual plant for seed to be produced.

A native of Madras, in the Palni and Nilgiri Hills, *Lysimachia leschenaultii* (D) is one of about two hundred species of a genus with its centres of diversity in eastern Asia and North America. It grows to about 12 inches (30 cm.) tall and bears purplish flowers in a dense raceme up to 9 or 10 inches (23–25 cm.) long. The plant is only sparsely branched from a fibrous root system and the fruits, which contain many seeds, are capsules opening by 5 valves. Better known species include *L. nummularia* from central Europe, *L. punctata* from Asia Minor, *L. thyrsiflora* from north temperate areas, and the Yellow Loosestrife, *L. vulgaris*, from temperate Asia and Europe.

PLUMBAGINACEAE

Plumbago rosea
A1 part of flowering stem × ⅔. A2 flower × 2.

LYTHRACEAE

Lagerstroemia speciosa, Queen of Flowers
B1 part of flowering stem × ⅔.
B2 ovary and style × 1⅓.

PRIMULACEAE

Primula prolifera
C1 flowering plant (stem cut) × ⅔.

Lysimachia leschenaultii
D1 part of flowering stem × ⅔.

Primula siamensis
E1 flowering plant × ⅔.

A1

B1

B2

C1

D1

E1

Plate 115   SOUTH EAST ASIA

The South East Asian genus *Durio* is made up of some twenty-seven species, all of which are characterized by spiny fruits and a seed enclosed in a fleshy aril, those of *D. zibethinus* (A) being the much sought after Durian fruit. An evergreen tree, with a wide distribution in Malaya and the East Indies, and usually cultivated, it begins to flower when only about seven years old, and the fruit takes about three months to ripen from pollination. The exquisite flavour of the Durian compensates for its almost intolerably offensive odour, which attracts elephants, tigers, deer, tapirs and other wild animals to the tree. Connoisseurs believe that the best fruit for eating are borne on the stout old branches (presumably because these can support the largest specimens) of pink-flowered trees when the flesh of the aril, which is the part eaten, is creamy to dark yellow in colour; smaller fruit borne on younger wood, or from white-flowered trees, are supposedly inferior. When fallen, the fruit decays rapidly and its edibility likewise deteriorates, so that after about four days the pulp becomes rancid and sour. There seems to be no satisfactory way of preventing this rapid decay as refrigeration has had only partial success and it seems likely that the Durian will continue to be worth travelling to taste.

One of the eight species found in tropical Asia and Africa, *Bombax ceiba* (B), the Silk-cotton Tree (see also plate 57), is a native of India and the drier parts of Burma, ascending to about 4000 feet (1220 m.) in the Himalaya; it is also found in Ceylon, Yunnan, Thailand, Indo-China, Indonesia and northern Australia. The sides of its sepals are hairy, as are both surfaces of the petals, which are also somewhat fleshy and shiny and often curl back upon themselves.

B. ceiba usually has about 60 stamens united into 5 bundles which alternate with the petals. Another bundle of about 12–15 stamens surrounds the ovary in the centre of the flower. In February, after the leaves have fallen, the dark brown buds open and brightly coloured flowers emerge. These flowers are mauled by mynahs and other birds, apparently for the same mysterious reason that sparrows will tear primroses in Europe, as pollination is effected by bees. When the fruits ripen in May, the seeds which are released when the capsule opens, tend to be blown away in a tangle of silky hairs, the source of kapok used for stuffing cushions and other soft items. The wood is used for making matchsticks, dug-out canoes and other light construction work. The name *Bombax ceiba* was first used by Linnaeus primarily for the Asiatic species later named *Bombax malabaricum* and *Salmalia malabarica*, the one described here. Subsequently the name *B. ceiba* was applied exclusively to a tropical American species now called *Bombacopsis quinata*.

The related *B. insigne* (C) differs from the Silk-cotton tree in having longer rose or white petals and more numerous stamens (about 400–700 as against 60–110 in *B. ceiba*) as well as longer capsules. It was first illustrated by Nathaniel Wallich (1786–1854) in his three volume work entitled *Plantae Asiaticae Rariores*. *B. insigne* grows in Burma, throughout the Andaman Islands and into parts of India.

The genus *Bombax* (syn. *Salmalia*), as defined by André Robyns in his monograph (1963), consists of eight Old World species; the tropical American species are placed in the genera *Pseudobombax, Eriotheca, Bombacopsis, Pachira, Rhodognaphalon* and *Rhodognaphalopsis*.

BOMBACACEAE

Durio zibethinus, Durian
A1 part of branch with flowers × ⅔.
A2 scales × 10.
A3 fruit and leaf on part of branch × ⅔.

Bombax ceiba (syn. *B. malabaricum, Salmalia malabarica*), Silk-cotton Tree
B1 flowering twig × ⅔. B2 leaf × ⅔.
B3 spines on trunk × ⅔. B4 open fruit × ⅔.

B. insigne
C1 flowering twig × ⅔.
C2 leaves on part of branch × ⅔.

A3

B1

B2

B3

B4

C1

C2

Plate 116   SOUTH EAST ASIA

A glowing fountain of a tree whose blossoms are used to decorate the horns of cattle during certain festivals, *Firmiana colorata* (B) grows to a height of about 80 feet (25 m.) and is native from India and Ceylon to Thailand and Sumatra; in Java it has been introduced. Its bark is grey or grey-green and the almost hairless leaves are more or less lobed. The flowers, springing from the naked axils near the tips of the branches in short, sometimes clustered, racemes, are the tree's most notable feature, and appear between March and May, after the leaves have fallen. They vary in colour from orange-red to grey-brown, and in size, though the relationship between depth of lobing and overall length remains more or less constant. The botany of the flowers is intriguing since, though they are structurally hermaphrodite, the organs of only one sex develop in any one flower. Male and female may occur on the same branch, but each local cluster is functionally either one sex or the other. The cluster illustrated is identifiable as male by the way in which the stalked stamens protrude far beyond the mouth of the flower, which itself consists of a calyx only, there being no petals. The female flowers can be recognized by their 5 carpels, borne on a stalk beyond the mouth of the flowers with their lobed stigmas and a number of abortive stamens below (see B2 and 4). The developing carpels split open well before the seeds inside are ripe, a characteristic typical of many members of *Sterculiaceae*, and it is not until the carpel-wall has dried out and become papery enough to form a wing for the seed, that they are ready for wind dispersal.

The yellowish flowering shoots and slightly downy leaves of the 30 foot (9 m.) *Eriolaena candollei* (A) are found from Bhutan, Burma and Yunnan, into Thailand, Cambodia and Vietnam. The specific epithet represents an interesting example of mutual recognition between botanists, in that Wallich took the opportunity of his discovery to return an earlier gesture of admiration embodied in de Candolle's *E. wallichii*.

About fifteen species are contained in the genus *Pterocymbium*, all of them with fruit bearing a single seed at the base of a humped wing. *P. tinctorium* (E) has a distribution that ranges from Burma to Java and the Philippines. The red- or purple-flowered Javanese type illustrated is sometimes classified as var. *javani-cum*, in distinction to the green-flowered var. *tinctorium*, although first described as a separate species, *P. javanicum*. Species of this genus resemble those of *Firmiana* in the sexuality of the flowers and in the early stage, sometimes even before fertilization, at which the carpels open. *P. tinctorium* may attain a height of 80 feet (25 m.) and occurs scattered through open forest, especially where they are periodically subjected to dry conditions.

A tree with wide distribution in the tropics, including South East Asia, and with many local names, was given its Latin name, *Thespesia populnea* (C), by Daniel Carl Solander (1736-1782), who discovered it on Tahiti during Captain Cook's first voyage, because of the sacred character attributed to it by the Tahitians (*thespesios* meaning 'divinely decreed') who planted it around places of worship. The resemblance of its leaves to those of the poplar, led Linnaeus to give it the epithet *populnea*. This tropical genus contains about fifteen species, and, of these, *T. populnea* has the widest distribution. It is an evergreen, sea-side or strand tree, about 50 feet (15 m.) in height and is much valued for the shade cast by its dense foliage and spreading crown. The flowers—yellow with a rich maroon eye—are brilliant but short-lived and contrast prettily with the 6 inch (15 cm.) leaves; as they wither, they fade through pink to purple. The fruits are green at first but later turn black and remain on the tree for a long time. Fruit and flowers yield a yellow dye, the bark and heartwood a red one. In habit it resembles an *Hibiscus* but the close-set, not radiating, stigmas distinguish it.

Elaeocarpus grandiflorus (D) is indeed large-flowered in comparison to some species in the genus but in any other context, the overall length of 1 inch (2·5 cm.) achieved by the jagged, cream-coloured petals and bright red sepals would appear unremarkable, especially on a tree 25 feet (7·6 m.) tall. The species is found in Thailand and Indo-China as well as Java, usually by rivers, and bears ellipsoidal, yellowish green fruit. Material presented to Kew by Sir George Leonard Staunton (1737-1801), a member of Macartney's Embassy to China in 1792, and who 'discovered it in his voyage to China, but in what country is not mentioned', flowered there for the first time in 1852.

STERCULIACEAE

Eriolaena candollei
A1 inflorescence and young leaf × $\frac{2}{3}$.
A2 style and ovary × 2.
A3 sectioned stamen column × 2.
A4 part of fruiting stem × $\frac{2}{3}$.

Firmiana colorata
B1 flowering shoot with male flowers × $\frac{2}{3}$.
B2 female flower × $\frac{2}{3}$.
B3 ovary with lobed style and abortive stamens × 2.
B4 fruit × $\frac{2}{3}$. B5 leaf × $\frac{2}{3}$.

Pterocymbium tinctorium var. *javanicum*
E1 fruiting twig × $\frac{2}{3}$. E2 leaf × $\frac{2}{3}$.
E3 male flowers × $\frac{2}{3}$. E4 male flower × 2.

MALVACEAE

Thespesia populnea
C1 flowering shoot × $\frac{2}{3}$.

ELAEOCARPACEAE

Elaeocarpus grandiflorus
D1 flowering shoot × $\frac{2}{3}$. D2 stamen × 4.

A3

A2

A1

A4

B1

B2

B3

B4

B5

C1

D1

D2

E1

E2

E3

E4

Plate 117   SOUTH EAST ASIA

Like all the plants illustrated on this plate, the members of the *Rafflesiaceae* are parasites. Their reproductive structures bear little resemblance to those of other plants and it may be mistaken to use such words as 'petals' and 'sepals' in describing them; several of their features recall those of fungi but the fact that they possess seeds distinguishes them clearly from the spore producing groups. The vegetative organs, which consist of a network of threads that penetrate the tissues of the host plant, are so inconspicuous that the plants only become visible with the appearance of the flowers. These may measure as much as 3 feet (91 cm.) in diameter, and are the largest known flowers. The ring of 4 to 5 conspicuous 'petals', which have a thick, fleshy consistency, sometimes surround a corona-like collar. At the base of the 'corolla-tube' there may be a mushroom-shaped column which supports the stamens or encloses the ovary, its cap decorated with upright cones of tissue. The fruit is a large berry.

The genus *Rafflesia* contains about fourteen species from Malaya and the East Indies, of which the enormous red- and cream-flowered Sumatran *R. arnoldii* has become well known through the models of the plant to be seen in museums, and its reputation as possessing the largest flower in the world. The difficulty of preserving the enormous and fleshy flowers and the relative rarity of its discovery in its tropical jungle habitat means that our knowledge of the structures and variations that occur within the genus is limited. Species are impossible to identify by their superficial resemblances, since it is the structures inside the flowers that distinguish them. The species illustrated (C) is thought to be hitherto undescribed, but cannot be known by anything more than the noncommittal '*Rafflesia* species' until a botanist has examined all the possibilities. When it is certain that the plant requires to be described and named, it will then be given a Latin description, and this, preferably in association with an illustration, will be published in a recognized botanical publication. If this *Rafflesia* is a new species, it might well be named in honour of Dr W. Meijer, who, in 1963, appears to have discovered it first on Mount Kinabalu in Sabah, or of Mr W. R. Price, who made an expedition to see it in his eighty-first year and upon whose colour photograph the plate opposite is based. The 14 inch (37 cm.) flowers grow at ground level from the root or stem of the host plant, a species of vine in the genus *Tetrastigma*. Inside the 'corolla' are visible the white cap of the column and the red cones with which it is decorated. The stamens, or the stigmas if the flower is female, are situated under the rim of the cap, although the plant photographed in this case was male.

Another total parasite that lives on the roots of tropical plants and whose way of life has endowed it with a similar superficial resemblance to fungi is *Balanophora celebica* (A). The species has an underground, creeping rootstock or rhizome from which separate male and female inflorescences arise, sometimes needing to rupture the rhizome in order to emerge. Some seventy-nine other species exist, all without chlorophyll and varying in colour between red, yellow, brownish and white, ranging from Madagascar, through South East Asia, to Japan, Polynesia and Australia.

The chlorophyll in the leaves of *Lepeostegeres beccarii* (B) indicates that this plant is only semi-parasitic and, to a certain extent, manufactures its own food materials. It forms a shrub and its stems reach a length of about 7 feet (2 m.) and spring from a sucker-like 'haustorium' attached to the tissues of the host. The flowers, which are grouped in clusters surrounded by a series of carmine bracts and, in this respect, resemble the capitula of some daisies, *Compositae* species, have green and claret-coloured corollas whose 6 free lobes, yellowish on the inside, curve back as the flower opens to contrast with the purple of the unopened buds. Each inflorescence measures about 6 inches (15 cm.) in length and contains 20 to 30 flowers (further illustrations of members of this family appear on the following plate). A number of fleshy fruits cluster within the bracts after flowering. The species was discovered by the Italian botanist Odoardo Beccari (1843–1920) when collecting in Borneo between 1865 and 1868; it is also found in Malaya.

BALANOPHORACEAE

Balanophora celebica
A1 female flowering plant × ⅔.
A2 male flowering plant × ⅔.
A3 male flower × 3.

LORANTHACEAE

Lepeostegeres beccarii
B1 part of flowering branch × ⅔.
B2 leafy shoot × ⅔.

RAFFLESIACEAE

Rafflesia species
C1 flower × ⅔.

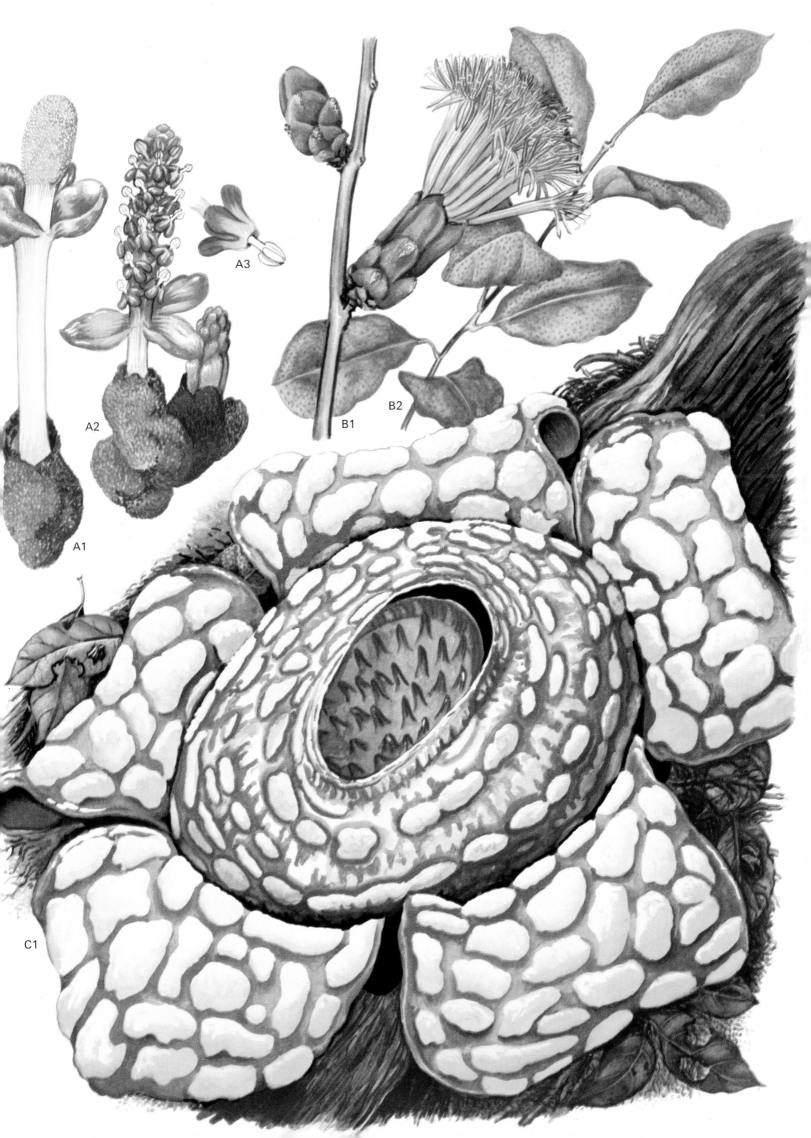

A1

A2

A3

B1

B2

C1

Plate 118   SOUTH EAST ASIA

The Mistletoe family, *Loranthaceae*, is not, as one might think, restricted to temperate regions: the majority of its thirty-six genera and one thousand three hundred species occur in the tropics, a number of them far more spectacular than the *Viscum* species with which we are familiar in north-western Europe. Most species are semi-parasitic and shrubby, attached to the host by a sucker-like outgrowth called a 'haustorium', though even this is not invariably so: the sole species in the Australian genus *Nuytsia* (plate 135), for instance, forms a tree 30 feet (9 m.) tall with roots in the ground, parasitizing the surrounding herbage. Foliage is usually evergreen and has a leathery texture peculiar to the family.

A Malaysian and Indonesian species, and the only one in its genus, *Loxanthera speciosa* (C) has flowers which are generally found in 3's and borne in the leaf-axils, with lobes that curl away from the opening flower in a way typical of the family as a whole. Their tips are tinged black or yellow and in bud, the reddish purple tube is constricted above the point where the stamens arise. The plant bears ellipsoidal fruits about $\frac{3}{4}$ inch (19 mm.) in length.

About one hundred and fifty species of *Amyema* are known, with a total range from tropical Africa, through Malaysia, to Australasia. *A. fasciculatum* (A), although first described from Java, was also discovered in the Philippines in the late 1830's by Hugh Cuming. Its little clusters of reddish, sometimes yellow-tipped, flowers commonly grow from points on the stem from which leaves have fallen. The 4 or 5 lobes of the corolla curl back and expose their green inner surfaces.

Said to be closely related to the families *Euphorbiaceae*, *Tiliaceae* and *Passifloraceae*, the *Flacourtiaceae* is a mostly tropical or subtropical family of trees and shrubs. The Kepayang, *Pangium edule* (B) grows to a height of 80 feet (25 m.) and, typical of many tropical trees, the base of its trunk usually develops large buttresses. The undersurfaces of the shiny green leaves, the flower stalks and the sepals are covered with a felt of rust-coloured hairs; only the older trees produce leaves of the shape illustrated, those of the younger plants having 4 or 5 lobes. Mature leaves may exceed 20 inches (50 cm.) in length. The flowers have pale creamy-green petals, divided from the reproductive organs by a ring of scales, and the sexes are separated on different trees. The fruits, 12 inches (30 cm.) long and 5 inches (12·5 cm.) in diameter, and with a coarse brown skin $\frac{1}{3}$ inch (8·4 mm.) thick, soften as they ripen until, when they fall, they are reduced to a mush in which are embedded the triangular, white seeds. All parts of the tree yield prussic acid, but this can be washed out to render the seeds and leaves edible. The seeds contain an oil that is particularly useful for cooking in areas where coconut-oil is scarce.

The Mangosteen (D) is one of those fruits that make life bearable, for the traveller in the right part of the tropics, between the last uneasy dream of the siesta and the first 'Campari' of the evening. The 40 foot (12 m.) evergreen trees, being difficult to propagate, as cuttings do not root easily and seeds do not stay viable for long, are rarely found outside their native tropical Asia, but once a tree is mature it produces abundant fruit, of which the delicious snow-white, oily pulp of the seed is eaten. The species, *Garcinia mangostana*, can be easily identified from other fruit trees by its characteristically semi-drooping habit and by the yellow latex that wells from the tissues when broken, but specific differentiation amongst the four hundred or so members of the genus is not so easy. Male trees of the Mangosteen have only rarely been found and it would seem that the females set fruit without fertilization.

LORANTHACEAE

Amyema fasciculatum
A1 part of flowering branch × $\frac{2}{3}$.

Loxanthera speciosa
C1 part of flowering shoot × $\frac{2}{3}$.

FLACOURTIACEAE

Pangium edule, Kepayang
B1 male flowering shoot × $\frac{2}{3}$.
B2 female flower × $\frac{2}{3}$. B3 fruit × $\frac{2}{3}$.

GUTTIFERAE

Garcinia mangostana, Mangosteen
D1 female flowering shoot × $\frac{2}{3}$.
D2 fruit × $\frac{2}{3}$. D3 fruit sectioned × $\frac{2}{3}$.

A1

B1

B2

B3

C1

D1

D2

D3

Plate 119   SOUTH EAST ASIA

All tropical and subtropical areas support *Phyllanthus*, a genus which contains about six hundred species. Some bear their flowers around the margin of what appears to be a leaf, but which is in fact, a flattened and modified stem, while others like *P. pulcher* (A), have normal shoots with flowers in the axils of true leaves. Botanists recognize that the flowers of *P. pulcher* spring from a shoot, while an untrained eye might suppose them to arise along the length of a dissected leaf. The tiny flowers of this species provide a good example of the benefits obtained from using a hand-lens when examining some plants, for much of their beauty is lost when seen only with the naked eye; when magnified, they may well compete with some of the more popular orchids. *P. pulcher* forms a shrub 2 to 5 feet (0·6–1·5 m.) high with separate male and female flowers which remain fresh for a long period and have characteristically ragged edges. Introduced into cultivation in Europe by Thomas Christy (1832–1905), the plant occurs in the wild from Sikkim and Burma to Thailand and south and east to Sumatra, Java and Borneo.

Botanical authority is divided over the two species which comprise the genus *Reinwardtia*, a woody member of the flax family. *R. indica* (B) has 3 stigmas and a more twiggy and spreading habit than *R. cicanoba* (syn. *R. tetragyna*) which has 4 stigmas and is found in Nepal, Sikkim and western China; *R. indica* has a wider range in the Himalaya and extends into peninsular India, Thailand and western China. It might be better to regard *R. cicanoba* as a variety of the illustrated plant. The genus is also interesting because, like *Lythrum* and *Cuphea*, also with polymorphic flowers, the plants have three different types of flowers according to the lengths and disposition of the stamens and stigmas. Sir Henry Collett wrote a letter from Simla to J. D. Hooker on 28 March 1884, stating his discovery of the three flower types, making drawings and sending glued dissections of them to Kew for display, where they can still be seen.

The genus *Dipterocarpus*, with seventy-five species contains some very large trees which grow to over 200 feet (61 m.) tall. Characteristically, they have small crowns of diffuse foliage borne at the end of the buttressed and lofty unbranched trunks; the bark of many species contains ducts which ooze resin when damaged. This exudate, called 'damar', is of great commercial value, especially that yielded by certain species of another genus, *Hopea*, which is exported for use in the paint and linoleum industries; Sabah alone exported more than 2800 tons (2845 tonnes) in 1961. Another source of damar is the important genus *Shorea*, with one hundred and eighty species; a few of these, including *S. mecistopteryx*, also produce 'illipe nuts' which contain some of the oils used in the chocolate industry.

Native in central and western Java and Bali, *Dipterocarpus trinervis* (C) sometimes grows gregariously and forms pure stands of the one species, a rare occurrence in tropical forests. The trees, which are found in a wide range of altitudes up to about 4000 feet (1220 m.), may attain a height of 230 feet (70 m.) or more. They have large leaves, up to 20 inches (50 cm.) long and 10 inches (25 cm.) broad, and bear numerous flowers at all times of the year. The local inhabitants use the oil obtained from the fruit as a body lotion and in some areas the timber is reserved for sacred purposes, such as the construction of temples.

It appears that the seeds of *Saurauia*, a genus of some three hundred species found in tropical America and Asia, are not long-lived, which partly explains why these not unattractive shrubs are rarely found in glasshouse collections. According to available information, *S. subspinosa* (E) is restricted to Upper Burma where, in 1924, George Forrest collected the species from near Htawgaw at an altitude of about 6000 feet (1830 m.). Very similar to the more westerly species *S. napaulensis*, its leaves have approximately 10–12 nerves joining the midrib at a narrow angle, whereas those of *S. napaulensis* have 40 nerves subtending a wide one; the leaves are sometimes twice as long as those shown and have an attractive reticulate pattern on the undersurface.

Citrus, a genus of about twelve species, has its natural range in South East Asia, reaching southern China, although it is now cultivated in all parts of the world. Many members of this family, the *Rutaceae*, have compound leaves unlike those of orange, lime, lemon and grapefruit; however, these usually have a joint between the blade and the leaf stalk which possibly indicates that their ancestors also possessed the usual divided leaves. The fruit, botanically a berry, has a leathery skin containing many glands filled with aromatic oils and the flesh consists of numerous enlarged cells full of 'juice'. The Lemon is *C. limon*; the Grapefruit, *C. paradisi*; the Tangerine, Satsuma and Mandarin Oranges, *C. reticulata*; and the Sweet Orange, *C. sinensis*.

A native of the East Indies, the Lime, *C. aurantifolia* (D), features more in the commerce of tropical markets than temperate, where it tends to be replaced by the lemon, which can be stored for a longer period without losing its freshness. Spaniards introduced the lime into the Americas in the 1500's, bringing it from Europe where it was introduced by the Arabs in the 13th century. Today a commonly encountered citrus fruit in all tropical areas, it is grown commercially in Mexico and the West Indies. The fruit of the lime differs from that of the lemon in being always green, more or less globular and about 1¾ inches (4·5 cm.) in diameter, while that of the lemon is yellow and ellipsoidal. Noted for their use in flavouring and mixing with drinks, the oil from their skin is used in perfume and the fruits may be candied or made into marmalade.

Probably a native of Cochin-China, *C. aurantium* (F), now known as the Seville Orange, found its way to Europe from the Far East about 1000 A.D., in the paniers of beasts using the Silk Route. Known in Europe some five hundred years before the Sweet Orange, *C. sinensis*, was introduced from China, the Seville Orange is normally too sour to eat, but is ideal for making into preserves. It is also the major flavouring ingredient in the liqueur Curacao.

EUPHORBIACEAE

Phyllanthus pulcher
A1 flowering shoot × ⅔.
A2 female flower and base of leaf × 8.

LINACEAE

Reinwardtia indica (syn. *R. trigyna*)
B1 flowering shoot × ⅔.
B2 flower, with all but one petal removed × 1⅓.

DIPTEROCARPACEAE

Dipterocarpus trinervis
C1 flowering shoot × ⅔.
C2 stamens and ovary × 2. C3 fruit × ⅔.

RUTACEAE

Citrus aurantifolia, Lime
D1 flowering shoot × ⅔. D2 ovary × 2⅔.
D3 fruit × ⅔. D4 fruit sectioned × ⅔.

C. aurantium, Seville Orange
F1 flowering shoot × ⅔. F2 fruit × ⅔.

ACTINIDIACEAE

Saurauia subspinosa
E1 part of flowering shoot × ⅔.

A1

B1 B2

C1

C2

C3

D1 D2

D3

D4

E1

F1 F2

Plate 120   SOUTH EAST ASIA

About fifteen of the forty or so species in the genus *Mangifera* bear edible fruits but by far the most widely cultivated, the source of the Mango now so commonly grown throughout the tropics, is *M. indica* (D). A native of the woodlands of north-east India and Burma, the species has been cultivated for at least four thousand years on the subcontinent, where it now occupies an estimated two million acres (809,400 hectares). About 500 B.C. it appears to have spread to Malaysia and the Far East; five hundred years later it was taken by the Arabs to East Africa. Later still, the Portuguese introduced the fruit into West Africa and the Americas, and only as recently as the late 18th century did it reach the West Indies where now it is also extensively grown. The evergreen trees thrive best at altitudes of below 2000 feet (610 m.) in areas where there is a marked dry season. There are between 1000 and 6000 flowers in each panicle, which consists of a mixture of about 60 % male flowers and 40 % hermaphrodite flowers. Only 33 % of the hermaphrodites are usually ever pollinated, and only 0·25 % of those ever produce mature fruit. Ripe mangoes are rich in vitamins and the sweet juiciness of their orange flesh has a flavour sometimes slightly reminis-cent of turpentine. Certain cultivars are spoilt for eating by the conspicuous fibres that surround the capsule and penetrate the flesh. Unripe mangoes are used for chutney.

The largest-flowered *Hoya*, a popular genus of climbers for cultivation under glass, with waxy, long-lasting and fragrant flowers, is *H. sussuela* (A), a native of Borneo and the Moluccas. As many as fourteen individual flowers are to be found in each inflorescence, each flower measuring up to 3 inches (7·5 cm.) across; they are very fragrant and long-lived and, like the leaves and stems, downy with minute hairs. The species was introduced into Europe by its discoverer Sir Hugh Low and won the prize for the best new plant at the 1848 exhibition in Regent's Park Gardens.

Hoya purpureofusca (B) is a little known woodland climber, first collected in the Panarang area of Java by Thomas Lobb. Its leaves, like those of *H. cinnamomifolia*, resemble the leaves of the cinnamon plant. Another Javan species first sent to Europe by Thomas Lobb, but discovered by Carl Ludwig Blume (1796–1862), is *H. coriacea* (C) which is notable for the texture of its leaves, somewhere between leathery and fleshy.

ASCLEPIADACEAE

Hoya sussuela (syn. *H. imperialis*)
A1 part of flowering stem × ⅔.

H. purpureofusca
B1 part of flowering stem × ⅔.

H. coriacea
C1 part of flowering stem × ⅔.

ANACARDIACEAE

Mangifera indica, Mango
D1 part of flowering shoot × ⅔. D2 fruit × ⅔.

Plate 121   SOUTH EAST ASIA

The melastomes, a family usually identifiable by the 3 to 9 longitudinal leaf veins common to all genera, include a number of species with brightly coloured flowers and strangely shaped stamens. *Sonerila margaritacea* (A) is one of a genus of one hundred and eighty species found in the warmer parts of Asia, this particular plant being native to Burma. The material shown, which is known as var. *argentea*, is sometimes to be encountered in hothouse collections; the white or cream markings on the upper surfaces of the leaves are generally smaller than those illustrated here.

Also seen sometimes in greenhouses with a very warm and humid atmosphere, *Medinilla magnifica* (C) grows to a height of 3 feet (91 cm.) or more and bears impressive pendant inflorescences, each consisting of 7 or more trusses springing from a single well-grown shoot. The species is a native of the Philippines. *Medinilla* is a large tropical genus; many species have flowers that are smaller than those of *M. magnifica*, but there are others with equally showy inflorescences which have yet to be introduced to cultivation.

The genus *Fagraea* of about fifty species contains sun-loving plants found either at the edges of forest clearings or as 'epiphytes (which are plants that grow on others, especially trees, not as parasites but for support) from South East Asia to northern Australia and the Pacific islands. The epiphytic roots clasp the trunks of trees and, given enough time, will descend to the forest floor. *F. auriculata* (E), found from Burma across to the East Indies, is a large, usually epiphytic, species with leaves from 4 inches to about 2 feet (10–61 cm.) long and fleshy, leathery flowers $\frac{1}{4}$ inch (6 mm.) thick and sometimes as much as a foot (30 cm.) in both width

and depth. The latter open in the morning and last for two days, during which time they turn from a greenish white to cream yellow. Their scent has been likened to a 'coarse musk'. Pollination is by insects and birds which, later in the season, feed on the reddish pulp in which the seeds of the lead-coloured fruits are embedded.

Named after Jean Baptiste Louis Théodore Leschenault de la Tour (1773–1826), *Hypericum leschenaultii* (D) is a representative in mountainous areas of the tropics of what is normally a northern temperate genus. It is an extremely variable species, decreasing in height and becoming more compact the higher and more exposed its habitat. Leschenault discovered the species in Java after accompanying the Baudin Expedition of 1800–1804, when he stayed on in the East Indies after falling ill. The species is also native to Sumatra.

In a family consisting mainly of trees and shrubs, some of them, the olive and ash for example, famous for their fruit or timber and others, for instance the lilacs and *Forsythia*, for their flowers, the genus *Jasminum* is a group of about three hundred scandent climbers. *J. rex* (B) grows as a climber in certain areas of dry woodland in south-eastern Thailand. Material was first collected by Henry James Murton, the King of Siam's gardener, in 1882, the year in which he died aged 29, but it was not until 1929, following a request to Kew for identification of the plant by a Thai gentleman in whose garden it had been growing, that the species became known formally to science. From Kew it has been propagated and sent to many other gardens for, although the flowers are without the characteristic jasmine scent, their size and grace make the plant a most desirable one to grow.

MELASTOMATACEAE

Sonerila margaritacea var. *argentea*
A1 flowering shoot × $\frac{2}{3}$. A2 flower × 2.

Medinilla magnifica
C1 part of stem with inflorescence × $\frac{2}{3}$.
C2 flower × $1\frac{1}{3}$. C3 stamen × 2.

OLEACEAE

Jasminum rex
B1 inflorescence × $\frac{2}{3}$.
B2 shoot with leaves and buds × $\frac{2}{3}$.
B3 section of the upper part of the corolla tube showing the style and 2 stamens × $1\frac{1}{3}$.

HYPERICACEAE

Hypericum leschenaultii
D1 flowering shoot × $\frac{2}{3}$.

LOGANIACEAE

Fagraea auriculata
E1 flowering stem × $\frac{2}{3}$.

A1

B2

B1

B3

2

C1

D1

E1

C3

Plate 122   SOUTH EAST ASIA

All the *Gesneriaceae* on this plate belong to the family's Old World subfamily, the *Cyrtandroideae*, not the New World *Gesnerioideae*, though a number of the genera are significantly similar. For instance, the genus *Aeschynanthus* which occurs in Indonesia, Malaysia and tropical China may be considered, both because of its epiphytic habit and the shape of its corolla, as the Old World equivalent of *Columnea*, a genus found only in tropical America. *A. tricolor* (C), discovered by the Cornishman Thomas Lobb (1820–1894) in Borneo and introduced into England by Sir Hugh Low (1824–1904), has the bright corolla colours associated with the genus. Also discovered by Lobb in Java, *A. longiflorus* (A) is characterized by a long corolla with constricted mouth. It is notable for the long capsular fruit, which contain plumed seeds. By analogy with *Columnea*, whose adherent anthers allow for the efficient deposition of pollen on birds' heads, the anthers of *Aeschynanthus*, which often adhere in pairs, may indicate, together with its red flowers, that this genus is also pollinated by birds.

Introduced into Europe via the botanic gardens of Germany, and a late arrival in Britain and America, the widely cultivated *Chirita lavandulacea* (F) conspicuously lacks an adequately documented scientific history. The genus *Chirita* occurs in Indonesia, Malaysia, and southern China and this particular species appears to be a native of Indo-China; it differs from the related *C. hamosa* in having bearded anthers and a broader corolla tube. Its decorative value lies in its translucent and hairy leaves which set off the trusses of pale lavender flowers.

Didissandra atrocyanea (E), one of a small genus confined to India, Malaya and China, is remarkable for its peculiar pimpled leaves, dark purple flowers and brownish hairs. The elongated fruits are pointed at the end, and may exceed $1\frac{1}{2}$ inches (38 mm.) in length. Among sister species, *D. quercifolia* is a somewhat larger rosette-plant with oak-like leaves, while in *D. castaneifolia* they resemble those of the Sweet Chestnut.

Originally from Bengal, but now widespread as a cultivated climber in many parts of the tropics, *Thunbergia grandiflora* (B) has the virtue of producing large green leaves which quickly cover unsightly objects and large blue flowers which, during the long flowering season, decorate the screen formed by the foliage. *Thunbergia* is included by some in a separate family, the *Thunbergiaceae*, but considered by most as part of the *Acanthaceae*. It appears to be somewhat intermediate between this family and the *Bignoniaceae*. The genus is named after Carl Peter Thunberg (1743–1828), sometime Professor of Botany at Uppsala and an early traveller to South Africa and Japan.

Also a member of the *Acanthaceae* but, as the illustration shows, with very different flowers from *T. grandiflora*, *Phlogacanthus guttatus* (D) belongs to an Indo-Malaysian genus of thirty shrubby species. This species is found in Bengal, Khasia and the Assam Hills and it is known as Beeja in some areas.

GESNERIACEAE

Aeschynanthus longiflorus
A1 flowering shoot × $\frac{2}{3}$.
A2 fruit × $\frac{2}{3}$. A3 seed × $6\frac{2}{3}$.

A. tricolor
C1 part of flowering stem × $\frac{2}{3}$. C2 flower × 2.

Didissandra atrocyanea
E1 flowering plant × $\frac{2}{3}$. E2 hairs on leaf × $6\frac{2}{3}$.

Chirita lavandulacea
F1 part of flowering stem × $\frac{2}{3}$. F2 flower × 2.

ACANTHACEAE

Thunbergia grandiflora
B1 flowering shoot × $\frac{2}{3}$.
B2 stamens, style and stigma × $1\frac{1}{3}$.
B3 anther × $2\frac{2}{3}$.

Phlogacanthus guttatus, Beeja
D1 flowering shoot × $\frac{2}{3}$.
D2 ovary and style × $2\frac{2}{3}$. D3 stamen × $2\frac{2}{3}$.

A1

B1

C1

C2

A3

B3

B2

D3

D2

D1

E1

E2

F1

F2

Plate 123 SOUTH EAST ASIA

Although the plants of the banana family look something like palm trees, they are in fact herbaceous plants—the visible and false trunk being made up of sheathed leaf bases. Their true stems grow and branch underground, throwing up leafy shoots, through the shaft of which the inflorescence passes. The palm-like appearance is sometimes heightened by the large leaves which get torn along their veins by the weather. These leaves make a useful thatch, wrapping material and a convenient umbrella for those caught in forest downpours. After flowering and fruiting, the whole shoot dies but further ones grow up from the rhizomes.

The Japanese Banana, *Musa basjoo*, illustrated opposite (A), is one of the thirty-five species of *Musa* and is a native of the Ryukyu Archipelago between Japan and Formosa. Like *M. textilis*, which provides manilla hemp, the Japanese Banana is grown for the fibre in its leaf stalks. The first flowers produced are functionally female and later ones functionally male, pollination being effected by birds and bees attracted by the abundance of nectar at the base of the flowers. The habit sketch (A6) shows a fruiting shoot near the end of its life on the left and a new one on the right. This species is one of the hardiest and, with polythene protection, is grown outside in the south-west of Britain; a plant first flowered at Kew in 1890. It will reach a height of about 10 feet (3 m.).

The Plantain, *M. × paradisiaca*, a complex hybrid in origin, may grow 25 feet (7·6 m.) tall and is cultivated for its fruit, used in the tropics like a potato and boiled, baked or roasted. A similar hybrid, *M. × sapientum* is the Banana of international trade which is used mainly as a fruit but is equally at home cooked in hot savoury dishes. Bananas, as wild plants, have their origins in the islands of South East Asia and the western Pacific and recent studies have shown the cultivated plants to have a complicated ancestry. But the commercial centres of banana cultivation are now often far removed from tropical Asia, and the Caribbean area has a particularly large annual output of banana-stems.

The demands of North American and European markets have created a highly organized and specialized system of banana transportation. Private growers cut the heavy stems of still green fruits and transport them to coastal depots. There they are weighed and if accepted by a banana contractor, packed—usually in boxes to minimize bruising and other damage—before being loaded onto the flat-bottomed banana boats. Speed of trans-shipment is essential and loading may continue through the night. The load is allowed to partially ripen in incubators en route and the process is completed under controlled conditions of humidity and temperature, in special ripening rooms just prior to retailing. Contrary to popular opinion and as anyone in the banana trade will tell, gold-yellow bananas are unripe, the sweet and full flavour only being found in fruit flecked and mottled with brown spots.

The improvement of banana strains, by sexual breeding, conflicts with the commercial requirement of seedless fruit and existing strains are increased by cuttings of the rhizome. Most wild bananas are denizens of sheltered forest habitats and, because banana plantations frequently fail to provide such conditions, disaster sometimes strikes. There is nothing more heartbreaking or dismal than field upon field of flattened banana plants after the passage of a tropical storm, even though modern cultivars are less liable to collapse than their wild ancestors.

Close relatives are *Heliconia* (plate 189), *Strelitzia* (plate 84) and *Ravenala*—The Traveller's Tree genus—with its spectacular fan-shaped series of leaves borne on top of a trunk sometimes 90 feet (27 m.) tall which, like those of palms, is composed of dead leaf-bases. This last genus, which contains only two species, has a curiously disjunct distribution in Guyana and Madagascar. The name *Musa* is derived from the Arabic plant name *mouz* and, although thus of barbarous origin, was adopted by Linnaeus on the pretext that it could be regarded as commemorating Antonius Musa, physician to the first Emperor of Rome, Augustus (64–14 B.C.).

MUSACEAE

Musa basjoo, Japanese Banana
A1 part of leaf $\times \frac{2}{3}$.
A2 fruits on inflorescence axis $\times \frac{2}{3}$.
A3 functionally male flowers $\times \frac{2}{3}$.
A4 stamen $\times 2\frac{2}{3}$. A5 male flower $\times 1\frac{1}{3}$.
A6 habit sketch $\times \frac{1}{18}$.

A2

A3

A4

A5

A6

Plate 124   SOUTH EAST ASIA

Gingers are important culinary herbs: the ground and dried rhizomes of *Curcuma domestica* (often known as *C. longa*) yield turmeric; the perfume zedoary is obtained from the tubers of *C. zedoaria*; ginger is simply the dead rhizome of *Zingiber officinale*; and the cardamom comes from the dried fruit of *Elettaria cardamomum*, which produces its fruits on leafless shoots arising from the rhizomes. An evolutionarily advanced group, the gingers are in many ways parallel to the orchids, but differ fundamentally in the organization of the flower and the development of a different type of single stamen.

The flowers characteristic of the *Zingiberaceae* are highly specialized; for example, what look like petals are often sterile and modified stamens, called staminodes. In *Hedychium*, a genus of about fifty species abundant in Madagascar, Indonesia, Malaysia and south-west China, the flowers have a long tube and 2 staminodes fused to form a 2-lobed lip; another 2 staminodes look like petals on either side of it (the 3 petals are relatively inconspicuous narrow appendages). This is illustrated opposite by *H. flavescens* (A). There is one functional stamen and, fitting into a groove along the upper surface of its filament is the style with its stigma projecting just beyond the single fertile stamen (A2). The flowers are aggregated into more or less dense heads sheathed by inflorescence bracts which hide the ovary containing 3 cavities. When the fruits, which open by 3 valves, have ripened, and the inflorescence bracts have withered, 3 aril-covered seeds can be seen lying attached to the central axis of the ovary, as shown in the illustration from *H. spicatum* (A4). *H. spicatum* is a native of Nepal and *H. flavescens* of Madras and Bengal. These, and several other species, are commonly grown in tropical countries and under glass in temperate areas. They spread by means of rhizomes and the plants often form dense stands. When the plants blossom, the superb perfume of their flowers permeates the surrounding area.

Globba winitii (B) was first discovered in 1924 by a Siamese forestry officer in Lampung Province, north-west Thailand. It represents its genus as one of the most northerly ranging of the fifty species which occur throughout Indonesia and Malaysia, and extend to southern China.

The flowers consist of a 3-lobed calyx, a long bent corolla tube crowned by 3 greenish yellow lobes, and 2 waxy, yellowish staminodes. Another arrow-shaped staminode points upward to the spurred stamen, the filament of which houses the style as in *Hedychium*. *G. winitii* has striking magenta inflorescence bracts and the undersurfaces of the leaves are whitish and covered with fine hairs.

While Africa is relatively poor in most members of this family, the genus *Kaempferia*, which contains about seventy species, is found there, as well as tropical Asia. *K. candida* (C), a Burmese plant, has been collected in the Shan Hills at an altitude of about 3000 feet (910 m.) where it grows in dry forest areas. Its inflorescence appears before the leaves and in the illustrated species, the leaves were unknown at the time the plant was described. Called 'sanun-byu' by the local inhabitants, the large flowers of this species are said to be very fragrant but the root system (see plate), unlike many *Zingiberaceae*, does not in this case contain aromatic constituents.

All aerial parts of *Kaempferia elegans* (E) die down in the dry season; the plant flowers and vegetates during the wet season. Its leaves and stature vary somewhat and specimens may have broader leaves than those on the plant illustrated. *K. elegans* is a native of Thailand, east Bengal, Burma and parts of the Malay Peninsula.

Zingiber gives its name to the whole ginger family and the genus itself includes some eighty to ninety South East Asian and Australian species. The rhizomes of the best known species, *Z. officinale*, are grown commercially. When harvested, they are first killed by exposure to the sun or immersion in boiling water, and then marketed, whole or ground up as flavouring, or candied as a sweetmeat. The species illustrated opposite, *Z. spectabile* (D), was first discovered in Malacca but later collected in other parts of the Malay Peninsula. Characteristically rigid and waxy, the bracts which enclose the flower are yellowish at first but later become scarlet in some specimens. Unlike those in *Hedychium*, the inflorescences are borne at ground level on separate shoots from the leaves. The flowers are described as cream with buff and purple reticulate markings, passing to pale yellow with gingery-red and purple-black reticulations.

ZINGIBERACEAE

Hedychium flavescens
A1 part of flowering shoot × $\frac{2}{3}$.
A2 stamen and style × $1\frac{1}{3}$.
A3 habit sketch × $\frac{1}{10}$.

H. spicatum
A4 fruiting head × $\frac{2}{3}$.
A5 2 seeds covered by red arils × $1\frac{1}{3}$.
A6 seed × $2\frac{2}{3}$.

Globba winitii
B1 part of flowering shoot × $\frac{2}{3}$.
B2 stamen and style × 2.

Kaempferia candida
C1 flowering plant × $\frac{2}{3}$.

Zingiber spectabile
D1 flowering stem × $\frac{2}{3}$.
D2 habit sketch × $\frac{1}{18}$.

Kaempferia elegans
E1 part of flowering shoot × $\frac{2}{3}$.
E2 back of flower × $\frac{2}{3}$.

A1

A2

A3

A4

A5

A6

B1

B2

C1

D1

D2

E1

E2

Plate 125   SOUTH EAST ASIA

The peculiar tasselled spadix of *Arisaema fimbriatum* (A) surprised many when it flowered for the first time in England in 1884 at the Chelsea nursery of William Bull from material which originated in the Malay Peninsula. Most aroids possess a club- or finger-like spadix similar to that of *Sauromatum venosum* (C2 opposite). The tassels on the spadix are assumed to represent highly modified flowers which have lost their reproductive capacity. It has been suggested that the spadix may trail over surrounding vegetation and with the tassels, allow a multitude of creeping insects to enter the spathe and gain access to the fertile flowers situated within the fused basal portion. While the illustrated species comes from Thailand and the Malay Peninsula, a similar spadix is found in *A. album* from Thailand and *A. ornatum* from Sumatra. Unlike these species, *A. filiforme*, with a range in Java, Sumatra and Borneo, has a whip-lash spadix which lacks tassels.

The interior of the spathe in *Sauromatum venosum* (C) is speckled—like certain lizards, if the generic name has any significance, since *sauros* is Greek for lizard. As a rule, the speckling is finer towards the fused part of the spathe, but there are individuals in which they are almost unspeckled, except perhaps in the basal area. The genus contains about six species distributed from western South East Asia into tropical Africa and is allied to the similar sized Mediterranean and central Asian genus *Eminium*, although this latter genus lacks the tiny, club-shaped modified flowers near the base of the spadix, see C2 opposite. Originally thought to come from north-west India alone, *S.*

venosum is now known to have a wide range in tropical Africa where it used to pass under the name *S. nubicum*. The inflorescence appears before the leaves and the spathe reaches a majestic length of 1 to 2 feet (30-61 cm.). The leaves, which emerge later, have 6 to 12 leaflets. The fruits, about 200 in all, develop from the simple and reduced female flowers situated at the very base of the spadix, and as they ripen, they become purplish and are crowded together at the end of a short stalk, invested in what remains of the spathe. The sterile club-shaped flowers previously mentioned are borne above the female, then there is a group of male flowers while the rest of the spadix consists of fleshy sterile material. The corm, if cut open when dried, is seen to contain a hard, floury food reserve, and is the means by which the plants survive during dry periods; yet, as long as water is provided, these corms are capable of producing an inflorescence, even if kept out of the soil. This has been exploited when, under such names as the Voodoo Lily, the species has been offered for sale for growing on window-sills.

Densely shaded parts of forests in Burma and East Pakistan shelter *Tacca aspera* (B), which grows to a height of 18 to 24 inches (46-60 cm.). The closely related *T. cristata* has narrower leaves and is more widely distributed through the Malay Peninsula into Sumatra and Borneo, and *T. leontopodioides* (syn. *T. pinnatifida*), unlike the illustrated species, has attractively dissected leaves. It has a range from tropical Asia to Tahiti in Polynesia and its rhizomes are an important source of East Indian or Tahiti Arrowroot.

ARACEAE

Arisaema fimbriatum
A1 part of flowering plant (stem cut) $\times \frac{2}{3}$.

Sauromatum venosum (syn. *S. guttatum*), Voodoo Lily
C1 flowering plant $\times \frac{2}{3}$.
C2 spadix $\times \frac{2}{3}$. C3 part of leaf $\times \frac{2}{3}$.

TACCACEAE

Tacca aspera
B1 leaf and inflorescence $\times \frac{2}{3}$.

A1

B1

C3

C1

C2

Plate 126　SOUTH EAST ASIA

Purplish leaves, veined with red, a bi-lobed spur and a gently curving flower lip characterize *Anoectochilus albolineatus* (A) and distinguish it from the closely allied *A. geniculatus*, in which the spur is not bi-lobed and the lip is strongly bent. *A. albolineatus* is found at altitudes of 3500 to 5000 feet (1070–1520 m.) in Thailand and many parts of Malaysia. As with most species of this genus, the sides of the flower lip are fringed (see A2) while the tip of the lip expands into a blade with 2 lobes. The lip of another closely related species, *A. griffithii* from Sikkim, however, is scarcely fringed at all and the tip is deeply lobed. Some forty species with a distribution from India and Ceylon, throughout Malaya, the East Indies and many Pacific islands into Japan, make up the genus *Anoectochilus*.

Carl Linnaeus was the first to give *Phalaenopsis amabilis* (B) a binomial. Working from material collected by Pehr Osbeck on his voyage of 1750–1752, he placed this plant, which had first been described by Georg Everhard Rumpf (?1628–1702) on Amboina, in the genus *Epidendrum*. Carl Blume, however, moved the species to a genus of its own in 1825, naming it *Phalaenopsis*, meaning 'with the appearance of a moth'. This genus is widely distributed in the Himalaya and China, through South East Asia to northern Australia. Containing about forty species, it has a centre of diversity in Malaya and the East Indies. *P. amabilis*, characteristic within the genus, of an essentially Philippine group, has long appendages which arise from the tip of a flower lip, varying in shape and structure from plant to plant.

Hugh Cuming (1791–1865) discovered a second species of *Phalaenopsis* in 1838 and later, in 1848, Thomas Lobb discovered a third. From that time the discovery of new species has quickened and today *Phalaenopsis* enthusiasts have founded such societies as the International Phalaenopsis Society and the Phalaenoptimists which carry out much hybridization.

Examination of herbarium specimens shows the extent of variation in leaf width and, to a lesser degree, flower size in both *Cymbidium atropurpureum* (C) and *C. finlaysonianum*, and the value of maintaining them as distinct species becomes questionable. *C. atropurpureum* was at one time erroneously known as a variety of *C. pendulum*; later it was more correctly classified as a variety of *C. finlaysonianum* which, although closely related, has thicker leaves and somewhat larger flowers. Plants of the illustrated species growing in Borneo have rich purple 'sepals' and 'petals'; those growing in Java have paler purple to olive-green flowers and in Malaysia the flower colour is intermediate to these extremes. The species was first cultivated in Europe about 1901, while *C. finlaysonianum*, found in the same areas, was introduced many years earlier, about 1857. Its splendid fruits, $2\frac{1}{2}$ inches (64 mm.) long, are filled with coarse fibres which support the many thousands of tiny seeds.

The showy red inflorescences of *Renanthera coccinea* (frontispiece) continue to bloom for several months. Indeed, the extended duration of the flowering period, characteristic of *Renanthera* species, has been exploited to produce hybrid genera such as × *Aranthera* (*Renanthera* crossed with *Arachnis*), × *Renanthopsis* (*Renanthera* with *Phalaenopsis*), and × *Renantanda* (*Renanthera* with *Vanda*). Perhaps the best known plant in this genus of about thirteen species which occurs throughout South East Asia and into the Solomon Islands, and certainly the most widely grown, *R. coccinea* is a native of Thailand, Indo-China and southern China. It grows in trees and its shoots occasionally reach a length of 20 feet (6 m.), although an average of 6 to 10 feet (1·8–3 m.) is more usual. Leaves, 4 to 6 inches (10–15 cm.) long clasp the stem and the 2 to 4 long, branching inflorescences each bear between 100 and 150 flowers, which spread horizontally in a spectacular blaze of bright red. Each flower is about $3\frac{1}{2}$ inches (9 cm.) across, with the upper 'petals' and 'sepals' somewhat mottled in yellow. Originally described by the Portuguese missionary botanist, João de Loureiro (1715–1791), *R. coccinea* was introduced into western hothouses in the early 1800's. It flowered, after much difficulty, for the first time in England during 1827 and still has a reputation for being shy to bloom. Long cultivated in tropical China, it is now also grown in many parts of the Malay Peninsula and, especially, in Singapore.

The famous Victorian pot-plant, *Aspidistra*, finds a close relative in *Tupistra*, a small genus of about seven species with a range from the Himalaya, through Burma into Malaya, China and Japan. Henry Nicholas Ridley (1855–1956) discovered *T. grandis* (D), a native of Perak, in dense forest on a hill called Bujong Malacca. He splendidly described, in 1900, the flowers he found inside the fleshy inflorescence, likening them to 'nearly black basins with recurved edges, from the centre of which arise small white fungi, on stout stalks (the pistils). The buds and tips of the petals and sepals are deep purple, almost black, and the contrast with the ivory-white pistil is most striking'. Each flower is subtended by a bract and each of the 6 fused petals has a stamen, with the filament fused to the perianth, opposite. Flowering from the base upwards, the inflorescence varies in length from 5 to 7 inches (13–18 cm.) and 3 or 4 blossoms open each day. One of the most southerly members of the tribe *Aspidistreae*, *T. grandis* was introduced into cultivation at the Singapore Botanic Garden about 1898, and to Kew in 1899, where it flowered for the first time in Europe later that year.

Peliosanthes is a genus of about fifteen species found from the Himalaya east to Formosa and south to Java. Some botanists place it clearly with the lily family, the *Liliaceae*, while others prefer to class it with the *Haemodoraceae*—the family which includes *Anigozanthos*, the Kangaroo-paws (plate 144), and several other natives of Australia. *P. teta*, *P. graminea* (E) and *P. teta* var. *angustifolia* have all been clearly distinguished by Ridley but one must either question the validity of these names or conclude that the plants are variable in cultivation. The species illustrated has the characteristics of *P. graminea* but its leaves are more like those of *P. teta*. Further collections and possibly field study are required to elucidate their differentiation. The rich blue fruits of *P. teta* (E3) are not dissimilar to those of *P. graminea*.

ORCHIDACEAE

Anoectochilus albolineatus
A1 flowering plant × $\frac{2}{3}$. A2 lip of flower × 2.

Phalaenopsis amabilis
B1 flowering plant × $\frac{2}{3}$.

Cymbidium atropurpureum
C1 flowering plant × $\frac{2}{3}$.

LILIACEAE

Tupistra grandis
D1 flowering plant (stem cut) × $\frac{2}{3}$.
D2 part of opened corolla with 2 stamens × $1\frac{1}{3}$.

Peliosanthes graminea
E1 leaves and inflorescence × $\frac{2}{3}$.
E2 flower × $5\frac{1}{4}$.
E3 fruit and sectioned fruit of *P. teta* × $2\frac{2}{3}$.

A2

A1

B1

C1

D1

D2

E1

E2

E3

Plate 127   SOUTH EAST ASIA

The different ways in which the flowers are formed, to allow different methods of pollination by various animals, suggest to botanists that orchids represent the most highly developed type of monocotyledon.

A great deal has been written about shoot and flower structure, ecological behaviour and adaptations of orchid flowers to particular insect and bird visitors. It is necessary to read Charles Darwin's *The Various Contrivances by which Orchids are fertilised by Insects* and other authoritative books and periodicals (such as *Orchid Review*) to do orchid-biology full justice. The recently published *The Biology of the Orchids* (1967) by C. H. Dodson and R. J. Gillespie deals with this subject in an interesting way.

Coelogyne is a large genus of some two hundred species found growing as epiphytes from the Himalaya into south China and Malaysia and as far as the New Hebrides. *C. pandurata* (B) grows on old trees in humid, lowland habitats and river valleys in Borneo, Sumatra and Malaya. This species, with its greenish, scented flowers, is easily cultivated if given appropriate conditions.

Also growing in Borneo, Sumatra and Malaya, the Kinta Weed, *Vanda hookerana* (C) favours swampy or coastal areas where it is often found scrambling over small shrubs. Unfortunately, tin-mining and the clearance of woodland in the Kinta Valley of Perak, Malaya, have recently reduced the numbers of this *Vanda* in an area once so rich in the species as to give it its common name. The spotting of the lip is a variable feature of the species and white-flowered plants are known. Another common name for *V. hookerana* (and also for *V. teres*) is Bone Plant because both species have slender leaves, which are also used in the preparation of a hot poultice for aching joints, but the success of this remedy is questionable.

Many species of *Vanda* hybridize easily and there are hundreds of cultivated varieties. According to figures published in 1959, *V. hookerana* is a parent of some nineteen valuable hybrids and continues to breed more. One of the most common Malayan garden-orchids is *Vanda* 'Miss Joaquim' (*V. hookerana* × *V. teres*) named after the lady in whose garden it appeared in 1893; its characters are intermediate to those of the parents, and it has a freer flowering tendency. By the 1920's it had become immensely popular in Malaya, and in 1925 the first cuttings were sent to Hawaii, where it has since provided a basis for a prosperous florist trade in cut orchid flowers.

The fifteen species of *Arachnis* occur from Burma, through Malaya, and into Indo-China. Known as the Common Scorpion Orchid due to the shape of its flowers, *A. flos-aeris* (A) is a native of Java, Sumatra, Borneo and of Malaya, where, according to Holttum (1964), it is not so common. These plants scramble over other vegetation and form large clumps in limestone areas; they tend to flower only in sunny habitats. Two varieties are sometimes recognized, var. *gracilis* from south-west Malaya, and var. *insignis* from Sumatra. Both varieties are said to lack the musty odour of the true species, having a much sweeter smell and the former also bears fewer flowers.

Bulbophyllum, with about nine hundred species, is a large genus, found principally in Asia but also in other continents. *B. medusae* (D) comes from Borneo, Sumatra and Malaya, where it is an epiphyte on rocks and trees. The curious 'flower' is in fact an inflorescence of flowers, each with an elongated group of perianth lobes. It is so named because Lindley obviously likened the inflorescence to the Medusa's head of Greek mythology. *B. medusae* is said to be slower growing and less common than other species, such as *B. vaginatum*, which is also found in Malaya.

The genus *Dendrobium* is equally large, and its species are found in all tropical areas, especially in Asia. *D. anosmum* (E) is confined to the East Indies and, less commonly, to Malaya, where it is usually found in trees in limestone districts. It will not flower well unless there is a regular dry season in which the stems can ripen suitably to produce flowers. A larger variety, native in the Philippines, was discovered and introduced into England in 1839 by Hugh Cuming.

ORCHIDACEAE

Arachnis flos-aeris, Common Scorpion Orchid
A1 part of flowering stem × $\frac{2}{3}$. A2 shoot × $\frac{2}{3}$.

Coelogyne pandurata
B1 flowering plant with old and new pseudobulbs × $\frac{2}{3}$.

Vanda hookerana, Kinta Weed, Bone Plant
C1 part of flowering stem with leaves and aerial root × $\frac{2}{3}$.

Bulbophyllum medusae (syn. *Cirropetalum medusae*)
D1 flowering plant with pseudobulbs × $\frac{2}{3}$.

Dendrobium anosmum (syn. *D. superbum*)
E1 part of flowering stem with leaves × $\frac{2}{3}$.

A1

A2

B1

C1

D1

E1

Plate 128   AUSTRALASIA

The stately buttercups of New Zealand deserve to be better known, forming as they do an important element of the country's alpine flora. With their large decorative flowers and seed capsules, they are unlike most other species. The genus *Clematis*, with its two hundred and fifty species, is chiefly distributed in temperate parts of the world but both the Australian and New Zealand species are restricted to their individual geographical areas. The genus *Hibbertia* is not a member of the *Ranunculaceae* but belongs to the *Dilleniaceae*, a family mainly confined to the southern hemisphere.

Because the flowers of the buttercup genus *Ranunculus* are relatively simple in structure and easily obtainable in northern temperate areas, they are often studied in schools. The common wild buttercups of Europe and America are too weedy for garden plants, but the cultivation of those from the southern hemisphere presents a more interesting challenge. Species such as *R. lyallii* (C), which is native to the Southern Alps, South Island, New Zealand have deep green, glossy leaves shaped like saucers, and large waxy flowers. Known popularly in New Zealand as the Mount Cook Lily, it grows in the shade of rocks and of other plants and flourishes in stony soil near torrents at altitudes of 1500 to 5000 feet (450–1500 m.). In contrast to the common meadow buttercup, this plant can grow to a total height of 5 feet (1·5 m.) and its leaves may reach 15 inches (38 cm.) in diameter. Like so many mountain plants, the species is difficult to cultivate, requiring abundant moisture combined with excellent drainage. In nature, *R. lyallii* flowers from October to January, the New Zealand spring and early summer. It was discovered by David Lyall (1817–1895), a naval surgeon, naturalist and explorer, after whom it is named. It first flowered at Kew in 1886 from seed germinated late in 1882.

At higher altitudes, 3500 to 6500 feet (1050–1980 m.), is found the yellow-flowered *R. insignis* (B) in both the North and South Islands of New Zealand. It grows usually in habitats sheltered from the drying sun but, in areas with a high percentage of cloudy days, may be found in more exposed places. Its flowers are a little smaller than those of *R. lyallii* and its other organs are more variable. Mr J. Barker of Geraldine, New Zealand produced hybrids some years ago from the two species, and these have since become popular cultivars, bearing numbers of large cream coloured flowers. However, these hybrids are sterile and must be propagated vegetatively. For more about these buttercups and their diversity of habit, see *Alpine Ranunculi of New Zealand* by Dr F. J. F. Fisher (1965), attractively illustrated by K. R. West.

Those species and cultivars of *Clematis* found in northern temperate gardens are Eurasian or North American in origin. *C. alpina*, with its solitary nodding blue flowers, comes from Europe. Of other cultivated species, the yellow-flowered *C. tangutica*, comes from north-west China and *C. texensis*, with somewhat similar but scarlet flowers, from Texas. The very popular hybrid *C. × jackmanii*, with large velvet purple flowers in terminal clusters, is derived from *C. lanuginosa*, a large white-flowered species from China, and *C. viticella* with rose-purple flowers, from southern Europe and western Asia.

As in all species of *Clematis*, it is the coloured sepals that form the 'flowers', there being no true petals; in the Australian and New Zealand species, these sepals are usually tinged with white or yellow-green. *C. microphylla* (D), a tall climber with leaves that vary in size and shape, is found from Queensland, through New South Wales, Victoria and South Australia, into Tasmania, especially near coasts and rivers. The fruits of *Clematis* have a plumed tail which develops from the style and may in *C. microphylla* be 3½ inches (9 cm.) long. The masses of plumed feathery fruits make it a most attractive plant, especially when climbing small trees or trailing over boulders and shrubs.

One of about a hundred species in a genus found throughout Australasia and in several Pacific islands, *Hibbertia scandens* (A) is restricted to the eastern areas of Queensland and New South Wales. By twining it attains a height of 4 feet (1·2 m.) or more and its leaves, which are silkily hairy beneath, measure up to 3 inches (7·5 cm.) in length. The genus is named after George Hibbert (1757–1837), a patron of the arts who had a collection of exotic plants in his garden at Clapham. Introduced into Europe about 1790, the species is grown under glass in a number of botanic gardens, its rich yellow flowers borne on twining woody stems providing a splash of colour in winter and early spring.

DILLENIACEAE

Hibbertia scandens (syn. *H. volubilis*)
A1 part of flowering branch with bud × ⅔.

RANUNCULACEAE

Ranunculus insignis
B1 part of flowering stem × ⅔.

R. lyallii, Mount Cook Lily
C1 part of flowering stem and leaf × ⅔.
C2 fruiting head on part of stem × ⅔.
C3 fruit × 2⅔.

Clematis microphylla
D1 part of flowering stem × ⅔. D2 sepal × 2.
D3 fruiting heads × ⅔. D4 fruit × 2.

A1

B1

C1

C2

C3

D1

D2

D3

D4

Plate 129   AUSTRALASIA

Australasian members of the pea family tend to have altogether more brightly coloured flowers than their counterparts in the northern hemisphere. The black and red crescents of *Clianthus*, the intense colouring found among the species of *Hovea*, and the yellow, or orange and red flowers of *Gompholobium* are all examples. The species of *Acacia*, the Wattles, have less flamboyant flowers but they are produced in such quantity as to turn the whole bush or tree into a mound of gold.

Despite the different appearance of their flowers, the rose family, *Rosaceae*, is related to the pea family and is represented in this plate by *Rubus parvus* (G), one of five members of the bramble genus in New Zealand and the only one there with undivided leaves. It is restricted to the north-west of South Island in lowland forest and river flats where its thorny stems and bronze foliage form tangled masses over the ground, and its white flowers are followed by juicy red and edible 'blackberries'. It is one of the few New Zealand plants to develop autumnal tints. Easy to get involved with and difficult to shake off, it is commonly known as Bush Lawyer. More widespread on both North and South Island, at the edges of forests, the liana *R. australis* trails its thick, tough, 30 foot (9 m.) stems with its fragrant white flowers borne in panicles up to 8 inches (20 cm.) long.

A fanciful resemblance of the pods of *Gompholobium* to a club has given the genus its name (*gomphos*, 'club', *lobos*, 'pod'); all but one of the twenty-five species are Australian, the exception coming from New Guinea. Discovered by Robert Brown in Western Australia and introduced into western Europe in 1803 by Peter Good, *G. polymorphum*, as its epithet suggests, is a protean plant, capable of taking the form of a small, erect shrub, a twiner or a ground creeper. The stems vary from 6 to 12 inches (15–30 cm.) in length and the leaves can be divided into 3 or 9 leaflets, which themselves often vary in shape. The flowers too, vary in colour from orange-yellow to deep crimson.

The name of the 18th century Irish botanist, John Templeton, is commemorated in the Australian genus of ten species, *Templetonia*. *T. retusa* (B), also known as Bullock Bush, is native to Western Australia where it grows only in coastal districts and forms a shrub 3 to 5 feet (0·9–1·5 m.) high with coarse, hard leaves.

There are two species of *Clianthus*: *C. formosus* (D) is found in Australia, *C. puniceus* in New Zealand. Sturt's Desert Pea, as the Australian plant is known, was first discovered by the explorer William Dampier (1652–1715) when, as captain of H.M.S. 'Roebuck', he visited the islands off the coast of north-western Australia that came to be called Dampier's Archipelago. In 1818, the botanist and explorer Allan Cunningham also found it there. Later still it was found to grow on the mainland as well, in fact across the whole of the dry hot areas. It is a creeping plant and the beauty of the

large, scarlet, rarely white, flowers, each with a bulbous velvet-black eye, is enhanced by the pale grey-green foliage with its silky hairs. The New Zealand species was first cultivated by the Maoris. It forms a soft woody shrub with spreading or trailing branches and bears scarlet or pink flowers; there is said to be a white flowered form that grows true from seed. The species is found only on North Island and, in recent years, has become extinct in several of its former localities.

As famous as *Clianthus* and almost as characteristic of Australasian flora is the genus *Sophora*, whose fifty species have a total range from Chile to New Zealand and across the Indian Ocean to east Africa. Yellow Kowhai, *S. tetraptera* (A), is restricted to North Island and grows to a height of about 42 feet (12·8 cm.). It is noted for its golden blossoms, set off by its dark green, pinnately divided leaves. Each flower, with its sulphur yellow petals and golden sepals, contains copious nectar on which the birds feed. The long-lasting fruits resemble corky strings of beads, each fruit containing 5 to 8 seeds. The wood, too, is much sought after, being extremely durable. *S. microphylla*, which occurs both on North and South Island, and on Chatham Island, has leaves with 20–40 pairs of leaflets usually about ⅓ inch (8 mm.) long. The finer foliage of this plant possibly makes it even more decorative than *S. tetraptera*. Sir Joseph Banks and Daniel Solander brought back from New Zealand viable seed of both these species in 1771 and they were thus the first New Zealand plants introduced into European gardens.

Anthony Pantaleon Hove, a Polish collector sent out by Sir Joseph Banks from Kew in 1780's and 1790's, is remembered in the genus *Hovea*, which consists of twelve Australasian species. The most widespread and variable of these is *H. longifolia* (C), which occurs in all parts of the region except Western Australia. It forms a shrub about 10 feet (3 m.) tall, with erect, twiggy branches whose narrow, coarsely textured leaves frequently have an underside of rust coloured hairs. The variety illustrated opposite, var. *lanceolata*, was at one time given the rank of a species. The rich violet flowers, borne in the axils of the leaves, later give way to short, inflated pods, covered with a dense mat of rusty hairs (C2).

The natural habitat of the tall shrubby *Acacia cultriformis* (E), discovered by Allan Cunningham in New South Wales, is rocky ground and dry, forest scrub. It has, nevertheless, been much cultivated for its showy flowers and curious, almost triangular, 'leaves' or phyllodes which clothe the angular branches and in whose axils arise the inflorescences consisting of 5 to 20 yellow globes, each of which is made up of 20 or 30 tiny flowers. These, on dissection, reveal 5 small, rounded sepals, 5 petals about $\frac{1}{17}$ inch (1·5 mm.) long, and numerous stamens (which en masse make the flowers so showy) with a single ovary in the middle (see plate 130, A2).

LEGUMINOSAE

Sophora tetraptera, Yellow Kowhai
A1 part of flowering stem × ⅔.
A2 fruit × 1.

Templetonia retusa, Bullock Bush
B1 flowering shoot × ⅔.

Hovea longifolia var. *lanceolata*
C1 flowering stem × ⅔. C2 standard petal × ⅔.
C3 fruit × ⅔.

Clianthus formosus, Sturt's Desert Pea
D1 part of flowering stem × ⅔.
D2 flower, with petals removed × ⅔.
D3 fruit × ⅔. D4 habit sketch × $\frac{1}{15}$.

Acacia cultriformis
E1 flowering twig × ⅔. E2 fruit × ⅔.

Gompholobium polymorphum
F1 flowering stem × ⅔.

ROSACEAE

Rubus parvus, Bush Lawyer
G1 flowering twig × ⅔. G2 fruiting twig × ⅔.
G3 base of underside of leaf showing thorns × 2.

A1

A2

B1

C2

C1

C3

D3

D1

D2

D4

E2

E1

F1

G1

G2

G3

Plate 130   AUSTRALASIA

The flora of Australasia, like its fauna, is extraordinary for the number of organisms it contains that are found nowhere else in the world. Of the five genera of the subdivision *Papilionoideae* represented opposite, for instance, three are known only from Australia, one only from New Zealand, and one is common to both areas but occurs in no other part of the world.

Baron Karl von Hügel, an early collector of plants in the Swan River area in 1833, proposed the generic name *Hardenbergia* after his sister, Countess von Hardenberg. Like the other two species in the genus, *H. violacea* (F), the False Sarsaparilla, which is found in southern and eastern Australia, has purple, pink or white flowers. The Native Wisteria, *H. comptoniana*, another well known species, represents the part of the genus that is characterized by having 3–5 leaflets, rather than the single leaf found on the species illustrated.

Like all the dozen or so species in its genus, *Kennedia beckxiana* (C) grows in coastal or moist habitats. It forms a twining, ground-level herb with red flowers that appear either singly or in pairs, and long, flat fruits containing greyish brown seeds. This species is a native of Western Australia and is related to the scarlet-flowered Running Postman, *K. prostrata* and the peculiar gold- and black-flowered Black Bean, *K. nigricans*. The generic name commemorates John Kennedy (1759–1842), a nurseryman of Scottish origin, partner in the once celebrated Vineyard Nursery of Lee and Kennedy at Hammersmith, Greater London, and horticultural adviser to the Empress Josephine of France.

Neither so well known nor so widely cultivated as certain other members of its genus, such as the Heartleaf Flame-pea, the Holly Flame-pea, *Chorizema ilicifolium* (B) is a small Western Australian shrub with orange and red flowers. *Swainsona galegifolia* (D) belongs to a genus of about fifty species, including both annuals and perennials, found in New Zealand and Australia, the species illustrated coming from eastern and southern Australia. Still within the same subfamily, *Notospartium glabrescens* (E) has twigs that are leafless but covered, when in flower, with masses of pale lilac blossom, and when in fruit, with silvery clusters of pods. It is found in certain valleys on New Zealand's South Island.

Cassia, a genus of another of the three subfamilies in the *Leguminosae*, the *Caesalpinioideae*, is a large one with five to six hundred species of tropical and subtropical trees and shrubs throughout the world, perhaps best known for the laxative senna, yielded by the dried leaves or pods of *C. senna*. *C. artemisioides* (G), an eastern and southern Australian species, is characterized by finely divided, silvery foliage. The third subfamily, the *Mimosoideae* is represented by *Acacia*, the majority of Australian species of which are, scientifically speaking, leafless: what would appear to be leaves to a layman are in fact 'phyllodes'—photosynthetic structures developed from a flattened stem or leaf stalk. True leaflets are produced by seedlings but are later lost, although in many species they continue to be developed throughout the life of the plant. Queensland Wattle, *A. podalyriifolia* (A), has numerous relatives throughout the continent (there are about six hundred species in Australia), among them the Blackwood, the Silver Wattle and the Kangaroo Thorn.

LEGUMINOSAE

Acacia podalyriifolia, Queensland Wattle
A1 part of flowering shoot $\times \frac{2}{3}$.
A2 single floret $\times 6\frac{2}{3}$. A3 flower-head $\times 4$.

Chorizema ilicifolium, Holly Flame-pea
B1 part of flowering stem $\times \frac{2}{3}$.
B2 flower $\times 2\frac{2}{3}$.

Kennedia beckxiana
C1 flowering and fruiting stem $\times \frac{2}{3}$.
C2 flower $\times 1\frac{1}{3}$.

Swainsona galegifolia
D1 flowering stem $\times \frac{2}{3}$.
D2 front view of flower $\times 1\frac{1}{3}$.
D3 side view of flower $\times 1\frac{1}{3}$.

Notospartium glabrescens
E1 flowering stem $\times \frac{2}{3}$.
E2 flower $\times 2\frac{2}{3}$. E3 fruiting stem $\times \frac{2}{3}$.
E4 pod $\times 1\frac{1}{3}$. E5 seed $\times 2$.

Hardenbergia violacea, False Sarsaparilla
F1 flowering stems $\times \frac{2}{3}$. F2 flower $\times 2$.

Cassia artemisioides
G1 flowering stem $\times \frac{2}{3}$. G2 flower $\times 2$.

Plate 131   AUSTRALASIA

The families represented opposite include a number of small but characteristic Australian genera. The majority of those in the *Pittosporaceae* and the whole of the *Tremandraceae* and *Byblidaceae* are found only in that continent.

The genus *Pittosporum*, with one hundred and fifty tropical and subtropical species, has a distribution outside Australia, though one of the better known members is the Australian Mock Orange or Native Laurel, *P. undulatum* (G). This tree, with its glossy evergreen foliage and fragrant cream-coloured flowers, has been a popular ornamental tree in places free from frost ever since it was first cultivated, by Sir Joseph Banks in 1789. It grows wild from New South Wales to Tasmania and is usually found as a small tree, though it can reach a height of 80 feet (24 m.), depending on whether it occurs in a moist, woodland habitat or in dry, rocky, open country. Its specific epithet refers to the undulating margins of the leaves. The plant has a number of uses: growing, it can be employed as a hedging plant or wind-break; about 2 ounces of a fragrant oil reminiscent of a mixture of jonquil and jasmine can be obtained from 100 lb. (45 kg.) of petals; an aromatic gum is yielded by the bark. The whitish close-grained wood is sometimes substituted for box as a medium for wood-engraving, and is used in the manufacture of golf clubs and the like. When first described by Etienne Pierre Ventenat (1757–1808), the species was mistakenly thought to be native to the Canaries. It is now naturalized in Hawaii, to which it was probably introduced by W. H. Purvis in 1875.

Along the edges of forests and streams in North Island, New Zealand, and Kermadec Island in the south-west Pacific, is found the Karo, *P. crassifolium* (E), a small tree up to 30 feet (9 m.) in height. The undersides of the leathery 2 to 4 inch (5–10 cm.) leaves, as well as the leaf and flower stalks, bear a white or buff felt, which, with the dark brown bark and terminal umbels of deep purple-red blooms, gives the species a considerable attraction. The flowers are functionally unisexual, the male borne in clusters of 5 to 10, the female singly or in pairs. It is hardy in the milder parts of Britain.

The commonest of Australia's three species of *Sollya*, named after Richard Horsman Solly (1778–1858), an English plant physiologist and anatomist, is *S. fusiformis* (F). This is a trailing twiner which, though introduced into Britain as early as 1830—when it was known as *S. hetero-phylla*—and easily grown in a cool greenhouse, has never received the recognition that its charm deserves. From a woody base it reaches a height of about 8 feet (2·4 m.) and bears, between October and December, small drooping terminal cymes of 4 to 12 bell-shaped flowers in a soft but striking blue. It was discovered by Jacques Julien Houtton de La Billardière, botanist to d'Entrecasteaux's expedition of 1791–1794, and

occurs on gravels and clays in Western Australia from the Darling Range to the south coast.

In the same region is found another delicate and ornamental genus, *Marianthus*, whose capsular fruits resemble those of *Pittosporum*, though their walls are membraneous rather than woody or leathery. The dense white clusters of the tall twiner *M. candidus* (A), with their attractive sharply pointed spreading petals and narrow erect claws, flower among rocks in December. The young leaves are toothed or lobed, the older entire and up to about 4 inches (10 cm.) in length. A sister-species, *M. coeruleo-punctatus*, whose flowers are of a pale violet spotted in a darker shade, was one of the earliest of the genus to be introduced into England, being sent as seed from the Swan river in 1839 by William Morrison.

Cheiranthera cyanea (B) is a low, hairless, twiggy undershrub, rarely exceeding 12 inches (30 cm.) in height, found in the scrubby woodlands of New South Wales, Victoria and South Australia. It has showy blue flowers and linear leaves, either minutely toothed or entire, about $\frac{3}{4}$ to $1\frac{1}{2}$ inches (20–40 mm.) in length.

About twenty species are contained in the genus *Tetratheca*. The Pink Eye, *T. ciliata* (C), widespread in South Australia, Victoria and northern Tasmania, is a decorative plant, seen at its best, as are all of its genus, when massed in clumps. It flowers in October and favours sandy soils in scrub, open woodland and heath. The numerous erect slender stems, their younger parts clad with hair, rise to a height of about 3 feet (91 cm.) from a woody stock. The leaves are usually arranged in whorls of 3 and are rounded, tough in texture, and scattered and edged with hairs.

The botanist and collector James Drummond (1783–1863) was the first to discover *Byblis gigantea* (D). Belying its epithet, it grows to a height of only 2 feet (61 cm.), and has very thin, sometimes channelled leaves clothed with two kinds of gland; those on stalks secrete a sticky mucilage which traps small insects, while the tiny sessile glands appear to have a digestive function, though some have doubted this. The similarity to the Sundews, *Drosera* (see plates 16 and 75), is striking. These glistening glands were fancifully likened to tears by R. A. Salisbury, who named the genus after Byblis, daughter of Miletus (the son of Apollo), who fell in love with her twin brother and, when he ran away, collapsed in tears and was changed into a fountain. The single delicately textured flowers borne on axillary peduncles vary in size and are purplish in colour. They are followed by capsular fruits containing numerous seeds. Specimens, introduced into Britain as seed in 1899, first flowered at Kew in 1900. Both *Byblis* and the South African genus *Roridula*, which it closely resembles, appear to have some affinity with the *Pittosporaceae*.

PITTOSPORACEAE

Marianthus candidus
A1 portion of stem with flowers and buds $\times \frac{2}{3}$.

Cheiranthera cyanea (syn. *C. linearis*)
B1 flowering shoot $\times \frac{2}{3}$.

Pittosporum crassifolium, Karo
E1 part of flowering stem $\times \frac{2}{3}$.
E2 fruit $\times \frac{2}{3}$.

Sollya fusiformis
F1 flowering shoot $\times \frac{2}{3}$. F2 flower $\times 1\frac{1}{3}$.

Pittosporum undulatum, Mock Orange, Native Laurel
G1 flowering shoot $\times \frac{2}{3}$.

TREMANDRACEAE

Tetratheca ciliata, Pink Eye
C1 part of flowering stem $\times \frac{2}{3}$.
C2 flower $\times 2\frac{2}{3}$. C3 anther $\times 3\frac{2}{3}$. C4 leaf $\times 2$.

BYBLIDACEAE

Byblis gigantea
D1 flowering stem and leaves $\times \frac{2}{3}$.
D2 stamens, style and ovary $\times 2$.

A1

B1

C1

C2

C3

C4

D1

D2

E1

E2

F1

F2

G1

Plate 132   AUSTRALASIA

A number of attractive garden species with white, cream, green or purple flowers belong to the genus *Ptilotus*. *P. exaltatus* (E), the Pink Mulla Mulla, is a stiff, erect perennial usually 2 to 3 feet (61–91 cm.) in height, found in most parts of Australia, though plants from the west region are generally taller with longer inflorescences and less hairy than their eastern counterparts. A smaller example of the same genus, *P. spathulatus* (F) is a prostrate perennial, 3 to 6 inches (7·5–15 cm.) tall, that grows from a thick, woody rhizome and occurs, usually in dry scrub, in Tasmania and the warm temperate regions of southern and western Australia. At the base, a rosette of stalked, rounded leaves contrasts with the narrower stem leaves. The small nuts or achene fruits are clothed in a loose coat and fall from the plant when ripe. Species of this genus are usually propagated from cuttings since the seeds are often infertile or slow to germinate.

The Parakeelyas are somewhat fleshy herbs with flowers that open quickly in response to sunshine. One hundred and fifty or so species make up the genus *Calandrinia* and occur in Australia and, in the New World, from Canada to Chile. The Broad-leaved Parakeelya, *C. balonensis* (B), named after the Balonne river in Queensland where it was first collected, is one of approximately thirty Australian species and grows as an annual or perennial in arid areas of southern Australia and the Northern Territory. The plant reaches a height of 6 to 15 inches (15–38 cm.) and has fleshy leaves and large long-lasting flowers.

The Spotted Emu Bush, *Eremophila maculata* (A), is an erect shrub with lance-shaped leaves that are hoary when young but become smooth as they mature. The yellowish or reddish flowers are mottled on the inside and supported on pedicels which, though reflexed, hold them erect. The plant is native of the drier areas of eastern and southern Australia, and is sometimes to be seen in gardens. *Eremophila* is an Australian genus of about forty-five species and was introduced to England prior to 1820. All its members have flowers with a tubular base and 2-lipped upper section.

The highly aromatic Mint bushes, the collective popular name of the genus *Prostanthera*, occur in bewildering array in Australia, to which all fifty species are endemic, although some have been introduced to cultivation. The Victorian Christmas Bush, *P. lasianthos* (D), which, despite its common name is also found in New South Wales and Tasmania, is a coarse-leaved shrub or small tree that grows at the edges of forests and streams and blooms from September to January.

A plant that effectively illustrates the relationship between hairiness in flora and aridity in environment is the rare *Lachnostachys verbascifolia* (C) which, like the other ten species in the genus, is restricted in range to Western Australia. These plants are commonly called Lambs' Tails or Blanket Plants and, as can be seen opposite, *L. verbascifolia*, which grows in sandy places, especially the 'sand plains', has spikes of small flowers which are almost hidden by a woolly felt.

MYOPORACEAE

Eremophila maculata, Spotted Emu Bush
A1 part of flowering twig × $\frac{2}{3}$.
A2 style and ovary × $1\frac{1}{3}$. A3 anther × $5\frac{1}{3}$.

PORTULACACEAE

Calandrinia balonensis, Broad-leaved Parakeelya
B1 part of flowering plant × $\frac{2}{3}$.

VERBENACEAE

Lachnostachys verbascifolia
C1 part of flowering stem × $\frac{2}{3}$.
C2 flower × $2\frac{2}{3}$. C3 massed stellate hairs × 10.

LABIATAE

Prostanthera lasianthos, Victorian Christmas Bush
D1 part of flowering stem × $\frac{2}{3}$.

AMARANTHACEAE

Ptilotus exaltatus, Pink Mulla Mulla
E1 flowering plant × $\frac{2}{3}$.

P. spathulatus
F1 flowering plant × $\frac{2}{3}$.
F2 flower with 2 petals removed × 4.

A3

A2

A1

B1

C2

C3

C1

D1

E1

F1

F2

Plate 133 AUSTRALASIA

Fuchsia provides a good example of discontinuous distribution in a genus: its major area is in Central and South America, but four species are also found in New Zealand and a further one in Tahiti. Australia contains two remarkable genera which, almost above all others, characterize the Australian flora. One is the Flannel Flower, a woolly umbellifer which has achieved fame on postage stamps; the other is *Cephalotus*, a pitcher plant with leaves very like those of *Nepenthes*, but with flowers which betray no affinity between these two carnivores. *Cephalotus*, with a restricted distribution in West Australia, has been placed in a family of its own.

One of the truly arborescent fuchsias, *Fuchsia excorticata* (A) reaches a height of 36 feet (11 m.) in the lowland and foothill forests of both the islands of New Zealand. The bark is flaky and when the trunk is freshly exposed it contains chlorophyll. As is common among fuchsias, the leaves may be suffused with purple and pale on the undersurface. The flowers, which bloom from August until December, are sometimes borne on naked branches, while the fruits, $\frac{1}{4}$ inch (6 mm.) long are blackish-purple berries and appear from September to January.

Among the rocks or sand above the high-water mark in coastal areas of North Island, New Zealand, *Fuchsia procumbens* (E) flourishes. A creeper which bears its purple and red flowers erect (unlike most species) from December to February, it was discovered by Richard Cunningham in 1834 near the village of Matauri opposite the Cavallos Islands. It was introduced into European gardens before 1870.

The New Zealand fuchsias show a remarkable diversity of habit for such a small number of species: *F. excorticata* is a tree, *F. colensoi* a shrub, *F. perscandens* a liana and *F. procumbens* a prostrate creeper.

A member of the *Umbelliferae*, *Actinotus* comprises fifteen species found in Australia, Tasmania and New Zealand. The Flannel Flower, *A. helianthii* (C), grows in Queensland and New South Wales, reaching a height of 3 feet (91 cm.). It favours sandstone or granite soils and sandy places under eucalyptus. Like many woolly plants, the vestiture of the Flannel Flower affords protection against the heat and dryness of the air.

The west Australian *A. leucocephalus* has less leafy, more diffusely branched stems, and its inflorescence is smaller and more hairy. *A. minor*, from New South Wales, is less conspicuous and has flowering heads of only about $\frac{1}{2}$ inch (13 mm.) diameter, and leaves of the same size. Even smaller is the Tasmanian *A. bellidioides*, a tiny rosette herb, no taller than an inch (2·5 cm.), with miniature flowering heads about $\frac{1}{4}$ inch (6 mm.) in diameter.

Cephalotus follicularis (D) is the only species in the family *Cephalotaceae*. It grows in damp sandy areas and swamps—the Albany Swamps and around the King river—in south-west Australia. Commonly called the Fly-catcher Plant, its leaves are modified into pitchers, which serve as insect traps. First discovered by La Billardière in 1792, it was found again by Robert Brown in 1801 during Flinders' voyage around Australia. *C. follicularis* was introduced at Kew in 1823 and flowered there in August of 1827. The species resembles *Nepenthes*, *Sarracenia* and *Darlingtonia*, other unrelated carnivorous pitcher plant genera.

Young *Cephalotus* plants have a deep taproot, with a rosette of leaves around the top, while in older plants, such as the one illustrated opposite, the rootstock may fork and have a smaller rosette of leaves. Foliage leaves begin to grow during July and August; by September or October they have reached full development, rarely exceeding 5 inches (13 cm.) in length. The pitcher leaves, although they begin their development in June or July, do not mature until December or January, when they reach about 2 inches (5 cm.) in length and $\frac{3}{4}$ inch (19 mm.) in diameter. The flowers are borne on a short inflorescence at the end of a long stalk which is triangular in cross section at the base. The pitchers, which trap ants and similar creatures, contain a fluid with digestive properties, but because test plants have appeared to flourish and flower without such secondary nutrition, it is possible that *Cephalotus* is not an obligate carnivore.

Ceratopetalum gummiferum (B) is one of five species found from New Guinea to eastern Australia. The *Cunoniaceae*, to which *Ceratopetalum* belongs, is related to the saxifrage family, *Saxifragaceae*. The generic name is derived from the Greek *keras* 'horn' and *petalon* 'petal', a reference to the petal tip which resembles the horns of a deer. Also popularly known as the Christmas Bush from its use as a decorative plant in Australia at that time of the year, it may form a tree 60 feet (18 m.) or more in height, in New South Wales where it grows. The lacerated petals are small, and inconspicuous. The persistent sepals, however, which enlarge when the plant is fruiting, give the Christmas Bush its cheerful red colour.

ONAGRACEAE

Fuchsia excorticata
A1 part of flowering branch × $\frac{2}{3}$.
A2 flower × $1\frac{1}{3}$.

F. procumbens
E1 part of flowering stem × $\frac{2}{3}$.
E2 shoot with fruit × $\frac{2}{3}$.

CUNONIACEAE

Ceratopetalum gummiferum, Christmas Bush
B1 part of flowering branch × $\frac{2}{3}$. B2 flower × 2.
B3 petal × 6.

UMBELLIFERAE

Actinotus helianthii, Flannel Flower
C1 part of flowering branch × $\frac{2}{3}$.
C2 flower × $4\frac{2}{3}$.

CEPHALOTACEAE

Cephalotus follicularis, Fly-catcher Plant
D1 flowering plant × $\frac{2}{3}$.

A2

A1

B3

B1

B2

C1

C2

D1

E1

E2

Plate 134   AUSTRALASIA

The shrubby types of veronica (*Hebe*) grown in north temperate gardens have a habit not unlike that of *Pimelea ferruginea* (A) but come from an entirely different, though predominantly Australasian, family. The genus *Pimelea* contains about eighty species, most of which are found in Australia, though some occur in New Zealand or as far north as New Guinea and the Philippines. Some of the species resemble the members of the northern genus *Daphne* in the same family, the *Thymelaeaceae*, but few of them are as sweetly scented. *P. ferruginea* varies in flower colour from pale pink to deep red and has been collected in many parts of Western Australia. Another pretty species, this time from Tasmania, is *P. nivea*, which has small rounded leaves with white undersides borne along extended stems and cream-coloured flowers somewhat larger than those of *P. ferruginea*. Commonly called the Qualup Bell, *P. physodes*, a shrub about 2 feet (61 cm.) tall, has an unusual appearance with leaves arranged up the stems in 4 neat rows. Inconspicuous heads of nodding flowers are found hidden inside a nodding involucre of large purple to greenish bracts.

A number of varieties of *Pimelea prostrata* (B) have been described, the plants showing much vegetative diversity in different habitats. It is a New Zealand species with a habitat range from the coast to rocky subalpine areas and requires intensive study to assess the validity of the different varieties described. Some of the more striking are var. *alpina,* which has tiny crowded leaves giving the appearance of mossy shoots, var. *prostrata* with larger leaves but a low prostrate habit, and var. *erecta*, with long, large-leaved, erect shoots about 10 inches (25 cm.) tall. A vigorous rock plant, perhaps assignable to var. *prostrata*—the plant on which the illustration opposite was based—grows at Kew. A shower of green foliage, which in summer bears masses of tiny white delicately scented flowers, is its main attraction. Botanists in New Zealand have noted that some flowers of this species are hermaphrodite, like those depicted here, while others may be functionally male or female, perhaps depending on the plant and habit. Investigation into this feature would also be valuable.

Jonas Carlsson Dryander (1748–1810), a Swedish botanist and one time Librarian to Sir Joseph Banks, is commemorated in the genus *Dryandra*. Found only in the south-western regions of Western Australia, it comprises some fifty-six species with flowers similar to those of the related genus *Banksia* (see below) but differing in having less woody seed capsules and more dense heads of flowers surrounded by basal bracts. *D. drummondii* (C) has flowers that are pale yellow inside and covered with gingery perianth hairs on the outside. The outer flowers of the head open first—the gingery perianth lobes curling back to expose the yellow style and stigma—then the process proceeds inwards towards the middle of the head. Young leaves are frequently covered with hairs which may be lost as the leaf matures. It forms a rosette plant with a short stem and is closely related to *D. calophylla*, with which it has been confused, but lacks the lateral subterranean shoots and smaller flowering heads of that species. Both are found in the Swan river area of south-western Australia.

The famous English naturalist and patron of science Sir Joseph Banks (1743–1820) who sailed with Captain Cook on his first voyage to the Pacific is honoured in the genus *Banksia*, which contains some fifty species found throughout Australia and into New Guinea. Its dense inflorescence spikes, which open from the bottom upwards, have been estimated to contain more than 1000 flowers each. One of the first species described, *B. serrata* (D), grows wild in New South Wales, where Banks and Solander discovered it in Botany Bay in 1770, and in Victoria and Tasmania. The outside of the broader tips of the perianth lobes are hairy and often bluish grey, as shown opposite, but as the flowers open and the lower portions of the lobes and style predominate, a yellow colour becomes more prominent. *B. littoralis* develops into a tree up to 60 foot (18 m.) tall and is found in swampy areas of Western Australia, near King George's Sound. The inflorescences form dignified spikes of yellow. The majority of species are western in distribution, *B. serrata* being one of the relatively few from the east.

In the bud the stigmas of *Grevillea* species become coated with pollen and so, when the flowers open, serve to present the pollen to visiting insects. The genus is a fairly large one with some two hundred and fifty species in all, most of them Australian, though a few occur in New Guinea and the New Hebrides; there is another minor concentration in New Caledonia. In flower *Grevillea* resembles *Hakea*, but differences in the fruit easily distinguish the two genera. *G. alpina* (E) is found in Tasmania, Victoria and New South Wales and has flowers in combinations of yellow and red or pink and red. It was first grown at Kew in 1857 and still grows there in the Australian House.

The Red Spider Flower, *G. punicea* (F), was introduced into western Europe from its native New South Wales in 1825 or even earlier. It is a variable species, as are a number in the genus, and both large- and small-leaved plants are often found.

THYMELAEACEAE

Pimelea ferruginea
A1 flowering stem × $\frac{2}{3}$. A2 flower × $2\frac{2}{3}$.

P. prostrata
B1 flowering stem × $\frac{2}{3}$. B2 flower × $4\frac{2}{3}$.

PROTEACEAE

Dryandra drummondii
C1 part of flowering plant × $\frac{2}{3}$.

Banksia serrata
D1 inflorescence and leaves on part of branch × $\frac{2}{3}$.
D2 open flower × 2.
D3 perianth lobe and stigma × 4.
D4 flower in bud × 3.

Grevillea alpina
E1 flowering stem × $\frac{2}{3}$. E2 flower × 2.

G. punicea, Red Spider Flower
F1 flowering and fruiting stem × $\frac{2}{3}$.
F2 flower opening × 2.
F3 open flower × 2.
F4 anther in tip of perianth lobe × $6\frac{2}{3}$.
F5 young fruit on part of stem × $\frac{2}{3}$.

A2

A1

B1

B2

C1

D2

D3

D4

D1

E1

E2

F1

F2

F3

F4

F5

Plate 135   AUSTRALASIA

With its blue, or blue and white, flowers, *Viola hederacea* (B) remains a recognizable violet, unlike some other Australasian members of its family. In the wild, the small, dainty flowers are to be found, sometimes in spectacularly large numbers, in moist and shady spots at altitudes of up to 7000 feet (2100 m.) among the mountains of eastern and southern Australia and Tasmania. Among the Australasian violets it is the most widely cultivated species and its creeping stolons make garden propagation easy.

Although it is also a member of the family *Violaceae*, *Hybanthus monopetalus* (A) deviates considerably from the familiar violet form, particularly in the shape of the flowers, whose exaggerated lower lips much exceed the smaller lateral petals and sepals. The plant grows in scrub or dry grassland in the same region as the previous species and reaches a height of about 18 inches (46 cm.) if ungrazed. The genus *Hybanthus* contains about one hundred and fifty widely spread tropical and nontropical species.

Discovered by Baron Karl von Hügel, an Austrian botanist who explored the Swan River Colony area in 1833, *Hibiscus huegelii* (D) is a variable and ornamental species that occurs in southern and western Australia. The thickets, up to 7 feet (2·1 m.) tall, which this plant tends to form are generally not found amongst the more arid and jarrah-like vegetation, but by the sides of rivers and streams. The blooms, which appear in September, are sometimes used for house decoration, but do not last long when cut.

Of the same family as *Hibiscus*, but entirely confined to New Zealand *Hoheria* (the name is derived from *Houhere*, one of the Maori names for these plants) is a genus of trees notable for the masses of white blossom with which in season, the branches are weighed down. The species are well worthy of cultivation wherever the local winter climate will permit. *H. lyallii* (E) is found in the South Island in small groups, sometimes as high as the sub-alpine zone in the mountains, and usually near streams. It grows to a height of about 18 feet (5·5 m.) and has densely hairy leaves, twigs and inflorescences. Flowering occurs between November and January and fruiting follows from January to March.

Despite its appearance, that of a free-growing tree, sometimes up to 40 feet (12 m.) tall, *Nuytsia floribunda* (C) is a parasite in the mistletoe family. Confined to Western Australia it is called the Christmas Tree because of the masses of bright orange blossom at Christmas time. Its apparent independence is accounted for by the fact that it is a root parasite attached underground to surrounding species, even grasses. Many adult plants of *Nuytsia* have developed from suckers and they are frequently found in groups. The name was given by Robert Brown in commemoration of Pieter Nuyts, a Dutch navigator who touched on Western Australia (Nuyt's Land) and sailed across the Australian Bight in 1627. There is only the one species in the genus.

VIOLACEAE

Hybanthus monopetalus (syn. *H. filiformis*)
A1 flowering plant × ⅔. A2 flower × 2.

Viola hederacea
B1 flowering plant × ⅔.

LORANTHACEAE

Nuytsia floribunda, Christmas Tree
C1 part of flowering stem × ⅔.
C2 part of leafy stem × ⅔.
C3 flowers and bud × 1⅓.

MALVACEAE

Hibiscus huegelii
D1 flowering shoot × ⅔.
D2 stamens, style and ovary × 1⅓.

Hoheria lyallii
E1 part of flowering twig × ⅔.
E2 apex of style × 6.

A2

A1

B1

C1

C2

C3

D1

D2

E1

E2

Plate 136   AUSTRALASIA

Although the *Epacridaceae* are found in Indo-China, Malaysia and parts of Oceana and South America, its main centre is in Australia and New Zealand, where it replaces the heather family, *Ericaceae*, to which it is closely related. Like heathers, the epacrids often grow in heaths and bogs. The family is broadly divisible into the genera resembling *Epacris*—heather-like shrubs without sheathing leaves and with stems lacking ring-scars; and those shrubs resembling the woody members of *Liliaceae* with sheathing leaves and stems marked with conspicuous ring-scars, (see *Richea* opposite).

There are about forty *Epacris* species distributed in New Caledonia, New Zealand, Tasmania and south-east Australia. The sparsely branched, variable *E. impressa* (A), growing from 1–4 feet (0·3–1·2 m.) tall, bears white, pink or red flowers from April or May until about November. The species was first discovered in 1793 by La Billardière who sailed with D'Entrecastaux in search of La Pérouse, a famous French sailor-explorer who vanished, and occurs in New South Wales, Victoria, and Tasmania, the pink form being the State Flower of Victoria.

Growing in the same states, but also in Queensland, *E. obtusifolia* (B) is a smaller species rising to 3 feet (91 cm.). Found in moist heathy places, its fragrant white flowers have fringed petals, giving them an attractive fluffy appearance. Another white-flowered and scented species, *E. microphylla* (E), has small pointed leaves on slender stems. It occurs in the same areas as the previous species, but a plant from Tasmania with larger leaves has sometimes been included, though it is generally split off nowadays, as a separate species, *E. gunnii*.

One of eleven species found in mainland Australia and Tasmania (unless one considers the genus *Leucopogon* as insufficiently distinct, as do many botanists) *Styphelia tubiflora* (C) comes from New South Wales, and with its red flowers it forms an attractive plant. In temperate regions it may be grown in a cool greenhouse and its cultural requirements are like those of *Epacris*: a peaty, sandy soil but with careful watering. The generic name comes from the Greek *styphelos* 'hard', a reference to the stiff leaves.

There are one hundred and fifty *Leucopogon* species, perhaps better included in *Styphelia*, ranging from Malaysia, through Australasia into New Caledonia. A native of Queensland and New South Wales, *L. melaleucoides* (G) exhibits once more the fringed petals so characteristic of certain epacrids.

The ten *Richea* species, nine from Tasmania and one from Victoria, bear a superficial resemblance to woody monocotyledons. With their somewhat southerly distribution, they prove half hardy in cultivation in Britain, and can be grown in milder regions such as Cornwall and parts of Ireland. The petals of these plants, which should not be confused with the capparaceous *Ritchiea* (see plate 52), are fused together into a little cap which is pushed off the flower as the stamens elongate, and thus never open. *R. dracophylla* (F) is a small, branched shrub, between 5 and 17 feet (1·5–5·2 m.) tall, which occurs only in Tasmania, growing in gullies and forests in the mountains. The sheathing leaves are crowded characteristically at the ends of the naked brown branches and the white inflorescences are subtended by pink or brownish bracts which are shed as the flowers develop. When ripe, the capsular fruit are brown and hard and contain many small seeds.

Another Tasmanian species, *R. scoparia* (D), has white flowers tinted pink or orange. Popularly known as the Kerosene Bush from its strong and pungent smell in flower, this species grows to 5 feet (1·5 m.) tall and has a thin reddish-brown flaky bark. Unlike the closely related *R. gunnii*, also from Tasmania, the leaves of the Kerosene Bush decay very gradually, persisting for a long time on the stems, and as in all richeas, the open flowers appear to lack petals as they are shed as a 'cap' at an early stage of flowering. The genus commemorates the French naturalist Claude Antoine Gaspard Riche (1762–1797), who was a fellow member with La Billardière of the D'Entrecastaux expedition and who got lost in the bush at Esperance Bay, Western Australia. Fortunately he survived by eating berries and turned up alone just as the expedition, having failed to find him by means of a search party under La Billardière, was about to leave.

EPACRIDACEAE

Epacris impressa
A1 part of flowering stem × ⅔.

E. obtusifolia
B1 part of flowering stem × ⅔. B2 flower × 2.
B3 leaf × 2.

Styphelia tubiflora
C1 part of stem with flowers and buds × ⅔.
C2 flower × 1⅓.

Richea scoparia, Kerosene Bush
D1 part of flowering stem × ⅔.

Epacris microphylla
E1 flowering stems on part of branch × ⅔.
E2 immature red leaves on part of stem × ⅔.

Richea dracophylla
F1 part of flowering branch × ⅔. F2 flower × 2.
F3 stamens, style and ovary × 2⅔.

Leucopogon melaleucoides
G1 part of flowering branch × ⅔.
G2 flower × 2⅔. G3 fruits on part of stem × ⅔.
G4 fruit × 2⅔.

A1

B1

B2

B3

C1

C2

D1

E1

F1

F2

F3

G1

G2

G3

G4

Plate 137   AUSTRALASIA

The genus *Eucalyptus* is a large one in number of species (about five hundred) as well as containing the largest hardwood trees in the world; trees over 350 feet (107 m.) have been recorded in *E. regnans*. The leaves produced by seedlings and young plants, the juvenile foliage, is usually quite different from that of adult plants which shows relatively little variation. Likewise, the flowers which usually consist of a mass of whitish stamens are remarkably uniform but the shape and form of the flower buds and the fruits have proved very useful in the recognition of species. The value of eucalypts as timber trees in subtropical and Mediterranean climates is now widely recognized and large plantations are coming to maturity in many of the warmer parts of the world. In Australia, the wood is employed for every possible use, including the cellulose industry, while the aromatic leaves yield oils employed in medicine, perfumery and the manufacture of organic chemicals. A number of species also produce nectar and pollen of great value to bee-keepers.

Typical woodland in Australia is composed of eucalypts, light in undergrowth and shading, though in places the trees grow as isolated standards in rich grassland or form an important component in tall rain forest. Members of the genus are given a variety of general names depending, in part, on the type of bark they possess, for example, 'Gums' are eucalypts whose bark is shed in plates or strips, 'Ironbarks' have deeply fissured, dark coloured, hard surfaces that never peel, and 'Stringy-barks' have untidy, fibrous barks.

Possibly the most colourful of all the species, and one of the most widely cultivated, the Red-flowered Gum, *E. ficifolia* (A) is a relatively small tree with an erect habit that grows to a height of about 30 feet (9 m.), and shows a considerable amount of variation, possibly due to hybridization. In its native Western Australia it flowers from December to February.

A species that provides a good example of the exceedingly tough wood common to many eucalypts is the Yate, *E. cornuta* (C), whose timber has a tensile strength of 17·5 tons per square inch (27·6 kg. per square mm.), only 3 tons (3·05 tonnes) less than wrought iron. It is a medium-sized species, up to about 60 feet (18 m.) in height and its bark is smooth and pale in the upper parts of the tree but darker and more fibrous lower down. The specific epithet alludes to its well developed, horn-like calyx cap (*cornus* 'horn'), which is shed as the flowers open; the blooms, produced in January or February, are plentifully supplied with nectar of great value to

apiarists. In Australia, it is confined to the southernmost areas of Western Australia but, although not the best of plantation trees, it has been successfully introduced into many other parts of the world.

Eucalyptus macrocarpa (E), the Blue Bush, is, despite the fact that it is usually gnarled in habit and rarely more than 13 feet (4 m.) tall, a highly valued decorative shrub, with an attractive mealy bloom to its foliage, and a contrasting dark grey bark on the older stems. The plant was discovered by James Drummond in Swan River Colony about 1839 and first described by Sir William Hooker in 1842. In the same year, the first specimens were raised from seed at Kew, and these bloomed some five years later.

Found in coastal and lowland forest on both islands of New Zealand, *Metrosideros fulgens* (D) is a flaky-barked liana with stems up to 30 feet (9 m.) long and 4 inches (10 cm.) in diameter, clothed with small leaves. The flowering heads and short-lived petals appear at the tips of the branches between February and June but the fruits do not ripen until November to December the following season. The heartwood of several of the sixty species in the genus, yields a hard timber known as 'rata', valued as a fine wood for turning. *Metrosideros* occurs throughout Australasia, Oceana and South Africa, and in parts of Malesia and Chile.

Several of the thirty-five heather-like species of *Darwinia*, all native to Australia, are easily recognized by their prominent nodding 'flowers', which consist in fact of a series of large, coloured bracts completely obscuring the several tiny true flowers at the base of the involucre. *D. meeboldii* (F) was described in 1942, and named after Alfred Karl Meebold (1863–1952), a German botanist, novelist, poet and traveller who collected in the plant's native area, west of the Stirling Range. It grows to a height of 5 or 6 feet (1·5–1·8 m.).

As the name implies (*kalos*, Greek for beautiful and *stemon* for stamen), it is in the long colourful stamens that the beauty of the flowers of *Callistemon*, a genus from Australia and New Caledonia, resides. They are commonly called Bottle-brushes and many, among them the long flowering, brilliant red *C. citrinus* var. *splendens* are widely cultivated and grace glasshouses in temperate areas. *C. brachyandrus* (B) is a tall bush with spreading branches, the flowers either compacted or spread out along the stem, usually for a length of about 2 inches (5 cm.). The inflorescence is never terminal and the continuing growth of the stem leaves the fruit to develop on the older wood.

MYRTACEAE

Eucalyptus ficifolia, Red-flowered Gum
A1 flowering shoot × ⅔. A2 fruits × ⅔.

Callistemon brachyandrus
B1 part of stem with flowers, old flowers and fruits × ⅔.
B2 flower × 2. B3 fruit × 2.

Eucalyptus cornuta, Yate
C1 budding and flowering shoot × ⅔.
C2 fruit × ⅔.

Metrosideros fulgens (syn. *M. florida*, *M. scandens*)
D1 flowering stem × ⅔. D2 fruiting twig × ⅔.

Eucalyptus macrocarpa, Blue Bush
E1 part of flowering stem × ⅔. E2 anther × 6.

Darwinia meeboldii
F1 flowering shoot × ⅔.

A1

A2

B3

B2

B1

C2

C1

D1

D2

E1

E2

F1

Plate 138   AUSTRALASIA

The family *Rutaceae* includes many familiar garden and crop plants, among them the *Citrus* fruits, *Choisya*, *Ruta* (the culinary rue), *Dictamnus* (dittany) and *Skimmia*. The Australian species, however, particularly those genera in the tribe *Boronieae*, are less well known outside the continent where they comprise a characteristic element of the flora, adapted, as they often are, to life in arid surroundings. All the genera represented here, with the exception of *Phebalium* which has one additional species in New Zealand, are endemic to Australia, and all belong to the *Boronieae*.

Known locally as Native Fuchsias, the eleven or so species of *Correa*, named in commemoration of the Portuguese botanist José Francesco Corrêa da Serra (1751–1823), are found in the temperate parts of Australia. George Bentham, in his *Flora Australiensis* (1863–1878), which is still the only work to cover the entire flora of the continent, included *C. reflexa*, *C. reflexa* var. *cardinalis* (C), *C. rubra* and *C. backhousiana* (A) in a species complex which he called *C. speciosa*. Today *C. reflexa* and *C. backhousiana* are considered separate species and the plant, which was known as *C. cardinalis*, is considered a variety of the former. First introduced into western Europe about 1804, it has striking scarlet and yellow flowers and reaches a height of about 3 feet (91 cm.).

Correa backhousiana (A) was named after James Backhouse (1794–1869), a Quaker who collected plants in Australia while on a mission to inspect the penal settlements and report their conditions. He found the species at Cape Grim on the north-west coast of Tasmania in 1833, but it also grows on the islands of the Bass Strait. The greenish yellow flowers and rusty-coloured undersides of the leaves, caused by a woolly vestiture, make the species highly ornamental. Some species are hardy in the mildest parts of western Europe, but in Britain, *C. backhousiana* is generally grown under glass.

The forty species of *Phebalium* mostly form shrubby plants, often with hairy or scaly stems and leaves. *P. squamulosum* (E), a native of New South Wales and Victoria, grows about 2 feet (61 cm.) tall and one of its variants (shown opposite) has larger flowers than most and scurfy fruits. Introduced into Britain about 1824,

this species, like *P. squameum* (syn. *P. billardieri*) which was introduced about 1822, is one of the more commonly cultivated. Another species from New South Wales is *P. rotundifolium* (G) which was first found in the Hunter's river area by Allan Cunningham. It exemplifies those species in the genus which do not possess the typical scurfy scales.

The English botanist James Crowe (1750–1807) of Norwich is commemorated by *Crowea*, a small genus of four Australian species that differs from the related genus *Eriostemon*, which is also closely related to *Phebalium*, in having long, hairy anther-appendages. *C. saligna* (B), which was introduced from its native New South Wales in about 1790, is valued for its large, reddish flowers. It is a cool glasshouse plant and grows to about 3 feet (91 cm.) in height.

The genus *Boronia*, with about seventy species, was named after Francesco Borone (*c.* 1769–1794), a Milanese, first a servant to Sir James Edward Smith (1759–1828) on his Italian journey, then successively botanical assistant to Afzelius in West Africa and to John Sibthorp (1758–1796). Sibthorp, who travelled widely and botanized in Greece and the Levant, originated the magnificent *Flora Graeca* (1806–1840), but the preparation of the text and its publication were due to the diligence of Smith and John Lindley. The purplish brown and yellow flowers of *B. megastigma*, the Scented Boronia, have often been used in the same way as lavender, placed between linen to keep it sweetly fragrant. Together with the rosy flowered *B. heterophylla* and the carmine *B. elatior*, it has been frequently cultivated. *B. granitica* (D) is a compact shrub that grows up to 6 feet (1·8 m.) tall and is often found in granite fissures. It was discovered near Howell in New South Wales in 1905 by J. H. Maiden and J. L. Borman.

Chloanthes contains ten species found in Australia and New Zealand and although it is traditionally classified in the family *Verbenaceae*, it is sometimes separated today in a small family, together with a few related genera, the *Dicrastylidaceae* (syn. *Chloanthaceae*). The erect, shrubby perennial *C. parviflora* (F) is found in Queensland and New South Wales and grows to a height of 2 feet (61 cm.). It is distinguishable from *C. stoechadis* mainly by its shorter, broader corolla.

A1

A3

A4

B2

B1

C1

D1

E2

E3

E1

F2

F1

G2

G1

Plate 139   AUSTRALASIA

A tall, woody climber with twining stems and pinnately divided leaves, *Pandorea pandorana* (C) is one of eight species with a total range from Malaya to Melanesia and Australasia; *P. pandorana*, however, is limited to east and south Australia, including Tasmania, and New Guinea. The climbing habit, the compound leaves and the slightly trumpet-shaped flowers, as well as the capsular fruits up to about 3 inches (7·5 cm.) long, are characteristic of this family, especially the flat, winged seeds that the fruits contain. Another Australian species found along the coasts of New South Wales and Queensland is *P. jasminoides* and together they are known locally as Wonga Wonga Vines and cultivated as attractive coverings for trellises and the like.

In moist and shaded spots in the rain forests of the mountains and coastal areas of New South Wales and Victoria is found *Fieldia australis* (F), a gesneriad and the sole species in its genus. This unspectacular yet attractive and slightly woody perennial was discovered in 1804 by a pioneer explorer of the Blue Mountains, George Caley, a collector for Sir Joseph Banks. His specimen was later deposited, with the rest of his collection, at the British Museum and the species was subsequently rediscovered by Allan Cunningham, who named it after his friend Barron Field, at one time Judge of the Supreme Court of New South Wales. Nevertheless, it was left to Charles Moore of the Sydney Botanic Garden to send live plants to Kew in 1857, where the first flowers in Europe were grown the following year. It forms a tall, climbing shrublet that clings to mossy bark, especially the trunks of tree-ferns, by means of roots that it can put out at need. The leaves are noteworthy as they grow in pairs of unequal length.

A discovery that dates back to Captain Cook's first voyage of exploration in the Pacific is that of *Rhabdothamnus solandri* (G), found by Dr Daniel Carl Solander, a botanist who acted as Sir Joseph Banks' assistant during the expedition. The plant has the distinction of being not merely the only species in its genus, but also the only gesneriad in New Zealand, where it is restricted to North Island. The shape of its 5 unequal corolla lobes, which resemble those of the New World species *Columnea jamaicensis*, led Solander to mistake it for a representative of that genus and the plant was at one time known as *C. scabrosa*. Tauropo, as it is called locally, forms a many branched shrub, standing about 6 feet (1·8 m.) tall, with slender-stalked, grey-green leaves scattered with stiff hairs. The flowers which spring singly from the leaf axils, vary in colour from bright orange to yellow,

veined with red. After the original discovery by Solander in 1769, the species was rediscovered by Allan Cunningham in 1826 and introduced into England in 1831.

Another botanist on an early expedition to Australasia, Leschenault de la Tour, who accompanied Captain Baudin's expedition to Australia (1800–1804), is honoured in the genus *Leschenaultia*, which contains twenty species endemic to Australia. The most famed of these is the Blue Leschenaultia, *L. biloba* (B), a delicate shrub or subshrub 2 to 3 feet (61–91 cm.) tall, with slender, grey-green leaves and indescribably blue flowers whose pointed lobes are veined with parallel, transverse lines. The hills of the Darling Range in Western Australia, where this species occurs, are noted for their spectacular beauty when this plant is in flower. Other species are almost as attractive with red, yellow or white flowers which provide splendid blazes of colour but which usually require careful cultivation when grown in gardens.

Trigger-plants are so called because of the rapid flick of the column when touched or triggered-off by a visiting insect. This column protrudes from the flower and bears the stamens and stigma. In the 'cocked' position it is kinked at the base and sticks out to one side between two of the petals. Then, when an insect attempts to take nectar from the flower, the sensitive base, irritated by its touch, straightens instantaneously and swings the stamens and stigma through an arc, hitting the animal and showering it with pollen. As the flower ages, the stamens shrivel but the stigma protrudes from the end of the column, ready to be brushed by insects already covered in pollen. A number of small appendages and colour markings situated at the entrance to the throat of the corolla, serve as a nectar guide for the insects. *Stylidium breviscapum* (A), to whose genus 90% of the *Stylidiaceae* belong, is a Western Australian species known as the Boomerang Trigger-plant. It is a creeping plant and the old stems develop thickened nodes from which grow wiry, black roots. Another species from the same area is the 16 inch (41 cm.) tall *S. spathulatum* (D). The rosette of leaves at its base is covered with green, yellow or brown glandular hairs. The fleshy leaves that cluster about the base of the scape of *S. crassifolium* (E) have given it the name of Thick-leaved Trigger-plant. It grows to a height of 2 feet (61 cm.) and comes from the same part of Australia as the two previously mentioned species, where it is found near wet flushes and drying creek beds, especially following bush fires.

STYLIDIACEAE

Stylidium breviscapum, Boomerang Trigger-plant
A1 flowering shoots × ⅔.
A2 old stem with wiry roots × ⅔.

S. spathulatum
D1 flowering plant × ⅔. D2 flower × 2.

S. crassifolium, Thick-leaved Trigger-plant
E1 part of flowering stem × ⅔.
E2 base of plant with roots × ⅔.

GOODENIACEAE

Leschenaultia biloba, Blue Leschenaultia
B1 flowering stem × ⅔.

BIGNONIACEAE

Pandorea pandorana, Wonga Wonga Vine
C1 flowering shoot × ⅔.
C2 fruit × ⅔. C3 seed × ⅔.

GESNERIACEAE

Fieldia australis
F1 part of flowering stem × ⅔.

Rhabdothamnus solandri, Tauropo
G1 flowering shoot × ⅔. G2 anthers × 2.

A1

A2

B1

C1

C2

C3

D1

D2

E1

E2

F1

G1

G2

Plate 140   AUSTRALASIA

One of a number of ornamental Australasian daisies now grown in American and west European gardens, *Celmisia hookeri* (D) is a large tufted plant inhabiting mountain grassland and open scrub and confined to north-east Otago, South Island, New Zealand. The upper sides of the somewhat leathery leaves are dark green and hairless, the undersides, with their prominent midribs and veins, are covered, like the flower stalks and involucral bracts, with a white or buff coloured felt. Another species that deserves wider cultivation, though it suffers the drawback, in a gardening context, of developing to its fullest only under subalpine conditions, is *C. coriacea*, discovered on the South Island by J. G. A. Forster (1754–1794) while on Captain Cook's second voyage. The leaves are about the same length as those of the preceding species but more leathery, and hairy on both the upper and lower sides. The flowering heads measure about 4 inches (10 cm.) in diameter and have white outer and yellow inner florets. *C. traversii* is found only in the subalpine pastures of the northern part of South Island and has leaves with a hairless upper surface with purple midrib, and a brownish, velvety undersurface. The flowering stalks are similarly covered with a brownish velvet, and the sheathing portions of the basal leaves are lined with silky white hairs. The genus *Celmisia* has sixty-five species from Australia, Tasmania and New Zealand.

Certain species of the New Zealand genera *Haastia* and *Raoulia* (not illustrated) bear the common name Vegetable Sheep because the large, dense clumps of these cushion plants could easily be mistaken, at a distance, for sheep. The tussocks, which consist of numerous small branches closely packed together to afford mutual protection against the weather, are coloured pale brown by the hairs which cover the small leaves. Tussocks may measure about 5 feet (1·5 m.) in diameter and, over the whole surface, each shoot produces a single, minute flower, only a millimetre or so across. *Raoulia* has smaller leaves than *Haastia* and also differs in having anther sacs which are attenuated into tail-like streamers. All three species of *Haastia* are endemic to New Zealand, although only one, *H. pulvinaris*, has the Vegetable Sheep habit.

Similarly most of the twenty-five species of *Raoulia* are endemic to New Zealand but there are also one or two in New Guinea.

Brachycome, a genus of some seventy-five species, includes the delicate Swan River Daisy, *B. iberidifolia* (B), a wiry annual that has been cultivated in western Europe since about 1843. The ray-florets may be white, pink or blue, with darker coloured disc-florets.

Also found in the same area, and indeed in all states of Australia, *Helichrysum bracteatum* (E) is a coarse, erect perennial growing to a height of about 3 feet (91 cm.) with branching stems that terminate in large yellow, brown, white or purple capitula, the colour derived from the chaffy involucral bracts that also make the heads 'everlasting', and are responsible for the plant's common names of Everlasting Flower and Yellow Paper Daisy. In Britain the species flowers throughout the summer and into the autumn, until killed by frost.

Craspedia consists of about seven Australian or New Zealand species. *C. uniflora* (A) occurs in Tasmania, temperate Australia and New Zealand, usually as an annual, but sometimes perennial, with tufted leaves at the base and smaller leaves clasping the stem. The spherical inflorescences, the origin of the common names Bachelor's Buttons and Billy Buttons, are yellow in this species but whitish in others, and made up of numerous clusters of florets, each of which consists of 3 to 8 blooms surrounded by 4 or 5 oval bracteoles. The whole is itself surrounded at the base by several somewhat leafy bracts. After the flowers have withered, the fruits or achenes develop, with a plumed pappus of hairs.

A native of sandy habitats in New South Wales, *Ammobium alatum* (C) is another member of the daisy family with a curious habit, the coarse stems being enlarged by the addition of membranous wings. The small heads of flowers are surrounded by a number of rows of papery involucral bracts, the outer unstalked, the inner stalked, making the inflorescences everlasting, like those of *Helichrysum*. The achenes bear a pappus of 2 scales and 2 bristles. The species, one of two, both endemic to Australia, was discovered in 1804 by Robert Brown and introduced to Britain eighteen years later.

COMPOSITAE

Craspedia uniflora, Bachelor's Buttons, Billy Buttons
A1 flowering plant × $\frac{2}{3}$.
A2 flower head from below × $\frac{2}{3}$. A3 floret × 4.

Brachycome iberidifolia, Swan River Daisy
B1 flowering stem × $\frac{2}{3}$. B2 ray-floret × $3\frac{1}{4}$.
B3 disc-floret × 6.

Ammobium alatum
C1 part of flowering stem × $\frac{2}{3}$.
C2 floret and bracteoles × 6.
C3 fruiting head × $\frac{2}{3}$.
C4 fruiting floret and bracteoles × 6.
C5 leaves and part of rootstock × $\frac{2}{3}$.

Celmisia hookeri
D1 part of flowering plant × $\frac{2}{3}$.
D2 ray-floret × $1\frac{1}{3}$. D3 disc-floret × $1\frac{1}{3}$.

Helichrysum bracteatum, Everlasting Flower, Yellow Paper Daisy
E1 part of flowering stem × $\frac{2}{3}$. E2 floret × 4.

A1 A2 A3 B1 B2 B3 C1 C2 C3 C4 C5 D1 D2 D3 E1 E2

Plate 141   AUSTRALASIA

The only member of a genus classified by some botanists in the same family as the rushes, *Juncaceae* (plates 7 and 25), and by others with the Black Boys, *Xanthorrhoeaceae* (plate 142), *Calectasia cyanea* (B) grows in the two southern parts of Australia, separated for over a thousand miles (1610 km.) by the Great Australian Bight. Commonly called the Blue Tinsel Lily, it is a variable plant, usually forming a wiry densely branched shrublet about 12 inches (30 cm.) or more tall. These branches are clothed with the sharply pointed leaves and the remains of the previous year's foliage. The single flowers, which appear between September and November, are borne at the ends of the twigs and their shiny, papery 'petals', and bright yellow stamens turning red or brown with age, are held horizontally when the flower is fully open. The fruit does not open to release the single seed, but is retained indefinitely within the hardened perianth tube, which protects it from a harsh environment and ensures that germination does not occur immediately. This 'delayed germination', an adaptation often found in arid places, has the advantage of preventing the destruction of a whole population of seedlings, which would probably occur in adverse conditions if all the seeds germinated at the same time. The plants from western Victoria and southern South Australia have a more extensive rhizome system, also differing in one or two other ways and have recently been differentiated from the Western Australian populations as var. *intermedia*.

Most of the twenty or so species of the Fringed-lily genus, *Thysanotus*, are found in Australia. The generic name comes from the Greek *thysanos* meaning a fringe, referring to the 3 inner lobes of the perianth which are edged with hair-like appendages. The flowering stalks of these tufted rhizomatous plants are longer than the grass-like leaves and sometimes branched. In the illustrated species, *T. multiflorus* (A), the inflorescence stalks vary from 12 to 18 inches (30–46 cm.) tall and are usually unbranched as shown, although a second branch may arise below the terminal cluster of flowers. The species grows in Western Australia, particularly on the Darling Range and has purple flowers with very thin outer 'petals', and unlike many other species, has only 3 stamens in each flower; *T. juncifolius* (syn. *T. junceus*) from New South Wales and Victoria, for example, has flowers with 3 short and 3 longer stamens. The flowers of all Fringed-lilies are short-lived, soon withering into small twisted remnants, and in order to identify the species, one needs to examine the roots, the basal leaves, as well as the flowers.

The two species of the genus *Xeronema*, one from New Zealand and the other from New Caledonia, are striking herbs with clusters of iris-like leaves and a long inflorescence stalk bearing a one-sided mass of bright red flowers. Both are rare plants but well worth cultivation although they take some time to reach the flowering stage. In New Caledonia *X. moorei* grows amongst ultra-basic rocks at altitudes between 3000 and 6000 feet (900–1830 m.). This plant, named after its discoverer Charles Moore (1820–1905), one time director of the Royal Botanic Garden, Sydney, was introduced as a cool glasshouse plant into Europe in 1875 by J. Linden. The flowers are highly valued for their decorative appearance and they retain their colour for a month or more. The other member of the genus, *X. callistemon* (C) was found in 1924 on Poor Knight's Island off the northern coast of New Zealand and was first described for science two years later. It is very similar to *X. moorei* and the two may be no more than geographical subspecies. The flower heads, up to 12 inches (30 cm.) long, are borne at the end of an inflorescence stalk of about 2 feet (61 cm.); as many as 11 separate inflorescences have been produced from the same plant in cultivation. Within the lily family, Dr John Hutchinson has related *Xeronema*, as well as *Thysanotus*, to the same tribe as *Asphodelus* and *Asphodeline* (see plate 41).

There are some twenty-five species in the genus *Astelia*, distributed throughout Australasia and Oceana into New Guinea. While a few species inhabit the ground, most of them are noted epiphytes, perched on branches high in trees, a very unusual feature in the *Liliaceae*. Male and female flowers are borne on separate plants in dense cream or purplish panicles which, in some species, may be 5 feet (1·5 m.) long. The female plants are later decorated with many small shiny berries which vary in colour from red, through yellow to dull green and, being sweet and edible, once formed part of the diet of the Maoris and other Polynesians, and indeed are still eaten. The Perching Lily, *A. solandri* (D) is also known by its Maori name 'Kowhara-whara'. It is a grass-like epiphyte in trees from North Cape, North Island to Westland, South Island, New Zealand, at altitudes up to 3300 feet (1000 m.). The sweetly scented flowers appear in January and February, the male inflorescences being about a foot (30 cm.) long and the female ones slightly smaller. The fruits which take about twelve months to mature, are eaten by birds who help to distribute the seeds, as they fly from tree to tree; thus new colonies are formed.

LILIACEAE

Thysanotus multiflorus
A1 flowering plant (stem cut) × $\frac{2}{3}$.

Xeronema callistemon
C1 flowering plant (stem cut) × $\frac{2}{3}$.
C2 habit sketch × $\frac{1}{15}$.

Astelia solandri, Perching Lily
D1 male inflorescence and leaves × $\frac{2}{3}$.
D2 male flower × $2\frac{2}{3}$.
D3 fruiting inflorescence × $\frac{2}{3}$.
D4 fruiting flower × $2\frac{2}{3}$.

XANTHORRHOEACEAE

Calectasia cyanea, Blue Tinsel Lily
B1 part of flowering shoot × $\frac{2}{3}$.
B2 petal × $2\frac{2}{3}$.

A1

B2

B1

C1

C2

D1

D2

D3

D4

Plate 142   AUSTRALASIA

Of the monocotyledons which form a conspicuous part of the Australasian vegetation *Cordyline*, the Palm-lily genus, with its small lily-like flowers, borne on plants with a palm-like habit, is one of the most characteristic. So too is the genus *Dianella* with its panicles of small flowers, its berry fruits and its tough, lance-shaped leaves. *Xanthorrhoea*, the genus of Grass-trees or Black Boys, is a unique group found only in Australia and allied to the rushes, *Juncaceae*. Black Boys have a novel method of manufacturing their own trunks: in the absence of the usual wood and bark they exude resin which cements the leaf bases together.

Cordyline, a genus of about fifteen species found in warm temperate areas, has a centre of diversity in Australasia and Oceana. Its habit resembles that of *Dracaena* but the former has a conspicuously bracteate inflorescence, ovaries with 6 to 15 ovules in each chamber (as opposed to 1 in *Dracaena*) and a creeping rootstock. A native of Queensland and New South Wales, *C. stricta* (A) is sometimes grown in glasshouses in the cool temperate areas of western Europe. Slender panicles of lilac to bright blue flowers arise from its slender corrugated stems topped with delicate foliage. The creeping rootstock must be periodically trimmed or it may produce too many shoots.

A species more frequently encountered in cultivation is New Zealand's *C. australis*, which is hardy enough to grow in the warmer parts of western Europe, such as southern Ireland and Cornwall, where the isolated plants suggest a tropical environment. In their native habitat they attain a height of up to 40 feet (12 m.) and bear spear-shaped evergreen leaves up to 3 feet (91 cm.) long in clusters at the ends of branches. They form an important component in certain semi-arid types of New Zealand vegetation and their resistance to dessication and rough treatment is impressive. One account tells of felled *C. australis* trees which languished on a beach for eight months, swamped by tides and beaten by fierce sun, only to be washed up on fresh soil where they began to root and sent out shoots once more. Chips of the 'wood' produced by felling have also been known to root and become established. It was probably early European colonists who coined the term 'Cabbage-tree' for the species, as the tender young parts were used as a vegetable, in the same way as the 'hearts' of palm-shoots are eaten in parts of the world.

There are fifteen species of *Xanthorrhoea* found only in Australia. These slow-growing plants have the appearance of dense clumps of grass borne on tree trunks. These 'trunks' consist of innumerable old leaf-bases impregnated with exuded resin. When the leaves first emerge they are erect, as they age they bend over and produce the characteristic habit shown opposite. The individual leaf is long, thin and brittle and when viewed in cross-section it may be square, triangular or almost flat. From the centre of the crown of leaves emerges a naked stalk on which is borne a dense spike of flowers, each of which is embedded in a ring of short, erect, chaffy bracts together with a less numerous and usually longer type of bract. The 6 petals are so short that they scarcely emerge above the general level of the bract although the 6 white stamens protrude well above the bract level and are set off against the dull brown bracts. The withered perianth continues to invest the pale brown fruit which contains a number of flat, black seeds; these are released, when the capsule opens, by means of three valves.

When young, *X. australis* (C) has no trunk, but later it may produce one up to 20 feet (6 m.) in height, often with several branches. A crown of greyish leaves encircles the flowering spike, in this species longer than the stalk that supports it. Found in Queensland, New South Wales, Victoria, South Australia and Tasmania, it thrives in open scrub, open woodland or dry heath. *X. arborea*, with a trunk up to 6 feet (1·8 m.) tall, has a more slender flowering spike; smaller still are *X. minor* and *X. macronema* which at no stage possess a trunk and consequently only attain a height of 2 to 3 feet (61–91 cm.).

The genus *Kingia* from Western Australia, with only one species, is quite as curious as *Xanthorrhoea* and is also similar in appearance but its flowering-spike is fat and clustered, resembling that of certain South American bromeliads.

Open woodland is the most common habitat of the thirty species of *Dianella*, a genus of Australasian and Oceanic distribution. Long narrow leaves spring from a stout rhizomatous rootstock and large panicles of white or blue flowers are followed by globular or egg-shaped berries, often bright blue in colour. *D. tasmanica* (B), as its name suggests, is a native of Tasmania. It is valued for its bright blue fruit which hangs for several weeks on delicate stalks and, like most species in this genus, it has shiny and rigid leaves with spiny edges. The clumps may grow to a height of 5 feet (1·5 m.).

AGAVACEAE

Cordyline stricta
A1 part of flowering stem × ⅔. A2 flower × 4.
A3 lower stem and leaves × ⅔.

LILIACEAE

Dianella tasmanica
B1 fruiting plant × ⅔.
B2 part of panicle × ⅔. B3 flower × 2⅔.

XANTHORROEACEAE

Xanthorrhoea australis
C1 inflorescence and leaves × ⅔.
C2 leaf tip × 1⅓. C3 flower × 2.
C4 fruit × 2. C5 habit sketch × 1/70.

A1

A2

A3

B1

B2

B3

C1

C2

C3

C4

C5

Plate 143   AUSTRALASIA

Kangaroo-paws are found only in Australia and representatives of two of the genera are shown on this and the following plate. Unusually for monocotyledons, they have hairy flowers which are long-lasting and a perianth which is divided asymmetrically. *Blandfordia*, another genus found only in Australia, is noted for its brightly coloured bell-shaped flowers. In *Crinum*, with species found throughout the world, one sees the type of monocotyledon more familiar to the eyes of north temperate plantsmen: short-lasting flowers, often with white or pastel colours.

Named after George Spencer-Churchill (1766–1840), Marquis of Blandford and later the 5th Duke of Marlborough, the genus *Blandfordia* has four species, commonly called Christmas Bells. *B. punicea* (A) is found only on Tasmania, where it grows in sandy places or acidic moorland from the coast up to about 4000 feet (1220 m.). The coarse leaves are narrow with rough edges and about 18 inches (46 cm.) long whereas the leafy flower stalk grows to 3 feet (91 cm.). It is terminated by a cluster of yellow and scarlet flowers, each about $1\frac{3}{4}$ inches (44 mm.) long—scarlet outside, except for the yellow margins of the 3 inner perianth lobes, and yellow inside. The capsular fruit, about $1\frac{1}{2}$ inches (38 mm.) long, are often surrounded by the withered remains of the perianth. Two lovely species from New South Wales are *B. nobilis* and *B. grandiflora*, but these have fewer flowered heads than *B. punicea*.

Of the hundred or so species of *Crinum* found in tropical and subtropical parts of the world, only five or six occur in Australia. Growing in coastal areas of North Australia and Queensland, *C. asiaticum* has stalkless, or nearly stalkless white flowers with long exserted stamens. This species also occurs as far west as northern India and on some of the Pacific islands. Its wide distribution, especially where it grows near the coast, may partly be explained by the corky covering to the seeds which undoubtedly helps in water dispersal. *C. flaccidum* (B) from New South Wales and South Australia, was discovered near the Macquarie Ranges. It was introduced to Britain about 1819 by Barron Field, a New South Wales Supreme Court Judge. Unlike *C. asiaticum*, the 5–8 flowers are stalked although borne on an inflorescence stalk of about the same length, 18 inches (46 cm.). The perianth lobes of its fragrant white flowers are the broadest of all the Australian species. In Australia, the crinums are a variable group and require further study.

Macropidia is closely related to the larger genus of Kangaroo-paws, *Anigozanthos* (plate 144) but has a superior ovary with single-seeded carpels and irregularly fragmenting fruit while the latter has an inferior ovary with carpels several-seeded and a fruit opening by 3 small apical valves. The Black Kangaroo-paw, *M. fuliginosa* (C), is a native of Western Australia and the only species in the genus. The leaves, up to 12 inches (30 cm.) long, spring from a short thick rhizome and the flowering stems grow up to 4 feet (1·2 m.) tall, the upper parts and flower buds being covered with black woolly hairs. J. Drummond noted, when sending his discovery to Europe, that the plant 'is a real mourning flower', yet as the perianth expands, the blackness gives way to a yellow or whitish coloration, due to the hairs on the inside.

LILIACEAE

Blandfordia punicea, Christmas Bells
A1 part of flowering stalk with leaves × $\frac{2}{3}$.
A2 fruit × $\frac{2}{3}$.

AMARYLLIDACEAE

Crinum flaccidum
B1 inflorescence and leaves × $\frac{2}{3}$.

HAEMODORACEAE

Macropidia fuliginosa (syn. *Anigozanthos fuliginosus*, *M. fumosa*), Black Kangaroo-paw
C1 part of flowering and budding stems × $\frac{2}{3}$.
C2 lower part of stem, leaves and roots × $\frac{2}{3}$.
C3 flower × 2.
C4 detail showing black and yellow hairs × 8.
C5 black hair × 24.

A1

2

B1

C1

C2

C3

C4

C5

Plate 144   AUSTRALASIA

The exotic blooms of *Anigozanthos* species are as characteristically Australian as the haunting paintings of Sidney Nolan. Australia, a continent so long separated from other land masses, has evolved its own unique fauna and flora: animals with strange habits, plants with often fantastic appearances.

Further east, in New Zealand, an equally distinctive flora has evolved, often dominated by ferns and small-flowered berry-bearing shrubs. While many agaves and yuccas occur in the New World, New Zealand possesses its own colourful counterpart in the genus *Phormium*. Just over two hundred years ago, during Captain Cook's first voyage, *P. tenax* was discovered.

Anigozanthos, the Kangaroo-paw genus, comprises about ten species confined to Western Australia, with very strangely formed flowers. The perianth is inserted on top of the ovary and 6 protruding stamens are inserted at the top of the tube which is split on the lower side. There are more than 2 seeds to be found in each of the 3 cavities in the ovary. The common Green Kangaroo-paw, *A. manglesii*, is the State Flower of Western Australia, and has red stems and a red base to the otherwise dark green tube of the flower, with pale green reflexed segments. It is named after Robert Mangles, an Englishman in whose garden at Whitmore Lodge, Berkshire, it was raised in 1833 from seeds sent by the governor of the Swan River Colony, Western Australia. It does not persist in cultivation for many years, unlike other species which flourish and produce large clumps.

Anigozanthos flavidus, the Albany Kangaroo-paw (A), is a variable species and the flowers appear green, yellowish or red, depending on the number of the red, branched hairs present on the outside of the perianth; the grey interior makes a peculiar contrast to the greens and reds of the outer parts. Plants of this species grow up to 6 feet (1·8 m.) tall.

The Black Kangaroo-paw, *Macropidia fuliginosa* is shown on the previous plate and, like the Albany Kangaroo-paw, is found only in Western Australia. Other strange and beautiful plants in this family, also confined to Western Australia, are *Blancoa canescens*, the Red Bugle, with pendulous dull red tubular flowers and *Conostylis*, a genus of about twenty-five species with usually yellowish woolly flowers and a tufted habit.

The two species of the New Zealand Flax genus, *Phormium*, are native in New Zealand and one of them is also found in Norfolk Island. The dull red flowered *P. tenax* tends to be the larger species with leaves often 6–9 feet (1·8–2·7 m.) long and flowering stalks from 12–15 feet (3·7–4·6 m.) long. *P. colensoi* (B), illustrated here, is generally smaller with much yellower flowers. The two species are most easily distinguished by their 3-angled capsules: those of *P. tenax* are stout, erect and straight while those of *P. colensoi* are long, twisted and droop. Both species are found throughout New Zealand but the former is more common in lowland and swamp habitats, while the illustrated plant grows in open heath and montane scrub. Hybrids between them are known. The leaves of both plants contain fibres which are strong and used for plaiting and cordage, although those of *P. tenax* are superior in length and strength. These fibres were extensively used by the Maoris, before the colonisation of New Zealand by Europeans, for making clothes and cord. Their quality excited the admiration of Sir Joseph Banks on Captain Cook's first voyage immediately after landing in New Zealand in 1769, being as he said 'of a strength so superior to hemp. . . shining almost as silk and surprisingly strong'. Hence J. R. and G. Forster gave the genus the name *Phormium* (from the Greek *phŏrmiŏn*, a mat or a plant used for mat-making, this from *phŏrmŏs*, anything plaited of rushes or reeds) with reference to its textile use. The epithet *colensoi* commemorates the Reverend William Colenso (1811–1899), a printer who went out to New Zealand in 1833 and there translated and printed the New Testament into the Maori language. He was ordained in 1844 as a missionary and became a pioneer New Zealand botanist. *P. tenax* grows well in the British Isles, particularly in the west of England and in Ireland, where splendid clumps grow in the grounds of Malahide Castle near Dublin, and at National Botanic Gardens, Glasnevin, Dublin.

Belonging to the same family as New Zealand Flax, *Doryanthes excelsa* has leaves about 4 feet (1·2 m.) long, borne in a cluster of 100 or more, and a single inflorescence stalk up to 18 feet (5·5 m.) tall. The globular inflorescence, about 1 foot (30 cm.) in diameter, is composed of several small clusters of 3–4 maroon-red flowers, with petals of about $5\frac{1}{2}$ inches (14 cm.) long and stamens of about 4 inches (10 cm.). This native of New South Wales, as can be imagined, is an imposing sight. It was first flowered in Europe in 1814 in the glasshouse of Charles Long, at Bromley Hill, Kent.

HAEMODORACEAE

Anigozanthos flavidus, Albany Kangaroo-paw
A1 part of flowering stem and leaves × $\frac{2}{3}$.
A2 anther × 4. A3 flower × $1\frac{1}{3}$. A4 hair × 6.

AGAVACEAE

Phormium colensoi
B1 inflorescence and leaves × $\frac{2}{3}$.
B2 habit sketch × $\frac{1}{14}$.
B3 style and ovary × $1\frac{1}{3}$. B4 flower × $1\frac{1}{3}$.
B5 fruits × $\frac{2}{3}$. B6 seed × 2.

A1

A2

A3

A4

B1

B2

B3

B4

B5

B6

Plate 145   AUSTRALASIA

Many Australasian orchids are terrestrial plants, and are often small. In the tropical parts of Queensland and Northern Territory epiphytic types appear, but as much of Australia is dry and arid, the terrestrial types predominate.

Caleana nigrita (D), called Flying Ducks, is a native of Western Australia in jarrah and mallee country, where its colouring makes the plant scarcely noticeable against the ironstone ground on which it grows. The sepals and petals are inconspicuous, but the column is pouch-like and a hinged lip fits the mouth of this pouch. The lip is irritable, and when at rest is poised above the mouth of the pouch. When an insect enters the pouch, the lip flicks down vertically to trap the animal. Inside the pouch the trapped animal picks up pollen before it is able to escape, and in this way pollination is facilitated. The lip is sufficiently sprung to grip a needle or pin when clamped over the pouch-like column. The genus *Caleana* comprises five species found in Australia and New Zealand, and commemorates George Caley (c. 1770–1829), who began as a stable-boy but, thanks to Sir Joseph Banks' encouragement, became an important plant collector.

The eighty species in the genus *Caladenia* range from Malaysia through Australasia into New Caledonia; over half are natives of Western Australia. Most have a single hairy leaf and characteristically elongated spidery petal lobes. *C. filamentosa*, the Red Spider Orchid (G), flowers between July and September in a range extending from south Queensland through New South Wales, Victoria and Tasmania into South Australia and Western Australia. It is a variable species, sometimes having yellow flowers, sometimes having extra-small purple flowers.

The Beard Orchid is aptly named, the lip being ciliate and much resembling a little beard. This species is *Calochilus robertsonii* (C), one of eleven found in Australia, New Zealand, New Guinea and New Caledonia. Found in New South Wales, Victoria, Tasmania and Western Australia, the Beard Orchid blooms in October or November and may grow to 18 inches (46 cm.).

Corybas rivularis (F) is a native of New Zealand, where it is found in both the North and South Islands. The species is one of fifty in Australasia and the Indomalaysian area. *C. rivularis* is hardly more than $2\frac{1}{2}$ inches (6·4 cm.) tall, and very delicate, growing in damp wooded ravines from sea level to about 2000 feet (610 m.). The long filamentous tips to the petals and lateral sepals and the attenuated leaf tip distinguish this species from others in New Zealand.

The most widespread *Pterostylis* species in New Zealand is *P. banksii* (E) which grows up to 18 inches (46 cm.) high in shady places, and is very variable. Flowering in October or November, only a solitary flower being produced on each plant, the blooms are inconspicuous amongst the grassy foliage, being green with a reddish tinge. There are about ninety-five species in the genus with a range from New Guinea into Australasia and New Caledonia.

The genus *Elythranthera* comprises two species native to Western Australia. *E. brunonis* (H), known as the Purple Enamel Orchid because of its glossy flowers, is a widespread and common plant flowering between August and December. Efforts to introduce it into gardens have been repeatedly unsuccessful.

Cymbidium canaliculatum (A) grows in Queensland, New South Wales and Western Australia, and is frequently epiphytic. The purplish-red and green flowers are borne in racemes about 12 inches (30 cm.) long and the leaves are the same length. First discovered by Robert Brown in the Cape York area, *C. canaliculatum* was introduced into cultivation by John Veitch (1839–1870) during the period 1864–1866 when he travelled in Australia and the South Sea Islands. (He was one of the first Europeans to reach the summit of Fujiyama when he visited Japan in 1860.)

Dendrobium discolor (B), sometimes called *D. undulatum*, is a native of Queensland and Northern Territory. The tropical nature of this species is attested by its cultivation in Java. The racemes are sometimes longer than 18 inches (46 cm.) and bear 30 or more flowers with attractively crisped petals. The leaves are thick and leathery, and rooted on rocks these plants may grow very large, up to 10 feet (3 m.) tall.

ORCHIDACEAE

Cymbidium canaliculatum
A1 flowering plant (stem cut) × $\frac{2}{3}$.

Dendrobium discolor (syn. *D. undulatum*)
B1 flowering spike × $\frac{2}{3}$.
B2 upper stem of pseudobulb with leaves × $\frac{2}{3}$.

Calochilus robertsonii, Beard Orchid
C1 part of flowering stem × $\frac{2}{3}$.

Caleana nigrita, Flying Ducks
D1 flowering plant × $\frac{2}{3}$.
D2 flower with closed lip × $\frac{2}{3}$.

Pterostylis banksii
E1 part of flowering stem × $\frac{2}{3}$.
E2 different view of flower × $\frac{2}{3}$. E3 fruit × $\frac{2}{3}$.

Corybas rivularis
F1 flowering plant × $\frac{2}{3}$. F2 flower × 2.

Caladenia filamentosa, Red Spider Orchid
G1 part of flowering stem with bud × $\frac{2}{3}$.

Elythranthera brunonis, Purple Enamel Orchid
H1 flowering plant × $\frac{2}{3}$.

A1

B2

B1

E3

E1

E2

C1

D2

D1

G1

F1

F2

H1

Plate 146   OCEANA

The humid mountain forests of the Hawaiian islands are the home of an as yet unexplained concentration of woody lobelias, mostly belonging to endemic genera. Their often limited or local distribution parallels the situation in the *Lobelia* species of the East African mountains, where remoteness and isolation appear to have led to a diversity of distinct but clearly related species.

The four species in the rare genus *Brighamia* grow, or in some cases, grew, only on the islands of Lanai, Molokai, Maui, Niihau and Kauai, either on sea-cliffs, sometimes within range of the spray, or on the sides of steep inland ravines. The smooth, fleshy and tapering trunk of *B. rockii* (D) is about 15 feet (4·6 m.) in height, and filled with watery sap. It ends in a disproportionately small, cabbage-like cluster of thick leaves from whose centre arise the flower stalks. The flowers, of which there may be as many as 15 on one plant, are reminiscent of those of *Hippobroma* (plate 172) and are said to have a scent of violets. Despite a superficial appearance to the contrary, the flowers are bilaterally symmetrical, 2 of the corolla lobes being a little longer than the others. The white anthers can be seen at the entrance to the corolla tube. The fruit takes the form of a capsule, about ¾ inch (2 cm.) long when mature.

Named after the Marquis de Clermont-Tonnerre, sometime Minister of the French Navy, *Clermontia* contains twenty-seven known species, all of them confined to the Hawaiian islands. The many-branched *C. parviflora* (B) is a variable shrub about 9 feet (2·7 m.) tall with 3 to 20 variously sized flowers hanging in clusters from the old leaf axils. The species grows in rain forest at altitudes of between 600 and 3000 feet (180–2750 m.) on the mountains of Hawaii and Oahu. *C. arborescens* (A) is an altogether larger plant, growing to a height of 25 feet (7·6 m.), with massive, fleshy, strongly arched flowers that are among the largest in the genus. The fruits mature into orange-yellow spherical berries holding pale yellow seeds. All parts of the plant exude a copious latex when cut. *C. arborescens* is a common plant in the moist forests of Maui and Molokai and is found, although more rarely, on Lanai.

A tall forest tree from Fiji, *Elaeocarpus storckii* (C) is notable for its large, handsome, drooping flowers and for the resin, which, like other species in the genus, it secretes from its tissues. The fruit (see C2) takes the form of a deep-purple drupe with 3 to 5 chambers, each containing a single seed. Polynesia is, in fact, the easternmost limit for the genus—to the west it stretches through Australasia into tropical Asia; a South East Asian species is shown on plate 116.

CAMPANULACEAE

Clermontia arborescens
A1 part of flowering stem × ⅔.
A2 staminal tube with 2 stamens removed and showing style and stigma within × ⅔.
A3 united anthers × 1⅓.

C. parviflora
B1 part of flowering stem × ⅔.

Brighamia rockii
D1 leaves and inflorescences at top of trunk × ⅔.
D2 habit sketch × 1/36.

ELAEOCARPACEAE

Elaeocarpus storckii
C1 flowering shoot × ⅔. C2 fruit × ⅔.

A3

B1

A1

C2

C1

D2

D1

Plate 147   OCEANA

Of all the Hawaiian *Leguminosae*, few species are more attractive than *Strongylodon lucidus* (B) with its showy red flowers and twining woody habit. *Hibiscus insularis* (A) is another decorative species, as is the relative of the heathers, *Paphia vitiensis* (C) from Fiji. *Eugenia gracilipes* (D) is one of several species in the genus to which the Clove, *E. caryophyllus*, a plant native to the Moluccas, belongs.

The genus *Strongylodon* contains twenty species with an overall distribution from Madagascar, islands of the Indian Ocean, including Ceylon, New Guinea and the Mascarenes, to the Philippines and Oceana. It is related to *Mucuna* (see plate 112), with *S. lucidus* (B) occurring on all the larger Hawaiian islands, Tahiti and Fiji. The species is a tall 20 to 30 foot (6–9 m.) twining climber, often found in dense woodland at altitudes between 2000 and 3000 feet (610–910 m.). The main stem may measure 4 to 6 inches (10–15 cm.) circumference, and the 3 glossy leaflets, the largest measuring up to 8 inches (20 cm.) long, are subtended by stipules. In summer the graceful and colourful pendant inflorescences may measure as much as 20 inches (51 cm.) in length, consisting of many clusters of 2 to 3 crimson flowers, and greenish red campanulate calyces. The pods are brown and slightly compressed, measuring up to $4\frac{3}{4}$ inches (12 cm.) and containing 1 or 2 round black seeds. 'Nukuiiwi' is the native Hawaiian name for the species, derived from 'nuku' beak, and 'iiwi', a native red feathered bird with a curved bill. At one time in the past the strong, pliable stems were used as swings by the Hawaiians.

Hibiscus insularis (A) is a good example of a rare, highly localized species which is now almost extinct in the wild. It is endemic to Philip Island, a small isle about four miles (6.4 km.) from Norfolk Island, itself a remote and very small landmass surrounded by ocean about midway between New Caledonia and New Zealand. Philip Island has never been inhabited by man but owing to goats and pigs, and a lesser extent rabbits, landed there by man to form a source of fresh meat in years gone past, the vegetation has been almost completely removed and destroyed. Whereas the island was once covered with a rich vegetation it is now a virtual desert with the soil washing away into the sea at every storm of rain. Only a very few native plants remain (and these are prevented from regeneration by the few wild rabbits), amongst them the last three or four bushes of *H. insularis*. There is no doubt that they should be protected before they become extinct, a fate which has overtaken another Philip Island endemic, an attractive genus in the *Leguminosae* which contained only the one species, *Streblorrhiza speciosa*. Fortunately perhaps, *H. insularis* is now well established in cultivation, but in terms of conservation this is a poor substitute for the wild plant.

Eugenia comprises about one thousand tropical and subtropical species, with *E. jambos*, the Rose-apple of Malaysia, *E. uniflora*, the Surinam Cherry of South America, and *E. caryophyllus*, the Clove of the East Indies. The fleshy berry is the edible part of most species but Cloves are the dried flower buds, and these were known to the Chinese by at least 2 B.C. A trade in Cloves became established between the East Indies and Europe, and by 8 A.D. the commodity was well known, if expensive. For most of the 1500's the Portuguese monopolized the Moluccan produce, as did the Dutch from 1605 until the early 19th century, when they took over the administration of the East Indies. Despite efforts to stop the spread of the crop, French plantsmen introduced Cloves from Ceram to Mauritius and Réunion in 1772, and to Cayenne in the New World about 1789, thus beginning the end of the monopoly. In 1818 Cloves were introduced to Zanzibar from Mauritius and often by the enforced planting of Cloves under threat of land confiscation, Cloves became one of Zanzibar's chief products, of which today she is the world's leading grower.

E. gracilipes (D) is more decorative than useful, forming a graceful tree with delicate foliage and drooping branches, and terminal slender racemes of 3 to 7 pale yellow or pink-tinged flowers. It is found only in the Fiji islands, where it is called 'Lutulutu'. Other Fijian species include *E. malaccensis*, the Malay Apple, which has deep purple, crimson or even white flowers and reddish fruits about $3\frac{1}{4}$ inches (8 cm.) long, much valued for eating.

Paphia vitiensis (C) is one of about fifteen species in a genus found in New Guinea, Queensland and Fiji. This Fijian plant was the first *Paphia* ever to be described, and formed the basis for the genus. It is a shrub or small tree about 4 to 23 feet (1·2–7 m.) tall, sometimes epiphytic in the case of small plants, with hairy young shoots and alternating leaves which are obscurely toothed and roughly elliptical in outline. The somewhat tubular flowers later give way to a purplish berry. The species is found on the higher mountains of Viti Levu at an altitude of about 4000 feet (1220 m.), where it was collected by Seemann in 1860.

MALVACEAE

Hibiscus insularis
A1 flowering and budding shoots × $\frac{2}{3}$.

LEGUMINOSAE

Strongylodon lucidus
B1 part of flowering shoot × $\frac{2}{3}$.
B2 fruiting shoot × $\frac{2}{3}$. B3 seed × $\frac{2}{3}$.

ERICACEAE

Paphia vitiensis
C1 part of flowering shoot × $\frac{2}{3}$.

MYRTACEAE

Eugenia gracilipes (syn. *Syzygium gracilipes*)
D1 flowering shoot × $\frac{2}{3}$. D2 fruit × $\frac{2}{3}$.

B1

B2

D1

D2

B3

Plate 148   OCEANA

Although the genus to which it belongs is, unlike two of the other genera on this plate, by no means confined to Oceana, *Capparis spinosa* var. *mariana* (D) is a characteristically Pacific plant occurring on many islands in the area between Hawaii, the Marianas, the Solomon Islands and Henderson Island. A straggling, mostly prostrate shrub, without spines (by which the stems of a number of the other two hundred and fifty species in *Capparis* climb), it prefers reasonably dry conditions or semi-arid habitats such as the shoreline, limestone cliffs or dry lava-fields. It produces fragrant white flowers that open only at night and wither, fading into pink, soon after sunrise, but which appear throughout the year, although borne in greatest profusion after the autumn rains. They are then followed by berries containing seeds embedded in an unpleasant orange pulp. Ethnobotanically, it is a most interesting plant for it appears that this Pacific variety of the well known Mediterranean Caper, *C. spinosa*, was early introduced to the Pacific by man, possibly to the Marianas by the Spanish in the 16th century, and from there it has gradually spread to occupy its present area, yet maintaining its rather uniform appearance. In the Hawaiian islands the species bears the common name Puapilo.

About forty species belong to *Barringtonia* and are all Old World in distribution. *B. samoensis* (A) is a shrub or small tree, reaching up to about 40 feet (12 m.) in height but sometimes more, found on the south-eastern islands of Indonesia, New Guinea, Micronesia and Samoa. The genus is closely related to the South American *Lecythis*, whose fifty or so species produce spectacular, woody, urn-like fruits that make ideal water containers.

Some of the loveliest of Pacific climbing plants belong to *Oxera*, a genus found only on the islands of New Caledonia. Discovered by La Billardière, *O. pulchella* (B) differs botanically, like its fellow species, from the related *Clerodendrum*, plates 60 and 104, in having only 2 stamens and deeply lobed, drupaceous fruit. Only one or two of the twenty-five species have yet been introduced to cultivation, *O. pulchella* being one.

Named in honour of William Carruthers (1830–1922) who collaborated with B. C. Seemann (1825–1871) in his study of Pacific flora, *Carruthersia scandens* (C) is a climber found on Fiji, with flowers that are borne between December and March and fruit up to 3 inches (7·5 cm.) in width. Despite Seemann's comment that it would 'prove a desirable acquisition to our gardens', *Carruthersia* still finds no place in collections of tropical plants. Our illustration is based, in part, on the plate Seemann published in his *Flora Vitiensis* which in turn was copied from a coloured drawing done from life by an amateur artist at that time resident in Fiji, Miss Mary Pritchard.

LECYTHIDACEAE

Barringtonia samoensis
A1 flowering shoot × ⅔.

VERBENACEAE

Oxera pulchella
B1 flowering shoot × ⅔.

APOCYNACEAE

Carruthersia scandens
C1 flowering shoot × ⅔.

CAPPARACEAE

Capparis spinosa var. *mariana* (syn. *C. sandwichiana*), Puapilo
D1 part of flowering stem × ⅔.
D2 fruit and peduncle × ⅔.

A1

B1

C1

D1

D2

Plate 149   OCEANA

Growth at high altitudes in conditions of exposure to daily warmth and noctural frost, extreme dryness of the air, and intense insolation, produces a similar habit in certain types of plant found in Hawaii, East Africa and the Andes of South America. Comparison of *Argyroxiphium sandwicense* (A) with *Senecio brassica* and *S. adnivalis* on Tropical Africa plates 56 and 65 respectively, shows the similarity of habit, despite the geographical distances separating the species: a characteristic rosette of leaves in a cabbage-like array, each leaf often covered with woolly hairs, and a towering inflorescence of daisy flowers.

Further details of the East African species are given with the relevant plates, but here we can note that the habit ameliorates the daily warming and cooling and minimizes the harmful effects of large doses of ultra-violet and infra-red rays from the sun. Why such large plant forms have evolved is hard to say. It might seem that a small perennial daisy with potential for vegetative spread, and perhaps only a single flowering head, might better suit the harsh environment than these vegetable giants, and indeed such small herbs are found together with the giants. But the tree-daisies do exist and are a characteristic feature of high altitude vegetation in the Andes, East Africa and Hawaii.

The Silversword, *Argyroxiphium sandwicense*, is found only on the islands of Hawaii and Maui, where it grows at altitudes of between 5000 and 12,000 feet (1500–3660 m.) in the volcanic ash and cinders of Mauna Loa, Mauna Kea, Hualalai and Haleakala. In the early stages of growth the narrow leaves are arranged about the dark-brown stem in what is more or less a sphere, the stem being about 6 inches (15 cm.) long and hidden from view by the silvery shining leaves. Once the shoot has a diameter of about 24 inches (61 cm.), the inflorescence develops, normally in June–October, and may grow to between 5 and 6 feet (1·5–1·8 m.) tall. The infloresence shown opposite is a small one. The flower heads (capitula), as such, are not attractive, but the combined effect of the yellow and maroon flowers massed in a towering structure above a basal rosette of shiny white leaves, makes the species one of the wonders of the Pacific plant-world.

The inflorescence stalk is hollow at the base and, like the leaves, is covered with silvery hairs. Higher up the stalk becomes pithy and is covered with glandular hairs, as are all parts of the upper inflorescence, save the tips of the bracts, which have silky hairs. According to Otto Degener, the glandular hairs tend to prevent crawling insects from reaching and self-pollinating the flowers, pollination being carried out by flying insects, thus increasing the chance of cross-pollination which is more satisfactory. A single plant may have as many as 500 nodding capitula, each on a stalk bearing 2–6 narrow bracts of about the same length as itself. An individual capitulum has 20 to 30 dark-green involucral bracts, up to 20 maroon-coloured female outer-flowers, each with a 3-toothed ray, and up to 400 yellow inner-flowers which are hermaphrodite. When ripe, the numerous achene fruits are black and just over $\frac{1}{2}$ inch (1 cm.) long.

There has been a drastic decrease in the number of Silversword plants found in nature, partly because of a 'phycitid moth' and fly, which in the larval state destroy large amounts of ripening seed on the plants, and partly because of thoughtless exploitation when the dried plants were shipped to east Asia as ornaments in the years around 1915. Degener states that in the 1890's tens of acres of Silversword could be found on Haleakala, yet in 1927 there were none. As the species is easy to grow from seed in the natural habitat, germination occurring after about a fortnight, it is to be hoped that numbers of the species can be increased artificially in protected plots of land, safe from grazing animals and the ravages of insect pests. It is important that stocks are maintained and not allowed to dwindle as the plants die after flowering, and successive years of poor seed-harvest might threaten the species with extinction. Recently Maui seed has been introduced onto Hawaii to offset the diminishing numbers of Hawaiian Silverswords, but as the Maui Silversword is a different plant confusion may arise as a result of hybrids occurring.

The Silversword is closely associated with the last days of the famous plant-hunter David Douglas, who collected its seed on 8 January 1834 shortly before his death on 11 July of the same year. The circumstances by which he met his death are still not completely known, and at the time some held that he was murdered for his money, having been pushed into the animal-pit in which he was found gored to death.

An indication of the extreme dryness of the air in Silversword habitats is to be found in observations made by Douglas on 12 January, on the summit of Mauna Kea, at 13,784 feet (4200 m.) when he commented that, as a result of the aridity, his hands and feet began to peel, and his eyes became sore and bloodshot.

Wilkesia gymnoxiphium (B), a most ornamental daisy, is named after Captain Charles Wilkes, commander of the United States Exploring Expedition (1838–1842) which visited Hawaii in 1840. With a habit superficially resembling a bamboo, this daisy is known only from the barren slopes of Kauai at altitudes of 3000–5000 feet (910–1500 m.), where it flowers during June and July. After fruiting, the plants die, and regeneration follows from seed and already established seedlings. *W. gymnoxiphium*, the Iliau, grows to about 12 feet (3·6 m.) tall and is usually unbranched. The long leafless stem consists of large numbers of nodes, about $1\frac{1}{4}$ inches (3 cm.) in diameter, and is woody with a white pithy core. There are 10 or more leaves in whorls at the apex of the stem, each whorl being fused at the base for a short distance (see B2). In bud, the leaves are compacted together into a sharp, erect spearhead, but as they expand they eventually release themselves and droop as shown in the habit sketch. The leaves are shiny and have a densely hairy margin, but are otherwise hairless.

The inflorescence is composed of whorls of 6 to 10 capitula on stalks, subtended by an equivalent number of bracts which are fused to each other at the base. There may be up to 20 such whorls of capitula with a single-stalked capitulum at the end of the inflorescence. Each nodding capitulum contains about 180 pale yellow, tubular flowers which are hermaphrodite, and its stalk and receptacle are covered with glandular hairs. The achene fruits, which are produced in large numbers, are dark brown when ripe.

COMPOSITAE

Argyroxiphium sandwicense, Silversword
A1 part of flowering stem × $\frac{2}{3}$.
A2 leaf × $\frac{2}{3}$. A3 habit sketch × $\frac{1}{18}$.

Wilkesia gymnoxiphium, Iliau
B1 part of flowering stem × $\frac{2}{3}$.
B2 whorl of leaves showing basal fusion and insertion on stem × $\frac{2}{3}$.
B3 habit sketch × $\frac{1}{18}$.

A3

A2

A1

B3

B1

B2

Plate 150   NORTH AMERICA

The dating of fossils by the particular geological formation in which they are found has led to the belief that magnolias and their allies are among the earliest of primitive flowering plants. Strange to think that at the time of the decline of giant reptiles, or even before, the blooms of magnolia ancestors may have graced trees and shrubs. These flowers may also have been pollinated by clumsy beetles which ate the pollen, as happens still with certain modern plants. Illiciums and magnolias are closely related and regarded as primitive, while calycanthi are more advanced, evolved to some intermediate state between magnolias, dillenias and roses. The Birthwort family (*Aristolochiaceae*), to which Wild Ginger belongs, have highly evolved methods of attracting pollinators to weirdly shaped, smelly flowers, yet retain traits which ally them to more primitive plants such as buttercups and barberries.

The Sweet or Swamp Bay, *Magnolia virginana* (D), grows wild along the Atlantic coastal plain of North America, ranging from Massachusetts to Florida and westwards into Texas. In the north it rarely grows more than 26 feet (8 m.) high but in the south, may be 80 feet (24 m.). It grows in wet woodland, or even as pure stands in the Florida swamps and bears comparatively small, fragrant, white flowers which soon drop after turning a dirty yellow. Introduced to Europe in 1688 as plants sent from John Banister (1650–1692) to Bishop Compton, it was the first species of magnolia to become a garden plant in Europe. Admirers of this species thought its fragrance rivalled that of the rose, but when Sir Joseph Banks introduced *M. denudata*, the Yulan, from China in the 1780's, the Sweet Bay became less popular, and the beauty of such species as *M. liliflora,* introduced in the 1790's, *M. sieboldii* introduced in the 1860's, and the floriferous *M. stellata* (plate 90), all from the Far 'East, eclipsed the American species, with the exception of *M. grandiflora*.

The Bull Bay or Southern Magnolia, *M. grandiflora*, is at once characterised by its white flowers up to 8 inches (20 cm.) in diameter and its large evergreen leaves, and may form a tree as much as 80 feet (24 m.) high. It ranges from North Carolina and Florida, westward to Arkansas and Texas. It was first introduced into Europe about 1711, when the one-time Mayor of Nantes, Réné Darquistade, cultivated the species in his manor La Maillardière, in France. Records show that this plant was nearly destroyed by fire and the falling of a brick wall when La Maillardière was attacked during the civil war in 1793, but local botanists and gardeners obtained plants from it by layering, and helped the original tree to recover so that it was still alive in 1848. In England, a plant was said to have borne flowers in 1737, in the garden of Sir Charles Wager (1666–1743) at Parsons Green, Fulham. Since that time, *M. grandiflora* has been grown in British gardens. Probably the oldest tree now growing is one in the University botanic garden at Padua in Italy, a plant dating from 1750. Other North American magnolias include the Cucumber Tree, *M. acuminata* with greenish yellow flowers and the Umbrella Tree, *M. tripetala* with white flowers and conspicuous red cone-shaped fruits.

Of the two species of *Liriodendron*, one is Chinese (*L. chinense*) and was discovered at the beginning of this century, and the other is the North American Tulip Tree, *L. tulipifera* (E), which has been known for three hundred years and is illustrated here. The Tulip Tree is a woodland species which grows up to 200 feet (61 m.) high in the wild. The flowers are individually showy but, being mainly greenish yellow, are generally inconspicuous amongst the foliage of the tree. The leaves look as if the tip has been cut off and the fruiting carpels, arranged in a cone, are equally distinctive, being winged and samara-like. This species has a distribution from Massachusetts and Vermont, to Ontario and Wisconsin and south to Louisiana and Florida. Its unusual leaves, pretty cup- or tulip-shaped flowers and comely habit, as well as its yellow autumn colouring, make it a widespread ornamental park tree.

The curious flowers of the Wild Ginger genus *Asarum* are borne near the ground and are pollinated by beetles and small flies. There are seventy or so species in the temperate regions and they are plants with a thick creeping rootstock from which annual shoots arise. Each shoot bears 2 leaves and is terminated by a flower. *A. caudatum* (B) is a native of moist shaded woods of Pacific North America, from the Santa Cruz Mountains just south of San Fransisco, north to British Columbia, where it is rarely found above 5000 feet (1520 m.). Its strange brownish purple flowers, with their 3 lobes drawn out into 2 inch (5 cm.) long tails, may be easily overlooked, concealed beneath the canopy of heart-shaped leaves. It is similar to *A. hartwegii*, also from western America, but differs in having a more slender rootstock with fewer scales and shorter horns on the anthers.

The Spice Bush, *Calycanthus occidentalis* (A), is the only member of its genus in western North America. It forms a bush up to 10 feet (3 m.) high and is found in parts of California, in moist places near lakes and ponds or beside streams, rarely ascending above an altitude of 4000 feet (1200 m.). It was introduced into Europe in 1831 by David Douglas. The perhaps better known Allspice, *C. floridus*, with smaller but more fragrant and deeper coloured flowers, is found in the south-eastern coastal states of the U.S.A.

The only New World *Illicium* is *I. floridanum* (C), the Polecat Tree, which grows to a small tree about 20 feet (6 m.) tall and has a smooth dark brown trunk, slightly furrowed. It is easily recognised because of the peculiar star-shaped flowers, star-shaped ring of fruits and aromatic odour when its leaves are crushed. Its range is across south-east U.S.A. from western Florida to eastern Louisiana. *I. verum* from China, is the Star-anise, the fruits of which are used for flavouring and the generic name, from *illicere* 'to allure' refers to their fragrance. The Japanese Star-anise, *I. anisatum*, has, however, poisonous seeds.

CALYCANTHACEAE

Calycanthus occidentalis, Spice Bush
A1 part of flowering branch × $\frac{2}{3}$. A2 petal × $1\frac{1}{3}$.

ARISTOLOCHIACEAE

Asarum caudatum, Wild Ginger
B1 part of flowering shoot with previous year's leaves and new leaves × $\frac{2}{3}$.
B2 flower × $1\frac{1}{3}$. B3 stamens, style and ovary × 2.

ILLICIACEAE

Illicium floridanum, Polecat Tree
C1 part of branch showing flowers and buds × $\frac{2}{3}$.
C2 carpels × 2. C3 anther × 6.

MAGNOLIACEAE

Magnolia virginiana, Sweet or Swamp Bay
D1 part of flowering branch × $\frac{2}{3}$.
D2 carpels × $1\frac{1}{3}$. D3 stamen × $2\frac{2}{3}$.

Liriodendron tulipifera, Tulip Tree
E1 part of flowering branch × $\frac{2}{3}$.
E2 stamen × $2\frac{2}{3}$. E3 carpels × $1\frac{1}{3}$. E4 petal × $1\frac{1}{3}$.

A2

A1

B1

B3   B2

C1

C2   C3

E1

E2

D1   D2   D3

E3   E4

Plate 151   NORTH AMERICA

'Mr Jones' pond was . . . covered with great white lilies . . . they poured from their leaves like candle fat, ran molten, then cooled on the water.' *Nymphaea*, the genus referred to in this quotation from Laurie Lee, and the yellow-flowered *Nuphar*, are the genera that contain the majority of the temperate waterlily species. In the tropics, however, several other fine flowered genera, such as the *Euryale*, *Victoria* and *Nelumbo*, exist. The various, equally useful, though less dramatic, species of *Ribes* decorate gardens and produce edible fruits like the currants and gooseberry; North America is particularly rich in species of this genus, many of which were introduced to cultivation in Europe by David Douglas.

The largest flowered species of the twenty-five in the genus *Nuphar* found in the temperate north is *N. polysepala* (A). Known popularly as Cow Lily and Great Yellow Pond-lily, the species was discovered by C. C. Parry in the sub-alpine lakes of Colorado. Its range extends from Alaska to California and Colorado where it is found in ponds and slow flowing water. Its floating leaves are dull green and thick, measuring about 16 inches (40 cm.) in length and 10 inches (25 cm.) wide, with a blunt tip and a sinus 4 inches (10 cm.) deep. The leaf stalks may be up to $\frac{3}{4}$ inch (15 mm.) thick and there are no submerged leaves. The round flowers stand out of the water with 7 to 9 large chrome yellow sepals tinged with red, thick in texture and about 2 inches (5 cm.) long. The petals are smaller and somewhat hidden, being about the same length as the stamens which are arranged in 5-7 rows. These have greenish yellow filaments and prune-coloured anthers that curve backwards slightly and surround the prominent, expanded stigma whose top is patterned with radiating stigmatic lines. The Klamath Indians used to collect the pods by boat as the seeds provided an important farinaceous food in winter, either roasted in the fire and made into a sort of popcorn on hot griddles, or ground into a mealy substitute for flour.

Two species of the genus *Nelumbo* exist, one in the Old World and one in the New. *N. pentapetala* (D) is found in still waters from New York and southern Ontario, south throughout the eastern States to Florida and Texas and into Central America, the West Indies and Colombia. It has acquired several common names such as Lotus Lily, Pondnuts, Wonkapin and Water Chinquapin. The first man to flower the species in Britain was Edward Sylvester of Chorley, Lancashire, who discovered, through an accidental malfunctioning in a heating system, that it flowers at a lower temperature than the Old World Sacred Lotus, *N. nucifera*. Although the yellow blooms of the illustrated plant are smaller and less fragrant than those of the pink Sacred Lotus, their size—10 inches (25 cm.) diameter on stalks 3 feet (90 cm.) long—make it the largest flowered plant in North America, with *Magnolia grandiflora* a close second. The

leaves are round and up to 28 inches in diameter (71 cm.), with the stalk attached in the very centre. This genus differs from *Nuphar* and *Nymphaea* in many ways but especially in its inverted, conical fruiting body, about 4 inches (10 cm.) across at the top. The nut-like and edible fruits are situated in pits all over this broad surface.

The underwater stems of *N. pentapetala*, like those of the Asiatic species, are hollow and tubular. The long-stalked leaves rise from the nodes and are borne high above the surface of the water, being overtopped only by the flowers. A number of coloured cultivars of *N. nucifera* exist, as well as several forms with double and quadruple flowers; its fruits are renowned for their longevity: between 1843 and 1855, Robert Brown germinated fruits one hundred and fifty years old. Even more remarkable were the fruits found by the Japanese palaeobotanist, I. Ohga, in the peat deposits of Manchuria. Though these deposits were estimated to be about a thousand years old, confirmed by radio-carbon dating, Ohga obtained perfect germination when the fruits were planted in 1924.

The Flowering Currant, *Ribes sanguineum* (C), is a popular member of its genus, first discovered in 1793 by Archibald Menzies, surgeon and naturalist on Captain Vancouver's Expedition of 1790-1795. It was, however, left to David Douglas, who came across the species near Fort Vancouver in 1825, to introduce it to Britain, where plants raised from seed sent by him flowered in 1828. Modern cultivated stocks tend to have larger and more intensely red or pink racemes than the wild plant. The shrub owes its popularity to the blaze of colour it produces in April, its easy propagation, and its tolerance of the smoke and grime of cities. It grows to a height of 6 to 8 feet (1·8-2·4 m.) and the branches, downy when young, bear lobed leaves with toothed edges. When the dusky red flowers have faded, they may be followed by small black fruits with a bluish bloom. About one hundred and fifty other species exist, mostly in the temperate north.

Another discovery of Archibald Menzies, dating from an earlier voyage in 1789, is the delightful early flowering shrub *R. speciosum* (B), the Fuchsia-flowered Gooseberry, which was introduced from California in 1828 by Alexander Collie, and again by Douglas in 1830. The flowers are given their fuchsia-like appearance by the long, protruding stamens. Later, translucent red gooseberries, ornately covered with long, dark red bristles, grow among the thorny stems. The shrub reaches a height of 3-6 feet (0·9-1·8 m.) and is clothed in small, 3-lobed leaves of a shiny deep green colour. The plant is a native of California from Santa Clara County to northern Lower California. Its early spring flowering period has deprived it of the recognition it deserves in places like Britain, where winter frosts may destroy the blooms.

NYMPHAEACEAE

Nuphar polysepala, Cow Lily, Great Yellow Pond-lily
A1 flower with leaf $\times \frac{2}{3}$.

Nelumbo pentapetala (syn. *N. lutea*), Lotus Lily, Water Chinquapin, Pondnuts, Wonkapin
D1 flower with leaves $\times \frac{2}{3}$.
D2 anther showing appendage $\times$ 2.
D3 fruit $\times \frac{2}{3}$.

GROSSULARIACEAE

Ribes speciosum, Fuchsia-flowered Gooseberry
B1 flowering shoot $\times \frac{2}{3}$. B2 flower $\times 1\frac{1}{3}$.
B3 fruiting twig $\times \frac{2}{3}$. B4 fruit $\times 1\frac{1}{3}$.

R. sanguineum, Flowering Currant
C1 flowering shoot $\times \frac{2}{3}$.

A1

B1

B2

B3

B4

C1

D1

D2

D3

Plate 152   NORTH AMERICA

Widely cultivated in both North America and Europe (into which it was introduced late in the 17th century) for the flowers, fruits and autumnal foliage it provides in decorative succession, the Cockspur Thorn, *Crataegus crus-galli* (B) forms a tree up to 30 feet (9 m.) in height with a short trunk and broad flattened crown of brownish-red spiny branches and lustrous dark green leaves. In Texas, at the southern limit of its range, the flowers, which are borne in clusters with either hairless or pubescent stalks, appear in April, but in New England, at the northern limit, they are not seen until June. Spherical to pear-shaped fruits, dull red when fully ripe and mealy inside, follow and persist on the tree, apparently having no attraction for birds, until the next spring. In autumn the leaves, which are variable in shape though generally oval, turn orange or scarlet. The wood beneath the grey scaly bark is hard, heavy and close-grained; the longest spines were at one time used as fasteners for sacks and the like. It is likely that many park specimens given the name *C. crus-galli* are in fact hybrids that include this species among their recent ancestors. The same may also apply to a large number of the hundreds of species described from North America: it has recently been estimated that there are no more than two hundred good species in the genus throughout all the northern temperate regions.

The twenty-five species, chiefly confined to North America, in the genus *Amelanchier* pose a similar problem, though on a much smaller scale. As in *Crataegus*, recognition of the species has proved most difficult, once again perhaps because of natural hybridization. One result is that their botanical nomenclature has become confused and they form what is known as a taxonomically critical group. However the genus does contain some lovely garden material, one of the best known species for this being *A. canadensis* (C), commonly called Shad Bush or Service Berry. It forms a shrub usually with several upright trunks that grow to a height of about 26 feet (8 m.). The species is found from Maine, New Hampshire and south-west Quebec, south as far as Georgia, but is most abundant in the Alleghany Mountains of North Carolina and Tennessee. In woodland it often occurs in the company of oaks, hickories, sugar maples and birches. In the south the flowers, which appear just before or with the new leaves, bloom in March but they do not appear further north for another month or so. The fruits, which may be sweet and edible, are borne earlier than almost any other wild fruit and ripen in early summer. Finally, in the autumn, the foliage is notable for the beautiful colours it develops. *A. canadensis* was introduced into western Europe by the Duke of Argyll in 1746 and has been cultivated as an ornamental tree ever since, although not seen as often as one might expect.

Introduced into Europe some sixty years later and valued at the time as a hardy late-flowering species, the Prairie Rose, *Rosa setigera* (D), is a native of eastern and central North America from Ontario to Texas. A climber with stems 6 to 12 feet (1·8–3·6 m.) long, it inhabits, as its common name implies, scrub and open country. Its synonym, *R. rubifolia*, first used by R. Brown in 1811, should not allow the species to be confused with the purple-leaved European *R. rubrifolia*, which was given its name by Dominique Villars in 1789.

Rosa palustris (A), the Swamp Rose, is found in swamps and marshes and near streams in an arc from Nova Scotia through Minnesota to the Gulf of Mexico. It grows as a many branched shrub to a height of 6 feet (1·8 m.) with flowers that are borne singly or in small groups late in the year; the fruits that follow remain on the plant for a long time. Unlike those of *R. setigera*, the styles are neither exserted nor fused into a column. The Swamp Rose was brought to Europe in 1726. Other noteworthy North American roses include *R. nutkana*, the Nootka Rose, from the west, which has bright red flowers 2 inches (5 cm.) in diameter, and the eastern *R. carolina* with purplish clusters of fragrant, slightly smaller flowers.

North America is also the home of several interesting and attractive members of the black-berry genus *Rubus* with flowers somewhat reminiscent of a rose. *R. odoratus*, for example, has rose-purple flowers 1½ inches (4 cm.) across, and *R. deliciosus* even larger ones, though in this case white.

ROSACEAE

Rosa palustris, Swamp Rose
A1 flowering shoot × ⅔.
A2 fruiting stem showing autumn colour of leaves × ⅔.

Crataegus crus-galli, Cockspur Thorn
B1 part of flowering branch × ⅔.
B2 flower × 2⅔. B3 anther × 10⅔.
B4 fruiting twig showing autumn foliage × ⅔.

Amelanchier canadensis, Shad Bush, Service Berry
C1 flowering twig with new leaves × ⅔.
C2 flower with 2 petals removed × 4.
C3 twig with fruit and mature leaves × ⅔.
C4 sectioned fruit × 4.
C5 autumn leaves on twig × ⅔.

Rosa setigera (syn. *R. rubifolia*), Prairie Rose
D1 flowering shoot × ⅔.

A1

A2

B1

B2

B3

B4

C1

C2

C3

C4

C5

D1

Plate 153   NORTH AMERICA

One of the earliest to be imported of the many North American pea plants now commonly grown in Europe, the False Acacia, *Robinia pseudoacacia* was first grown about 1590 in the garden of the Louvre, by Jean Robin (1550–1629), Henry IV of France's gardener and eponym of the genus. The tree, a native of eastern North America, reaches a height of about 85 feet (26 m.), has a deeply fissured bark when mature, and extremely delicate foliage, each leaf being divided into 7–19 rounded leaflets, and, because of this, has become familiar in parks and avenues. In June, the fragrant white or pinkish racemes, 5 inches (12·5 cm.) long, hang from the smaller twigs amongst the leaves; later these are replaced by legume fruits about 4 inches (10 cm.) in length.

Sir John Colliton of Exmouth brought the Rose Acacia, *R. hispida* (A), to England from his estate in Carolina, the plant being native to the south-eastern States, in 1741 and by 1790 it was being grown by a number of gardeners, though usually as a standard grafted onto False Acacia stock. By 1863, three varieties were under cultivation but today the tendency is to allow the plant to revert to its normal habit as a straggling and stoloniferous shrub, when it grows to a height of 6 feet (1·8 m.). It has bristly branches with leaves divided into 7–13 coarse leaflets, and pendulous racemes of flowers that appear periodically from May to the end of summer. In the wild, the flowers are followed by bristly pods 3 inches (7·5 cm.) long, but these are rarely seen in cultivation. The distribution of the twenty species of *Robinia* extends from the eastern U.S.A. to Mexico.

One of those genera with a disjunct distribution that spans the Pacific, with species in eastern Asia and North America, is the genus *Apios* which contains ten species. *A. americana* (B), the Cinnamon Vine, is a climber found in moist woods from south-eastern Canada to Minnesota and Colorado to Texas and Florida with dense, sometimes elongated, racemes of fragrant brownish purple flowers. The leaves, in whose axils the flowers are borne, consist of 5 to 7 leaflets. The related *A. priceana* is a rare plant from Kentucky and Tennessee that bears greenish white flowers and springs from underground tubers about 7 inches (17·5 cm.) in diameter (larger than those of *A. americana*).

None of the two thousand species estimated to belong to the widely distributed genus *Astragalus* is more beautiful than *A. coccineus* (C), a native of the desert fringes at altitudes between 2000 and 7000 feet (610–2100 m.) in south-eastern California and south and west Arizona. It is a stemless, tufted perennial with thick silky hair on all its parts, the erect racemes of 3 to 8 scarlet flowers contrasting vividly with the rosettes of silky, divided leaves by which each is surrounded. The curved pods, about 1 inch (2·5 cm.) long, are also silky. In winter, the leaves die down leaving the crown of the plant protected by a dense mat of persistent leaf stalks. A very similar plant, but with less hairy parts and pinkish purple flowers, called *A. newberryi*, is found on dry gravelly hillsides in Idaho, Oregon and New Mexico as well as the States mentioned above.

Some of the two hundred American and Mediterranean species in the genus *Lupinus* rank among the finest of all herbaceous plants. *L. ornatus* (E) (including its variety *obtusilobus*) is a species from altitudes of between 5500 and 10,000 feet (1670–3050 m.) in Washington, Idaho and California. It has a handsome way of combining both form and colour, having spreading shoots clothed with silvery foliage and densely flowered blue or pinkish lilac racemes, in bloom between June and September. The plant, which rarely exceeds 18 inches (46 cm.) in height, was discovered by David Douglas and first grown by the Horticultural Society of London, from seed introduced by him in 1827. *L. villosus* (D) is a little-cultivated species native to dry sandy habitats from South Carolina to Florida, with flowers that vary in colour from white through rose to purple. Unlike the majority of lupins, it has undivided leaves.

No wild lupins, however, surpass the numerous and multicoloured Russell Lupin cultivars (named after their original raiser George Russell) in vigour, size and density of inflorescence, and variety of colour. The Russell Lupins are the result of the crossing of two western North American species, *L. arboreus* and *L. polyphyllus*. All lupins require good drainage and are sensitive to both limy and freshly manured soils.

LEGUMINOSAE

Robinia hispida, Rose Acacia
A1 flowering shoot × ⅔.
A2 flower with all but one petal removed × 1⅓.
A3 wing petal × 1⅓.

Apios americana (syn. *A. tuberosa*), Cinnamon Vine
B1 flowering shoot × ⅔.

Astragalus coccineus
C1 flowering plant × ⅔. C2 pod × ⅔.

Lupinus villosus
D1 flowering plant × ⅔. D2 pod × ⅔.

L. ornatus
E1 part of flowering plant × ⅔.
E2 standard petal × 2.
E3 wing petal × 2. E4 leaflet × 2.
E5 part of stem with unripe pods × ⅔.

A1
A2
A3
B1
C1 C2
D1 D2
E1 E2 E3 E4 E5

Plate 154   NORTH AMERICA

The genus *Eschscholzia* is represented on this plate by its best known species, *E. californica* (A), the Californian Poppy. This genus, which contains some ten species, all native to western North America, from the Columbia River to New Mexico, commemorates Johann Friedrich Gustav von Eschscholz (1793–1831), a surgeon, entomologist and botanist. It was discovered in 1792 by Archibald Menzies (1754–1842) and was at first thought to be a member of the Greater Celandine genus, *Chelidonium*. Only when Count Romanzoff's expedition round the world enabled Ludolf Adalbert von Chamisso and von Eschscholz to refind the species near San Francisco, was there sufficient accurate information available for it to be placed in a new genus. However, it was David Douglas who first sent seed to England, after which the species gained its well deserved popularity as a garden plant. In nature, it varies according to the area in which it grows; a typical dune and coastal type is perennial and bears yellow flowers, while an inland perennial type has orange flowers which vary in size and intensity of colour, depending on the season. There is another perennial dune type in the Monterey area, with roughish grey leaves, while an annual type grows in southern California and the San Joaquin Valley. As in many members of the poppy family, the 2 sepals fuse to form a protective cap on the outside of the flower bud and in *Eschscholzia* this is lifted off almost intact by the expanding petals.

Argemone, a genus of some ten species, is found from the south-eastern to the western United States, as well as in the Caribbean area, and with one species endemic to Hawaii. *A. mexicana* (B), which originated in Mexico, has now entrenched itself as an attractive but troublesome weed in many tropical parts of the world, probably because the seeds set easily and the plants are well protected from grazing animals by being spiny and containing a bitter-tasting yellow latex. Gerard gives a whimsical account of the derivation of its colloquial name, Devil's Fig, from the fruit which 'doth much resemble a figge in shape and bignesse, but so full of sharpe and venomous prickles, that whosoever had one of them in his throte, doubtless it would send him packing either to heaven or to hell'. The species is also known as the Golden

Thistle of Peru, a glaring botanical and geographical error.

Platystemon species are found in western North America, the home of most of the species on this plate and an area which seems to provide a concentration of poppy genera found nowhere else in the world. Depending on interpretation, this genus contains either about sixty species or a single variable one. Another discovery of Archibald Menzies during his travels around the world as a member of Captain Vancouver's Expedition, *P. californicus* (C) is an annual and, like all the plants in the genus, its leaves are arranged in whorls, thus differing from other poppies, and the carpels forming the ovary are only partly fused. These sometimes separate when in fruit, a characteristic unique to this poppy. Commonly called Cream Cups, the plant grows throughout California and on the desert fringes in Utah, Arizona and the Baja Peninsula. As with many Californian plants, it was introduced into England by David Douglas.

Two *Romneya* species, found only in California and north-western Mexico, commemorate T. Romney Robinson, an Irish astronomer and friend of Thomas Coulter (1793–1843) who first discovered the genus and whose name is also linked in the name of the plant illustrated opposite, *R. coulteri*, the Matilija Poppy (D). This species grows in coastal scrub and canyons below about 4000 feet (1220 m.) from the Santa Ana Mountains region to San Diego County. The related *R. trichocalyx* is treated by some botanists as a variety of *R. coulteri*, although its flowers are slightly smaller, its leaves more narrowly lobed and its calyx hairy. Often found growing in chaparral in Ventura and San Diego Counties, it spreads also into Lower California. Hybridization does occur between the two species and the progeny are sometimes cultivated in gardens.

A single species, *Stylomecon heterophylla* (E) comprises the Californian genus *Stylomecon*. At one time the species was included in *Meconopsis* and thought to be a second outlying species in that mainly Sino-Himalayan genus, like the Welsh Poppy, *M. cambrica*, in Europe. It was later considered sufficiently different, however, to be separated on its own. Discovered by David Douglas in 1833, it grows from Lake County in tne San Joaquin Valley, through the foothills of the Sierra Nevada to the Baja Peninsula.

PAPAVERACEAE

Eschscholzia californica, Californian Poppy
A1 flower, buds, fruit and leaves × $\frac{2}{3}$.
A2 stamens in position on petal × 2.
A3 style and ovary × 2. A4 seed × 8.

Argemone mexicana, Devil's Fig, Golden Thistle of Peru
B1 flowering stem × $\frac{2}{3}$. B2 style × 4.
B3 fruiting stem × $\frac{2}{3}$. B4 top view of fruit × 2.
B5 seed × 8.

Platystemon californicus, Cream Cups
C1 flowering and budding stem × $\frac{2}{3}$.
C2 petal × 2. C3 stamen × 2.
C4 fruiting stem × $\frac{2}{3}$. C5 young fruit × 2.

Romneya coulteri, Matilija Poppy
D1 flowering shoot × $\frac{2}{3}$.
D2 style and ovary × 2. D3 stamen × 4.

Stylomecon heterophylla
E1 buds, flower, immature fruit and leaves × $\frac{2}{3}$.
E2 side view of flower × $\frac{2}{3}$. E3 petal × $1\frac{1}{3}$.
E4 stamens, style and ovary × $2\frac{2}{3}$.
E5 young fruit × 2.

A1

A3

A4

B1

B2

B3

B4

B5

C1

C2

C3

C5

D1

D2

D3

E1

E2

E3

E4

E5

Plate 155   NORTH AMERICA

The European traveller in North America will recognize many shrubs belonging to genera also found in the Old World such as *Viburnum*, *Lonicera*, and *Cornus*, but he will probably be unfamiliar with species of the endemic genus *Garrya*, or those of *Hamamelis*, although the latter does have some east Asian species.

Comprised of about one hundred and fifty species, *Viburnum* has centres of diversity in Asia and North America. A number have inflorescences in which the outer flowers consist of an enlarged and attractive corolla but possess only reduced and functionless reproductive organs; the small inner flowers of the inflorescence contain the functional sexual organs. This division of labour between reproductive and attractive flowers goes some way towards the more highly evolved, but similar, inflorescence construction found in most daisies and many umbellifers. Only two North American species, *V. alnifolium* and *V. trilobum*, resemble the European species *V. opulus*, the Guelder Rose, in having large sterile marginal flowers. In other characteristics *V. alnifolium* (A), a native of eastern North America from Nova Scotia and New Brunswick westward to Ontario and southward into the mountains of North Carolina, is more like *V. lantana*. It is very difficult to cultivate, and, since its introduction into European horticulture in 1820, has appeared only sporadically in gardens. The shaded and very moist natural habitats occupied by *V. alnifolium* are not easy to imitate. This is a pity for the white spring flowers and the red (later black) fruits and red autumnal leaves make it a very ornamental plant, which reaches a height of 10 feet (3 m.). Hobblebush, its common name, arose through its habit of rooting at the tips of its low growing branches, forming hoops which have been known to dismount riders and trip up the unwary.

An inhabitant of the coastal ranges from Del Norte County to Santa Barbara County, the California Honeysuckle, *Lonicera ledebourii* (D) was introduced into Europe about 1838. It forms an erect growing shrub up to 9 feet (2·7 m.) tall, and is notable for the 2 broad bracts around each pair of flowers; these are later replaced by purple-black fruits. The closely allied *L. involucrata* has smaller corollas and stamens projecting from the corolla tube.

Three species possessing 2-lipped corollas and thin walled capsule fruits comprise the North American genus *Diervilla*. They are sometimes united to form one genus with the twelve east Asian species of *Weigela*, which have larger, more symmetrical corollas and thick walled capsules, but it is customary to keep them separate.

Diervilla sessilifolia (B) grows in the Allegheny Mountains, Tennessee, North Carolina and Georgia. It is distinguished from the more widespread and northerly *D. lonicera* by its 3- to 7-flowered clusters (instead of 3) and its stalkless (instead of distinctly stalked) leaves. *D. lonicera* ranges from Quebec, Manitoba and Newfoundland, through New York, Illinois and Virginia. Both species spread into colonies about 3 to 4 feet (0·9-1·2 m.) high. The genus commemorates a French surgeon, N. Dièrville, who travelled in eastern Canada at the end of the 17th century and introduced *D. lonicera* into cultivation in France.

Broadly defined, *Cornus* comprises about sixty species separated into five main groups which some botanists regard as sections, others as separate genera. *Cornus nuttallii* (C), a native of western North America from British Columbia to southern California, is common in the coastal ranges below 6000 feet (1830 m.) as far south as Monterey. A component of the famous Redwood forests of northern California, it may grow into a tree about 100 feet (30·5 m.) tall. The large creamy involucral bracts make the flower heads, which can be up to 6 inches (15 cm.) in diameter, splendid in the late spring, while its red autumnal leaves and gaudy fruiting heads are equally attractive. David Douglas discovered *C. nuttallii* about 1826 but it was only recognized as a separate species in 1836 by Thomas Nuttall (1786-1859) whom it commemorates. In 1837 it was illustrated on one of Audubon's renowned bird plates and was first described in the accompanying text of this book. Nuttall sent seed to England, but the plant never became widely grown. Introduced at Kew in 1904 it first flowered in 1909 and continues to flourish. For those who divide *Cornus* into several genera, the correct name of this species is *Benthamidia nuttallii*.

The *Garryaceae*, which comprises about fifteen species in the single genus *Garrya*, is thought to be related to the *Cornaceae*. It commemorates an employee of the Hudson Bay Company, one Nicholas Garry, who collected plants in the Fort Vancouver area and helped Douglas during his travels in western America. *G. elliptica* (E), the type species, was discovered by Archibald Menzies in 1792 and introduced into England by David Douglas from California in 1828. Characteristic of the chaparral and similar dry types of vegetation, it occurs in the outer coastal ranges from Oregon and California southward to the Santa Cruz Islands. It forms shrubs up to about 20 feet (6 m.) tall and, when in flower, the foliage of the male trees may become smothered in pollen.

A genus of woody plants confined to eastern North America and eastern Asia, China and Japan, the witch hazel genus, *Hamamelis* has pinnately veined leaves and 4-petalled flowers. First collected in Missouri in 1845 by George Engelman (1809-1884) and subsequently found in Arkansas and Oklahoma, *H. vernalis* (F) remained unnamed and undescribed until 1911 when Professor Charles S. Sargent (1841-1927) accomplished the task. Sargent was largely responsible for the development of the Arnold Arboretum in New England. He was appointed Director in November 1873, soon after one hundred and twenty-five acres (5·6 hectares) became available for the purpose of forming an arboretum according to the will of Mr James Arnold, a Massachusetts merchant. *H. vernalis* flowers on leafless shoots from midwinter to spring, whereas the other American species, *H. virginiana*, which has longer petals, flowers in autumn while in full leaf. The flowers vary in colour from dark red, through orange, to orange and yellow, while the leaves also show variation in degree of hair covering. In nature it grows along the courses of streams in gravelly valleys forming 6 foot (1·8 m.) tall thickets by means of underground stems, but rarely ascending the valley sides. Its petals are very narrow, strapshaped and spirally-coiled in bud, like those of

other witch hazels, and are smaller than those of the Asiatic species.

The Sweet Gum, *Liquidambar styraciflua*, which ranges from Central America and Mexico through Florida and Texas northward to Indiana and Connecticut, also belongs to the witch hazel family. In a wild state it may be up to 150 feet (45 m.) high and it produces an easily worked timber useful for making furniture. Also known as American Red-gum or Satin Walnut, the tree has palmately veined leaves which are fragrant when crushed, with autumnal colours ranging from purple to rose and crimson, or yellow to orange, to make it a spectacular parkland tree. However, the flowers, which lack petals, are inconspicuous. The generic name, from the Latin *liquidus* and Arabic *ambar*, refers to the fragrant resin obtained from the bark of *L. orientalis*.

CAPRIFOLIACEAE

Viburnum alnifolium, Hobblebush
A1 flowering twig × ⅔. A2 fruiting twig × ⅔.

Diervilla sessilifolia
B1 part of flowering stem × ⅔.
B2 flower and calyx × 2⅔. B3 fruiting twig × ⅔.
B4 fruit × 1⅓.

Lonicera ledebourii, California Honeysuckle
D1 flowering and fruiting shoot × ⅔.
D2 flower × 1⅓. D3 fruit × 1⅓.

CORNACEAE

Cornus nuttallii (syn. *Benthamidia nuttallii*)
C1 part of flowering branch × ⅔.
C2 inner flower × 2⅔. C3 fruiting head × ⅔.
C4 fruit × 1⅓.

GARRYACEAE

Garrya elliptica
E1 male catkins on twig × ⅔.
E2 female catkin on twig × ⅔.
E3 male flower × 6. E4 female flowers × 6.
E5 fruiting twig × ⅔. E6 fruit × 2⅔.

HAMAMELIDACEAE

Hamamelis vernalis
F1 flowering twig × ⅔.
F2 mature leaves on part of stem × ⅔.
F3 side view of flower × 2.
F4 face view of flower × 2.

A1

A2

B1

B2

B3

B4

C1

C2

C3

C4

D1

D2

D3

E1

E2

E3

E4

E5

E6

F1

F2

F3

F4

Plate 156   NORTH AMERICA

The genus *Dodecatheon*, most of whose fifty or so species, popularly known as Shooting Stars, are from western North America and typically found in cool, shaded spots, is notable for the colour contrasts provided by the exserted stamens and reflexed, cyclamen-like petals of the numerous flowers, which are borne on a single stalk springing from a leafy rosette. *D. pulchellum* (D) frequents damp meadows at altitudes of up to 7000 feet (2130 m.) from Alaska to California and from Wisconsin to Missouri. The nodding flowers, borne on a stalk up to 20 inches (51 cm.) long, vary in number from 3 to 25 and appear between April and June; the corolla tube is maroon and yellow, the stamens a contrasting yellow and the petals, magenta to lavender. The capsular fruits contain numerous small seeds.

The genus *Oenothera* consists of over a hundred and twenty species when accepted in a broad sense, although some botanists break it into many smaller groups such as *Megapterium, Pachylophus, Camissonia* etc., and most of them are North American, though a few also occur in South America and the Caribbean. All have long tubular flowers that open by night and are ideally suited to pollination by moths. The Glade Lily or Missouri Primrose, *O. missouriensis* (F), found in dry, open habitats, often on chalky soils or rocky outcrops, from Nebraska, Kansas and Missouri to Texas, may be either an almost stemless plant, or a spreading one with a stem as much as 20 inches (51 cm.) long. The few but lovely flowers have extremely long corolla tubes that may be easily mistaken for flower stalks, the true flower stalks, situated beneath the ovaries which lie almost next to the stem, being very short. The sepals all tend to curl in the same direction. At the end of the flowering period, which lasts from May to July, equally attractive reddish, winged fruit are produced.

Oenothera caespitosa ssp. *marginata* (E) is a small, very pretty plant, usually stemless and hairy, found in gravelly places or amongst sagebrush. The flowers, scented and white, but fading to pink when spent, combine attractively with the variable, divided leaves. This species occurs from Washington and Oregon to New Mexico and inhabits environments as diverse as the desert slopes of California and mountain sides at altitudes of up to 10,000 feet (3050 m.). It manifests great diversity in hair-covering and capsule and, in 1965, was divided by the monographer Philip Munz into nine subspecies.

Clarkia amoena (C) is a member of a genus of about forty species, mostly found in western North America but also occurring as far south as Chile, which was named in honour of Captain William Clarke (1770–1838) who, with Captain Lewis, explored the Rocky Mountains in 1806. As defined by Lewis & Lewis in 1955, *C. amoena* is a variable species ranging from Vancouver Island to California and divisible into five subspecies, of which the type (ssp. *amoena*) is endemic to coastal slopes and bluffs of California. Commonly called Farewell to Spring, and sometimes placed in the genus *Godetia*, named after the Swiss botanist C. H. Godet (1797–1879), it forms an erect or sprawling shrublet up to 3 feet (91 cm.) tall and is very hairy all over. The fan-shaped petals are pink to lavender or whitish in colour, the stamen filaments white to lavender. The plants known in gardens as Godetias are derived from *C. amoena*. A member of the genus more familiar in cottage gardens is *C. unguiculata* (syn. *C. elegans*), introduced about 1832 from its native California, which flowers between June and August and ranges in colour from pink to red-purple or white.

The two hundred and fifty species of the genus *Cuphea*, found throughout tropical and subtropical America, are characterized by brightly coloured flowers, often of peculiar construction, and sticky hairs on the leaves and other organs. *C. lanceolata* (A) is a stately and colourful plant about 3 feet (91 cm.) in height with clammy leaves. Originally a native of Mexico, where it flowers late in the year, it was first grown in England about 1796, in the Apothecaries' Garden at Chelsea. After the 1830's, however, the species was lost to cultivation in England and it only returned when Kew received material from German sources in the 1860's; since then, it has continued to be grown at Kew. A more familiar glasshouse plant is *C. ignea* which bears cigar-shaped flowers of scarlet tipped with black and white. The plant was brought to Europe from Mexico in 1848.

One of the finest of all North American plants, and consequently one of the first to be shipped to Europe where it has been cultivated since 1626, *Lobelia cardinalis* (B) stands about 3 feet (91 cm.) tall, bearing between July and September, a long, scarlet inflorescence. In the wild, it inhabits woodland clearings and similar moist places from New Brunswick and Michigan south to the Gulf States. Though hardy in western Europe, it has gained a reputation for delicacy as a result of its being confused with the tender *L. splendens* from the southern States and Mexico, which is often sold under the name *L. cardinalis*.

LYTHRACEAE

Cuphea lanceolata
A1 part of flowering and fruiting stem × ⅔.
A2 flower, sectioned × 2. A3 fruit × 1⅓.

CAMPANULACEAE

Lobelia cardinalis
B1 part of flowering stem × ⅔.
B2 flower × 2. B3 style and anthers × 2⅔.

ONAGRACEAE

Clarkia amoena (syn. *Godetia amoena*), Farewell to Spring
C1 part of flowering stem × ⅔.
C2 stamen × 2⅔.

Oenothera caespitosa ssp. *marginata* (syn. *O. marginata, Pachylophus marginatus*)
E1 flowering plant × ⅔.

O. missouriense (syn. *Megapterium missouriense*), Glade Lily, Missouri Primrose
F1 flowering shoot (decumbent habit) × ⅔.
F2 part of fruiting stem × ⅔.

PRIMULACEAE

Dodecatheon pulchellum (syn. *D. pauciflorum*)
D1 flowering plant (stem cut) × ⅔.
D2 flower × 2. D3 fruit × ⅔.

A3 A1 B2 B3 C1 C2 D3 D2 D1 B1 E1 F1 F2

Plate 157   NORTH AMERICA

This plate demonstrates the fascinating variety of forms exhibited by North American members of the *Crassulaceae* family, especially those found in the area from California south into Mexico.

The two hundred species of the genus *Echeveria* begin their range in the southern states of the U.S.A. and extend as far as the northern Andes. *E. subrigida* (A), a splendid flowering plant well worth cultivating, was discovered in 1892 by C. G. Pringle in the Tultenango Canyon, its only known habitat, in Mexico. First cultivated in the Missouri Botanic Garden, it was introduced to Kew in 1905 and flowered there for the first time in 1911. Like the majority of echeverias, it is easy to grow, requiring only protection from frost during the winter. The plant was originally classified as a *Cotyledon* species.

Discovered by Dr J. A. Purpus (1860-1932) in southern Mexico in 1907, during his explorations of 1907-1908 in the mountains of Puebla State, *E. setosa* (D) is distinguished from the rest of its genus by its succulent, hairy leaves, which are arranged in dense rosettes of a hundred or more. It was introduced simultaneously into cultivation at Washington and Darmstadt, and flowered first in Germany in 1909. Flowers were produced at Kew in 1914 from German material obtained from Erfürt.

Named in honour of its discoverer, the Reverend Dr Nevius, *Sedum nevii* (B) grows in the eastern U.S.A. from Illinois to Alabama and, which is unusual among sedums, favours moist habitats. Flowering shoots spring from its small dense rosettes in June. Commoner in gardens, *S. glaucophyllum*, with which the illustrated species is often confused, differs from *S. nevii* in having more, longer and flatter inflorescences, smoother foliage and more densely clustered leaves.

Although discovered in Vera Cruz State of Mexico by Eric Walther in 1935, and known to be cultivated in the vicinity, the natural habitat of *S. morganianum* (C), Donkey's Tail, has never been ascertained. Its trailing branches, which sometimes reach 3 feet (91 cm.) in length and are clothed in fleshy sharply pointed leaves, are seen at their best when grown in hanging baskets; the flowers secrete large amounts of nectar. The species is easily propagated by leaf offsets. *S. morganianum* takes its name from Dr Meredith Morgan of Richmond, California, under whose care it first flowered in 1938.

The Mexican *Pachyphytum bracteosum* (E) is one of the most attractive of the twelve species in its genus. Fleshy stems, 12 inches (30 cm.) tall in old specimens, rise from rosettes of smooth, thick leaves and bear red-petalled flowers in April and May. Other pachyphytums, such as *P. heterosepalum* from Puebla State of Mexico have spreading sepals and some, such as *P. compactum* from Hidalgo State, have smaller inflorescence bracts than *P. bracteosum*.

Dudleya species, which commemorate William Russel Dudley (1849-1911), Professor of Botany at Stamford University, occur in western North America from Oregon to Mexico and number about forty species in all, though many hybridize freely and are consequently variable. *D. greenei* (F) is native to Santa Cruz, Santa Rosa and the Santa Catalina and San Miguel Islands, in California. The stems are about 2 inches (5 cm.) thick in old plants and may branch to form clumps 4 feet (3·7 m.) broad; inflorescences appear between May and July. The plant is closely related to *D. caespitosa*.

CRASSULACEAE

Echeveria subrigida
A1 inflorescence and leaf × $\frac{2}{3}$.

Sedum nevii
B1 flowering plant (stem cut) × $\frac{2}{3}$.

S. morganianum, Donkey's Tail
C1 flowering shoot × $\frac{2}{3}$. C2 flower × $2\frac{2}{3}$.
C3 petal and stamens × $2\frac{2}{3}$. C4 leaf × $1\frac{1}{3}$.

Echeveria setosa
D1 part of flowering plant × $\frac{2}{3}$.

Pachyphytum bracteosum
E1 part of flowering plant × $\frac{2}{3}$.

Dudleya greenei (syn. *D. regalis, Cotyledon greenei*)
F1 part of flowering plant × $\frac{2}{3}$.

A1

B1

C1

C2

C3

C4

D1

E1

F1

Plate 158 NORTH AMERICA

No other region contains such a wide range of carnivorous plants as North America. Genera not illustrated on this plate include *Darlingtonia*, which feeds on insects drowned in the water of its deep pitchers; *Pinguicula*, whose broad leaves roll over on top of the prey caught on their sticky surfaces; *Drosera*, which has on its leaves numerous small sticky tentacles in which insects become entangled; and *Utricularia*, which sucks minute aquatic animals into sensitive little bladder-traps on its submerged leaves.

The sole species in the genus *Dionaea*, *D. muscipula* (A), Venus' Fly-trap, occurs in damp, mossy spots in the south-eastern states of the U.S.A., where it was discovered about 1760 by Arthur Dobbs, Governor of North Carolina. The leaves consist of a stalk and a terminal blade which, modified into two toothed jaws normally open at an angle of 40° to 50°, forms the trap; in young leaves, the trap is folded back upon the stalk, and it only becomes terminal when the mature leaf has completed its expansion. The 2 sets of teeth with which the jaws are edged, interlock when closed to prevent the escape of larger prey. Closure of the jaws is actuated by an insect touching the 3 or more irritable prongs, arranged in a roughly triangular pattern, with which each is provided; the prongs are hinged at the base to allow the jaws to close tightly. Over the remaining surface of the inner face of each jaw are scattered many small digestive and alluring glands, most of the latter situated just inside the marginal teeth.

Once triggered off, a strong force set up by tensions in the leaf tissue causes the jaws rapidly to enclose the insect, which is then destroyed by juices secreted by the digestive glands, and its broken down substance absorbed through the leaf. Experiment has shown that the number of stimuli necessary to close the jaws varies in direct proportion to the length of the intervals between stimuli: thus two stimuli within twenty seconds of one another, four at one minute intervals and six at two minute intervals will all induce closure. This argues that the build up of some chemical substance may be required for jaw closure.

These remarkable leaves intrigued botanists from an early date. Some, like Linnaeus, believed that the capture of insects was a chance occurrence (any plant with sticky hairs may catch numbers of small insects) and not part of a sophisticated system for obtaining nourishment. Others, like Erasmus Darwin, postulated that the leaves were a 'plant armament' against predatory animals. This trapping device is not, in fact, unique to *Dionaea*, for similar jaws are found on the rootless aquatic *Aldrovanda vesiculosa* found from southern France to Japan.

Sarracenia, a genus of ten species whose range extends along the Atlantic seaboard from Labrador to Florida and west into Minnesota and Wisconsin, commemorates Michel Sarrasin de l'Etang (1659–1734), a French physician at Quebec who sent the first specimens to Joseph Pitton de Tournefort, the celebrated 17th century botanist, for description. *S. purpurea* (C), the most widespread species, was found by John Tradescant in Virginia and brought alive by him to Europe in 1640. The plant grows in *Sphagnum* bogs or floats at the edges of pools. Rosettes of pitchers, which are formed by the whole of every leaf, spring from short rhizomes buried in the sodden moss. Scattered over the outer surfaces of the pitchers are warts and nectar glands by which small animals are lured to their mouths. The inner surfaces are divided into an upper, glandular zone with downward pointing hairs, an alluring and more densely glandular zone with a velvety texture, a glassy glandular zone and, lowest of all, a zone of downward pointing hairs which serve to trap the lured creatures. The width and development of these zones vary according to the development of the pitcher. Accumulated rainwater drowns what is trapped and the subsequent digestion takes place partly by means of juices secreted by the pitcher walls, partly by the action of bacteria.

The pitcher-lids were originally thought to help in the conservation of water but, as was soon discovered, the lids are virtually immobile. Experimental proof that digestion occurs in the pitchers was provided in 1874 by J. H. Mellichamp of Bluffton, South Carolina, who, in a letter to Asa Gray, the father of American botany, described how he had placed pieces of venison in them and watched the breakdown of the meat.

The presence of animals lured to the pitchers attracts in turn predatory creatures such as spiders and ichneumons. There is also a harmless species of mosquito that lays its eggs in the pitcher-water and is thought to breed nowhere else. The moth *Exyra rolandiana* lays its eggs in a single pitcher; on hatching, each larva migrates to a nearby pitcher and then proceeds to eat its way through pitcher, flower, fruit and all. The peculiar leaves of this plant have given rise to a host of vernacular names, among them Sidesaddle Plant and Devil's Boots.

Sarracenia leucophylla (B), better known as *S. drummondii*, produces stalked flowers similar to those of *S. purpurea* between April and September in sandy and boggy spots along the coasts of Georgia and north-western Florida. The pitchers, which may grow up to 18 inches (46 cm.) in height, often overtop the flowers and have lids attractively patterned in red and white.

DROSERACEAE

Dionaea muscipula, Venus' Fly-trap
A1 young growing plant × $\frac{2}{3}$.
A2 flowering plant (stem cut) × $\frac{2}{3}$.
A3 open 'trap' × $1\frac{1}{3}$. A4 closed 'trap' × $1\frac{1}{3}$.
A5 'trap' hairs × 8.

SARRACENIACEAE

Sarracenia leucophylla (syn. *S. drummondii*)
B1 flowering plant × $\frac{2}{3}$.
B2 front view of flower × $\frac{2}{3}$.

S. purpurea, Sidesaddle Plant, Devil's Boots
C1 flowering plant × $\frac{2}{3}$.
C2 style and stamens × $1\frac{1}{3}$.

Plate 159   NORTH AMERICA

Something of the great diversity of violets in North America, where leaf shape, habit and flower colour vary considerably from species to species, is shown on this plate. The common Wild Pumpkin is also illustrated.

Distributed through the North Coast Range from Mendocino County, California to Salem, Oregon, *Viola hallii* (B), Hall's Violet, is a rare plant that favours open woodland at altitudes of between 1000 and 6000 feet (300–1830 m.). The partially buried stems, rising from a short root-stock, bear leaves dissected into linear segments that make a graceful foil for the flowers which bloom between April and May. The species commemorates Professor Elihu Hall who first collected it, on the campus of Willamette University, Salem.

The Stream Violet, *V. glabella* (C), occurs in woodland and near watercourses from Monterey County, California, north into Alaska, and in Japan, at altitudes of up to 8000 feet (2440 m.). The plant, which grows to a height of between 3 and 12 inches (7·5–30 cm.), has kidney-shaped leaves that are often softly hairy all over. Particularly fine stands are said to exist about Portland and in Oregon.

Immediately distinguishable by its soft, silkily haired leaves, the Fern-leaved Violet, *V. vittata* (A), grows beside ponds and in bogs in a relatively restricted area from the Gulf states to Texas and Florida. It propagates itself by forming runners, and flowers in March.

Other distinctive species in the genus include *V. pedata*, Bird's-foot Violet, a variable purple-flowered plant with leaves deeply divided by 3 clefts, found in New England and the southeastern states; *V. triloba*, which has variously 3-lobed leaves and occurs in woodland over much the same area; and *V. pedatifida*, a prairie species with palmate, 3-clefted leaves and red-dish-violet flowers that is found from Ohio to Saskatchewan and New Mexico.

Cucurbita foetidissima (D), known as Wild Pumpkin, Missouri Gourd, or Calabazilla, is often encountered trailing along roadsides and on railway embankments and the like in Missouri, Nebraska, Texas, California and Mexico. The triangular, strongly smelling leaves are borne on far-creeping, rough stems which, in June and July, also support the large yellow marrow-like flowers. The fruits contain a substance called saponin which has the power to foam water. The plant is anchored in the dry, sandy soil by a stout perennial root which may be as much as 12 inches (30 cm.) in diameter and 6 to 9 feet (1·8–2·7 m.) in length. Another of North America's several cucumbers, *Sicyos angulatus*, Bur Cucumber, is unusual in having uninflated knobbly fruits covered in hairs and spines. This species climbs by means of branched tendrils and may extend itself over several metres in this way. The plant is native from Quebec through Minnesota into Texas, Florida and Arizona.

Another genus of trailing or climbing plants, *Marah* consists of seven species, all confined to the Pacific coast, with turgid spiny capsular fruits up to about 6 inches (15 cm.) in length. Solitary female flowers and male flowers in racemes or panicles rise from the axils of the 5- to 7-lobed leaves. The name *Marah*, given to the genus by Kellogg, a pioneer Californian doctor and botanist with Swedenborgian interests, comes from the Hebrew and means 'bitter'. He had in mind a passage in *Exodus* (15:23), describing the plight of the Israelites wandering in the waterless desert of Shur: 'And when they came to Marah, they could not drink of the waters of Marah, for they were bitter: therefore the name of it was called Marah'.

VIOLACEAE

Viola vittata, Fern-leaved Violet
A1 flowering plant × $\frac{2}{3}$.

V. hallii, Hall's Violet
B1 flowering plant × $\frac{2}{3}$.

V. glabella, Stream Violet
C1 flowering plant × $\frac{2}{3}$.

CUCURBITACEAE

Cucurbita foetidissima, Wild Pumpkin, Missouri Gourd, Calabazilla
D1 male flowering shoot × $\frac{2}{3}$.
D2 female flower × $\frac{2}{3}$. D3 style × $\frac{2}{3}$.
D4 fruit × $\frac{2}{3}$. D5 seed × $\frac{2}{3}$.

A1

B1

C1

D1

D2

D3

D4

D5

Plate 160   NORTH AMERICA

The genera *Mammillaria* and *Opuntia* provide some of the most widely and easily cultivated cacti, usually producing flowers with a minimum of attention. The former takes its name from the series of tubercles, or nipple-like protuberances, with which the small globe-shaped stems are covered. The latter, with its variously shaped spiny joints is the epitome of all cacti. The Ocotillo (*Fouquieria*) is a curious plant found only in North America and Mexico and, with the related genus *Idria*, recalls the *Didiereaceae* of Madagascar (see plate 70).

One of two or three hundred species in the genus, which occurs in south-western North America, the West Indies, Colombia and Venezuela, *Mammillaria elongata* (A) is native to central Mexico, where it is found most abundantly in Hidalgo State. The whitish tips to the spreading aggregates of cylindrical green stems take their colour from the short-lived covering of wool with which the young areoles are clothed. Each areole has 15 to 20 curved radial spines and sometimes 1 central spine, which may be white, yellow or brown. The colour of the spines can greatly alter the appearance of the plant and a number of varieties based on differences of spine-colour exist. The bell-shaped flowers open between March and April. *M. elongata* is frequently found as a house plant but is often overwatered and therefore prone to rot.

Of the two hundred and fifty or so species of *Opuntia* known to science, all are native to the Americas, though a few have become naturalized throughout the warmer parts of the world, some as troublesome weeds; one species, *O. ficus-indica*, the Prickly Pear, is widely grown for its edible fruits but its origin is lost in cultivation.

A plant variable in spininess, flower colour, shape and size of stem-joint and fruit, *O. lindheimeri* (C) grows in thickets of sometimes quite considerable extent in Louisiana, Texas and north-east Mexico. The species, which may reach 12 feet (3·7 m.) in height, usually has a pronounced trunk but also occurs with a prostrate habit. Each young bluish-green stem-joint bears numerous narrow fleshy leaves that soon fall to reveal areoles with 1 to 6 spines, the larger central, the smaller spreading. The flowers, which vary in colour from red to yellow, are replaced by an oblong or pear-shaped fruit some

2¼ inches (5·6 cm.) in length. A species with low bushy habit and elongated fruits that occurs in certain parts of Texas and appears to be intermediate between *O. lindheimeri* and *O. macrorhiza* (see below) and may well be a hybrid has been called *O. leptocarpa*.

Opuntia macrorhiza (D), a native of dry prairie from Missouri and Kansas to Texas, somewhat resembles *O. compressa* (syn. *O. humifusa*), a low spreading cactus found from as far north as Massachusetts to Georgia, but has woody roots and only 3, or sometimes no, spines at each areole. The yellow flowers may be tinged with red.

Opuntia imbricata (syn. *O. arborescens*) commonly called the Tree Cactus or Candelabrum Cactus, is an example of those opuntias, none of which are illustrated here, that have cylindrical instead of flattened stem-joints. The species, easily identifiable by its dense, branching joints and papery spine-sheaths, grows to a height of 6 feet (1·8 m.) and has a trunk about 2¼ inches (5·6 cm.) thick. Woolly areoles give rise to from 6 to 20 barbed spines, the longest of which measures about 1¼ inches (31 mm.). The purple or pink flowers produce a dry yellowish fruit that remains attached to the plant for many months. In summer, the new stem-joints bear quite large leaves. Live joints, when broken, give off a smell of witch hazel and may be easily detached from the plant, thus giving it a vegetative means of propagation. Dead, woody stem-joints are sold as curios or candlesticks.

Fouquieria comprises ten species of which *F. splendens* (B), the Ocotillo, is the best known. A tawse-like appearance is given to the plant by the somewhat grooved spiny stems, which reach a height of 20 feet (6 m.) and are only slightly branched at the base. The leaves vary in size and shape according to whether they are borne on long or short branches. The capsular fruits measure ⅔ inch (1·6 cm.) long and contain seeds with wings which soon become fractured into fringes of hair. Placed closely together, Ocotillo plants make effective natural fences and the stems yield a sort of wax, as well as a gum and a resin. The species grows in desert and semi-desert, from Texas, Arizona and southern California into Mexico and the scarlet flowers are very conspicuous in a wet season.

CACTACEAE

Mammillaria elongata
A1 flowering plant × ⅔.
A2 flower sectioned × 4.
A3 areole × 5⅓.

Opuntia lindheimeri
C1 flowering stem × ⅔.
C2 fruiting stem × ⅔. C3 areole × 1⅓.

O. macrorhiza
D1 flowering stem × ⅔. D2 areole × 2⅔.
D3 habit sketch × 1/18.

FOUQUIERIACEAE

Fouquieria splendens, Ocotillo
B1 flowering shoot × ⅔.
B2 leafy part of stem × ⅔.
B3 habit sketch × 1/22.

A2

A3

A1

B2

B3

C3

C2

C1

B1

D2

D1

D3

Plate 161   NORTH AMERICA

The genera represented opposite all contain decorative North American species found to a certain extent in temperate gardens the world over. The genus *Zenobia* is generally considered today to contain one species from eastern North America, with two forms—one with glaucous leaves and the other with them simply green. As yet little cultivated, these plants deserve wider recognition for their fragrant, lily-of-the-valley-like flowers and clusters of fruit covered with a bluish white bloom. *Z. pulverulenta* (A), which has been grown in Britain since about 1801, is a native of damp woods on the eastern coastal plain from Virginia to South Carolina. Like many genera in the *Ericaceae*, this genus commemorates a character of classical antiquity, the courageous 3rd century Queen of Palmyra Zēnŏbia Augusta.

The genus *Kalmia*, with about eight American species, commemorates the Finnish botanist Pehr Kalm (1715–1779) who, between 1747 and 1751, collected specimens of the genus whilst travelling in North America, although plants had already reached Britain by 1730. The exquisite pink flowers with little swellings or pouches on the outside, very evident on the buds, seem to have pleased the discriminating Ruskin, who described them as 'bosses in hollow silver, beaten out apparently in each petal by the stamens instead of a hammer'. In fact the unusual shape arises from the special pollination mechanism; the anthers develop, tucked into little 'pockets' on the corolla so that the growing filament bends like a bow; when the flowers open, visiting insects dislodge the anthers, releasing the tension on the 'bow' which springs towards the centre of the flower covering the underside of the insect with pollen which is then dusted onto the stigma of another flower. Mountain-laurel or Calico Bush, *K. latifolia* (B), grows in woods on sandy or rocky, non-calcareous soils throughout eastern North America, from Ontario and New England south to Missouri and Georgia. Usually evergreen, it forms a shrub or small tree, usually about 10 feet (3 m.) tall, sometimes rising to 20 feet (6 m.), and given adequate moisture, will produce many trusses of pink flowers in spring.

The Mayflower or Trailing Arbutus, *Epigaea repens* (C) occurs from eastern Canada south to Florida, while the very similar *E. asiatica* grows in the mountains of Japan—yet another example of the affinity between the flora of eastern Asia and North America. The Mayflower forms a creeping sub-shrub about 6 inches (15 cm.) high, with a stem rooting at intervals, bearing clusters of 5 to 6 flowers at the ends of shoots in April and May. In a letter to Sir Joseph Hooker on 2 May 1874, the great American botanist Asa Gray noted how rarely this plant produces fruit. It was introduced into Britain in 1736 but has never been easy to grow as it is susceptible to late frosts and mild winters, needing cool conditions in leafy soil; nor is it easy to cultivate in gardens in its native States. The pretty pinkish or white flowers have a waxy texture and are so attractive as to have caused enthusiastic gardeners to decimate the wild populations in many parts of North America in an attempt to grow the species in their own gardens. The name, from Greek *ĕpi* 'upon', *gaea* 'earth', refers to its low growth. Tradition has it that the Pilgrims, when they landed at Plymouth, Massachusetts, saw *E. repens* in flower and christened it 'Mayflower' after the gallant vessel which had transported them across the Ocean.

Another plant with lily-of-the-valley-like flowers, the delicate little heather *Cassiope lycopodioides* (D) is in all ways suited to the desolate and bitter habitats in which it grows. It ranges eastward from the Aleutian Islands and the islands in the Bering Straits across Alaska, south to British Columbia at altitudes of about 4000 feet (1220 m.), and west to eastern U.S.S.R. and Japan. The resemblance of the stem of this plant, with its rows of small leaves, to that of a clubmoss or *Lycopodium* species, explains the specific epithet; the generic name, after Cassiŏpē the mother of Andromeda, was chosen by David Don because Linnaeus had previously named the related Bog-rosemary after Andromeda herself. In all there are about twelve, very low-growing and evergreen species in the genus.

Named after Jean François Gaultier (1708–1751), a physician and amateur botanist from Quebec, the genus *Gaultheria* contains some two hundred species found from the south of India, through the western Himalaya, around the basin of the Pacific, into eastern North America and eastern Brazil, with a conspicuous centre of species diversity in the Andes. Salal, *G. shallon* (E), grows to about 6 feet (1·8 m.) tall in favourable habitats, spreading by underground suckers and forming a dense growth, often used in America and elsewhere as game-cover. The pink to white, urn-shaped flowers appear in May or June, each being subtended by a hood-like bract. The fruits, which contain many small seeds, are dark purple, juicy and edible; they are not berries, as they appear, but capsules surrounded by persistent calyces which have become fleshy. Salal is found in mixed evergreen forest, Redwood forest and coastal scrub in California, north through Oregon into British Columbia. It was introduced to the west by David Douglas in 1826 and is very satisfactory for cultivation in moist shaded spots where other plants may not grow; it has become naturalized in some parts of Europe.

The monotypic family *Clethraceae*, with about one hundred and twenty species, is allied to the *Ericaceae* although the petals of its flowers are not fused into a single unit. Ranging from North Carolina to Florida and Alabama, *Clethra tomentosa* (F) flowers late in the summer and produces fragrant white blossom, massed into inflorescences up to 6 inches (15 cm.) long. It is sometimes classified as a variety of *C. alnifolia* with greyish, felted leaves although the latter is more widespread and variable, with unfelted leaves and which flowers about a month earlier. Both species thrive best in moist habitats but the illustrated plant is more interesting for cultivation even though it is frost-sensitive.

The *Pyrolaceae* may be considered as the herbaceous off-shoot of the *Ericaceae*. It is confined to north temperate and arctic areas and contains three genera, of which *Pyrola* with about twenty species, is one. In America, the Common Wintergreen, *P. minor* (G), occurs in cool woods or thickets almost throughout the continent. Across the Atlantic, it is found from Britain and Iceland, across to the Caucasus and into the eastern Himalaya; as may be expected, such a widespread species is variable throughout its range. The capsular fruit contain many tiny seeds which can be easily dispersed by the wind; this may explain the widespread distribution.

ERICACEAE

Zenobia pulverulenta
A1 flowering shoot × ⅔.
A2 flower with corolla removed × 2⅔.
A3 stamen × 5⅓. A4 fruit × 2⅔.

Kalmia latifolia, Calico Bush, Mountain-laurel
B1 flowering shoot × ⅔. B2 bud × 1⅓.
B3 flower × 1⅓.

Epigaea repens, Mayflower, Trailing Arbutus
C1 flowering shoot × ⅔.

Cassiope lycopodioides
D1 flowering plant × ⅔.

Gaultheria shallon, Salal
E1 part of flowering shoot × ⅔.
E2 flower with corolla removed × 2⅔.
E3 stamen × 5⅓. E4 style and ovary × 2⅔.
E5 fruiting twig × ⅔. E6 fruit × 2.
E7 sectioned fruit × 2.

CLETHRACEAE

Clethra tomentosa
F1 part of stem with flowering shoot × ⅔.
F2 immature fruit × 5⅓.

PYROLACEAE

Pyrola minor, Common Wintergreen
G1 part of flowering and fruiting plant × ⅔.
G2 flower × 2⅔. G3 petal and stamen × 3⅓.

A1

A2

A3

A4

B1

B2

B3

C1

D1

E1

E2

E4

E5

E6

E7

F1

F2

G1

G2

G3

Plate 162   NORTH AMERICA

A magnificent and decorative tree growing to a height of 45 feet (14 m.), *Catalpa bignonioides* (A), the Common Indian Bean, is a native of river banks and other moist habitats in the southern states of the U.S.A. from Georgia to Mississippi and exists as a feral plant further north. The large rounded leaves, which may be up to 12 inches (30 cm.) long, have pointed tips and hairy undersides. The panicles, up to 12 inches (30 cm.) tall and roughly pyramidal in shape, contain numerous flowers but only a few mature fruit, full of winged seeds, are produced. Nectar is not confined to the flowers but is also secreted by glands in the angles of the leaf-veins. The species was introduced into England in 1726 by Mark Catesby (1682–1749), an Essex man who imported a number of plants from North America following his two visits to the New World. One of the largest specimens to have been recorded in Britain was one grown at Wilton House, Wiltshire, which is said to have reached 53 feet (16 m.) in height. The *Catalpa* genus, like *Campsis* (see below), includes east Asian as well as North American species, thus underlining the relationship that exists between the floras of the two areas.

It was Mark Catesby who first noticed how well the flowers of the Trumpet Creeper, *Campsis radicans* (B) are adapted to suit the nectar-seeking hummingbirds by which they are pollinated: the brilliant red corollas serve to attract the birds, while their fleshy texture ensures that they are not damaged by the probing beaks. The species is a native of moist woodland and waysides from New Jersey to Florida and Texas, and may be found clinging to brickwork by its ivy-like aerial roots. Its climbing stems extend 30 feet (9 m.) or more and give rise to shoots at whose ends are borne the clusters of flowers. The slightly flattened fruits contain numerous winged seeds about $\frac{5}{8}$ of an inch (1·5 cm.) long that somewhat resemble those of *Catalpa* species. *C. radicans* was introduced into

Europe in the late 1630's. The other species of the genus is a native of China, long cultivated in Japan. The two have hybridized in cultivation, producing the hybrid group known as *C. × tagliabuana*, members of which are stated to be commoner in southern Massachusetts than either parent, 'climbing over houses, barns, out-buildings and garden fences in complete abandon'.

Further west, along the watercourses of the Mojave and Colorado Deserts and in other similarly arid areas, grows another bignoniaceous shrub, *Chilopsis linearis*, commonly known as the Desert Willow because of the resemblance of its narrow leaves to those of true willow species. It reaches a height of about 18 feet (5·5 m.) with many stems and slender twigs, and bears small panicles of lavender, pink or whitish flowers speckled with purple. The corollas are shaped more or less like those of *Catalpa* species, though the crisped edges of the lobes give the impression of having been nibbled away. The slender fruits contain many winged seeds.

Nine species from the warmer parts of the Americas belong to the genus *Proboscidea*. Of these the most distinctive is the Unicorn Plant, *P. louisianica* (C), whose common name refers to the shape of the immature fruit, which is elongated at the tip into a long curved horn. The woody inner portion of the fruit can be seen, after the disappearance of the initial fleshy covering, to consist of 2 valves, each with a horn 8 inches (20 cm.) long, that split apart to release the ripe seeds. The plant is an annual and densely hairy, with spreading stems up to 3 feet (91 cm.) long bearing large rounded leaves on long stalks. Though often cultivated to the north of its native area, the south-west of the U.S.A., it requires too much sun and warmth during the July to September flowering period to be able to flourish in a western European summer.

BIGNONIACEAE

Catalpa bignonioides, Common Indian Bean
A1 flowering shoot × $\frac{2}{3}$.
A2 twig with pods showing seeds × $\frac{2}{3}$.
A3 seed × 2.

Campsis radicans, Trumpet Creeper
B1 flowering shoot × $\frac{2}{3}$. B2 pod × $\frac{2}{3}$.
B3 seed × $\frac{2}{3}$.

MARTYNIACEAE

Proboscidea louisianica, Unicorn Plant
C1 flowering and fruiting shoot × $\frac{2}{3}$.
C2 fruit lacking pulpy outer shell × $\frac{2}{3}$.
C3 leaf × $\frac{2}{3}$.

A2

A1

A3

B1

B2

B3

C2

C1

C3

Plate 163 NORTH AMERICA

The *Hydrophyllaceae* or Water-leaf plants, to which family the *Phacelia* and *Nemophila* belong, are so called because they have soft leaves and delicate parts which quickly wilt when picked.

There are about two hundred species of *Phacelia*, some annuals and some perennials, found from North America to the Andes. The flowers have a 2-part style and anthers which turn inside out when releasing the pollen. The annual *P. viscida* (A) grows in southern California from Monterey County to Los Angeles County and in the Channel Islands, from sea level to about 3000 feet (910 m.). The plants are found in sandy places, in chaparral and among sage-scrub, and grow 1–2 feet (30–61 cm.) high. The flowers may be white, blue or bi-coloured. Its distribution overlaps the larger-flowered, clammy-stemmed and more southerly annual, *P. grandiflora*.

A much smaller genus than *Phacelia*, *Nemophila* has about twelve species all of which are annual. They are found in west and south-eastern North America. *N. maculata* (B) is restricted to the Sierra Nevada and Coast Range of California and grows below about 7500 feet (2280 m.). It has been given the common name of Fivespot because the flowers always have 5 large purple blotches whereas Baby Blue-eyes, *N. menziesii*, is typically bright blue but variable, indeed, so variable that some authorities have concluded that it should really be treated as a group of several different species. For instance, *N. atomaria* applies to a form with pale blue flowers dotted purple or black and *N. liniflora* distinguishes a form with white or pale blue flowers with a black centre.

Lewisia is a genus of some twenty western American perennial species; it belongs to the *Portulacaceae*, a family related to the *Cactaceae*. Because of their thick and fleshy roots, which are sometimes eaten, certain plants in this genus show great resistance to desiccation. *L. rediviva*, it is reported, can easily withstand two years of drought. The genus commemorates Meriwether Lewis of the famous Lewis and Clark expedition across North America in 1804–1806.

Lewisia tweedyi (C), one of the largest flowered lewisias, is an alpine plant found in the Wenatchee Mountains of Washington State, a range between the Rockies and the Cascades. It grows on Mount Stuart between 6000 and 7000 feet (1830–2130 m.). The species has a large tuberous rootstock and succulent leaves. When cultivated it is treated like an alpine.

Known as Virginia Bluebell or Cowslip, *Mertensia virginica* (F), belongs to a genus of some fifty species, found mostly in northern temperate areas, but also as far south as Afghanistan and Mexico. This familiar plant, a native of the U.S.A., is well-distributed from New York and Ontario through Minnesota and South Carolina, to Alabama, Arkansas and Kansas. Its height varies from 9 inches (23 cm.) to about 2 feet (61 cm.), according to where it is found. Its typical habitats are in woods and wet meadows, but it is easily cultivated as a spring flowering garden plant.

Linanthus is a genus of forty to fifty species, ranging throughout western North America and as far south as Chile, although California with thirty-four native species is its centre of distribution. This genus differs from the closely related *Gilia* in having opposite leaves on leafy stems, instead of alternately inserted leaves confined to the basal parts of the stem. In addition, the corolla of *Linanthus* tends to be salver-shaped rather than funnel-shaped as in *Gilia*, and, at the microscopic level, its chromosomes are smaller than those of *Gilia* although they are the same in number. *L. grandiflorus* (E) is an annual of the central Californian coast. Its white or lavender-coloured flowers with orange anthers are visited and pollinated by bumble bees.

The genus *Monarda* is named after the Spaniard, Nicolas Monardes (1493–1588), the author of the first book on American plants (*Historia medicinal de las cosas que se traen de nuestras Indias occidentales* of 1569, translated in 1577 with the more exciting title *Joyfull Newes out of the Newe Founde Worlde*), which contained the first descriptions of that delightful or deadly herb, tobacco. *Monarda* contains some twelve species and extends throughout North America into Mexico; it is one of the genera with 2 stamens, and these mature well before the style becomes receptive to pollen. *M. fistulosa* was introduced into Britain in 1637 by John Tradescant the younger, while *M. didyma* (D) had to wait until 1744 for its introduction by Peter Collinson, as seed sent by John Bartram of Philadelphia; the plant flowered the year after sowing. One of its common names, Oswego Tea, was given to the plant because it was collected from the area known as Oswego on Lake Ontario and its leaves were used in the preparation of a tea. Authors differ as to whether the flowers are pollinated by butterflies with long mouthparts or by hummingbirds.

At least seven hundred species of *Salvia* exist and the genus is the largest in the *Labiatae*. Like *Monarda*, only 2 stamens are present, but where the anthers join the top of the filament, it is generally T-shaped with one arm longer than the other and an articulation at the point of junction. When a bee, hummingbird or other pollinator pushes against one arm, it levers the other onto the pollinator and dusts him with pollen. In most species, in fact, one of the anther arms is sterile and acts only as a lever (see detail of flower, G2). The styles mature well after the pollen is shed and the stigma always has 1 of its 2 lobes longer than the other. Unlike species found elsewhere, the stigma has the upper lobe longer than the lower in species native to Central or South America. *S. elegans* (G) is found throughout Mexico, with a variety called *sonorensis* restricted to the Sonora and other areas of north-west Mexico.

A2

B2

B3

B4

B1

C1

A3

A1

D2

D1

D3

E1   E2

E3

F2

F1

G1

G2

Plate 164   NORTH AMERICA

Though not always hardy plants, and needing an open position and plenty of sun, the Beard Tongues, *Penstemon* species, include a number of colourful and ornamental bedding types. They range in size from such species as the Mexican *P. barbatus* which grows up to 4 feet (1·2 m.) in height, and the even taller *P. isophyllus,* up to 6 feet (1·8 m.) to the 4 to 5 inch (10–13 cm.) *P. davidsonii* and *P. fruticosus* var. *scouleri.* Among other colourful North American members of this same family are *Collinsia* species, named after the Philadelphia botanist Zaccheus Collins (1764–1831), and the genus *Castilleja,* whose vividly coloured bracts have given rise to the general name Indian Paint Brushes.

One of the neatest and showiest rock garden pentstemons, *P. fruticosus* var. *scouleri* (A) is a small alpine plant with lanceolate leaves and flowers, erect or obliquely held, with a pronounced and hairy lower lip. A native of the north-western U.S.A. and southern British Columbia, the species was introduced into Europe in the 1880's and has proved hardy there.

A species found over a wide range in the central states of the U.S.A., *P. bradburii* (B) has elliptical leaves, the upper, which are more pointed than the lower, each subtending 1 or 2 flowers on a common peduncle. These flowers, which are slightly flattened vertically, vary in colour from purple-lilac to white. As in all penstemons, there are 5 stamens (the name is derived from the Greek *penta*, five and *stemon*, a stamen), 4 growing in pairs of unequal length, the 5th reduced to a staminode with a yellowish hairy or pimpled tip. Both stamens and staminode are fused to the inside of the corolla base. *P. bradburii* first appeared for sale in England in 1813, when it was catalogued as *P. grandiflorus* in recognition of the impressive inflorescences of foxglove-like flowers. It was not until the following year that Frederick Traugott Pursh (1774–1820) formally described the plant by its present name.

A native of the Rocky Mountains, discovered by Thomas Nuttall, *P. humilis* (E) is a variable species 6 to 12 inches (15–30 cm.) tall that flowers between May and July. The shortly-branched erect stems are clothed with hairless, mainly basal leaves and end in panicles of pale red-purple to azure flowers with inflated corolla tubes borne in 3 or more whorls.

The Texan *P. baccharifolius* (F) was first described in 1852, after its discovery by Charles Wright. Its almost unbranched stems grow to a height of 18 inches (46 cm.) and bear showy scarlet flowers in groups of 3. The stalkless leaves are somewhat rigid, coarsely serrated and hairless and their resemblance to those of some species of *Baccharis* gave rise to the epithet.

The greater number and most diverse of the hundred or so species of the Monkey Flower genus, *Mimulus*, are to be found in North America. *M. cardinalis* (C), one of the better known, inhabits shady places near streams, or dripping cliff-faces, in mountains throughout California, north to Oregon, east to Utah and south to northern Mexico. Where the branches are allowed to spread, the plant may attain a height of 3 feet (91 cm.). The leaves are stalkless and covered with soft hair, and each of the upper ones subtends a single flower on a long stalk. The calyx is sometimes ribbed and dotted in red, while the corolla, its cylindrical tube almost enclosed by the calyx, may be bright scarlet and rose, or pink and yellow.

A species with a curious history is *M. moschatus*, a sad little plant from western North America with yellow flowers that was much cultivated in Europe in the latter half of the 19th century for its strong smell of musk. However, about the turn of the century, for no apparent reason, all the cultivated plants lost their smell. As no scented wild plants have since been found, it is possible that the form cultivated may have derived from a small, abnormal population, or even from a single individual.

One of the most handsome Butterworts, *Pinguicula macrophylla* (D) grows at altitudes of 4500–9000 feet (1370–2740 m.) on moist banks and ledges in the oak and pine forests of Mexico's western mountains. The leaves, sticky on the surface, trap small flies and then curl inwards from the edges to secrete the digestive juices by which the insects' bodies are broken down prior to absorption. *P. macrophylla*, sometimes referred to by its synonym *P. caudata* when cultivated, resembles *P. colimensis* but has a looser, less crowded leaf rosette and narrower corolla lobes.

SCROPHULARIACEAE

Pentstemon fruticosus var. *scouleri* (syn. *P. scouleri*)
A1 part of flowering plant × ⅔.
A2 part of opened corolla showing stamens and style × 1⅓.
A3 stamen × 5⅓.

P. bradburii
B1 part of flowering stem × ⅔.

Mimulus cardinalis
C1 part of flowering stem × ⅔.

Pentstemon humilis
E1 part of flowering plant × ⅔.

P. baccharifolius
F1 part of flowering stem × ⅔.

LENTIBULARIACEAE

Pinguicula macrophylla (syn. *P. caudata*)
D1 flowering plant × ⅔.
D2 part of leaf showing glands × 1⅓.

A3

A2

A1

B1

C1

D2

D1

E1

F1

Plate 165 NORTH AMERICA

Rare in the wild, *Stokesia laevis* (A) occurs here and there in pine woodlands from South Carolina through Louisiana and Alabama to Florida. It grows 8 to 24 inches (20-61 cm.) tall and has blue flower heads of variable size, often smaller than the one illustrated, the outer florets having a 5-toothed ray. The genus commemorates Jonathan Stokes (1755-1831), author of *Botanical Materia Medica* (1812) and was introduced into England about 1770 when James Gordon, a nurseryman who died in about 1780, sent plants to Kew, where it is still grown. It makes a fine summer bedding plant if given ample water.

Their decorative attributes and their wide tolerance of habitat conditions have made some of the twenty-five *Rudbeckia* species useful garden plants, and several of the more commonly encountered ones are described below. A tall yellow-flowered plant with divided, sparsely hairy leaves, *R. laciniata* ranges from Manitoba, Saskatchewan and Quebec through the New England States to the southern states and as far west as Colorado and Arizona; a garden variety, *hortensia* bears double flowers. Found in the midwest from Ohio to Missouri, *R. speciosa* displays large yellow flower heads with orange-brown to brown-purple bands and in recent years has been grown as a polyploid plant. Black-eyed Susan, *R. hirta*, with a short, stocky habit and hairy leaves and stems, has pale to dark yellow flower heads, tinged with orange, brown or maroon. A close relative, *R. fulgida*, with purple coloured stems and leaves and orange-brown flowers with a central cone of maroon disc-florets, has a wider range, being found from Manitoba and British Columbia through Wisconsin and Illinois to the southern United States. *R. bicolor* derives its name from the yellow flower heads with bands of dark purple running round the bases of the ray-florets. It has conspicuously hairy leaves and occurs from Texas to Florida. The illustrated *R. amplexicaulis* (C), a native of Texas, Kansas and Louisiana, is characterized by leaves which clasp the stem and flower heads which are variable in size. Its common name, Coneflower, is derived from the way in which its disc-florets are arranged around a column in the centre of the inflorescence. Other members of the *Compositae* have even more exaggerated cones, that of *Ratibida columnifera*, for example, being up to 2 inches (5 cm.) long. The genus *Rudbeckia* commemorates Olof Rudbeck (1660-1740), a Swedish professor who befriended Linnaeus.

A native from Wisconsin and Ontario, through New York and New Jersey south to Louisiana and Florida, *Liatris spicata*, the Button Snakeroot (D), grows on prairies and along highways and railroad tracks. Each flowering head consists of 4 to 14 flowers, normally rose-purple but occasionally white, arranged on an axis. The genus contains about forty species, some of which have hybridized with others.

The genus *Gaillardia* is named after a French botanist, Gaillard de Merentonneau, and has about twenty-five species in North America and another two in South America. Found on waste ground and waysides from Colorado to New Mexico, and from Texas, Minnesota, Nebraska and Oklahoma into Louisiana and Kansas, *G. pulchella* (E), also called Indian Blanket or Firewheels, is said to have been introduced east of the Mississippi River. The variety *picta* has somewhat more succulent leaves and colourful flower heads. *G. aristata*, a yellow-flowered species sometimes found in gardens, was introduced from the Rocky Mountains in 1826; it is a native of Colorado, Oregon and British Columbia.

Helenium autumnale belongs to a related genus and has a wide distribution, being found in many parts of the U.S.A. and Canada. It is therefore naturally tolerant of a variety of habitats and a useful garden plant, especially prized for its plentiful flower heads which range in colour from bronze and mahogany to red and yellow, with reflexed marginal rays; the variety *grandiflorum* has larger flowers.

Represented by the single species *L. texana* (B), the genus *Lindheimera* occurs very locally in Texas and Oklahoma. It is named after Ferdinand Jacob Lindheimer (1801-1879) who discovered it in 1846. A small Mexican species was included at one time in this genus, but is better classified as *Dugesia mexicana* as its leaves are more divided and form a rosette, although the flowers of the two species are rather similar.

Aster is a large genus of some five hundred species found in the Americas, Africa and Eurasia from which the Michelmas Daisy has arisen. The numerous garden daisies of this name are largely varieties of several North American and Asian species, notably the bright blue-violet-flowered *A. novae-belgii* ranging from Newfoundland down the east coast to Georgia; the blue- or violet-flowered *A. laevis* extending from Maine to Georgia and Louisiana; and the purple-flowered *A. novae-angliae* with a range from Quebec to South Carolina and Colorado. A particularly useful Eurasian species has been the yellow- and purple-flowered *A. amellus*. Commonly found in moist woodland from Ontario and Quebec, through Michigan, Illinois and Indiana, to Massachusetts and south to Georgia, *A. macrophyllus* (F), the Large-leaved Aster, bears its delicate pale lilac flower heads on stems about 18 to 24 inches (46-61 cm.) tall.

COMPOSITAE

Stokesia laevis
A1 part of flowering stem × ⅔.
A2 portion of leaf showing undersurface × 8.

Lindheimera texana
B1 flowering and fruiting shoot × ⅔.
B2 ray-floret × 2⅔.
B3 disc-floret and style × 2⅔.

Rudbeckia amplexicaulis, Coneflower
C1 part of flowering and budding stems × ⅔.
C2 disc-floret (from cone) × 4.
C3 ray-floret × 1⅓.

Liatris spicata, Button Snakeroot
D1 flowering spike and leaves × ⅔.
D2 floret × 2⅔.

Gaillardia pulchella, Indian Blanket, Firewheels
E1 part of flowering stem × ⅔.
E2 ray-floret × 2⅔.

Aster macrophyllus, Large-leaved Aster
F1 part of flowering stem with leaf × ⅔.
F2 disc-floret × 4. F3 ray-floret × 2⅔.

A1

A2

B1

B2

B3

C1

C2

C3

D1

D2

E1

E2

F1

F2

F3

Plate 166   NORTH AMERICA

The genus *Sagittaria* is spread over most of the world except for Africa and Australasia, although only two of the twenty or so species occur outside America. In general most plants can produce 3 types of leaf according to the conditions under which they grow. Completely submerged leaves, usually the first to be produced, are strap-shaped or terete; floating leaves have linear, elliptical or ovate blades, generally with a pointed tip; leaves held above water are usually shaped like arrow-heads giving the genus both its scientific and popular names.

Sagittaria rigida (E) grows in the shallows of swamps and ponds from Quebec to the southern states of the U.S.A., and has become naturalized in Europe. A number of forms, with differences largely dependent on locality, have been recognized. *S. rigida* never, apparently, produces arrow-shaped leaves. The inflorescence measures from 4 to 32 inches (10–80 cm.) in length and bears 2 to 8 flowers in whorls up the stem, the upper (male) blooms with stalks $1\frac{1}{4}$ inches (3 cm.) long, the lower (female) without. This distribution of male and female flowers on the stem is constant throughout the genus. All flowers have about 3 white perianth segments approximately $1\frac{1}{4}$ inches (3 cm.) long. The filaments of the stamens are covered with tiny scales and the beaked fruits, each about $\frac{1}{8}$ of an inch (3 mm.) long, have winged margins.

The Italian botanist Giulio Pontedera (1688–1757) is commemorated in a purely American genus of four species, *Pontederia*. *P. cordata* f. *cordata* (A), Pickerel Weed, from the marshes and shallow waters of Nova Scotia to those of Florida, has 40 inch (102 cm.) stems growing from creeping rhizomes. The leaves, which vary from form to form within the species, are usually heart- to lance-shaped, those of the form illustrated being more triangular, with straighter sides, than most. Each of the clustered panicles of blue flowers produces an achene-like fruit enveloped in the remains of the perianth. The species is gregarious and often forms large colonies, attractive when in flower.

Another attractive, though dangerous, plant is *Eichhornia crassipes*, a floating fresh-water species with long fibrous hanging roots and clusters of upward-thrusting leaves, the stalks of which are swollen with spongy buoyant tissue. Its main beauty lies in the candles of lilac to pale blue flowers which have given it its popular names of Water Hyacinth and Water Orchid. The characteristic that makes it so widely feared, not only in its native tropical America but in Africa, Java and Australia too, is the speed at which its lateral shoots reproduce: one raft of connected brother plants may cover several hundred square metres of water; a section of such a raft, detached and blown by the

wind, will colonize new areas. *E. crassipes* is thought to have been introduced to the Sudanese Nile early in 1957; by 1958 it had spread along 620 miles (1000 km.) of river, a rate of advance of 1140 yards (1·4 km.) a day upstream and 1 mile 970 yards (2·5 km.) downstream (approximately 6 inches (15 cm.) a minute). By November 1958 steamers were taking twelve days to complete what had previously been an eleven day voyage, irrigation pumps were so frequently blocked as to be almost useless, and the incidence of bilharzia and malaria was increasing. Herbicides have had some effect but the plant continues to grow. There are four other species of *Eichhornia*, all of them American.

Entirely different in habit are the hundred or so species of *Sisyrinchium*, whose centre of diversity lies in South America, though it is also well represented in North America. A typical species is *S. campestre* (D), which grows in tufts up to 16 inches (41 cm.) tall and bears small pale blue or white flowers which later produce capsules that turn straw-coloured when dry. The colour of the flowers together with its prairie, glade and open woodland habitat, have given the species its popular name Prairie Blue-eyed Grass. It is found through the central states of the U.S.A. from Wisconsin in the north to Texas in the south. A sister species, *S. bermudiana*, native to moist woodland from Quebec to Florida, illustrates a phenomenon often noticed in the comparison of the North American and European floras: material of the same species found in western Ireland is indistinguishable from that found in America.

Iris fulva (C), the Copper Iris, has stems about $4\frac{1}{2}$ feet (1·4 m.) tall with almost evergreen leaves 3 feet (91 cm.) in length. The coppery-orange flowers, which between April and May ornament swamps from Illinois and Missouri to Georgia and Louisiana, measure about $3\frac{1}{2}$ inches (9 cm.) across. *I. fulva* is closely related to *I. hexagona*, a blue-violet-flowered species from the south-eastern states, distinguishable from the former by its narrower 'standard' petals.

Native to grassy open places in Washington and Oregon, *I. tenax* (B) has lilac to violet flowers flushed down the centre of each 'fall' petal with a yellow streak. The always single-flowered stems grow to a height of about 12 inches (30 cm.). The strong fibrous leaves are stated to be used by Indians to make snares and nets. A very similar species bearing 2 yellow flowers on each stem and found in open coniferous forests in California, *I. hartwegii* is held by some botanists to be simply a colour form of *I. tenax*. The ease with which certain species of iris (*I. hartwegii* among them) hybridize with one another in the natural state is a striking and much studied phenomenon.

PONTEDERIACEAE

Pontederia cordata f. *cordata*, Pickerel Weed
A1 part of flowering stem with leaf $\times \frac{2}{3}$.
A2 flower $\times 2\frac{2}{3}$. A3 radical leaf $\times \frac{2}{3}$.

IRIDACEAE

Iris tenax
B1 part of flowering plant $\times \frac{2}{3}$.
B2 stamen and style $\times 2$. B3 fruit $\times \frac{2}{3}$.

I. fulva, Copper Iris
C1 part of flowering stem with bud and withered flower $\times \frac{2}{3}$.

Sisyrinchium campestre, Prairie Blue-eyed Grass
D1 flowering plant $\times \frac{2}{3}$.

ALISMATACEAE

Sagittaria rigida (syn. *S. heterophylla*)
E1 flowering plant with off-shoot $\times \frac{2}{3}$.
E2 male flower $\times 2\frac{2}{3}$. E3 stamen $\times 5\frac{1}{3}$.
E4 female flower $\times 2\frac{2}{3}$.

B3

A2

A3

A1

B1

B2

C1

E3

E2

E1

D1

E4

Plate 167 NORTH AMERICA

As well as members of the true lily genus, *Lilium*, the woodlands of eastern and western North America provide some of the prettiest examples of related genera suitable for growing in gardens. *Uvularia*, found only in the east, consists of four or five species, generally known as Merrybells or Bellworts, and is related to the east Asian genus *Tricyrtis* (see plate 107). *U. grandiflora* (A) is a native of moist woodlands from Quebec to North Dakota and south to Oklahoma and Georgia, and in April and May, when the plant has reached a height of about 20 inches (51 cm.), it bears 1-4 pendulous flowers partially hidden amongst the foliage of arching stems. Later in the season these stems may grow to 3 feet (91 cm.) tall. Another species, *U. perfoliata*, resembles *U. grandiflora* but has glands and rough projections on the insides of the perianth segments, and seems to prefer somewhat acid not limestone soils.

The genus *Trillium* contains about thirty species and the most ornamental are those from North America, although species are found in the Himalaya and other parts of eastern Asia. Leaves, sepals and petals are all clearly arranged in groups of three. Painted Trillium, *T. undulatum* (C), extends from Quebec to Manitoba in Canada south to Wisconsin in the west and upland Georgia in the east and grows to a height of about 16 inches (41 cm.). Flowering occurs in May and June, when the leaves are some 4 inches (10 cm.) in length; the sepals are shorter and less colourful than the wavy-edged petals. This species was introduced into cultivation in 1811.

Trillium erectum (D), introduced into western Europe somewhat earlier, in 1759, when Philip Miller grew it in his garden at Chelsea, grows to the same height as the previous species but has a less westerly distribution. The 4 inch (10 cm.) long flower stalk rises from a rosette of 3 stalkless leaves, and the sepals almost equal the petals in length. One of its common names, Stinking Benjamin, refers to the unpleasant scent of its flowers.

The species most cultivated in western Europe, *T. grandiflorum* was introduced to Kew in 1799 by Francis Masson (more famed for his travels and plant collecting in South Africa) but was probably grown before that by other collectors. It also comes from eastern North America and has large white or rose coloured petals which are sometimes doubled, even in nature.

The genus *Erythronium*, although it possesses a number of attractive species, such as the Dog's-tooth Violet, *E. dens-canis*, on the Eurasian side of its distribution, reaches its climax of development in North America's Pacific mountains where many species worth cultivating are found.

A native of shady woodlands on the Sierra Nevada in California, *E. multiscapoideum* (B) bears its nodding flowers with their showy perianth segments between March and May. In 1896 it was exhibited in London. Another Californian species, *E. grandiflorum*, lacks the mottled leaves of the illustrated plant and has golden flowers, but resembles it in most other respects. *E. grandiflorum*, which blooms in June and July, was discovered by David Douglas about 1828 and first flowered in the London Horticultural Society's Chiswick garden in 1835 or 1836.

Also a native of California, *Calochortus pulchellus* (F), the Star Tulip or Golden Lantern, belongs to a genus of sixty species confined to the western and central parts of the continent from British Columbia to Central America. It grows in woodland and thicket vegetation, usually at altitudes of above 700 feet (210 m.). The conspicuously fringed perianth segments are twisted at an angle to one another, their edges overlapping. Flowering occurs in May and June and the capsules later produced have 3 broad wings. Not all members of this genus have nodding flowers: *C. venustus*, one of the Mariposa Lilies, for instance, carries its white, yellow, purple or red perianths, blotched with dark red, erect on stems about 24 inches (61 cm.) tall. It is one of the best known species and easiest to grow. *C. kennedyi*, like *C. venustus* from California, is less easy to grow, being a plant of dry desert slopes, but has spectacular, erect flowers, orange to vermillion-scarlet in colour and blotched at the base with deep purple.

To the south of the area so far discussed, the flora takes on a more tropical aspect. Typical of this region are the exotic but ephemeral Mexican Tiger-lilies, of the genus *Tigridia*. Probably because the flowers are so short-lived, lasting no more than a day, or even less, these plants are less widely cultivated than their appearance demands. *T. pavonia*, with flowers in shades from white to red-purple according to variety, is the species most often found in gardens. It flowers in late summer and has 2 ranks of sheathing leaves 10-15 inches (25-38 cm.) long, each blade concertinaed along the veins. *T. pavonia* is native to southern and central Mexico and was introduced into Europe as early as 1799.

A northern Mexican plant, found by C. G. Pringle in Chihuahua in 1887, *T. pringlei* (E) forms a 2- to 4-leaved herb with leaf blades strongly folded along the veins. A succession of blooms, bell-shaped at the base, are produced from the 5 or 6 sheathing bracts, one at a time on each stem.

LILIACEAE

Uvularia grandiflora
A1 flowering plant × $\frac{2}{3}$.
A2 4 stamens, style and ovary × $1\frac{1}{3}$.

Erythronium multiscapoideum
B1 part of flowering plant × $\frac{2}{3}$.

Trillium undulatum, Painted Trillium
C1 flowering plant (stem cut) × $\frac{2}{3}$.

T. erectum, Stinking Benjamin
D1 flowering plant × $\frac{2}{3}$.
D2 stamens and ovary × $1\frac{1}{3}$.

Calochortus pulchellus, Star Tulip, Golden Lantern
F1 part of flowering plant × $\frac{2}{3}$.
F2 flower, petal removed × $1\frac{1}{3}$.
F3 edge of perianth segment × 4.

IRIDACEAE

Tigridia pringlei
E1 part of flowering stem × $\frac{2}{3}$.
E2 base of stem and bulb × $\frac{2}{3}$.

A2

A1

B1

C1

D1

D2

E1

E2

F1

F2

F3

Plate 168   NORTH AMERICA

Approximately three hundred *Agave* species occur from the southern U.S.A. into South America, many of which are peculiar in having long life-cycles, only flowering after sixty to a hundred years spent in the vegetative condition; when they are produced, the inflorescences are sometimes of a spectacular size. *A. attenuata* (B) has flowers held at right angles to the inflorescence axis, while the bracts are orientated with the axis throughout the curving inflorescence. The specimen illustrated is short-stemmed, but when fully grown, the species has a stem 3 to 4 feet (91–122 cm.) tall with leaves up to about 3 feet (91 cm.) in length. Hooker described how the inflorescence may produce many plantlets instead of flowers and this is quite a common phenomenon in the genus; the plant illustrated produced ripe fruits at the base of the inflorescence and plantlets towards the tip. *A. attenuata*, a native of Mexico, first flowered in Britain in 1861.

A native of coastal regions of Georgia, Alabama and Mississippi, *Yucca recurvifolia* (A) is allied to *Y. gloriosa* and as an intermediate between the two species, *Y. recurvata*, is occasionally found; some botanists regard *Y. recurvifolia* as a variety of *Y. gloriosa*. Introduced into Britain in 1794, it is quite hardy and is occasionally seen in private gardens, and, for example, grows at the Royal Botanic Gardens, Kew. Its gracefully recurved leaves are quite thin and flat on the upper surface for most of their length. *Y. gloriosa*, a native of coastal areas from North Carolina to Florida, has thicker, stiffly erect leaves.

Some forty species of *Yucca* occur in the southern United States, Mexico and the West Indies. They differ from *Agave* in having perianth segments and stamens which are inserted at the base instead of the top of the ovary, as in *Agave*. The pollination of yuccas is highly specialized and with the flowers only open at night, it involves nocturnal visits from *Pronuba* moths. The female moth has specially adapted mouth-parts, unique to this group, with which she collects pollen. After gathering a pollen-ball, she flies to another flower and deposits her eggs in the ovary by means of a long ovipositor; she then climbs to the top of the ovary and spreads the pollen she had previously collected over the stigma, thus ensuring pollination. The ovules then begin to develop in the ovary in sufficient number both to feed the developing grubs and provide some viable seed. In this remarkable way the continuation of both the yucca and its moth is ensured from generation to generation.

AGAVACEAE

Yucca recurvifolia (syn. *Y. pendula*, *Y. recurva*)
A1 habit sketch × $\frac{1}{7}$.
A2 part of flowering shoot × $\frac{2}{3}$.
A3 nocturnal flower fully opened × $\frac{2}{3}$.
A4 stamen × 2. A5 style and ovary × $1\frac{1}{3}$.

Agave attenuata
B1 flowering plant (stem cut) × $\frac{1}{6}$.
B2 flowers on part of stem × $\frac{2}{3}$.
B3 petal tip × $1\frac{1}{3}$.
B4 flower with 3 stamens and 3 petals removed × $1\frac{1}{3}$.
B5 bract × $1\frac{1}{3}$.

A1

A2

A3

A4

B1

B2

B3

B4

B5

5

Plate 169   CENTRAL AND SOUTH AMERICA

Victoria amazonica (A) is the largest and most remarkable water-lily known. In the words of Richard Spruce (1817–1893), the famous botanical explorer of South America: '. . . the impression the plant gave me, when viewed from the bank above, was that of a number of green tea-trays floating, with here and there a bouquet protruding between them; but when more closely surveyed, the leaves excited the utmost admiration, from their immensity and perfect symmetry. A leaf, turned up, suggests some strange fabric of cast-iron, just taken from the furnace, its ruddy colour, and the enormous ribs with which it is strengthened, increasing the similarity.'

The enormous water-lily was first discovered in 1801 by Thaddaeus Haenke (1761–1817), a Bohemian botanist, doctor and mineralogist. Employed by the Spanish government in Peru, he died there and little of his work ever became known. Indeed his discovery of this superb species remained unknown until 1848. Aimé Bonpland was the second botanist to find the species, in 1820 when he was travelling in the area where the rivers Parana and Paraguay converge. Eduard Friedrich Poeppig also found the water-lily in the course of his travels up the Igaripes, a tributary of the river Amazon, in 1832, and the following year he published a description under the name *Euryale amazonica*, mistakenly allying the plant to a species found in South East Asia and China; but the two are now placed in different genera. Sir Robert Hermann Schomburgk (1804–1865) found *V. amazonica* when travelling up the Berbice river in British Guiana in 1837, and he too was amazed by its wonderfully large leaves and flowers. He also noted how a particular type of beetle, now considered a pollinator of the plant, was associated with the flowers. Thomas Bridges (1807–1865) first introduced viable seeds, from the Moxos Province of Bolivia, which were germinated and grown at Kew for a short time in 1846. Not until 1849 were seeds successfully germinated and seedlings distributed in any number from Kew to gardens such as those at Chatsworth House and Syon House. The Duke of Devonshire's enterprising gardener, Joseph Paxton (1802–1865), obtained a seedling from Kew in August 1849 and had it in flower that November. Its remarkable growth led Paxton to design a new conservatory and the veining of the leaves 'like transverse girders and supports' suggested the principles of a construction he adopted when designing the biggest glasshouse of all time, the Crystal Palace, for the Great Exhibition of 1851. The generic name commemorates Queen Victoria.

In the botanic gardens of temperate areas, the plant is grown from seed each year, although in nature it is a perennial. Thus it attains its mammoth dimensions in the period of about seven months. Not surprisingly, it requires a large amount of very rich compost in which to grow.

The flowers and leaves spring from a stout rhizome of about 8 inches (20 cm.) diameter, which penetrates the mud with its roots. Young leaves are at first crumpled and about the size of a child's head, but after about three days they begin to resemble a round tea-tray. After seven days the leaves are fully expanded and about 6 feet (1·8 m.) across. In the wild, leaf size is influenced by the depth of water, for this determines the length of leaf stalks, which in turn determines how closely the leaves grow around the rhizome. Shallow waters tend to produce shorter leaf stalks and small, more crowded leaves; and in cultivation, reduced light also diminishes leaf size. The upper surface of the leaf resembles a large number of small low mounds, while the underside is correspondingly pocked with numbers of depressions between the massive ribs and struts which are the veins.

The stalks are about 10 to 18 feet (3–5·5 m.) long and the pear-shaped flower-bud is about 8 inches (20 cm.) in length. The 4 sepals are more or less prickly on the outside and their dull purple to green surfaces open to reveal the white, more delicate petals. By mid-morning the mature bud opens, and by early afternoon the flower reaches the condition illustrated opposite. Some flowers have as many as 60 petals, but usually only one flower opens on a plant at a time. The flower remains open through the night and until early afternoon of the following day when the petals become completely reflexed and radiate out. The stamens remain erect for a while but these too finally reflex and expose the innermost series of staminodes which form a barricade over the entrance to what one might call the 'inner flower'. Details of this inner flower are shown opposite.

The fruits themselves sink into deeper water to mature and the spongy tissue surrounding the seed cavities forms a pulp when the fruit has ripened. When ripe, the fruit resembles an olive-brown coloured urn covered with large elastic prickles, and it opens by releasing the stopper of the urn, splitting and showing the greenish black seeds embedded in the pulp. These edible seeds are about the size of a pea and known locally as 'Mayz de l'Eau', or water maize, for they contain a floury starch from which excellent pastry is made.

After germination the first leaf is grass-like, the second is arrow-headed, and the third and subsequent leaves are circular in outline but dissected where the leaf stalk is inserted (A5), until in mature leaves the groove is marked by two small indentations in the upturned rim of the leaf. These indentations serve as overflow channels when heavy rains fall, preventing suffocation as the leaf breathes through its upper surface.

The other species of the genus is *V. cruziana*, named after a General Santa Cruz, which has a more southern distribution, in Paraguay, Bolivia and Argentina. The species differ in the underside leaf colour—more blue in *cruziana* and more red in *amazonica*. There are also other botanical differences. In 1961 a hybrid named 'Longwood Hybrid' was raised from the two species at Longwood Gardens, Pennsylvania.

NYMPHAEACEAE

Victoria amazonica, Royal Water-lily
A1 flower × $\frac{2}{3}$ against part of leaf.
A2 long section of bud × $\frac{2}{3}$: petals surrounding red-tipped staminodes; below the stamens, the dish-shaped stigma surface has a small central cone of tissue and a rim of fused finger-like objects pointing down from above; the ovary is between the stigma and the flower stalk.
A3 cross section of ovary showing the vertically arranged cavities in which the seeds mature × $\frac{2}{3}$.
A4 stamen of the type immediately outside the staminodes × 2.
A5 seedling with early leaf stages × $\frac{2}{3}$.
A6 habit sketch × $\frac{1}{22}$.

A6

A5

A1

A3

A4

A2

Plate 170   CENTRAL AND SOUTH AMERICA

The inflorescences of *Brownea grandiceps* (A), a rather rare tree 30 to 40 feet (9–12 m.) tall found in certain areas of Venezuela, are essentially the same in structure as those of a rhododendron: unopened flowers at the tip of each inflorescence are protected by velvety bracts which continue to persist amongst the open flowers (see A2). Before they mature, the young leaves, like those of all the other species in the genus *Brownea* and in the related genus *Amherstia*, plate 113, are soft, drooping, limp and reddish. The species bears the common names Rose of Venezuela and Rosa del Monte. The genus commemorates Patrick Browne (1720–1790), author and botanist, who pioneered the study of natural history in Jamaica.

Members of the genus *Erythrina*, whose hundred or so species occur throughout the tropics and subtropics, are characterized by spiky inflorescences composed of numerous elongated pea-flowers in shades of red or orange that appear before the leaves, transforming the bare tree into a glowing spectacle. A native of the Peruvian Andes, *E. poeppigiana* (C), commonly called Mountain Immortelle, is often used as a shade plant on coffee and cacao plantations and has thus spread northwards into Panama, Colombia, Venezuela and the West Indies, and south into Brazil, Bolivia and Ecuador. Its specific epithet commemorates Eduard Poeppig (1798–1868).

Calliandra haematocephala (D) is a perplexing plant with a complex history and problematical nomenclature. The name used above was given in 1855 by Justus Carl Hasskarl (1811–1894) to material grown at Bogor, Java from seed sent from the Calcutta Botanic Garden; the plant was, however, unknown in the wild, as George Bentham pointed out in 1875, when he wrote that he could relate *C. haematocephala* to no other Old World species. A relative, however, was provided for *C. haematocephala* when Henry Hurd Rusby (1855–1940) described a wild plant collected in Bolivia in 1892 as *C. inaequilatera*; indeed the two 'species' were found to be almost identical and botanists are still uncertain whether *C. haematocephala* had its origin in the Americas. A possible explanation of its presence in the Old World is that it was taken there by a plant lover attracted by the red powder puffs that decorate the plant's flowering branches. This seems more credible than postulating either that two almost identical species should have arisen independently through evolution in both the Old and New Worlds, or that a single species should have a distribution that is not only peculiarly disjunct but also consists in part of plants known only in cultivation. Wild plants have been collected in Peru, Bolivia and Brazil but do not appear to be common in any of those areas. Material from Peru is cultivated and flowers in the Palm House at Kew.

By far the greater number of species in the family *Aristolochiaceae*, which contains some three hundred and fifty species in all, belong to the genus *Aristolochia*. Many, such as *A. ridicula*, possess flowers so grotesque as to defy description. Other species, like *A. ruiziana* with its deep purple and white flowers, are strikingly coloured or, like *A. weddellii*, have exaggerated, overhanging upper lobes. A considerable range in flower-size is also manifested, with *A. gigantea* (B) at the larger end of the scale and *A. fimbriata* and several Mediterranean species at the smaller. *A. gigantea*, a native of Brazil, is cultivated at Kew, where it grows high in the roof of the Palm House and flowers annually. It was discovered between 1817 and 1820 by Carl Friedrich Philipp von Martius (1794–1868), South American explorer and initiator of the massive *Flora of Brazil*. The specimen illustrated was introduced into Kew by Sir Frank Crisp (1843–1911) in 1910. The species should not be confused with the equally large-flowered *A. grandiflora*, a native of Mexico, certain parts of Central America, Jamaica and Trinidad, which has a long thin dangling appendage attached to the lower lobe.

LEGUMINOSAE

Brownea grandiceps, Rose of Venezuela, Rosa del Monte
A1 part of flowering stem × ⅔.
A2 flower × ⅔. A3 subtending bract × ⅔.

Erythrina poeppigiana, Mountain Immortelle
C1 flowering twig and leaf × ⅔.

Calliandra haematocephala
D1 part of flowering stem with fruit × ⅔.
D2 group of flowers × 2. D3 flower × 2.

ARISTOLOCHIACEAE

Aristolochia gigantea
B1 part of flowering stems × ⅔.
B2 sectioned base of corolla showing stamens × ⅔.

Plate 171   CENTRAL AND SOUTH AMERICA

A good example of an endemic family, that is one restricted to a single geographical area—in this case South America from Mexico to Peru—*Tropaeolaceae* is best known in temperate gardens for its annuals, most of which have red or yellow flowers, though blue-flowered species also exist. The peppery-tasting leaves of *T. majus* and *T. minus*, the Garden Nasturtiums, can be used as salads, and their pickled seeds and pods make an acceptable substitute for capers. *Tropaeolaceae* has affinities with the geranium, balsam and oxalis families, the last of which is also represented on this plate.

The Canary Creeper, *Tropaeolum peregrinum* (A), is a climbing annual probably introduced into Europe in 1755 from Ecuador or Peru, where it is common in the Tarma district and such localities as Cuzco and Chincheros, often at altitudes of above 10,000 feet (3050 m.). The smaller, lower petals have fringed margins. The common name may be derived from the rather far-fetched idea that the plant when in flower resembles a bush full of canaries, but more probably refers to the fact that the plant was first cultivated on the Canary Islands, and reached Europe from there. *T. peregrinum* should not be confused with the South African species *Senecio tamoides* (see plate 83), which is also known as Canary Creeper.

Another annual climber, but distinguished by its edible, tuberous rootstock, *T. tuberosum* (D) is a native of Peru and Bolivia, where it is known to the Indians as anu. The plant was introduced into Europe in 1827 and is still cultivated in some parts. In Europe, as in the Andes, the rootstock is boiled and sweetened before being eaten.

Many of the eight hundred species in the genus *Oxalis* are characterized by having bulbous or tuberous underground stems that allow them to remain dormant for part of the year in areas with an unfavourable, usually a dry, season. A number, such as *O. deppei* and *O. tuberosa*, also have edible tubers, known as oca, that are tastier and consequently more widely grown than anu; after a few days in the sun, which removes the bitterness imparted by crystals of calcium oxalate, oca is ready to eat, either raw or in stews. The importance of those tuber-bearing plants (collectively known as chunu) still cultivated on the ancient Inca terraces of Andean Peru to the Indians' diet is indicated by the local proverb 'Stew without chunu is like life without love'. Oca, along with two other tuberous natives of the region, the Potato and Ullucu or Melloco (*Ullucus tuberosus*), has in fact been grown in an area centred on the basin of Lake Titicaca since before the time of the Incas, as motifs on pottery of the Tiahuanaco period show. This long history of cultivation may have something to do with the fact that *O. tuberosa*, like the Potato, does not set seed but is propagated from the tubers: Indian farmers may have depressed the tendency to set seed by the selection and vegetative propagation of high yielding plants. When roasted or boiled, the tubers are said to taste like Sweet Potato, or Chestnuts.

It is an obvious general rule that flowers with, for instance, short, rather than medium or long, styles will tend to be pollinated by pollen from anthers borne at an equivalent height. In other words, the mechanism of pollination allows fertilization only between particular flower types through the activity of particular bee or butterfly pollinators. Dissection of the flowers of *O. ortgiesii*, another Peruvian species, shows stamens arranged in two tiers, and stigmas of an intermediate height (see F2). It follows that, given short, medium and long styles, the species contains three possible combinations of anther/stigma height and therefore a triple opportunity for cross-fertilization. A number of other *Oxalis* species have three types of flower, each type borne on separate plants; yet others have two types; and some, as is the case of the majority of flowering plants, have flowers with a fixed anther/stigma relationship. There are also species of *Oxalis* that may not be cross-pollinated, but may become self-pollinated within a permanently closed corolla.

Further species on this plate illustrate some of the differences evolved within the genus. *O. dispar* (B), for example, is a species from Guyana that, together with *O. acetosella*, the European Wood Sorrel (see plate 14), shows the more usual characters associated with oxalises: stalked leaves with 3 leaflets, and stalked flowers with 5 petals and 5 sepals.

The Brazilian *O. rusciformis* (C) has exaggeratedly flattened leaf stalks with 3 leaflets that are much reduced or, in some specimens, altogether lacking. These leaflets fold up if touched. The leaf stalks parallel the structure of the stems of the liliaceous genus *Ruscus*, Butcher's Broom (plate 41), in which these organs have become green and flattened and taken on the role of food manufacture.

The cymose inflorescences typical of the genus can be seen clearly on *O. ortgiesii*; the organs that resemble tentacles, armed with suckers, are what is left of the inflorescence after the flowers have fallen. As in most oxalises, the leaves curl up at night into what has been called a 'sleep position'. The red pigment on the undersides of the leaf is even more marked in some other species, and may cover the entire leaf.

O. ptychoclada (E), also from Peru, manifests itself, according to A. W. Hill, in two different forms of plant, those growing in deep soil having more or less normal leaf stalks and leaves, while those found amongst rocks are distinctly succulent. It may be, however, that Hill was confusing two different species, or possibly the true species with the less succulent *O. ptychoclada* var. *trichocarpa* as many *Oxalis* species are notoriously difficult to identify, especially those in the plexus of succulent or semi-succulent species allied to *O. carnosa*, of which *O. ptychoclada* is one. As in *O. rusciformis*, the leaf stalks have undergone an adaptive change and become circular in cross section, and succulent. The stem is woody at the base and this, together with the succulent leaf stalks, helps the species to survive in arid conditions.

TROPAEOLACEAE

Tropaeolum peregrinum (syn. *T. canariense*), Canary Creeper
A1 part of flowering and fruiting stem × ⅔.
A2 flower × 1⅓.

T. tuberosum, Anu
D1 part of fruiting and flowering stem × ⅔.
D2 dissected flower × 1⅓. D3 fruit × 1⅓.

OXALIDACEAE

Oxalis dispar (syn. *O. insipida*)
B1 part of flowering stem × ⅔.
B2 flower × 1⅓.
B3 pedicels of flowers, cut to show latex × 2⅔.

O. rusciformis (syn. *O. fruticosa*)
C1 flowering shoot × ⅔.
C2 leaves in position on petiole × 2.

O. ptychoclada
E1 flowering shoot × ⅔. E2 flower × 2.

O. ortgiesii
F1 part of flowering stem × ⅔.
F2 dissected flower × 4.
F3 underside of part of leaf showing coloration and hairs × 1⅓.

Plate 172   CENTRAL AND SOUTH AMERICA

Illustrated opposite are a few of the many tropical American species of campanulas and gentians, which are vastly different from the creeping bellflowers of European meadows or the alpine gentians of the Himalaya and China. *Hippobroma* is presumed closely related to the strange Hawaiian genus *Brighamia* (see plate 146), while *Centropogon* and *Siphocampylus* are two conspicuous tropical American lobelia genera. Of the two further plants to be described, *Hypsela* has a curious distribution in the southern hemisphere and the *Lisianthius* species are a group of woody or shrub-like gentians.

The only member of the genus *Hippobroma*, *H. longiflora* (A) (also known as *Isotoma longiflora* and *Laurentia longiflora*) is extremely poisonous. It is easy to understand how it earned its generic name, which translated from the Greek, means 'horse' *hippŏs* 'poison' *brŏmŏs*. Glandular hairs cover the plant surface; it is sticky to the touch and the juice causes inflammation of the skin and eyes. Found in lowland areas from the southern United States, southward to Brazil and Peru, and widespread in the West Indies, it is a perennial herb 6 inches to 2 feet (15-61 cm.) tall and notable for its almost symmetrical, star-shaped, white corolla with a long narrow tube. *H. longiflora* was cultivated in Paris prior to 1823 and was introduced into England from there.

The two hundred and thirty species of *Centropogon*, a genus of shrubs and robust herbs, are confined to the Caribbean area and the American tropics from Mexico to Bolivia. *C. cornutus* (D) (which has long been known as *C. surinamensis* or *C. fastuosus*) has the widest distribution of any *Centropogon*, spreading from the Lesser Antilles, through Trinidad and Panama over Guyana to Peru, Chile, Bolivia and Brazil. It has alternate leaves, its fruits are berries, and the flowers range in colour from carmine to pale purple. When growing without the support of other vegetation it forms a shrub up to 9 feet (2·7 m.) tall, but when scrambling through bushes and trees it may reach a height of 30 feet (9 m.). Its protruding, bearded anthers should not be confused with the stigma. *C. cornutus* was introduced into England as early as 1786 from the West Indies.

Found in tropical America from Costa Rica to Peru, the genus *Siphocampylus* consists of some two hundred and fifteen shrubs and robust herbs. Related to *Lobelia,* it differs in that the corolla tube is not split down the back. The leaves are normally arranged in 3's and the capsular fruits open by 2 valves. A native of Bolivia, *S. orbignianus* (F) is named after its discoverer, the French botanist Alcide Dessalines d'Orbigny (1802-1857). A shrub 3 to 6 feet (0·9-1·8 m.) high, the tube of its flower is reddish, while the pointed lobes are greenish or yellow.

A curious type of discontinuous southern distribution is displayed by the genus *Hypsela*. *H. reniformis* is found only in South America; *H. rivalis* occurs only in New Zealand; *H. sessiliflora* and *H. tridens* appear only in Australia. The South American species, *H. reniformis* (B) occurs in damp maritime habitats up to 14,400 feet (4390 m.) in the Peruvian Andes, Bolivia, Ecuador, Chile and into southern Argentina. The high mountain habitat of the plant is reflected in its generic name from the Greek *hypsĕlos* meaning 'high'. As growing conditions vary the plant may be dwarf and prostrate (B2) or larger and more erect (B1). A glabrous creeping herb, it forms dense mats of prostrate stems rooting at the nodes, and its small pinkish flowers are borne in the leaf axils. Gardeners have confused this species with *Selliera radicans*, in the *Goodeniaceae* family. The latter has a similar creeping habit, but its leaves are gradually narrowed at the base. *H. reniformis* was introduced into cultivation from Chile in 1926 by Harold F. Comber (1898-1969), and one of his herbarium specimens was consulted in preparing this illustration.

The fifty *Lisianthius* species, a group of woody and shrub-like gentians, extend from Mexico and the West Indies into tropical South America. Commonly called 'Flor de Muerto' because it is favoured as a decoration for graves in southern Mexico, *L. nigrescens* (C) grows to about 5 feet (1·5 m.) and may be crowned by a large diffuse inflorescence 2 to 3 feet (61-91 cm.) tall. The illustration, depicting merely a small portion of this inflorescence, shows the characteristically drooping blue-black flowers. Discovered near Papantla, Mexico, by Christian Julius Wilhelm Schiede (1798-1836), it is also known from Guatemala.

Found in Jamaica where it occurs only in the Parish of Hanover on Dolphin Head Mountain, *L. umbellatus* (E), a shrub 8 to 12 feet (2·4-3·5 m.) tall in nature, has leaves clustered at the tips of its branches and scented, densely clustered, yellow and green flowers. *L. capitatus*, closely allied to *L. umbellatus* (some would say conspecific), has almost sessile instead of shortly stalked flowers. More widely distributed in Jamaica, *L. capitatus* occurs in the Parishes of Trelawny, St Ann, Portland and St Thomas. These plants are locally common in limestone woodland margins at altitudes of between 1000 and 3000 feet (305-915 m.). William Purdie (1817-1857), a plant collector for Kew, introduced *L. capitatus* into cultivation from Jamaica in 1843. The six other *Lisianthius* species have loosely branched inflorescences or solitary flowers which are yellow and narrowly funnel-shaped. The commonest of these is *L. longifolius*. All the species mentioned above are found only in Jamaica.

CAMPANULACEAE

Hippobroma longiflora (syn. *Isotoma longiflora, Laurentia longiflora*)
A1 part of flowering stem with fruit × ⅔.
A2 stamens and style × 2⅔.

Hypsela reniformis
B1 flowering plant, large and erect × ⅔.
B2 flowering plant, dwarf and prostrate × ⅔.

Centropogon cornutus (syn. *C. surinamensis, C. fastuosus*)
E1 part of flowering stem × ⅔.

Siphocampylus orbignianus
F1 part of flowering stem × ⅔.

GENTIANACEAE

Lisianthius nigrescens, Flor de Muerto
C1 part of inflorescence × ⅔.

L. umbellatus
D1 part of flowering stem × ⅔.

A2

B2

B1

A1

C1

D1

E1

F1

Plate 173   CENTRAL AND SOUTH AMERICA

The four hundred species in the genus *Passiflora* are mainly American in distribution, though there are a few native to the Old World. The botanic name *Passiflora* (earlier, *Flos passionis*) and the generic common name, Passion Flower, refer to the symbolism associated with the plant by early Spanish friars and missionaries in tropical America, who 'made it an epitome of our Saviour's Passion' and saw in the five anthers a resemblance to the five wounds received by Christ when nailed to the cross. In the triple style are seen the three nails employed; one for each of the hands, the other for the feet. In the central receptacle one can detect the pillar of the cross, and in the filaments (of the corona) is seen a representation of the crown of thorns on the head. The calyx was supposed to resemble the *nimbus*, or glory, with which the sacred head is regarded as being surrounded (H. Friend, *Flowers and Flower Lore*; 1884).

Small green flowers, variable in size and lacking petals characterize *Passiflora suberosa* (A). This variable species, commonly called Meloncillo, is found in Texas, Mexico, the West Indies, Central America and South America as far south as Paraguay and Argentina. Leaf size and shape vary considerably, both entire and lobed leaves often occurring on the same plant. The flowers, borne like the tendrils in the leaf axils, may occur singly or in cymes. Like other members of the genus, it has a circle of filaments or fringe called a corona arising between the petals and the stamens which serves to attract insect and bird pollinators. Older stems develop a conspicuous corky bark.

Granadilla, *Passiflora quadrangularis* (B), grows in Mexico, throughout Central America and the West Indies, and in northern South America. Both the fleshy roots of this perennial climber and the juicy white rather tasteless flesh of the fruit are edible; the latter can be made into jam or mixed with ice-cream. Unripe fruits may be used like marrow and the outer rind is sometimes candied. When ripe, the fruits—elongated berries about 12 inches (30 cm.) in length and 6 inches (15 cm.) in diameter—are yellowish green, sometimes tinged with pink. Outside its natural range, the Granadilla may have to be hand pollinated before it will set fruit, since the normal pollinating agents are absent. Petals, varying in colour from pale to deep dull red, form the attractive flowers, which measure up to 7 inches (17·5 cm.) in diameter. *P. quadrangularis* takes its specific epithet from its characteristically square-sectioned, 4-winged stems.

Discovered in 1837 by George Gardner and flowered for the first time in Britain in 1868 by Philip Frost, *P. cincinnata* (E) is native to many parts of Brazil, Paraguay and Argentina and is also found in Venezuela and Colombia, probably as an introduction. The leaves are variable in shape. The Passion Fruit, *P. edulis*, has much the same range but is now grown in many tropical areas and is a commercial crop in Australia, Hawaii and parts of South America. The flesh of the berry, which measures about 3 inches (7·5 cm.) in diameter, is aromatic and gelatinous and surrounded by firm yellow or purple skin. The flowers are about 5 inches (12·5 cm.) in diameter and have purple and white corona filaments that contrast attractively with the white petals.

The *Loasaceae* family is characteristic of the flora of the Andes but also found in other parts of tropical America, and in southern Africa and Arabia. Many species are twiners, often with hairy leaves that sting virulently when touched. The flowers, hermaphrodite and often yellow, occur singly or in cymes and are symmetrical with 5 boat-shaped petals that may be fused or free. In some genera, such as *Loasa*, the ovary is surrounded by conspicuous, sometimes brightly coloured staminodes that secrete nectar. The ovaries ripen into spirally twisted capsules. None of the species has economic value, but many are strangely attractive and, as they are hardy, deserve more attention in temperate gardens.

Though first discovered by Berthold Carl Seemann (1825–1871), near Gonzanama in Ecuador, *Loasa vulcanica* (D) was not introduced into Britain until 1876, when it was rediscovered by Edouard François André (1840–1911), who reported being stung fiercely by the plant while collecting it. The red, white, and yellow staminodes contrast strikingly with the white petals, and the plant would be well suited to British gardens.

Fuchsia simplicicaulis (C) is one of about a hundred members of a genus that occurs throughout Central and South America with outlying species in New Zealand and Tahiti. This species, like most of those from America, is adapted to pollination by hummingbirds. Pendant flowers arise from the axils of the whorls of 3 or 4 leaves that characterize the species. The plant was discovered by Ruiz and Pavon during their exploration of Peru, first illustrated in their uncompleted *Flora*, and introduced into cultivation by William Lobb. The Mexican species *F. fulgens* (F) has large and rather untidy leaves and drooping racemes of colourful flowers. *F. fulgens* was probably introduced into Britain in 1837 by Theodore Hartweg, though it may have been cultivated in the country as early as 1830.

According to Felix Porcher, writing in 1874, *F. triphylla*, discovered and introduced by Charles Plumier (1646–1704), was the first fuchsia to be cultivated. Later, however, this species was lost to cultivation until a certain Thomas Hogg reared seedlings in his New York nursery in 1873 and on identification, these were found to be *F. triphylla*. The variable *F. magellanica*, now widely cultivated and in some places naturalized, was introduced into Europe about 1788, purchased, some say, by a nurseryman from the wife of a sailor in Wapping, London. Prior to 1830 most cultivated fuchsias were small-flowered, an interesting example being the Mexican *F. microphylla*, but these types lost favour when species such as *F. fulgens*, *F. cordifolia*, *F. corymbiflora* and *F. venusta* became available. English growers began to hybridize these recent introductions about 1837; by 1840 about five hundred varieties were in cultivation and forty years later over one thousand five hundred were known. The Victorian era drew to a close while the craze for fuchsias, which only passed with the coming of the Great War, was at its height. Interest in the genus revived in the 1930's and has not waned since, fuchsias remaining popular basket and cool greenhouse plants. The generic name commemorates the German herbalist Leonhart Fuchs (1501–1565), albeit he never saw a plant of the genus nor knew of its existence.

A1

A2

A3

B1

B2

B3

C1

D1

E1

F1

3

Plate 174   CENTRAL AND SOUTH AMERICA

Attractively coloured leaves and the ease with which, in appropriate conditions, the plants may be propagated, have made begonias favourite house and greenhouse subjects. The genus *Begonia* itself, found in all parts of the tropics and subtropics but particularly abundant in the Americas, contains about nine hundred species and makes up the greater portion of the entire family *Begoniaceae*. *B. haageana* (A) is notable not only for its pink flowers with red hairs and its foliage, red bronze on the undersides, but also for the series of errors that led to its taking the name it now bears. First found on Santa Catharina Island, Brazil, by D. Scharff, it was introduced to Kew in a batch of unidentified seed sent by the horticultural firm of Haage and Schmidt, whose wish it was that any new species the collection might be found to contain should be named after Scharff, from whom it came. They were, however, forestalled for on 14 July 1888 the *Gardeners' Chronicle* published a description of the plant as *B. haageana*, thus giving publication and priority to a name which, by the international rules that govern botanical nomenclature, could not be unmade. The *Botanical Magazine* of December 1888 only helped to establish the mistake when, though describing the plant as *B. scharffii* within, used *B. haageana* on the dust cover.

A rare member of a tropical American genus distinguished by long, graceful stamens and sepals covered with a livid mustard-coloured vestiture, *Steriphoma paradoxa* (C) is a native of the forests of Guatemala, Venezuela and Colombia at altitudes of between 2500 and 4000 feet (760–1220 m.). The Mexican and Guatemalan plant *S. clara*, known locally as Barba de Leon, appears to be a separate species. Further south, on Trinidad and in Venezuela, *S. elliptica* grows to a height of 12 feet (3·7 m.), has leaves with a hairy underside and sepals of a more reddish orange colour than those of the illustrated plant. The most splendid species so far discovered, *S. urbanii*, with petals 2 inches (5 cm.) and stamens 4 inches (10 cm.) in length, occurs in Ecuador.

A plant that is becoming a popular summer bedder in temperate areas and belongs to the same family as *Steriphoma* is *Cleome hassleriana* (B), often called the Spider Flower. The seeds of this South American plant, which should be germinated under glass and only planted out in the summer, are now offered by several seedsmen and are well worth cultivating, though the plant requires the shelter of a wall or hedge if it is not to be damaged during windy or rainy spells. Together with *C. speciosa* and *C. spinosa*, from the West Indies and Central America, it has usually been lumped by gardeners under the name *C. spinosa*, a very variable group of plants.

Members of *Marcgravia*, a genus of some fifty or so tropical American climbers, are characterized by their having two different types of shoot. Climbing shoots have small, round, greenish yellow or bronze leaves that press themselves close to the surface supporting the plant. Once the shoot has reached the top of a tree or a point where the light is sufficient for its needs, it loses its climbing tendency and becomes a flowering shoot—pendulous, with stalked, spirally arranged and leathery leaves, and ending in an umbel of flowers.

Several species of *Marcgravia* have been illustrated in the past but few until now have shown the flowers in the same position relative to the inflorescence as that shown opposite (D1). They do not always, as most illustrations indicate, hang down, but may be held erect; so, at least, the evidence of a photograph and report from Dr C. D. Adams in Jamaica prove in the case of *M. brownei* (D). More observation of wild populations of *Marcgravia* would show whether the position of the flowers differs in other species and whether the posture changes according to the age of the inflorescence. This is not so academic a point as might appear: it is usually held that hummingbirds feed from the sac-like nectaries slung from the tip of the inflorescence and that in so doing their heads become dusted with pollen; in the case of *M. brownei* this is clearly unlikely. It is more probable that the birds dip into the nectar-sacs whilst hovering above the flowers and so receive the pollen on their breasts. The unopened flower has a corolla of fused petals resembling a small cap; this cap, inside which are numerous stamens surrounding a large ovary crowned with a blunt stigma, is lost at an early stage of flowering.

BEGONIACEAE

Begonia haageana
A1 flowering shoot and leaves × ⅔.

CAPPARACEAE

Cleome hassleriana, Spider Flower
B1 part of flowering and fruiting stem × ⅔.
B2 fruit × 1⅓. B3 seed × 4.
B4 leafy part of stem × ⅔.

Steriphoma paradoxa
C1 flowering shoot.

MARCGRAVIACEAE

Marcgravia brownei
D1 flowering twig × ⅔. D2 corolla × 1⅓.
D3 flower, after shedding corolla × 1⅓.
D4 entrance to nectary × 2.
D5 climbing shoot × ⅔.

A1

B3

B4

B2

B1

D1

D2

D3

D4

D5

C1

Plate 175   CENTRAL AND SOUTH AMERICA

With the possible exception of *Rhipsalis,* cacti, as native plants, are confined to the Americas. Succulent species from the Old World, such as some euphorbias or asclepiads, unlike cacti, usually exude a milky liquid when pricked or damaged. The classical habitat of the 'cactus' is hot semi-desert, but species extend north and south of Central America to British Columbia and Patagonia respectively, and ascend to over 10,000 feet (3050 m.) in the Andes.

Cactus plants are modified to withstand dry conditions by having a tough-skinned fleshy stem, which varies in shape; leaves usually reduced to spines; and great powers of regeneration after drought. The flowers usually arise singly, from or near a group of spines borne on a cushion-like swelling or 'areole'; they may be large in relation to the plant as a whole and show no adaptation to arid conditions. The fruit is a berry, which in a number of genera including *Opuntia,* plate 160, the Prickly Pear, is edible.

The characteristic spines of cacti are thought to have several functions. They conserve a quiet layer of air around the stem which helps reduce water loss; they are centres upon which dew condenses; they decrease harmful levels of insolation on the stem; they protect the plant from predators; and they help the spread of cacti by becoming entangled in the plumage or coats of animals, for cacti will regrow from broken-off pieces or cuttings. Botanists believe that the spine-bearing 'areoles' represent condensed shoot systems or branches.

The Saguaro (D), the State Flower of Arizona, grows to about 36 feet (11m.) high after some one hundred and fifty years and may weigh 7–8 tons (7100–8100 kg.). About 95% of the weight of a well-watered plant is due to its water content. The roots are shallow but spread widely, the plants growing best in coarse rock debris; they may be found up to altitudes of about 4500 feet (1370 m.) but are less stately there than at lower altitudes. The seedlings develop very slowly at first, only $\frac{1}{4}$ to $\frac{1}{2}$ an inch (7–14 mm.) annually for several years, then more rapidly, reaching a height of about 2 feet (0·6 m.) in twenty years, 9 feet (2·7 m.) in thirty-five years and 25 feet (7·6 m.) in eighty years. At about twenty-five years old they start fruiting. The white flowers grow at the ends of the stems, usually in May, and are pollinated during the daytime by insects and Western White-winged Doves, and at night by bats. The fruits, ovoid at first, split when ripe into 4 sections with conspicuous crimson pulp in which are embedded thousands of shiny black seeds. These fruits are very rich in sugar and eagerly sought by both birds and Indians, who pick them using long poles, and make them into jam and jelly. *Carnegiea gigantea* is the only species of the genus. It is found in the south western United States (Arizona and south east California) and the Sonora district of Mexico and commemorates Andrew Carnegie (1835–1919), the Scottish-born American industrialist and philanthropist. The name Saguaro (sa-wha-ro) is of Indian origin.

The Night-blooming Cereus, (E), is one of the twenty or so species of the genus *Selenicereus.* They extend from southern U.S.A., through Central America and the West Indies, into northern South America. The large white flowers open at night, whence the botanic name from the Greek *sĕlēnē* 'moon' and the common name of the illustrated species. All the plants of this genus trail or climb and have elongated, ribbed or angled stems, and are found clambering amongst rocks or along the trunks and branches of trees. The species illustrated is a native of Jamaica and Cuba, but widely cultivated throughout tropical America where it has become naturalized. The Night-blooming Cereus is distinguished from the other species by having tawny or whitish hairs springing from the areoles on the ovary and flower-tube.

The twenty or so species of *Pereskia* are among the few cacti still producing true, well-developed leaves. They are found from Mexico and the West Indies to South America. The disposition of the leaves supports the view that the areoles of cacti represent a condensed shoot system. The Barbados Gooseberry or Lemon Vine, *P. aculeata* (C), was cultivated at Hampton Court in 1696, and has been cultivated at Kew since 1760, where it now regularly bears its fragrant blossom. In nature, it forms an erect shrub, but older plants become untidy and develop vining branches up to 30 feet (9 m.) long. The branches climb by means of the hooks on the stems, while the woody trunk is densely armed with wicked-looking spines. Sometimes valued for its edible pale yellow fruits, its leaves are also used as a pot-herb in Brazil. A number of varieties exist differing in leaf shape and colour.

A native of Brazil, *Rhipsalis capilliformis* (A) shows the habit of most plants in the genus. The genus has its centre of distribution in southern Brazil but one species, *R. baccifera,* extending in America from Florida to Brazil and Peru, also occurs in tropical Africa and Ceylon, apparently, but not indubitably, native. It may have been introduced from America by man or birds. *Rhipsalis* may be an exception to the otherwise all American distribution of cacti.

Schlumbergera truncata (B) is a native of the montane parts of Rio de Janeiro State including the Organ Mountains in Brazil. It was introduced in 1818, and its cultivars have since become popular house plants, bearing masses of rose, salmon, orange, purple or white flowers. Many authorities include this species in the genus *Zygocactus* as *Z. truncatus,* separating that from *Schlumbergera* on account of its reflexed petals. The origin of the Christmas Cactus, *S.* × *buckleyi,* probably dates from about 1852 when the hybridizations were made. The contemporary grower, W. Buckley, stated the hybrid arose from a cross between a variety of *S. truncata* and *S. russelliana* (then called *Epiphyllum russellianum*), and this statement has been recently verified (1964) by W. L. Tjaden, who synthesised *S.* × *buckleyi* from *truncata* and *russelliana.*

CACTACEAE

Rhipsalis capilliformis
A1 part of flowering branch with buds × $\frac{2}{3}$.
A2 flower on part of stem × 4.
A3 part of fruiting stem × $\frac{2}{3}$.
A4 fruit of *R. baccifera* in section × 2.

Schlumbergera truncata
B1 part of flowering branch × $\frac{2}{3}$.
B2 part of leaf showing areole × 2.

Pereskia aculeata, Barbados Gooseberry, Lemon Vine
C1 part of flowering branch × $\frac{2}{3}$.
C2 areole (stem hook) × $3\frac{1}{4}$.

Carnegiea gigantea, Saguaro
D1 upper part of stem with flowers and buds × $\frac{2}{3}$. D2 areole × 1.
D3 habit sketch of plant × $\frac{1}{105}$.

Selenicereus grandiflorus
(syn. *Cactus grandiflorus, Cereus grandiflorus*), Night-blooming Cereus
E1 part of flowering branch × $\frac{2}{3}$.
E2 flower-tube scale × $2\frac{2}{3}$. E3 areole × 4.

A1

A2

A3

A4

B2

B1

C2

C1

D2

D3

D1

E1

E2

E3

Plate 176   CENTRAL AND SOUTH AMERICA

Both the plants illustrated on this plate played important roles in South American civilization before the Spanish conquest: cacao seeds were used as currency in ancient Mexico and provided a drink valued by the Amerindian aristocracy; the Hand-flower Tree, whose stamens resemble a red hand, was the focus of a religious cult.

Since the days of the great Indian civilizations, *Chiranthodendron pentadactylon* (B) has been known as the Hand-flower Tree (macpalxochi quahuitl) or, as in modern Guatemala, Monkey's Hand (mano de mico). At the time of the conquest, the Mexican Indians regarded it with superstitious awe, believing that only one specimen of the tree existed and that to propagate it would offend the gods. The plant had probably been an early introduction to Mexico from Guatemala where many were found growing around Guatemala City in 1801. The first Hand-flower trees to be cultivated by Europeans were grown in Mexico from cuttings obtained by José Mariano Mociño (1757-1820) and Martin de Sessé y Lacasta (d. 1809) during a great expedition made on behalf of the King of Spain from 1787 and, although the first seeds introduced into Europe, by Humboldt and Bonpland at the beginning of the following century, did not germinate, by 1813 the plant was being grown in Madrid, Paris and Montpellier. Slightly later Aylmer Bourke Lambert (1761-1842), Vice-President of the Linnean Society for forty-six years and author of the sumptuous *A Description of the Genus Pinus* (1803-1824, plus subsequent editions), brought it to England where its first recorded flowering occurred in 1859.

The tree may reach a height of 45 feet (14 m.) with a trunk 16 inches (41 cm.) in diameter, and bears large solitary flowers opposite the leaves, whose undersurfaces in contrast to the almost naked upper surfaces are covered with clusters of star-shaped brownish hairs. Each lobe of the bell-shaped calyx has a deep well on the inside at the base and is downy. The sepals are leathery in texture; there are no petals. The base of the fused filaments of the long red stamen column, which terminates in the 5 red anthers arranged in the form of a hand with five fingers from which the species takes it name, forms a tube from which the style protrudes and which conceals the ovary. The latter matures into a narrow capsule some 6 inches (15 cm.) long, hairy within and containing small black shiny seeds. At the base of the staminal column on the outside are 5 yellowish staminal lobes that alternate with the sepals.

The thirty species in the genus *Theobroma* are all originally native to Central and South America but some are now widely cultivated in other rainy tropical areas. *T. cacao* (A), Cacao, is a tree 18 to 40 feet (5·5-12 m.) tall found in rain forests where it often grows by watercourses, since it requires not only temperatures of between 80° and 90°F (26·7°-32·2°C), but much free flowing water near its roots. After germination the seedlings form a single shoot 3 feet (91 cm.) long which then throws out from its tip 3 to 5 radial, almost horizontal branches, initiating a process of growth that recurs throughout the life of the plant. Foliage is also produced in well defined flushes. The largest leaves may measure 2 feet (61 cm.) in length and 8 inches

(20 cm.) in width, and occur towards the middle of the tree. Up to 50 small whitish pink flowers may be produced each season from the dense cymose clusters that appear on the old wood of the trunk. The petals are curious in shape, having pouches at the base and reflexed, spoon-shaped tips. Though all flowers are hermaphrodite and have 5 small stamens, the plant does not cross-pollinate easily in cultivation.

The fruits, whose outer casings are often marked by 5 to 10 furrows running lengthwise, may measure 12¾ inches (32·4 cm.) and vary in shape from almost spherical to cylindrical. When mature, they may be green, yellow, red or red-purple, depending on variety. The seeds, tightly packed in 5 rows around the central axis of the fruit, are surrounded by a shiny pulp which in cultivation is removed during a six to seven day period of fermentation under banana leaves. Unless picked, the pods remain attached to the tree and do not release the seeds until the fruit wall has decayed. Between 250 and 450 dry, fermented seeds are needed to make 1 pound (0·45 kg.) of cocoa.

All of the several varieties of cacao now in existence are thought by some authorities to have originated on the lower eastern slopes of the Andes overlooking the Amazon basin. The tree was introduced into the West Indies by the Spanish about 1525, into the area around the Gulf of Guinea sometime in the following century, and into the Philippines in 1670. However it only reached Ghana, now the world's major producer, in 1879. Uganda's Cocoa crop was started in 1901 with seedlings sent from Kew.

The name 'cacao', which applies to the actual plant and seed, is derived from the Nahuatl word 'cacahuatl', though the modern Mexicans use the corrupt form of the word 'cacahuate' for both Cacao and Pea-nut (*Arachis* species *Leguminosae*). The name 'cocoa' refers to the cacao seeds after roasting and grinding, and 'chocolate' (from 'xocoatl') to a similar product from which the fats have not been removed. The drink known to the Indians of Central America at the time of the conquest as 'xocoatl' was far removed from anything commercially produced from cacao seeds today: xocoatl was a strong decoction of cacao seeds in water, flavoured with honey, maize, chile and other substances and sometimes coloured with red-brown Annatto (the dye from the seed pulp of *Bixa orellana* (*Bixaceae*)). This was then whipped into a foaming beverage which must have had the consistency of the froth on a glass of Guinness. This drink, consumed in vast amounts by the noblemen of Mexico, their consumption increasing with their rank, made the Cacao the most highly esteemed tree among the Amerindian races.

Cacao had other uses too. According to Garcia Icazbalceta, 10 seeds were sufficient, in the money system based upon it, to buy a rabbit, while a hundred would have bought a slave. Netzahualcoyotl, King of Tetzcuco, is recorded to have received an annual payment of 2,744,000 fanegas (1 fanega equals 88 lb. (40 kg.)—an indication of the great wealth of the society he ruled. Even as late as 1850, copper coinage had not replaced cacao seeds in Yucatan, and in 1923 the late Dr Paul Standley reported that the seeds still had value in rural Mexico.

STERCULIACEAE

Theobroma cacao, Cacao
A1 flowering and fruiting trunk with leaves × ⅔.
A2 flower × 5⅓.
A3 petal and stamen × 8.
A4 stamen × 8. A5 staminode × 9¼.
A6 fruit partly opened × ⅔.

Chiranthodendron pentadactylon (syn. *C. platanoides, Cheirostemon platanoides*), Hand-flower Tree, Monkey's Hand.
B1 flowering shoot × ⅔.
B2 leaf hairs × 8.
B3 single stellate hair × 16⅔.

A1

A2

A3

A4

A5

A6

B1

B2

B3

Plate 177 CENTRAL AND SOUTH AMERICA

Pavonia, a genus of some two hundred species found throughout the tropics and subtropics, commemorates José Antonio Pavon, an early collector of plants in Peru and Chile which he explored with Hipolito Ruiz Lopez for the Spanish government. *P. multiflora* (B), a native of Brazil growing in the forests in the vicinity of Rio de Janeiro, was discovered by Auguste de St Hilaire (1779–1853) and introduced into Europe in the 1830's or 1840's.

One of about a hundred very widely distributed tropical and subtropical species in its genus, *Abutilon insigne* (A) was introduced from Colombia in 1851 by Lucien Linden; in Europe it requires hothouse treatment. The flowers may be whitish or rose and have a network of deep red veins across the surfaces of the petals. Buds covered with rich brown, star-shaped hairs enhance the appearance of the shoots and the blooms tend to hang away from the foliage on trailing stems, giving the plant a graceful habit.

The exact provenance of the commonly grown *Abutilon megapotamicum* (F) is not known with any certainty, though the specific epithet refers to the Rio Grande of Brazil. The plant has delicate arching stems, and red calyces that combine with the 'bottle-brush' of fused stamens which emerges from the funnel-shaped corolla as the flower expands to full size to give the species a fuchsia-like appearance. Some cultivars have variegated yellow and green leaves.

A number of technical characters distinguish *Coryneabutilon* from *Abutilon*. Probably the best known of the four or so species in this Chilean genus is *C. vitifolium* (C), introduced into Europe in 1836 by the enthusiastic horticulturist Captain Cottingham and germinated in 1844 by William Lobb. Although fairly hardy and still sometimes cultivated against a southern wall in southern English gardens, like many soft-wooded shrubs

it is liable to succumb during a severe winter. Fortunately the plant is easily propagated from seed.

Both South Africa and the warmer parts of the Americas have members of the genus *Sphaeralcea*, which contains about sixty species. *S. umbellata* (E) is a native of Mexico where it was collected in 1840 by Henri Guillaume Galeotti (1813–1858) (hence the synonym *S. galeottii*). Its deep red flowers, which fade to pale rose in the centre, are sometimes confused with those of *S. rosea*, though the latter has larger flowers, variable in colour from white through rose to maroon. *S. umbellata* grows to a height of about 20 feet (6 m.) and bears drooping umbels of flowers on long peduncles.

Clusia grandiflora (D) is a native of Guyana and forms a shrub up to 20 feet (6 m.) tall with somewhat leathery leaves about 12 inches (30 cm.) in length. There are usually 3 or 4 flowers, borne at the end of the shoot. A feature often found in the genus and present in *C. grandiflora* is the raised (umbonate) surface on the inner face of the petals. Male flowers are characterized by a dense ring of stamens, all of which curve into the centre of the flower, which is occupied by a boss of reduced and depressed stamens covered with a shiny viscid resin. Each female flower has a fat central ovary capped by several radiating stigmatic arms flattened against its top. This ripens to a globose fruit about 5 inches (12·5 cm.) long. The woody capsule opens by means of lateral slits to expose the seeds and the fleshy orange arils around them. The majority of specimens collected from the wild are, like that illustrated, male flowering shoots; the females are either less conspicuous or, perhaps, less numerous. *Clusia* is about one hundred and fifty species strong and appears to be exclusively American.

MALVACEAE

Abutilon insigne
A1 flowering shoot × ⅔. A2 sepal × 2.

Pavonia multiflora
B1 part of flowering stem × ⅔.
B2 flower with some petals removed × 1⅓.
B3 stamens and styles × 1⅓.

Coryneabutilon vitifolium (syn. *Abutilon vitifolium*)
C1 part of flowering stem × ⅔.

Sphaeralcea umbellata (syn. *S. galeottii*)
E1 part of flowering stem × ⅔.
E2 stamens and styles × 1⅓.

Abutilon megapotamicum (syn. *A. vexillarium*)
F1 flowering shoot × ⅔. F2 petal × 1⅓.

GUTTIFERAE

Clusia grandiflora
D1 part of flowering stem × ⅔.

A1

A2

B2

B3

B1

C1

D1

E1

E2

F1

F2

Plate 178   CENTRAL AND SOUTH AMERICA

Like many members of its family the *Zygophyllaceae*, which is often associated with dry and salty habitats, Lignum Vitae, *Guaiacum officinale* (E), grows in dry scrub near coasts; it is one of about six species in a genus found in the West Indies and the warmer parts of the Americas. The species, which has long been known for the density and durability of its wood and the medicinal properties of its leaves, fruits and wood shavings, was, by 1514, a trade monopoly of the Spanish, who introduced it into Europe. The first scientific documentation of its medicinal value in English came from Sir Hans Sloane (1660–1753), who, in 1687 and 1688, practised medicine in Jamaica. He mentions the plant in his two volume work, published in 1707 and 1725, *A Voyage to the Islands Madera, Barbados, Nieves, St Christophers and Jamaica, with the Natural History of the Herbs and Trees, Four-footed Beasts, Fishes, Birds, Insects, Reptiles etc., of the last of those islands.* Today the decorative value of the bicoloured wood, pale brown on the outside, chocolate on the inside, is exploited to make table-ware and carvings. It also forms a useful park tree, growing to a height of about 25 feet (7·6 m.) and having a rounded crown so smothered with deep blue blossoms during the flowering season that the leaves may be entirely hidden. *G. officinale* is found along the Pacific coasts of Central America, the coasts of Venezuela and Colombia, and throughout the Caribbean, where it has become the National Flower of Jamaica.

Stigmaphyllon ciliatum (A) is a climbing plant bearing golden yellow blossom found in British Honduras and northern South America, often in coastal areas. The genus *Stigmaphyllon*, which contains about sixty species, occurs throughout the West Indies and tropical America. Its botanical name refers to the extraordinary leaf-like stigmas, on the 3 styles, that arch over the 3 long stamens (see A2).

Well known as a climbing plant in both tropical and subtropical regions, and in conservatories elsewhere, *Bougainvillea* is named after Louis Antoine de Bougainville (1729–1811), who circumnavigated the world between 1766 and 1769 and claimed Tahiti and the other Society Islands for the French. The eighteen species in the genus are all natives of South America but are now found under cultivation throughout the tropics. *B. glabra* (B), a native of Brazil, shows how the inflorescences are formed of 3 flowers surrounded by 3 purple bracts, the latter being what are commonly termed the 'flowers'.

Discovered in Mexico near Tabasco and brought to Europe by Linden, *Deherainia smaragdina* (F) deserves wider cultivation for its curious green flowers and the contrasting chocolate-coloured hairs on the stems and leaves. It forms a shrub or small tree up to about 20 feet (6 m.) tall and inhabits dense rain forest on the coast or, more rarely, at high altitudes inland. The elongated egg-shaped fruits are green and somewhat shiny, and measure about 3 inches (7·5 cm.) in length. *D. smaragdina*, which ranges from British Honduras and Honduras through Guatemala into Mexico, is the better known of the two species in the genus, which commemorates Pierre-Paul Dehérain (1830–1902), once a naturalist at the Museum of the Jardin des Plantes, Paris; the epithet comes from the Latin *smaragdus*, 'emerald', in reference to the unusual colour of the flowers. The other species is *D. cubensis*, which occurs on Cuba and, unlike the continental species, has leaves edged with spines.

A native of the West Indies, *Jatropha integerrima* (C) is a shrub or small tree with woody stem, variously lobed leaves, and flowers in cymes, the first branch produced usually bearing a female flower, later branches male flowers. One of the commonest members of the genus, which contains about one hundred and seventy-five species, is the deciduous *J. podagrica*: it occurs both as a weed in the tropics and as a glasshouse plant in temperate regions, where it is cultivated for its heads of bright orange-red flowers. The plant is remarkable for its swollen stem which gives it the appearance of a miniature Baobab tree.

The complex, strangely shaped flowers borne by species of *Dalechampia* provide an excellent example, like those of the daisies, of how a whole inflorescence can come close to resembling a single flower. Set off by 2 large pink, green or red bracts, the inflorescence in this genus consists, from above, first of a mass or 'cushion' of yellow, highly modified and sterile male flowers (D3), then a series of 9 to 12 functional male flowers (D4), with small bractlets, and finally a series of 3 naked female flowers (D5), in the lowest position. The genus contains over a hundred species, many of which are native to the warmer parts of the Americas. That illustrated is the Mexican *D. roezliana* (D), which was introduced into living collections in Britain from Ghent by William Bull.

MALPIGHIACEAE

Stigmaphyllon ciliatum
A1 part of flowering shoot × ⅔.
A2 flower with petals removed × 2⅔.

NYCTAGINACEAE

Bougainvillea glabra
B1 flowering shoot × ⅔.
B2 sectioned flower showing attachment to inflorescence bract × 4.
B3 inflorescence bract × 1⅓.

EUPHORBIACEAE

Jatropha integerrima
C1 flowering stem × ⅔.
C2 stamens of male flower × 3⅓.
C3 petal × 3⅓.

Dalechampia roezliana
D1 flowering shoot with fruit × ⅔.
D2 inflorescence × 1¼.
D3 sterile 'cushion' of modified male flowers and bractlets × 2⅔.
D4 male flower, buds and bractlets × 2⅔.
D5 female flower × 2⅔.

ZYGOPHYLLACEAE

Guaiacum officinale, Lignum Vitae
E1 flowering shoot × ⅔. E2 fruits × ⅔.

THEOPHRASTACEAE

Deherainia smaragdina
F1 flowering stem × ⅔. F2 flower × 1.

A1

A2

B1

B2

B3

C1

C2

C3

D1

D2

D3

D4

D5

E1

E2

F1

F2

Plate 179 CENTRAL AND SOUTH AMERICA

Joseph Libon (1821–1861) introduced *Pilocarpus pennatifolius* (A), one of about twenty tropical American species in its genus, into France from the Sao Paulo district of Brazil in 1847. Only later were the leaves discovered to contain an oil and alkaloid—pilocarpine—that has pharmaceutical properties, inducing a flow of saliva and perspiration. Similar properties are also common to a number of peppers, members of the rutaceous genus *Zanthoxylum*, and to *Moniera* species and, as these were called by the popular name 'jaborandi', the same was applied to this species of *Pilocarpus*. It has in fact been claimed since that *P. pennatifolius* represents the true jaborandi of tropical American medicine. A closely related plant from Paraguay with longer flower stalks and larger petals than typical *P. pennatifolius* was named *P. selloanus* by Engler but later treated by Emil Hassler as a variety of the Brazilian species. Typical *P. pennatifolius*, which has smaller flowers in a tighter raceme, occurs in the Matto Grosso area of Brazil, in the northern part of the species' range. This is the plant illustrated.

Its large, woody, rounded fruits have given *Couroupita guianensis* (B), member of another tropical American genus of some twenty species, its common name of Cannon-ball Tree for, when fallen, they greatly resemble spent cannon shells. Preserving the plant's military aura, the sound of fruits falling in the forest has been described as similar to rifle fire. Each fruit, before the tissues break down to produce the dirty red pulp which surrounds the seeds, contains 6 cavities. In the unripe state, the pulp makes a refreshing drink but when ripe has an extremely disagreeable smell, though this does not deter numerous monkeys, beetles and ants from visiting the plant. As many as a hundred large waxy, sweetly scented flowers, which can be smelt some distance away, may be borne on a single inflorescence arising directly from the bark, but relatively few of them ever produce fruit. *C. guianensis* occurs mainly from Brazil to Panama and is widely cultivated in Central and South America as well as in some parts of the Old World. The generic name is derived from the Carib 'Kurupittumu'.

The Monkey-pot Tree, *Lecythis ollaria*, is another interesting member of the *Lecythidaceae* family. Its spherical fruits with rounded apertures are used to trap monkeys, which find their hands caught after reaching inside for sugared bait. The Brazil-nut, *Bertholletia excelsa*, also belongs to the same family.

Feijoa sellowiana (C) is one of two Brazilian species notable for having stamen filaments which, unlike those of other members of the *Myrtaceae*, are held erect in the flower bud. Its elongated fruits are edible and bear some resemblance to guavas. The flowers of the plant illustrated are atypical, being borne within the bush on older, leafless twigs, perhaps because this particular specimen was grown out of doors in England and the slight extra warmth afforded by the interior of the bush was needed to allow them to develop. Given some protection, the plant seems to be quite hardy and is well worth cultivating. *Feijoa sellowiana* was discovered by Friedrich Sellow while collecting in Brazil and Uruguay, its native homes, between 1821 and 1829. The generic name commemorates Joao da Silva Feijo, a minor Portugese botanist who worked in Brazil. Some botanists hold the opinion that *Feijoa* and the closely allied *Acca* are not generically distinct.

RUTACEAE

Pilocarpus pennatifolius, Jaborandi
A1 part of flowering stem × $\frac{2}{3}$.
A2 flower × 4. A3 immature fruits × $\frac{2}{3}$.

LECYTHIDACEAE

Couroupita guianensis, Cannon-ball Tree
B1 flowering shoot × $\frac{2}{3}$. B2 leafy twig × $\frac{2}{3}$.
B3 inner stamens × $2\frac{2}{3}$. B4 outer stamens × $2\frac{2}{3}$.
B5 fruit × $\frac{2}{3}$. B6 habit sketch × $\frac{1}{18}$.

MYRTACEAE

Feijoa sellowiana
C1 flowering shoot × $\frac{2}{3}$.
C2 sectioned flower × $2\frac{2}{3}$.
C3 leafy shoot × $\frac{2}{3}$.

A1

A2

A3

B1

B2

B3

B4

B5

B6

C1

C2

C3

Plate 180 CENTRAL AND SOUTH AMERICA

Although plants belonging to the periwinkle family *Apocynaceae* and the bindweed or Morning Glory family *Convolvulaceae* are often similar in their superficial appearance, both families containing a number of trumpet-flowered climbers with white milky sap, there are several distinguishing features that make their identification fairly simple. The leaves of the *Convolvulaceae* are usually alternate, the petals very rarely overlap and are twisted in the bud, and the anthers are normal, in contrast to members of the *Apocynaceae*, whose anthers are curiously shaped and have long terminal appendages, whose petals generally overlap, at least in the bud, and whose leaves are usually borne opposite one another.

Some fifteen species of *Allemanda* grow in South America and the West Indies, the illustrated *A. violacea* (A) being a native of Brazil, where its roots are used in the treatment of fevers. This plant, with its rich purple flowers which fade as they age, differs from most other cultivated species in not having yellow flowers. It was introduced into England in the 1850's. Perhaps better known, *A. cathartica* of Guyana and northern South America was introduced as early as 1785 and is still widely cultivated as a hothouse plant. Like *A. violacea*, it is a climber but can be trained, in the tropics, to form a beautiful yellow-flowered hedge. The species of *Allemanda* share two features with most other members of their family: they are poisonous and they exude a white latex when the tissues are broken.

The seven *Plumeria* species are native to the warm regions of the Americas, Frangipani, *P. rubra* (C), being found wild in an area from southern Mexico to Costa Rica, although it is also now grown in many other tropical countries for its deliciously fragrant flowers. Growing in dry rocky habitats, it forms a tree 12 to 20 feet (3·7–6 m.) high with unusually stout branches, and may be deciduous in areas with a seasonal climate. The flowers, borne in inflorescences which sometimes exceed 8 inches (20 cm.) in diameter, vary in colour and may be white, yellow, pink or red. The fact that they are long-lived and very fragrant combine to make them popular cut flowers for decoration. The paired, elongated fruits grow at right angles to the stalk and on splitting open along one side to reveal flat, plumed seeds very similar to those of *Strophanthus* (see plates 61 and 103). The white-flowered form should be distinguished from *P. alba* which has smaller flowers, narrower leaves and is a native of the Caribbean islands. *P. rubra*, also known as Red Jasmine and West Indian Jasmine, is often associated with burial grounds

and Buddhist temples in the Old World. According to some authorities, the popular name Frangipani, which is common to several species, refers to an Italian of that name and a perfume distilled by him from the flower.

Mandevilla splendens (E) is one of about a hundred and fourteen species in a genus found throughout Central and tropical South America. A Brazilian species, occurring in the wild at altitudes of about 3000 feet (905 m.) in the Organ Mountains near Rio de Janeiro, it was introduced to the west in 1841. The genus commemorates Henry John Mandeville (1773–1861), once British Minister in Buenos Aires, who introduced Chilean Jasmine, *M. laxa* (syn. *M. suaveolens*) into cultivation in Britain in 1837.

Mandeville, together with William Thomas Horner Fox Stangeways, 4th Earl of Ilchester (1795–1865), also introduced to Britain the Blue Dawn-flower, *Ipomoea learii* (D), which is really only a cultivated form of the widespread and variable *I. acuminata*. It was widely reported that, following its introduction, a plant in a Chelsea nursery grew to a length of 40 feet (12 m.) and bore a total of 60,000 flowers. It is a pity that such a lovely species cannot be grown outside a glasshouse in temperate areas. *I. acuminata* is pantropic in distribution and was first described from Santa Cruz in the West Indies; it belongs to a genus of five hundred species.

Other notable members of the genus *Ipomoea* include *I. pes-caprae*, a very common and widespread tropical shore plant, and *I. batatas*, the Sweet Potato, which has swollen, edible tubers. The name *I. hederacea* has been used for the strains of Morning Glory that reached such a height of popularity in Japan in the 1830's that single seeds could command high prices among enthusiasts.

About five species of the endemic South American genus *Pyrostegia* exist, of which a well known representative is the Brazilian *P. venusta* (B), the Welted Trumpet-flower, introduced into Britain in 1815. *P. venusta* is a rampant climber which, in sunny conditions, bears the pendulous clusters of bright orange flowers that have given the genus its name (from the Greek *pyr* 'fire' and *stĕgē* 'roof', referring to the colour and shape of the upper lip of the flower). Although at its best out of doors, it must be grown in a hothouse in temperate areas. The style bears at its apex 2 thin, flattened plates which are spread apart in the newly opened flower, exposing the stigmatic surfaces. The plates close together as the style and stamens mature. Other trumpet-flowers, members of the *Bignoniaceae*, are illustrated on the following plate.

APOCYNACEAE

Allemanda violacea (syn. *A. blanchetii*)
A1 part of flowering stem $\times \frac{2}{3}$.

Plumeria rubra, Frangipani, Red Jasmine, West Indian Jasmine
C1 flowering shoot $\times \frac{2}{3}$.
C2 shoot with young leaves $\times \frac{2}{3}$.

Mandevilla splendens
E1 part of flowering stem $\times \frac{2}{3}$.
E2 young climbing shoot $\times \frac{2}{3}$.

BIGNONIACEAE

Pyrostegia venusta, Welted Trumpet-flower
B1 part of flowering stem $\times \frac{2}{3}$.

CONVOLVULACEAE

Ipomoea learii, Blue Dawn-flower
D1 part of flowering stem $\times \frac{2}{3}$.
D2 stamens and style with cut base of corolla $\times 2$.
D3 part of stem with old flower and leaf $\times \frac{2}{3}$.

A1

B1

C1

C2

D3

D2

D1

E1

E2

Plate 181   CENTRAL AND SOUTH AMERICA

The beautiful flowering trees of the *Bignoniaceae* are an important and attractive element in the forest vegetation of tropical America and include such plants as the *Tabebuia* species, smothered with tubular pink or yellow blossoms in the spring and the Jacarandas with their delicately divided foliage and splendid erect clusters of blue or violet flowers. By way of contrast there is the gnarled and spiny Calabash Tree with its large glossy green gourds and also numerous climbing and twining plants with brightly coloured and often curiously formed flowers.

The six species of *Eccremocarpus* are all found in western South America. David Don considered the illustrated species, *E. scaber* (C) sufficiently different from the others to put it in a new genus which he called *Calampelis* but this is now treated as a monotypic section of the genus *Eccremocarpus*. *E. scaber* grows in Argentina and in the mountains of the central provinces of Chile, where it is known as 'chupachupa'. It was introduced into cultivation in 1824 and is now frequently grown as a half-hardy climbing plant in northern temperate gardens. There are several cultivars differing in flower colour.

The *Pithecoctenium* species, about twelve in all, are native in Mexico, the Caribbean and tropical South America. These woody climbing plants have fibrous ribs which peel off the branchlets and spiny capsular fruit. When ripe, the fruit splits around a suture which joins the 2 woody valves together (sometimes likened to 'two shallow trays') which then fall away to expose a partition (septum) supported by a circular band of tissue (see illustration B2). When the septum separates from this band, remaining connected at one end, the movement shakes the numerous winged seeds (B3) from their compressed position against it and so disperses them. Illustrated opposite, *P. cynanchoides* (B) is native in Brazil, through Paraguay and Uruguay, into Argentina. The tips of the spines covering the surface of its fruit are bright yellow, making the strange dangling opened fruits unmistakable when seen in woodland vegetation. The generic name comes from the Greek *pithēkŏs* 'ape', *ktĕniŏn* 'little comb' and refers to the spiny fruit.

Intermediate between *Bignoniaceae* and *Polemoniaceae*, the genus *Cobaea* is now put into a family of its own, *Cobaeaceae*. The eighteen species, found from Mexico through Central America into the Andes, are divided into two sections—thirteen species in the section *Cobaea*, all with bell-shaped flowers, and the remaining five in the more localized section *Rosenbergia*, characterized by having corollas split almost to the base into long, narrow dangling petals. The genus commemorates a Jesuit missionary in Mexico and Peru, Bernabé Cobo (1582–1657).

Known as Violet Ivy, *C. scandens* (A), of the section *Cobaea*, is native to Mexico, though it is now cultivated in many tropical areas and was probably introduced into Europe in 1787. When young, the flowers are green and evil-smelling but as they mature they lose their foul odour and usually turn purple, though some cultivars have white flowers. This climber grows rapidly in suitable conditions, and can cover large areas with its foliage interspersed with flowers. Bat-claw marks found on the flowers of species related to *C. scandens* suggest that they are pollinated by vegetarian bats of the *Phyllostomidae* group, as reported by Grant and Grant in 1965. These authors also note that, while birds bring about limited pollination of Violet Ivy, owing to the shape of the corolla, it is not basically bird-, moth- or bee-pollinated.

C. hookerana (D) is illustrated in the *Botanical Magazine* of 1869, plate 5757, but under the name *C. penduliflora*, having been incorrectly identified. Real *C. penduliflora* and *C. hookerana* are both natives of the montane forests of Venezuela, but the former has stamens longer than the corolla lobes, whereas the latter's stamens are shorter. *C. penduliflora* is found around Caracas, but the precise origin of *C. hookerana* is not known, as the species was described and illustrated in cultivation. The detailed differences between these two species may, as Hemsley noted, be due to variation, and be more apparent than real. The pendulous flowers of species in the section *Rosenbergia* to which *C. hookerana* belongs are visited at night by hawkmoths, attracted by the nectar contained within the flowers; the wings of the moths pick up pollen from the stamens of one flower and transport it to the stigmas of others. Ernst (1880), who studied these night-flowering plants, found that the stigma only becomes receptive to pollen, and the anthers only release pollen, after sunset. The next morning the stamens curl up, the stigma loses its receptivity, and when eventually the flower withers, the developing fruit is slowly withdrawn into the dense and shady foliage, where it ripens.

These different methods of pollination in the two sections of *Cobaea* illustrate the biological significance of the taxonomy of the group.

COBAEACEAE

Cobaea scandens, Violet Ivy
A1 part of flowering stem with young and mature flowers × $\frac{2}{3}$.
A2 side view of flower × $\frac{2}{3}$.
A3 style and ovary × $1\frac{1}{3}$. A4 anther × 2.
A5 fruit and seed × $\frac{2}{3}$.

C. hookerana
D1 part of flowering stem × $\frac{2}{3}$.

BIGNONIACEAE

Pithecoctenium cynanchoides
B1 part of flowering stem × $\frac{2}{3}$.
B2 part of fruiting stem × $\frac{2}{3}$. B3 seed × $\frac{2}{3}$.

Eccremocarpus scaber, Chupachupa
C1 part of flowering stem × $\frac{2}{3}$.
C2 part of fruiting stem × $\frac{2}{3}$. C3 seed × $6\frac{2}{3}$.

B1

B2

A1

A2

A5

B3

C1

C2

C3

D1

Plate 182   CENTRAL AND SOUTH AMERICA

Diversity within the coffee family, *Rubiaceae*, reaches its zenith in the tropics, where many spectacular shrubby and arborescent types are to be found. *Portlandia*, *Rondeletia* and the rarely illustrated *Ferdinandusa* are examples of attractive South American genera. *Petrea*, like *Verbena* a member of the *Verbenaceae*, contains of a number of beautiful species that can be grown under glass in temperate areas.

Petrea, named in honour of Robert James Petre (1713–1743), patron of botany and horticulture, is made up of about thirty species of trees, shrubs and woody vines found in northern Mexico, Central America, the Caribbean Islands, Brazil, Bolivia, Peru and Paraguay. Climbing species may reach a height of 30 feet (9 m.). The genus is characterized by short-lived deciduous corollas and blue calyces that remain on the plant until they come to form the wings by which the fruits are dispersed. *P. kohautiana* (A) was first collected by Franz Kohaut on Martinique between 1819 and 1821 and is also found on others of the Windward Islands, some of the Leewards and Hispaniola. The plant is often confused with two other woody vines, *P. volubilis* and *P. racemosa*, though these, natives respectively of Mexico and Central America, and Brazil and Paraguay, differ in having axillary, instead of terminal, racemes and in the hairness of the calyces. The '*P. volubilis*' found in various American and European botanic gardens is often *P. kohautiana*.

A very good rockery plant, though susceptible to English winters, with a creeping habit and brilliant scarlet flowers, *Verbena peruviana* (D) is a native of Argentina and Brazil but also occurs in pampas in other parts of the continent. The flowers, each with 5 unequal lobes and about $\frac{1}{2}$ inch (13 mm.) in diameter, grow in dense terminal corymbs up to 2 inches (5 cm.) across. The small-flowered *V. officinalis*, which is said to have been used in the religious ceremonies of the Druids and Romans, and was once believed to be a specific against eye-diseases, is one of the few Old World species among the two hundred and fifty in the genus: the majority are natives of tropical and temperate America. The summer

bedding verbena, with crimson, pink, white or lilac flowers, is *V. × hybrida*, a complex hybrid between *V. peruviana*, *V. incisa* and *V. teucrioides*, all of which are South American.

A tropical American genus found from Mexico to Colombia and in the West Indies, *Rondeletia* commemorates Guillaume Rondelet (1507–1566), professor at Montpellier, a physician and naturalist who was one of thé most successful and influential 16th century botanical teachers, among his students being J. Bauhin, Felix Platter, Clusius, de L'Obel, Dalechamps and Rabelais. It consists of about one hundred and ten trees and shrubs, most of which have leathery leaves, and small flowers varying in colour between white, yellow and red, according to species. Many species have relatively restricted ranges: Jamaica, for example, has between twenty and thirty species. *R. odorata* (B), a native of Panama and Cuba, is a shrub with a maximum height of 6 feet (1·8 m.) and attractive clusters of slightly scented orange and vermilion flowers. In Cuba where it grows in rocky places near the sea, the plant tends to become rather untidy and straggly.

In 1827, Johann Baptist Emanuel Pohl (1782–1834) commemorated Prince Ferdinand of Austria in the genus *Ferdinandea*, altered later to *Ferdinandusa*. Approximately twenty species, with white or red narrow, funnel-shaped flowers, grow in South America and the West Indies. Found in marshy areas in certain provinces of Brazil, *F. speciosa* (C) is a small but spectacular tree that produces terminal corymbs of red flowers and reddish-black, capsular fruits, and deserves greater recognition as a glasshouse plant.

The Mexican, Central American and Caribbean genus *Portlandia*, named after the keen botanist and gardener Margaret Cavendish Bentinck, Duchess of Portland (1715–1785), contains twenty-five species with large white or crimson, funnel-shaped flowers. Often grown as a glasshouse plant, *P. albiflora* (E), which has slightly scented white flowers and dark green foliage, is one of the six species confined to Jamaica, where it forms a shrub or small tree up to 15 feet (4·6 m.) in height.

VERBENACEAE

Petrea kohautiana
A1 part of flowering branch × $\frac{2}{3}$.
A2 flower × $3\frac{1}{3}$. A3 female parts × $3\frac{1}{3}$.

Verbena peruviana (syn. *V. chamaedryfolia*)
D1 part of flowering stem × $\frac{2}{3}$.
D2 flower × $2\frac{2}{3}$.

RUBIACEAE

Rondeletia odorata
B1 part of flowering stem × $\frac{2}{3}$.
B2 flower × $2\frac{2}{3}$.

Ferdinandusa speciosa
C1 part of flowering stem and part of stem with leaves × $\frac{2}{3}$.
C2 detail of tips of petal and stamen × 4.
C3 part of fruiting stem × $\frac{2}{3}$.

Portlandia albiflora
E1 flower, bud and leaves on part of stem × $\frac{2}{3}$.
E2 detail of stamens and style × $1\frac{1}{3}$.

A1

B1

B2

C2

C3

C1

D2

E2

D1

E1

Plate 183   CENTRAL AND SOUTH AMERICA

The Potato, *Solanum tuberosum*, which now holds an unrivalled position among edible plants and whose output exceeds that of all other world crops in both volume and value, did not achieve this supremacy without first overcoming considerable public opposition, nor without the help of governmental propaganda. The prejudice against the plant among the public of 17th and 18th century Europe may be attributed to the fact that other members of the same family, with which Europe was already familiar, were associated in the public mind with witchcraft and murder: the Mandrake, *Mandragora officinarum* (see plate 38), for instance, was supposed to have a man-shaped root with mysterious sexual powers and to shriek as it was dragged out of the earth; while Henbane, *Hyoscyamus niger* and Deadly Nightshade, *Atropa bella-donna*, were known to contain poisonous drugs. At the same time a lingering distrust of tobacco, introduced from the Americas with the Potato, held back acceptance of the vegetable. Attempts to combat such feelings were made by, among others, Frederick the Great of Prussia and Louis XVI of France; the latter sponsored Potato banquets and placed guards on his Potato fields to arouse curiosity among his subjects and stimulate interest in the crop. It was not, however, until the latter half of the 18th century, two hundred years after the Potato was first brought to Spain from the northern Andes, that it became an important food plant in Europe. Though the plant was introduced into North America as early as 1621 and was re-introduced in 1719 by Irish immigrants, it is Europe that today produces some 90% of the world crop. The unexposed tubers are in fact the only edible part of the Potato plant; exposed, green tubers and other organs contain the harmful 'solamine'.

The twelve species of the genus *Juanulloa*, non-edible relatives of the Potato, range from Mexico to tropical South America and they take their name from Jorge Juan and Antonio Ulloa, co-authors in 1748 of *Relacion Historica del Viaje a la America Meridional*. *J. mexicana* (B), a native of Mexico as its epithet implies, is usually found as an epiphyte on trees but is not a parasite and will grow in earth. The tubular orange or red corollas never open more widely than that shown on the plate.

Discovered by Louis Feuillée in the mountains of Chile between 1707 and 1712 and recorded by him under its vernacular name, *Cestrum parqui* (E) was introduced into Britain in 1787 and became one of the twelve out of one hundred and fifty or so species to be cultivated as an ornamental plant. All of these shrubs or small trees are from the warmer parts of the Americas, including the Caribbean. *C. parqui* forms an upright shrub with yellowish green flowers that are fragrant at night. In colder areas, it may be propagated by cuttings if the fruits fail to mature.

Datura rosei (D)—named after its collector, J. N. Rose, not after the colour of the corolla—is one of a small but striking genus of some ten species especially common in tropical America but also found in warm temperate regions. The species depicted is often confused with another having red flowers, *D. sanguinea*, but may be distinguished from the latter by its corolla tubes, which are about 7 inches (17·5 cm.) in length, and by its tomentose and toothed, rather than puberulent, entire or wavy-edged leaves. *D. rosei* is found only in the mountains of Ecuador, while *D. sanguinea* extends from Ecuador to the Peruvian Andes. Both grow to a height of about 10 feet (3 m.). Two other species, *D. stramonium* and *D. metel*, contain the hallucogenic alkaloid 'daturine', said to have been used by thieves to stupify their victims. The genus as a whole is divided into three subgenera; *Datura*, *Dutra*, and *Brugmansia*.

The tribe within the *Solanaceae* formed by the genus *Salpiglossis* differs from the rest of the family in having 2 to 4 fertile stamens as against the typical 5. A native of Chile, *S. sinuata* (C) is an annual long cultivated as an ornamental plant that manifests a wide variation in flower colour. In fact a number of species described, such as *S. atropurpurea* and *S. picta*, appear to be no more than colour variants of *S. sinuata*.

The thirty species of the genus *Brunfelsia*, named after the 16th century German herbalist Otto Brunfels, are shrubs or small trees found in tropical America and the Caribbean. Purple, violet and blue flowered species such as *B. calycina* (A), which takes its name from the comparatively large, tubular calyx, are almost scentless, whereas the white and yellow flowered species give off a strong perfume at night, evidently to attract moths. Variety *macrantha*, shown here, the showiest of the several within the species, is a native of Chile.

SOLANACEAE

Brunfelsia calycina var. *macrantha*
A1 flowering shoot × $\frac{2}{3}$.
A2 older flower in profile × $\frac{2}{3}$.

Juanulloa mexicana
B1 part of flowering shoot × $\frac{2}{3}$.
B2 opened corolla × $1\frac{1}{3}$.

Salpiglossis sinuata
C1 flowering plant (stem cut) × $\frac{2}{3}$.

Datura rosei
D1 flower and bud on part of stem × $\frac{2}{3}$.
D2 stamen, style and ovary × $\frac{2}{3}$.

Cestrum parqui
E1 part of flowering stem with leaves × $\frac{2}{3}$.
E2 sectioned corolla × $2\frac{2}{3}$.

A1

A2

B1

B2

D1

D2

C1

E1

E2.

Plate 184   CENTRAL AND SOUTH AMERICA

Any visitor to the American tropics is likely to encounter at least a few plants of the *Acanthus* family, in the form of the gaily coloured inflorescences of the *Pachystachys* and *Aphelandra*, the coloured leaves of *Fittonia* or the bright flowers of *Ruellia*. Not only will these American genera be found, but Old World genera like *Barleria* and *Thunbergia* which have escaped from cultivation and become naturalized. The *Acanthaceae* is in many ways a tropical counterpart of the more temperate *Labiatae* and *Scrophulariaceae*.

Ruellia is a genus of shrubs and herbs, all American, with its centre of diversity in Brazil, and named after Jean Ruel (1474–1537), a French botanist. *R. macrantha* (B) is native to Brazil, in Minas, Sao Paulo and the Matto Grosso areas. With its large flowers and its stature of 4 to 6 feet (1·2–1·8 m.), it makes an attractive—if not spectacular—plant. Most species in this genus have symmetrical funnel-shaped flowers which are usually quite large and have only small bracts on the inflorescence.

The genus *Fittonia* comprises three species and is named after the sisters Elizabeth and Sarah Mary Fitton, authors of the 'anonymous' but once popular *Conversations on Botany* of 1817. The pale yellow flowers are inconspicuous with only 1 or 2 emerging from among the inflorescence bracts at any one time, but the purple or white veined leaves have made the species popular in the glasshouse. *F. gigantea* (E) is found only in Peru, while *F. verschaffeltii* occurs in Peru and Colombia and *F. argyroneura* in Colombia, Bolivia and Peru.

Species of *Pachystachys* are found throughout tropical America including the Caribbean area and number about seven. *P. coccinea* (C), Cardinal's Guard, is a native of French Guiana but is cultivated in several tropical countries and has sometimes escaped and become naturalized, as in Jamaica. It is a woody herb about 3 feet (91 cm.) tall and the scarlet torches of flowers are attractive to hummingbirds, which feed from them. The clustered inflorescence of flowers surrounded by bracts and bracteoles is characteristic of many acanthaceous plants.

The Shrimp Plant, *Drejerella guttata* (A), one of the twelve species of the genus, is a native of Mexico. It was first introduced into Europe in the early 1920's and into Britain in the 1930's. It has since become a popular household and conservatory plant because it bears conspicuous persistent, reddish bracts, out of which the white or pinkish flowers appear. This plant is perhaps better known to most people under its synonym, *Beloperone guttata*. Yet another synonym for the plant is *Calliaspidia guttata*. It should be noted that *Drejerella* and *Beloperone* are included by some botanists in *Justicia*.

The three to four hundred species of *Calceolaria* are largely temperate and often lovely plants which occur from Mexico, deep into Patagonia in South America. The most notable feature is the pouch or sac-like lower lip of the corolla, formed by the fusion of 3 lobes. The upper lip is smaller, formed by the fusion of the remaining 2 lobes, and the stamens are reduced to 2. The species may be large shrubs or small herbs, hardy enough for summer bedding or more tender glasshouse plants. The flowers are usually yellow. *C. purpurea* (D), a native of Chile in the Santiago region, is a herb up to about 2 feet (61 cm.) in height with many small purple flowers. It was introduced into Britain in 1826.

The genus *Lophospermum* comprises about six Mexican species. *L. erubescens* (F) is also known as *Asarina erubescens* and *Maurandia erubescens*. The corolla is funnel-shaped with 5 lobes and 4 stamens inserted above the base of the corolla whereas the exclusively European genus *Asarina* has a 2-lipped corolla. *L. erubescens* grows wild in Mexico, Jamaica, Venezuela and Colombia, but may sometimes be an escape from cultivation. It is like a softly hairy, creeping foxglove (*Digitalis*).

ACANTHACEAE

Drejerella guttata (syn. *Beloperone guttata, Calliaspidia guttata*), Shrimp Plant
A1 part of flowering stem × $\frac{2}{3}$. A2 stamens × 2.

Ruellia macrantha
B1 flowering shoot × $\frac{2}{3}$. B2 anther × 2.

Pachystachys coccinea, Cardinal's Guard
C1 part of flowering stem × $\frac{2}{3}$. C2 anthers × $2\frac{2}{3}$.

Fittonia gigantea
E1 part of flowering stem with leaves × $\frac{2}{3}$.
E2 corolla × $2\frac{2}{3}$.

SCROPHULARIACEAE

Calceolaria purpurea
D1 part of flowering stem and stem with leaves × $\frac{2}{3}$.

Lophospermum erubescens (syn. *Asarina erubescens, Maurandia erubescens*)
F1 part of flowering stem with leaves and immature fruit × $\frac{2}{3}$.
F2 opened corolla × 1. F3 anthers × 4.

B1

B2

C1

C2

D1

E1

E2

F1

F2

F3

Plate 185   CENTRAL AND SOUTH AMERICA

Gesneriads occur in spectacular abundance in the American tropics, an area where rainfall may exceed 200 inches (500 cm.) a year, where dense mists envelop an ever moist tangle of living and rotting trees and climbers, and where temperatures seldom drop below 80°F (26·7°C). Despite the expensive glasshouses and indoor culture needed to grow them outside this environment, their flowers, startlingly intense in colour, and the velvety or multicoloured foliage have made these plants very popular in North America. The majority are creepers or vines that put out roots from the joints (nodes) along the stem where the leaves are inserted; in tropical forest, where plants are in constant competition for nutrients and space, a creeper is well adapted to occupy any temporarily vacant niche. Furthermore, plants that can climb up and over others away from the shadowy forest floor and into the light may have a selective advantage over more immobile types. The genera *Hypocyrta*, *Sarmienta* and *Columnea* all contain species found high in trees or climbing up trunks near clearings through the forest.

Found among the moss on tree trunks in Costa Rica and Guatemala, *Hypocyrta nummularia* (C) is the one Central American species in an otherwise South American genus allied to the genera *Alloplectus* and *Columnea*. The peculiarly formed corolla, typical of *Hypocyrta* species, with its pouch-like lower side and small mouth is, as B. L. Burtt has said, reminiscent of certain deep-sea fishes.

The genus *Columnea* is found from Mexico throughout Central America and south to Bolivia in the west and northern Brazil in the east. Some of the hundred and twenty species are large-leaved and shrubby, others small-leaved and creeping. The asymmetrical flowers, red, yellow, or a combination of both, are adapted to pollination by hummingbirds; because of the copious nectar secreted by the flowers, the plant is known in some areas as 'liane de syrup'. The red or white berries are slightly sweet and contain numerous seeds.

Like many other species in the genus, *C. argentea* (H) has a very restricted distribution, in this case a few localities in Jamaica. It is an attractive species with silvered, silkily haired leaves and sepals, and silky lemon-coloured corollas. *C. fendleri* (F) is a native of Venezuela and allied to another Venezuelan species, *C. scandens*, which has a less elongated corolla tube. The illustrated species was described from a plant collected by August Fendler (d. 1883) at Tovar de Aragua.

All the twenty species in the genus *Sinningia*

are Brazilian. *S. speciosa* is the 'gloxinia' of horticulturalists, the name having been attached to it erroneously in 1817 by Conrad Loddiges; true *Gloxinia* is in fact a quite unrelated genus. A small shrubby plant with relatively large leaves, reddish beneath, *S. barbata* (G), the Bearded Sinningia, differs from the majority of sinningias in having no tubers; the flowers are also more strongly pouched than those of most species. It has been cultivated in Europe since the 1860's, at the beginning of which decade it was discovered by D. H. Wawra in Brazil. Recently it has been introduced into cultivation in the United States.

The diminutive species *S. pusilla* (D) can be grown in a thimble and is probably the smallest member of the *Gesneriaceae*. Groups of these plants rooted on old tree-fern trunks look most attractive. *S. concinna* is somewhat similar but has more intense purple flowers, a mouth-shaped, not bilobed, stigma, and a spurless corolla tube. The generic name commemorates Wilhelm Sinning, a gardener at the Botanic Garden of the University of Bonn in the 19th century.

The genus *Kohleria* comprises some sixty species with a wide range of flower colour from white to red found throughout tropical America. It should not be confused with the temperate grass genus *Koeleria*. *Kohleria bogotensis* (E), an erect and very hairy plant which may reach a height of 2 feet (61 cm.), was introduced into cultivation in 1844 from Colombia and is much used for hybridization.

A native of Chile, where it grows on the trunks of trees and on rocks, *Sarmienta repens* (A) is the sole species in its genus. The plant is notable for its peculiar small urn-like corollas. In cultivation it has been found that a cool period of three months at a temperature of about 43°F (6°C) is necessary to induce flowering. *Sarmienta* is named after Martin Sarmiento, a Spanish philosopher-botanist. *Mitraria coccinea*, also the sole species in its genus, is a very similar plant but has larger flowers and has 4 perfect stamens, instead of the 2 found in *Sarmienta*.

The genus *Trichantha* consists of about twelve species, natives of Panama, Colombia and Ecuador. Though included in *Columnea* by some botanists, the almost symmetrical flowers are of a more flimsy texture than those of that genus and have small peg-like appendages, in the sinuses between the lobes of the corolla, which are conspicuous when the flower is in bud. *T. elegans* (B) from Ecuador was introduced into Britain in 1861, when it was confused with *T. minor*. Its finely divided sepals make the plant most attractive.

GESNERIACEAE

Sarmienta repens
A1 part of flowering and fruiting plant × $\frac{2}{3}$.

Trichantha elegans
B1 part of flowering stem × $\frac{2}{3}$.

Hypocyrta nummularia
C1 flowering shoot × $\frac{2}{3}$.
C2 flower and calyx × 2.
C3 dissected flower × 2.

Sinningia pusilla
D1 flowering plant × $\frac{2}{3}$.
D2 flower × $3\frac{1}{3}$. D3 fruit × $3\frac{1}{3}$.

Kohleria bogotensis
E1 part of flowering stem × $\frac{2}{3}$.

Columnea fendleri
F1 flowering stem × $\frac{2}{3}$.
F2 dissected flower × $1\frac{1}{3}$.
F3 lower part of corolla × $1\frac{1}{3}$.

Sinningia barbata, Bearded Sinningia
G1 part of flowering stem with leaves × $\frac{2}{3}$.
G2 opened corolla showing stamens × 1.
G3 stamen × 4.

Columnea argentea
H1 part of flowering stem × $\frac{2}{3}$.
H2 anthers in joined position × 2.

Plate 186   CENTRAL AND SOUTH AMERICA

The daisy family is one of the largest plant groups in the world and its great diversity is displayed, in the American tropics, in the intensely coloured, jewel-like flowers of the zinnias, the equally bright colours of the dahlias, the luxuriance of the *Tithonia* species and the climbing *Mutisia* species with their gay firework-like flowers and strange grasping leaves. The woody shrubs of the genus *Stifftia* found in the Brazilian forest have fruiting heads which would put to shame those of the temperate dandelion and the giant Andean *Espeletia* species (unfortunately not described in this book) closely parallel the *Argyroxiphium* species of Hawaii (plate 149) and the tree-senecios of East Africa (plate 56) in monumental habit.

There are about twenty species of *Zinnia* found in the southern United States and as far south as Brazil and Chile. In Mexico they were cultivated in Aztec gardens long before the Spanish conquest. The genus commemorates Johann Gottfried Zinn (1727-1759), a professor at Göttingen University. It was not until 1753 that *Zinnia peruviana* (A) was introduced into Britain by Philip Miller of the Chelsea Physic Garden who had received seeds from Paris.

The parent of the annual zinnia is the variable *Z. elegans* which first reached Britain in 1796. The cultivated plant called '*Z. pumila*' is nothing more than a dwarf form of *Z. elegans*, for the true *Z. pumila* is a completely different species with a tufted habit and small greyish leaves. Wild *Z. elegans* has purple to lilac coloured flowers, but the cultivars have a wider colour range, including white, buff, rose, violet and scarlet. Other zinnias found in cultivation are *Z. angustifolia* and *Z. linearis* which has small narrow leaves but trusses of vivid orange flowers. *Z. peruviana*, like *Z. linearis*, is found in Mexico, but it also extends into Arizona, through Guatemala and Honduras into the West Indies, and south through Colombia and Ecuador into Peru and Argentina. It is precisely this wide distribution that caused plants in the southern range of the species to be called *Z. peruviana*, while the northern ranging plants were erroneously called *Z. pauciflora* for a long time.

Like zinnias, dahlias were favourite garden plants of the Aztecs. The genus comprises some twenty species found in Mexico and Central America, and they all have clustered tuberous roots. The Spaniard Vincente Cervantes (1759-1829) was the first to send dahlia seed to Europe, where it was received in 1789 by Cavanilles at the Royal Gardens at Madrid. In 1791 Cavanilles described as *Dahlia pinnata* a semi-double purple form, dedicating this new genus to a Swedish botanist Anders Dahl (1751-1789). In 1794 he described two more forms also cultivated at Madrid: both were single, but *D. coccinea* (D) was red and *D. rosea* rose. Later introductions from Mexico soon after 1800 led to a great increase in the number of forms available in European gardens, particularly in Germany.

The explanation for the great variability so quickly manifested is that the original introductions came not from the wild but were the products of hybridization in Mexico between species with magenta or ivory coloured flowers and others with scarlet or orange flowers. These hybrids possessed combinations of pigments unknown in any wild species and by 1818 almost all the colours known today had been obtained. The introduction of *D. juarezii*, the Cactus Dahlia, sometime between 1864-1872, increased the variability in the form of the flower. The majority of cultivars are propagated by vegetative methods, so as to preserve their characteristics. Dahlia tubers, which at one time had been thought of as a supplement to potatoes in the Europe, proved unpalatable. *D. coccinea* is known as 'Cocoxochitl' in its native habitat.

The genus *Tithonia* is some ten species strong and occurs in Mexico, Central America and the West Indies. *T. rotundifolia* (B), growing to a height of 9 feet (3 m.) in suitable habitats, is widely cultivated in such countries as Sierra Leone, Sudan, Kenya, Malawi and Rhodesia. Its natural range extends from Mexico to Costa Rica, but it seems to have been introduced fairly widely in the Caribbean area. In Europe, it was introduced into cultivation from Vera Cruz by William Houston (d. 1733).

The closely related *T. diversifolia*, sometimes called the Mexican Sunflower, is a more robust plant than *T. rotundifolia*. It grows to a height of about 15 feet (4·5 m.) in many parts of Mexico, Central America and the West Indies, where it appears to be native. In Kenya it is used as a hedge plant and in parts of Asia the attraction of its large showy flower heads is some recompense for the nuisance it causes as a weed.

Mutisia is named after the Spanish explorer and botanist José Celestino Mutis (1732-1808), the founder of a botanical institute at Malaquita, Colombia, where his team of artists made some 6000 drawings of South American plants, the first of which were published in 1955. It is an essentially South American genus remarkable in that many of the sixty or so species are climbers —a habit rare in *Compositae*—with the end of the midrib of the leaf lengthened into a tendril; the flower heads are large and showy. *M. decurrens* (C) was introduced by Richard Pearce in 1859 after he had collected it in South America. It is a native of Chile and is also found in Argentina in the San Martin de los Andes area, scrambling amongst other vegetation. Grown against a south facing wall at Kew, *M. decurrens* often produces a number of its attractive flowers each year. As its name indicates, *M. ilicifolia* (E) has leaves very like those of holly (*Ilex*). It was collected in 1831 by Hugh Cuming, and was introduced a year later from the Valparaiso area of Chile, where it is commonly found growing amongst shrubs. It is a variable species, especially with regard to the wings up the stem, the hairs of the undersides of the leaves, the shape of the involucral bracts, and the number and size of the ray-florets, which may be pale pink to rose in colour.

Stifftia, a genus of about seven species found only in the northern parts of South America, commemorates A. J. Stifft (1760-1836), a physician to the Imperial Court of Austria. *S. chrysantha* (F) is a native of Brazil, where it was collected by George Gardner (1812-1849), amongst others, in 1837; Gardner writes that it was common in the woods around Rio de Janeiro at that time. It is also found in Sao Paulo. Another species from the Manaus and Amapa regions of Amazonia is *S. uniflora*, described in 1935; although its white flowers are inconspicuous, the same cannot be said for its lovely rose-coloured pappus hairs.

COMPOSITAE

Zinnia peruviana (syn. *Z. pauciflora*)
A1 part of flowering stem with buds × $\frac{2}{3}$.
A2 top view of flower × $\frac{2}{3}$.
A3 ray-floret × 2. A4 disc-floret × 2.
A5 involucral bract × 2.

Tithonia rotundifolia
B1 flowering stem with buds × $\frac{2}{3}$.
B2 ray-floret × 2.
B3 disc-floret and receptacular scale × $2\frac{2}{3}$.
B4 achene × 2.

Mutisia decurrens
C1 flowering stem × $\frac{2}{3}$.

Dahlia coccinea, Cocoxochitl
D1 flowering stem with bud × $\frac{2}{3}$.
D2 back view of flower × $\frac{2}{3}$.
D3 ray-floret × 2.
D4 disc-floret and receptacular scale × $1\frac{1}{3}$

Mutisia ilicifolia
E1 flowering stem × $\frac{2}{3}$.

Stifftia chrysantha
F1 flowering stem × $\frac{2}{3}$. F2 flower × $1\frac{1}{4}$.

A1 A2 A3 A5

B1 B2 B3 B4

C1

D1 D2 D3 D4

E1

F1 F2

Plate 187   CENTRAL AND SOUTH AMERICA

Most plants in the Spiderwort family, the *Commelinaceae*, are succulent herbs found in the warmer parts of the world, with jointed stems, grass-like leaves and flowers that are so delicate that they only last a few hours on a warm day and soon dissolve, as a result of chemical changes speeded up by the heat, into a watery mass. Under a microscope, the protoplasm in the hairs of the stamens can be seen moving.

One of the largest cultivated species in the family is *Tradescantia virginiana*, to which the common name of Spiderwort is particularly applied, in allusion to its once supposed ability to cure spider bites. A number of other hardy garden tradescantias are hybrid descendants of this, *T. ohiensis* and *T. subaspera*; the group so formed which contains plants of considerable horticultural value, has been given the name *T.* × *andersoniana* by W. Ludwig and Rohweder. The generic name commemorates John Tradescant (d. 1638), 'that painful industrious searcher and lover of all nature's varieties', as a contemporary described him.

T. sillamontana (E), a native of north-eastern Mexico, is notable for having a covering of long white hairs on the leaves and stem, and hairless stamen-filaments. An easy plant to grow, it has been cultivated in the U.S.A. under a variety of names, including *Cyanotis veldthoutiana*, *T. villosa*, *T. velutina*, and *T.* 'White Gossamer'. The name given pre-eminence here is that used to describe it by Eizi Matuda in the 1930's, the specific epithet referring to Cerro de la Silla, where it was found; in 1960 it was again described, from cultivated specimens, by Harold E. Moore, who named it *T. pexata*. There are about sixty species in the genus *Tradescantia* and they occur in both North and South America.

The thirty or so species of the genus *Dichorisandra* are confined to the American tropics and characterized by racemose inflorescences, anthers that open by pores instead of slits, and arillate seeds. *D. reginae* (B), a native of central Peru, differs from most species in having leaves arranged in 2 ranks, instead of a spiral. Introduced into Belgium in 1890, and exhibited at the Brussels Exposition the following year, it caught the eye of the Queen of the Belgians, and was named *Tradescantia reginae* in her honour. However, so enthusiastic were they to name the plant, the authors described sterile material and not until the 1950's, when the flowers were first examined, at Cornell University, did it become apparent that the species was not a *Tradescantia* at all, nor even a horticultural form of *Dichorisandra*, but a true *Dichorisandra*

species, and that the characteristic silvery-white transverse markings on the foliage were not, as had previously been thought, a product of cultivation.

One of a genus of about five species, the Wandering Jew, *Zebrina pendula* (D), is widely grown as a house plant and is found as an escape from cultivation in places as far from its probable native home—tropical Central America and Mexico—as Ghana, Sierra Leone and Ethiopia. The species grows under shrubs, amongst grasses and in similar shady habitats. The generic name refers to the zebra-like stripes on the leaves.

A plant found in cultivation long before it received its scientific name, *Setcreasea purpurea* (C) was brought to Darmstadt Botanic Garden by Carl Alfred Purpus (1853–1941), who had collected in Mexico, the plant's presumed home. The plant remained unstudied and undescribed until 1955, when living Darmstadt material was christened by B. K. Boom. It is now cultivated in many parts of the world and, like a number of plants in the family, is easily propagated from stem cuttings. The coloration, usually violet-purple, of the leaves, the stem and the bloom that covers the surface may vary according to conditions of growth.

Of the two species in the genus *Cochliostema*, one, *C. odoratissimum*, grows only in Colombia, and the other, *C. jacobianum* (A), only in Ecuador. Both are epiphytes found in moist rain forest. *C. jacobianum*, discovered and introduced by Lucien Linden, was on display at the Paris Exhibition of 1867 and reached Britain the following year, when J. D. Hooker ranked it as 'amongst the grandest stemless Monocotyledons known'; we might extend the scope of the comparison to include all seed plants. In nature, the leaves are said to attain a length of 4 feet (1·2 m.), with a sheathing base about 10 inches (25 cm.) wide from between whose leaves, at various points, emerge numerous inflorescence stalks, each about 12 inches (30 cm.) tall. So peculiar are the flowers that Brenan, in his tentative classification of the family made in 1966, placed the species in a tribe of their own. There are 3 sepals and 3 petals; 2 staminodes covered with purple-blue hairs and 1 with yellow; and a reddish-purple, pointed, bilobed hood, derived in all probability from the fused filaments of the 3 stamens, enclosing the 3 anthers. The latter are each twisted like a corkscrew, a unique feature referred to in the generic name, which comes from the Greek *kokhlos* 'snail' and *stēma* 'stamen'.

COMMELINACEAE

Cochliostema jacobianum
A1 part of flowering stem and leaf × ⅔.
A2 fringing hairs on petal × 4.
A3 habit sketch × 1/15.

Dichorisandra reginae
B1 part of flowering stem with leaves × ⅔.
B2 section of flower × 2⅔.
B3 anther showing pores through which pollen is released × 4.

Setcreasea purpurea
C1 flowering shoots × ⅔. C2 flower × 2.
C3 stamen × 6. C4 stamen hair × 12.
C5 withered flower × 4.

Zebrina pendula, Wandering Jew
D1 part of flowering stems × ⅔. D2 flower × 2⅔.

Tradescantia sillamontana (syn. *T.* 'White Gossamer', *T. villosa*, *T. velutina*, *T. pexata*, *Cyanotis veldthoutiana*)
E1 part of flowering stem × ⅔. E2 stamen × 6.

A1

A2

A3

B1

B2

B3

C3

C4

C5

D1

D2

E1

E2

Plate 188   CENTRAL AND SOUTH AMERICA

Commonly known as Spanish Moss or Old Man's Beard, *Tillandsia usneoides* (A) is one of about four hundred *Tillandsia* species among which it is remarkable for lacking the usual cup-shaped, water-storing rosette of leaves. A covering of absorbent scales, however, on the surface of the plant compensates for this. As moisture fills the air-spaces between these scales, the grey shoots, which hang in festoons from trees and telegraph wires in subtropical and tropical America from the south-eastern United States to Chile and central Argentina, take on a greenish tinge. The shoots, which may be several feet long, bear tiny blue or pale green flowers, are used as nesting material by birds which thus help the plant to spread vegetatively.

Tillandsia lindeniana (C), which has a relatively large rosette of leaves, is more characteristic of the genus as a whole. Its showy bracts and exceptionally large flowers make the species valuable horticulturally: several varieties, among them var. *tricolor* with its red flowers and bracts and white 'eye', are grown in gardens. A native of the Andes in Ecuador and Peru, it was introduced into Europe via France, where it was shown at the Paris Exhibition of 1867.

The multicoloured drooping inflorescence with pink or red bracts, pink calyx, yellowish green petals usually tipped with purplish blue, and protruding stamens make *Billbergia nutans* (B) a spectacular pot-plant. The species, one of about fifty in the genus, was first described from a plant which flowered at Kew in 1870. It grows in Brazil, Uruguay, Paraguay and Argentina.

Ochagavia comprises four or five Chilean species of limited distribution. *O. lindleyana* (D) was brought to Europe around 1851 and has become common in cultivation. *O. elegans* occurs only on the island of Juan Fernandez.

A native of Colombia, where it occurs in the Andes and in clumps amongst swamp and at the edges of streams along the Rio Pirparana and Rio Paca, *Pitcairnia corallina* (E) is notable for the lobes of its petals, which never open widely, but are edged with a fine white margin. One variety, var. *viridis*, has leaves only 1¼ inches (3 cm.) wide and yellow green inflorescences. Some two hundred and fifty tropical American species and one African—*P. feliciana*, which grows in rock crevices in Guinea and was at first thought to comprise a new genus in the *Liliaceae*—make up the genus.

In the same family, the Pineapple, *Ananas comosus*, forms on the ground rosettes of long spiny leaves out of which rises a stalk 2 to 4 feet (0·6–1·2 m.) tall bearing a large many-flowered inflorescence crowned with a tuft of leaves. The fruit, technically called a 'syncarp', has all its parts united into a fleshy body, of which the major part, the swollen pulpy stem, becomes juicy and edible on reaching maturity. Seeds are rarely produced under cultivation. The plant was introduced into England about 1690 and is naturalized in many parts of the Old World. There are many commercial cultivars.

The tallest members of the *Bromeliaceae* family are contained in the genus *Puya*; the Colombian *P. gigas*, for example, can grow to a height of 30 feet (9 m.), and the Chilean species *P. berteroniana* and *P. alpestris,* both of which have blue flowers and are cultivated in Britain, to 10 to 12 feet (3–3·6 m.) and 3 to 4 feet (0·9–1·2 m.) respectively. In some species the lower halves of the branches of the inflorescence are crowded with flowers, while the upper halves are bare; birds alight on this sterile part to seek nectar in the cup-shaped flowers and in so doing pollinate them.

BROMELIACEAE

Tillandsia usneoides, Spanish Moss, Old Man's Beard
A1 flowering plant × ⅔.

Billbergia nutans
B1 flowering stem × ⅔.
B2 flower and calyx × 1⅓.

Tillandsia lindeniana
C1 plant growing in position on tree trunk × ⅔.

Ochagavia lindleyana
D1 part of flowering plant × ⅔.

Pitcairnia corallina
E1 inflorescence and leaf × ⅔.

Plate 189   CENTRAL AND SOUTH AMERICA

Approximately one hundred and fifty species of *Heliconia* are native to the American tropics, South East Asia and Polynesia. The African genus *Strelitzia* (plate 84) contains fused perianth segments and many ovules in each chamber while *Heliconia* perianth segments are only partly fused and each chamber contains a single ovule. Similar to bananas in appearance, Wild Plantains (*Heliconia*) are large herbs with 2-ranked leaves and rigid inflorescences dominated by conspicuously coloured, 2-ranked, boat-shaped spathes. Each of these sheaths a compactly branching cluster of flowers and, later, the capsular blue fruits.

Distributed throughout the Caribbean, *Heliconia psittacorum* (A), which reaches a height of 3 feet (91 cm.), is sometimes divided according to habit and leaf shape into var. *robusta* and var. *silvestris*. *H. bihai* is a much larger plant, often reaching a height of 12 feet (3·7 m.) and bearing enormous inflorescences 2 feet (61 cm.) long and 1 foot (30 cm.) wide. It bears a series of scarlet and yellow spathes but the flowers themselves are an inconspicuous whitish shade. Another West Indian species, *H. caribaea*, is distinguished by its red spathes which contrast sharply with its whitish flowers and blue fruits. Its inflorescences may be 8 to 10 feet (2·4–3 m.) above the ground and the unwary person who tries to cut through its stalks may easily be doused by an unexpected shower as the spathes often collect and hold considerable quantities of water.

Clusters of cream flowers surrounded by mottled purple leaves and leaf stalks covered with fine hairs make *Calathea angustifolia* (B) a popular addition to the glasshouse. It is said to have been cultivated in St Petersburg and Berlin before 1858 and has certainly been growing at Kew for more than sixty years. *Calathea* may have originated in Central America

but this is not known with any certainty. Many of the one hundred and fifty or so species—all confined to tropical America—have patterned leaves which make them valued as decorative household plants.

Stromanthe sanguinea (C) bears lax clusters of waxy, bright pink flowers which are very beautiful, but also incredibly difficult to interpret botanically. One of the thirteen species native to South America, *S. sanguinea* was introduced into Britain from Europe though it is originally from Brazil. By 1852 the species had flowered at Kew and it has continued to do so ever since.

Named after Bartolomme Maranti, an obscure Neapolitan botanist who published at Venice in 1559 and died in Naples sometime after 1570, the genus *Maranta* comprises a total of twenty-three tropical American species, many of which are ornamental with variegated leaves. *M. bicolor*, a Brazilian plant, has leaves with purple undersides and pale green patches between the midrib and margin of the dark green upper surfaces. *M. leuconeura*, however, has pale green leaves with white or dark green patches and there are many cultivars of this species in a variety of colour patterns. *Maranta* leaf patterns may be easily confused with those of the aroids *Caladium*, *Dieffenbachia* and *Philodendron*. The former bear thin, delicate leaves while the latter have leaves which are stout and leathery or fleshy and the flowers are distinctively different. The crushed rhizome of the West Indian Arrowroot, *M. arundinacea* (D), contains an easily digested form of starch which gives the plant its value. This species is found from Mexico through Central America and the Caribbean as far south as Paraguay. Its variegated leaves give it usefulness as a decorative plant in some areas and it may reach a height of 10 feet (3 m.).

MUSACEAE

Heliconia psittacorum
A1 part of flowering stem × ⅔.
A2 fruiting stem and leaf (stem cut) × ⅔.
A3 fruit × 2⅔.

MARANTACEAE

Calathea angustifolia
B1 lower part of stem with flowering and new shoots × ⅔.
B2 flower × 1⅓.
B3 leaf showing purple underside × ⅔.
B4 portion of underside of leaf × 1⅓.

Stromanthe sanguinea
C1 part of flowering plant × ⅔.
C2 flower with sepals removed × 4.
C3 immature fruit × 1⅓.

Maranta arundinacea, West Indian Arrowroot
D1 flowering stem × ⅔.
D2 root × ⅔.

Plate 190   CENTRAL AND SOUTH AMERICA

South America, with its forests, mountains, plains and full complement of climatic conditions, is the home of spectacular and often little known plants of the *Amaryllidaceae* which could fill a book with illustrations.

Confined to the Peruvian Andes, the five species of *Urceolina* are bulbous plants with curiously shaped flowers which hang down on slender pedicels, the lower part a stalk-like tube swelling abruptly into an urn-like upper part—probably giving rise to the generic name (from the Latin *urceolus* 'little pitcher'). The stalked leaves usually develop later than the flowers. The famous collectors, Ruiz and Pavon discovered *U. urceolata* (C), in the Huanuco region of Peru in the late 1700's, calling it *Crinum urceolatum*. In this species the leaves and flowers develop together, as is evident from the plate published in their *Flora* (1802) but not from the figure of the plant in *Botanical Magazine*, Pl. 5464 (1864). It was introduced from Peru by Richard Pearce and flowered at Kew in 1864, four years before he died in Panama.

Sometimes called the Blue Amaryllis or Empress of Brazil, the remarkable *Worsleya procera* (E) can be regarded with equal right as an isolated member of the *Hippeastrum* genus (commonly confused with *Amaryllis*), or as an independent genus. Among its special features are its bulb with an extraordinary, long aerial neck up to 5 feet (1·5 m.), and its lilac flowers. It was discovered around 1860 by a Monsieur Binot of Rio, who found it growing at 4000 feet (1220 m.) on a nearby mountain but it was first described in 1863 by P. E. S. Duchartre (1811–1894). It was not until 1899, however, that Arthington Worsley (1861–1943), an English civil engineer who was also a keen gardener, visited the Organ Mountains above Petropolis and re-introduced it into cultivation. In the wild, *W. procera* grows on steep moist cliffs with the necks of the bulbs projecting horizontally or hanging from the cliff. Bulbs were first flowered in Worsley's glasshouse at Isleworth and he raised the plant from home-produced seed, growing it on top of drainpipes filled with rock, stone-chippings and a little oak-leaf mould. In California, it is now being grown successfully in the open.

There are about five Chilean species of *Leucocoryne*, which is distantly related to the onion (*Allium*) except that it has 3 fertile stamens instead of 6. The other 3 are represented by 3 projecting staminodes, which suggested the derivation of the generic name from the Greek *leukos* 'white', *koryne* 'club'. Ranging from Coquimbo to Valparaiso, *L. ixioides* (D) was probably first grown in Britain in 1820 by John Walker in his London collection at Southgate and was named *Brodiaea ixioides* by Hooker in 1823. In 1927, Clarence Elliott (1881–1969) of Stevenage found it growing near Coquimbo 'in misty sweeps by the mile and by the million'; he collected many bulbs and sent them back to England, naming the plant Glory of the Sun by analogy with Glory of the Snow (*Chionodoxa*). In nature the species is very variable and the deliciously fragrant flowers can be lilac (as shown), dark blue, blue- and red-throated, or white.

Philesia has but one species, *P. magellanica* (A), with a habit so unlike that of most monocotyledons that out of flower it might be mistaken for a *Vaccinium*. It was first found along the Straits of Magellan by Philibert Commerson on the Bougainville Expedition of 1767–1769 to South America and the Pacific. However, it was Messrs Veitch's collector, William Lobb, who introduced the plant to Europe, and in 1853 Messrs Veitch successfully exhibited it at the Chiswick Flower Show. The species extends from the southern tip of South America up the west coast as far as Valdivia and Chiloe. It forms a multi-branched bush up to 4 feet (1·2 m.) high, with small evergreen leaves and pendulous dark rose flowers of waxy texture. Crossed with the related genus *Lapageria* it has produced the bigeneric hybrid × *Philageria*. *Philesia* and six allied genera sometimes included in the Lily family are now often put in a family of their own, the *Philesiaceae*, with some nine species all confined to the southern hemisphere.

Before 1837 *Bomarea* was usually included in *Alstroemeria*; since then it has been accepted as a distinct genus in the *Alstroemeriaceae* with about one hundred and fifty species found in tropical America and Mexico. The distinction is made chiefly on account of the climbing habit of many species and the fact that the outer 3 perianth segments are much shorter than the inner 3.

Bomarea caldasii (B) was discovered by Humboldt and Bonpland in 1802 in the mountains near Quito, Ecuador, during their memorable explorations in South America. It commemorates another botanical explorer, the brilliant Francisco José de Caldas (1771–1816), who was a mathematician and astronomer as well as botanist and zoologist and might have continued the work of his master, José Mutis (see plate 186), in Colombia had he not been executed in October 1816 for his part in a revolt against the Spanish government. Not until the 1860's, when Richard Pearce sent material to Veitch's of Exeter, was this species introduced into Europe. It is common at altitudes of 6000 to 12,000 feet (1830–3660 m.) in the Andes of Colombia and Ecuador, scrambling over other vegetation and conspicuous with its umbels of bright pendulous flowers. Depending on the locality where they are found, the flowers may be yellow, with the inner perianth segments slightly spotted, or orange to reddish, and densely spotted on the inside. It is fortunate that this species is hardy in milder parts of Europe such as Malahide Castle, near Dublin, Ireland, and is easily grown from seed.

LILIACEAE

Philesia magellanica (syn. *P. buxifolia*)
A1 part of flowering stem × ⅔.

ALSTROEMERIACEAE

Bomarea caldasii (syn. *B. caldasiana*, *B. kalbreyeri*)
B1 part of flowering stem × ⅔.

AMARYLLIDACEAE

Urceolina urceolata
C1 flowering plant (stem cut) × ⅔.

Leucocoryne ixioides, Glory of the Sun
D1 flowering stem with leaves × ⅔.
D2 dissected flower × 1⅓.

Worsleya procera (syn. *Hippeastrum procerum*, *Amaryllis rayneri*), Empress of Brazil, Blue Amaryllis
E1 part of flowering stem and leaf × ⅔.
E2 habit sketch of plant × 1/15.

A1

B1

C1

D2

D1

E2

E1

Plate 191   CENTRAL AND SOUTH AMERICA

This plate illustrates the palms, or *Palmae,* from both the New and the Old Worlds. Found in all tropical and subtropical areas, some are hardy enough to grow in temperate climates. Their habitat is extremely varied: they thrive in the sun and in the shade, in deserts and swamps, on mountains and near the sea. The largest species rise to a height of 100 feet (30 m.), while others creep along the ground in the absence of other supporting vegetation. Some communities rely on the palm as the basis of their rural economy as, for example, the Coconut on many Pacific islands and the Sago Palm in South East Asia.

Palm trunks have no bark and, once formed, they cannot increase in diameter like Dicotyledon or Gymnosperm trees such as Oak or Pine. Most attain their maximum girth before the stem grows upwards. Cells may swell, however, and give the impression of lateral growth, as in the Pot-bellied Palm. The trunk acquires its structural rigidity by means of a peripheral ring of fibre-bundles which also constitute the food- and water-conducting system of the plant.

Most palms have a constant number of leaves in the crown at the top of the trunk. In species which have congested leaves and long leaf-sheathes, such as *Roystonea* species, there is an apparent elongation of the trunk called the 'crownshaft'. The leaf blade may be divided into segments on either side of the midrib, or 'rachis', in the feather-palms or into segments with a common point of insertion on a short midrib at the end of the leaf stalk in the fan-palms. The broken bands of tissue which connected the once undivided segments of the leaf may remain attached to the leaf in the form of long trailing strands. Dead leaves may persist for long periods on the trunk as in *Washingtonia* or completely abscise as in *Cocos.*

The many-branched inflorescences of palms bear numerous flowers, which appear below the crown of leaves, as in *Chamaedorea* and *Roystonea,* within the crown, as in *Cocos,* or terminating the trunk above the crown as in *Corypha.* The inflorescence is usually sheathed by 2 or more bracts, and on emerging, the flowers may be arranged on a central axis with or without side branches. Most of the flowers are unisexual, with male and female occurring on the same tree, as in *Cocos,* or on separate trees, as in such species as *Chamaedorea oreophila. Corypha* inflorescences are sometimes huge, and appear only once in the plant's lifetime after which, worn out by the effort of producing these structures, the plant promptly dies.

The sole species of *Nypa* is *N. fruticans* (A), which grows on steep banks in brackish estuaries from the Bay of Bengal and Ceylon throughout Malaysia, to Queensland and the Solomon Islands. Unlike most palms, *Nypa* never develops long aerial shoots and the bases of the leaves have air-spaces which serve to buoy up the leaf rosette on the tidal mud-flats where the plants grow. Before opening, the spathe surrounding the inflorescence turns red and increases in temperature (smelling of hot-water bottles, according to Corner, 1966). *Nypa* leaves are used for thatch and when tapped, the inflorescence yields syrup. On the evidence of fossil fruits found in London Clay, the ancient delta mud of an Eocene river, we know that this species has existed since the Cretaceous Period, which occurred over one hundred million years ago.

Cocos is also monotypic, and *C. nucifera* (B), which probably originated in the western Pacific, is cultivated throughout the tropical world. As the plant needs an ample supply of moisture but must also be well drained, it is frequently found on sand in coastal areas. Most parts of the plant have some value in tropical rural economy. The leaves are used for thatch, the growing point or 'cabbage' can be eaten as a vegetable (although this usually kills the tree) and the young fruit contains a refreshing juice. The seed of the mature fruit is thickly lined with the endosperm which is commonly known as coconut flesh; the fruit is invested in a husk which comprises coir when broken down and the seed shells make useful receptacles. Copra—dried coconut flesh—is an important commercial product because it yields high quantities of vegetable oil.

There are two species of *Washingtonia* (J). Both are native to desert stream beds and oases in California, Arizona and Mexico. The characteristic fan-leaves and persistent dead leaves form a 'skirt' under the crown of leaves, and this accounts for the popularity of the genus as an ornament in areas suitable for its cultivation. They grow to 65 to 75 feet (20–23 m.) and produce better 'skirts' in sheltered habitats.

Colpothrinax is a monotypic genus represented by the Pot-bellied Palm, *C. wrightii* (H), found only in Cuba. The swollen trunk is a constant feature and is thought to be produced by pronounced cell expansion at the time of maximum growth of the plant.

Lodoicea maldivica (G) is the sole species of the genus *Lodoicea* and it only occurs in the Seychelles Islands in the Indian Ocean. As Corner (1966) observes, the dispersal of the 40 lb. (18 kg.) fruits is a mystery, since they sink in water and cannot roll uphill, yet the trees grow on hillsides and hilltops in the islands. *L. maldivica* towers to 100 feet (30 m.), with leaves up to 16 feet (5 m.) long. This giant produces the largest fruit in the plant kingdom—3 feet (91 cm.) in circumference—which is even more remarkable when compared with the $\frac{1}{6}$ inch (5 mm.) size of some of the smallest palm seeds. This plant is often known as 'Coco de Mer'.

Features of a savannah or semi-desert vegetation, the thirty or so species of the Doum Palm genus, *Hyphaene* (F), are found in Africa, Arabia, Madagascar and India. They are among the few palms to show regular branching of the trunk. The pulp surrounding the fruits is made into a syrup and the bony endosperm, which resembles ivory, is carved into domestic articles such as needles and ornaments. The species *H. thebaica* was cultivated by the ancient Egyptians.

The fourteen species of *Roystonea* are found from Venezuela through the Caribbean into Florida. *R. regia* (E) is a graceful, decorative tree often planted in rows down avenues; its smooth columnar trunk looks most imposing and is crowned by shading leaves. All the species except *R. oleracea* have the pinnae of the leaves arranged along the midrib in several ranks, giving the leaves an untidy appearance.

Chamaedorea is a large American genus of about one hundred species occurring from Bolivia and Brazil in the south to Mexico in the north. Most species are reedy in character but diverse in size. The male and female flowers are borne on different plants, and the inflorescence may be paniculate, as in *C. oblongata* (C) from Venezuela, or spicate, as in *C. oreophila* (D) from Mexico.

PALMAE

Nypa fruticans
A1 habit sketch $\times \frac{1}{190}$.

Cocos nucifera, Coconut
B1 habit sketch $\times \frac{1}{150}$.

Chamaedorea oblongata
C1 habit sketch $\times \frac{1}{18}$.
C2 portion of main stem with fruiting stem $\times \frac{2}{3}$.

C. oreophila
D1 habit sketch $\times \frac{1}{18}$.
D2 part of stem with male inflorescence $\times \frac{2}{3}$.
D3 male flower $\times 8$. D4 part of leaf $\times \frac{2}{3}$.

Roystonea regia
E1 habit sketch $\times \frac{1}{210}$.

Hyphaene species, Doum Palm
F1 habit sketch $\times \frac{1}{170}$.

Lodoicea maldivica (syn. *L. sechellarum*),
Coco de Mer
G1 habit sketch $\times \frac{1}{250}$.

Colpothrinax wrightii, Pot-bellied Palm
H1 habit sketch $\times \frac{1}{180}$.

Washingtonia species
J1 habit sketch $\times \frac{1}{195}$.

A1

B1

C2 C1

D1 D3 D4

E1

F1

G1

H1

J1

Plate 192   CENTRAL AND SOUTH AMERICA

In tropical areas, such as Central and South America, orchids are frequently found growing on trees or high on rocks, and these plants are described as being epiphytic. Epiphytic orchids do not draw nutriment from the plants on which they perch, but benefit by being situated nearer to the light in forest which is often very shaded at ground level. In temperate areas, most orchids are terrestrial with tuberous roots acting as storage organs. The roots of epiphytic orchids are of three kinds: those that anchor the plant to its support; those that collect humus beneath and around the plant and absorb nutrients from the surface of the support; and aerial roots that hang down from the plant, manufacture food materials, and absorb water from damp air through a spongy outer layer called the 'velamen', having a role much the same as leaves. Orchids are more prominent in tropical floras and are often larger and more elaborate than their temperate cousins.

The epiphytic orchid *Ornithidium coccineum* (A) is one of about sixty species of *Ornithidium* found from Mexico, throughout the Caribbean and into tropical South America. This species is found in central South America and on islands such as Cuba and Puerto Rico, where it grows on trees in montane forest. The generic name comes from the Greek *ornis* 'bird', referring to the elongated curved column of the flower as shown in the illustration.

Although the fifty or so species of *Brassia* are confined to tropical America, the genus commemorates William Brass (d. 1783) who collected plants in west tropical Africa in 1782-1783, for three wealthy patrons—Banks, Fothergill and Pitcairn. *B. longissima* (B) was at first regarded as a variety of *B. lawrenceana* but is now accepted as a distinct species on account of its very much longer tail-like 'sepals'. It is a native of Costa Rica and first flowered in cultiva-

tion in England in 1868. *B. brachiata* is a similar species also of great ornamental merit.

The genus *Zygopetalum* comprises about twenty species found in Central and South America. Its name, from the Greek *zygŏn* 'yoke', refers to the somewhat yoke-like swelling at the lip (lower petal). Probably introduced to Britain in 1837, *Z. intermedium* (E), a terrestrial species, is found wild in Brazil and has been confused with *Z. mackaii*.

The four hundred or so species of *Epidendrum* come from tropical America and are mostly epiphytic, whence the generic name from the Greek *ĕpi* 'upon' and *dĕndrŏn* 'tree'. They display much variation in both habit and floral characters. The range of *E. ciliare* (C) extends from Mexico and Puerto Rico, southward to Brazil. The specific epithet and vernacular name of Eyelash Orchid, derive from the fringed (ciliate) margin of the lip. It was among the first of the epiphytic orchids to be successfully grown in Britain and was introduced as long ago as 1790, being cultivated in the Royal Garden at Kew in 1794 where it is still grown. In nature this fragrant-flowered species grows on rocks or on trees up to altitudes of about 6000 feet (1830 m.) and the plants vary considerably in size.

The genus *Laelia* comprises about thirty species found in Central America and eastern South America. The name *Laelia*, referring to one of the vestal virgins of ancient Rome, was chosen by Lindley simply as a pleasant and convenient designation, without any special relevance, apart from the delicacy and beauty of the flowers. The Flor de San Miguel, *L. anceps* (D), is a native of Mexico and possibly Honduras. It was introduced into Britain about 1834 from Mexico and has become one of the most important of orchids in cultivation. In nature it grows on rocks and trees at the fringes of dense forest.

ORCHIDACEAE

Ornithidium coccineum
A1 flowering plant × ⅔. A2 flower × 2.

Brassia longissima
B1 flowering plant × ⅔. B2 lip and column × 1⅓.

Epidendrum ciliare, Eyelash Orchid
C1 inflorescence and leaf × ⅔.
C2 lip and column × 1⅓.

Laelia anceps, Flor de San Miguel
D1 inflorescence and leaf × ⅔. D2 column × 3⅓.
D3 anther and pollinia × 6.

Zygopetalum intermedium
E1 inflorescence and leaf × ⅔. E2 column × 1⅓.

A1

A2

B1

B2

C1

C2

D1

D2

D3

E1

E2

ABBREVIATIONS OF AUTHORS' NAMES
USED IN THE BOTANIC INDEX

Names used in the botanic index

Dates are not given for living authors

Adams – J. M. F. Adams 1780–1833
Agnew – A. G. Agnew
Ait. – W. Aiton 1731–1793
Ait. f. – W. T. Aiton 1766–1849
All. – C. Allioni 1725–1804
Allan – H. H. B. Allan 1882–1957
Andr. – H. C. Andrews *floreat* 1794–1830
André – E. André 1840–1911
Anthony – J. Anthony
Anway – J. C. Anway
Arn. – G. A. W. Arnott 1799–1868
Aschers. – P. F. A. Ascherson 1834–1913
Aubl. – J. B. C. F. Aublet 1720–1778
auct. – auctor, auctores: authors
Audubon – J. J. Audubon 1785–1851

Bab. – C. C. Babington 1808–1895
Bailey – L. H. Bailey 1858–1954
Baill. – H. E. Baillon 1827–1895
Bak. – J. G. Baker 1834–1920
E. G. Bak. – E. G. Baker 1864–1949
Bal. – B. Balansa 1825–1891
Balb. – G. B. Balbis 1765–1831
Balf. – J. H. Balfour 1808–1884
Balf. f. – I. B. Balfour 1853–1922
Ball – J. Ball 1818–1889
P. W. Ball – P. W. Ball
Bally – P. R. O. Bally
Banks – Sir J. Banks 1743–1820
Barbey – W. Barbey 1842–1914
Bartling – F. G. Bartling 1798–1875
Bartram – W. Bartram 1739–1823
Batsch – A. J. G. K. Batsch 1761–1802
Batt. – J. A. Battandier 1848–1922
Bean – W. J. Bean 1863–1947
Beauv. – A. M. F. J. Palisot de Beauvois 1752–1820
Beauverd – G. Beauverd 1867–1942
Becc. – O. Beccari 1843–1920
Beck – G. Ritter Beck von Mannagetta und Lerchenau 1856–1931
Benoist – R. Benoist
Benth. – G. Bentham 1800–1884
Bentvelzen – P. A. J. Bentvelzen
Berg – O. K. Berg 1815–1866
Berger – A. Berger 1871–1931
Bergius – J. P. Bergius 1730–17?u
Bernh. – J. J. Bernhardi 1774–1850
Berth. – S. Berthelot 1794–1880
Bertol. – A. Bertoloni 1775–1869
Betche – E. Betche 1851–1913
Bickn. – E. P. Bicknell 1859–1925
Bieb. – F. A. Marschall von Bieberstein 1768–1826
Blake – S. F. Blake 1892–1959
Blanche – E. Blanche 1824–1908
Blanco – M. Blanco 1780–1845
Blume – C. L. Blume 1796–1862
Boiss. – P.-E. Boissier 18.0–1885
Bojer – W. Bojer 1797–1856
Bolle – C. A. Bolle 1821–1909
Bolus – H. Bolus 1834–1911
L. Bolus – L. Bolus
Bonnier – G. E. M. Bonnier 1853–1922
Bonpl. – A. J. A. Bonpland 1773–1858
Boom – B. K. Boom
Bor. – A. Boreau 1803–1875
Bornm. – J. F. N. Bornmüller 1862–1948
Bouché – C. D. Bouché 1809–1881
Bowles – E. A. Bowles 1865–1954
N. E. Br. – N. E. Brown 1849–1934
R. Br. – R. Brown 1773–1858
Brandegee – T. S. Brandegee 1843–1925
Bremek. – C. E. B. Bremekamp
Briq. – J. I. Briquet 1870–1931
Britten – J. Britten 1846–1924
Britton – N. L. Britton 1859–1934
Brongn. – A. T. Brongniart 1801–1876
Brot. – F. da Avellar Brotero 1744–1828
E. A. Bruce – E. A. Bruce *floreat* 1910–1955
Buch.-Ham. – F. Buchanan, Lord Hamilton 1762–1829
Buchanan – J. Buchanan 1819–1898
Buckl. – S. B. Buckley 1809–1884
Buek – J. N. Buek 1779–1856

Buhse – F. A. Buhse 1821–1898
Bull – W. Bull 1828–1902
Bullock – A. A. Bullock
Bunge – A. von Bunge 1803–1890
Bunting – G. S. Bunting
Bur. – E. Bureau 1830–1918
Burchell – W. J. Burchell 1781–1863
Burm. – J. Burman 1706–1779
Burm. f. – N. L. Burman 1734–1793
B. L. Burtt – B. L. Burtt
Burtt-Davy – J. Burtt Davy 1870–1940
Bury – P. S. Bury *floreat* 1831–1837
Buser – R. Buser 1857–1931

Caldas – F. J. Caldas 1771–1816
Camus – E. G. Camus 1852–1915
Capuron – R. Capuron
Carey – W. Carey 1761–1832
Carr. – E. A. Carrière 1818–1896
Cass. – A. H. G. de Cassini 1781–1832
Cav. – A. J. Cavanilles 1745–1804
Chaix – D. Chaix 1730–1799
Cham. – A. L. von Chamisso 1781–1838
Chatel. – J. J. Chatelain 1736–1822
Cheeseman – T. F. Cheeseman 1846–1923
Cheval. – A. J. B. Chevalier 1873–?1956
Chevall. – F. F. Chevallier 1796–1840
Chiov. – E. Chiovenda 1871–1940
Chittenden – F. J. Chittenden 1873–1950
Chodat – R. H. Chodat 1865–1934
Choisy – J. D. Choisy 1799–1859
Christm. – G. F. Christmann *floreat* 1777–1788
Clausen – R. T. Clausen
Cockayne – L. C. Cockayne 1855–1934
Coem. – H. E. L. Coemans 1825–1871
Cogn. – C. A. Cogniaux 1841–1916
O. F. Cook – O. F. Cook 1867–1949
Coll. – Sir H. Collett 1836–1901
Compton – R. H. Compton
Correa – J. F. Correa da Serra 1751–1823
Coss. – E. S.-C. Cosson 1819–1889
Coste – H. J. Coste 1858–1924
Court. – R. J. Courtois 1806–1835
Craib – W. G. Craib 1882–1933
Crantz – H. J. N. von Crantz 1722–1799
Cronq. – A. Cronquist
Croom – H. B. Croom 1797–1837
Cunn. – A. Cunningham 1791–1839
R. Cunn. – R. Cunningham 1793–1835
Curt. – W. Curtis 1746–1799
Cyr. – D. Cirillo (Cyrillus) 1739–1799

Dammann – E. Dammann & Co. *floreat* 1880
Dandy – J. E. Dandy
Danguy – P. A. Danguy 1862–1942
Danser – B. H. Danser 1891–1943
Davis – K. C. Davis 1867–1936
DC. – A. P. de Candolle 1778–1841
A.DC. – A. de Candolle 1806–1893
Decne – J. Decaisne 1807–1882
De Coincy – A. H. C. de la F. de Coincy 1837–1903
Delavay – J. M. Delavay 1834–1895
Desr. – L. A. J. Desrousseaux 1753–1838
Desv. – A. N. Desvaux 1784–1856
Diels – F. L. E. Diels 1874–1945
Dietr. – F. G. Dietrich 1768–1850
Dinsmore – J. E. Dinsmore 1862–1951
Don – D. Don 1799–1841
G. Don – G. Don 1798–1856
Domin – K. Domin 1882–1953
Dougl. – D. Douglas 1798–1834
Drake – E. Drake del Castillo 1855–1904
Druce – G. C. Druce 1850–1932
Drumm. – J. Drummond 1783–1863
Duby – J. E. Duby 1798–1885
Duchartre – P. E. S. Duchartre 1811–1894
Ducke – A. Ducke 1876–1959
Dugand – A. Dugand
Dumort. – B. C. J. Dumortier 1797–1878
Dunal – M. F. Dunal 1789–1856
Dunn – S. T. Dunn 1868–1938
Durand – E. M. Durand 1794–1873

Durande – J. F. Durande 1730–1794
Duthie – J. F. Duthie 1845–1922
Dyer – W. T. Thiselton Dyer 1843–1928
R. A. Dyer – R. A. Dyer 1900–1937
Dykes – W. R. Dykes 1877–1925

Eastw. – A. Eastwood 1859–1953
Eggers – H. F. H. Eggers 1844–1903
Ehrenb. – C. G. Ehrenberg 1795–1876
Ehrh. – J. F. Ehrhart 1742–1795
Eichl. – A. W. Eichler 1839–1887
Ell. – S. Elliot 1771–1830
Ellis – J. Ellis 1710–1776
Endl. – S. L. Endlicher 1804–1849
Engelm. – G. Engelmann 1809–1884
Engler – H. G. A. Engler 1844–1930
Esch. – J. F. Eschscholz 1793–1831

Fedde – F. K. G. Fedde 1873–1942
O. Fedtsch. – O. A. Fedtschenko 1845–1921
Feer – H. Feer 1857–1892
Fenzl – E. Fenzl 1808–1879
Fernald – M. L. Fernald 1873–1950
Fisch. – F. E. L. von Fischer 1782–1854
C. Fischer – C. E. C. Fischer 1874–1950
Fomin – A. V. Fomin 1869–1935
Ford – N. Ford
Forrest – G. Forrest 1873–1932
Forsk. – P. Forskål 1732–1763
G. Forst. – J. G. A. Forster 1754–1794
J. R. Forst. – J. R. Forster 1729–1798
Foster – Sir M. Foster 1836–1907
Foug. – A. D. Fougeroux 1732–1789
P. Fourn. – P. Fournier 1877–1964
Fr. – E. M. Fries 1794–1878
Franch. – A. Franchet 1834–1900
Franco – J. do A. Franco
R. E. Fries – K. R. E. Fries 1876–1966
Th. Fries – Th. M. Fries 1832–1913
Fritsch – K. Fritsch 1864–1934
Froehner – A. Froehner

Gaertn. – J. Gaertner 1732–1791
Gamble – J. S. Gamble 1847–1925
Gams – H. Gams
Gand. – M. Gandoger 1850–1926
Garcke – F. A. Garcke 1819–1904
Gardner – A. Gardner 1812–1849
C. A. Gardner – C. A. Gardner
Gaudich. – C. Gaudichaud-Beaupré 1789–1854
Gaudin – J. F. A. T. G. P. Gaudin 1766–1833
Gay – J. E. Gay 1786–1864
C. Gay – C. Gay 1800–1873
Gerrard – W. T. Gerrard *floreat* 1862
Gilg – E. Gilg 1867–1933
Gilib. – J. E. Gilibert 1741–1814
Gill. – J. Gillies 1747–1836
Gleason – H. A. Gleason
J. F. Gmelin – J. F. Gmelin 1748–1804
Godr. – D. A. Godron 1807–1880
Gouan – A. Gouan 1733–1821
Graebner – K. O. R. P. P. Graebner 1871–1933
Graells – M. de la P. Graells 1818–1898
Graham – R. Graham 1786–1845
R. A. Graham – R. A. Graham 1915–1958
Gray – S. F. Gray 1766–1836
A. Gray – A. Gray 1810–1888
M. L. Green – M. L. Green
Greene – E. L. Greene 1843–1915
Gren. – J. C. M. Grenier 1808–1875
Griff. – W. Griffith 1810–1845
Gris – J. A. A. Gris 1829–1872
Griseb. – A. H. R. Grisebach 1814–1879
Groenwald – J. W. Groenwald
Groenl. – J. Groenland 1824–1891
Guss. – G. Gussone 1787–1866

F. J. Hanb. – F. J. Hanbury 1851–1938
Hance – H. F. Hance 1827–1886
Hanstein – J. L. E. R. von Hanstein 1822–1880

Hara – H. Hara
Harms – H. A. Th. Harms 1870–1942
Harris – W. Harris 1860–1920
Harvey – W. H. Harvey 1811–1866
Hassk. – J. C. Hasskarl 1811–1894
Hausskn. – H. K. Haussknecht 1838–1903
Haw. – A. H. Haworth 1768–1833
Hayek – A. von Hayek 1871–1928
Hayne – F. G. Hayne 1763–1832
HBK – F. A. von Humboldt, A. Bonpland, C. S. Kunth
Hedberg – O. Hedberg
Heldr. – T. von Heldreich 1822–1902
Heller – A. A. Heller 1867–1944
Hemsl. – W. Botting Hemsley 1843–1924
Henry – Louis Henry 1853–1913
Herbert – W. Herbert 1778–1847
F. Hermann – F. Hermann
Heywood – V. H. Heywood
Hiern – W. P. Hiern 1839–1925
Hill – J. Hill 1716–1775
Hillebrandt – F. Hillebrandt 1805–1860
Hoffm. – G. F. Hoffmann 1761–1826
Holttum – R. E. Holttum
Honck. – G. A. Honckeny 1724–1805
Hoog – T. & C. J. H. Hoog
Hoogl. – R. D. Hoogland
Hook. – W. J. Hooker 1785–1865
Hook. f. – J. D. Hooker 1817–1911
Hoppe – D. H. Hoppe 1760–1846
Hornem. – J. W. Hornemann 1770–1841
Hort. – Hortorum: of the gardens
Hose – J. Hose ?–1800
Houtt. – M. Houttuyn 1720–1798
Huber-Morath – A. Huber-Morath
Huds. – W. Hudson 1730–1793
Hueg. – Baron K. von Huegel 1794–1870
Huet – A. L. P. Huet 1814–1888
Hultén – E. Hultén
Humb – A. von Humboldt 1769–1859
Hunter – W. Hunter 1755–1812
Hutchins. – J. Hutchinson

Iinuma – Y. Iinuma *floreat* 1832

Jack – W. Jack 1795–1822
Jacq. – N. J. Jacquin 1727–1817
Jalas – J. Jalas
James – E. James 1797–1861
D. A. Johansen – D. A. Johansen
I. M. Johnston – I. M. Johnston 1898–1960
Jord. – A. Jordan 1814–1897
Juss. – A. L. de Jussieu 1748–1836

Karst. – G. K. W. H. Karsten 1817–1908
Kearney – T. H. Kearney 1874–1956
Kellogg – A. Kellogg 1813–1887
Kennedy – P. B. Kennedy 1874–1930
Kensit – E. G. Kensit 1879–1916
Ker – (Ker-Gawl) J. Gawler (né J. B. Ker) 1764–1842
King – Sir G. King 1840–1909
Kit. – P. Kitaibel 1757–1817
Klotzsch – J. F. Klotzsch 1805–1860
Knuth – R. G. P. Knuth 1874–1957
Koch – W. D. J. Koch 1771–1849
K. Koch – K. H. E. Koch 1809–1879
Koehne – E. Koehne 1848–1918
Koern. – F. Koernicke 1828–1908
Korsh. – S. I. Korshinsky 1861–1900
Kostermans – A. J. G. H. Kostermans
Kotschy – T. Kotschy 1813–1866
Kränzl. – F. W. L. Kränzlin 1847–1934
Krug – C. W. L. Krug 1833–1898
Kunth – C. S. Kunth 1788–1850
Kuntze – K. E. O. Kuntze 1843–1907

L. – C. Linnaeus (C. von Linné) 1707–1778
L. f. – C. von Linné 1741–1783
Labill. – J. J. H. de La Billardière 1755–1834
Lacaita – C. C. Lacaita 1853–1933
Lam. – J. B. A. P. de M. de Lamarck 1744–1829

Lane – I. E. Lane
Lange – J. M. C. Lange 1818–1898
Larreát. – J. D. Larreátegui *floreat* 1795
Lecoq – H. Lecoq 1802–1871
Ledeb. – C. F. von Ledebour 1785–1851
Lehm. – J. G. C. Lehmann 1792–1860
Leicht. – M. Leichtlin 1831–1910
Lem. – C. Lemaire 1801–1871
Léonard – J. Léonard
Less. – C. F. Lessing 1809–1862
L'Hérit. – C. L. L'Héritier de Brutelle 1746–1800
Libosch. – J. L. Liboschitz 1783–1824
Liebl. – F. K. Lieblein 1744–1810
Lind. – J. Linden 1817–1898
Lindau – G. Lindau 1866–1923
Lindl. – J. Lindley 1799–1865
Link – J. H. F. Link 1767–1851
Lipsky – V. I. Lipsky 1863–1937
Lodd. – C. Loddiges 1738–1826
Lour. – J. Loureiro 1715–1791
Lourteig – A. Lourteig
Ludwig – W. Ludwig

Macb. – J. F. Macbride
Macf. – J. Macfadyen 1798–1850
Mackensen – B. Mackensen 1863–1914
Maiden – J. H. Maiden 1859–1925
Maire – R. C. J. E. Maire 1878–1949
Makino – T. Makino 1862–1957
Malte – M. O. Malte 1880–1933
Marloth – R. Marloth 1855–1931
Marsh. – H. Marshall 1722–1801
Mart. – K. F. P. von Martius 1794–1868
Martelli – U. Martelli 1860–1934
Masson – F. Masson 1741–1805
Mast. – M. T. Masters 1833–1907
Maton – W. G. Maton 1774–1835
Matsum. – J. Matsumura 1855–1928
Mattüschka – H. G. von Mattüschka 1734–1779
Matuda – E. Matuda
Maw – G. Maw 1832–1912
Maxim. – K. J. Maximowicz 1827–1891
McVaugh – R. McVaugh
Medic. – F. K. Medicus 1736–1808
Meisn. – C. F. Meisner 1800–1874
Merr. – E. D. Merrill 1876–1956
Mert. – F. K. Mertens 1764–1831
Merxm. – H. Merxmueller
Mey. – C. A. Meyer 1795–1855
E. Mey. – E. H. F. Meyer 1791–1858
Mez – K. C. Mez 1866–1944
Michx – A. Michaux 1746–1802
Mickel – J. L. Mickel
Miers – J. Miers 1789–1879
Mikan – J. C. Mikan 1769–1844
Mildbr. – G. W. J. Mildbraed 1879–?1954
Mill. – P. Miller 1691–1771
J. Miller – J. Miller (J. S. Mueller) ?1715–1790
Milne-Redhead – E. W. B. H. Milne-Redhead
Miq. – F. A. W. Miquel 1811–1871
Moench – C. Moench 1744–1805
Moldenke – H. N. Moldenke
Molina – J. I. Molina 1740–1829
Moore – T. Moore 1821–1887
H. E. Moore – H. E. Moore
Moran – R. V. Moran
Morr. – C. J. E. Morren 1833–1886
Morton – C. V. Morton
Ch. des Moulins – Charles des Moulins 1797–1875
Muell. Arg. – J. Mueller of Aargau 1828–1896
F. Muell. – F. von Mueller 1825–1896
Muir – J. Muir
Munz – P. A. Munz
Murr. – J. A. Murray 1740–1791

Nakai – T. Nakai 1882–1952
Napper – D. M. Napper
Naudin – C. Naudin 1815–1899
Nees – C. G. D. Nees von Esenbeck 1776–1858
Nelson – J. G. Nelson 1818–1882
Nicholson – G. Nicholson 1847–1908
Nied. – F. J. Niedenzu 1857–1937
Norl. – T. Norlindh

Nutt. – T. Nuttall 1786–1859
Nyman – C. F. Nyman 1820–1893

O'Brien – J. O'Brien 1842–1930
Oliv. – D. Oliver 1830–1917
E. G. H. Oliver – E. G. H. Oliver
W. R. B. Oliver – W. R. B. Oliver 1883–1957
Opiz – P. M. Opiz 1787–1858
Orbigny – A. D. d'Orbigny 1802–1857
Orph. – T. G. Orphanides 1817–1886
Osbeck – P. Osbeck 1723–1805
Ostenf. – C. H. Ostenfeld 1873–1931
Otto – F. Otto 1783–1856

Palibin – I. V. Palibin 1872–1949
Pall. – P. S. Pallas 1741–1811
Panc. – J. Pančić 1814–1888
Par. – Rev. C. S. P. Parish 1822–1897
Pav. – A. Pavon 1750–1844
V. Pavlov – N. V. Pavlov
Pax – F. Pax 1858–1942
Paxt. – J. Paxton 1802–1865
H. W. Pearson – H. H. W. Pearson 1870–1916
Pellegrin – F. Pellegrin
Pennell – F. W. Pennell 1886–1952
Perry – T. A. Perry *floreat* 1850
Pers. – C. H. Persoon 1762–1836
Peterm. – W. L. Petermann 1806–1855
Peters. – O. G. Petersen 1847–1937
Petrie – D. Petrie 1846–1925
Petrov. – S. Petrovitsch 1839–1889
Peyritsch – J. J. Peyritsch 1835–1889
Pfitz. – E. H. H. Pfitzer 1846–1906
Phil. – R. A. Philipi 1808–1904
Phillips – E. P. Phillips 1884–1967
Pierre – J. B. L. Pierre 1833–1905
Piers – F. Piers
Planch. – J. E. Planchon 1823–1888
Podlech – D. Podlech
Poeppig – E. F. Poeppig 1798–1868
Pohl – J. B. E. Pohl 1782–1834
Poir. – J. L. M. Poiret 1755–1834
Pollard – C. L. Pollard 1872–1945
Polunin – N. Polunin
Pomel – A. N. Pomel 1821–1898
A. E. Pors. – A. E. Porsild
Porter – T. C. Porter 1822–1901
Pospichal – E. Pospichal 1838–1905
Praeger – L. Praeger 1865–1953
Prain – Sir D. Prain 1857–1944
C. Presl – C. B. Presl 1794–1852
Pugsl. – H. W. Pugsley 1868–1947
Purpus – J. A. Purpus 1860–1932
Pursh – F. T. Pursh 1774–1820

Raddi – G. Raddi 1770–1829
Radius – J. W. M. Radius 1797–1884
Radlk. – L. A. T. Radlkofer 1829–1927
Raf. – C. S. Rafinesque-Schmaltz 1783–1840
Raffill – C. P. Raffill
Ramat. – T. A. J. d'Audibert de Ramatuelle 1750–1794
Rauh – W. Rauh
Räusch. – E. A. Räuschel *floreat* 1772–1797
Redouté – P. J. Redouté 1761–1840
Regel – E. A. von Regel 1815–1892
Rehd. – A. Rehder 1863–1949
Reichb. – H. G. L. Reichenbach 1793–1879
Reichb. f. – H. G. Reichenbach 1823–1889
Reinw. – C. G. C. Reinwardt 1773–1854
Rendle – A. B. Rendle 1865–1938
Retz. – A. J. Retzius 1742–1821
Reyn. – A. Reynier 1845–1932
Reynolds – G. W. Reynolds 1895–1967
Rich. – L. C. M. Richard 1754–1821
A. Rich. – A. Richard 1794–1852
Richardson – Sir J. Richardson 1787–1865
Ridley – H. N. Ridley 1855–1956
Rob. – B. L. Robinson 1864–1935
Rodigas – E. Rodigas 1831–1902
Roem. – J. J. Roemer 1763–1819
Roemer – M. J. Roemer *floreat* 1835–1847

Roessler – M. Roessler 1754–1829
Rohrb. – P. Rohrbach 1847–1871
Rohweder – O. Rohweder
Rolfe – R. A. Rolfe 1855–1921
Ronn. – K. Ronniger 1871–1954
Roscoe – W. Roscoe 1753–1831
Rose – J. N. Rose 1862–1928
Roth – A. W. Roth 1757–1834
Rottb. – C. F. Rottboell 1727–1797
Rouy – G. C. C. Rouy 1851–1924
Roxb. – W. Roxburgh 1751–1815
Royle – J. F. Royle 1779–1858
Rozhkova – O. L. Rozhkova
Ruiz – H. Ruiz Lopez 1754–1815
Rümpl. – T. Rümpler 1817–1891
Rusby – H. H. Rusby 1855–1940
Ryd. – P. A. Rydberg 1860–1931

Safford – W. E. Safford 1859–1926
St Hil. – A. de Saint Hilaire 1779–1853
St John – H. St John
Salisb. – R. A. Salisbury 1761–1829
Salm-Dyck – J., Prince and High Count Salm-Reifferscheidt-Dyck 1773–1861
Sarg. – C. S. Sargent 1841–1927
Sasaki – S. Sasaki 1888–1960
Sav. – L. Savatier 1830–1891
Sch. Bip. – C. H. Schultz Bipontius 1805–1867
Scheidweiler – M. J. Scheidweiler 1799–1861
Schelpe – E. A. C. L. E. Schelpe
Schinz – H. Schinz 1858–1941
Schlecht. – D. F. L. Schlechtendal 1794–1866
Schmidt – F. W. Schmidt 1764–1796
F. Schmidt – F. Schmidt 1832–1908
Schneevoogt – G. V. Schneevoogt 1775–1871
Schneid. – C. K. Schneider 1876–1951
Schnizl. – A. Schnizlein 1814–1868
Schönland – S. Schönland 1860–1940
Schott – H. W. Schott 1794–1865
Schousb. – P. K. A. Schousboe 1766–1832
Schrad. – H. A. Schrader 1767–1836
Schreb. – J. C. D. von Schreber 1739–1810
Schrenk – A. von Schrenk 1816–1876
Schrödinger – R. Schrödinger 1857–1919
Schult. – J. A. Schultes 1773–1831
Schultz – C. H. Schultz 1805–1867
Schum. – K. M. Schumann 1851–1904
Schumach. – H. C. F. Schumacher 1757–1830
Schur – P. J. F. Schur 1799–1878
Schwant. – G. Schwantes 1881–1960
Schweickerdt – H. G. W. J. Schweickerdt
Schwein. – G. A. Schweinfurth 1836–1925
Schweinitz – L. D. von Schweinitz 1780–1834
Scop. – G. A. Scopoli 1723–1788
Sealy – J. R. Sealy
Seaton – H. E. Seaton 1869–1893
Seem. – B. C. Seemann 1825–1871
Sell – P. D. Sell
Ser. – N. C. Seringe 1776–1858
Seub. – M. A. Seubert 1818–1878
Sibth. – J. Sibthorp 1758–1796
Sieb. – P. F. von Siebold 1796–1866
Sieber – F. W. Sieber 1789–1844
Silva – A. R. Pinto da Silva
Simonk. – L. tol Simonkai 1851–1910
Sims – J. Sims 1792–1838
J. Sims – J. Sims 1749–1831
Skeels – H. C. Skeels 1873–1934
Sm. – J. E. Smith 1759–1828
B. Smith – L. B. Smith
C. P. Smith – C. P. Smith 1835–1892
W. W. Smith – Sir W. W. Smith 1875–?1956
Sobrinho – L. G. Sobrinho
Soland. – D. C. Solander 1736–1782
Solereder – H. Solereder 1860–1920
Solms – H. Graf zu Solms Laubach 1842–1915
Sond. – O. W. Sonder 1812–1881
Soulange-Bodin – E. Soulange-Bodin 1774–1846
Sowerby – J. D. Sowerby 1787–1871
Spach – E. Spach 1801–1879
Splitg. – F. L. Splitgerber 1801–1845
Sprague – T. A. Sprague 1877–1958
Spreng. – C. P. J. Sprengel 1766–1833
Standl. – P. C. Standley 1884–1963

Staner – P. Staner
Stapf – O. Stapf 1857–1933
Stearn – W. T. Stearn
Stern – Sir F. C. Stern 1884–1967
Sternb. – C. Graf von Sternberg 1761–1838
Steud. – E. G. Steudel 1783–1856
Stev. – C. von Steven 1781–1863
Stoker – F. Stoker ?1879–1943
Summerhayes – V. S. Summerhayes
Sw. – O. Swartz 1760–1818
Sweet – R. Sweet 1783–1835
Swingle – W. T. Swingle 1871–1952

Tausch – I. F. Tausch 1793–1848
G. Taylor – Sir G. Taylor
Thell. – A. Thellung 1881–1928
Thoms. – T. Thomson 1817–1878
Thonn. – P. Thonning 1775–1848
Thunb. – C. P. Thunberg 1743–1828
Tisch. – A. Tischer
Torr. – J. Torrey 1796–1873
Tratt. – L. Trattinick 1764–1849
Traub – H. P. Traub
Triana – J. Triana 1828–1890
Turcz. – N. S. Turczaninow 1796–1864
Turrill – W. B. Turrill 1890–1961

Urban – I. Urban 1848–1931

Vahl – M. H. Vahl 1749–1804
J. Vahl – J. L. M. Vahl 1796–1854
Valeton – T. Valeton 1855–1929
van Steenis – C. G. G. van Steenis
Vatke – G. C. W. Vatke 1849–1889
Velen. – J. Velenovsky 1858–1949
Vent. – E. P. Ventenat 1757–1808
Vickery – J. W. Vickery
Vig. – R. Viguier 1880–1931
Vill. – D. Villar(s) 1745–1814
Vis. – R. de Visiani 1800–1878
Voss – A. Voss 1857–1924
Vuillet – A. Vuillet 1883–1914

Waldst. – F. A. Graf von Waldstein-Wartemberg 1759–1823
Wall. – N. Wallich 1786–1854
Wallr. – K. F. W. Wallroth 1792–1857
Walp. – W. G. Walpers 1816–1853
Walt. – T. Walter 1740?–1789
E. Walther – E. Walther 1892–1959
Warburg – O. Warburg 1859–1938
F. K. Ward – F. Kingdon Ward 1885–1958
Wats. – S. Watson 1826–1892
H. C. Wats. – H. C. Watson 1804–1881
W. Wats. – W. Watson 1858–1925
W. C. R. Wats. – W. C. R. Watson 1885–1954
Webb – P. B. Webb 1793–1854
Weber – G. H. Weber 1752–1828
Wehrhahn – H. R. Wehrhahn 1887–1940
Weimark – H. Weimark
Welw. – F. M. J. Welwitsch 1806–1872
Wendelbo – P. Wendelbo
Wenderoth – G. W. F. Wenderoth 1774–1861
Wendl. – H. Wendland 1823–1903
C. West – C. West
Weston – R. Weston 1773–1806
Whyte – R. Whyte *floreat* 1892
Wight – R. Wight 1796–1872
Wildeman – E. A. T. de Wildeman 1866–1947
Willd. – C. L. Willdenow 1765–1812
Willis – J. H. Willis
Willmott – A. J. Willmott 1888–1950
Wils. – E. H. Wilson 1876–1930
E. Wimmer – E. G. Wimmer
Wittm. – M. C. L. Wittmack 1839–1929
Woodson – R. E. Woodson 1904–1963
Woot. – E. O. Wooton 1865–1945
C. H. Wright – C. H. Wright 1864–1941
Wurmb – F. van Wurmb *floreat* 1779

Zucc. – J. G. Zuccarini 1797–1848

INDEX OF BOTANIC NAMES

Illustrated plants are indicated by *

421

INDEX OF COMMON NAMES

Illustrated plants are indicated by *